Handbook of Research on Learning in the Age of Transhumanism

Serap Sisman-Ugur
Anadolu University, Turkey

Gulsun Kurubacak
Anadolu University, Turkey

A volume in the Advances in Educational Technologies and Instructional Design (AETID) Book Series

Published in the United States of America by
IGI Global
Information Science Reference (an imprint of IGI Global)
701 E. Chocolate Avenue
Hershey PA, USA 17033
Tel: 717-533-8845
Fax: 717-533-8661
E-mail: cust@igi-global.com
Web site: http://www.igi-global.com

Copyright © 2019 by IGI Global. All rights reserved. No part of this publication may be reproduced, stored or distributed in any form or by any means, electronic or mechanical, including photocopying, without written permission from the publisher. Product or company names used in this set are for identification purposes only. Inclusion of the names of the products or companies does not indicate a claim of ownership by IGI Global of the trademark or registered trademark.
Library of Congress Cataloging-in-Publication Data

Names: Sisman-Ugur, Serap, 1981- editor. | Kurubacak, Gulsun, 1964- editor.
Title: Handbook of research on learning in the age of transhumanism / Serap
   Sisman-Ugur and Gulsun Kurubacak, Editors.
Description: Hershey PA : Information Science Reference, [2020]
Identifiers: LCCN 2018054445| ISBN 9781522584315 (hardcover) | ISBN
   9781522584322 (ebook)
Subjects: LCSH: Learning--Research. | Learning, Psychology of. |
   Education--Effect of technological innovations on. | Educational
   technology.
Classification: LCC LB1060 .H34577 2019 | DDC 370.72--dc23 LC record available at https://lccn.loc.gov/2018054445

This book is published in the IGI Global book series Advances in Educational Technologies and Instructional Design (AETID) (ISSN: 2326-8905; eISSN: 2326-8913)

British Cataloguing in Publication Data
A Cataloguing in Publication record for this book is available from the British Library.

All work contributed to this book is new, previously-unpublished material. The views expressed in this book are those of the authors, but not necessarily of the publisher.

For electronic access to this publication, please contact: eresources@igi-global.com.

Advances in Educational Technologies and Instructional Design (AETID) Book Series

Lawrence A. Tomei
Robert Morris University, USA

ISSN:2326-8905
EISSN:2326-8913

Mission

Education has undergone, and continues to undergo, immense changes in the way it is enacted and distributed to both child and adult learners. In modern education, the traditional classroom learning experience has evolved to include technological resources and to provide online classroom opportunities to students of all ages regardless of their geographical locations. From distance education, Massive-Open-Online-Courses (MOOCs), and electronic tablets in the classroom, technology is now an integral part of learning and is also affecting the way educators communicate information to students.

The **Advances in Educational Technologies & Instructional Design (AETID) Book Series** explores new research and theories for facilitating learning and improving educational performance utilizing technological processes and resources. The series examines technologies that can be integrated into K-12 classrooms to improve skills and learning abilities in all subjects including STEM education and language learning. Additionally, it studies the emergence of fully online classrooms for young and adult learners alike, and the communication and accountability challenges that can arise. Trending topics that are covered include adaptive learning, game-based learning, virtual school environments, and social media effects. School administrators, educators, academicians, researchers, and students will find this series to be an excellent resource for the effective design and implementation of learning technologies in their classes.

Coverage

- E-Learning
- Educational Telecommunications
- Digital Divide in Education
- Hybrid Learning
- Curriculum Development
- Instructional Design Models
- Virtual School Environments
- Collaboration Tools
- Adaptive Learning
- Higher Education Technologies

IGI Global is currently accepting manuscripts for publication within this series. To submit a proposal for a volume in this series, please contact our Acquisition Editors at Acquisitions@igi-global.com or visit: http://www.igi-global.com/publish/.

The Advances in Educational Technologies and Instructional Design (AETID) Book Series (ISSN 2326-8905) is published by IGI Global, 701 E. Chocolate Avenue, Hershey, PA 17033-1240, USA, www.igi-global.com. This series is composed of titles available for purchase individually; each title is edited to be contextually exclusive from any other title within the series. For pricing and ordering information please visit http://www.igi-global.com/book-series/advances-educational-technologies-instructional-design/73678. Postmaster: Send all address changes to above address. Copyright © 2019 IGI Global. All rights, including translation in other languages reserved by the publisher. No part of this series may be reproduced or used in any form or by any means – graphics, electronic, or mechanical, including photocopying, recording, taping, or information and retrieval systems – without written permission from the publisher, except for non commercial, educational use, including classroom teaching purposes. The views expressed in this series are those of the authors, but not necessarily of IGI Global.

Titles in this Series

For a list of additional titles in this series, please visit: www.igi-global.com/book-series

Handbook of Research on Ecosystem-Based Theoretical Models of Learning and Communication
Elena A. Railean (Siberian Federal University, Russia & Moscow State Pedagogical University, Russia & Free International University of Moldova, Moldova)
Information Science Reference • copyright 2019 • 401pp • H/C (ISBN: 9781522578536) • US $245.00 (our price)

Comparative Perspectives on Inquiry-Based Science Education
Stuart Bevins (Sheffield Hallam University, UK) Louise Lehane (St. Angela's College, Ireland) and Josephine Booth (Sheffield Hallam University, UK)
Information Science Reference • copyright 2019 • 298pp • H/C (ISBN: 9781522554394) • US $185.00 (our price)

Opening Up Education for Inclusivity Across Digital Economies and Societies
Patricia Ordóñez de Pablos (The University of Oviedo, Spain) Miltiadis D. Lytras (Effat University, Saudi Arabia) Xi Zhang (Tianjin University, China) and Kwok Tai Chui (City University of Hong Kong, China)
Information Science Reference • copyright 2019 • 352pp • H/C (ISBN: 9781522574736) • US $185.00 (our price)

Cultural and Social Implications of Artificial Intelligence in Education
Dennis Anderson (St. Francis College, USA) and Robert Niewiadomski (Hunter College, USA)
Information Science Reference • copyright 2019 • 305pp • H/C (ISBN: 9781522577935) • US $185.00 (our price)

Mobile Technologies in Educational Organizations
Alona Forkosh Baruch (Levinsky College of Education, Israel & Tel Aviv University, Israel) and Hagit Meishar Tal (Holon Institute of Technology, Israel)
Information Science Reference • copyright 2019 • 320pp • H/C (ISBN: 9781522581062) • US $195.00 (our price)

An Invariant-Based Approach to Second Language Acquisition Emerging Research and Opportunities
Elena Orlova (Lobachevsky State University of Nizhny Novgorod, Russia)
Information Science Reference • copyright 2019 • 164pp • H/C (ISBN: 9781522582205) • US $145.00 (our price)

Performance-Based Assessment in 21st Century Teacher Education
Kim K. Winter (Western Carolina University, USA) Holly H. Pinter (Western Carolina University, USA) and Myra K. Watson (Western Carolina University, USA)
Information Science Reference • copyright 2019 • 295pp • H/C (ISBN: 9781522583530) • US $175.00 (our price)

701 East Chocolate Avenue, Hershey, PA 17033, USA
Tel: 717-533-8845 x100 • Fax: 717-533-8661
E-Mail: cust@igi-global.com • www.igi-global.com

Death is actually resurrected; apparently absence; eternity in truth. Hz. Mevlana

for all of our lost loved ones...

This book is dedicated to the memory of our late fathers, Ali Sisman and Cemalettin Kurubacak, and our late siblings for the love and care.

Editorial Advisory Board

Alan Bruce, *Universal Learning Systems, Ireland*
Yücel Güney, *Anadolu University, Turkey*
Badrul Khan, *KDW, USA*
Figen Kılıç, *Mersin University, Turkey*
Mayte Martin, *Universal Learning Systems, Ireland*
Santosh Panda, *Indira Gandhi National Open University, India*
Ramesh Sharma, *Indira Gandhi National Open University, India*
John Traxler, *University of Wolverhampton, UK*

List of Reviewers

Okan Aksu, *Trakya Univeristy, Turkey*
Hakan Altınpulluk, *Anadolu University, Turkey*
Aras Bozkurt, *Anadolu University, Turkey*
Martin Ciupa, *Mindmaze, Switzerland*
Teresa L. Coffman, *University of Mary Washington, USA*
Celal Murat Kandemir, *Osmangazi University, Turkey*
Mary Beth Klinger, *University of Maryland University College, USA*
Mehmet Emin Mutlu, *Anadolu University, Turkey*
M. Recep Okur, *Anadolu University, Turkey*
Erdem Öngün, *Trakya University, Turkey*
Harun Serpil, *Anadolu University, Turkey*
Thomas Stanley, *Nevada Learning Academy, USA*
Esra Pınar Uça Güneş, *Anadolu University, Turkey*
Hasan Uçar, *Bilecik Seyh Edebali University, Turkey*
İlker Usta, *Anadolu University, Turkey*

List of Contributors

Abramov, Polina Shafran / *University of Louisville, USA* 32
Aksu, Okan / *Trakya University, Turkey* 157
Altinpulluk, Hakan / *Anadolu University, Turkey* 205
Banger, Gürcan / *Railway Systems Cluster, Turkey* 307
Bozkurt, Aras / *Anadolu University, Turkey* 224, 252
Chaturvedi, Devendra Kumar / *Dayalbagh Educational Institute, India* 363
Chauhan, Sumit / *ABES Engineering College, India* 363
Coffman, Teresa L. / *University of Mary Washington, USA* 134
Doğan, Ezgi / *Anadolu University, Turkey* 185
Ergül, Işıl Boy / *Yıldız Teknik Üniversitesi, Turkey* 291
Goksel, Nil / *Anadolu University, Turkey* 224
Gulati, Muskan / *ABES Engineering College, India* 363
Güler, Emel / *Anadolu University, Turkey* 116
Gupta, Mayank / *Tata Consultancy Services, India* 363
Istifci, Ilknur / *Anadolu University, Turkey* 274
Istvan, Zoltan / *Transhumanist Party, USA* 28
Karadeniz, Şirin / *Bahçeşehir University, Turkey* 291
Karaman, Faruk / *Konya Food and Agriculture University, Turkey* 98
Karatop, Buket / *Istanbul University-Cerrahpasa, Turkey* 116
Klinger, Mary Beth / *College of Southern Maryland, USA* 134
Kurubacak, Gulsun / *Anadolu University, Turkey* 1
Misra, Pradeep Kumar / *Chaudhary Charan Singh University, India* 171
Mutlu, Mehmet Emin / *Anadolu University, Turkey* 47
Öngün, Erdem / *Trakya University, Turkey* 346
Ossiannilsson, Ebba S. I. / *ICDE OER Advocacy Committee, Sweden* 78
Rastogi, Rohit / *ABES Engineering College, India* 363
Şahin, Ferhan / *Anadolu University, Turkey* 185
Sharma, Pallavi / *ABES Engineering College, India* 363
Singhal, Parv / *ABES Engineering College, India* 363
Ucar, Hasan / *Bilecik Seyh Edebali University, Turkey* 237
Uğur, Serap / *Anadolu University, Turkey* 1
Urgan, Suzan / *Ondokuz Mayıs University, Turkey* 328
Vita-More, Natasha / *University of Advancing Technology, USA* 18
Yadav, Vishwas / *ABES Engineering College, India* 363
Yampolskiy, Roman V. / *University of Louisville, USA* 32

Table of Contents

Foreword xxi

Preface xxii

Acknowledgment xxxi

Section 1
Introduction

Chapter 1
Artificial Intelligence to Super Artificial Intelligence, Cyber Culture to Transhumanist Culture:
Change of the Age and Human 1
    Serap Uğur, Anadolu University, Turkey
    Gulsun Kurubacak, Anadolu University, Turkey

Section 2
Radical Futuristics

Chapter 2
Ability to Advance Knowledge and Capacity to Achieve the Impossible 18
    Natasha Vita-More, University of Advancing Technology, USA

Chapter 3
According to Zoltan Istvan: Transhumanism and Future 28
    Zoltan Istvan, Transhumanist Party, USA

Chapter 4
Automatic IQ Estimation Using Stylometric Methods 32
    Polina Shafran Abramov, University of Louisville, USA
    Roman V. Yampolskiy, University of Louisville, USA

Section 3
Technology and Learning

Chapter 5
Exocortex as a Learning Technology 47
Mehmet Emin Mutlu, Anadolu University, Turkey

Chapter 6
Transhumanism and Innovative Leadership: A Question of Quality 78
Ebba S. I. Ossiannilsson, ICDE OER Advocacy Committee, Sweden

Chapter 7
Ethical Issues in Transhumanism 98
Faruk Karaman, Konya Food and Agriculture University, Turkey

Chapter 8
Using Artificial Intelligence in Massive Open Online Courses: A Conceptual View to Wise
MOOCs 116
Emel Güler, Anadolu University, Turkey
Buket Karatop, Istanbul University-Cerrahpasa, Turkey

Chapter 9
Transforming the Classroom Experience Through Transhumanism: Education as the Learning
Organization 134
Mary Beth Klinger, College of Southern Maryland, USA
Teresa L. Coffman, University of Mary Washington, USA

Chapter 10
Artificial Intelligence in the Era of Transhumanism Smart Phones 157
Okan Aksu, Trakya University, Turkey

Chapter 11
The Role, Influence, and Demand of Pedagogies in the Age of Transhumanism: Critical
Reflections 171
Pradeep Kumar Misra, Chaudhary Charan Singh University, India

Chapter 12
Being a Post-Learner With Virtual Worlds 185
Ferhan Şahin, Anadolu University, Turkey
Ezgi Doğan, Anadolu University, Turkey

Chapter 13
Innovative Learning Approach in the 21st Century: Personal Learning Environments 205
Hakan Altinpulluk, Anadolu University, Turkey

Chapter 14
Artificial Intelligence in Education: Current Insights and Future Perspectives 224
    Nil Goksel, Anadolu University, Turkey
    Aras Bozkurt, Anadolu University, Turkey

Chapter 15
Online and Distance Education in the Era of Rampant Technological Revolution 237
    Hasan Ucar, Bilecik Seyh Edebali University, Turkey

Chapter 16
From Distance Education to Open and Distance Learning: A Holistic Evaluation of History,
Definitions, and Theories 252
    Aras Bozkurt, Anadolu University, Turkey

Chapter 17
A Case Study on Pre-Service English Teachers' Perceptions of Self-Efficacy and Integration of
Information-Communication Technologies 274
    Ilknur Istifci, Anadolu University, Turkey

Chapter 18
Educational Technologies in the Age of Transhumanism 291
    Şirin Karadeniz, Bahçeşehir University, Turkey
    Işıl Boy Ergül, Yıldız Teknik Üniversitesi, Turkey

Section 4
Business, Management, Law, and Health

Chapter 19
Business Management Learning: Research for the Age of Transhumanism 307
    Gürcan Banger, Railway Systems Cluster, Turkey

Chapter 20
Transhumanism and Positive Psychological Capital in Organizational Behavior 328
    Suzan Urgan, Ondokuz Mayıs University, Turkey

Chapter 21
An Evaluation of Transhumanist Bill of Rights From Current and Future Perspective: The
Adventure of Technohumanism and Rights 346
    Erdem Öngün, Trakya University, Turkey

Chapter 22
Statistical Resultant Analysis of Psychosomatic Survey on Various Human Personality Indicators:
Statistical Survey to Map Stress and Mental Health 363
    Rohit Rastogi, ABES Engineering College, India
    Devendra Kumar Chaturvedi, Dayalbagh Educational Institute, India
    Pallavi Sharma, ABES Engineering College, India
    Vishwas Yadav, ABES Engineering College, India
    Sumit Chauhan, ABES Engineering College, India
    Muskan Gulati, ABES Engineering College, India
    Mayank Gupta, Tata Consultancy Services, India
    Parv Singhal, ABES Engineering College, India

Compilation of References 384

About the Contributors 439

Index 446

Detailed Table of Contents

Foreword xxi

Preface xxii

Acknowledgment xxxi

Section 1
Introduction

Chapter 1
Artificial Intelligence to Super Artificial Intelligence, Cyber Culture to Transhumanist Culture:
Change of the Age and Human 1
    Serap Uğur, Anadolu University, Turkey
    Gulsun Kurubacak, Anadolu University, Turkey

The 21st century is a period in which technological developments constantly present new innovations. This broad spectrum, from computers to mobile technologies, from augmented reality to virtual reality, from wearable technologies to artificial intelligence, is radically changing societies' economies, education systems, governments, and even cultures. Artificial intelligence studies have reached a point where people discuss how a human-like intelligence would be. This leads to the emergence of systems that regulate the work, daily lives, communications, jobs, and even family budgets of people. These developments also change the living standards and styles of individuals. The cultural texture that technology has restructured is now called "cyber" beyond digital. But how will the future technologies affect this cultural change and what kind of change awaits?

Section 2
Radical Futuristics

Chapter 2
Ability to Advance Knowledge and Capacity to Achieve the Impossible 18
    Natasha Vita-More, University of Advancing Technology, USA

This chapter focuses on human achievement as accomplished with the use of technology to explore humanity's most daunting challenges. While ancient Promethean myths echo a threat of the human use of technology, transhumanism offers a social construct to inform and mitigate many impending threats. The aim is to encourage life-long learning—ongoing, voluntary, and self-motivated pursuit of knowledge—through immersive and educational platforms for ethical leadership in a world of rapid change. Notably, there are counter arguments to an intervention of the human condition, which often expose themselves as biases of moral perception that, in due course, fall short. Yet, humans continue to be fueled by curiosity and a need for amelioration to transcend limits. What is lacking and most imminently necessary to deal with the exponentially increasing technology in our midst, and to society's varied perceptions and reactions, is straightforward knowledge and guidance in navigating towards the telos of our humanity.

Chapter 3
According to Zoltan Istvan: Transhumanism and Future 28
   Zoltan Istvan, Transhumanist Party, USA

Radical science and technology are changing everything around us. The area of transhumanism is growing dramatically in size and impact - and the impact on our species is enormous. In just a decade, many things can change how we live our lives. The upcoming innovation will be amazing. Transhumanists believe that we must protect ourselves from our natural genes, unless they bind us to remain forever as animals. We believe that our outdated instincts can easily tempt us to know right from wrong, practical from impractical. If you look closely, the human body and its biology constantly highlights our many imperfections. Transhumanism seeks to improve the human body through science and technology - that is, to help people develop. This is a strange cultural and philosophical position for a movement. And yet, change is exactly what transhumanism aspires to.

Chapter 4
Automatic IQ Estimation Using Stylometric Methods 32
   Polina Shafran Abramov, University of Louisville, USA
   Roman V. Yampolskiy, University of Louisville, USA

Stylometry is a study of text linguistic properties that brings together various fields of research such as statistics, linguistics, computer science and more. Stylometry methods have been used for historic investigation, as forensic evidence and an educational tool. This chapter presents a method to automatically estimate individual's IQ based on quality of writing and discusses challenges associated with it. The method utilizes various text features and NLP techniques to calculate indexes which are used to estimate individual's IQ. The results show a high degree of correlation between expected and estimated IQs in cases when IQ is within the average range. Obtaining good estimation for IQs on the high and low ends of the spectrum proves to be more challenging and this work offers several reasons for that. Over the years stylometry benefitted from wide exposure and interest among researches, however it appears that there aren't studies that focus on using stylometry methods to estimate individual's intelligence. Perhaps this work presents the first in-depth attempt to do so.

Section 3
Technology and Learning

Chapter 5
Exocortex as a Learning Technology.. 47
   Mehmet Emin Mutlu, Anadolu University, Turkey

Exocortex is a hypothetical technology where the human brain can connect to a brain implant or a computational environment which is in the state of a wearable device, using two-way brain-computer interface, in order to augment the cognitive powers of the human brain such as perception, storage, recollection and processing. Exocortex is expected to be a part of everyday life in the 2030s. Exocortex technology is supported by parallel technologies such as brain reading, uploading knowledge into the brain from the outside, brain-computer interface, brain-to-brain interface, which are now undergoing prototype applications. In this study, by discussing the potential of exocortex technology in its use for learning processes, as a result of handling it with the "learning experiences management" approach, the opportunities it provides specifically for lifelong learners are examined. In the results and recommendations section of the study, a foresight is given for the scientific research projects that can be performed for this purpose.

Chapter 6
Transhumanism and Innovative Leadership: A Question of Quality... 78
   Ebba S. I. Ossiannilsson, ICDE OER Advocacy Committee, Sweden

Rethinking leadership at all levels is required to reach the goals of learning and education in 2030 through which learners will take the lead in orchestrating the process and manner of their own learning and in choosing their personal learning journeys. The fourth industrial revolution will continue to change the ways we act, perform, live, work, and learn. Therefore, there is a need for a social revolution that includes the understanding of transhumanism and its effects. The term "cutting edge" does not concern technology as much as it concerns humans. Accordingly, transhumanism is crucial for a sustainable ecosystem of learning with and through technology and digital transformation, which encompasses all levels of institutions—macro, meso, and micro. This chapter is focused on future trends, issues, and challenges in management and leadership as well as on issues and challenges in communication, which is essential in both leadership and smart learning.

Chapter 7
Ethical Issues in Transhumanism.. 98
   Faruk Karaman, Konya Food and Agriculture University, Turkey

Transhumanism seems to be inevitable. There seems to be no way to stop the developments leading humanity to transhumanism. As Heidegger puts, technological determinism rules, rather than social determinism. In other words, the technology controls the society, not the other way around. Therefore, in a short time period, people will be forced to face the challenges of transhumanism. It is therefore the right time to prepare for those challenges before they became mainstream. Tomorrow, it will be too late. Academicians, educators, politicians, philosophers, intellectuals, psychologists … etc. all should concentrate on the issue. This chapter will try to answer such questions and many others. A philosophical approach is used. After all, ethics is a branch of philosophy. Since, this is a futuristic topic, it is hard to find first-hand data and conduct survey analysis etc. Therefore, this is a theoretical chapter.

Chapter 8
Using Artificial Intelligence in Massive Open Online Courses: A Conceptual View to Wise
MOOCs 116
   Emel Güler, Anadolu University, Turkey
   Buket Karatop, Istanbul University-Cerrahpasa, Turkey

It can be said that the reflection of the philosophy of Transhumanism on education creates a threat to the survival of human civilization or, on the contrary, focuses on technologies that try to create opportunities to overcome basic human limitations. MOOCs are still a major tool in the ongoing development of opportunities to teach the whole community. With MOOCs, interactive student-oriented large audiences can be reached instantly. The MOOCs, which offer great opportunities, should be made intelligent by the interaction of the curricula and the learner in order to achieve more effective results. As MOOCs are student-friendly, it is important that, when preparing training materials, the curriculum is formulated strategically. It is important that stakeholders' views are involved in decision-making using artificial intelligence techniques because learning is too important to be left to coincidence.

Chapter 9
Transforming the Classroom Experience Through Transhumanism: Education as the Learning Organization.. 134
    Mary Beth Klinger, College of Southern Maryland, USA
    Teresa L. Coffman, University of Mary Washington, USA

This chapter examines the intersection of transhumanism and the use of technology as a cognitive tool in education. Transhumanism is explored as a pedagogical philosophy to transform the limits of self by using educational technology tools to expand global networked knowledge. These tools include technologies that stimulate learning to expand and extend cognitive and metacognitive capabilities. The role of pedagogy is to create educative experiences that provide meaningful opportunities for students to cultivate deeper conceptual understandings. Students learn necessary skills and develop knowledge to improve conceptual competencies and cognitive capabilities. When human thought and capabilities are used in conjunction with technology as a cognitive instructional tool, the learning experience is transformed. The potential exists to extend the conceptual competencies of the learner, thus realizing the transhumanists' goal of transforming learning experiences and improving student potential.

Chapter 10
Artificial Intelligence in the Era of Transhumanism Smart Phones 157
    Okan Aksu, Trakya University, Turkey

The relationship between humans and machines has been a controversial topic throughout history. In the past, technology was viewed as a mere change in people's living conditions while today it is evident that it affects the nature of humanity itself. This very change can range from microscale structures, such as human DNA, to bigger structures, such as limbs. We have been aware that it is just the beginning for this change. According to the theory of transhumanism, further changes on the human body are expected with the rapid developments in technology. These changes will naturally not be limited to the human body. The increasing amount of interaction between humans and machines will result in the execution of more complicated and difficult tasks by machines instead of humans, which is the focus of the present study. There are many points where the humans and machines meet with technological developments, one of which is the thinking function of humans and its possible transfer to machines. The thinking capacity of machines is known as artificial intelligence.

Chapter 11
The Role, Influence, and Demand of Pedagogies in the Age of Transhumanism: Critical Reflections... 171
    Pradeep Kumar Misra, Chaudhary Charan Singh University, India

Whether pedagogies play a role in the age of transhumanism is a question that has no certain answers. There are some who say that pedagogies do not play any role in transhumanism while some say that pedagogies appear to play a role in this movement. Agreeing to the later observation, this chapter proposes that pedagogies have a relationship with transhumanism and will play a very important role in the transhumanistic societies of the future. Extending these arguments and observations, present paper assesses the role, influence and demand of pedagogies in the age of transhumanism. In this quest, present chapter: defines pedagogy and discusses its importance; enumerates the relationship between pedagogy and transhumanism; analyses the role of pedagogies in the age of transhumanism; looks upon the influence and demand of pedagogies in the age of transhumanism; and predicts the future of pedagogies in transhumanistic societies.

Chapter 12
Being a Post-Learner With Virtual Worlds 185
    Ferhan Şahin, Anadolu University, Turkey
    Ezgi Doğan, Anadolu University, Turkey

Transhumanism, which emerges as a movement of thought, stands out with the developments such as artificial organs, brain-to-brain knowledge and learning transfer and smart robots in the 21st century. One of these technologies, where we see early applications with the goal of reaching the post-human, is the virtual worlds. Some features of the post-humans, which can now be experienced through 3 dimensional immersive virtual worlds in a certain scale, also reveal the fact that the existing virtual worlds are a limited simulation of a transhumanist future. While the virtual worlds and transhumanism perspective is expected to be effective in various areas of human life, it will be inevitable for these effects to manifest themselves in learning processes. In this sense, evaluation of surrounding learning by virtual worlds is the main objective of this chapter. For this purpose, virtual worlds in transhumanism age were tried to be evaluated under learning context by using anime series and film samples which are yet considered as sci-fi.

Chapter 13
Innovative Learning Approach in the 21st Century: Personal Learning Environments 205
    Hakan Altinpulluk, Anadolu University, Turkey

The ease of access to information, which has become evident with the development of communication technologies such as the internet, has brought about revolutionary changes in education. With the development of Web 2.0 technologies, the strengthening of social networks and the process of the learners taking responsibility for their own learning, personal learning environments (PLEs) have emerged. PLE is a connectivism and network-based learning environment where the learning process is more flexible and the management of learning is in charge of the learner instead of the teacher or other person. It is regarded to be the learning environment for the future generations consisting of components that keep the learner active at all times as open, flexible, social network-based and cooperative Web 2.0. environments. In this section, definition of PLE, its ways of use, its advantages over the other learning systems, limitations and recommendations for use, are listed.

Chapter 14
Artificial Intelligence in Education: Current Insights and Future Perspectives............................ 224
    Nil Goksel, Anadolu University, Turkey
    Aras Bozkurt, Anadolu University, Turkey

Though only a dream a while ago, artificial intelligence (AI) has become a reality, being now part of our routines and penetrating every aspect of our lives, including education. It is still a field in its infancy, but as time progresses, we will witness how AI evolves and explore its untapped potential. Against this background, this chapter examines current insights and future perspectives of AI in various contexts, such as natural language processing (NLP), machine learning, and deep learning. For this purpose, social network analysis (SNA) is used as a guide for the interpretation of the key concepts in AI research from an educational perspective. The research identified three broad themes: (1) adaptive learning, personalization and learning styles, (2) expert systems and intelligent tutoring systems, and (3) AI as a future component of educational processes.

Chapter 15
Online and Distance Education in the Era of Rampant Technological Revolution 237
    Hasan Ucar, Bilecik Seyh Edebali University, Turkey

Developments in information and communication technologies have reached an all-time high. These improvements have accelerated the transformation of higher education milieus on all sides. Accordingly, higher education institutions have begun to be delineated by these technological developments, activities, and practices. This technoculture era has started a new interaction among communication technologies, teachers, and learners. Herein, transhumanism regards changes in societies through these technological interactions and transformations. The worldwide technological transformation is approximating all societies and cultures to Marshall McLuhan's notion of a global village day by day as a consequence of the technology paradigm. The heydays of the developments in technologies affect all human beings at all points from living, learning, communicating to eating and even thinking styles. Taking these points into account, this chapter will explore how these variables may influence the online distance education milieus in terms of technoculture and transhumanism perspectives.

Chapter 16
From Distance Education to Open and Distance Learning: A Holistic Evaluation of History,
Definitions, and Theories... 252
    Aras Bozkurt, Anadolu University, Turkey

As pragmatist, interdisciplinary fields, distance education (DE) and open and distance learning (ODL) transform and adapt themselves according to changing paradigms. In this regard, the purpose of this study is to examine DE and ODL from different perspectives to discern their future directions. The study concludes that DE and ODL are constantly developing interdisciplinary fields where technology has become a significant catalyst and these fields become part of the mainstream education. However, mainstreaming should be evaluated with caution, and there is a need to revisit core values and fundamentals where critical pedagogy would have a pivotal role. Besides, there is no single theory that best explains these interdisciplinary fields, and therefore, there is a need to benefit from different theoretical approaches. Finally, as a result of constant changes, we should keep the definition of both DE and ODL up-to-date to better explain the needs of the global teaching and learning ecosystem.

Chapter 17
A Case Study on Pre-Service English Teachers' Perceptions of Self-Efficacy and Integration of
Information-Communication Technologies 274
    Ilknur Istifci, Anadolu University, Turkey

The aim of this study is to find out pre-service English language teachers' ICT self-efficacy perceptions and ICT integration in their lessons. The data were collected from 60 pre-service English teachers in one of the state universities in Turkey via a questionnaire developed by Ekici, Ekici, and Kara. Semi-structured interviews were also carried out with some volunteering pre-service teachers. The questionnaire data were analyzed using the Statistical Package for Social Sciences (SPSS 22). Interview data were analyzed finding emerging themes and categorizing them using constant comparison method. The results showed that they use ICTs in their lessons mostly especially in practicum or macro and micro teaching sessions and they have high self-efficacy on ICT use in language education. Results also revealed some problems they encounter while using ICTs in language teacher education and their suggestions on how to improve their use. Based on the results, certain implications were drawn from the study in order to organize future teacher education programs that utilize ICTs.

Chapter 18
Educational Technologies in the Age of Transhumanism 291
    Şirin Karadeniz, Bahçeşehir University, Turkey
    Işıl Boy Ergül, Yıldız Teknik Üniversitesi, Turkey

Transhumanism has created drastic changes in many different sectors, especially in education as it is directly related to how we grow and shape our lives. Transhumanist technologies, especially augmented reality (AR), virtual reality (VR), and artificial intelligence (AI), play an important role in education and provide new opportunities by facilitating the communication between students and teachers and students and other students in order to obtain fruitful learning outcomes. In this chapter, transhumanist technologies used in teaching and learning will be discussed with a critical analysis, and how these technologies can change the way people learn will be explained through the lens of transhumanism.

Section 4
Business, Management, Law, and Health

Chapter 19
Business Management Learning: Research for the Age of Transhumanism 307
    Gürcan Banger, Railway Systems Cluster, Turkey

The Transhumanist future will be an age of data dominance, pervasive computing, artificial intelligence, smart machines, and autonomous mobile robots accompanied by a vast speed and ever-increasing acceleration of change. The pervasive and ongoing change requires a fundamental re-invention of business management which should coincide with the conditions of the converging transhumanism age. The main feature of the future management paradigms that differ from the traditional style will undoubtedly be the artificial intelligence with several applications of machine learning and humans' collaborative work with associate-like autonomous robots. Managers at all levels will have to adapt to the world of artificial intelligence and smart environment. The transhumanist manager should learn and get equipped with the necessary management requirements. The new learning platforms, methods, techniques, and media should be researched to get prepared for a transhumanist business management future with a faster alacrity to compensate for the speed of the technological progress.

Chapter 20
Transhumanism and Positive Psychological Capital in Organizational Behavior 328
   Suzan Urgan, Ondokuz Mayıs University, Turkey

The efforts to extend the human life have been one of the most discussed topics in all periods of history. Advances in science and technology lead the way to these pursuits. Especially with the developments related to artificial intelligence, it is thought that in many fields, human life will change radically in the future. Transhumanism refers to studies that are performed for the human to live a good life psychologically, physiologically and socially through extending the life span. The ability of a person to live a better life depends on his harmony with hope, optimism, resilience and self-efficacy, which indicate his positive psychological capital, as much as the progress in science and technology. With the study, transhumanism and positive psychological capital have been examined in the framework of organizational behavior, and how life in the future might be has been stated.

Chapter 21
An Evaluation of Transhumanist Bill of Rights From Current and Future Perspective: The Adventure of Technohumanism and Rights 346
   Erdem Öngün, Trakya University, Turkey

Science and technology are now radically changing human beings and how they help create various future forms of advanced sapient and sentient life in a transhumanist future and their related rights. In that process, the issue of transhumanist rights for such forms attract a great attention that is worth rethinking. Transhumanist Bill of Rights mainly covers "sentient entities" such as human beings, including genetically modified humans, digital intelligences, cyborgs, intellectually enhanced, previously non-sapient animals, any species of plant or animal enhanced to possess the capacity for intelligent thought, and other advanced sapient life forms. In that respect, the main concern of this chapter basically centers around the question to what extent transhumanist rights will be compatible and applicable enough to meet the needs of all sentient entities and forms on universal basis in a transhumanist world, which stands on the line between a dystopian and utopian future.

Chapter 22
Statistical Resultant Analysis of Psychosomatic Survey on Various Human Personality Indicators: Statistical Survey to Map Stress and Mental Health 363
   Rohit Rastogi, ABES Engineering College, India
   Devendra Kumar Chaturvedi, Dayalbagh Educational Institute, India
   Pallavi Sharma, ABES Engineering College, India
   Vishwas Yadav, ABES Engineering College, India
   Sumit Chauhan, ABES Engineering College, India
   Muskan Gulati, ABES Engineering College, India
   Mayank Gupta, Tata Consultancy Services, India
   Parv Singhal, ABES Engineering College, India

Machines are getting intelligent day by day. Modern science has gifted us many boons but simultaneously the mental, physical and spiritual disorders have surprisingly disturbed smile, peace and definite attitude and lifestyle of individual and all human beings. The stress has been the biggest challenge against mankind like nuclear weapons, global warming, and epidemics. It leads towards tension, frustration, and depression and ultimately in extreme cases towards the suicide or murder of innocents. The happiness index, safety of individual, living parameters have drastically challenged us and India specially has pathetic situation among global quality of life (QoL) index. This chapter is an effort to define a simulated model and framework for the subjective quality of stress into quantitative parameters and mathematically analyzing it with help of popular machine learning tools and applied methods. Using machine intelligence, authors are trying to establish a framework which may work as an expert system and may help the individual to grow self as better human being.

Compilation of References 384

About the Contributors 439

Index 446

Foreword

There is little doubt we live in times of profound and unprecedented change. The challenges and risks equal the opportunities as a deep and sustained transformation of everything we mean by human occurs around us. We may be the first humans to recognize that we hold the destiny of life itself on this planet – as well as our own survival as a species – in our own hands. How we approach this awesome responsibility requires deep resources in terms of values, norms and beliefs – as well as a profound grasp of the imperative to learn (and learn how to learn) so that we can go beyond information and knowledge to the bedrock of wisdom itself. Transhumanism is a movement that recognizes the extraordinary potential of technology and digital realities to allow us to transcend our current limitations and achieve ever more astounding levels of human performance and quality of life. Is this merely science fiction? Is it a Faustian deal fraught with danger? Is it an illusion that blunts our human need for mutual care and emotional warmth, replacing this with cybernetic peril?

We cannot begin to answer these questions unless we face squarely the issues posed. This valuable book confronts us with the realities of the potential we have unleashed for technologies to impact our lives, functions and relationships. The spectacular rise of Artificial Intelligence alone brings us face to face with undreamt of possibilities for human freedom, or enslavement. In the world of learning – both formal and informal – the implications are vast and pervasive. This book gives us an expert guide through the opportunities and challenges. In a curious way, these extraordinary technologies bring us both forward to a luminous future of creative options but also back to questions first posed when our ancestors contemplated the galaxies above them or the basic moral questions that underline our humanity. Transhumanism – however we view it – does not determine our fate as we become passive spectators on our own lives. It confronts us with choices. And choice is what makes us sustainably human – it is what we pass on to those we love. Choices between servile adaptation to a hostile universe, or a boundless sense that emancipatory learning is what the educator's task is ultimately about.

Let these chapters enthrall and stimulate and challenge you. While you always remember that going beyond humanity does not abandon life but dares us to live it even more fully and passionately.

Alan Bruce
Universal Learning System, Ireland

Preface

Dr. Ramesh Sharma highlighted that since the time humans have started teaching and learning, there has been a persistent question such as, "what is the appropriate pedagogy to teach this?" Many methods of teaching have been proposed and designed. Much research has gone into learning styles and design thinking about how to promote advanced learning with the help of technologies. Whether the learning is happening in face-to-face classrooms or through distance education mode or fully online or via mobile devices, learning effectiveness has been the prime concern. With the introduction of modern ICT, traditional educational approaches have been transformed both qualitatively and quantitatively. From knowledge receiver, the learner of today is knowledge generator. It has resulted in a significant shift in educational pedagogy and theory. The chapter addresses such issues as how online facilitation, classroom learner behavior, learner engagement, teacher's perception and teaching can be improved by new pedagogies in the age of transhumanism.

Therefore, learning about technologies, with technologies and for technologies must be one of the most important focuses of transhumanism. Not only can transhumanism radically change human habits, but also learning practices. Therefore, the aim of this handbook is to foresee a futuristic view of how transhumanism can achieve the sustainability in the context of human learning to prevent human intelligence in the future. The foundation of a revolutionary transformation on human learning will be established for the social networks. Thus, transhumanism must be sustainable, and transform humans through ecological learning environments.

This book, consisting of 24 chapters, is divided into four sections: Introductions; Radical Futuristics; Technology and Learning; and Business, Management, Law and Health;

- **Chapter 1: Artificial Intelligence to Super Artificial Intelligence, Cyber Culture to Transhumanist Culture – Change of the Age and Human by Serap Uğur, Gülsün Kurubacak**

The 21st century is a period in which technological developments constantly present new innovations. This broad spectrum, from computers to mobile technologies, from augmented reality to virtual reality, from wearable technologies to artificial intelligence, is radically changing societies' economies, education systems, governments and even cultures. Artificial intelligence studies have reached to a point where people discuss how a human-like intelligence would be. This leads to the emergence of systems that regulate the work, daily lives, communications, jobs, and even family budgets of people. These developments also change the living standards and styles of individuals. The cultural texture that technology has restructured is now called "cyber" beyond digital. But how will the future technologies affect this cultural change and what kind of change awaits?

Preface

- **Chapter 2: Ability to Advance Knowledge and Capacity to Achieve the Impossible by Natasha Vita-More**

This chapter focuses on human achievement as accomplished with the use of technology to explore humanity's most daunting challenges. While ancient Promethean myths echo a threat of the human use of technology, transhumanism offers a social construct to inform and mitigate many impending threats. The aim is to encourage life-long learning—ongoing, voluntary, and self-motivated pursuit of knowledge—through immersive and educational platforms for ethical leadership in a world of rapid change. Notably, there are counter arguments to an intervention of the human condition, which often expose themselves as biases of moral perception that, in due course, fall short. Yet, humans continue to be fueled by curiosity and a need for amelioration to transcend limits. What is lacking and most imminently necessary to deal with the exponentially increasing technology in our midst, and to society's varied perceptions and reactions, is straightforward knowledge and guidance in navigating towards the telos of our humanity.

- **Chapter 3: According to Zoltan Istvan, Transhumanism, and Future by Zoltan Istvan**

This chapter is compiled from the articles on huffingtonpost.com.written by Istvan. Transhumanism is an international movement that aims to use technology to overcome ageing and eventually biological death. Transhumanists advocate research into technologies that can enhance human intellectual, physical and psychological capabilities, such as brain implants, bionic eyes and exoskeleton body suits. Humans are handicapped by our biology. We operate tens of thousands of years behind evolution with our inherited instincts, which means our behavior is not suited towards its current environment. Futurists like to say evolution is always late to the dinner party. We have instincts that apply to our biology in a world that existed ages ago; not a world of skyscrapers, cell phones, jet air travel, the Internet, and CRISPR gene editing technology. We must catch up to ourselves. We must evolve our thinking to adapt to where we are in the evolutionary ascent. We must force our evolution in the present day via our reasoning, inventiveness, and especially our scientific technology. In short, we must embrace transhumanism—the radical field of science that aims to turn humans into, for lack of a better word, gods.

- **Chapter 4: Automatic IQ Estimation Using Stylometric Methods by Polina Abramov, Roman Yampolskiy**

Stylometry is a study of text's linguistic properties that has multiple applications in the world of academia, education, forensics, security and more. Over the years stylometry benefitted from wide exposure and interest among researchers, however there aren't many studies that focus on using stylometric methods to estimate individual's intelligence. This research presents a method to automatically estimate individual's IQ based on quality of writing and discusses challenges associated with it. The method utilizes several text features and NLP techniques to estimate individual's IQ. The results show a high degree of correlation between expected and estimated IQs in cases when IQ is within the average range. Obtaining good estimation for IQ scores that fall outside of average range proves to be more challenging and this work offers several explanations for that.

- **Chapter 5: Exocortex as a Learning Technology by Mehmet Emin Mutlu**

Exocortex is a hypothetical technology where human brain can connect to a brain implant or a computational environment which is in the state of a wearable device, using two-way brain-computer interface, in order to augment the cognitive powers of the human brain such as perception, storage, recollection and processing. Exocortex is expected to be a part of everyday life in the 2030s. Exocortex technology is supported by parallel technologies such as brain reading, uploading knowledge into the brain from the outside, brain-computer interface, brain-to-brain interface, which are now undergoing prototype applications. In this study, by discussing the potential of exocortex technology in its use for learning processes, as a result of handling it with the "learning experiences management" approach, the opportunities it provides specifically for lifelong learners are examined. In the results and recommendations section of the study, a foresight is given for the scientific research projects that can be performed for this purpose.

- **Chapter 6: Transhumanism and İnnovative Leadership – A Question of Quality by Ebba Ossiannilsson**

Rethinking leadership at all levels is required to reach the goals of learning and education in 2030 through which learners will take the lead in orchestrating the process and manner of their own learning and in choosing their personal learning journeys. The fourth industrial revolution will continue to change the ways we act, perform, live, work, and learn. Therefore, there is a need for a social revolution that includes the understanding of transhumanism and its effects. The term "cutting edge" does not concern technology as much as it concerns humans. Accordingly, transhumanism is crucial for a sustainable ecosystem of learning with and through technology and digital transformation, which encompasses all levels of institutions—macro, meso, and micro. This chapter is focused on future trends, issues, and challenges in management and leadership as well as on issues and challenges in communication, which is essential in both leadership and smart learning.

- **Chapter 7: Ethical Issues in Transhumanism by Faruk Karaman**

Transhumanism seems to be inevitable. There seems to be no way to stop the developments leading humanity to transhumanism. As Heidegger puts, technological determinism rules, rather then social determinism. In other words, the technology controls the society, not the other way around. Therefore, in a short time period, people will be forced to face the challenges of transhumanism. It is therefore right time to prepare for those challenges before they became mainstream. Tomorrow, it will be too late. Academicians, educators, politicians, philosophers, intellectuals, psychologists … etc all should concentrate on the issue. This chapter will try to answer such questions and many others. A philosophical approach is used. After all, ethics is a branch of philosophy. Since, this is a futuristic topic, it is hard to find first-hand data and conduct survey analysis etc. Therefore, this is a theoretical chapter.

- **Chapter 8: Using Artificial Intelligence in Massive Open Online Courses – A Conceptual View to Wise MOOCs by Emel Güler, Buket Karatop**

It can be said that the reflection of the philosophy of Transhumanism on education, which creates a threat to the survival of human civilization or, on the contrary, focuses on technologies that try to create opportunities to overcome basic human limitations. MOOCs are still a major tool in the ongoing development and at the same time learning the great opportunities, teaching and even offering the whole

Preface

community. With MOOCs, interactive student-oriented large audiences can be reached instantly. The MOOCs, which offer great opportunities, should be made intelligent by the interaction of the curricula and the learner in order to achieve more effective and effective results. As MOOCs are student-friendly, it is important that, when preparing training materials, the curriculum is formulated, and strategically, it is important that stakeholders' views are involved in decision-making using artificial intelligence techniques. Because learning is too important to be left to coincidence.

- **Chapter 9: Transforming the Classroom Experience Through Transhumanism – Education as the Learning Organization by Mary Beth Klinger, Teresa L. Coffman**

This chapter examines the intersection of transhumanism and the use of technology as a cognitive tool in education. Transhumanism is explored as a pedagogical philosophy to transform the limits of self by using educational technology tools to expand global networked knowledge. These tools include technologies that stimulate learning to expand and extend cognitive and metacognitive capabilities. The role of pedagogy is to create educative experiences that provide meaningful opportunities for students to cultivate deeper conceptual understandings. Students learn necessary skills and develop knowledge to improve conceptual competencies and cognitive capabilities. When human thought and capabilities are used in conjunction with technology as a cognitive instructional tool, the learning experience is transformed. The potential exists to extend the conceptual competencies of the learner, thus realizing the transhumanists goal of transforming learning experiences and improving student potential.

- **Chapter 10: Artificial intelligence in the Era of Transhumanism Smart Phones by Okan Aksu**

The relationship between humans and machines has been a controversial topic throughout history. In the past, technology was viewed as a mere change in people's living conditions while today it is evident that it affects the nature of humanity itself. This very change can range from microscale structures, such as human DNA, to bigger structures, such as limbs. We have been aware that it is just the beginning for this change. According to the theory of transhumanism, further changes on human body are expected with the rapid developments in technology. These changes will naturally not be limited to the human body. The increasing amount of interaction between humans and machines will result in the execution of more complicated and difficult tasks by machines instead of humans, which is the focus of the present study. There are many points where the humans and machines meet with technological developments, one of which is the thinking function of humans and its possible transfer to machines. The thinking capacity of machines is known as Artificial Intelligence.

- **Chapter 11: The Role, Influence, and Demand of Pedagogies in the Age of Transhumanism Critical Reflections by Pradeep Kumar Misra**

Whether pedagogies play a role in the age of transhumainsim, is a question that has no certain answers. There are some who say that pedagogies do not play any role in transhumainsim while some say that pedagogies appear to play a role in this movement. Agreeing to the later observation, this chapter proposes that pedagogies have a relationship with transhumansim and will play a very important role in the transhuamanistic societies of future. Extending these arguments and observations, present paper assesses the role, influence and demand of pedagogies in the age of transhumanism. In this quest, present chapter: defines pedagogy and discusses its importance; enumerates the relationship between pedagogy and transhumanism; analyses the role of pedagogies in the age of transhumanism; looks upon the influence and demand of pedagogies in the age of transhumanism; and predicts the future of pedagogies in transhumanisitc societies.

- **Chapter 12: Being a Post-Learner With Virtual Worlds by Ezgi Doğan, Ferhan Şahin**

Transhumanism, which emerges as a movement of thought, stands out with the developments such as artificial organs, brain-to-brain knowledge and learning transfer and smart robots in the 21st century. One of these Technologies, where we see early applications with the goal of reaching the post-human, is the virtual worlds. Some features of the post-humans, which can now be experienced through 3 dimensional immersive virtual worlds in a certain scale, also reveals the fact that the existing virtual worlds are a limited simulation of a transhumanist future. While the virtual worlds and transhumanism perspective is expected to be effective in various areas of human life, it will be inevitable for these effects to manifest themselves in learning processes. In this sense, evaluation of surrounding learning by virtual worlds is the main objective of this chapter. For this purpose virtual worlds in transhumanism age were tried to be evaluated under learning context by using anime series and film samples which are yet considered as sci-fi.

- **Chapter 13: Innovative Learning Approach in 21st Century – Personal Learning Environments by Hakan Altınpulluk**

The ease of access to information, which has become evident with the development of communication technologies such as the internet, has brought about revolutionary changes in education. With the development of Web 2.0 technologies, the strengthening of social networks and the process of the learners taking responsibility for their own learning, personal learning environments (PLEs) have emerged. PLE is a connectivism and network-based learning environment where the learning process is more flexible and the management of learning is in charge of the learner instead of the teacher or other person. It is regarded to be the learning environment for the future generations consisting of components that keep the learner active at all times as open, flexible, social network-based and cooperative Web 2.0. environments. In this section, definition of PLE, its ways of use, its advantages over the other learning systems, limitations and recommendations for use, are listed.

- **Chapter 14: Artificial Intelligence in Education – Current Insights and Future Perspectives by Nil Göksel, Aras Bozkurt**

Though only a dream a while ago, artificial intelligence (AI) has become a reality, being now part of our routines and penetrating every aspect of our lives, including education. It is still a field in its infancy, but as time progresses, we will witness how AI evolves and explore its untapped potential. Against this background, this chapter examines current insights and future perspectives of AI in various contexts, such as Natural Language Processing (NLP), Machine Learning, and Deep Learning. For this purpose, Social Network Analysis (SNA) is used as a guide for the interpretation of the key concepts in AI research from an educational perspective. The research identified three broad themes: (1) adaptive learning, personalization and learning styles, (2) expert systems and intelligent tutoring systems, and (3) AI as a future component of educational processes.

- **Chapter 15: Online and Distance Education in the Era of Rampant Technological Revolution by Hasan Uçar**

Developments in information and communication technologies have reached an all-time high. These improvements have accelerated the transformation of higher education milieus on all sides. Accordingly, higher education institutions have begun to be delineated by these technological developments, activities, and practices. This technoculture era has started a new interaction among communication technologies, teachers, and learners. Herein, transhumanism regards changes in societies through these technological interactions and transformations. The worldwide technological transformation is approximating all societies and cultures to Marshall McLuhan's notion of a global village day by day as a consequence of the technology paradigm. The heydays of the developments in technologies affect all human beings at all points from living, learning, communicating to eating and even thinking styles. Taking these points into account, this chapter will explore how these variables may influence the online distance education milieus in terms of technoculture and transhumanism perspectives.

- **Chapter 16: From Distance Education to Open and Distance Learning – A Holistic Evaluation of History, Definitions, and Theories by Aras Bozkurt**

As pragmatist, interdisciplinary fields, distance education (DE) and open and distance learning (ODL) transform and adapt themselves according to changing paradigms. In this regard, the purpose of this study, is to examine DE and ODL from different perspectives to discern their future directions. The study concludes that DE and ODL are constantly developing interdisciplinary fields where technology has become a significant catalyst and these fields become part of the mainstream education. However, mainstreaming should be evaluated with caution, and there is a need to revisit core values and fundamentals where critical pedagogy would have a pivotal role. Besides, there is no single theory that best explain these interdisciplinary fields, and therefore, there is a need to benefit from different theoretical approaches. Finally, as a result of constant changes, we should keep the definition of both DE and ODL up-to-date to better explain the needs of the global teaching and learning ecosystem.

- **Chapter 17: A Case Study on Pre-Service English Teachers' Perceptions of Self-Efficacy and Integration of Information-Communication Technologies by İlknur İstifçi**

The aim of this study is to find out pre-service English language teachers' ICT self-efficacy perceptions and ICT integration in their lessons. The data were collected from 60 pre-service English teachers in one of the state universities in Turkey via a questionnaire developed by Ekici, Ekici and Kara (2012). Semi-structured interviews were also carried out with some volunteering pre-service teachers. The questionnaire data were analyzed using the Statistical Package for Social Sciences (SPSS 22). Interview data were analyzed finding emerging themes and categorizing them using Constant Comparison Method. The results showed that they use ICTs in their lessons mostly especially in practicum or macro and micro teaching sessions and they have high self-efficacy on ICT use in language education. Results also revealed some problems they encounter while using ICTs in language teacher education and their suggestions on how to improve their use. Based on the results, certain implications were drawn from the study in order to organize future teacher education programs that utilize ICTs.

- **Chapter 18: Educational Technologies in the Age of Transhumanism by Şirin Karadeniz and Işıl Boy Ergül**

Transhumanism has created drastic changes in many different sectors, especially in education as it is directly related to how we grow and shape our lives. Transhumanist technologies, especially Augmented Reality (AR), Virtual Reality (VR) and Artificial Intelligence (AI) play an important role in education and provide new opportunities by facilitating the communication between students and teachers and students- students in order to obtain fruitful learning outcomes. In this chapter, transhumanist technologies used in teaching and learning will be discussed with a critical analysis, and how these technologies can change the way people learn will be explained through the lens of transhumanism.

- **Chapter 19: Business Management Learning – Research for the Age of Transhumanism by Gürcan Banger**

The Transhumanist future will be an age of data dominance, pervasive computing, artificial intelligence, smart machines, and autonomous mobile robots accompanied by a vast speed and ever-increasing acceleration of change. The pervasive and ongoing change requires a fundamental re-invention of business management which should coincide with the conditions of the converging Transhumanism Age. The main feature of the future management paradigms that differ from the traditional style will undoubtedly be the artificial intelligence with several applications of machine learning and human's collaborative work with associate-like autonomous robots. Managers at all levels will have to adapt to the world of artificial intelligence and smart environment. The transhumanist manager should learn and get equipped with the necessary management requirements. The new learning platforms, methods, techniques, and media should be researched to get prepared for a transhumanist business management future with a faster alacrity to compensate for the speed of the technological progress.

- **Chapter 20: Transhumanism and Positive Psychological Capital in Organizational Behavior by Suzan Urgan**

The efforts to extend the human life have been one of the most discussed topics in all periods of history. Advances in science and technology lead the way to these pursuits. Especially with the developments related to artificial intelligence, it is thought that in many fields, human life will change radically in the future. Transhumanism refers to studies that are performed for the human to live a good life psychologically, physiologically and socially through extending the life span. The ability of a person to live a better life depends on his harmony with hope, optimism, resilience and self-efficacy, which indicate his positive psychological capital, as much as the progress in science and technology. With the study, transhumanism and positive psychological capital have been examined in the framework of organizational behavior, and how life in the future might be has been stated.

- **Chapter 21: An Evaluation of Transhumanist Bill of Rights From Current and Future Perspective – The Adventure of Technohumanism and Rights by Erdem Öngün**

Preface

Science and technology are now radically changing human beings and how they help create various future forms of advanced sapient and sentient life in a transhumanist future and their related rights. In that process, the issue of Transhumanist Rights for such forms attract a great attention that is worth rethinking. Transhumanist Bill of Rights mainly covers "sentient entities" such as human beings, including genetically modified humans, digital intelligences, cyborgs, intellectually enhanced, previously non-sapient animals, any species of plant or animal enhanced to possess the capacity for intelligent thought, and other advanced sapient life forms. In that respect, the main concern of this chapter basically centers around the question to what extent transhumanist rights will be compatible and applicable enough to meet the needs of all sentient entities and forms on universal basis in a transhumanist world, which stands on the line between a dystopian and utopian future.

- **Chapter 22: Statistical Resultant Analysis of Psychosomatic Survey on Various Human Personality Indicators – Statistical Survey to Map Stress and Mental Health by Rohit Rastogi, Devendra Kumar Chaturvedi, Pallavi Sharma, Vishwas Yadav, Sumit Chauhan**

Machines are getting intelligent day by day. Modern science has gifted us many boons but simultaneously the mental, physical and spiritual disorders have surprisingly disturbed smile, peace and definite attitude and life style of individual and all human beings. The stress has been the biggest challenge against mankind like nuclear weapons, global warming and epidemics. It leads towards tension, frustration and depression and ultimately in extreme cases towards the self suicide or murder of innocents. The happiness index, safety of individual, living parameters have been drastically challenged us and the India specially has pathetic situation among global quality of life (QoL) index. This chapter is an effort to define a simulated model and framework for the subjective quality of stress into quantitative parameters and mathematically analyzing it with help of popular machine learning tools and applied methods. Using machine intelligence, authors are trying to establish a framework which may work as an expert system and may help the individual to grow self as better human being.

This publication can be used for researchers, mentors, facilitators and tutors as well as learners. As it covers the management, communication, pedagogy, technology/computing, evaluation, biology/genetics/psychology, and sociology/intelligent social networks-based future trends, issues and challenges of learning in the age of transhumanism, the chapters answer their questions in this context. Therefore, this publication is a course supplement book in not only sociology, computer science, psychology, etc. but also open education, open and distance education, online education, online learning, transformative online learning, and transformative learning. In addition, it is a unique resource for the researchers, scholars and professionals and lifelong learners. This proposed book is a reference book, and also a welcome addition to academic libraries' collections in natural and life science as well as social science.

In short, according to Sharma (R. Sharma, personal communication, May 21, 2018), online education has transformed traditional education over distance from postal delivery of simple resource materials to learners to an entirely new format where interactivity, collaboration, and competence assessment are the key integral components. Pedagogies have never been as important and essential as they are today to help teachers, tutors, and designers effectively make the transition to online education. Teachers need guides on how to design and implement educational interactions: between teacher and learners and/or among learners in order to facilitate learning through group discussion and project teams. Teaching methods, models, and theories are currently in processes of significant change due to new developments in technologies and socio-economic realities. It is essential to study, identify and apply suitable pedagogical responses. As online education becomes increasingly learner oriented, suitable new learning designs become all the more important. Not only does the book address such issues as how online facilitation, classroom learner behavior, learner engagement, teacher's perception and teaching can be improved by new pedagogies in the age of transhumanism; but also as how culture, business management, artificial intelligence, mental heaths, future of human, etc. can be transform today's life.

Acknowledgment

We have many individuals to thank for their impressive on the book. First, we would like to praise the people at IGI Global. The book developmemt team and other our editors, provided framework for the revision; they also suggested areas that could be strengthened and were invaluable in shaping the book. They helped make critical decisions about the transformative structure of the book, and provided useful feedback on stylistic issues.

We would also to express our appreciations to the Editorial Advisory Board (EAB) members. The EAB Members helped on the book included Ramesh Sharma, Alan Bruce, Mayte Martin, Badrul Khan, Santosh Panda, John Traxler, Yücel Güney and Figen Kılıç. The excellent advice from these people helped shape the book. We would also thanks the following reviewers for their careful and thoughtful work: Mehmet Emin Mutlu, Esra Pınar Uça Güneş, M. Recep Okur, Celal Murat Kandemir, Harun Serpil, Aras Bozkurt, Hakan Altınpulluk, Martin Ciupa, Thomas Stanley, Hasan Uçar, Erdem Öngün, Okan Aksu, İlker Usta, Mary Beth Klinger and Teresa L. Coffman.

We would particularly like to thank all of the authors of the individual chapters for their excellent contributions. Special mention in this regard must go to Natasha Vita-More, Zoltan Istvan, Roman Yampolskiy, Polina Abramov, Mehmet Emin Mutlu, Ebba Ossiannilsson, Martin Ciupa, Thomas Stanley, Faruk Karaman, Emel Güler, Buket Karatop, Mary Beth Klinger, Teresa L. Coffman, Okan Aksu, Pradeep Kumar Misra, Ezgi Doğan, Ferhan Şahin, Hakan Altınpulluk, Nil Göksel, Aras Bozkurt, Hasan Uçar, İlknur İstifçi, Şirin Karadeniz, Işıl Boy Ergül, Gürcan Banger, Suzan Urgan, Erdem Öngün, Rohit Rastogi, Devendra Kumar Chaturvedi, Pallavi Sharma, Vishwas Yadav and Sumit Chauhan.

The final words of thanks belong to our parents and families: This book is dedicated to the memory of our late fathers, Ali SISMAN and Cemalettin KURUBACAK, and our late siblings for the love and care. Also, to our mothers, Azime SISMAN and Oznur KURUBACAK. Serap SISMAN UGUR would like to thank her husband, Bulut UGUR, and her sons, Emir Kaan and Emin Alp as well as her brother, Yavuz SISMAN. Gulsun KURUBACAK MERIC would like to thank her husband, Münir MERIC, and her daughter, Canem, and her son, Can, as well as her daughter-in-law, Gamze.

Serap Sisman-Ugur
Anadolu University, Turkey

Gülsün Kurubacak
Anadolu University, Turkey

Section 1
Introduction

Chapter 1
Artificial Intelligence to Super Artificial Intelligence, Cyber Culture to Transhumanist Culture:
Change of the Age and Human

Serap Uğur
Anadolu University, Turkey

Gulsun Kurubacak
Anadolu University, Turkey

ABSTRACT

The 21st century is a period in which technological developments constantly present new innovations. This broad spectrum, from computers to mobile technologies, from augmented reality to virtual reality, from wearable technologies to artificial intelligence, is radically changing societies' economies, education systems, governments, and even cultures. Artificial intelligence studies have reached a point where people discuss how a human-like intelligence would be. This leads to the emergence of systems that regulate the work, daily lives, communications, jobs, and even family budgets of people. These developments also change the living standards and styles of individuals. The cultural texture that technology has restructured is now called "cyber" beyond digital. But how will the future technologies affect this cultural change and what kind of change awaits?

DOI: 10.4018/978-1-5225-8431-5.ch001

INTRODUCTION

The 21st century is a period in which technological developments constantly present new innovations. This broad spectrum, from computers to mobile technologies, from augmented reality to virtual reality, from wearable technologies to artificial intelligence, is radically changing societies' economies, education systems, governments and even cultures.

Artificial intelligence studies have reached to a point where people discuss how a human-like intelligence would be. This leads to the emergence of systems that regulate the work, daily lives, communications, jobs, and even family budgets of people. These developments also change the living standards and styles of individuals. The cultural texture that technology has restructured is now called "cyber" beyond digital. But how will the future technologies affect this cultural change and what kind of change awaits?

Transhumanism aims at eliminating undesirable or unnecessary aspects of human physical and / or cognitive abilities, such as aging and illness (More, 1990). It is known as an international intellectual and cultural movement suggesting that technology and science should be utilized for this aim. Future is shaped by technology and in the future, a new human-like form invention with its semi-human semi-robot body, as well as an artificial intelligence and improved minds are waiting for us. In this case, the structure of societies will also change and cultural differentiations will be inevitable. Of course, there will be some people who will willingly accept this transformation but there will also be people who will refuse it or do it out of pure need. There will be those who experience this transformation in their body. In addition, there will be those who will support or will be against this experience. The new cultural structure, which will come along with such an era, has already begun to take its shape.

In this study, the predictions of futuristic researchers about how technologies will affect the daily life in the coming years are examined and the effects of these developments on culture are discussed.

From Artificial Intelligence to Artificial Superintelligence

The concept of artificial intelligence, which emerged with the idea of enabling the computers and robots to think, represents the human effort to imitate the human brain, which is considered the most complex structure of the world. Intelligence is the process of thinking, reasoning, perceiving objective facts, comprehension, judgment and conclusion (Uğur and Kınacı, 2006). Artificial intelligence is the intelligence in non-organic systems that can mimic these features. Basically, it works as multi-probability decision-making structures. Artificial intelligence is also known as intelligent machinery and intelligent computer program making science and engineering (Luger, 2002).

The aim of artificial intelligence is to simulate the intelligence of a human being through a computer, to make a decision that is similar to learning to a certain extent, to create a strategy of choice. Artificial intelligence generally consists of methods that aim to model the thinking system of humans, the model/mode of work of the brain or the biological evolution of nature. Especially, techniques to solve real-life problems, which have evolved over the last two decades and cannot be solved intuitively or solved by mathematical techniques, are called artificial intelligence techniques (Russell & Norvig, 2016).

The prominent ones are;

1. Knowledge-based expert system approach
2. Artificial neural networks approach
3. Fuzzy logic approach

4. Non-traditional optimization techniques
5. Genetic algorithm
6. Simulated annealing
7. Hyprid algorithms
8. Object-oriented programming
9. Geographic information systems
10. Improvement of decision support systems
11. Soft computing (Tektaş, Akbaş and Topuz, 2002)

Briefly, with artificial intelligence, systems that perform certain human behaviors, such as taking objects and placing them in specific places, and simulating the process of human thinking related to a particular area of expertise such as data calculation, medical diagnosis, can be created. Although important developments in artificial intelligence have been provided nowadays, the level of research is still not at the desired level. Artificial intelligence researchers continue to introduce new inventions and innovations for the development of artificial intelligence.

Artificial general intelligence is the artificial intelligence that can process human cognitive systems and processes in depth and can perform different kinds of tasks well. It is an intelligent enough system to simulate the wide range of human intelligence, rather than focusing on reality in the width of the human mind (Techopedia, 2018).

The state of technology; developed technologies and software; advances in portable, wearable and integrated devices, in the light of such data, to make predictions about the future of artificial general intelligence is a complex, big, difficult issue. In terms of the level of human intelligence, the realization of artificial super intelligence can be seen as an ambiguous subject just as measuring human intelligence (Yapmolskiy & Fox, 2012; Everitt, Goertzel & Potapov, 2017).

Today, evaluating the revolutions of artificial general intelligence and autonomous machines in business life has become a common topic in the discussions of technologists and futurists. By the end of the 21st century, humanity is predicted to be in a much different state (Goertzel, 2007B; Everitt, Goertzel & Potapov, 2017). Artificial superintelligence can be defined as an intelligence that can manifest itself as an entity capable of performing the same operations as human intelligence (Yampolskiy, 2015). When the technology required to implement the human-level artificial intelligence in a digital computer is developed, artificial intelligence will become one step ahead by becoming closer to humanoid features (Bostrom, 1998).

Artificial superintelligence is used as a term that refers to the time when computers' abilities will surpass humans'. "Artificial intelligence", which has been widely used since the 1970s, expresses the ability of computers to mimic human thinking process. Artificial superintelligence takes it one step further and depicts a world in which a computer's cognitive ability is superior to a human (techopedia). The Turing test, developed years ago, is still used to discuss whether computers can simulate human speech and thought, or whether others can think that a communicating computer is actually a human being. (Copeland, 2000; Saygin, Cicekli ve Akman, 2000).

It is important to set the right target and the right programming for the goals. As a result of failure to identify and program the desired destinations correctly, instability in programmed targets, the emergence of some illegal groups, there may emerge groups opposing the artificial super-intelligence. Hence, artificial superintelligence should be framed and dealt as a technique rather than a political challenge (Sotala and Yampolskiy, 2015).

Artificial superintelligence will result in unrequited financial assistance from the state to support the producer or consumer, due to the advanced technologies and updates it will require. One can say that artificial superintelligence and minds to be created can be easily copied. As artificial intelligence is a software, they can be copied easily and quickly. They require hardware to be stored. Similarly, these requirements apply to human installation. In addition to hardware, the marginal cost of creating an installation or an artificial copy cannot be denied. It can now be predicted that it would be difficult to develop artificial super-intelligence at the human level. However, when the developments are taken into consideration, it is necessary to be prepared for these technologies that are awaiting us in the future.

There are challenges to sustainability for artificial general intelligence and artificial superintelligence. The changing fluxes of energy, matter and knowledge can be interpreted as different faces of these challenges. It is argued that artificial general intelligence can affect production technologies and economic decisions deeply and can be influenced by the socio-economic and ecological context in which they develop (Goertzel, 2007A).

Culture, Digital Culture, Cyber Culture

Humanity has gone through various periods since its existence. Man produces what is appropriate for the environment in which he lives. Bashkow (2004) states that the cultural boundaries between countries today are highly permeable due to the new neocolonic economic structures, regional change systems, migration, border regions, media, evangelism and tourism.

Unlike other periods in the 21st century, digital technologies do stand out. Now computers and what they produce are also in question. A multilayered process of cultural transformation has been initiated with the shaping power of advances in technology, media and communication. The proliferation of digital communication tools, especially online communication means, refers to the extensive digital change in culture (Hepp, 2010). Castells states that social networks identify technology and society, and that these networks change the cultural processes radically, while creating the social morphology of the society (Castells, 2004). With the discovery and expansion of the internet, which is one of the most important developments in the cultural formation of the century we live, communication has become electronic; societies have transformed into a network society; information has been digitized and digital culture has been included in literature (Güzel, 2016).

The new media has the characteristics of digitalism, interaction, multi-media, hypermetality and modularity. These characteristics of the new media distinguish it from the traditional media. Digitalism refers to the new media being numerical(digital) based. New media technologies are produced with digital technology different from mass media produced by traditional analog technology in a quantitative sense (Törenli, 2005: 87). Interaction means that the contents are produced by the users; shared and disseminated by the users. In traditional media, individuals are readers / viewers. Individuals do not have a decisive participation in mass media content. Multi-media feature refers to the inclusion of multiple media (radio, television, newspaper, etc.) on new media platforms. New media users can play music, watch videos, read books, play games, chat with friends and share content on a single platform.

Cyber culture is a modern phenomenon that has emerged worldwide due to the use of computer networks for communication, entertainment and business purposes. The Cyber culture notion defines the production and application of culture through internet technologies. Cyber culture as an increasingly expanding concept shows how individual and digital technologies interact, and how they coexist. Cyber culture can be seen as lifestyles in cyberspace or lifestyles shaped by cyber space. In this context, cyber culture involves thinking about how new technologies change human life and representations, images and meanings in life (Bell 2007). Cyber culture has a structure that constantly evolves in a virtual environment and has a rapid change and makes people feel that they need to follow it, or that they will be left behind the life updates (Demir, 2017).

Rheingold (1993) draws attention to the existence of computer-related and addictive cultures that attract millions of people. The emergence of new cultural forms and products with digital media and the transformation of culture have led to the emergence of cyber culture. The mediator of cyber culture is not a society, but a screen or a tool.Email, online interview, blog, virtual games, social media messaging, online shopping, bill payment; these digital actions constitute this culture.

At the point reached today, it can be seen how the visual media, in particular, affects individuals and distributes information through discourses, images and symbols. This new culture realizes its existence through the media and begins to shape itself with the new norms and values that this culture presents. Since it imposes popular preferences of the masses and the form of capitalist industry, it is the determinant and performer of mass culture in line with continuous consumption. The consumed things are not the things needed, but the things that are desired (Karakoç, 20007; Taylan and Arklan, 2008; Karaduman, 2017).

A new field has been created in interpersonal communication and information sharing through new media and networks. In this area, activities such as learning from friends, sensitivity to intellectual property, diversification of cultural expressions, gaining valuable skills in modern life and a stronger sense of citizenship can be realized (Acun, 2011).

The media of the 21st century are now shaped by social networks. Social media, which is a network in which messages are generated by digital systems, is one of these virtual reality environments. It is a combination of global network systems called social media such as Facebook, Instagram, Twitter, LinkedIn. Social media is not only in the form of content sharing, such as photographs and videos, but also in forms of communication such as blogs, online social forums, and chat tools. The new communication networks, which are formed due to the development of technology, cause the formation of new everyday reality and the formation of new cultural structures by breaking the order of reality and transferring its remanufactured form to the society. This reality, according to Jean Baudrillard, is the "hyperreality" created by the loss of the natural meaning of truth. Thanks to the digital age, the Internet shortens distances and a new world of cyber culture is created with the use of social media. As Baudrillard states "Nowadays, the system is being dragged into a totally uncertain environment, and all reality is exploited by code and simulation-specific hypersensitivity." (Nunes, 1995).

In a constantly changing and renewed cyber culture with technology, one may think that they are free and one can also see real life as an illusion or simulation. The most important aspect of cyber culture is that it does not reflect a single culture. "Through visualized reality, technology places the individual into a universe he believes to be true. Because the individual sees this universe. But this universe is a completely fictional world of images. Image-based facts are fictional as they are being produced and consumed. For example, television reflects the existing reality to the image, thus providing a single effective reality and makes it inevitable to look at itself (Bayrı 2011)".

Transhumanist Culture

It can be stated that Transhumanist technologies began to be developed with human's desire to dominate nature. Clothing used to cover oneself up, warm-up, and increase body resistance can also be said to be examples of transhumanist technologies. Although one is unable to realize, the technologies such as sunglasses, reading glasses, prescription glasses and contact lenses, robot hands, prosthetic leg, eye tracking devices that are becoming widespread, nowadays are also transhumanistic technologies. By the 21st century, transhumanist technologies will be able to be integrated not only to the human body but also to every area of human life. Furthermore, when this integrated process started or when it will end has become unobservable. This is what makes it scary. Transhumanist reflection is an important concept in the process of human development.The keys in this transformation are science and technology. It is a key factor in observing many developments from regenerative medicine to nanotechnology, improving quality of life, extending life span and mind loading (Transhumanist Decleration, 1998; More, 2013; Uğur, 2018; Vigo, 2018).

It is evident that humanity will thrive with transhumanist technologies in the next centuries and that transhumanist culture will shape this humanity and become the life itself. More stated that the new form of humanity became a major focus of the quest for happiness along with transhumanism and pointed out how the speed of technological, cultural and economic change continues to accelerate and deepen (Hansell, 2011). Transhumanism proposes a biological intervention to change the body, the value of which is based on the addition of physical properties, prolong its biological life and transfer it to non-biological platforms to protect the brain rather than cyborgization (Vita-More, 2013). There are some arguments in Transhumanism that point out the fact that one should focus on the continuity of memory for the personality/self development of individuals (Schneider, 2009; Hughes, 2013; Bostrom, 2015). Transhumanism, which plays a critical role in the development of the personal self, will have a critical importance in changing the social identity and cultural structure of the societies of individuals.

METHODOLOGY

This research was designed with hermeneutical research. The hermeneutic model is suggested for the investigation of the accumulation and outcome acquired by humanity since its existence and in order to investigate the society, the explanatory model is suggested. Hermeneutical or interpretive thinking is essentially an effort to understand the words, behaviors, or any other creative activity of a human being produced by another human being. Nothing human-fiction in the form of hermeneutic thinking is capable of isolating one from the perspective of the constructor, from his identities, from his experiences, and from the cultural practices of his society. In this context, the social disciplines, which investigate both the subject and the human world, meet at certain midpoints with hermeneutical thinking (Gadamer, 2008). Hermeneutics focuses on social explanation as the understandability of social events. In this study to be conducted within this context, the discourses of the researchers who are considered experts and authorities in their field were examined in order to describe the relationship between technology and society and to predict the possible changes that the technology may cause in the society. Based on the transhumanist ideologies obtained from the content analyzes of these discourses, the predictions for the social and cultural structure of the coming centuries were developed. In addition, structuring of new ideologies around the nature of learning and learning itself in the context of transhumanist culture was discussed.

RESULTS AND DISCUSSION

Looking at the evolution of artificial intelligence from its birth to the present day, its growth with the innovations in hardware technologies stands out. It can be said that the width in the areas of use of artificial general intelligence is moving towards transhumanism, when we look at the discourses of futurist technologists of the processes that will begin with the development of artificial superintelligence. The report titled "The Malicious Use of Artificial Intelligence: Forecasting, Prevention,and Mitigation" and which mentions the opinions of 26 different experts as well as Elon Musk, Michio Kaku, Ray Kurzweill, Stephen Hawking, Bill Gates, Roman Yampolskiy, Yuval Harari, Joschua Bach (2018) was included in the study in order to conduct content analysis of the discourses of the experts in the field of technology, singularity, artificial intelligence and transhumanism. These discourses, especially those related to the social and cultural structure of technology, were kept within the scope.

Elon Musk

According to Elon Musk, robots may be out of human control until the end of our age. Michio Kaku states that we need to cooperate with them to prevent a dystopia that robots control the world. It can be said that this explanation corresponds to the idea of Musk which is "we should become a robot-human(cyborg)" (Vanderelst & Winfield, 2018). Jones (2014) states that Musk considers artificial intelligence to be the greatest existential threat in the long term. Musk states that "In my opinion, if something poses a risk to the public, the government deserves a chance to state its opinion since its job is to ensure the welfare of its people"(Caughill, 2017B).

Musk's prediction of the need to be cyborg can be interpreted as him leaning towards the idea of transhumanist society. Transhumanism emphasizes the human beings bettered and improved through technology.These improvements can also take place with genetic regulation and interventions.

Michio Kaku

For artificial intelligence, Kaku says it is a technology that needs to be followed very carefully. Artificial intelligence software technology is rapidly evolving, although it is being used as a new concept. In 5-10 years, robots can be doctors, lawyers or engineers. This means "Expert artificial intelligence systems can be integrated into wristwatches, walls or internet-supported contact lenses and will be available at any time." In fact, Kaku states that virtual reality will become more important in the coming years and will be encountered in many different areas, from augmented reality practices to shopping. "With augmented reality, there will be internet connection in contact lenses. This way,, you will be able to search all products quickly and see which product is the cheapest or which one is the most popular. Any information about any product can be accessed with a single movement of the eye." (Anthony, 2003; BigThink, 2012; Gough, 2018). When Google Glass is taken as an example, one cannot deny the fact that this is not impossible to do.

He now shares the same idea as Elon Musk on the fact that it will not be very difficult for the humans who have made changes in their body for years to transform into a Cyborg. Just as the Tattoo applications performed from past to present, in-ear implants and artificial retinas are also reflections of this process.

The people will democratically vote on how much they want to develop this technology. Kaku says that the impact of technology in the short term will be "more democracy" and implies that the quality of democracy will be as high as those who vote. He states that in the future there will be nations but they will lose their importance.

There will be nations, because we have a common language and culture within a nation. As for taxation, and currency, let's not forget that collecting taxes, raising profits within national borders, will gain more global, regional qualification. In 2100s, besides the local culture, there will be "planet culture" as a second culture. We already see this: Planet culture football and rock'n roll. The music the younger generations listen to and the clothes they wear are the same everywhere. In other words, the social life will be like this in Type-I civilization. (Creighton, 2014; Gürdilek, 2016).

One hundred years later, when we become Type-1 civilization, some people may be genetically engineered and some may be mechanically enhanced. In this context, the person who has given up the change made on himself, in fact, will be the one to perform the transhumanist suicide. Transhumanist suicide concept; refers to freeing one's own spirit / improvements / developments to be performed on the mind / and the effort to turn into an organic human being.

The current concept of death will only apply to the organic man. On the other hand, the Transhuman's death will be associated with transforming into an organic man. Transhuman body transfer will have features such as mind transfer, but it will not be destroyed but will be archived. Once it gives up these features, it will then have the feature to be perished by being transformed into an organic human being.

Given the change in culture from digitalism to cyber, these predictions of Kaku may be deemed valid. With the developments in the field of robotics, the human body and mind combined with artificial superintelligence will lead to new virtual worlds, new cyber environments and new cultural structures and this cultural structure will be transhumanist culture. In transhumanist culture, humanity will have body, mind and genetic structure improved by technology. But consciousness and soul will remain outside of this. This can be considered as a separate discussion and research topic.

Ray Kurzweil

According to Kurzweil, it would be possible to develop cloud connection systems for non-biological organs and even to connect the human brain to wireless storage systems. At this point, the singularity will come along with the hybridization of man.

Kurzweil says "The singularity will lead us to a place where computers have human intelligence, where we hold them in our brains, connect them to the cloud and expand our existence. This is not a future scenario; this is already happening and will continue to gain momentum. All these developments will form the cybernetic society." (Ergün, 2017).

Like Kaku, Kurzweil predicts that virtual reality and real life will be intertwined in the following years. According to Kurzweil, virtual reality will be able to take on different personalities both physically and emotionally; before the 2030s, virtual reality will occupy everything and there will be no need for physical working environments. This will be a stage in the formation of the new social structure. It is also possible to say that new virtual office structures will be formed with virtual reality. (Caughill,

2017A; Galeon, 2017A; Creighton, 2018). These developments can eliminate the situation of living together and working in certain places. According to Kurzweil's prediction, only a few people who want to maintain their natural state in some natural habitats will be able to live as we do today. This will cause the emergence of a new cultural structure.

Within the scope of this prediction, it can be said that the human form can be said to live as an organic human. These organic people may be considered as an elite group to manage the transhumans. Otherwise, the concept of organic human will remain a theory. Because the transhumanist structure will want everyone in the society to have the same structure in order to maintain its existence. Therefore, the need for the power and management to remain in the hands of the organic human in every condition is an inevitable fact.

Stephen Hawking

Stephen Hawking, who is seen as one of the best physicists ever after Einstein, thinks that early versions of artificial intelligence are useful, but he thinks a full-scale artificial intelligence is dangerous. According to Hawking, the possibility of developing a very talented AI is frightening. As a result, a super-intelligent AI can be extremely good at achieving his goals and if these goals aren't compatible with ours, we're in "trouble" (Pan, 2016; Caughill, 2017B; Kharpal, 2017).

Once people develop artificial intelligence, such intelligence can redesign itself in its own way and develop at an ever-increasing pace. I believe there is no deep difference between what can be achieved with the biological brain and what can be achieved with a computer. Therefore, I think that theoretically, computers can mimic human intelligence and transcend it.

According to Hawking, artificial intelligence can be thought of as a way of life that will leave humans behind. So much so; this implies that the necessity of finding a second planetary home for humans is due to concerns about the growing population and the immediate threat of artificial intelligence (AI) development. In a future where there is artificial intelligence integrated with humans or separate, the restructuring of a society culture to change is also inevitable.

Bill Gates

In recent years, the development of AI has become quite a divisive issue. Bill Gates has also been expressing his concerns about artificial intelligence for a long time. Gates thinks AI's development will be the cause of humanity's death. Gates also states that "The machines will help us in many areas but at this stage they will not be at the level of super intelligence. If we manage this well, then we can get positive results. But in the years to come, I think they will not be smart enough to worry us. I agree with Elon Musk and others and I don't understand why people are not worried about it."(Dredge, 2015; Rawlinson, 2015).

Gates' concerns are about the threat of human extinction. He points out the importance of being cautious to avoid such a scenario. Of course, human beings are experienced in adapting to the outcomes of the time coming along with the changing ages. It is necessary to be prepared for future changes both individually and socially. Transhumanism can be considered as the best preparation tool at this point.

Roman Yampolskiy

Like Elon Musk or Stephen Hawking Dr Yampolskiy also has concerns for the future of artificial intelligence. In particular, this is a concern within the scope of the idea of developing an artificial intelligence beyond machine learning and human capacity, and this is due to the growth of artificial superintelligence. When expressing his thought on this issue, he draws attention to ethical concerns and if there is an artificial intelligence at or above the level of human intelligence, he wonders how to control it. Restricting access to the real world of intelligent machines with artificial superintelligence is a widely recommended solution for AI security issues. Yampolskiy proposes an artificial intelligence limitation protocol to be used for this purpose. (Yampolskiy, 2012).

According to Yampolskiy, as the artificial intelligence systems become more skillful in the near future, we will begin to see more automatic and increasingly sophisticated social engineering attacks. In the near future, it is expected that the increase of artificial intelligence-supported cyber attacks, network penetration, personal data theft and smart computer viruses will spread just like an epidemic. This situation can be interpreted as a sign that societies will need new structuring on their security and confidentiality of their information and personal privacy. In this context, it may be thought that transhumanist technologies will be needed in social information security studies.

Yuval Noah Harari

Harari had made a similar statement. He said that artificial intelligence could reach a level that they can hack into people. According to Harari the human body and mind will be rebuilt in the coming years. This foresees that the importance of "data" in the 21st century will increase and that it will become a new product in the economy. Not only industrial production materials, textile, automotive, machinery, but also human body and mind will be managed to be improved. Data will become the world's most important asset. Those who manage the data will determine what life conditions and life itself will turn into. Those who have control of the data will define not only humanity but also the future of human life. According to Harari's claims, the data will be valuable in the future as much as the land was in the past. In the industrial age that emerged through the industrial revolution, the machines exceeded the value of the land. With a large number of machines under the control of a small number of people, classes began to form.Society structure and cultures transformed. This is how the capital and the working class were born. Nowadays, data has started to replace machines.Likewise, if the control of the data gets into the hands of a small number of people, then humanity will be divided into different species, not classes (Makridakis, 2017; Harari, 2016; Dickson, 2018; Harari, 2018).

According to Harari, a digital dictatorship system may emerge in the future with the power of biotechnology, artificial intelligence and machine learning. Dictatorship does not create decision-making mechanisms by disseminating information to different institutions as in a democracy, it concentrates all knowledge and power on a single point and conducts the works. People can be dominated by digital dictatorships if the center of democracy cannot adapt to structures that enable data processing (Dickson, 2018). In these days when we are close to the year 2020, the investments made by countries using these technologies to the power of data and technology, which are the power of the future, are obvious.

Harari predicts that humanity will be divided into two groups as super-humans and useless, unqualified humans. Unqualified people will have economic value and no political power. According to Harari, the three biggest threats are the nuclear war, climate change and destructive technologies. The best scenario is to get better health care and have more free time. The worst-case scenario is the digital dictatorships, where all power is left in the hands of a small elite group who monitors everyone (Harari, 2018).

In this context, of course, the states will have great responsibilities. Societies also play a critical role in this new structure as binders, decision makers and selectors. Human behavior, social and cultural structures reshaped by social media will continue to develop in the future in the context of technology.

Joscha Bach

The MIT Media Laboratory and the Evolutionary Dynamic Officer of the Harvard Program, Joscha Bach, states that they cannot foresee how the technologies that will provide efficiency and sustainability together with the developing automation technologies will have an impact on wage-based economic systems. He also states that the artificial intelligence that cannot be controlled cannot be calculated by the modern day algorithms, and therefore the sociological dimension of the developments in artificial intelligence should not be ignored (Bach, 2015A; Bach, 2015B).

According to Basch, if it is possible to build Artificial Intelligence at the human level, this would mean that we have solved the puzzle of the human mind. The biological system will not provide a system that is prone to the limits of the human brain, but the artificial brains will probably be in a form that is better scaled than the biological ones. However, the limits of artificial superintelligence will mostly depend on the speed of first evolution, and artificial intelligence cannot go beyond human intelligence (Bach, 2015B).

The Malicious Use of Artificial Intelligence: Forecasting, Prevention and Mitigation Report

Moreover, a report on the future of artificial intelligence was prepared by 26 experts from 14 different institutions including University of Oxford's Future of Humanity Institute, University of Cambridge Centre for the Study of Existential Risk, Elon Musk's OpenAI company and Electronic Frontier Foundation in 2018. The author of this 100-page report titled The Malicious Use of Artificial Intelligence: Forecasting, Prevention,and Mitigation Report, Miles Brundage, Research Assistant at the Institute of Human Rights, Oxford University, states that "not only the Artificial intelligence systems reach human performance levels but exceeds them significantly." In the report, in addition to AIs taking the place of humans in the physical sense, researchers also report the dangers of them taking the place of humans in the digital media. The report also included dystopian scenarios, such as the proliferation of autonomous vehicles causing "deliberate" accidents, coordinating attacks of micro-drones or transformation of facial recognition systems into assassins.

According to the report, when we look at the genetic studies, within a few years, genetic engineering and other forms of biological engineering can lead to us making extensive changes not only in our physiology, immune system and life expectancy, but also in our intellectual and emotional capacity. As a matter of fact, when the Human Connectome Project which aims to completely map the human brain is successful, it can be said that our brains can be transferred to mechanical avatars like Japanese animes.

CONCLUSION AND SUGGESTIONS

The change of cultural structure that technology and societies have been going through throughout history is more rapid now than in the past. With the increasing use of artificial intelligence applications in the social media widely used in the 21st century, the rapid increase in the dissemination of cyber culture, the development of intelligent social media applications along with artificial superintelligence can be interpreted as an indication that it can increase the interconnectedness of real culture with cyber culture. One of the final results of this change can be considered as the formation of transhumanist culture.

Observation of the reflections of virtual and augmented reality and artificial intelligence applications integrated in blockchain applications to be used with equipment such as mobile devices, wearable technologies, which play an active role in the formation of this momentum, in cyber world and cyber culture can be seen as manifestations of the transhumanist culture that will take place with these developments.

Transhuman will benefit from technology in many different processes, from living to learning. The new cultural structure will be shaped with the change that the individuals will be experiencing due to the new technologies and the existence of transhumans in society. Of course, it is unclear where integrated technologies will begin and end in the future, which can be seen as part of what the futurists find alarming. With that being said, strategic structuring will provide a controlled development of these developments in the right areas.

REFERENCES

Acun, R. (2011). Her Dem Yeniden Doğmak: Online Sosyal Ağlar ve Kimlik. *Milli Folklor Dergisi, 89*, 66–77.

Andersson, J. (2018). That Very Big Computer Known as Human Civilisation-Yuval Noah Harari, Homo Deus–A Brief History of Tomorrow. *Archives Européennes de Sociologie, 59*(3), 429–434. doi:10.1017/S0003975618000267

Anthony, M. (2003). Visions Without Depth: Michio Kaku's Future. *Journal of Futures Studies, 7*(4), 55-66.

Bach, J. (2015A). Modeling motivation in MicroPsi 2. In *International conference on artificial general intelligence* (pp. 3-13). Springer. 10.1007/978-3-319-21365-1_1

Bach, J. (2015B). *Why Artificial Intelligence won't just be a bit smarter than humans*. Retrieved from http://bach.ai/why-ai-wont-be-just-a-bit-smarter-than-humans/

Bashkow. (2004). A Neo-Boasian Conception of Cultural Boundaries. *American Anthropologist, 106*(3), 443-458.

Bayrı, D. (2011). *Gözün Egemenliği Tarihin Sonu mu? Özne: Baudrillard Sayısı, 14*. Kitap.

BigThink. (2012). *Michio Kaku Describes Virtual Reality Glasses*. Access: https://bigthink.com/michio-kaku-describes-virtual-reality-glasses

Bostrom, N. (1998). How long before superintelligence? *Int Journal of Future Studies, 2*.

Bostrom, N. (2003). Ethical issues in advanced artificial intelligence. *Science Fiction and Philosophy: From Time Travel to Superintelligence*, 277-284.

Bostrom, N. (2005). A history of transhumanist thought. *Journal of Evolution and Technology / WTA, 14*(1).

Bostrom, N. (2014). *Superintelligence: Paths, Dangers, Strategies*. Retrieved from https://www.researchgate.net/publication/285393594_Nick_Bostrom_Superintelligence_Paths_Dangers_Strategies

Castells, M. (2004). *The network society A cross-cultural perspective*. Edward Elgar.

Caughill, P. (2017A). *Ray Kurzweil's Most Exciting Predictions About the Future of Humanity*. Access: https://futurism.com/ray-kurzweils-most-exciting-predictions-about-the-future-of-humanity

Caughill, P. (2017B). *Stephen Hawking Believes Humankind Is in Danger of Self-Destruction Due to AI*. Access: https://futurism.com/stephen-hawking-believes-humankind-danger-self-destruction-ai

Cellan-Jones, R. (2014). Stephen Hawking warns artificial intelligence could end mankind. *BBC News, 2*.

Clifford, C. (2016). Elon Musk: robots will take your jobs, government will have to pay your wage. *CNBC.com, 4*.

Copeland, B. J. (2000). The turing test. *Minds and Machines, 10*(4), 519–539. doi:10.1023/A:1011285919106

Creighton, J. (2014). *The Kardashev Scale – Type I, II, III, IV & V Civilization*. Access: https://futurism.com/the-kardashev-scale-type-i-ii-iii-iv-v-civilization

Creighton. (2018). *The "Father of Artificial Intelligence" Says Singularity Is 30 Years Away*. Access: https://futurism.com/father-artificial-intelligence-singularity-decades-away

Daly, B. M. (2004). *Transhumanism: Toward a brave new world?* Academic Press.

Demir, A. (2017). Siber Kültür ve Hiper Gerçeklikte Değişen Yaşam. *AJIT-e, 8*(29), 87. doi:10.5824/1309-1581.2017.4.005.x

Dickson, B. (2018). *AI, big data and the future of humanity*. Access: https://bdtechtalks.com/2018/01/31/yuval-harari-wef-ai-big-data-digital-dictatorship/

Dredge, S. (2015). *Artificial intelligence will become strong enough to be a concern, says Bill Gates*. Access: https://www.theguardian.com/technology/2015/jan/29/artificial-intelligence-strong-concern-bill-gates

Eden, A. H., Moor, J. H., Søraker, J. H., & Steinhart, E. (2015). *Singularity Hypotheses*. Springer.

Everitt, T., Goertzel, B., & Potapov, A. (Eds.). (2017). *Artificial General Intelligence: 10th International Conference, AGI 2017, Melbourne, VIC, Australia*, August 15-18, 2017, *Proceedings* (*Vol. 10414*). Springer.

Gadamer, H. G. (2008). *Philosophical hermeneutics*. Univ of California Press.

Galeon, D. (2017A). *Ray Kurzweil: AI Will Not Displace Humans, It's Going to Enhance Us*. Access: https://futurism.com/ray-kurzweil-ai-displace-humans-going-enhance

Galeon, D. (2017B). *Stephen Hawking: "I Fear That AI May Replace Humans Altogether"*. Access: https://futurism.com/stephen-hawking-ai-replace-humans

Goertzel, B. (2007A). *Artificial general intelligence* (vol. 2; C. Pennachin, Ed.). New York: Springer. doi:10.1007/978-3-540-68677-4

Goertzel, B. (2007B). Human-level artificial general intelligence and the possibility of a technological singularity: A reaction to Ray Kurzweil's The Singularity Is Near, and McDermott's critique of Kurzweil. *Artificial Intelligence, 171*(18), 1161–1173. doi:10.1016/j.artint.2007.10.011

Gürdilek. (2016). *Michio Kaku'nun gözünden gelecek 20 yıl*. Access: https://kurious.ku.edu.tr/wp-content/uploads/2016/02/20160212103512-kule_37_michio_kaku.pdf

Güzel, E. (2016). Dijital Kültür ve Çevrimiçi Sosyal Ağlarda Rekabetin Aktörü:'Dijital Habitus'. *Gümüşhane Üniversitesi İletişim Fakültesi Elektronik Dergisi, 4*(1), 83–103.

Hansell, G. R. (2011). *H+/-: Transhumanism and its Critics*. Xlibris Corporation.

Harari, Y. N. (2016). *Homo Deus. A Brief History of Tomorrow*. Harvill Secker.

Harari, Y. N. (2018). *21 Lessons for the 21st Century*. Random House.

Hawking, S., & Mlodinow, L. (2017). *The Grand Design*. Academic Press.

Hawking, S., Russel, S., Tegmark, M., & Wilczek, F. (2015, January 5). Stephen Hawking: are we taking artificial intelligence seriously. *The Independent*.

Hepp, A. (2010). *Cultural studies und Medienanalyse: eine Einführung*. Springer-Verlag. doi:10.1007/978-3-531-92190-7

Hughes, J. (2013). Transhumanism and personal identity. *The Transhumanist Reader: Classical And Contemporary Essays On The Science, Technology, And Philosophy Of The Human Future*, 227-233.

Huxley, J. (1968). Transhumanism. *Journal of Humanistic Psychology, 8*(1), 73–76. doi:10.1177/002216786800800107

Kaku, M. (2017). Discussion question: Are human brains big enough? *Confronting Complexity*, 310.

Kaku, M. (2018). *The Future of Humanity: Terraforming Mars*. Penguin.

Karaduman, N. (2017). Popüler kültürün oluşmasında ve aktarılmasında sosyal medyanın rolü. *Erciyes Üniversitesi Sosyal Bilimler Enstitüsü Dergisi, 31*(43), 113–133.

Karakoç, E. (2007). *Medya aracılığıyla popüler kültürün aktarılmasında toplumsal değişkenlerin rolü* (Doctoral dissertation). Selçuk Üniversitesi Sosyal Bilimler Enstitüsü.

Kharpal, A. (2017). *Stephen Hawking says A.I. could be 'worst event in the history of our civilization'*. Access: https://www.cnbc.com/2017/11/06/stephen-hawking-ai-could-be-worst-event-in-civilization.html

Kurzweil, R. (2010). *The singularity is near*. Gerald Duckworth & Co.

Kurzweil, R. (2015). Superintelligence and singularity. *Science fiction and philosophy: From time travel to superintelligence*, 146-170.

Luger, G. F. (2002). *Artificial Intelligence: Structures and Strategies for Complex Problem Solving* (4th ed.). Addison-Wesley.

Makridakis, S. (2017). The forthcoming Artificial Intelligence (AI) revolution: Its impact on society and firms. *Futures*, *90*, 46–60. doi:10.1016/j.futures.2017.03.006

Metin, O., & Karakaya, Ş. (2017). Jean Baudrillard Perspektifinden Sosyal Medya Analizi Denemesi. *Afyon Kocatepe Üniversitesi Sosyal Bilimler Dergisi*, *19*(2), 109–121.

More, M. (1990). Transhumanism: Towards a futurist philosophy. *Extropy*, *6*, 6–12.

More, M. (2010). True transhumanism. In H+/-: Transhumanism and Its Critics. Bloomington, IN: XLibris.

More, M. (2013). The philosophy of transhumanism. *The transhumanist reader: Classical and contemporary essays on the science, technology, and philosophy of the human future*, 3-17.

More, M., & Vita-More, N. (Eds.). (2013). *The transhumanist reader: Classical and contemporary essays on the science, technology, and philosophy of the human future*. John Wiley & Sons. doi:10.1002/9781118555927

Musk, E. (2017). Making humans a multi-planetary species. *New Space*, *5*(2), 46–61. doi:10.1089pace.2017.29009.emu

Nadimpalli, M. (2017). Artificial intelligence risks and benefits. *Artificial Intelligence*, *6*(6).

Nunes, M. (1995). Jean Baudrillard in cyberspace: Internet, virtuality, and postmodernity. *Style (Fayetteville)*, 314–327.

Pan, Y. (2016). Heading toward artificial intelligence 2.0. *Engineering*, *2*(4), 409–413. doi:10.1016/J.ENG.2016.04.018

Rheingold, H. (1993). *The virtual community: Finding commection in a computerized world*. Addison-Wesley Longman Publishing Co., Inc.

Robbins, J. (2016). When Smart Is Not: Technology and Michio Kaku's The Future of the Mind. *IEEE Technology and Society Magazine*, *35*(2), 29–31. doi:10.1109/MTS.2016.2554439

Russell, S. J., & Norvig, P. (2016). *Artificial intelligence: a modern approach*. Pearson Education Limited.

Saygin, A. P., Cicekli, I., & Akman, V. (2000). Turing test: 50 years later. *Minds and Machines*, *10*(4), 463–518. doi:10.1023/A:1011288000451

Sotala, K., & Yampolskiy, R. V. (2014). Responses to catastrophic AGI risk: A survey. *Physica Scripta*, *90*(1), 018001. doi:10.1088/0031-8949/90/1/018001

Taylan, H. H., & Arklan, Ü. (2008). Medya Ve Kültür: Kültürün Medya Aracılığıyla Küreselleşmesi. *Sosyal Bilimler Dergisi*, *10*(1), 86.

Tektaş, M., Akbaş, A., & Topuz, V. (2002). *Yapay zeka tekniklerinin trafik kontrolünde kullanilmasi üzerine bir inceleme*. Retrieved from http://www.trafik.gov.tr/SiteAssets/Yayinlar/Bildiriler/pdf/C4-7.pdf

Törenli, N. (2005). e-Devlet'in ekonomi-politiğine giriş: Kullanıcı dostu ortamlarda "Sanallaşan" kamu hizmetleri. *Ankara Üniversitesi SBF Dergisi, 60*(01), 191–224.

Transhumanist Declaration. (1998). *The Transhumanist Declaration*. Retrieved from https://itp.uni-frankfurt.de/~gros/Mind2010/transhumanDeclaration.pdf

Uğur, A., & Kınacı, A. C. (2006). Yapay zeka teknikleri ve yapay sinir ağları kullanılarak web sayfalarının sınıflandırılması. XI. Türkiye'de İnternet Konferansı (inet-tr'06), Ankara, 1-4.

Uğur, S. (2018). Transhumanizm ve öğrenmedeki değişim. *Açıköğretim Uygulamaları ve Araştırmaları Dergisi, 4*(3), 58–74.

Vanderelst, D., & Winfield, A. (2018). The dark side of ethical robots. In *Proceedings of the 2018 AAAI/ACM Conference on AI, Ethics, and Society* (pp. 317-322). ACM. 10.1145/3278721.3278726

Vigo, J. (2018). *The Ethics Of Transhumanism And The Cult Of Futurist Biotech*. Retrieved from https://www.forbes.com/sites/julianvigo/2018/09/24/the-ethics-of-transhumanism-and-the-cult-of-futurist-biotech/#b3d29b04ac54

Vita-More, N. (2013). Aesthetics: bringing the arts & design into the discussion of transhumanism. *The transhumanist reader: Classical and contemporary essays on the science, technology, and philosophy of the human future*, 18-27.

Warwick, K. (2010). Implications and consequences of robots with biological brains. *Ethics and Information Technology, 12*(3), 223–234. doi:10.100710676-010-9218-6

Yampolskiy, R. V. (2012). Leakproofing Singularity-Artificial Intelligence Confinement Problem. *Journal of Consciousness Studies*.

Yampolskiy, R. V. (2015). *Artificial superintelligence: a futuristic approach*. Chapman and Hall/CRC. doi:10.1201/b18612

Yampolskiy, R. V., & Fox, J. (2012). Artificial general intelligence and the human mental model. In *Singularity Hypotheses* (pp. 129–145). Berlin: Springer. doi:10.1007/978-3-642-32560-1_7

Section 2
Radical Futuristics

Chapter 2
Ability to Advance Knowledge and Capacity to Achieve the Impossible

Natasha Vita-More
University of Advancing Technology, USA

ABSTRACT

This chapter focuses on human achievement as accomplished with the use of technology to explore humanity's most daunting challenges. While ancient Promethean myths echo a threat of the human use of technology, transhumanism offers a social construct to inform and mitigate many impending threats. The aim is to encourage life-long learning—ongoing, voluntary, and self-motivated pursuit of knowledge—through immersive and educational platforms for ethical leadership in a world of rapid change. Notably, there are counter arguments to an intervention of the human condition, which often expose themselves as biases of moral perception that, in due course, fall short. Yet, humans continue to be fueled by curiosity and a need for amelioration to transcend limits. What is lacking and most imminently necessary to deal with the exponentially increasing technology in our midst, and to society's varied perceptions and reactions, is straightforward knowledge and guidance in navigating towards the telos of our humanity.

INTRODUCTION

This chapter focuses on human achievement as accomplished with the use of technology as a means to explore humanity's most daunting challenges. To begin this journey, it is essential to understand that advancing knowledge is the primary undertaking of leaders in many fields, including academics, who benefit from sharing information. That benefit can be based on an innate desire to raise intellectual awareness. When a society has knowledge, it prospers. However, to prosper the knowledge must be based on researched studies that can be tested to reveal what types of knowledge cause a society to prosper, in what locations in the world, and within what time frames. In addressing human achievement, three distinct points need to be made that offer insight into why limits placed before us are often echoes of antiquity, the inequality of knowledge and the need for a straightforward approach to knowledge.

DOI: 10.4018/978-1-5225-8431-5.ch002

Ability to Advance Knowledge and Capacity to Achieve the Impossible

First, cultural beliefs concerning knowledge are often influenced by antiquity. Religion, philosophy, science, and the arts provide a foundation for the varied cultures throughout the world. However, knowledge is not equitably imparted across populations and their demographics. There are often differing opinions that evoke struggles and constraints on what type of knowledge and how much knowledge people ought to have, and who provides it—academic institutions, religious institutions, governments, open source shared environments, and/or word of mouth. What is reliable and how is the information being funneled to the public in a highly politicized world?

Second, it is an observable fact that not all populations will have the same level of knowledge and available technology within the same time frame. Social structures are governed by diverse laws and rules that either support or prevent the advancement of knowledge. While we must work toward encouraging education and fostering technology for those in need, there are often rigidly uncompromising beliefs that denounce and prevent such advancements. Why are some populations benefiting from knowledge and technology and others are not?

Third, education has changed and will continue to change as diverse learning models shape environments for reaching as many people as possible through varied communication channels. The fluid interaction between providing information and accessing information is readily available with online education and virtual learning, which adds significantly to mentoring, and hands-on team-based experiential projects. Yet, who is delivering the content and how balanced and straightforward is it?

An Influence of Antiquity

Long after the ancient Greeks (800 - 500 B.C.), philosophical theory, Socratic method, rhetoric and leadership training continue today to form fundamental structures for intellectual ruminations. Nevertheless, the ancient myths linger and have imprinted indelible warnings about humans using technology to tempt the Gods or to play God. This influence can be seen as exponential technologies are faced off with existential risks that alter aspirations into foreboding impossibilities rather than hopeful opportunities.

Mythology imparts a narrative that warned humans to beware of reaching to high are traveling too far. Consider the Creation Myth of Theogony, as written by the poet Hesiod during the 8th Century BCE. In this mythical branch of science of the origins of the universe, there was a void—a empty space. In "The Theologony of Hesoid", translated by Hugh G. Evelyn-White (1914), the query about the beginnings of our World were the architecture of the Grecian Gods:

(ll. 104-115) Hail, children of Zeus! Grant lovely song and celebrate the holy race of the deathless gods who are forever, those that were born of Earth and starry Heaven and gloomy Night and them that briny Sea did rear. Tell how at the first gods and earth came to be, and rivers, and the boundless sea with its raging swell, and the gleaming stars, and the wide heaven above, and the gods who were born of them, givers of good things, and how they divided their wealth, and how they shared their honours amongst them, and also how at the first they took many-folded Olympus. These things declare to me from the beginning, ye Muses who dwell in the house of Olympus, and tell me which of them first came to be. (Evelyn-White, 1914).

The "Chaos", a term used to mean empty space and could be interpreted as entropy in stasis, blossomed into Earth. Nevertheless, on Earth the humans were continually forewarned. Zeus, Prometheus, Pandora, all with their own characteristics (Black, 2013). While this is mythology and the Gods were fictional characters, their place in human history is relevant to fears about technology, and has formed the basis of science fiction narratives. Within human imagination, there is a precautionary tale that pulls us back from the precipice of challenging ourselves, least we make a mistake, fail, or cause emotional or financial damage to others. Perhaps, it starts with Mary Shelley's *Frankenstein* (published in 1818, revised in 1831), which is subtitled "The Modern Prometheus".

This recalls the ancient Greek myth of Prometheus, the Titan who stole fire from the gods and gave it to humankind (e.g, Hesiod's Theogony, Aeschylus' Prometheus Bound); in one version of the myth (Plato's Protagoras), fire was our unique "gift," analogous to other animal's claws, thick hides, or ferocious speeds. Since the myth of Prometheus may be read as an explanatory account and as a symbol for the ongoing human relationship to technology, Shelley's subtitle further implies that Frankenstein will share with Greco-Roman literature and with mythology more generally an interest in the question of how "technology" of different types helps define human culture, and, through it, our relationship to the natural world. (Rogers and Stevens, date, p. 1-2).

The name Prometheus is given to a fictional supervillain in DC Comics in "Dark Knight Rises" (Nolan, 2012) and a potential counterpart of Batman. The character's attributes include a pathological need to kill law officers, peak physical and cognitive powers, an arsenal of weapons, and powers of cybernetic enhancement (Buesing, 2017). The inference that Prometheus is a villain borrows from fears of interfacing technology with human biology. It suggests that giving fire to man is rogue behavior at best. Further the human curiosity to seek advancements in technology on the exponential curve posits a threat of global warming, natural catastrophic disasters, and the existential risk of humanity.

In Hesiod's Works & Days we are told that Zeus punished man for receiving the fire by instructing Hephaistos to create the first woman, Pandora, from clay and through her all the negative aspects of life would befall the human race - toil, illness, war, and death - and definitively separate mankind from the gods. (Cartwright, 2012).

A counter argument might claim that human existence has sustained over time due to human use of technology and that without fire, electricity, and computerized communication the World would be comparable to an endless Dark Ages. Another argument might asert that the human of the homo sapiens species is a stage and not the final outcome of the species evolutionary voyage, and that we must steer our own evolution beyond a reliance on biology to survive.

Consider human enhancement as a necessary process for species sustainability, that without vaccines, medical interventions, and life-prolonging cures, we could die off from a pandemic virus. When looking back over history, it is evident that the fragility of biology must be appended though technology. Smallpox, an ancient disease that is older than plague is identified to date back to the Pharaoh Ramses V (1149-1145) (Aberth, 2011, p. 73). This disease killed an estimated 60 million people in Europe in the 18th century, and an estimated 300 deaths in the 20th century; the Spanish Flu (1918-1919) killed between 50 and 100 million people worldwide (Oddee, 2007); and the Black Death (1340-1771) resulted in 75 million deaths (Aberth, 2011, p. 121). However, will merging with technology truly make us safe?

A parallel can be drawn between the vulnerability of human biology and the vulnerability of computer technology. Both systems have an infrastructure that is attacked by viruses. For biology it is the viruses and antigens that breakdown infection-fighting white blood cells. For the computer, it is the viruses that infect the algorithmic functioning. Because of humanity's deep seeded relationship with technology, currently in the form of the devices we use, it is essential to understand the risks and the benefits. The complexity of information networks and channels of delivery alerts us that accuracy is essential. We need the guidance and leadership of experts in their fields—from medical biology to computer science—to impart their knowledge and first-hand experience. Further, we need these experts to provide information without bias or moral distinctions, as an ethical responsibility for imparting knowledge. Relatedly, we need to recognize the seeding of ideas, nurturing, and the evolving nature of causality, as knowledge is tested and further developed. Breakthroughs occur more rapidly, and one researcher's discovery can become the source for another researcher's breakthrough within a few years or sooner. AI will speed this up as its ability to sort data from discoveries minimizes the time frame by years to days.

In this pace of acceleration, what is reliable when information is funneled through a highly politicized world? According to transhumanist studies in the fields of Computer Science, Cybersecurity, Technology Forensics, and data management, there is too much information streaming continually to effectively collect and organize (Singh, Nov 20, 2017). Because myths and fake news have penetrated channels of information, it is difficult to offer an absolute set of reliable facts in any field. It seems the only effective way to collect and organize the data is through narrow AI (Bainbridge, 2013). This is an action-oriented strategy used by financial institutions, medical facilities, and other industries to produce a streamlined bevvy of collected data that can be reviewed by experts. On the ethical side of this pace, the key issue for any business or institution is to make AI responsible in all its dimensions. Thus, making AI trustworthy is a top challenge:

Most executives know that artificial intelligence (AI) has the power to change almost everything about the way they do business — and could contribute up to $15.7 trillion to the global economy by 2030. But what many business leaders don't know is how to deploy AI, not just in a pilot here or there, but throughout the organization, where it can create maximum value. (PwC, n.d.).

Not Everyone Will Have Knowledge and Technologies, at First

The differences in people's financial and personal status is relative to each country and economic structure. The inequality across the world is daunting. Some have benefits of knowledge to build successful environments and others do not. It has been a human condition for eons. We may hope for a revolution to result in a globally equitable economic structure for all. Yet, we do not have enough knowledge to form a reasonable analysis of how to mitigate the inequalities among populations. There is conjecture, to be sure, but each field of study will inevitably end up with diverse speculations that simply do not add up because we cannot obtain all the variables needed to make a proper assessment. The data is simply too complex.

Let's look at the agricultural revolution for insight:

While the agricultural revolution certainly had something to do with the development of increasingly complex societies, there is considerable debate about why some agricultural societies ultimately developed into advanced civilizations while others did not. Indeed, in some cases, it seems like complex political orders were the cause rather than the consequence of the development of agricultural systems. Historians and anthropologists are still trying to understand what other variables were at play, such as large-scale irrigation projects, warfare, trade, geography, and competition. Each society grew more complex in response to its own set of environmental, social, and political stimuli. (Kahn Academy).

Governing structures are different throughout the world. It is reasonable to claim that a governing body intentionally prevents knowledge and technology to be provided to its citizens unethical or immoral. This action would be devious, detestable or deranged. In other words, it would have to be greed or madness that would cause intentionally restricting others to succeed. It is evident in some areas of the World, but not with democratic societies.

Thus, why would a person, a culture, or belief system claim that a technologically advantaged society is a bad thing, or those who "have" are a non-sharing elite? First, a technologically advantaged environment is usually the result of business strategy and hard work. The fact that this society "has" knowledge and technology usually means that their society is not governed by greed or madness. Second, we must question why those who have knowledge and technological advantages are called elite. Could there be a social construct in place that is not based on growth, but sequestered to a psychology of envy or a general fear of success? Does this stem from myths of antiquity?

Societies that do not restrain or censor innovation have developed strategic models for obtaining and furthering knowledge. Through these models, the entrepreneurial environment can assess technological advancements and determine best practices. These elites are pioneers of progress and looking at the issues of why politics obfuscates social change. It is common knowledge that there are background forces that filter information for their own benefit and thereby have a large influence on the public temperament.

Fixing politics will become much easier once a compelling, integrative vision of a sustainable transhumanist future has become widespread – a convincing account of how technology can be harnessed for profound positive progress; and energizing account that inspires coordinated action in support of that future. (Wood, 2018).

What is this compelling vision? Within the transhumanist agenda, there is deep concerted efforts to address why politics goes awry. The Center for the Governance of AI is part of the Future of Humanity Institute at Oxford University. Its focus is the political challenges as a result of transformative AI. Because the connection between distribution of knowledge and technology to politics may rely on AI to better coordinate actions for the future, we are once again looking at how transhumanists are exploring what needs to be done now for future productive outcomes. Rather than looking at the haves and have nots as separate populations, perhaps we might look at individuals and how they are contributing to uplift the human condition.

It hence makes sense to leave decisions on a deeply personal ethical level to individuals rather than making them society-wide policies. Global ethical policies will by necessity both run counter to the ethical opinion of many individuals, coercing citizens to act against their beliefs and hence violating their freedom and contain the temptation to adjust the policies to benefit the policymakers rather than the citizens. (Sandberg, 2001).

Ability to Advance Knowledge and Capacity to Achieve the Impossible

The potential advances in AI, molecular engineering, and automation, will be made at a faster pace and delivered to people around the world. Getting to people is challenging, and channels for delivery is necessary. But rather than having to deal with theft at boarders, molecular manufacturing can build products on the spot where products are needed—housing, food, cloths, clean water, etc. That future is not tomorrow, but the vision is here today, and that vision will come to fruition. We made it to the moon and we can discover solutions for human problems on Earth.

In 1970, in Zambia, Africa, Sister Mary Jucunda wrote to NASA and asked how they could justify spending billions of dollars on the space program while children were dying of starvation. Ernst Stuhlinger, a NASA rocket scientist responded with great empathy. He wrote to her and explained the benefits of the space program and included a reference to how seemingly wasteful acts often afford great rewards. The reference was about a wealthy Germany count in 1570 who helped many of the poor in the community. However when he donated money to build a lab for a glassworker to grind glass, the poor scorned him for wasting money on a mere hobby.

What transpired from the grinding of class was the invention of a microscope, which contributed to the elimination of the plague and other infectious diseases. Stuhlinger explained:

We need more knowledge in physics and chemistry, in biology and physiology, and very particularly in medicine to cope with all these problems which threaten [hu]man's life: hunger, disease, contamination of food and water, and pollution in the environment. (Siegel, 2017).

Advancing Knowledge

In some universities, a four-year university degree has shifted to a shorter, three-year and even two-year curricula, and with obtainable certifications in technical fields. Students now can select their degree areas and combine fields as interdisciplinary rather than being sequestered to one department or field. Life-long learning has endowed a fresh approach to education populated with adults whose careers encourage or require them to update their skills with refresher prep courses and certificate programs.

The ability to advance knowledge is all around us. Educational systems have altered the structure of the classroom from lecture hall and note-taking audience to a flexible 24/7 synchronous learning. The model is anytime, anywhere, online, on-ground, one-one-one mentoring, virtual, videotaped lectures, and chat rooms with whiteboards and other collaborative tools. The students are the customers or consumers and the educators are the knowledge providers. To best encourage and advance knowledge, the primary purpose is to ask the question: "Where is knowledge?" Once knowledge channels are identified, then we ask: "What could happen if the knowledge is wrong?" Predictive analytics uses the knowledge data that we have acquired to forecast or form conjecture about the information we do not have. To prescribe what we need to acquire, we then ask: "What should we do?" or "What are our options?"

Consider the scientific breakthroughs of two renown scientists, over 200 years apart in time, but whose innovation significantly changed the World.

Disciplines such as astronomy, chemistry, physics, geology, and biology have developed a robust combination of logical coherence, causal description, explanatory power, and testability, and have become examples of how reliable and deeply satisfying human knowledge can become. (Tooby and Cosmides, 1992, p. 19).

Newton provided theoretical evidence of gravitational fields in the esteemed "Principia", written in 1687 (Smith, 2008). Yet, without the prior work of Kepler or Galileo, Newton might not have arrived at his theory. Similarly, is Einstein developed the General Theory of Relativity (1915), which is arguably built upon Newton's research; however, because the science and technology had advanced between 1687 and 1915, Einstein had more available information to establish a new scope of reasoning. Here we have over a two-hundred-year difference of imparted new knowledge, both based on previous knowledge, and whose research evidences that new knowledge is achieved through the technology of their respective time frames.

At this point, strategizing about what knowledge is necessary to achieve a level of distinction is unveiled. Because the learning landscape is not static, all fields and their educators need to continually update their sources. Primary sources are foundational, and it is only when disruptive knowledge reveals new information that alters the value of the primary source; nevertheless, it is still of value. What does need attention are the second and tertiary sources that build off of the primary foundational knowledge and how new models for learning can bridge the gap between scholars and talent in the workforce.

The educator as entrepreneur is unique and sets into practice a relationship between learning and doing. As an example, Arizona State University (ASU) and Global Silicon Valley (GSV) host an annual summit called ASUGSV X[10] that is focused on leaders in education and tech talent. In short, it is a summit for educators to build out their curricula to meet industry standards; thereby, developing more efficient learning processes that will engage real-world scenarios that students can experience and better prepare them for building their careers. A far-reaching program that holds its summit in Brooklyn is the Close It Summit, which held the "SHIFT Happens: Work+Learn Futures.

U.S. News & World Report will join the Summit as a media partner, and Whiteboard Advisors and JobsFirst NYC will participate as leading strategic partners. Keynotes will include top CEOs from innovative Fortune 1000 companies, leading educational programs, and leading tech strategists. Attendance will continue to include industry, philanthropy, venture capital and national education and workforce leaders sharing their views of the shift in work and learn models with themes to include innovation, automation and technology. (Shulman, Feb 11, 2018).

One of the most recognized educational events referred to as the epicenter of edtech is the International Society for Technology in Education (ISTE) conference. These conferences are packed with innovation labs, team projects, project management, leadership, sharing knowledge, and where students can attend and gain a certification for credit. A slightly different approach in the entrepreneurial education sector is the Reimagine Education conference, which offers a $50,000 USD award for creating transformation educational initiatives, enhancing student learning outcomes and employability" (Shulman).

These projects offer potential, but we continue to ask who are the educators outside academic institutions? To prepare for lifelong learning, we need new curricula that is designed fall a varied demographics, including those who are in their later years. This is relevant to the social and economic sectors, as every day 10,000 baby boomers in the United States turn 65 and will until approximately 2030 (Heimlich, 2010). How are these people going to support themselves? Social security in the US is one way, but it may not be satisfying to not be part of the culture of entrepreneurs and innovators, educators and project leaders. Different countries have different statistics, but the fact is that people are living longer and may opt to continuing being a vital force in society—with a passion and purpose. Lifelong learning is an iterative process, we are never finished—we just keep getting smarter.

Ability to Advance Knowledge and Capacity to Achieve the Impossible

If the transhumanist era does bring about longer, healthier lifespans, then people need to be prepared to participate in the day-to-day activities of society, such as meeting others, continuing or changing a career, and socializing with others. New fields such as a living healthy project developer, life extension entrepreneur, and aging gracefully advisor. Predictive analytics helps to understand what could be ahead in the future for humanity and how to develop ethical AI to work with humans to strategize methods for designing sustainable environments, overcoming poverty, and improving upon the human condition.

Rather than throwing up our hands in the face of an uncertain future, transhumanists and other futurists seek to better understand our options (More, 2011).

Capacity to Achieve the Impossible - Amelioration to Transcend Limits

It is imminently necessary to deal with the exponentially increasing technology and to society's varied perceptions and reactions to AI, and there is a need for straightforward guidance in navigating towards the telos of our humanity. The greatest human achievements are hailed as overcoming unachievable odds through skill, courage and a committed focus. Some of these achievements are recognized as developed theories within science and technology, especially physics, astronomy and engineering, which led to electricity, space exploration, and medical breakthroughs. Other achievements have helped humanity understand what it means to be human through the creative expression of the mind and body through works of musical scores, architectural monuments, and in-depth narratives expressed in writing and the visual arts. Each era provides advances, some highly beneficial and some that have caused enormous grief and pain, but from all experiences we have gained the knowledge to take human ingenuity further than ever before (Vita-More, 2018).

This is quite lovely, but we have a problem. This problem is getting accurate information. For example, what is existential and why is it used to argue against supercomputing or the advancements in AI and instilling fears about robots? If we are the ones making the computers smart and the robots human-like, then is it us that we need to be wary of. Thus, are we Prometheus making the evolution of the homo sapiens out of the clay of our times? If so, are we doomed to be punished for all eternity?

As a philosophy transhumanism deals with fundamental nature of reality, knowledge, and existence. As a worldview, it offers a way of understanding the ecology of human integration with technology. As a business, its approach to the future brings to action strategic analyses of exponential technologies that are beneficial to entrepreneurs, innovators and investors. This process requires critical thinking and visionary narratives to assess how technology is altering human nature and what it means to be human in an uncertain world (Vita-More, 2018).

First-hand experience has afforded me an opportunity to be more aware of the questions people are asking today so that they can better understand their circumstances for the future. When questions repeat themselves over and over again, decade after decade, it is evident that the capacity to acquire and/or sustain knowledge is not working well. What types of questions are these and why have they not been answered effectively? Either the educational vehicle or the observer is amiss. It could be a referential gap in understanding of terms or phrases, or it could be that the sources providing information are obfuscated and/or contradictory.

As an example, if a person is concerned about exponential technology affecting what it means to be human, the question usually pertains to AI. But AI is narrow and is not exponential. The exponential factor, meaning continuing to grow (Moore's Law), expand and increase processing power is relative to artificial general intelligence (AGI) or Strong AI, not narrow AI. The haunting fear of AI is related to machine ethics and a forewarning from purveyors of fear. So, we have a society of people that are potentially missing out on the enormous benefits of AI in the fields of medicine, education, financial institutions, science research labs, etc. because they believe it is a threat to humans (Existential Risk). Once the emotions of society become entangled in fear, it is difficult to untangle. But we must sort it out through scholarship, effective learning models, entrepreneurs as educators, and vice versa. We can untangle it with our telos.

The vast knowledge held within any culture flourishes in a healthy society that prospers. The gift of fire gave incomparable benefits to humans—warmth, light, sustenance, and protection. As a practical matter, learning how to prepare for an uncertain future requires reliable sources, ethical leaders, and the skills to be able to identify deceptive information from authentic information. Not only this, we must navigate our own evolution and champion the challenges as we learn along the way.

Raise the level of uncertainty a bit and you're in a situation where there are several distinct possible futures, one of which will occur. In these situations, you can make good use of tools such as scenario planning, game theory, and decision-tree real-options valuation. At a higher level of uncertainty, we face a range of futures and must use additional tools such as system dynamics models. When uncertainty is at its highest and the range of possible outcomes is unbounded, we can only look to analogies and reference cases and try to devise resilient strategies and designs. (More 2011).

REFERENCES

Aberth, J. (2011). Plagues in World History. Lanham, MD: Rowman & Littlefield Publishers.

Aeschylus. (1975). *Prometheus Bound* (J. Scully & J. D. Herington, Trans.). Oxford University Press.

Bainbridge, W. (2013). Transavatars. In M. More & N. Vita-More (Eds.), *The Transhumanist Reader: Classical and Contemporary Essays on the Science, Technology, and Philosophy of the Human Future*. Hoboken, NJ: Wiley-Blackwell, John Wiley & Sons, Inc. doi:10.1002/9781118555927.ch9

Black, J. (2013). *Greek mythology and human origins*. Available: https://www.ancient-origins.net/human-origins-folklore/greek-mythology-and-human-origins-0064

Buesing, D. (2017, July 7). 5 DC Villains Who Destroyed The Justice League. *Comic Book Reader*. Retrieved from https://www.cbr.com/15-dc-villains-who-destroyed-the-justice-league/

Cartwright, M. (2013, April 20). Prometheus. *Ancient History Encyclopedia*. Retrieved from https://www.ancient.eu/Prometheus/

Heimlich, R. (2010, Dec. 29). *Baby Boomers Retire*. FactTank. Pew Research Center. Retrieved from http://www.pewresearch.org/fact-tank/2010/12/29/baby-boomers-retire/

More, M. (2011). *True Transhumanism. In H+/=: Transhumanism and Its Critics*. Metanexus Institute.

Nolan, C. (Dir.). (2012). *The Dark Knight Rises*. Retrieved from https://www.imdb.com/title/tt1345836/

Oddee. (2007, Oct. 15). *7 Worst Killer Plagues in History*. Retrieved from https://www.oddee.com/item_90608.aspx

Plato. (380 B.C.E.). *Protagoras*. Retrieved from http://classics.mit.edu/Plato/protagoras.html

PricewaterhouseCoopers (PwC). (n.d.). *2019 AI Predictions: Six AI priorities you can't afford to ignore*. PwC. Retrieved from https://www.pwc.com/AI2019#section3

Rogers, B. M., & Stevens, B. E. (2015). Introduction: The Past Is an Undiscovered County. In Classical Traditions in Science Fiction (pp. 1–2). Oxford, UK: Oxford University Press.

Shelly, M. (1818). *Frankenstein or The Modern Prometheus*. London: Lackington, Hughes, Harding, Mavor & Jones.

Shulman, R. D. (2018, Feb 11). If You Are An Education Entrepreneur In 2018. *Forbes*. Retrieved from https://www.forbes.com/sites/robynshulman/2018/02/11/10-conferences-you-should-attend-if-you-are-an-education-entrepreneur-in-2018/#a1d1cbd36d5d

Siegel, E. (2017, Oct. 26). Why Exploring Space And Investing in Research Is Non-Negotiable. *Forbes*. Retrieved from https://www.forbes.com/sites/startswithabang/2017/10/26/even-while-the-world-suffers-investing-in-science-is-non-negotiable/#538fabd21647

Singh, S. (2017, Nov. 20). *Transhumanism And The Future Of Humanity: 7 Ways The World Will Change By 2030*. Retrieved from https://www.forbes.com/sites/sarwantsingh/2017/11/20/transhumanism-and-the-future-of-humanity-seven-ways-the-world-will-change-by-2030/#498018347d79

Smith, G. (2008). Newton's *Philosophiae Naturalis Principia Mathematica*. In *The Stanford Encyclopedia of Philosophy*. Retrieved from https://plato.stanford.edu/archives/win2008/entries/newton-principia/

Tooby, J., & Cosmides, L. (1992). The Psychological Foundations of Culture. In J. Barkow, L. Cosmides, & J. Tooby (Eds.), *The Adapted Mind: Evolutionary Psychology and the Generation of Culture* (p. 19). New York: Oxford University Press, Inc.

Vita-More, N. (2018). Transhumanism: What is it? Academic Press.

Wood, D. (2018). *Transcending Politics: A Technoprogressive Roadmap to a Comprehensively Better Future*. London: Delta Wisdom.

Chapter 3
According to Zoltan Istvan:
Transhumanism and Future

Zoltan Istvan
Transhumanist Party, USA

ABSTRACT

Radical science and technology are changing everything around us. The area of transhumanism is growing dramatically in size and impact - and the impact on our species is enormous. In just a decade, many things can change how we live our lives. The upcoming innovation will be amazing. Transhumanists believe that we must protect ourselves from our natural genes, unless they bind us to remain forever as animals. We believe that our outdated instincts can easily tempt us to know right from wrong, practical from impractical. If you look closely, the human body and its biology constantly highlights our many imperfections. Transhumanism seeks to improve the human body through science and technology - that is, to help people develop. This is a strange cultural and philosophical position for a movement. And yet, change is exactly what transhumanism aspires to.

INTRODUCTION

Are you ready for the future?

We know that driverless test cars are on the road, and how doctors in France are replacing people's hearts with permanent robotic ones. Some researchers investigate already a billion-dollar market for brainwave readers/brain wave reading headsets. Using electroencephalography (EEG) sensors that pick up and monitor brain activity, NeuroSky's MindWave (2018) can attach to Google Glass and allow you to take a picture and post it to Facebook and Twitter just by thinking about it. With other headsets, you can play video games on your iPhone with your thoughts. In fact, more than a year ago, the first mind-to-mind communication took place. An Indian researcher projected a thought to a colleague in France and they got along with their headsets. They understand each other, trough to headsets. That mean is, telepathy became reality from science fiction.

DOI: 10.4018/978-1-5225-8431-5.ch003

According to Zoltan Istvan

The history of transhumanism—the burgeoning field of science and radical tech used to describe robotic implants, prosthetics, and cyborg-like enhancements in the human being and its experience—has come a long way since scientists began throwing around the term a half century ago.

The thriving pro-cyborg medical industry is setting the stage for trillion-dollar markets that will remake the human experience. Furthermore, this industry is continuously developing. For the last couple of decades, researches show that five million people in America suffer from Alzheimer's (Moore, 2015), but a new surgery that involves installing brain implants is showing promise in restoring people's memory and improving lives. The use of medical and microchip implants, whether in the brain or not, are expected to surge in the coming years. Some experts surmise as many as half of Americans will have implants by 2020. I already have one in my hand (Istvan, 2015A). Moreover, as the world becomes more technologically orientated, fewer people will want to carry around purses and wallets, when all this info can be contained in a microchip the size of a grain of rice that can be implanted in a person's hand. As a result, we can talk about that within a decade, half of humans will have microchip implants in them.

Are We Ready for the Transhumanist Future as a Human and Society?

Transhumanism is a social movement that aims to use science and technology to radically modify the human body—and modify the human experience, just like a future of contact lenses that see in the dark, endoskeleton attached artificial limbs that lift a half-ton, and brain chip implants that read your thoughts and instantly communicate them to others (Istvan, 2014). May be those developments are frightening and those also will be held. In fact, much of those technologies already exists. Some of them being sold commercially at your local superstore or being tested in laboratories right now around the world. So, in this case, how will change the artificial intelligence practices humanity in the future?

The answer for this question is; artificial intelligence will dramatically reshape humanity within 20 years. But the key to the survival of human beings is merging our brains with artificial intelligence by brain implants. We can't just create artificial intelligence and let it go freely, as it will become the dominant species on Planet Earth. We must merge with it, by making our brain be one with it in the cloud. Numerous companies in Silicon Valley are working on this technology right now.

In any case, humans and their advancing technology will create paths and plans of our universe that will transform us into other entities - transhuman beings. We are at the door of a new world and experience, and transhumanism is the future.

The human race is on the threshold of so much revolutionary change, and societies will also be affected by these changes. On the other hand, it is not hard to imagine that this transformation will be able to create a different and new structure in societies, too. What kind of change do you foresee in the social structure? Apparently massive changes will take place in the social structures of society. Another question is "If we can live 1000 years in the future, will we get married and have kids?". Because then marriage is "forever" and also, if we live thousands of years, we may not want kids. Kids would become robots anyway in the future, so it's not the same. Basically, social structures will fall away as we become machine entities. We will, however, probably find new social structures that work for AI beings and robots.

Within a decade, babies with augmented intelligence will be alive. There's already technologies out there that may improve or outright replace CRISPR gene editing technology. Even so, genetic editing of the human embryo is still here to stay. Through these technologies we will be able to eliminate hereditary disease and improve human performance. More importantly, we will be able to improve human intelligence and boost our own IQ and also increase the IQ of babies. This situation may be even potentially creating a new generation of Einsteins (Istvan, 2016).

Change in Daily and Business Life

Just like social structures, change will affect not only daily life but also business life. Then, next question is "How will this change affect daily life and business life?"

Daily life and business will be dramatically affected because of transhumanism. I don't believe many jobs will survive the onslaught of the robot revolution or complete automation. Probably, robots will be better than humans at everything, so they will quickly replace all human workers.

Entrepreneurs, venture capital firms and even business media are seeing new transhuman-oriented companies emerge and work to overcome death. The next generation of billionaires is likely to come from the biotech industry. However, transhumanist technology is much bigger than just biotechnology. All technology is reinventing the human being as we know it. The driverless cars will soon eliminate tens of thousands of fatalities worldwide from drunken driving accidents. The exoskeleton technology already brings in wheelchair users who get up and walk. Chip implants monitor our fluid and sugar content and tell our smartphones when and what we should eat and drink.

Transhumanism will soon prove to be the coolest and possibly most important industry in the world. The big business is pushing to hire engineers and scientists who can launch brand new health products to adapt to our changing biological self. And in fact we are changing. From deafness wiped out by cochlear implant technology, to stem cell rejuvenation of cancer-damaged organs, to creative babies born with genetics. This is no longer the future. That's here today.

Looking to the future, companies that use radical science and technology will make humans the healthiest and strongest bodies they can become (Istvan, 2015B).

So, what will humans do to survive?

Probably the government will have to give a Universal Basic Income, and then humans will live lives of luxury. So in the end, robots doing everything might be very nice and liberating.

Transhumanism and Learning

All these changes will impact learning, which is the critical process of human beings. Within 20 years, going to college won't exist. What will exist is downloading information into our brains via chip implants, similar to the Matrix movie. Why spend 10 years learning to play piano when you can play Motzart in minutes after downloading the information. Our brains will be plugged into the cloud, and we will educate ourselves there on everything. These effects can be seen on learning of human. On the other hand, there is also learning for transhuman. What will be the transhumans' learning like in the future?

Probably, transhumans learn by uploading information into their brain. But the more important question is how do they learn morals. I think as long as death and danger exist, our moral systems and sense of survival will determine our lives and why we learn and evolve. We essentially evolve to live better and avoid death. So most education and evolution of our species will focus on becoming a species that doesn't die and more perfect than we've ever been.

So, how can educational institutions be shaped in line with these changes?

Sadly, I don't believe education institutions can be shaped much longer. Take media for example. Media no longer leads—but Facebook does, Google does, Apple does. Media comes from them, even if they don't have many journalists. In the same way, education will come from major tech corporations which might even become larger than entire countries. I see major tech companies swallowing everything—all business and even most government. Let's just hope they continue to have our best interest in their hearts.

REFERENCES

Istvan, Z. (2014). *A New Generation of Transhumanists Is Emerging*. Retrieved from https://www.huffingtonpost.com/zoltan-istvan/a-new-generation-of-trans_b_4921319.html

Istvan, Z. (2015A). *Why I'm running for president—and got a chip implanted in my hand*. Retrieved from https://www.dailydot.com/via/zoltan-istvan-rfid-chip-implant/

Istvan, Z. (2015B). *Transhumanism Is Booming and Big Business Is Noticing*. Retrieved from https://www.huffpost.com/entry/transhumanism-is-becoming_b_7807082

Istvan, Z. (2016). *Why Haven't We Met Aliens Yet? Because They've Evolved into AI*. Retrieved from https://motherboard.vice.com/en_us/article/vv7bkb/why-havent-we-met-aliens-yet-because-theyve-evolved-into-ai

Moore, C. (2015). *Brain Implant Could Help People With Memory Loss*. Retrieved from https://alzheimersnewstoday.com/2015/10/06/brain-implant-help-people-memory-loss/

NeuroSky's MindWave. (2018). Retrieved from https://store.neurosky.com/

Chapter 4
Automatic IQ Estimation Using Stylometric Methods

Polina Shafran Abramov
University of Louisville, USA

Roman V. Yampolskiy
University of Louisville, USA

ABSTRACT

Stylometry is a study of text linguistic properties that brings together various fields of research such as statistics, linguistics, computer science and more. Stylometry methods have been used for historic investigation, as forensic evidence and an educational tool. This chapter presents a method to automatically estimate individual's IQ based on quality of writing and discusses challenges associated with it. The method utilizes various text features and NLP techniques to calculate indexes which are used to estimate individual's IQ. The results show a high degree of correlation between expected and estimated IQs in cases when IQ is within the average range. Obtaining good estimation for IQs on the high and low ends of the spectrum proves to be more challenging and this work offers several reasons for that. Over the years stylometry benefitted from wide exposure and interest among researches, however it appears that there aren't studies that focus on using stylometry methods to estimate individual's intelligence. Perhaps this work presents the first in-depth attempt to do so.

INTRODUCTION

Stylometry is a study of linguistic properties of the text which employs an analysis of various text features to study a document. Stylometry combines various fields of research such as statistics, linguistics, philology, psychology computer science and more. For quite some time stylometry has been used to assess one's development level for education purposes. However, per our investigation not many studies attempt to detect the IQ level of text's author. Despite wide availability of various text corpora, one of the biggest challenges for such research is finding the training and testing data. Ideally, for such research one would require not only the text corpora but also authors' IQ score, however due to privacy laws associated with such information, obtaining such data is deemed impossible.

DOI: 10.4018/978-1-5225-8431-5.ch004

One attempt to explore a correlation between the Quality of Writing (QoW) and the writer's IQ was made by Nawaf Ali (2014).However inability to obtain access to data required for the research forced him to change the original direction of research and settle for a simplified plan. In his study Ali is able to classify texts based on QoW using such features as occurrence of rare words, vocabulary richness, word's length and more. His results showed 99.8% accuracy when classifying texts of two highly distinct groups (Scientific Writing Samples vs School Students Writing) but proved more challenging when the borderline between intelligence groups was thinner, e.g. 4th-5th graders vs middle school students. A preliminary research "Automated IQ Estimation from Writing Samples" (A. Hendrix, R. Yampolskiy, 2017) introduces the idea of correlation between the vocabulary used in a written sample and the writer's IQ. This research shows the existence of such correlation and urges further research on the subject.

In "The Other IQ" (Simonton, 2009) Dean Keith Simonton talks about "historiometry" – a discipline in which the IQ assessment may be performed on participants that are long deceased, by applying quantitative analysis on historical data such as person's biography profiles, letters and political speeches.

This research might become the first and initial deep dive into the subject of stylometry based IQ assessment.

METHOD

In this research we are making an attempt to work arounds the difficulty of obtaining dataset of written samples with corresponding IQ scores by proposing a hypothesis. Our method utilizes the bell curve distribution of IQ scores.

We are going to compute stylometric features on the training set and plot their normal distribution. The proposed hypothesis is that if the normal distribution of the computed feature matches the IQ scores distribution, then we can use the IQ curve to estimate author's IQ.

In order to find a correlation between person's writing ability and IQ, we need to find a way to assess the quality of the written sample. A common way of doing it in stylometry is choosing several relevant text features and explore them. Our feature selection process relied on three aspects – previous research, experimentation and relevance. In her research on Linguistic Features of Writing Quality (McNamara, Crossley and McCarthy, 2010) Danielle McNamara et al. concluded that lexical features such as number of sentences, number of paragraphs, number of words per sentence and number of sentences per paragraph were not showing significant difference for high and low proficiency essays, hence those features were discarded. On the other hand, features such as lexical diversity and vocabulary proficiency showed correlation with individual's abilities. Multiple experiments were performed on more than 100 indices calculated by both our scripts and Coh-Metrix (Dowell, Graesser and Cai, 2016; Graesser, McNamara and Kulikowich, 2011; Graesser, McNamara, Louwerse and Cai, 2004; McNamara, Graesser, McCarthy and Cai, 2014; McNamara, Louwerse, Cai and Graesser, 2009) tool. Results that didn't show sufficient match between index's and IQ score's normal distributions were discarded. Lastly, multiple IQ test questions were explored and used as the guidance in selected appropriate features.

Selected Features

Lexical Aptitude Ration (LAR)

For this feature, we utilize a list of words (denoted as D) that is used by SAT for evaluation of vocabulary proficiency. The goal is to identify whether the author used any of those words in the text sample. Then given a text sample of length N, the formula for LAR is shown in Figure 1.

Lexical Diversity (LDMTLD)

LDMTLD is am measure of unique words used in the text. The simplest way to measure LD is to use type- type-token ratio (TTR) (Templin, 1957) that is defined as the number of unique words (called types) divided by the overall number of words in text (tokens). This measure, however, shows high sensitivity to text length. To reduce discrepancies caused by different lengths of text samples, we are going to use MTLD measure for Lexical Diversity, that was developed specifically to reduce the effect of text length. MTLD is calculated as the mean length of sequential word strings in a text that maintain a given TTR value (McCarthy and Jarvis, 2010).

Syntactic Complexity (SYNNP)

Measures the syntactic structure of the sentence. The sentence is considered less complex when, for instance, it has fewer verbs before the main verb of the main clause, when it is shorter or when it follows the simple syntactic pattern of actor-action-object. For this measure, we use Coh-Metrix SYNNP index which measures the mean number of modifiers per noun-phrase. A modifier is an optional element in a sentence and is said to modify (change the meaning of) another element in the structure, on which it is dependent. This is a good measure of working memory load.

Meaningfulness (WRDMEAc)

This metric is based on the meaningfulness ratings corpus developed by Toglia and Battig (Toglia and Battig, 1978) that provides ratings for 2627 words. As Coh-Metrix description states "Words with higher meaningfulness scores are highly associated with other words (e.g., people), whereas a low meaningfulness score indicates that the word is weakly associated with other words." (McNamara, Louwerse, Cai and Graesser, 2009). We use Coh-Metrix WRDMEAc index that calculates meaningfulness rating for content words only.

Figure 1. Formula for LAR

$$LAR = \left\{ \frac{CountDistinct(W)}{N}, W \in D \right\} \qquad (1)$$

DATA

SAT Vocabulary

A list of 5000 words for SAT preparation (SAT, 2014) is used to identify words for LAR feature.

Training Set

For training set we used Open American National Corpus (OANC) (ANC, 2018) that consists of texts of American English produced since 1990. The corpus includes both spoken and written text samples with written samples including technical articles, grant proposals, letters, essays and more. Only written texts are used in this research. The corpus has been preprocessed to exclude samples that are poorly written or constructed.

Test Set

Ideally, the test set would consist of text samples and the IQs of their authors. However, finding such set is a very hard task. This data is not publically available and not many people would willingly share it, especially if their IQ is relatively low. There are several people in the world with known IQ scores, for example, world renowned theoretical physicist Stephen Hawkings (IQ 160) and an American columnist and a writer Marylyn Von Savant (IQ 190). However, those are mostly people with an extraordinary high IQs which doesn't make for a balanced test dataset. Selecting a text sample for these people would also be challenging as the goal and the target audience of these texts can vary, thus creating very incoherent data set. For example, if this is a scientific paper written for the audience of scientists, the choice of language and the structure of the text will take that into an account. In such texts, we can expect frequent appearance of field-specific terminology that is not as common outside the academia world, formulas and overall structure that is specific to scientific articles. On the other hand, if this same author were to write an article to be understood by the general public, chances are that the author would chose a simplified way to express ideas in "layman's terms". This creates a potential of constructing a non-homogeneous dataset that is hard to evaluate and compare. To partially solve this issue, we used publicly available GRE sample essays as our test set (ETC, 2011), (ETC, 2018). There are several benefits in using these samples:

- The samples are written on a given subject with the expectation for them to be evaluated and graded, hence offer a more homogeneous dataset.
- The samples are written with the expectation to be evaluated and graded hence we can assume that the writer "did their best" when writing the text.
- The samples are written by a single person and didn't undergo any editing process.
- Each text sample has been evaluated and analyzed by a human and given a score. The score can be used as an IQ estimation and mapped to an expected IQ.

GRE scores for written samples go from 1 to 6 and are not as granular as IQ score. For this reason, each score is mapped to the range of IQ scores. Note that score 0 is also valid for GRE writing test, however, for the purpose of this research, we are discarding this score as it would indicate an empty text.

In order to map GRE scores to IQ scores we use a chart that interprets the meaning of IQ scores shown in Table 1. The chart is based on Resing and Blok (Resing and Blok, 2002).

GRE test is geared towards graduate students which are unlikely to have an IQ that is below average, hence mapping lower GRE grades to IQ ranges between 70 and 89 requires an additional explanation.

A close examination of GRE samples that received lower scores shows that those are cases where an examinee either ran out of time or appeared as non- native speaker. Even though most likely those are not individuals with low IQs, their text samples can serve as an estimation for low-IQ samples. Following above logic, the mapping of GRE scores to IQ score ranges looks as shown in Table 2.

This research doesn't attempt to claim that there is a reliable way to convert GRE scores to IQ scores. The authors are aware that these two tests are different and there is no known correlation between GRE and IQ score. We are using only the samples from the Analytical Writing portion of the test to construct a homogenous set of written essays and simulate IQ scores. Our final test set contains twelve GRE text samples - two samples for each GRE score.

PROCESS

Training

1. Preprocess OANC dataset.
2. Compute LAR, LDMTLD, SYNNP and WRDMEAc features.

Table 1. IQ scores interpretation

IQ	Intelligence Level
>130	Very Gifted
121-130	Gifted
111-120	Above Average
90-110	Average
80-89	Below Average
70-79	Cognitively Impaired

Table 2. Mapping GRE score to IQ ranges

IQ	Intelligence Level
131-160	6
121-130	5
111-120	4
90-110	3
80-89	2
70-79	1

3. Normalize computed features to match IQ range (40 - 160) and plot them as a normal distribution overlaid with the known IQ distribution curve. The first goal at this stage is to see how close the obtained distribution of text grades overlays with the IQ distribution curve.
4. Collect coefficients used in step 3 transformations. These coefficients are going to be used to transform test set results.

Testing

1. Compute LAR, LDMTLD, SYNNP and WRDMEAc features.
2. Use coefficients from Training step 3 to transform the indices of the testing set.
3. Evaluate the resulting score with respect to its proximity to the expected IQ range.

IMPLEMENTATION

OANC Dataset Preprosessing

OANC dataset contains large amount of text samples. Not all of them being relevant or useful for this research, hence certain degree of data preprocessing was required. The corpus includes text samples from various sources, including transcripts of spoken text. Due to the fact that this research focuses on written text, all spoken samples were removed from the training set. The original corpora contained 6516 written text samples. During the analysis process, several samples that contained unreadable characters were discovered. Those samples could not be processed by automatic tools, hence were excluded. Some of Coh-Metrix indices provide descriptive information regarding text sample, such as number of sentences, words and paragraphs. Out-of-norm values of those metrics can hint to poorly structured or poorly written text. For example, a text that contains only one sentence is either too short or completely lacks any punctuation, which would make it ineffective as part of training set. Coh-Metrix descriptive indices were examined to detect and remove such samples.

As a result of this preprocessing the remaining dataset that is being used as training set contains 5749 samples of written text.

Training Set Analysis

The calculation of the features on the training dataset was performed by our proprietary analytical program implemented in python using NLTK library and Coh- Metrix tool.

LAR Feature Calculation

We use our own implementation to compute LAR. Our python script utilizes NLTK (Natural Language Toolkit) python suite that implements Natural Language Processing functionality. The calculation of this feature requires a predefined list of words that are considered proficient. We used a SAT preparation list of 5000 words, which was stemmed using NLTK Porter Stemmer (NLTK, 2018). This stemming is done in order to allow for a more flexible lookup in which we are looking for a word's stem rather than its exact appearance. For example, the SAT list includes the word "abridgment". Our goal is to detect all the cases in which this word appears in its various forms, such as "abridged" or "abridge". This becomes possible if instead of comparing the exact word we compare only its stem - "abridg".

```
from nltk.stem.porter import PorterStemmer
if __name__ == "__main__":
    f = open('vocabulary.txt', 'r')
    out = open('vocabulary_stem.txt', 'w')
    porter_stemmer = PorterStemmer()
    for line in f:
        sline = line.split(' ', 3)
        out.write(porter_stemmer.stem(sline[0]) + '\n')
```

Now that we have the list of stems, we can calculate the LAR index. Each word is stemmed before being looked up in the vocabulary. In order to improve performance, we skip stop words, such as "a", "an", "the", "and" as we can safely assume those words are not going to be on the list. There is an additional logic to account for cases when the same stem appears more than one time in the sample. We only count it once.

```
def calculateLAR(text):
    count = 0
    d = {}
    duplicates = {}
    with open("vocabulary_stem.txt") as f:
        for line in f:
         line = line.rstrip()
            if line not in d:
                d[line] = line
    for word in text:
      if (word not in stopwords.words('english')):
            porter_stemmer = PorterStemmer()
         stemmed_word = porter_stemmer.stem(word)
            if stemmed_word in d:
                #skip duplicates
                if stemmed_word in duplicates:
                    continue;
                duplicates[stemmed_word] = True;
                count+=1
    return count/len(text)
```

Other Features Calculation

The resulting Coh-Metrix spreadsheet contains all 105 Coh-Metrix indeces that were calculated for each text sample. Out of those we select Lexical Diversity (LDMTLD), Syntactic Complexity (SYNNP) and Meaningfulness (WRDMEAc).

Features Transformation

Here the goal is to plot a normal distribution for each feature and to overlay it with the known IQ normal distribution. In order to do so, a linear transformation of a form ax+b is applied on each index to map its range to [40, 160] segment. This transformation is calculated separately for each index and performed using python script.

First we find the coefficients a and b by solving linear equation where min_value and max_value are the lowest and highest values of the given index.

```
def findCoefficients(min_value, max_value)
    return solve((40 - b - a*min_value, 160 - b - a*max_value), a, b)
```

Then, we apply the transformation on each feature value and move the transformed values so that their mean point aligns with the mean point of IQ standard deviation curve, which is equal to 100.

```
transformed_indices =
    list(map(lambda x:float(c[a])*x+float(c[b]), indices_arr))
diff = 100 - np.mean(transformed_indices)
final_indices = map(lambda x:x+diff, transformed_indices)
```

After finding the a, b and diff coefficients and applying the transformation, the resulting index values are plotted along with IQ normal distribution. This allows us to assess the degree in which two curves align. Figure 2 shows the resulting distribution for all 4 indices overlaid with the IQ Score normal distribution. Yellow curve represents the distribution of index values, while the red curve represents IQ bell curve.

Test Set Analysis

We are interested in calculating the same features for the samples from test set as the ones calculated for training set. As previously, the computation of LAR feature is performed by our proprietary analytical program implemented in python using NLTK and LDMLTD, SYNNP and WRDMEAc features are computed by Coh-Metrix tool. Having computed all four features for the test set, we used the coefficients that were calculated for the corresponding index from the training set in order to place the index value on the curve. This value is the Calculated IQ that we are going to compare for the Expected IQ. For example, for SYNNP index the calculation looks as follows:

Where SI denotes the test sample value of SYNNP feature and aSYNNP, bSYNNP and diffSYNNP are the coefficients calculated for SYNNP feature on the training set.

Figure 2. SYNNP, LDMTLD, WRDMEAc and LAR indices distribution (yellow) plotted with IQ normal distribution curve (red)

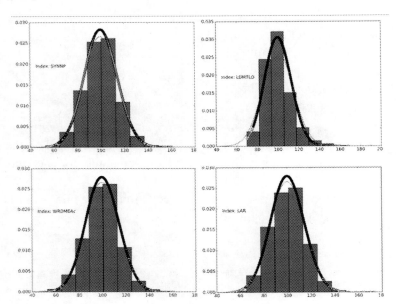

Figure 3. Calculated IQ formula

$$Calculated\ IQ = a_{SYNNP} * SI + b_{SYNNP} + diff_{SYNNP} \quad (2)$$

The final step of the process consists of assessing the proximity of Calculated IQ to the Expected IQ. Since our Expected IQ is expressed as a range, we performed the assessment by calculating the error between the Calculated IQ and the high and low boundary of the Expected IQ range. If the Calculated IQ falls within Expected IQ range, then the error value is equal 0. Any value that has the error value less than 10% from either boundary is considered acceptable.

RESULTS

The results of the analysis described in previous session are presented in Figure 4 and Figure 5. Figure 4 shows calculated IQ Scores based on each one of the chosen features – SYNNP, LDMTLD, WRDMEAc and LAR. The left most column lists the Expected IQ that is compared with the Calculated IQ. Figure 5 displays the results of this comparison by presenting the value of the error. The highlighted cells show all the results where the error is up to 10%.

Figure 4. Table of calculated IQ Scores

Exp. IQ	Sample Name	SYNNP	LDMTLD	WRDMEAc	LAR
70-79	Sample 1	72.20	75.55	67.69	84.98
	Sample 2	104.98	76.11	123.90	98.12
80-89	Sample 3	131.28	76.96	72.54	95.93
	Sample 4	113.32	72.42	81.55	91.60
90-110	Sample 5	121.32	86.88	83.68	108.70
	Sample 6	114.83	84.59	93.51	125.56
111-120	Sample 7	108.01	88.98	104.92	121.93
	Sample 8	109.74	92.79	124.72	101.74
121-130	Sample 9	103.36	76.14	111.63	94.82
	Sample 10	119.37	117.02	104.47	135.67
131-160	Sample 11	118.08	95.65	121.67	89.20
	Sample 12	124.14	87.02	75.10	102.62

Figure 5. Table of error values for calculated IQ scores

Exp. IQ	Sample Name	SYNNP	LDMTLD	WRDMEAc	LAR
70-79	Sample 1	0.00	0.00	3.30	0.00
	Sample 2	32.89	0.00	56.84	24.20
80-89	Sample 3	47.50	3.80	9.32	7.79
	Sample 4	27.32	9.47	0.00	2.92
90-110	Sample 5	10.29	3.46	7.02	1.18
	Sample 6	4.39	6.01	0.00	14.14
111-120	Sample 7	2.69	19.83	5.48	0.00
	Sample 8	1.13	16.41	3.94	8.34
121-130	Sample 9	14.58	37.08	7.75	21.64
	Sample 10	1.34	3.29	13.66	0.00
131-160	Sample 11	9.87	26.99	7.12	31.91
	Sample 12	5.24	33.57	42.67	21.67

The correlation between chosen features and IQ scores is visible in the obtained results even though not all of them fall within 10% margin. At least 60% of the results for each index estimate IQ level with up to 10% error with some indices showing particularly good results. For example, WRDMEAc feature provides good estimations on the author's IQ level in 75% of the cases. Notably, the results for samples that represent non-extreme IQ scores (90-120) show very good approximation with 3 out of 4 indices showing errors within 10% range and the remaining fourth index falling within 20%. As we observe the more "out of norm" IQ scores, the correlation is still noticeable but error values increase. For Sample 3 and Sample 4 we still see three out of four features giving a very close guess, but the error on the remaining fourth SYNNP feature gets almost up to 50%.

Figure 6. Table of calculated IQ scores for high IQ represent non-extreme IQ scores (90-120) show very individuals

Exp. IQ	Sample Name	SYNNP	LDMTLD	WRDMEAc	LAR
160 - 180	Anonymous M	107.90	88.64	93.27	112.37
	Garth Zietsman	100.98	101.26	94.91	99.12
	Marilyn vos Savant	110.72	101.39	117.42	98.08
	S. Hawkins	104.12	91.54	93.11	108.17

Weaknesses

Analyzing the results unveiled several weaknesses in our method. It is important to note that most of those weaknesses are present in standard IQ test as well and are not specific to our method, some of them, however, become more evident when using an automated method that does not involve an assessment by human.

Sample Length

Calculating text based metrics requires that a text sample is long enough to be analyzed. There is no single number of words that would be perfect for all cases, but from our experiments the minimum length requirement at which metrics give sensible results is around 300 words per text. Sample 2, for example consists only of 2 sentences and contains under 50 words, which without a doubt contributes to the difficulty in properly assess some of the features. It is interesting to note, that LDMTLD index for this sample shows an error that is less than 10%, which complies with the claim that this specific index was designed to not be dependent on the length of the texts.

Extreme IQ Scores

In cases when IQ score is very low or very high, our method can be hard to rely on. People with IQ lower than 70 are classified as people with mental disability and the expectation to obtain a text sample that can be analyzed using normal metrics might be unreasonable. Same with the opposite case – the higher IQ score gets, the harder it becomes to solely rely on features of the text. Standard IQ test suffer from similar deficiency. Figure 6 and Figure 7 display results of IQ estimations for several individuals who are known to have extremely high IQ scores. We used samples by S. Hawking (2016), Marilyn vos Savant (2018), Garth Zietsman (2010) and Anonymous M (personal info omitted for privacy reasons). The results are quite unsatisfying with error values varying between 20% and 40%.

Figure 7. Table of error values for calculated IQ scores for high IQ individuals

Exp. IQ	Sample Name	SYNNP	LDMTLD	WRDMEAc	LAR
160-180	Anonymous M	32.56	44.60	41.71	29.77
	Garth Zietsman	36.89	36.71	40.68	38.05
	Marilyn vos Savant	30.80	36.63	26.61	38.70
	S. Hawkins	34.93	42.79	41.81	32.39

Dependence on Language

The method in its current design is geared towards native English speakers as the indices are calculated based on English grammar rules. Furthermore, LAR feature relies on list of SAT words which is designed and used in United States, making the LAR index specific to American English. To make this method work for another language, one would need to calculate the same indices for that language. This limitation is not unique to our method. Regular IQ test is also language dependent, at least its verbal part, and requires an assessment using one's native language. In addition, just like regular IQ test, our method will potentially discriminate against individuals who are not using their native language to write the text sample. This isn't because of an inherent issue in our method design, but rather due to the fact that non- native speakers have a disadvantage when it comes to proficiency in foreign language as opposed to their native speaking peers. This can result in a less sophisticated text sample and lower IQ estimation.

CONCLUSION AND FUTURE WORK

This work presents one of the first attempts to use stylometry principles to estimate individual's IQ score. Results obtained using our method are very promising and can serve as a stepping stone for further research in this area. One of the main things that would help to move this work forward is obtaining or creating a dataset of text samples with corresponding IQ scores of their authors. To avoid privacy complication, such dataset can be fully anonymized as we are not interested in specific identities, but rather the correlation itself. Having such training dataset will potentially allow researchers to achieve more precise results.

Four specific features were used in this research, however there is a lot of other information that can be extracted from a text sample and used to improve the assessment. Coh-Metrix tool offers more than 100 different indices and it is worth exploring them and their correlation with author's intelligence as well. Perhaps the assessment of text length could be incorporated into the analyses of the text to account for the edge case where the sample is too short to rely on calculated indices values.

Additional step forward would be to find an efficient way to combine results of various features into a single number that would provide the final estimation. The process of combining multiple features into one will need to be intelligent enough to account for different situations. Our results show that some features provide better estimation than others in different circumstances, hence one should consider granting a different level of importance to each feature. The This can be done by assigning weights to each feature and calculating weighted average. The weights might need to be dynamic and change based on context. There is a potential to employ machine learning techniques such as genetic algorithm or neural networks to find the appropriate weight values.

REFERENCES

Ali, N. (2014). *Text stylometry for chat bot identification and intelligence estimation*. Academic Press.

ANC. (2018). *American National Corpus Project*. Available: http://www.anc.org

Dowell, N. M., Graesser, A. C., & Cai, Z. (2016). Language and discourse analysis with Coh-Metrix: Applications from educational material to learning environments at scale. *Journal of Learning Analytics*, *3*(3), 72–95. doi:10.18608/jla.2016.33.5

ETC. (2011). *Analytical Writing Sample Essays and Commentaries*. Available: https://www.ets.org/s/gre/accessible/gre_practice_test_2_writing_responses_18_point.pdf

ETC. (2018). *Sample Essay Responses and Rater Commentary for the Argument Task*. Available: https://www.ets.org/gre/revised_general/prepare/analytical_writing/argument/sample_responses

Graesser, A. C., McNamara, D. S., & Kulikowich, J. M. (2011). Coh-Metrix: Providing multilevel analyses of text characteristics. *Educational Researcher*, *40*(5), 223–234. doi:10.3102/0013189X11413260

Graesser, A. C., McNamara, D. S., Louwerse, M. M., & Cai, Z. (2004). Coh-Metrix: Analysis of text on cohesion and language. *Behavior Research Methods, Instruments, & Computers*, *36*(2), 193–202. doi:10.3758/BF03195564 PMID:15354684

Hawking, S. (2016). This is the most dangerous time for our planet. *The Guardian, 1*.

Hendrix, A., & Yampolskiy, R. (2017). *Automated IQ Estimation from Writing Samples*. MAICS.

McCarthy, P. M., & Jarvis, S. (2010). MTLD, vocd-D, and HD-D: A validation study of sophisticated approaches to lexical diversity assessment. *Behavior Research Methods*, *42*(2), 381–392. doi:10.3758/BRM.42.2.381 PMID:20479170

McNamara, D. S., Crossley, S. A., & McCarthy, P. M. (2010). Linguistic features of writing quality. *Written Communication*, *27*(1), 57–86. doi:10.1177/0741088309351547

McNamara, D. S., Graesser, A. C., McCarthy, P. M., & Cai, Z. (2014). *Automated evaluation of text and discourse with Coh-Metrix.* Cambridge, UK: Cambridge University Press. doi:10.1017/CBO9780511894664

NLTK. (2018). *NLTK Stem Package.* Available: http://www.nltk.org/api/nltk.stem.html

Resing, W. C. M., & Blok, J. B. (2002). The classification of intelligence scores. Proposal for an unambiguous system. *The Psychologist, 37,* 244–249.

SAT. (2014). *SAT Vocabulary Words.* Available: http://www.freevocabulary.com

Savant, M. V. (2018). *Logical Fallacies.* Available: http://marilynvossavant.com/logical-fallacies/

Simonton, D. K. (2009). The "other IQ": Historiometric assessments of intelligence and related constructs. *Review of General Psychology, 13*(4), 315–326. doi:10.1037/a0017141

Statistics How To. (2018). *What is a Normal distribution?* Retrieved from https://www.statisticshowto.datasciencecentral.com/probability-and-statistics/normal-distributions/

Toglia, M. P., & Battig, W. F. (1978). Handbook of semantic word norms. Mahwah, NJ: Lawrence Erlbaum.

Zietsman, G. (2010). *Idiotic Geniuses in Noesis.* Mega Society.

Section 3
Technology and Learning

Chapter 5
Exocortex as a Learning Technology

Mehmet Emin Mutlu
https://orcid.org/0000-0002-0949-4057
Anadolu University, Turkey

ABSTRACT

Exocortex is a hypothetical technology where the human brain can connect to a brain implant or a computational environment which is in the state of a wearable device, using two-way brain-computer interface, in order to augment the cognitive powers of the human brain such as perception, storage, recollection and processing. Exocortex is expected to be a part of everyday life in the 2030s. Exocortex technology is supported by parallel technologies such as brain reading, uploading knowledge into the brain from the outside, brain-computer interface, brain-to-brain interface, which are now undergoing prototype applications. In this study, by discussing the potential of exocortex technology in its use for learning processes, as a result of handling it with the "learning experiences management" approach, the opportunities it provides specifically for lifelong learners are examined. In the results and recommendations section of the study, a foresight is given for the scientific research projects that can be performed for this purpose.

INTRODUCTION

Exocortex is a hypothetical technology that is expected to be a part of everyday life in 2030's and can connect with brain-computer interface to a brain implant or a computational environment which is in the state of a wearable device, in order to augment the biological high-level cognitive processes of the human brain and assist a user's decisions and actions (Bonaci, Herron, Matlack, & Chizeck, 2014; Zappa, 2012).

In 1950's and 1960's, first theoretical researches that are aimed at augmenting human intelligence with the support of technology, revealed this problem for the first time (Ashby, 1952, 1956; Licklider, 1960; Engelbart, 1962). Since 1980's, science fiction writers started working on technologies providing a direct connection between human brain and cyberspace (Gibson, 1982, 1984; Vinge, 2034; Stross, 2004).

DOI: 10.4018/978-1-5225-8431-5.ch005

The humankind began the search for an external support in order to augment the brain's storage, recollection and processing power with the invention of writing (Donald, 1991, 1993) and smartphones, nowadays indispensable for our day-to-day information, are seen as a pre – exocortex technology (Hughes, 2007).

Exocortex technology is supported by parallel technologies such as brain reading, uploading knowledge to the brain from the outside, brain-computer communication, brain-to-brain communication, which are now undergoing prototype applications (Bonaci, et al., 2014; Sotala & Valpola, 2012).

Although exocortex is a vital topic for "learning", there is a limited number of studies existing in the literature. In this study, by discussing the potential of exocortex technology in its use for learning processes, as a result of handling it with the "learning experiences management" approach, the opportunities it provides specifically for lifelong learners are examined.

According to Dambrot (2016), conceptualization, design and specifications in an exocortex research include a set of future studies techniques proposed by Kosow and Gaßner (2008) for predicting, evaluating and discarding possible, probable and preferred futures:

- Backcasting: To anticipate the future scenario and define the measures necessary to achieve or prevent this scenario.
- Modified Delphi: Review publications and expert statements that examine the likelihood of a particular scenario, its potential impact and time frame, and the likely impact of trends and other variables.
- Scanning: Identifying emerging trends by investigating research articles, media, literature and other sources.
- Scenario: Manages the current uncertainty by framing perceptions about alternative future environments that may affect existing decisions.
- Technological Forecasting: Projecting that future technologies may be able to do.
- Technology Foresight: To identify both emerging and converging technologies that can generate the greatest socioeconomic benefits by anticipating future science and technology future scenarios.
- Trend Analysis and Extrapolation: Determine an ongoing change based on historical data and observations.
- Vision: Making your future images real and attractive enough to allow them to act as targets.

For this purpose, the major studies done on exocortex are reviewed in the "Background" section. Then, a conceptual design based on "learning experiences management" approach, in order for exocortex to support lifelong learning, was made in the "A Conceptual Design for Exocortex in Lifelong Learning" section. Proposed design contains methods and tools which are expected to take place in different temporal perspectives aimed at utilizing exocortex in learning experiences management. Thus, the use of exocortex in learning experiences management is examined respectively according to the technology's current state and near future state, developments expected to take place in ten years and twenty years. Then, the proposed system's implementation and evaluation in different temporal zones are given in the "Solutions and Recommendations" section. In the "Conclusion and Future Research Direction" section of the study, the results obtained by the discussion of the findings are given a place and a foresight is given for a realizable scientific research project for the development and implementation of the conceptual design given in this study.

BACKGROUND

Neocortex

Human brain differentiates from other living beings with its neocortex structure. Neocortex constitutes 80 percent of the human brain while not existing in reptiles and having only a minor part of the other mammals' brain. Neocortex is the source of cognitive skills like thinking, imagining, questioning, making an inference high-level cognitive mental processes that differentiates human beings from other living beings. Despite the brain's complex structure resisting against scientific researches for a long time, the fact that neocortex is formed by the numerous repetition simpler structures. Neocortex is actually a 2-4 millimeters-long shell. This shell creates a large part of the brain by folding on itself many times. This thin layer is constituted of cortical columns. Cortical columns are made up of six layers in themselves (Kurzweil, 2012).

Ray Kurzweil argues that cortical columns are pattern recognizers that contain about 60.000 neurons and neocortex is created with 300 million of those pattern recognizers. Each and every one of those pattern recognizers is specialized in recognizing a specific pattern. For example, some of them are very successful in recognizing horizontal lines, while some of them are very successful in recognizing skew lines and some of them using these are very successful in recognizing the letter "A". High-level recognizers using pattern recognizers that recognize letters are able to recognize the word "APPLE" before all the letters are completed. All pattern recognizers in the brain are able to work simultaneously and cause cognitive behavior in a higher level like storage, recollection and processing by recognizing all images, voices, tastes, textures and odors coming from all receptors (Kurzweil, 2012).

It took millions of years for this advanced form to shape. Humanity is now at the edge this form. While it is biologically impossible to increase the number of those pattern recognizers in our brains, advancing technology makes it possible to build computers containing pattern recognizers thousands times more than neocortex contains. It is assumed that human thinking capacity will increase infinitely as a result of its combination with other big pattern recognizers (Kurzweil, 2012). This hypothetical technology providing human brain to use these other structures as its own extension is named as exocortex.

Donald (1991), in his book "Origins of the Modern Mind", focuses on modern people's way of using their external symbolic storage and regulation systems (in a wide range of scale from cuneiform, hieroglyphics and ideographs to alphabetic languages, mathematics and then to computers today). According to Donald's perspective, these external symbolic systems cause the functional rearrangement of the human mind in its relationship with the world.

The externalization of the memory via external symbolic storage systems has changed the role of biological memory in the human brain's resource allocation method and creation of the modern culture by taking real memory architecture's place in thinking (Donald, 1993).

Hughes (2007) implies that the technologies in our daily lives are constructing an exocortex increasingly:

In a sense, we have been using external technology to enhance cognition and memory since the invention of written language. Today, about half of all American cell phone and laptop owners say they cannot imagine life without these devices. In a very tangible sense our electronic data and communications devices have become parts of our "exo-cortex," an integrated part of our brain. The next step is for these capabilities to move into direct communication with our neurons.

Researches Towards Augmenting Human Intelligence

Cybernetic developments in the 1950's have led the scientists in that period to introduce optimistic opinions about an evolution of people towards a symbiosis with computers. Dambrot (2016) has compiled the views of Ashby, Licklider and Engelbart's views on that period:

Ashby introduced his "Intelligence Amplification" thesis in his book "Design for a Brain" published in 1952 (Ashby, 1960). He described the self-coordinating capacity of interdependent cortical neurons in learning and organism-wide adaptive behavior and how this capacity might be applied to an artificial brain. Ashby extended these ideas in 1956 in his book "An Introduction to Cybernetics", addressing regulation and control of inborn and learned behaviors in biological systems, and how regulators and controllers can be built and amplified (Ashby, 1956).

J.R. Licklider described a result of humans and computers establishing flexible, cooperative behavior in decision-making and managing complex circumstances in 1960 in his book "Man-Computer Symbiosis". According to this, humans would engage in intellectual tasks – goals, hypotheses, criteria, and evaluations – with computers performing routine tasks that support human activities (Licklider, 1960).

In a report published in 1962, Douglas Engelbart defined the augmentation of human intellect as improving the depth, speed and quality of human comprehension and (problem) solving skills. This will ensure that complex problems of diplomats, executives, social scientists, life scientists, physical scientists, attorneys, and designers will be overcome (Engelbart, 1962).

The Emergence of the Term Exocortex

The external cortex was first described by Ben Houston in an online dictionary as follows (Houston, 2000):

exocortex (eks'o kor'teks) n. Latin--an organ that resides outside of the brain that aids in high level thinking. This term can apply to advanced wearable computer applications that significantly control/ influence a person's thought and behavior. This will not be a prominent term until prefrontal cortex neural implants become widespread.

According to Bonaci et al. (2014), the exocortex term specifies a wearable computer (or placed in the brain) that is used to augment a brain's biological high-level cognitive processes and assists a user's decisions and actions. It stems from computer science and evolutionary psychology, but it has been popularized by science-fiction writers.

Although the term was used in a science fiction work for the first time in 2004 by Charles Stross (Stross, 2004), first fictional devices fitting this definition of the exocortex were introduced in 1980's by William Gibson (Gibson, 1982, 1984) and later, by Vernor Vinge (Vinge, 2003).

William Gibson used the concept of "cyberspace" for the first time in his short story "Burning Chrome" (Gibson, 1982), then founded his work "Neuromancer" upon this concept. Readers have long thought that cyberspace was an early anticipation of the internet and virtual worlds that were not yet mature at the time. In reality, with Gibson's design, cyberspace is closer to the concept of exocortex as a digital medium ("matrix", a term used by Gibson himself) that people can directly get involved with their brains.

According to the blogger Dana Edwards, an exocortex can be accurately described as an external neocortex. (Edwards, 2017a). According to Edwards, exocortex also includes personal information management system and personal knowledge management system functions (Edwards, 2017b).

Today, intensive scientific studies in the field of "Augmented Cognition" are closely related to the hypothetical exocortex topic. According to Skinner et al. (2014), the field of Augmented Cognition (AugCog) provides a scientifically-grounded approach to addressing the intrinsic human information processing and manipulation challenges associated with complex and data-intensive digital systems, leveraging empirically-based HCI solutions that assess and account for human cognitive limitations. With projects supported by DARPA, the resulting developments in this area, where the results are usually available to military purposes, are expected to have a role in the design of interfaces between human beings and the exocortex in the future.

Related Emergent Technologies

It is projected that exocortex technology will be supported by emergent technologies such as brain reading, uploading knowledge to the brain from the outside, brain-computer interface, brain-to-brain interface, which are now undergoing prototype applications (Bonaci et al, 2014; Sotala & Valpola, 2012).

Brain – Computer Interface

Discoveries of the complex nature of the message flow in the brain began in the mid-1990's with the improvements in the Magnetic Resonance Imaging (MRI) device. Thus, according to Kaku (2014), more than what was known in all human history about the brain was learned in the last 15 years.

Radio waves are electromagnetic waves that can pass through tissues without damaging. By using this method, the MRI apparatus can acquire the perfect three-dimensional image of the tissue they pass through by the reflection of the electromagnetic waves in consequence of a physical phenomenon. It is possible to image the messages that are coming from and out of the brain, electrical signals that circulate in the brain and on neurons. With the MRI scans, the electrical flow can be traced within the brain's area of one tenth of a millimeter. These scans showed that a thought does not occur at a specific point, but occurs at numerous points at the same time throughout the brain and circulates in the form of electrical energy flow between those points. MRI can only image the static structure of the brain. In the mid-1990's, an important step was taken by the development of functional MRI (fMRI) capable of detecting oxygen in the brain. Since oxygen is necessary to provide energy for the neurons in the brain, the flow of electrical energy in neurons can be monitored by tracking the oxygen flow in the brain (Kaku, 2014).

Another way to examine the brain is EEG (electroencephalogram) device. EEG device provides to save electromagnetic waves that are emitted naturally from the brain by several electrodes plugged onto the brain region of the head. The human brain emits different electromagnetic waves while sleeping, dreaming, in the moments of relaxation, when angry, frightened or concentrated on a thought. EEG can instantly measure the electrical activity of these different states of the brain. MRI, as a very expensive device, gives a perfect three-dimensional image while being time consuming to acquire this image. EEG, as a cheap device, gives very sensitive results in terms of being temporal, but is insensitive to what part of the brain the signals are coming from (Kaku, 2014).

Skull that wraps the brain also significantly hinders the passage of electromagnetic waves out of the brain. Probes placed directly into the brain provide more responsive measurement in EEG waves in studies on the brain-damaged patients. The patient can move a cursor on the computer just by thinking by the fast computer analysis of the EEG waves spread while focusing on the cursor. It is made sure that patients learn the system by making a period of trial and error for this purpose. These studies have led to the emergence of the scientific field called brain-computer interface (BCI) (Graimann, Allison, & Pfurtscheller, 2009). Today, at this stage of the BCI research, users are able to use computers, manage artificial arms and robots, fly drones without placing any probes into the brain, with the analysis of the electromagnetic waves captured with electrodes placed over the head (Kosmyna, Tarpin-Bernard, & Rivet, 2015).

Brain Reading

When people focus on a particular image, the brain broadcasts EEG waves that can be associated with that image. In a study using this feature, the subjects were fitted with helmets measuring EEG waves for a certain period of time, and made focus on something, for example a car image, and EEG waves formed during this time were recorded. A dictionary of EEG waves for people's thoughts was obtained by repeating this process for a large number of pictures. Then EEG waves of the subject were measured by showing another car picture. The computer, by searching the EEG waves in the dictionary, can detect that the subject is thinking of a car (Kapoor, Shenoy, & Tan, 2008). Seeing a picture and thinking of a picture have the same effect, even if not the same intensity. If a large enough image-EEG wave library is created, it is possible to capture images portrayed in the eyes of people at a moment.

An improved practice of reading the images in brain with more accurate results was achieved with fMRI (Kay, Naselaris, Prenger, & Gallant, 2008). In a following study, by monitoring the activities of a brain reading a handwritten writing, it was able to understand writings (Schoenmakers, 2013).

A further research for brain reading, individuals were made to watch hours of videos while being connected to fMRI, and the electrical flows in the brain neurons at every moment of the videos were matched by capturing. As a result of the long-troublesome measurements, mathematical formulas determining the relationship between the video images and the electrical flashes within the brain's three-dimensional structure were obtained. As a result, when a subject is asked to think about a specific image, the computer can create a video piece closest to that image in its database with the help of the data coming from fMRI device at that moment. This system can create a video that will give a rough idea about the image in the eyes of the subject to an outsider person watching it (Nishimoto et al., 2011).

A similar study was conducted by Cowen et al. (2014) to identify the human faces, from the brain activities, that the individual sees. In this study, a large number of human face images are shown to the participant, the resulting brain activities are captured by fMRI and the patterns are determined by using a machine learning algorithm. Then the participant is shown an example picture of a face and the face is reconstructed by the computer with analyzing the activities captured at that moment.

In a recent study, it has been able to be caught the images individuals see in their dreams with fMRI (Horikawa, Tamaki, Miyawaki, & Kamitani, 2013).

Further results can be taken in brain reading because of capturing electromagnetic waves without them being absorbed by the skull with the measurements made by placing probes into brain by Electrocorticography (ECoG) method on brain damaged patients (Schalk, et al., 2008). For example, a patient with a probe plugged into the brain can transmit letters and numbers to a computer by thinking of them and, in this way, can write with a mental typewriter. Guger firm [Guger] markets an EEG spelling device that carries out the same process. It takes 10 minutes to learn to use this telepathic typewriter, and then 5 to 10 words per minute can be written by thinking. With these methods, not only are the thoughts realized by the brain in conscious state, but also the dreams seen during sleep can be caught and visualized, although roughly, by computer today with the help of EEG waves (Guger, 2017).

The methods in these practices are the first applications of a technology towards reading a person's thoughts at the moment, and they should be expected to be developed in order to produce faster and more sensitive results in the future. Thus making it will become possible to read and record thoughts. With the help of technology that will enable easier and more detailed reading of the brain in the future, it will be easier than ever to communicate remotely via brain waves with devices and tools around oneself. This, in a way, is the realization of affecting distant objects, in other words, telekinesis. Transmitting thoughts from distance via brain waves will provide people an infinite freedom. Individuals will be able to take a note, increase their house's temperature and shop from the internet by thinking while walking. This process will become as natural as talking on cell phone while walking (Kaku, 2014).

Uploading Knowledge to the Brain From the Outside

Brain Implants

Brain processes signals captured via interfaces. In the case of a deactivation of these interfaces, advancements take place about producing the signals synthetically and transmitting them directly to the brain. For example, "cochlear implants", developed for deaf patients, transform sound waves into electrical signals and transmit them directly to the auditory nerve (Mudry & Mills, 2013). Similarly, an image consisting of a limited number of pixels captured continuously with an image sensor in a spectacle can be transmitted through a chip to the responsible area of the brain, thus allowing the blind patients to see although being extremely blurry. With this technology called "retinal implant", the brain can learn to see from the window with this little sensitivity after a while by taking advantage of neuronal plasticity (Mills, Jalil, & Stanga, 2017).

Brain-to-Brain Communication (Synthetic Telepathy - Silent Communication)

A recently developed device called Transcranial Magnetic Stimulation (TMS) is used to temporarily stop the activity of particular parts of the brain by creating magnetic energy bursts. This device is useful in areas close to the skull because of electromagnetic waves being difficult to access deep into the brain by getting through the skull. With the aid of this device, certain muscular movements of the subject can be realized with the command given from the outside. In an experiment conducted at the University of Washington, the EEG waves measured while a subject performs hand movements have been forwarded to another laboratory on the internet and the second subject was made to move his hand with the help of TMS (Yoo, Filandrianos, Taghados, & Park, 2013).

Uploading Knowledge to the Brain

With a technique called deep brain stimulation (DBS), more complex stimulus can be given to brain with probes as thin as feather placed deep into the brain in patients with brain damage. Recently, artificial memories implanted into a mouse brain (Ramirez et al., 2013). In the case of using uploading knowledge to the brain from the outside world via deep brain stimulation with brain reading technology, it will be possible for the human brain to establish two-way communication with devices outside the body and therefore with other brains. With the development of these technologies in the next 30-40 years, it may be possible to transmit thoughts from the brain to the outside or from the outside to the brain by placing implants in the brain to stimulate and read the brain. These applications that will provide direct communication between the brains in the future are now referred to as "synthetic telepathy" (Kaku, 2014).

The possibilities that uploading knowledge to the brain will provide are endless. With this method, individuals can have experience in a subject without actually putting it into practice by uploading artificial custom memories to their brains. So, a user who wants to know about a country may have experience like a person who has lived there for years by uploading artificial memories about that country into the brain. With the help of this technology, individuals will be able to share their memories with others on the internet just like sharing a photo or a video. When students want to learn any subject, it will suffice only to upload the information and the experience on that subject to their brains. People will be able to realize lifelong learning in the true sense by learning effortlessly when they need in everyday life (Kaku, 2014).

Foresights About the Exocortex

The concept of exocortex is given place frequently in studies about the future of the technology with or without giving reference. These studies can be seen in hypothetical scientific fields, multi-participant European Union projects, national initiatives or popular science books.

Hypothetical Fields

"Mind uploading" ("brain uploading" or "whole brain emulation") is a hypothetical technology that expresses how the human mind is run as software on a computer by being transformed into digital form. Sandberg and Bostrom published a road map showing what the technological requirements for mind uploading are, and suggested that this could be done in the middle of the century (Sandberg & Bostrom, 2008).

Sotala and Valpola (2012) have proposed the approach of coalescing minds through the exocortex by connecting several brains the exocortex. The authors suggest a reverse split-brain operation for a hypothetical process of mind coalescence, where artificial connections are created between two or more brains. With this method, brains of more than one person will coalescence with the other brains through an exocortex. Thus, a mind upload will occur as the individual's personality moves towards exocortex by getting over the biological brain. The mind uploaded to exocortex will be duplicable and shareable. According to the authors, the bounds of personal identity will become unclear, or even unnecessary.

Dambrot (2016) offers a detailed architecture for an extreme hypothetical exocortex. According to the "exocortical cognition interface" architecture, human neocortex will be strengthened with neuroscience, neural prostheses and synthetic biology. On the other hand, a connection based on quantum physics is projected between the neocortex and an exocortex that has exopresence technologies and is able to connect artificial general intelligence.

European Union Projects

Normally, the human brain can process 120 thousand events unconsciously in a second and fewer than 10 events consciously at the same moment. In an approach proposed in a European Union project named UCepCortex, which aims to develop complex event handling technologies, a universal event cloud covering various types of events, from natural events originating from the universe and environment to artificial events originating from the internet of things and services, are addressed. The aim of the uCepCortex project is to develop an exocortex based on Ubiquitous Complex Event Processing (U-CEP) as an Artificial Cognitive System (ACS) and to investigate how to enhance human cognitive abilities, manage assistive robots, and their cooperation with humans via an exocortex system. The results of these events are made to be perceived by the human brain through an interface named BrainPort and is placed under the skin of the tongue as a tattoo (Ehresmann, von Ammon, Iakovidis, & Hunter, 2012).

Initiatives Originating From Russia

There are key initiatives aimed at anticipating technologies expected to occur in the 21st century in Russia and routing R&D activities in these fields. As one of those initiatives, "Neuroweb Initiative [Neuroweb]" is working on developing the interfaces between the internet and the human brain and transferring human thoughts on the internet (Neuroweb, 2017). "2045 Initiative [2045]", is found in 2011 to investigate neural interfaces, robots, artificial organs and systems. The purpose of the organization is "transferring the human personality to non-biological carriers, extending the lifetime and finding cyber immortality". The purpose of the organization between 2015-2020 is to produce "avatars" controlled by a "brain-computer" interface, between 2020-2025 is to transfer a brain to an "autonomous life support" robot, between 2030-2035 is to create a computer model of the brain and to transfer individual consciousness onto an artificial carrier, an in 2045 is to start a new era with people having a holographic body ("2045", 2017). Another initiative named "Global Education Futures [GEF]" aims to investigate the forms that education will take through 21st century. According to this organization, for example, by 2020s there will be a cognitive revolution and brain-to-brain communication protocols will be developed, the human idea transport protocol will be developed, the human body will be used as an interface to communicate with the digital environment and non-verbal neural communication will be an educational tool (GEF, 2017).

Exocortex in Popular Science

Future scientist Ray Kurzweil, one of the advocates of Singularity Theory and a member of the Transhumanism movement, discusses in detail the principles of neocortex in his works. According to Kurzweil, the neocortex contains 300 million pattern recognizers that provide us to perceive and make an inference of the world step by step in a hierarchical way. In the not too distant in the future, the number of those pattern recognizers will be increased thousands of times by the exocortex that will be articulated to neocortex. Kurzweil suggests concepts such as "hybrid thinking", "cloud-connected hybrid brains", and "thinking outside the brain" to express this situation (Kurzweil, 2012). In his book "Singularity is Near", Kurzweil, by highlighting the fact that biological intelligence is making no progress while the capacity of non-biological intelligence will double its capacity every year, projects that by the 2030's the non-biological portion of our intelligence will predominate, and by the 2040's the non-biological portion will be billions of times more capable (Kurzweil, 2005). Similarly, Michio Kaku comprehensively examines this topic in his book "The Future of the Mind" as a future scientist (Kaku, 2014).

In 1927, the biologist Julian Huxley (author Aldous Huxley's older brother) suggested that the term "transhumanism" to say that we should use technology to circumvent the limits of our body and brains. Transhumanism has become an internationally influential intellectual movement today (Hughes, 2006).

Transhumanism advocates that, with the technological developments that will take place, there will be an association between human and computer, and that the human kind will experience an evolution towards a transhuman entity with computers. After a point where artificial intelligence passes human intelligence, humanity will switch into a post-human or trans-human state by creating a symbiosis with machines (Bostrom, 2005).

Nick Bostrom of Oxford University emphasizes that human-machine common intelligence will evolve into a super-intelligence in the transhuman era, and says that the development of artificial intelligence, the realization of whole brain emulation, the creation of mind networks through the brain-computer interface of biological cognition are the paths reaching that super-intelligence (Bostrom, 2014). Bostrom describes the form exocortex will reach with the super-intelligence concept without referencing exocortex concept.

Future researcher Hutchinson gives place to a future scenario about the exocortex in his article entitled "The Future History of Consciousness" as follows (Hutchinson, 2012):

Imagine: it is a few years in the future, and machine learners will be reading through millions of books and journals, billions of web pages, trillions of pieces of information, to save, categorize, parse, summarize, and synthesize. Then in the blink of an eye, a natural language interface will be marketed, allowing you to have a discussion with this worldwide exocortex, a brain outside your brain holding the world's knowledge. A year later there is a brain-mind interface available that gives you instant access to the world brain. And then you can talk to anyone, anywhere, through this medium, with the power of thought alone.

A CONCEPTUAL DESIGN FOR EXOCORTEX IN LIFELONG LEARNING

It is clear that exocortex augmenting human's high level cognitive abilities will also make important changes in the human learning ability. However, there is no study approaching exocortex in terms of learning in the literature. Especially, Doswell's studies are among the most convergent researches on the topic of exocortex in the field of the use of current technologies in learning (Doswell, 2006, 2008; Doswell & Skinner, 2014; Doswell, Blake, & Butcher-Green, 2006). Doswell follows an approach to enhance human cognitive skills in the use of augmented reality technologies for learning, without using the term exocortex, and uses technology to design architects that will transmit the learning materials to the learner in the most effective way.

In this study about this chapter, the use of exocortex in realizing behaviors that cause learning will not take place. In other words, this is not a learning study that can be classified as technology supported learning, tutorial systems, virtual tutorials, augmented learning, ubiquitous learning or informal learning.

Learning Experiences Management

In this study, the use of exocortex technology in monitoring the learning experiences of the learners and helping the learners to understand and regulate their learning experiences can be seen. For this purpose, a conceptual design will be carried out based on "learning experiences management" approach in order to use the exocortex in learning.

Why Learning Experiences?

The learning experience "is a physical, mental, emotional, spiritual, religious, social or virtual event or activity that we have participated or are exposed to, which has gained, changed or strengthened new knowledge, behavior, skills, values or preferences." (Mutlu, 2014).

According to Sparrow, Liu and Wegner (2011), because of the "Google Effect", individuals live a digital amnesia. According to this view, the fact that an information is written somewhere removes the worry of forgetting it. Thus, individuals are more inclined to forget information that can be accessed by the Google search engine. Any information that is encountered in the online environment is erased from memory after it has caused gain, change or strengthening new knowledge, behavior, value or preference. Individuals see the Google search engine as an extension of their own memory. Just as it is easier to access a copy of a document on the internet than looking for it on the computer, it is easier to refer to Google than to try to recollect that information in our memory.

Accessing an information itself is different from accessing our experience with that information. Because the experience with a piece of information means relating that piece of information with our previous experiences, placing it on the conceptual map that we have, obtaining gains from the experience that we live with that information. In this case, recollecting the experience containing this piece of information is no longer just recollecting that information. Re-experiencing - overviewing the experience ensures that we realize what that information means to us (that we make sense of the learning experience that is part of that piece of information). So, it is more important to recollect how and when we used that information, what changes we did, how we combined it with other pieces of information, how we interpreted it or in what way we criticized it than the information itself (Mutlu, 2015e). With this reasoning, accessing to past experiences with the information is given priority over accessing the information. In order for this to happen, all of our experiences should be captured first.

Stages of Learning Experiences Management

An approach that enables individuals to manage their learning experiences is tried to be developed by Mutlu and his team with a series of projects starting in 2013. At the point these studies have come so far, learning experiences management approach includes the stages; a) capturing the experiences of life, b) interpreting life experiences, c) acquiring contexts from experiences, d) making sense of the learning experiences, and e) planning, monitoring, controlling and evaluating learning experiences (Mutlu, 2015b). The projects completed in the learning experiences management field from 2013 until now and the main results obtained by Mutlu and his team are given in Table 1.

In the following sections, the steps of the learning experiences management approach will be tried to be designed in such a way that it will get input as less as possible from the user and give output as much as possible to the user by applying the methods and technologies of today and near future in order to be used in the exocortex architecture to be designed in this study.

Table 1. Development of learning experiences management model

Completed Projects	Major Outcomes
Anadolu University Scientific Research Project (1301E014), named "Development and Implementation of a Digital lifelogging System for the Management of Lifelong Learning Experiences", conducted between 15 February 2013 and 15 August 2014	• In the conceptual design phase of the project, the "learning experiences management approach" was developed. • With the software developed during the following stages of the project, individuals can capture their life experiences directed to information work almost completely, and they can get them together in a dedicated computer by transferring via cloud. They can interpret their experiences in the form of activities / events, episodes and stories. They are able to determine the contexts of their life experience. They can access and make sense of their past learning experiences by browsing their life experiences. They can manage their learning experiences. • The approach's applicability in the three dimensions of learning and informal learning models is revealed.
The Scientific and Technological Research Council of Turkey – Type 3001 Project (114K579) named "The Design, Development and Implementation of a Multiple Device and Multiple Sensor Digital lifelogging System for Learning Experiences Management" conducted between 15 September 2014 and 15 March 2016	• Three different time perspectives of the interpretation of the experiences have been noticed. • The active usage of the lifelogging is also included in the model. • The life experiences context model was developed and used for the learning contexts. • The fact that contexts and content need to be examined separately, and content ontology have been revealed. • Reflective learning process and meta-cognitive regulation process are added to the model in order to make sense of the learning experiences and manage experiences respectively.
The Scientific and Technological Research Council of Turkey – Type 1001 Project (115K497) named "The Design, Development and Implementation of a Digital lifelogging System for Virtual Learning Experiences Management Supported With Artificial intelligence Technologies" conducted between 15 September 2015 and 15 September 2017	• Past screenshots can be accessed via key words. • Experiences can be separated by the computer in the format of activities/events, episodes and stories. • Similar experiences that took place in the past can be found by the computer. • The processes of adding context to and taking over context from experiences, and extracting context from experiences to context ontology are defined. • Context-experience graphs were created and their structure was observed. • Experience trees can be created and experience portfolios can be created and exported. • Experience plans are created and experiences were monitored and inspected, and detailed reports and analyses belonging to past experiences were acquired.

Capturing Life Experiences

Capturing the life experiences stage of the learning experiences management approach involves the processes of capturing, recording, re-accessing and browsing of the activities/events of experiences with the help of sensors (Mutlu, 2015b).

The most effective method to capture the life experiences is to use a lifelogging system. Lifelogging devices are located on individuals or with individuals in a portable or wearable format during the day in order to capture moments belonging to the experience. In the learning experiences management approach, this definition is extended a bit further, adding the ability to capture moments in fixed devices that an individual uses throughout the day, other than wearable or portable devices. Thus, lifelogging systems, with the help of the sensors they contain, will be dealt with as passive data capturing systems with the various sensors located on the devices they use/carry/wear during their experiences.

The main passive lifelogging devices are lifelogging camera, location capturer, screenshot of the computer, computer web cams, heart rate sensor, and Bluetooth sensor for determining users around. Passive capturing usually occurs intermittently every 30 seconds during the day. As an exception to

Exocortex as a Learning Technology

this situation, continuous capturers such as motion sensor and EEG sensor passive log data (Gurrin, Smeaton, & Doherty 2014).

Other than that, active lifelogging tools and sensors are used in order to capture the important context of the learning experience. These include the screen video, audio and video. With active capturing, continuous record is taken for 360 seconds, usually every 360 seconds until it is stopped after it is initiated by the user. The user can also use the passive capturer actively. Examples include behaviors like taking a camera image or a screenshot or taking notes actively (Mutlu, 2015d).

Lifelogging systems, with these sensors, capture the log data of the person, name them with time-stamped tags, and usually store them in the cloud environment. With the lifelog browsers developed for this purpose, the daily log data from a given date and hour can be accessed directly as well as displaying life experiences from a specific time period by listing.

The raw data captured increases gradually over time, both in terms of number and coverage, and "personal big data" occurs (Gurrin et al., 2014).

In two projects carried out by Mutlu and his team in 2013 and 2014, a variety of tools are developed in order to capture the life experiences of the individuals. In the first project, capturing screenshot and camera image tools for desktops, tablets and smartphones, and tools for image capture with wearable lifelogging camera are developed. In the second project, in addition to the previous ones, screen video, audio, video, location and note information capture is added. Also, lifelog browsers were developed in order to monitor these data and gain access to them (Figure 1).

Figure 1. Learning experiences management systems based on lifelogging
(Mutlu, 2015b; 2015c)

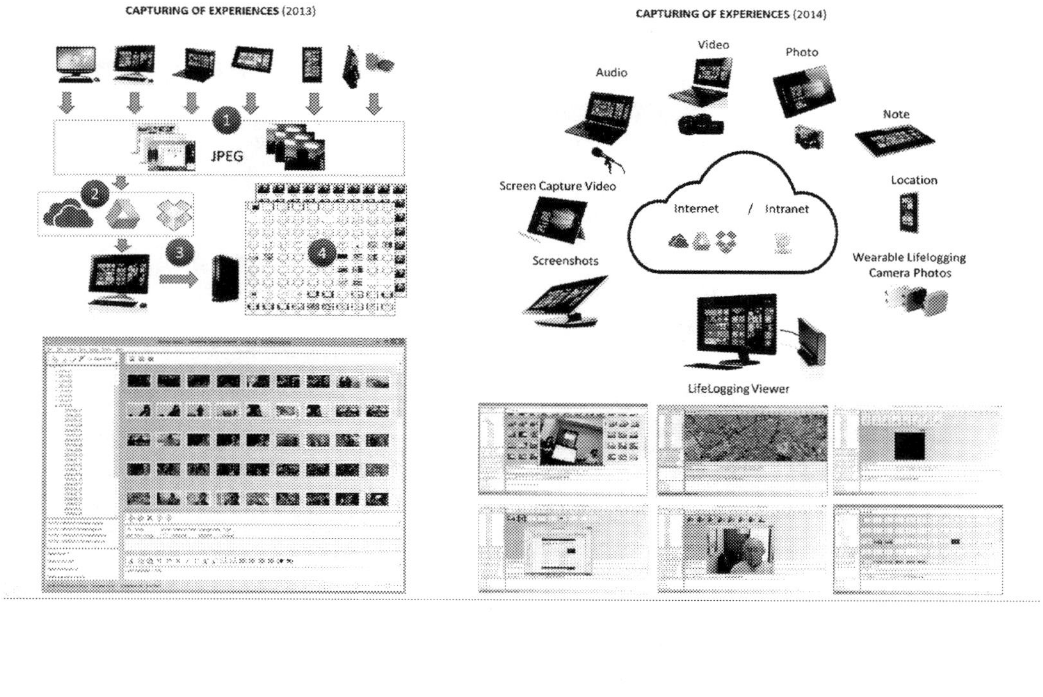

Interpreting Life Experiences

Interpreting life experiences involves the processes of determining the activities/events of experiences, creating their temporal hierarchies, creating their hierarchies' trees, recognizing and finding the similar ones in past experiences (Mutlu, 2014).

For this purpose, it is necessary to extract the characteristics from the data by applying the algorithms developed according to the data types on the captured log data. By taking advantage of these characteristics, it becomes possible to determine activities/events related to experiences, to create hierarchies of experiences, to create their trees by classifying experiences, to recognize experiences and to find their similar in past experiences.

Mutlu and his team have shown that life experiences can be classified by the individual with recognizing them as activities/events that may take hours starting from a few seconds, episodes lasting days, weeks or months and stories lasting for many years (Mutlu, Kayabas, Kip Kayabas, & Peri Mutlu, 2015f).

There are a number of techniques developed by lifelogging researchers to determine the daily events from their daily data. Gurrin et al provide a detailed list of these techniques (Gurrin et al., 2014). Daily events are usually determined by processing the camera images with image processing software and detecting scene changes. This allows the determination of operations/actions or contexts that accompany the experience more than determining the experience. With this method, for example, the event of working on computer (context) can be determined while no information is obtained about the report (the experience of writing report X) being written. For this purpose, log data coming from more than one sensor needs to be combined.

For different log data, different characteristic acquisition and classification approaches can be applied. For example, it is possible to determine daily actions and events by using the algorithms of; topic modeling for texts, pattern recognition techniques for images, sound type recognition technique for sound (music, speech, device, musical instrument ...), matching the captured passive-active log data, context fusion (location, content, movement, mental state ...) and lifelogging event determination (Gurrin et al., 2014). The user can also interpret the experience at active capture moments, depending on the preference.

By processing the data acquired from all these sources, tags acquired from a given moment usually provide clues to the actions taken and the events happening at that moment. These operations and actions should be processed with special algorithms to determine the experiences.

Examining the content in learning experiences is also gaining importance. For example, in a lifelogging project where only screenshots were captured, it was possible to extract text from images with OCR and to use texts to determine and classify experiences (Mutlu, 2016b).

Acquiring Contexts From Experiences

The stage of acquiring contexts from experiences includes the processes of determining the contexts that accompany experiences, creating a context based ontology and context-experience semantic network (Mutlu, 2015a).

There are contexts that accompany every life experience. Determination of the context/content accompanying experience, creation of context ontology, creation of context-experience semantic network allows to recognize the experiences, access the experiences, classify the experiences, query the experiences and make sense of the experiences. Context ontologies belonging to locations, people, events, assets, attributes, feelings and behaviors take place in LECOM (Life Experiences COntext Model), developed to examine the contexts accompanying the life experiences (Mutlu, 2015a).

Log data obtained from sensors are utilized directly or by combining in order to acquire the context values for a given moment. For example, to create the values that belong to the location context, location data can be used. To acquire the values for the people context, Bluetooth device recognition technique that scans users in the surrounding area and face recognition technique can be used. lifelog events can be determined separately from the camera images and screenshots to acquire events. Object recognition algorithms can be used to determine assets. To determine attributes, the sensor values showing the mental state and physical situation can be used. For feelings, heartbeat, galvanic skin response sensor and EEG records can be used. In order to determine the behaviors, lifelogging activity (walking, sitting, eating, sleeping, running, climbing, cycling, travelling via car, etc.) determination algorithms can be used (Gurrin et al., 2014).

The new context values acquired are searched in the context ontologies containing previously acquired context values and placed on the appropriate nodes in these ontologies (also containing the link information of the life experience they accompanied). The main draft of the context ontology should be created by the user and maintained from time to time. The context tree/trees occurring as experiences are lived will bring an autobiographical personal knowledge base of the individual's personal experiences.

The content accompanying life experiences are then later will be used frequently in making sense of the learning experiences. Therefore, the ontology of the text, image, audio and video content accompanying the experience also must be created separately. Content ontologies include field, topic and concept ontology. Fields are classified as working, learning, special interests, daily life etc. according to which life field of individual the content falls into. Topics and concepts are acquired by resolving the content. Users may have to create their own initial draft of content ontology and to do its maintenance from time to time. Content elements included in these context ontologies nodes in these ontologies will form the semantic knowledge base of the individual over time (Mutlu, 2015d).

Then the graphs of context/content-experience semantic networks can be created between experiences and contexts/contents that accompany these experiences. These networks allow an individual to make semantic queries on his/her experiences (Figure 2).

Making Sense of Learning Experiences

The first three stages of the learning experiences management approach include the processes necessary to capture, recognize/define, and classify life experiences. The next two stages of the approach aim to understand and manage the learning experiences using the data structures acquired in the first three stages.

A process is applied including stages; return to the experience, applying reflective learning process on the experience, obtaining gains from the experience in order to make sense of the learning experience contained in life experiences. Following tools are needed in this process (Mutlu, 2015e):

- **Accessing the Experience Again:** The user can access a past experience again by moving along the timeline, searching through keywords, selecting nodes across a network of experience, selecting nodes across the experience trees, selecting an experience among similar experiences, moving along the context network, moving along the content ontologies, selecting among the semantic query results etc. Experience can be scattered through a long period of discrete time intervals. This experience is displayed to the user by being turned into a continuous whole.

Figure 2. Context-experience graph
(Mutlu, 2015d)

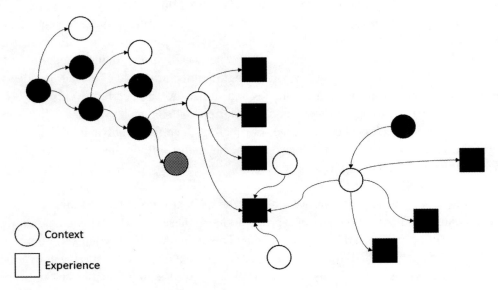

- **Animate the Experience:** Temporal occurrences of the experience, all the contexts that accompany the experience and the content is displayed.
- **Displaying the Experience Network:** Past experiences that each experience is affected by and subsequent experiences that each experience affected are displayed.
- **Displaying the Experience Tree:** The top experience hierarchy that the experience in belonging to and the lower experience hierarchies that are contained by the experience and sibling experiences (other experiences belonging to the same parent experience) are displayed.
- **Displaying Context/Content-Experience Networks:** Free movement is carried out along the context/content-experience network from experience to contexts or contents, from contexts or contents to experiences.
- **Making Semantic Queries on the Context/Content-Experience Networks:** Searching for the similar or related experiences, context or content is ensured in the personal experience pool.
- **Creating Activity/Event, Context and Content Based Experience Portfolios:** Packaging of the experience with the timeline is ensured in a way that can be used as evidence for the learning act.

The stage of making sense of the learning experience allows the individual to fully evaluate the experience with all its connections by visualizing any past experience.

Meta-Cognitive Regulation of Learning Experiences

It is ensured that meta-cognitive regulation of learning experiences at cognitive level are planned, monitored, supervised and evaluated at meta-cognitive level (Mutlu, 2016a). The following tools can be used in this stage.

Planning Experiences

Active planning: Activities/events that belong to the experiences can be planned actively in daily, weekly, monthly, and yearly in perspective by the user in a story/episode/activity hierarchy.

Recommend a plan: By learning from past experiences with the help of machine learning by the system, depending on the user's desire, can automatically recommend plans at any moment or collectively in a time perspective.

Monitoring the Experiences

Live monitoring: That day's experiences can be recognized/defined by being resolved live, daily experience analytics can be displayed and past similar experiences may be listed.

Recommend a behavior: Recommendations can be made for the next steps of the experience by learning from past experiences with the help of machine learning by the system.

Control of Experiences

Decision making: Start, suspend, complete, cancel, reschedule, terminate and continue decisions can be applied for the experiences planned by the user beforehand. Decisions can be reported to the system by the user and/or the status changes specified by the system are either approved or rejected.

Initiating unplanned experience: The user may indicate to the system that he or she will initiate an unplanned experience.

Evaluation of Experiences

Creating activity reports: Plans are evaluated with the reports obtained as a result of comparing and matching the inspected experiences with planned experiences.

Creating experience analytics: Yearly/monthly and daily experience analytics of stories/episodes and activities/events are created and displayed by the system.

In order to plan and evaluate the yearly, monthly, weekly, daily learning experiences, it may be necessary for the individual to carry out active work before these periods. The individual can update plans live when planning can be done anytime and anywhere. The operation in evaluation process that needs focusing is actively carried out at the end of the relevant periods. Activity/event reports and analytics should be available for display every time and everywhere. The monitoring and controlling of learning experiences are carried out live.

Hypothetical Design and Development of the System

A hypothetical design involving different temporal perspectives will be carried out so that the learning experiences management approach summarized in the previous section can be implemented with the help of an exocortex. The first of these temporal perspectives is an exocortex architecture that can be realized with near future technologies. Other temporal perspectives following this include the period up to next 10 years, and the period up to next 20 years.

The Architecture That Contains Technologies That Are Expected to Emerge Within a Few Years

In the next few years, two-way neural connections between the human neocortex and an exocortex may not be established. But by giving some basic commands mentally to a computation environment kept in a cloud and reflecting the results obtained by processing the daily data of the computation environment with the help of commands on the reality image of the individual's retina, emulation of the cycle of considering the problem and visualizing the result will be provided in the individual's mind.

Different interfaces can be used to communicate with an exocortex. For example, Katsevman, in a simple exocortex application developed by him, used text to speech voice synthesizing and voice recognition software with a Bluetooth connected microphone/speaker (Katsevman, 2008).

By 2018, in the next 1-5 years, it will be possible to give commands easily by thought with wearable BCI devices, improvements will take place in reviewing experiences with holographic mixed reality glasses and smart lenses, real-time results will be obtained due to the increase in processing power. According to these foresights, it may be possible to use EEG reader for the exocortex input unit (thought output device) and the holographic mixed reality goggles for the exocortex output unit (visual input device).

Progress has been made in EEG readers in recent years and they are being marketed as BCI consumer devices (van Erp, Lotte, & Tangermann, 2012). Among them the EEG readers of Emotiv (Emotiv, 2018) and NeuroSky (Neurosky, 2018) firms stand out (Swan, 2012).

Maharg (2016), who studies on legal education, indicates that it is possible to establish a connection with the cybernetic exocortex through the use of brain-computer interfaces marketed as user electronics, such as Emotiv Insight, which will have a significant effect on legal education and professional law skills, thus personal learning will have a transformation.

Nowadays, wearable EEG readers are able to capture the waves that the brain transmits and can perform basic physical and emotional assessments by analyzing these waves (Minguillon, Lopez-Gordo, & Pelayo, 2017). However, it is not possible to write fluently using these devices, for example, using a virtual keyboard. In order to overcome this problem, the cursor on a virtual keyboard in the front of the eye can be brought on the desired character with the head movements and can be selected it with the thought of "pushing", and writing with this method is possible. It is possible to do this with a wearable EEG device and holographic goggles.

With the Google Glass project at the beginning of 2010 (Google Glass [Glass], 2018) smart glasses that offer augmented reality emerged. In augmented reality, the glasses can mount images created by itself on the environmental image by evaluating the perceived data from its environment. Then glasses that allow mixed reality applications have been developed with Microsoft Hololens. In the mixed reality application, the images added on the true image of the environment can be made part of the environment. Thus, for example, when an artificial image is placed on the table, this image becomes a part of the table and the user can look around the table to see this image from every direction (Microsoft Hololens [Hololens], 2018).

- **Capturing Experiences:** In addition to the other sensors that people use, carry with themselves and on the devices they wear, it will become common to capture experience with augmented reality glasses such as Google Glass and mixed reality glasses such as Microsoft Hololens. Microsoft Hololens has four cameras to detect the environment, a depth sensor camera, and a separate camera for capturing a photo/HD video and four microphones (Hololens, 2018). With BCI, more mental and physical characteristics will be captured. Today, with the cheaper EEG readers, you can catch emotional situations such as instant fascination, long-term excitement, experiencing stress, dealing with a job, relaxation, taking care of something, focusing as well as physical situations such as frowning, smiling, grimacing, lifting eyebrows. EEG sensors also have very sensitive gyroscope, accelerometer and magnetometer on them (Emotiv, 2018). Disadvantages of these devices include lifetimes of 4-8 hours for EEG Reader and 4 hours for Hololens, and with Hololens weighing 579 gr and NeuroSky EEG reader weighing 130 gr, carrying a load weighing more than 700 grams in total over the head for a long time. All data captured by portable or wearable sensors will be saved in a portable computer via a personal area network (PAN) constructed with Bluetooth, and then will be transmitted wirelessly to exocortex. In the case where holographic glasses have enough power for this process, portable computer will be deactivated and sensors will use from holographic glasses to exocortex flow directly. The transmitter interface will transmit with 4.5G-5G in environments without Wi-Fi. Fixed devices capturing log data like desktop computers will transmit the captured log data themselves to exocortex directly.

- **Transmitting Commands to Exocortex and Browsing Past Experiences**: Although it is possible to give commands with Hololens through holographic cursor, hand movements and voice input, the command input in the proposed architecture will be carried out by wearable EEG reader. This process can be carried out in two ways. The first one is benefiting from visual commands determined by focusing on holographic symbols on the holographic glasses or from verbal commands entered with the help of virtual keyboard letters/numbers. In the near future, writing commands fast enough by thinking them in the mind will be provided. Commands will be transmitted to exocortex via holographic glasses or portable computers used as transmitter interface. After transmitting the received commands to exocortex, holographic glasses will be used in order to display the results obtained in exocortex. The glasses will reflect the image coming from exocortex upon the real world image. In the case of having enough resources, the glasses will get the results directly from exocortex; in the case of not having enough resources, the glasses will use 4.5G-5G connected portable computer as a transmitting interface. It has started to be realized that using holographic glasses with wearable EEG readers will provide more benefits (Lal, 2015). Logging analytics about from which devices and sensors log data came from to exocortex at that moment will be reflected to the holographic glasses in a hologram without the need of any command as long as there is connection.

- **Interpreting Experiences in Exocortex:** The exocortex components that are working on cloud will determine and tag the actions and activities at that moment by running activity determination algorithms on the captured log data. By using these tags, activities will be indexed in order to use them in searches, episodes including activities and stories including episodes will be determined. Episode trees and story trees will be updated alongside the experience trees belonging to experiences. Analytics belonging to the process of instantaneous interpreting of the experiences by exocortex will be reflected to the holographic glasses in a hologram without the need of any command as long as there is connection. So, for example, the temporal histogram of the past likes of a text that has been read before will be displayed in a side hologram and the user will carry out a "synthetic recollection" by accessing a document on this timeline.

- **Acquiring Context in Exocortex:** Components of exocortex working on cloud will detect the context values of the log data coming from sensors and will place them on context ontologies by running context determination algorithms. Context determination analytics will be reflected to the user live in this process. From time to time, the user can reorganize the context trees by accessing them. Thus, the user will be provided with clues from past experiences of basic contexts such as location, people, object, etc. with a personal augmented reality support.

- **Making Sense of Learning Experiences in Exocortex:** The user, at any time, can give commands for the processes of re-accessing a past experience in the experience pool, animating the accessed experience in a timeline, displaying the experience network, displaying the experience tree, displaying the context/content-experience networks, making semantic queries on context/content-experience networks experience and creating activity/event, context and content based experience portfolios, and the results of those commands will be reflected upon the real world in a hologram.
- **Meta-Cognitive Regulation of Learning Experiences in Exocortex:** The user can give commands for active planning, taking plan recommendations from the system, live tracking of the experiences, getting recommendations for the next behavior from the system, decision making about the experiences, starting an unplanned experience, displaying activity reports or experience analytics to exocortex and the results are reflected to the glasses in a hologram by the exocortex.

An exocortex diagram, including the five stages of the learning experience management approach, is shown in Figure 3.

An Architecture Using Technologies That Will Emerge Within Ten Years

As a result of the technological developments which will take place within ten years, communicating with computers at the speed of thought via brain-computer interfaces and displaying the results directly in the retina via virtual retinal projection will be possible.

- It will be possible to capture images + see the distance + see in the dark with smart lenses (Wong, 2016).

Figure 3. An exocortex architecture that can be applied in the near future for learning experiences management

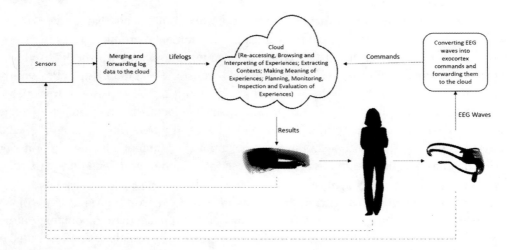

- It will be possible to capture all the conversations in the environment separately with smart headphones.
- As a result of the developments in processing power, developments will take place in making semantic queries on experiences, learning from experiences and guiding based on experiences with personal artificial intelligence. Image and object recognition and voice recognition will be carried out faster and more accurate.
- When capturing experiences, thoughts (even in the form of meaningless words) will be captured at the same time. Experiences captured at that moment will be tagged with thoughts, re-accessing to experiences will be easier. Thus, mental access to experiences outside the brain will be accelerated.
- Experiences and results will be displayed in mixed reality environment with virtual retinal projection.

Magic Leap founded in 2010 developed a virtual retinal projection method that is expected to create a turning point in 3-dimensional holographic imaging technology. In this method where the image is projected directly on the retina layer of the eye with micro fiber projections, if it has enough precision, it is impossible to distinguish the difference by the human eye between the actual image and the virtual image placed on it (Magic Leap, 2018).

An Architecture Using Technologies That Will Emerge Within Twenty Years

As a result of the technological developments which will take place within twenty years, it will be possible to share experiences and feelings with the brain-brain interface. Considering the expected developments in the non-biological part of the human intellect (Kurzweil, 2005) and expected developments on mental communication (Kaku, 2014), the following inferences can be made:

- All of the brain senses (sight, hearing, touch, taste, and smell) will be captured directly by the brain implants at a certain level.
- Past experiences may be stored in implant memories in the brain while they may be stored outside the brain via mental communication.
- Transactions may be done with the implant processors in the brain while they may be done outside the brain via mental communication.
- The results may be animated as images and sound directly in the brain.
- Experience and emotion sharing may be done/others' experiences may be utilized.
- Reliving past experiences in mind will be provided with exocortex
- Making sense of and managing experiences will be carried out by thinking. As the processes of accessing experience, bringing back experience (return to experience), animating experience and saving evaluation results will be carried out by synthetic cognition, the effectiveness biological thinking process will increase.
- Past experiences can be analyzed in great detail with powerful and fast algorithms and the individual will be provided with realistic reports about his/her performance.
- By tracking the experiences an individual lives at that moment, support aimed for increasing the individual's performance will be provided in order to carry out the individual's plans.

- Individuals may plan their future by discussing with the exocortex, inspect the experiences lived at that moment and evaluate their past. This mental dialog established with the exocortex will substitute inner voice that the individual uses when discussing to himself/herself.

SOLUTIONS AND RECOMMENDATIONS

In this section, the possibilities provided especially for lifelong learners by implementing "learning experiences management" approach in an exocortex environment will be discussed. For this purpose, with the present day use case for learning experiences management approach, future scenarios for using exocortex technologies belonging to different temporal perspectives in the future will be given a place.

In order to animate the hypothetical implementation of the learning experiences management approach in an exocortex environment, first of all, the implementation of learning experiences management approach according to the results taken from the projects in Table 1 is addressed as a future reality scenario written as first person narrative:

An Implementation Scenario Belonging to Learning Experiences Management Approach Today

My lifelog captures the passive screenshot and camera image of all of my work that I carry out in my computer. The screen video, video and voice records that I captured actively are added to the lifelog, too. Also, throughout the day, location information and the images captured by wearable lifelogging camera are added to the lifelog, too. Apart from these, I am tracking all records belonging to heart rate, sleeping state, walking and other exercises via smart phone and smart watch. I am combining all these information in a dedicated computer on a timeline by transmitting them through cloud.

Thus, I, too, have the 5R benefits of the lifelogging provide according to Sellen and Whittaker (2010):

- I can recollect easily the locations, people, behaviors, objects and events included in my experiences by examining the records of my experience (recollect).
- I can review and relive any experience by going back to any moment I want to recollect (reminiscing).
- I can easily access the information (document, correspondence, image, etc.) I am looking for in a past experience (retrieving).
- I can have more information about myself (my behaviors, environment, characteristics, etc.) by reviewing my past experiences (reflecting).
- I can review the plans, programs and trials that I have made in the past (remembering intentions).

I can make daily, monthly and yearly interpretations on my past, present and probable future experiences kept in my lifelog. It is possible for me to define and classify experiences, and encode contexts accompanying experiences by adding appropriate tags to those interpretations.

When needed, I can review and evaluate a learning experience by accessing a specific learning experience or images belonging to an experience series and other records with the help of experience interpretations and tags, and context tags. I can use time stamped images or videos of learning experience as an evidence for learning.

Exocortex as a Learning Technology

From time to time, I can carry out the processes of planning future experiences, tracking-inspecting current experiences and evaluating past experiences on the experience database by using interpretation possibilities for current and past experiences. Thus, I can easily manage all of my learning experiences in a meta- cognitive platform in lifelong learning and life-wide learning contexts.

A Scenario for the Implementation of the System in the Near Future

Image, voice, video, location, speed and biologic lifelog data provided by the fixed, portable and wearable devices I use are combined in my common time line by being established in the cloud by themselves. The system, while tracking my experiences at that moment, interprets my log data in a sub system and acquires contexts by recognizing my log data real-time with pattern recognition techniques. Thus, I can access my past experiences through an experience search engine while I am in action and at any time. I can make key words and other commands be transmitted in the search engine mentally and at the speed of thought by using holographic mixed reality goggles and wearable EEG reader together. Experiences and results found are reflected to my holographic mixed reality goggles wirelessly.

So, I can scan and access my past experiences, and reanimate my experiences at any time without being forced to take care of the processes of capturing, combining and defining experiences. This enables me to plan, inspect and evaluate my experiences in any time.

By tagging all of my experiences with the EEG reader data, I can save how much I was focused on my experience and, in a way that can determine my emotional state during the experience, my mental and emotional state, too. This way, when I go back to a past experience, I can see how much I was focused on the experience and how I felt during the experience.

A Scenario for the Implementation of the System Within the Next Ten Years

The angle of vision of the human eye (both eyes together) is, normally, horizontally 200°, vertically 135° (60 degrees upward and 75 degrees downward) (Dagnelie, 2011, p. 398). With the help of the cameras on the smart lens/goggles on me, I can capture all of my life experiences in video format in 3D and 8K and 60fps quality with having 270° horizontally and 190° vertically. At the same time, I capture images with the quality of 120 megapixel per second. With the aid of smart headphones, I can capture all the conversations in the environment separately and conceal all the voices except the voice belonging to the experience on focus. My smart lifelog designed as a small drone continuously shoots high quality 360 degree videos of my environment and provides the possibility of observing my experience from outside.

All the texts I have seen and all the conversation I have heard are translated to text simultaneously and recorded with my experience. With the help of sensors on joints, my body position is precisely determined and recorded. The movements of my body, feet and arms are captured with the motion sensors. My heart rate and blood pressure, my physical facial movements, mental and emotional state are captured and saved by being packaged with my experiences, with the help of biological sensors and brain wave reader respectively. So, the experiences which I did not focus on enough but I live in parallel with the experience that I focused on can be noticed and tracked separately.

Captured log data are saved to my personal cloud live by transmitting with the wireless communication infrastructure with 1 GB/s bandwidth. My exocortex defines and classifies all of my past experiences by scanning them real-time with the help of enhanced machine learning algorithms.

I can synthetically recollect my past experiences by transmitting commands to exocortex at the speed of thought with the help of EEG reader and can see my past experiences in my retina with the help of virtual retinal projection. I can easily access a similar of an image I saw, a text I read or a voice I heard in the past. Due to this function, my recollection capacity increases almost infinitely compared to past.

By focusing on a past experience, I can reanimate and watch the progress of that experience realistically. All these data are downloaded to my smart goggles with the same wireless communication infrastructure. When I need, I can have a look at the background experiences that I lived in parallel but could not focus enough at that time.

By tracking all of my experiences, my exocortex displays reports, analytics, and additional reference sources, similar and parallel past experiences, recommendations for the next step relating to my current experience. Exocortex can notice my planning, starting, suspending, canceling, terminating, rescheduling, continuing decisions about an experience and can update my plans. My exocortex can evaluate my past experiences, by comparison, singularly as activities/events, episodes or stories, or collectively with plans and decisions.

A Scenario for the Implementation of the System Within the Next Twenty Years

My exocortex, placed as an implant to my brain, saves the images and sounds captured in high resolution by the retinal implant and hearing implant in a high capacity memory in the implant by tagging them with the touching, taste and smell senses that are read from my brain.

My drone shaped lifelog watching me continuously in-flight, captures all the events in my environment and captures high resolution log data that can animate my experiences holographically in the future. My exocortex analyzes my experiences instantaneously on the implant and places them on its own memory as synthetic memories. My exocortex can share experience and feelings and can utilize others' experiences by connecting to the super-intelligence and the other individuals' open-to-share exocortex by the high speed wireless communication infrastructure.

As a result of the thinking activity about any experience that I want to recollect, my exocortex can bring this experience and similar ones, and can animate it in the brain as image and voice. Thus, I can relive my past experiences by animating them synthetically in my mind. Visualizing a few images of a past experience to do this is enough. In other words, synthetic recollection is taking the place of biological recollection. My exocortex can analyze my past experiences in detail and can give realistic reports about my whole past life with strong and fast algorithms.

My exocortex tracks very delicately my experiences that I live at that moment and can show the most appropriate information, memory and method right on time in order to increase my performance in my experience by comparing it with my plans. My exocortex has become my inner voice. I can make plans, inspect the experience that I live at that moment and evaluate my past experiences by speaking through my mind with my exocortex. Most of the times, I find myself discussing on a topic or searching for solutions to a problem with my exocortex. Also, my exocortex gives me cognitive support in solving problems by always being connected to the artificial super-intelligence.

CONCLUSION AND FUTURE RESEARCH DIRECTIONS

Because of the speed of technological change, individuals today have to forget in order to learn more information and skills, apply them and make way for the next learning. This causes individuals' minds to turn into graveyards of learning experiences, recollection capacities to decrease and possibility of utilizing their past experiences to perish. In most of the cases, thinking that new information and skill are obtained because of the differences in contexts, individuals are forced to relearn the same information and skills over and over again in actuality. With every new learning process, they are forced to overcome again the steps that they worked so hard to overcome in past learning experiences. However, even a quick review of past experiences will provide time and energy saving for new experiences, by triggering the recollection of mistakes. The edge of satisfying this need by biological memory and mental possibilities has come. From now on, exocortex and external mental instruments will be used. Although today's technology does not allow the exocortex to be accessible every time and everywhere, it is expected from this technology to be accessible in the near future and to mature gradually within the next 10-20 years.

In this study, by scanning the literature about exocortex, the structure, functions and the limits of a hypothetical technology allowing human cognitive skills to be supported outside of the neocortex is tried to be determined. Then, by examining the learning experiences management approach, how this approach can be applied with exocortex in the future by lifelong learners is discussed.

Scenarios about the future show that an exocortex system, appropriate for the learning experiences management to be applied every time and everywhere, consists of a storage system and software in a cloud environment using wearable mental communication and visual sharing technologies as the interface, and that is continuously connected in a two-way connection with high speed wireless.

Once this initial system is established, with an evolutionary advancement, this system is expected to be more robust, accelerated, and fluent every year with the technological developments in sensors, interface technologies, wireless data transmission infrastructure, faster and more efficient machine learning algorithms, and computing power and storage capacity of computers.

While individuals will make sense of and manage their past experiences lagged on a computer screen during this development at first, they will be able to make sense of and manage their past experiences every time and everywhere although in a slow manner by accessing them via an exocortex with mental communication in a few years. This development will continue its journey in ten years, and will enable individuals to access their past experiences every time and everywhere fluently and completely. Within the next twenty years, as a result of the developments in this area, exocortex will be almost inseparably integrated with the individuals' neocortex and the differences between biological recollection and synthetic recollection or cognitive activities carried out with brain and cognitive activities carried in exocortex will be insignificant.

An exocortex architecture for learning experiences management contains important benefits for lifelong learning in the near future. Among these; an individual's learning past being accessible lifelong and the interpretation pool that contains past experiences and becomes valuable with time, the personal knowledge base constructed by the contexts with experiences and context pool belonging to the information gathered in one's life stand out. Machine learning algorithms of exocortex make personal knowledge base more valuable gradually by determining, defining and classifying the individual's experiences and the learning experiences accompanying them. Thus, the individual will have the fluency and sharpness in recollecting, animating and evaluating lifelong learning experiences better than ever. This also reveal the objective tools in proving experiences. This dominance that the individual establishes over his/her past experiences will provide the possibility to "determine and evaluate one's own situation and conditions properly" that no one else possesses for planning the future, inspecting the current moment and evaluating the past experiences.

These benefits will increase gradually within ten years and a significant cognitive skill difference will emerge between individuals having an exocortex and individuals not having an exocortex. Within twenty years, the individual becoming a transhuman or a posthuman will be a matter of discussion because the capacity of exocortex will increase tens and hundreds of times compared to the capacity of neocortex.

The system has some possible drawbacks. Among these are the possibilities of the individual's biological cognitive skills lying fallow because of becoming more and more addicted to the cognitive skills the exocortex provides and the individuals losing their skill of working independently. Individuals' calculation skills degrading because of calculators becoming common and individuals' legible writing pencil skills degrading because of keyboard usage becoming common can be shown as examples. Another drawback is the violation of private life caused by the common usage of lifelog. The line about this matter has already been crossed with the surveillance cameras and car cameras becoming common. Wearable lifelogging devices or drone shaped in flight lifelog devices will be perceived as personal surveillance cameras for each individual in the future.

The proposed exocortex architecture can be guiding for studies aimed at constructing a synthetic autobiographical memory, too (Evans, Fox, & Prescott 2014).

The development by designing and evaluation by implementing, as part of a research project, of an exocortex based learning experiences management system in the near future whose design was carried out hypothetically in this study are necessary for the main idea of this study, namely, evolutionary development.

Such a research project may contain the following ideas and hypotheses:

- An applicable exocortex should be closely related to the individual's own experience history. In this case, an exocortex must contain an individual's lifelogging system.
- The fact that the designs related to exocortex are based on hypothetical technologies aiming 2030's is not an obstacle in making applicable designs for this purpose in today.
- The proposed system contains the possibility of access in every time and everywhere to the individual's lifelog kept in cloud environment. The biggest obstacles in realizing this design are providing the captured log data to be uploaded to cloud at the same speed, those data to be processed in real time in cloud environment and the results obtained according to the commands coming from the user in cloud to be downloaded to the user at the same speed.
- The fact that the individual gives command by thinking and sees the results in holographic mixed reality environment shows that the individual's neocortex can be connected with an exocortex with today's technology.
- With the proposed system, it is expected of the individual to utilize efficiently the learning experiences accompanying past life experiences and to increase the cognitive capacity in daily life.

In order to develop and experiment the necessary technologies for each stage in the exocortex architecture, that are capturing, interpreting, contextualizing, making sense of and managing experiences, which are suggested in this study, a research and development study is needed.

REFERENCES

2045.. 2017). *2045 Initiative*. Retrieved from http://2045.com/

Ashby, W. R. (1956). *An Introduction to Cybernetics*. London: Chapman & Hall. doi:10.5962/bhl.title.5851

Ashby, W. R. (1960). *Design for a Brain*. London: Chapman & Hall. doi:10.1007/978-94-015-1320-3

Bonaci, T., Herron, J., Matlack, C., & Chizeck, H. J. (2014). Securing the exocortex: A twenty-first century cybernetics challenge. In *Norbert Wiener in the 21st Century (21CW), 2014 IEEE Conference on* (pp. 1-8). IEEE. 10.1109/NORBERT.2014.6893912

Bostrom, N. (2005). A history of transhumanist thought. *Journal of Evolution and Technology / WTA*, *14*(1), 1–25.

Bostrom, N. (2014). Superintelligence: Paths, dangers, strategies. Oxford, UK: Oxford University Press.

Cowen, A. S., Chun, M. M., & Kuhl, B. A. (2014). Neural portraits of perception: Reconstructing face images from evoked brain activity. *NeuroImage*, *94*, 12–22. doi:10.1016/j.neuroimage.2014.03.018 PMID:24650597

Dagnelie, G. (2011). *Visual Prosthetics: Physiology, Bioengineering, Rehabilitation*. Berlin: Springer Science & Business Media. doi:10.1007/978-1-4419-0754-7

Dambrot, S. M. (2016). Exocortical Cognition: Heads in the cloud. In *Systems, Man, and Cybernetics (SMC), 2016 IEEE International Conference on* (pp. 004007-004014). IEEE.

Donald, M. (1991). *Origins of the modern mind: Three stages in the evolution of culture and cognition*. Cambridge, MA: Harvard University Press.

Donald, M. (1993). Precis of Origins of the modern mind: Three stages in the evolution of culture and cognition. *Behavioral and Brain Sciences*, *16*(4), 737–748. doi:10.1017/S0140525X00032647

Doswell, J. T. (2006). Context-aware mobile augmented reality architecture for lifelong learning. In *Advanced Learning Technologies, 2006. Sixth International Conference on* (pp. 372-374). IEEE. 10.1109/ICALT.2006.1652448

Doswell, J. T. (2008). Wearable Augmented Reality System Architecture: for Mobile Assistance and Training. In *Proceedings of X Symposium on Virtual and Augmented Reality (SVR 2008), Joao Pessoa, Brazil* (pp. 129-132). Academic Press.

Doswell, J. T., Blake, M. B., & Butcher-Green, J. (2006). Mobile augmented reality system architecture for ubiquitous e-learning. In *Wireless, Mobile and Ubiquitous Technology in Education, 2006. WMUTE'06. Fourth IEEE International Workshop on* (pp. 121-123). IEEE. 10.1109/WMTE.2006.261358

Doswell, J. T., & Skinner, A. (2014). Augmenting human cognition with adaptive augmented reality. In *International Conference on Augmented Cognition* (pp. 104-113). Cham, Switzerland: Springer International Publishing. 10.1007/978-3-319-07527-3_10

Edwards, D. (2017a). Thinking Outside the Brain – Why We Need to Build a Decentralized Exocortex - Part 2 [Blog entry]. Retrieved from https://steemit.com/technology/@dana-edwards/thinking-outside-the-brain-why-we-need-to-build-a-decentralized-exocortex-part-2

Edwards, D. (2017b). Personal knowledge management [Blog entry]. Retrieved from https://steemit.com/enigma/@dana-edwards/personal-knowledge-management

Ehresmann, A., von Ammon, R., Iakovidis, D. K., & Hunter, A. (2012). *Ubiquitous complex event processing in exocortex applications and mathematical approaches.* Retrieved from http://www.complexevents.com/2012/06/17/ubiquitous-complex-event-processing-in-exocortex-applications-and-mathematical-approaches/

Emotiv. (2018). *Emotiv Brainwear*. Retrieved from https://www.emotiv.com/comparison/

Engelbart, D. C. (1962). *Augmenting human intellect: a conceptual framework*. Retrieved from https://www.dougengelbart.org/pubs/augment-3906.html

Evans, M. H., Fox, C. W., & Prescott, T. J. (2014). Machines learning-towards a new synthetic autobiographical memory. In *Conference on Biomimetic and Biohybrid Systems* (pp. 84-96). Cham, Switzerland: Springer International Publishing. 10.1007/978-3-319-09435-9_8

GEF. (2017). *Global Education Futures*. Retrieved from https://edu2035.org/

Gibson, W. (1982). Burning Chrome. *Omni (New York, N.Y.)*, *4*(10), 72–77.

Gibson, W. (1984). *Neuromancer*. New York: Ace.

Glass. (2018). *Google Glass*. Retrieved from https://www.x.company/glass

Graimann, B., Allison, B., & Pfurtscheller, G. (2009). Brain–computer interfaces: A gentle introduction. In *Brain-Computer Interfaces* (pp. 1–27). Springer Berlin Heidelberg. doi:10.1007/978-3-642-02091-9_1

Guger. (2017). *Guger Technologies*. Retrieved from http://www.gtec.at/

Gurrin, C., Smeaton, A. F., & Doherty, A. R. (2014). Lifelogging: Personal big data. *Foundations and Trends in Information Retrieval*, *8*(1), 1-125.

Hololens. (2018). *Microsoft Hololens*. Retrieved from https://www.microsoft.com/en-us/hololens)

Horikawa, T., Tamaki, M., Miyawaki, Y., & Kamitani, Y. (2013). Neural decoding of visual imagery during sleep. *Science*, *340*(6132), 639–642. doi:10.1126cience.1234330 PMID:23558170

Houston, B. (2000). *Exocortex*. Retrieved from https://everything2.com/title/exocortex

Hughes, J. J. (2006). What comes after Homo sapiens? *New Scientist*, *192*(2578), 70–72. doi:10.1016/S0262-4079(06)61144-5

Hughes, J. J. (2007). The struggle for a smarter world. *Futures*, *39*(8), 942–954. doi:10.1016/j.futures.2007.03.002

Hutchinson, D. (2012). The Future History of Consciousness. Integral Review: A Transdisciplinary & Transcultural Journal for New Thought, Research, &. *Praxis (Bern)*, *8*(1), 62–67.

Kaku, M. (2014). *The Future of the Mind: The Scientific Quest to Understand, Enhance, and Empower the Mind*. New York: Doubleday.

Kapoor, A., Shenoy, P., & Tan, D. (2008). Combining brain computer interfaces with vision for object categorization. In *Computer Vision and Pattern Recognition, 2008. CVPR 2008. IEEE Conference on* (pp. 1-8). IEEE. 10.1109/CVPR.2008.4587618

Katsevman, M. (2008). *Exploring the exocortex: an approach to optimizing human productivity*. Retrieved from http://logarchy.org/exocortex.pdf

Kay, K. N., Naselaris, T., Prenger, R. J., & Gallant, J. L. (2008). Identifying natural images from human brain activity. *Nature, 452*(7185), 352–355. doi:10.1038/nature06713 PMID:18322462

Kosmyna, N., Tarpin-Bernard, F., & Rivet, B. (2015). Towards brain computer interfaces for recreational activities: Piloting a drone. In *Human-Computer Interaction* (pp. 506–522). Springer International Publishing.

Kosow, H., & Robert Gaßner, R. (2008). *Methods of Future and Scenario Analysis. Studies / Deutsches Institut für Entwicklungspolitik gGmbH. DIE Research Project Development Policy: Questions for the Future*. Bonn, Germany: German Development Institue.

Kurzweil, R. (2005, Sept. 24). Human 2.0. *New Scientist*, 32–37. PMID:16317855

Kurzweil, R. (2012). How to Create a Mind: The Secret of Human Thought Revealed. New York: Viking Penguin.

Lal, A. (2015, May 14). *VR and AR Need Brain-Computer Interfaces to Achieve Their Full Potential*. Retrieved from http://gadgets.ndtv.com/wearables/opinion/vr-and-ar-need-brain-computer-interfaces-to-achieve-their-full-potential-692413

Leap, M. (2018). *Magic Leap*. Retrieved from https://www.magicleap.com/

Licklider, J. C. (1960). Man-computer symbiosis. *IRE Transactions on Human Factors in Electronics, 1*, 4-11.

Maharg, P. (2016). Editorial: Learning/Technology. *The Law Teacher, 50*(1), 15–23. doi:10.1080/03069400.2016.1146454

Mills, J. O., Jalil, A., & Stanga, P. E. (2017). Electronic retinal implants and artificial vision: Journey and present. *Eye (London, England), 31*(10), 1383–1398. doi:10.1038/eye.2017.65 PMID:28548648

Minguillon, J., Lopez-Gordo, M. A., & Pelayo, F. (2017). Trends in EEG-BCI for daily-life: Requirements for artifact removal. *Biomedical Signal Processing and Control, 31*, 407–418. doi:10.1016/j.bspc.2016.09.005

Mudry, A., & Mills, M. (2013). The early history of the cochlear implant: A retrospective. *JAMA Otolaryngology-Head & Neck Surgery, 139*(5), 446–453. doi:10.1001/jamaoto.2013.293 PMID:23681026

Mutlu, M. E. (2014). Öğrenme Deneyimlerinin Yorumlanması (Interpreting of Learning Experiences). [In Turkish]. *Eğitim ve Öğretim Araştırmaları Dergisi, 3*(4), 21–45.

Mutlu, M.E. (2015a). Yaşam Deneyimleri İçin Bir Bağlam Modeli – LECOM (LECOM – A Context Model for Life Experiences). In *AB'15 – XVII. Akademik Bilişim Konferansı*. Anadolu Üniversitesi Eskişehir. (In Turkish)

Mutlu, M. E. (2015b). Design and Development of a Digital Life Logging System for Management of Lifelong Learning Experiences. *Procedia: Social and Behavioral Sciences*, *174*, 834–848. doi:10.1016/j.sbspro.2015.01.678

Mutlu, M.E. (2015c). Öğrenme Deneyimlerinin Yakalanması İçin Çoklu Algılayıcılı Bir Yaşam Günlüğü Sisteminin Geliştirilmesi [Development a Multisensor Lifelogging System for Capturing Learning Experiences]. In *IETC 2015 – 15. Uluslararası Eğitim Teknolojisi Konferansı*. İstanbul Üniversitesi. (in Turkish)

Mutlu, M.E. (2015d). Yaşam Günlüğünün Aktif Kullanımı [Active Usage of Lifelogging]. In *20. Türkiye'de İnternet Konferansı – İnet-Tr'15*. İstanbul Üniversitesi. (in Turkish)

Mutlu, M. E. (2015e). Öğrenme Deneyimi Portfolyo Sistemi Tasarımı [Design of Learning Experiences Portfolio System]. *Proceedings of INT-E 2015 International Conference on New Horizons in Education*. (in Turkish)

Mutlu, M. E. (2016a). Öğrenme Deneyimlerinin Yönetiminde Üstbilişsel Düzenleme [Meta-cognitive Regulations in Learning Experiences Management]. [In Turkish]. *Eğitim ve Öğretim Araştırmaları Dergisi*, *5*(2), 265–288.

Mutlu, M. E. (2016b). Sanal Ortamlardaki Öğrenme Deneyimleri İçin Bir Enformasyon Erişim Sistemi Tasarımı [An Information Retrieval System Design for Learning Experiences in Virtual Environments]. [In Turkish]. *Eğitim ve Öğretim Araştırmaları Dergisi*, *5*(2), 395–408.

Mutlu, M. E., Kayabas, I., Kip Kayabas, B., & Peri Mutlu, A. (2015f). Implementation of the Lifelong Learning Experiences Management Approach – Observations on the First Experiences. *Procedia: Social and Behavioral Sciences*, *174*, 849–861. doi:10.1016/j.sbspro.2015.01.680

NeuroSky. (2018). *NeuroSky – Body and Mind Quantified*. Retrieved from http://neurosky.com/

Neuroweb. (2017). *Neuroweb Iniative*. Retrieved from http://www.globalneuroweb.org/ru/

Nishimoto, S., Vu, A. T., Naselaris, T., Benjamini, Y., Yu, B., & Gallant, J. L. (2011). Reconstructing visual experiences from brain activity evoked by natural movies. *Current Biology*, *21*(19), 1641–1646. doi:10.1016/j.cub.2011.08.031 PMID:21945275

Ramirez, S., Liu, X., Lin, P. A., Suh, J., Pignatelli, M., Redondo, R. L., ... Tonegawa, S. (2013). Creating a false memory in the hippocampus. *Science*, *341*(6144), 387–391. doi:10.1126cience.1239073 PMID:23888038

Sandberg, A., & Bostrom, N. (2008). *Whole brain emulation: a roadmap*. Technical Report #2008-3, Future of Humanity Institute, Oxford, UK: Oxford University. Retrieved from https://www.fhi.ox.ac.uk/brain-emulation-roadmap-report.pdf

Schalk, G., Miller, K. J., Anderson, N. R., Wilson, J. A., Smyth, M. D., Ojemann, J. G., ... Leuthardt, E. C. (2008). Two-dimensional movement control using electrocorticographic signals in humans. *Journal of Neural Engineering*, *5*(1), 75–84. doi:10.1088/1741-2560/5/1/008 PMID:18310813

Schoenmakers, S., Barth, M., Heskes, T., & van Gerven, M. (2013). Linear reconstruction of perceived images from human brain activity. *NeuroImage*, *83*, 951–961. doi:10.1016/j.neuroimage.2013.07.043 PMID:23886984

Sellen, A. J., & Whittaker, S. (2010). Beyond total capture: A constructive critique of lifelogging. *Communications of the ACM*, *53*(5), 70–77. doi:10.1145/1735223.1735243

Skinner, A., Russo, C., Baraniecki, L., & Maloof, M. (2014). Ubiquitous augmented cognition. In *International Conference on Augmented Cognition* (pp. 67-77). Cham, Switzerland: Springer.

Sotala, J., & Valpola, H. (2012). Coalescing minds: brain uploading-related group mind scenarios. *International Journal of Machine Consciousness*, *4*(1), 293–312.

Sparrow, B., Liu, J., & Wegner, D. M. (2011). Google effects on memory: Cognitive consequences of having information at our fingertips. *Science*, *333*(6043), 776–778. doi:10.1126cience.1207745 PMID:21764755

Stross, C. (2004). Elector. *Asimov's Science Fiction*, *4*(9).

Swan, M. (2012). Sensor mania! The internet of things, wearable computing, objective metrics, and the quantified self 2.0. *Journal of Sensor and Actuator Networks*, *1*(3), 217–253. doi:10.3390/jsan1030217

van Erp, J., Lotte, F., & Tangermann, M. (2012). Brain-computer interfaces: Beyond medical applications. *Computer*, *45*(4), 26–34. doi:10.1109/MC.2012.107

Vinge, V. (2003). The Peace War. New York: Tor Books.

Wong, R. (2016, April 5). *Samsung patents smart contact lenses with a built-in camera*. Retrieved from https://www.sciencealert.com/samsung-just-patented-smart-contact-lenses-with-a-built-in-camera

Yoo, K. H., Filandrianos, E., Taghados, S., & Park, S. (2013). Non-invasive brain-to-brain interface (BBI): Establishing functional links between two brains. *PLoS One*, *8*(4), e60410. doi:10.1371/journal.pone.0060410 PMID:23573251

Zappa, M. (2012). *Envisioning emerging technology for 2012 and beyond*. Retrieved from http://www.demainlaveille.fr/wp-content/uploads/2012/01/envisioningtech.pdf

Chapter 6
Transhumanism and Innovative Leadership:
A Question of Quality

Ebba S. I. Ossiannilsson
https://orcid.org/0000-0002-8488-5787
ICDE OER Advocacy Committee, Sweden

ABSTRACT

Rethinking leadership at all levels is required to reach the goals of learning and education in 2030 through which learners will take the lead in orchestrating the process and manner of their own learning and in choosing their personal learning journeys. The fourth industrial revolution will continue to change the ways we act, perform, live, work, and learn. Therefore, there is a need for a social revolution that includes the understanding of transhumanism and its effects. The term "cutting edge" does not concern technology as much as it concerns humans. Accordingly, transhumanism is crucial for a sustainable ecosystem of learning with and through technology and digital transformation, which encompasses all levels of institutions—macro, meso, and micro. This chapter is focused on future trends, issues, and challenges in management and leadership as well as on issues and challenges in communication, which is essential in both leadership and smart learning.

INTRODUCTION

Transhumanism, which is often abbreviated as H+ or h+, is an international philosophical movement that advocates the transformation of the human condition by developing widely available sophisticated technologies that greatly enhance human intellect and physiology (Boström, 2005). Advocates of transhumanism study the potential benefits and dangers of emerging technologies that could overcome fundamental human limitations as well as the ethical limitations of using such technologies. Emerging technologies are those perceived as capable of changing the status quo. These technologies are generally new, but they include older technologies that are still controversial and relatively undeveloped in their potential. Rotolo, Hicks, and Martin (2015) considered that emerging technologies are characterized by

DOI: 10.4018/978-1-5225-8431-5.ch006

radical novelty, relatively fast growth, coherence, prominent impact, uncertainty, and ambiguity. They argued that emerging technologies could be defined as having a certain degree of coherence that persists over time as well as the potential to exert considerable influence on the socio-economic domain, which is observed in the composition of actors, institutions, and the patterns of interactions among them, including the associated processes of knowledge production. The predominant influence of emerging technologies, however, lies in the future; therefore, in the emergence phase, they are still somewhat uncertain and ambiguous. O'Reilly (2008) argued that emerging technologies include a variety of technologies, such as educational technology, information technology, nanotechnology, biotechnology, cognitive science, psychotechnology, robotics, and artificial intelligence. In short, the link between transhumanism and emerging technologies promises us freedom from the biological limitations inherent in our nature. It aims to enhance the physical, emotional, and cognitive capacities of humans, thus opening up new possibilities and horizons of experience.

Sisman-Uğur & Kurubacak (forthcoming) argued in the call and outline of this book, that:

[T]transhumanism must advocate the moral right to use technologies to extend individual capacities, to surpass natural limits, and to improve humans not only physically and psychologically but also educationally. In other words, cutting-edge technologies must be used to improve humans by enabling them to live longer, healthier, and more intellectual lives. At this point, transhumanists must be progressive, advocating the use of emerging technologies to improve not only human lives, including cybernetics, artificial intelligence, social networks, space colonization, cryonics, and curing aging but also human learning. Transhumanism, therefore, must be a sound philosophy by valuing scientific facts, reason, and logic above spiritual principles as well as viewing humankind as controlling its transformation and promoting rational thinking, freedom, tolerance, democracy, and concern for human beings. Improving human learning means improving the human organism so that it can transform beyond its natural and biological limits.

In contributing to this book, this chapter considers a futuristic view of how transhumanism can achieve sustainability in the context of human learning to promote human intelligence in the future. The objectives of this chapter are to emphasize the need for a social revolution in response to the influence of transhumanism and the fourth industrial revolution, which is much more than a technical and digital revolution. The fourth industrial revolution and its accompanying social revolution will change the way we act, perform, live, work, communicate, and interact with each other and society, and hence the way we learn. The term "cutting edge" does not concern to technology as much as it concerns humans. Accordingly, the influence of transhumanism is crucial in a sustainable ecosystem of learning with and through technology and digitization. The digital transformation encompasses all levels of institutions—macro, meso, and micro. This chapter is focused on future trends, issues, and challenges in management and leadership as well as on issues and challenges in communication, which is essential in both leadership and smart learning. Rethinking leadership at all levels is required to reach the goals of learning and education in 2030 through which learners will take the lead in orchestrating the process and manner of their own learning and in choosing their personal learning journeys. This chapter is informed by the author's research and experiences in this field as well as by the relevant current literature. This chapter delineates a position rather than providing case studies, although some models are presented.

In the following sections, the concept of transhumanism is described, followed by a discussion of current and future trends related to the needs of transformation of education. Next, the model of substitution vs. transformation (SAMR) is discussed as well as the concepts of digitization and digital transformation. Thereafter, challenges in management and leadership related to future trends are discussed. The issues in smart learning are then discussed. The chapter ends by considering future research directions and offering conclusions.

BACKGROUND

The rise of transhumanism has become obvious during the last two or three years. One major reason is that transhumanists advocate new approaches, methods, and techniques that have influenced and will continue to influence social, political, ethical, and spiritual issues. However, there are some major dilemmas within this philosophy, and it is not clear how to identify the global values, norms, and ethics that are related to the diverse needs of learners in the digital era. Therefore, it is urgent to establish appropriate learning modalities (i.e. methods, processes and procedures) for humans in addressing future priorities and needs and to predict future issues and challenges for transhumanism in the near future.

Transhumanism is defined as the use of technology for the improvement of humans. Moreover, transhumanism is a way of thinking about the future. The transhumanist movement has developed gradually over the past two decades, based on the rapid digitalization of global society in recent decades. Therefore, transhumanism can be viewed as an extension of the concept of humanism. As a movement, transhumanism aims to improve the human body through science by constantly pushing back biological limits by using cutting-edge technologies to repair and improve the human body beyond its natural abilities, such as in learning. In this context, new and emerging communication and information technologies will be ways to help human transformation. Hence, learning about technologies, with technologies, and for technologies is one of the most important focuses of transhumanism (Boström, 2005).

This new era in human development is being enabled by extraordinary technological advances (Rotolo, Hicks and Martin, 2015). Moreover, Schwab (2017) and Schwab, Davis, and Nadella (2018) argued that the fourth industrial revolution will continue to fundamentally change the ways in which we live, work, learn, and relate to one another. It has been argued that the fourth industrial revolution concerns more than technology-driven change and technological opportunities (World Economic Forum, 2017). It must also be aligned and integrated with a social revolution. Accordingly, the digital revolution must involve a social revolution that is based on the needs of humans and how they respond proactively in this new era. Thus, encompassing both digital and social revolutions, the fourth industrial revolution will affect the ways in which humans relate, interact, and communicate with each other. In addition, it has been argued that this revolution concerns not only technological innovation but also human empathy, collaboration, emotions, attitudes, competences, and values. Consequently, because the fourth industrial revolution is aligned with a social revolution, and the transhumanism movement will radically change human habits, including learning practices, it will change the ways in which we live, work, learn, and relate to one another.

CURRENT AND FUTURE TRENDS

As argued above we stand on the brink of both a technological and a social revolution that fundamentally will alter the way we live, work, and relate to one another. In its scale, scope, and complexity, the transformation will be unlike anything humankind has experienced. Although it is not yet clear how it will unfold, the response to it must be integrated and comprehensive, and it must involve all stakeholders in the global polity—from the public and private sectors to academia and civil society (Schwab, 2017; Schwab, Davis, Nadella, 2018; World Economic Forum, 2016 2017).

The United Nations Educational, Scientific, and Cultural Organization (UNESCO) Sustainability Goals (SDG), specifically SDG4, have emphasized and fostered global, lifelong, and life-wide learning. UNESCO's mandate stipulates that education should be available to all at anytime, anywhere, and through any device (UNESCO, 2015a, 2015b, 2015c). Its SDG4 goals are designed to empower and ensure inclusion, equity, equality, and quality in education. These goals are designed to be achieved through access, democracy, affordability, efficacy, and lifelong or ongoing learning (S. Järvelä, personal communication, October 25, 2018). In brief, the SDG4 are aimed to ensure inclusive equality, equity, quality education for all, and lifelong learning.

In Europe, the digital single market (2018) emphasized the global challenges, as globalization, demographic changes, technology, and digitalization. Furthermore, the digital single market stressed that global changes include speed and scale. In addition, they underlined the importance of investing in the future and of embracing and empowering digital citizens. Although knowledge, infrastructure, attitudes, and mindsets are of utmost importance, the main issue concerns digitalization or marginalization. A different approach is to become mainstreamed to ensure a competitive Europe. This approach should, according to the digital single market, build on a "rock and roll" way of working, which means accelerating the process of marketization, forming and collaborating in partnerships, destroying silo thinking, executing all means, including "walk the talk," that is, putting ideas into action. The digital single market also emphasized the importance of freedom, diversity, user-centeredness, and entrepreneurship. Thus, solutions need to build on technological development, investment in human resources, and user experiences. Thus, any solution should be comprehensive and consumer-oriented. In January 2018, the European Commission adopted the Digital Education Action Plan, which includes three priorities and 11 initiatives to support technology use and digital competence in education (European Commission, 2018). The three priorities and the 11 initiatives are elaborated below in the discussion on issues related to leadership:

Priority 1: Making better use of digital technology for teaching and learning
Priority 2: Developing digital competences and skills
Priority 3: Improving education through better data analyses and foresight

Other challenges in education and society include the influence and use of emerging technologies, such as block chain, 3D, the Internet of Things, cloud computing, artificial intelligence, learning analytics, robotization, and other developments in technology-enabled social and mobile learning (Rotolo, Hicks, & Martin, 2015). These challenges affect issues concerning transhumanism. Additionally, education is now facing a growing trend toward micro-credentials and the need for microlearning in workplaces and in continuing professional development. Hence, there are urgent calls for modern governance, as well as extensive and agile university reforms with dynamic, proactive leadership and management as well as innovative and inclusive open pedagogical approaches (Digital Single Market, 2018).

The following section presents selected models to consider for the digital and transhumanist transformation.

THE SUBSTITUTION VS. TRANSFORMATION MODEL

In the 21st century, a new era of technology has been reshaping everyday life, facilitating outdated processes, and giving rise to entirely new business sectors (Schwab, 2017; Schwab, Davis, & Nadella, 2018; World Economic Forum, 2016 2017). Some common catchphrases used to refer to this era are digitization, digitalization, and digital transformation. However, they are used synonymously, and there has been persistent confusion regarding the differences between them are significant and should be taken into account in discussing the kinds of changes that business is, or should be, making. Bloomberg (2018) provided an overview. Because the excitement about the digital transformation continues, the terms digitization and digitalization have only added to the confusion. In reality, these three terms have distinct meanings depending on the context in which they are discussed. However, this confusion is more than a question of semantics. In reality, these terms are confused in ways that do not consider the power and importance of the digital transformation, thus putting the very survival of the organizations in peril. In the context of transhumanism, is it worth elaborating these distinctions.

Digitization is a straightforward term and refers to encoding analog information into zeroes and ones so that computers can store, process, and transmit it. According to the *Gartner IT glossary* (2018), digitization is the process of changing from analog form to digital form. Hence, converting handwritten or typewritten text into digital form is an example of digitization, such as converting the music from a long-playing record (LP) or a video from a Video Home System (VHS) tape. Digitization is the process of making information available and accessible in a digital format. In contrast, digitalization is the application of digitized information in practice for the benefit of humans, such as customers. Finally, in the digital transformation, digitalization is used to create completely new business concepts. Because of digitization and digitalization, data are easily accessible for use across various platforms, devices, and interfaces. The digital transformation is the process of devising new business applications that integrate all digitized data and digitalized information. Consider the example of Netflix; once films were digitized, the path was paved for a completely new business model, such as movie streaming. Films have been the biggest "game changers" in the digital transformation. Definitions of digitization, digitalization, and digital transformation are provided in Table 1.

Table 1. Definitions of digitization, digitalization, and digital transformation

Concept	In short
Digitization	Refers to encoding analog information in zeroes and ones so that computers can store, process, and transmit it
Digitalization	The application of digitized information in practice
Digital transformation	Taking advantage of digitalization to create completely new business concepts

The distinctions between digitization, digitalization, and digital transformation are more than semantic. Parallels can be drawn between these distinctions and Puentedura's (2012) SAMR model. The SAMR model is the abbreviation of the four different stages of implementing technology in education: substitution, augmentation, modification, and redefinition (see Figure 1).

The four stages are described as follows: Substitution (S) occurs when technology acts as a direct substitute with no functional change (e.g., digitization is a move from analog to digital). Augmentation (A) occurs when technology acts as a direct substitute but with functional improvement. Hence, they are both correlated to enhancement. Real transformation requires modification (M), which occurs when technology allows for significant task redesign. Finally, redefinition (R) occurs when technology allows for the creation of new tasks that were previously inconceivable.

In relation to transhumanism, it is thus a question of what technology brings in the stages of modification and redefinition. As mentioned above in the discussion of future trends, the influences and uses of emerging technologies, such as block chain, 3D, the Internet of Things, cloud computing, artificial intelligence, learning analytics, robotization, and other developments in technology-enabled and social and mobile learning, influence the issues in transhumanism. Therefore, the main concerns are whether they serve as substitutions or transformations. According to Schwab (2017), Schwab, Davis, and Nadella (2018), and the World Economic Forum (2016), emerging technology will change the ways in which we live, work, learn, and relate to one another. Aligned with the social revolution, the application of emerging technology will change human habits, attitudes, communication, interactions, relationships, and mindsets. Accordingly, it makes sense not only to empower and embrace this development but also to be critical in anticipating its consequences.

Transhumanism must therefore advocate the moral right to use technology to extend human capacities, to surpass natural limits, and improve human lives not only physically and psychologically but also educationally. In other words, cutting-edge technologies must be used to improve human lives by enabling them to be longer, healthier, and more intellectual. At this point, transhumanists must be progressive. They must advocate the use of emerging technologies to improve not only human lives including

Figure 1. The model of four different stages of implementing technology in education
Source: Puentedura (2012)

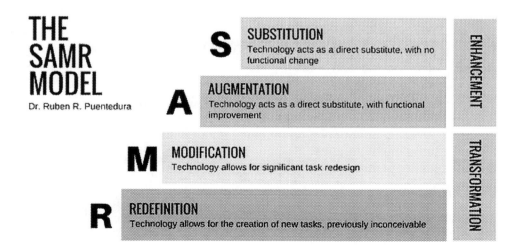

cybernetics, artificial intelligence, social networks, space colonization, cryonics, and curing aging, but also human learning. Transhumanism, therefore, must be based on a sound philosophy by that values scientific facts, reason, and logic above spiritual principles as well as seeing humankind as controlling its transformation. It must promote rational thinking, freedom, tolerance, democracy, and concern for all human beings. Human learning will be improved by transforming the human organism beyond its natural and biological limits. Accordingly, learning about technologies, with technologies, and for technologies must be one of the most important focuses of transhumanism. Transhumanism can radically change both human habits and learning practices. Therefore, it is also crucial to foresee that transhumanism can achieve sustainability in the context of human learning to promote human intelligence in the future. The foundation of a revolutionary transformation of human learning will be established by social networks. Thus, transhumanism must be sustainable in transforming humans in the contexts of ecological learning environments. In particular, senior management and leadership have a crucial role in this development and in agile processes in not only sustainability, policies, strategies, incentives, financing, and professional development but also in human resource-related issues and concerns. In the following section, the challenges of management and leadership in relation to future trends will be elaborated.

CHALLENGES OF MANAGEMENT AND LEADERSHIP IN RELATION TO FUTURE TRENDS

The main purpose of this handbook is to identify, discuss, and scrutinize the future trends, priorities, and needs of learning in the age of transhumanism. According to the editors (Sisman-Uğur & Kurubacak, forthcoming), the scholarship on learning in the age of transhumanism should address several issues and challenges arising from future trends, such as the following: management, communication, pedagogy, technology/computing, evaluation, and sociological/intelligent social networks. The challenges for leadership and management will be elaborated in this section.

In previous research by the Ossiannilsson (2017a, 2017b, 2018a, 2018b, 2018c), the next generation of leaders in the digital era must be in the forefront of responding to the rapid global change due to emerging technologies and to the digital explosion in societies. This need has been pointed out in the United Nations Sustainability Goals, especially SDG4 (2018), Education for All 2030, and the European Digital Education Action Plan 2020 based on the upcoming requirements of the fourth industrial revolution (Ossiannilsson, 2017a, 2017b, 2018a, 2018b, 2018c). Education and learning should, according to UNESCO SDG 4 for 2030 (UNESCO, n.d.) be available for all, at any time, from anywhere, and through any device. In this global, lifelong, and lifewide perspective, learners take the lead in orchestrating the process and manner of their learning, thus choosing their personal learning journey in its widest interpretation. There have been calls for modern governance arrangements and dynamic, proactive leadership and management (UNESCO, 2016). The Director-General of UNESCO (UNESCO, 2016 n.p) argued the following:

[A] fundamental change is needed in the way we think about education's role in global development because it has a catalytic impact on the well-being of individuals and the future of our planet.... Now, more than ever, education has a responsibility to be in gear with 21st-century challenges and aspirations and foster the right types of values and skills that will lead to sustainable and inclusive growth and peaceful living together.

Transhumanism and Innovative Leadership

The fourth industrial revolution, as argued above, has changed the ways we act, perform, live, work, and learn today (Schwab, 2017; Schwab, Davis, & Nadella, 2018; World Economic Forum, 2016). The consequences are that the digital transition encompasses all levels of an educational institution. Therefore, rethinking leadership and management is needed at all levels: macro, meso, micro, and nano (Ossiannilsson, 2018a, 2018b, 2018c).

Learning technologists and instructional designers have often taken responsibility for developing and merging technology and pedagogy for their mutual enrichment. Hence, these individuals are in an ideal position to influence institutional strategies. However, the often self-imposed role has not always been supported, recognized, or understood by senior leaders. Next-generation leadership involves staff at all levels in the institution in playing a strategic role in enabling, supporting, and facilitating effective institutional change. In open education, leadership is also a shared responsibility. In the Opening up Education framework, developed by the European Commission's Joint Research Institute, leadership is so crucial that it is an own, and one of the four transversal dimensions of open educational practices in higher education institutions (Inamorato dos Santos et al., 2016). The framework includes in total 10 dimensions of open education. In this framework, there are four transversal dimensions, and six core dimensions. The transversal dimensions are leadership, technology, quality, and strategy. The six core dimensions are pedagogy, recognition, collaboration, research, access, and content. Leadership affects all the other dimensions, and not only the other transversal dimensions but also each one of the core dimensions (see Figure 2).

Leaders at all levels can foster sustainable open education activities and initiatives through transparent top-down and bottom-up approaches. They can pave the way for creating openness by inspiring and empowering people. The greatest challenges probably are related to mindsets and attitudes because systemic

Figure 2. Smart learning is disruptive
Source: Inamorata dos Santos et al. (2016)

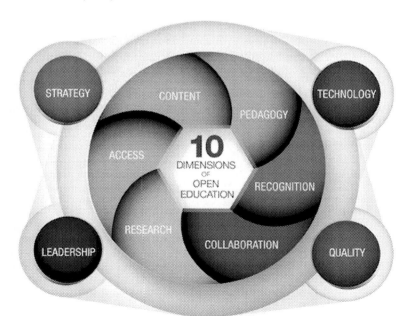

changes are required. Hence, human capital is crucial for cultural change, which includes ownership, inclusiveness, and participation. Thus, a key issue for leaders is to promote a culture that allows people to grow, take responsibility, and build trust throughout the organization as well as to promote a culture of passion and persistence (Ossiannilsson, 2017a, 2017b, 2018a, 201b). The cultivation of a culture of quality is crucial. Moreover, it must be in the interests of everyone (i.e., the nano level), and it must be encouraged by leaders (Ossiannilsson, 2017a, 2018a). Rethinking the culture of quality as it applies to open pedagogy, situated learning, and self-directed learning requires rethinking quality assurance. Recognized international quality models of open online education take a holistic approach that includes an ecosystem, focusing not only on the learning and teaching processes but also on policy, strategies, curriculum, course design, course delivery, infrastructure, and support for staff and students (Ossiannilsson et al., 2015). Quality dimensions also relate to efficiency, learner and faculty satisfaction and engagement as well as short- and long-term outcomes. In addition, the work and study conditions of learners and staff must be considered. Gulliksen, Lantz, Walldius, Sandblad, and Åborg (2015) argued that the consequences of competitive advantage, meeting student expectations, reorganization, and continuing professional capacity building for staff are often neglected. Thus, because it is neglected, digital transformation in working places usually fails. Digital tools are often not incorporated in a well-planned manner, and most are used as substitutions or augmentations (Puentedura, 2012). Many problems could be minimized or prevented if leaders and managers had insights and knowledge of the benefits of digitalization.

To promote, realize the potential, and be at the forefront of the digital transformation, the European Commission launched the action plan for Europe (2018), which has three priorities, setting out measures to help European member states to meet the challenges and opportunities of the digital age (European Commission, 2018):

Priority 1: Making better use of digital technology for teaching and learning
Priority 2: Developing digital competences and skills
Priority 3: Improving education through better data analyses and foresight

Achieving these priorities in the European Single Market (2018) requires strong senior leaders and managers who have insights into the development, potential, and consequences of transhumanism. Being a transhumanist leader requires planning and financing learning in the transhumanist age, not only assets and equipment but also continuous professional development, infrastructure, and research in the field of transhumanism, taking into account its potential and limitations. The following are some recommended actions for implementing the three priorities according to the European Commission (2018):

- Making better use of digital technology in teaching and learning (Actions 1 to 3)
    - **Action 1:** Connectivity in schools
    - **Action 2:** Self-reflection tool and mentoring scheme for schools (SELFIE)
    - **Action 3:** Digitally-signed qualifications
- Developing digital competences and skills (Actions 4 to 8)
    - **Action 4:** Higher education hub
    - **Action 5:** Open science skills
    - **Action 6:** EU code week in schools
    - **Action 7:** Cybersecurity in education
    - **Action 8:** Training in digital and entrepreneurial skills for girls

- Improving education through better data analysis and foresight (Action 9 to 11)
  - **Action 9:** Studies on ICT in education
  - **Action 10:** Artificial intelligence and analytics
  - **Action 11:** Strategic foresight

In addition, the D-transform project in Europe emphasized the crucial importance of senior management and leadership for the digital transformation to succeed. Hence, D-transform training programs for leaders in European universities were developed and implemented to focus on the major role played by emerging digital technologies and transhumanism in the necessary transformation of their institutions.

The premise is that e-education (digital pedagogy and training) can become a strategic tool for European universities, enabling them to be pedagogically more effective, more cost-effective, more attractive and able to meet the needs of the professional world with regard to youth training and life-long learning (D-transform (n.d)).

Cöster, Ekenberg, Gullberg, Westelius, and Wettergren (2017) emphasized that increased digitization, digital transformation, and change allow organizations to have better conditions than ever to succeed. However, they need to understand and utilize the potential of the digital era. Some are successful, but others not; digitalization is not an easy process. However, Cöster et al. explained how organizations could create value in the context of a digitized reality. They focused on what an organization is, what it needs, and how digitization could be a solution instead of a means. Their suggestions included goals, business models, strategies, organizations, decisions, and projects. They emphasized structure, efficient decision-making, and successful project implementation.

Experts in academia, the international organizational community, and industry are currently focusing on the real-world practices of digital transformation. For example, they are engaged in discussions on the ways in which artificial intelligence (AI), the Internet of Things, and even robotization could bring value to this evolution. It is therefore essential to clearly identify the values, norms, and ethics in relation to transhumanist approaches to learning. It is also essential to examine the qualifications and expectations of learners in the transhumanist age and how to support learning by technology.

Smart environments and smart cities are developed by empowering the potential of transhumanism. Hence, there are needs to live, work, perform, communicate, interact, relate, and learn in smart ways in an information and knowledge society. In the following section, smart learning will be elaborated with regard to its role in smart cities and smart environments. A framework for the ecologies of smart learning, smart learning environment and smart cities is also presented.

SMART LEARNING

The revolutionary transformation of human learning take place through social networks, and transhumanism can be fostered in ecological learning environments. Therefore, ecological learning environments should be agile, resilient, and sustainable. This new era in human development is being enabled by extraordinary technological advances. However, the fourth industrial revolution concerns more than technological opportunities; it also involves a social revolution (Schwab, 2017; Schwab, Davis, Nadella, 2018; World Economic Forum, 2016). The literature on smart learning environments indicates that previous research has focused on technology and pedagogy, and only a few studies have considered the citizen's learning perspective. Therefore, there is a need to define the elements, functions, and scenarios of smart learning environments, which could be addressed in models of smart learning environments and in best practice and case studies that build on the existing research. In both education and learning, the real opportunity is to look beyond technology to a systemic change in education and the ways in which smart learning spaces can foster and encourage the ecologies of smart learning for smart citizens in smart cities in the 21st century. A smart city is a place where traditional networks and services are made more efficient by the use of digital and telecommunication technologies for the benefit of its inhabitants and businesses. With this vision in mind, the European Union is now investing in information and communication technology (ICT) research and innovation, and it is developing policies to improve the quality of life of citizens and increase the sustainability of cities. The concept of the smart city goes beyond the use of ICT to reduce resource use and emissions. It extends to smart urban transport networks, upgraded water supplies and waste disposal facilities as well as efficient ways to light and heat buildings. It also encompasses an interactive and responsive city administration that ensures safe public spaces and meets the needs of an aging population (Digital Single Market, 2018). Figure 1 shows a framework for smart learning and its disruptions. Disruptive innovation, which is an artistic term coined by Clayton Christensen (1997), describes a process in which a product or service takes root initially in simple applications at the bottom of a market and then relentlessly moves upward in that market, eventually displacing established competitors. Several issues affect the growing number of reasons that smart learning is crucial both in the digital era and for transhumanism. In addition, there is a huge rise in the number of disruptions in several areas (see Figure 3). First, in response to the increasing development of openness in education, a large variety of delivery models have been proposed, such as Inamorata et al.'s 2016) framework, which is described above. Second, the use of social media in learning has disrupted the common communication model one to many. In addition, social media allow cross action spaces (Jahnke, 2017). Hence, it will be established via transhumanism, and it will affect learning. Third, the development of rich digital media will disrupt the dependency on texts. Fourth, user-generated media will disrupt models of provided content. Fifth, "bring your own device" (BYOD) will disrupt models of provided technology. Sixth, the rise of mobile learning will disrupt the fixed learning model.

In education and learning, real opportunities will arise in meeting the challenges of looking beyond technology to how smart learning spaces can foster and encourage smart learning in the 21st century. Smart learning environments will have positive effects on both personal and collaborative learning in smart cities and in communities. The educational sector will be challenged in implementing and adapting to the SDG4 goals, which are designed to empower and ensure inclusion, equity, and quality education. These goals will be achieved through access, democracy, affordability, efficacy, and equality. In addition, learners will be challenged in taking the lead in orchestrating the process and manner of their own learning and in choosing their personal learning journeys according to the widest interpretation of education (Hwang, 2014; Kinchuk et al., 2014; Koper, 2016, Traxler & Kukulska-Hulme, 2016).

The terms future learning environment, smart classroom, learning spaces, smart campus, and technology-enhanced learning are synonymous with smart learning environments. All these terms refer to utilizing information technology to build a personalized and adaptive learning environment. According to Hwang (2014), technology-enhanced learning can be perceived as a smart learning system. In smart learning environments, several systems are integrated and combined, such as intelligent tutoring, learning analytics, educational data mining, adaptive learning, and personalized learning (Yang et al., 2015). However, the literature on smart learning environments indicates that previous research has focused on

Figure 3. Smart learning and its disruptions
Source: Ossiannilsson (2018)

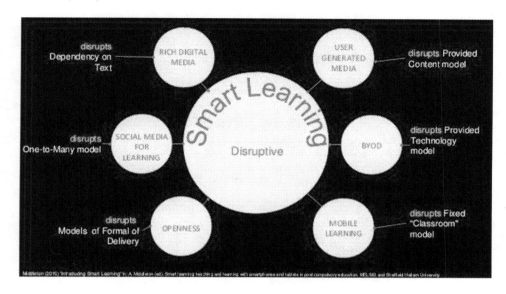

technology and pedagogy, and only a few studies have considered the citizen's learning perspective. Therefore, there is a need to define the elements, functions, and scenarios of smart learning environments based on the integration of formal and informal learning in physical and virtual spaces in community learning contexts. These needs could be addressed by focusing on models of smart learning environments models and by presenting best practice and case studies based on research. Based on the current literature review, informed by the author's research and experiences in this field and by the relevant literature, a the proposed framework for the ecologies of smart learning, smart learning environments, and smart cities is presented in Figure 4.

Innovation in educational systems, which is understood as the adoption of new services, technologies, and competences by educational organizations, can help to improve learning outcomes, enhance equity, and improve efficiency. Innovation is the most effective and sustainable when it is embraced by well-trained teachers and embedded in clear teaching goals. Further research is needed on how to best use digital means to reach educational objectives. Education can benefit by opening classrooms to real-life experiences and projects and by applying new learning tools, materials, and open educational resources. Learners can be empowered by online collaboration. The access to and the use of digital technologies can help reduce the learning gaps between students from high- and low-socioeconomic backgrounds. Personal teaching can result in the increased motivation of individual learners (Downes, 2016). However, the progress in integrating technology in education remains limited.

Digital advances have brought new challenges for pupils, students, and teachers not only in Europe but also worldwide. The algorithms used by social media sites and news portals can be powerful amplifiers of biased or "fake" news" moreover, data privacy has become a key concern in the digital society. Both young people and adults are vulnerable to cyber bullying and harassment, predatory behavior, and disturbing online content. The daily exposure to digital data that consist of inscrutable algorithms creates clear risks, which requires critical thinking and the ability to engage positively and competently in the digital environment. The constantly evolving need for media literacy, the wide mix of digital skills

Figure 4. The ecologies of smart learning, smart learning environment and smart cities
Source: Ossiannilsson (2018)

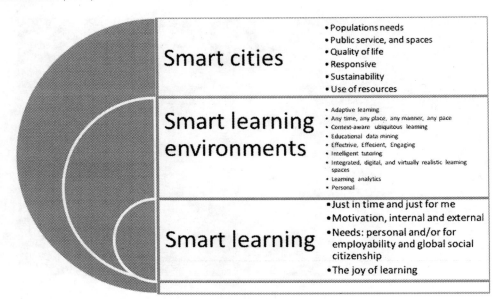

and competences required to ensure the safety, security, and privacy of the public and private sectors remains a challenge.

The ecologies of smart learning, smart learning environments, and smart cities empower the potential of global, lifelong, life-wide learning, ongoing learning, and education available to all, at anytime, anywhere, and through any device, according to the UNESCO SDG4. These goals, which were designed to empower and ensure inclusion, equity, and quality education, could be achieved through access, democracy, affordability, efficacy, and equality. Cöster et al. (2017) examined the use of technology by government agencies to collect and secure data, make intelligent decisions for personal service while considering ethics, legality, soft and hard infrastructures, human resources, and capacity building among others. They emphasized that citizens' experiences are a key driver in this journey.

Wheeler (forthcoming) argued that a rapidly growing area of technology that will significantly influence the future is AI and its potential effects on the future of learning and technological development. He and others believe that this subject must be explored. According to Wheeler, there are several philosophical debates about the nature of intelligence and the ways in which human intelligence differs from machine intelligence. One of the sources he cites is Tegmark's book, *Life 3.0* (2017), in which the author presents some compelling arguments for the future of AI. According to Wheeler, Tegmark argued that the benefits of AI will surpass the threats provided they are aligned with human intentions. One of the greatest concerns was not that computers might become sentient, or "evil," but a scenario in which the goals of "competent" AI would become misaligned with ours. His key argument is that the debate about whether computers will attain consciousness or emotional capability is spurious (Tegmark, 2017). The future co-existence with technology will be premised on the ability of computers to make life better for humanity, not to "out-think" us. For Tegmark, intelligence, whether human or artificial, is the ability to accomplish complex goals (good or bad). He argued that intelligence ultimately relies on information and computation, not on flesh and blood or on metal and plastic. Therefore, he reasoned, because of the exponential developments taking place in the world of technology, there is no barrier to computers eventually attaining and even surpassing human intelligence. However, Wheeler noted that regardless of whether the arguments are supported or not, it is interesting to note the comparisons between humans and machines. Arguably, all the above attributes, such as free will, emotion, abstract thinking, and intuitive action not only make us who we are but also create a permanent and unbridgeable divide between humans and computers.

FUTURE RESEARCH DIRECTIONS

Currently and in the near future, further research should be conducted on transhumanism, particularly in relation to leadership and quality. In addition, research should be conducted on emerging trends related to the digital transformation and their effects on individuals and educational systems as well as the ways we work, live, and learn in a smart global world. It is worth emphasizing that times are changing faster than ever today. Statistics have shown that business is also changing faster than ever. However, many people neglect important aspects of change, which include decision-making and disruptions in almost every sector. It is significantly more difficult to make a decision in a time of change than in a time of stability. In the latter, one can learn from the successes and failures in previous experience. In times of change, previous experiences cannot be applied to the situation because the landscape has changed. Clark (2015) recommended the following rule for navigating change in uncertain circumstances: do not apply the first solution that occurs. She meant that it is fine to accept the initial solution when the conditions are unchanged, and "two plus two still equals four." However, under conditions of change, relying on the same assumptions and action plans could be a damaging mistake. Instead, she recommended a framework for making smarter decisions in times of change and in smart environments. This simple framework consists of three steps:

Step 1: What worked previously?
Step 2: What has changed?
Step3: What solutions have others found to related problems?

According to Clark (2015), decision-making is critical in times of rapid change. By answering the questions in Clark's three-step framework, other solutions might become apparent. In order to innovate, mental agility must be cultivated. Accordingly, although everyone is responsible for the cultivation of his or her mental agility, leaders and senior managers have a crucial role in ensuring that its development is aligned with the fourth industrial and social revolution in the 21st century. Furthermore, leaders and senior managers have crucial roles in meeting the SDG as well as the SDG4, which are designed to empower and ensure inclusion, equity, equality, and quality in education through access, democracy, affordability, efficacy, lifelong learning, and ongoing learning.

CONCLUSION

The research and the issues discussed in this chapter on transhumanism and innovative leadership clearly concern the question of quality. My research on the next-generation leadership's role in achieving the goals of Education for All 2030 has revealed the urgent need for not only the modernization of the approach to education but also effective organizational leadership in the digital era. Leaders and managers can make a difference to higher education offers, services, processes, quality, and consequences. The cultivation of a culture of quality is critical. It must be in the interests of everyone, and it must be empowered and encouraged by leaders (Ossiannilsson, 2017a, 2017b, 2018a, 2018b); Innamorata dos Santos et al., 206; Wheeler, forthcoming).

To succeed in the era of new trends and emerging new technologies, a trusting relationship should be focused on the return on investment. The following measures are recommended to survive data breaches, emerging technologies, and new platforms:

- Understand the audience.
- Review the social media marketing strategy.
- Allocate time and budgets for new tools and technologies such as software and hardware as well as professional development and evaluation.
- Focus on what works.
- Strive to build trust with users in every campaign.

To meet the challenges of transhumanism, there is an urgent need for people who have the knowledge, abilities, competences, and attitudes to lead the process as well as to analyze and evaluate digital work environments by applying appropriate methods to analyze complex digital environments. Moreover, there are needs to analyze and evaluate the consequences of transhumanism and digital work environments by using appropriate methods to analyze the influence of complex digital environments on society.

ACKNOWLEDGMENT

This research received no specific grant from any funding agency in the public, commercial, or not-for-profit sectors.

REFERENCES

Bloomberg, J. (2018, April 29). Re: Digitization, digitalization, and digital transformation: confuse them at your peril [web log post]. *Forbes*. Retrieved from https://www.forbes.com/sites/jasonbloomberg/2018/04/29/digitization-digitalization-and-digital-transformation-confuse-them-at-your-peril/#1f02cf102f2c

Bostrom, N. (2005). A history of transhumanist thought. *Journal of Evolution and Technology*. Retrieved from https://nickbostrom.com/papers/history.pdf

Christensen, C. (1997). *The innovator's dilemma: When new technologies cause great firms to fail*. Boston: Harvard Business School Press.

Christensen, C., & Overdorf, M. (2000, March). Meeting the challenge of disruptive change. *Harvard Business Review*.

Clark, D. (2015). *Reinventing you and stand out*. Inc. Magazine.

Cöster, M., Ekenberg, L., Gullberg, C., Westelius, A., & Wettergren, G. (2017). *Organisering och digitalisering: Att skapa värde i det 21a århundradet* [Organization and digitalization: To empower value in the 21st century]. Liber.

D-Transform. (n.d). *Transforming universities for the digital age*. Retrieved from http://www.dtransform.eu/about-us/

Daniel, J. (2015). *Making sense of educational technology: From MOOCs to blended learning: What next? Journal of Open Education Research*.

Digital Single Market. (2018). *ITC2918, Investing in the future*. Retrieved from https://youtu.be/5UqvCXFjShs

Digital Single Market. (2018, March 19). *Smart cities*. Retrieved from https://ec.europa.eu/digital-single-market/en/policies/smart-cities

Downes, S. (2016). Personal and personalized learning. *EMMA Newsletter*. Retrieved from https://us8.campaign-archive.com/?u=17ce08681f559814caf1359d3&id=fa1770e58d&e=6fb1272e29

European Commission. (2018). *Communication from the Commission to the European Parliament, the Council, the European Economic and Social Committee and the Committee of the regions on the digital education action plan*. Brussels: European Commission. COM (2018) 22 final. Retrieved from https://ec.europa.eu/education/sites/education/files/digital-education-action-plan.pdf

Gartner. (2018). *IT Glossary*. Retrieved from https://www.gartner.com/it-glossary/digitization/

Gulliksen, J., Lantz, A., Walldius, Å., Sandblad, B., & Åborg, C. (2015). *Digital arbetsmiljö* [Digital work environment]. Report 2015:17: Stockholm (Arbetsmiljöverket). Retrieved from https://www.av.se/globalassets/filer/publikationer/rapporter/digital_arbetsmiljo-rap-2015-17.pdf

Hwang, G. J. (2014). Definition, framework and research issues of smart learning environments: A context-aware ubiquitous learning perspective. *Smart Learning Environments, 1*(1), 4. doi:10.118640561-014-0004-5

Hwang G. J., & Tsai, C. C. (2011). Research trends in mobile and ubiquitous learning: A review of publications in selected journals from 2001 to 2010. *Br. J. Educ. Technol., 42*(4). doi:10.1111/j.1467-8535.2011.01183.x

Inamorato dos Santos, A., Punie, Y., & Castaño-Muñoz, J. (2016). Opening up education: A support framework for higher education institutions. *JRC Science for Policy Report, EUR 27938 EN*. Retrieved from http://publications.jrc.ec.europa.eu/repository/bitstream/JRC101436/jrc101436.pdf

Jahnke, I. (2016). *Digital didactical designs: Teaching and learning in cross action spaces*. New York: Routledge.

Kinshuk, C., Chen, N.-S., Cheng, I.-L., & Chew, S. W. (2016). Evolution is not enough: Revolutionizing current learning environments to smart learning environments. *International Journal of Artificial Intelligence in Education, 26*(2), 561–581. doi:10.100740593-016-0108-x

Koper, R. (2014). Conditions for effective smart learning environments. *Smart Learning Environments*, *1*(1), 5. doi:10.118640561-014-0005-4

Learning with "e"s. (2018a, Sept. 24). Re: Digital learning in organizations [Web log post]. Retrieved from http://www.steve-wheeler.co.uk/2018/09/digital-learning-in-organisations.html

Learning with "e"s. (2018b, Dec. 14). Re: Humans, machines and learning [Web log post]. Retrieved from http://www.steve-wheeler.co.uk/2018/12/humans-machines-and-learning.html

Liu, D., Huang, R., & Wosinski, M. 2017). *Smart learning in smart cities: Lecture notes in educational technology*. doi:10.1007/978-981-10-4343-7_2

Mercer, C. (2014). Religion and transhumanism: The unknown future of human enhancement. Santa Barbara, CA: Praeger.

O'Reilly. (2008). *The shape of things to come. Emerging Technology Conference.*

Ossiannilsson. (2017a). Leadership in global open, online, and distance learning. In J. Keengwe & P. H. Bull (Eds.), *Handbook of research on transformative digital content and learning technologies* (pp. 345–373). Hershey, PA: IGI Global. Retrieved from https://altc.alt.ac.uk/blog/2017/12/its-time-for-the-next-generation-of-leadership/#comments

Ossiannilsson. (2017b, Dec. 16). Re: It is time for the next generation of leadership [Web log post]. Retrieved from https://altc.alt.ac.uk/blog/2017/12/its-time-for-the-next-generation-of-leadership/#comments

Ossiannilsson. (2018a). Leadership: In a time when learners take ownership of their own learning. In K. Buyuk, S, Kocdar, & A. Bozkurt (Eds.), Administrative leadership in open and distance learning programs (pp. 1–33). Hershey, PA: IGI Global.

Ossiannilsson. (2018b). Visionary leadership for digital transformation: In a time when learners take the ownership of their own learning. *Distance Education in China: An International Forum, 5*, 22-34.

Ossiannilsson. (2018c, Sept. 26). The case for mobile learning [web log post]. Retrieved from https://virtuallyinspired.org/?s=leadership

Puentedura, R. R. (2012). *The SAMR model: Background and exemplars*. Hippasus. Retrieved from http://www.hippasus.com/rrpweblog/archives/2012/08/23/SAMR_BackgroundExemplars.pdf

Rotolo, D., Hicks, D., & Martin, B. R. (2015, Aug. 9). What is an emerging technology? *Research Policy*, *44*(10), 1827–1843. doi:10.1016/j.respol.2015.06.006

Schwab, K. (2017). *The fourth industrial revolution*. World Economic Forum.

Schwab, K., Davis, N., & Nadella, S. (2018). *Shaping the fourth industrial revolution*. World Economic Forum.

Sisman-Uğur, & Kurubacak, G. (2019). *Handbook of research on learning in the age of transhumanism*. Hershey, PA: IGI Global.

Tegmark, M. (2017). *Life 3.0: Being human in the age of artificial intelligence*. London: Penguin Books.

Thompson, J. (2017). Transhumanism: How far is too far? *A Multidisciplinary Journal of Biotechnology and the Body, 23*(2), 1–14.

Traxler, J., & Kukulska-Hulme, A. (Eds.). (2016). *Mobile learning: The next generation.* London: Routledge.

UNESCO. (2015a). *The Incheon Declaration. Education 2030. Towards inclusive and equitable quality lifelong learning for all.* Retrieved from http://unesdoc.unesco.org/images/0023/002338/233813m.pdf

UNESCO. (2015b). Education 2030. The Incheon Declaration and framework for action for sustainable goal 4. Retrieved from http://unesdoc.unesco.org/images/0024/002456/245656E.pdf

UNESCO. (2016, Sept. 9). *Education needs to change fundamentally to meet global development goals.* Retrieved from http://www.unesco.org/new/en/media-services/single-view/news/education_needs_to_change_fundamentally_to_meet_global_devel/

UNESCO. (2016, Sept. 9). Education needs to change fundamentally to meet global development goals. Retrieved from http://www.unesco.org/new/en/media-services/single-view/news/education_needs_to_change_fundamentally_to_meet_global_devel/

UNESCO. (n.d.). *Sustainable development goal 4 and its targets.* Retrieved from https://en.unesco.org/education2030-sdg4/targets

United Nations. (2018). Sustainable development goal 4. Progress of goal 4 in 2018. Retrieved from https://sustainabledevelopment.un.org/sdg4

Wheeler, S. (forthcoming). Digital learning in organisations. London: *Kogan Page.*

World Economic Forum. (2016). The fourth industrial revolution: What it means and how to respond.

World Economic Forum. (2017, March 28). *The digital revolution is not about technology – it's about people.* Retrieved from https://www.weforum.org/agenda/2017/03/the-digital-revolution-is-not-about-technology-it-s-about-people/

ADDITIONAL READING

Adams Becker, A., Brown, M., Dahlstrom, E., Davis, A., DePaul, K., Diaz, V., & Pomerantz, J. (2018). *NMC Horizon Report: 2018 Higher Education Edition.* Louisville, CO: EDUCAUSE.

Chen, N. S., Cheng, I. L., & Chew, S. W. (2016). Evolution is not enough: Revolutionizing current learning environments to smart learning environments. *International Journal of Artificial Intelligence in Education, 26*(2), 561–581. doi:10.100740593-016-0108-x

Ferguson, R., Barzilai, S., Ben-Zvi, D., Chinn, C. A., Herodotou, C., Hod, Y., ... Whitelock, D. (2017). *Innovating pedagogy 2017: Open University innovation report 6.* UK: Milton Keynes: The Open University.

OECD. (2016). *Innovating education and education for innovation: The power of digital technologies and skills*. OECD.

Traxler, J. (2013). Mobile learning: Shaping the frontiers of learning technologies in global context. In R. Huang, Kinshuk, & J. M. Spector (Eds.), Reshaping learning: New frontiers of educational research. Berlin; Heidelberg: Springer.

UNESCO. (2013). *Policy guidelines for M-learning*. Retrieved from http://unesdoc.unesco.org/images/0021/002196/219641e.pdf

KEY TERMS AND DEFINITIONS

Artificial Intelligence (AI): The simulation of human intelligence processes by machines, especially computer systems. These processes include learning (i.e., the acquisition of information and rules for using the information), reasoning (i.e., using rules to reach approximate or definite conclusions), and self-correction.

Digital Transformation: Digital transformation is the process of devising new business applications that integrate all digitized data and digitalized applications. Taking advantage of digitalization to create completely new business concepts. Because of digitization and digitalization, data are easily accessible for use across various platforms, devices, and interfaces.

Disruption: Disturbances or problems that interrupt an event, activity, or process. Events, activities, or processes are often used or understood differently than they were at the beginning. Disruptive innovation, which is an artistic term coined by Clayton Christensen, describes the process by which a product or service is initially offered in simple applications at the bottom of a market and then moves relentlessly upward in the market, eventually displacing established competitors.

Innovative Leadership: The innovative leader's focus is on the big picture and on working with creative thinkers who contribute to enhancing that vision. The innovative leader needs to be able to communicate her/his vision and generate enthusiasm for it. The leader's team needs to be able to see the vision and be willing to invest their time and resources into making it happen. Innovative leaders know that leadership by demand is far less effective in encouraging creativity and innovation than leadership through motivation and inspiration. The innovative leader needs to have confidence in her/his team and their ability to work together to achieve the vision.

Internet of Things (IoT): The network of devices, vehicles, and home appliances, such as electronics, software, actuators, and connectivity, which allows these devices to connect, interact, and exchange data.

Quality in Open Online Learning: In education and learning, quality is usually defined as teaching methods that successfully help learners develop the knowledge and skills they will require in the digital age. the short answer to the question of quality in open online learning. A longer definition requires examining, at least briefly, institutional and degree accreditation, internal (academic) quality assurance processes, differences in quality assurance between traditional classroom teaching and online and distance education, the relationship between quality assurance processes and learning outcomes, and quality assurance that fits the purpose, all of which are necessary for meeting the goals of education in the digital age.

Smart Learning: Learning anytime and anywhere based on individual cognitive ability. It takes place by using an advanced electronic device. Smart learning is also called advanced distributed learning, e-learning, online leaning, hybrid learning, and blended learning.

Transhumanism (H+ or h+): An international philosophical movement that advocates the transformation of the human condition by developing and making sophisticated technologies widely available for the enhancement of human intellect and physiology.

Chapter 7
Ethical Issues in Transhumanism

Faruk Karaman
Konya Food and Agriculture University, Turkey

ABSTRACT

Transhumanism seems to be inevitable. There seems to be no way to stop the developments leading humanity to transhumanism. As Heidegger puts, technological determinism rules, rather than social determinism. In other words, the technology controls the society, not the other way around. Therefore, in a short time period, people will be forced to face the challenges of transhumanism. It is therefore the right time to prepare for those challenges before they became mainstream. Tomorrow, it will be too late. Academicians, educators, politicians, philosophers, intellectuals, psychologists ... etc. all should concentrate on the issue. This chapter will try to answer such questions and many others. A philosophical approach is used. After all, ethics is a branch of philosophy. Since, this is a futuristic topic, it is hard to find first-hand data and conduct survey analysis etc. Therefore, this is a theoretical chapter.

INTRODUCTION

One certain fact about the future is that it is uncertain. It is almost impossible to predict the future. There are infinite number of possibilities and before time passes it is hard to determine which possibility will come true. Therefore, research topics such transhumanism are difficult to conduct. Uncertainty means risk and risk should be managed.

Maybe, all will go well and side effects of technology will not appear. However, it is better to be prepared for pessimistic scenarios. If cures are found for the negative effects of technology, only the positive sides will be left and then a much more desirable future is ahead. For the time being an healthy dose of pessimism is what is needed in that possible problems can be detected via being pessimist.

As time passes, the number of possibilities will shrink to a few. Then, maybe some of the fears about the technology will prove to be ungrounded and then the documents like this will be thought to be overly pessimistic. But, this is just a possibility. Alternatively, a very dystopic future world may arise and the majority of people may suffer.

DOI: 10.4018/978-1-5225-8431-5.ch007

Ethical Issues in Transhumanism

It is not wise to wait for risks to happen before taking any action. Then, it will be too late and it will most probably be impossible to correct anything. Although, it is hard to predict all of the risks, ethicists should work hard to analyze the possible side effects. Also, many more people should be trained as technology ethicists. Given the unemployment threat from the technology, this is one of the areas for secure employment.

This is not the first time that technology used as a destructive weapon. In fact, some of the scenes from science-fiction movies direct humans' attention to the negative effects of the technology. Such movies give clues about how ethical conduct should be in that most of them are based on some ethical problems. There is a tendency to underestimate these movies but they can help humans in understanding what the future will be like.

Messages about the positive attributes of the technology are delivered to the people by means of media by the representatives of the technology companies. There is no shortage of such positive and optimistic messages. However, negative views can not be heard and read by majority of people. For example, side effects of cell phones are not researched enough even though quite a lot of time has been passed since the first introduction of them.

Transhumanism-related new technology is first introduced in medical practices. Almost no one can criticize new but controversial applications for desperate patients. Thus, these new techniques find application in the treatment of deadly diseases. After, they prove to be successful, then they spread to more normal people and at a point they become mainstream.

Anyway, it is necessary for human being to make predictions about the future. If it is known where the events are heading to, the situation about the current time will be better understood. Maybe some predictions will prove to be wrong, but even so they will be helpful in understanding the technology environment, its positives and side effects.

BACKGROUND

Due to the rapid technological developments, transhumanism is fast becoming a reality. Each year, enhanced people are seemingly appearing as a close possibility rather than science-fiction. Although, the ordinary people are not fully aware of the phenomenon, experts know the issue well.

In fact, the great majority of technological developments follow an exponential path. Initially, the developments are very slow, but then it accelerates gradually. Finally, technological change is very rapid. The case of transhumanism is no different. Today, transhumanism is not a top agenda among leading media outlets, however in the future, it will be much different.

Transhumanism present numerous opportunities for humanity but there are also a lot of ethical problems to be solved. After becoming a synthesis of biological and non-biological portions will humans stay as human or transform into a new type of creature? What will happen to those who do not want to be enhanced and prefer to stay as classical humans? Will they be able to finance their lives and find jobs in a world where super-humans called transhumans set the rules?

Some experts predict that humans will be divided into two different species, one is enhanced, the other is un-enhanced. This may cause social clashes, wars, famine etc. Will classical humans have place in future's world or will everyone be forced to transform into the new form of the humans? Some people may find transhumanism against to their religious beliefs and resist the transformation. In that case, enhanced people will have a definite advantage in passing exams, learning new material and finding new jobs.

In emerging countries such as Turkey, the issues about transhumanism are not well-known since such countries have much more fundamental problems such as economic problems. In fact, enhanced awareness is needed even in developed countries. This study aims to contribute to the ethical discussions surrounding transhumanism.

Transhumanism is actually an old idea and can be witnessed even in the early stages of civilization. The idea of super-humans or super-heroes can be found in ancient literature. However, nowadays humanity is close to reach that old goal and super-humans may take the stage, thanks to ever-advancing technology (Harari, 2018). In fact, transhumanism will not come with one single step but there will be a chain of events leading to transhumanism.

There are numerous ethical issues related to the topic. For the first time in the history, human being is set to merge with the advanced technology and will have a non-biological portion. There are religious, cultural and democracy-related complex issues. So far, humans thought that they were superior to all other animals and now transhumans are to be appeared and take that superiority away.

It is now not a topic of science-fiction but a topic of ordinary scientific research (Joy, 2000). As time passes, it will become an old-fashioned topic since the majority of humans will have become transhumans or enhanced humans. The technological change is so fast that, this can occur earlier that it is predicted (Yamamoto and Karaman, 2005). Then, there will be little value of analyzing ethical issues since transformation will be almost complete (Ford, 2015).

These days are critical days in the transformation. Transhumanism has not become widespread yet although there are small examples of application. Enhanced people are not all around. The currently living people may be just last representatives of classical biological human being. After they die, the scene will be much different. Even some of today's humans may become enhanced and become transhuman. This is just a turning point after which events will be much different.

Even this book and this chapter will soon become outdated in the face of fast and accelerating events. Today, transhumanism is being discussed but tomorrow it will be widely accepted by the majority of the people. In fact, it may be even too late to discuss what transhumanism should be and not. Enhanced people will appear and they will set the norm. Classical biological humans will need to be protected from the enhanced people. But who will do that? Enhanced people or classical humans?

In fact, technology-related elitism is not a new phenomenon. Information and Communication Technologies (ICT) has performed this previously (Yamamoto and Karaman, 2006). Each new technology causes inequality among humans and new elites appear. They are the winners of the new technology. There are also losers.

Three great religions, namely Judaism, Christianity, and Islam all labels humans as the most valuable being in the universe. Now, as the technology advances artificial intelligence (AI) becomes superior to human being in numerous areas and humans' only response is said to becoming transhuman. This seems against the traditions of religions and can be considered to be part of End-Time concept in these religions ("End time." 2018).

MAIN FOCUS OF THE CHAPTER

Issues, Controversies, Problems

Academic Studies and AI

In academic studies, there are problems related to the artificial intelligence, Just like the AI replaces humans in low-skilled labor, academic field is also not immune to its effects. Increasingly, it becomes more difficult to find viable research topics. This is the result of the advances in technology. Thus, analyzing the effects of the technology itself becomes the sole solution to find a proper research topic. After this field is fully analyzed it become much more difficult to conduct academic research.

In the previous industrial revolutions, muscle power of humans were being replaced by machinery and people found jobs in the service sector and used their intellectual abilities. However, artificial intelligence aims the intellectual capabilities of human being (Karaman, 2012). Intelligence is no longer the kingdom of humanity. Academic studies are among the most advanced intellectual activities. But they are also vulnerable in the face of AI (Ford, 2015).

Today, AI's effect is not fully observed in academia. However, in the future it will be hard to find new research topics and AI-based systems will produce research papers. Of course, at the beginning, some human researchers will supervise them and those humans will become champions of academic research. To conduct research, AI and big data will become necessary and research will be much more expensive.

For sure, the change will not occur suddenly. It will take time for AI to replace human researchers. This is one of the most sophisticated area for humans. After the academic research is transferred to the AI, there will not be much left for humans to show their talents. Few researchers using the top expensive AI research products will be stars of the university environment and other researchers will become totally useless (Ford, 2015).

It may be thought that this may occur far into the future and not soon. However, there is an accelerating change and improvement in the technology in general (Harari, 2018). Those recently graduated the universities may witness AI's takeover the research projects from human being. It is already occurring. People deal with similar research topics and their numbers are limited. Industry 4.0 for example. A concept is introduced and suddenly all research are interested in Industry 4.0.

One reason is of course globalization and advanced level of communication. But, another reason is the AI itself (Joy, 2000). As technology advances and becomes more prevalent, almost every research has a technology component. This causes standardization of the general information and research topics. This is the early stages of AI's takeover of research projects from humans.

Humans can not compete with AI in some particular areas such as chess. However, AI takes over more and more areas known as humans' superiority. Then, transhumanists' solution is making humans transhuman or enhanced humans. Transhumans may continue to compete with AI for a longer time and therefore conduct research projects.

Becoming transhuman poses numerous ethical problems. Not everyone will prefer to become transhuman. Some will prefer to stay as biological humans or so to say "plain vanilla" humans. Their reason may be cultural, ideological or religious. So, even the technology advances, everyone will not become transhumans. The surrounding technologies may be expensive for the ordinary people. Thus, a deep level of inequality will occur after transhumanism technologies become available for market.

In other words, becoming transhuman is not much different than owning the best AI when it comes to costs. Thus, either the owners of the most sophisticated AI or first select transhumans will be the stars in the academic research field. Then, so many academicians will not be needed anymore. A few select starts will discover all needed and the rest will just follow their research (Harari, 2018).

These days are the last times for the classical academic research. When AI becomes powerful enough, all research will standardized since best research from best AI will soon become the standard. This will be end of the academic research practice as it is widely known. Academic research is expensive and time consuming. A centralized AI-based research will be much more efficient and cheap.

Academicians has two basic roles: Teacher and researcher. It seems that they will lose both to the AI but the research function may be replaced by the AI sooner than the teaching function. Teaching will persist a little bit more because it includes human interaction. Academic research will be easier for the AI to replace than teaching. Today, the last products of human intellect are being prepared as research projects.

When the academic papers or chapters are analyzed, it can be seen that they became more standardized over the time. This is a direct consequence of technological developments. Technology is both used in the production of the research material but also the AI technology is one of the main consumers of the research products. For current AI to consume the research products, they should be standardized. Of course, in the future, much more sophisticated AI may be developed and the need for standardization may go away.

Technology and Unemployment

If the enhancing technologies are not considered, human being is far behind in the race against the technology. Following the path of Moore's Law, each year computers become faster and cheaper, while human intellect is limited by its biological design ("Moore's law." 2018). In the future, there likely to be a serious problem of unemployment for un-enhanced people.

To help alleviate the problem, a solution is basic income ("Basic income." 2018). Although, there is no country universally supplying basic income, in the future it is likely that many countries will introduce such means of support to their citizens. Rich countries may have this privilege, however poor countries will be unable to defend their people from ever-improving technology (Ford, 2015).

To find sources to finance basic income, technology titans should be taxed. However, no country has such a power since these companies may shift operations to those countries with low or no taxes. Even so, governments may find ways to finance basic income and people may live with ample leisure time. That will support companies with operations related to the leisure-time activities.

It will be hard to learn how to live without working after hundreds of years of tradition of work. For many people, the meaning of life is closely related to work environment (Joy, 2000). Maybe, some people will continue to go to offices even though no payment is made to them. All of these developments will occur very fast and it will be very hard to adapt to them ("Technological unemployment." 2018).

Even so, basic income is better than starvation. Governments need to support their citizens in front of technology, they can't stay inactive. New generations may better adapt to basic income and enjoy their leisure time. In fact, work will not disappear totally and some very highly sophisticated jobs will continue to exist. However, only very select people will be able to get these jobs.

Ethical Issues in Transhumanism

Education will also lose its meaning and higher education will not be enough to get jobs. A totally new societal framework is needed to be established for people to adapt to this new situation. Primary and secondary education should be completely re-designed to prepare children for this brave new world of advanced technology and ample leisure time.

Smartphones and Enhanced People

Traditionally a new generation was characterized by 20-25 years. However, recently, it is calculated as merely 5 years. Every few years a new technological breakthrough is witnessed. The last revolution was the smartphone revolution. It swept through all the landscape and changed everything. Now, very little children can't do without a smartphone. They are totally a new generation. But when they are grown up, their experience with the technology will be outdated.

Smartphones are last technological breakthrough and last decade the news media was full of these phones. Huge investments have been made to develop smartphones and it is nearing the stage of maturity. Many people can not imagine a life without these gadgets. Almost every year a new phone is purchased and they are not cheap. They can be easily broken ans stolen. However, people embraced this technology much more than many other technologies.

People using smartphones are examples of enhanced humans although no mechanical equipment is transplanted into their bodies. Smartphones are the early stages of enhancement. After, really enhanced people will follow. Already, some people uses under-skin RFIDs as a replacement of their identification card ("Radio-frequency Identification." 2018).

Children uses smartphones starting from very early ages. These children, when they grow up will be the first candidates to use implanted RFIDs. They will see it as a natural improvement and follower of their smartphone. People are not cognizant of the fact that how enhanced they are. They are ready to become transhumans and smartphones are preparing them for such a future.

Enhanced people will be a natural continuation of people using smartphones. They are just smartphones embedded into human bodies. At least at the beginning. Today, smartphones can not be criticized or ethical issues can not be addressed. Likewise, in the future, the ethical issue related to the enhanced people will not be so visible. People will rush to install a newer enhanced version paying big amounts of money. Smartphone-mania gives clues about how will transhumanism be.

Technological Singularity

A standard $1,000 computer sold in 2030 is expected to have a processing power of a human brain (Kurzweil, 2006). Such computers will most likely behave like humans given the fact that there will be advances in areas such as deep learning and tomorrow's computers will most likely be massively parallel just like human brain.

The concepts from the 20'th century are still around and 21'st centuries concepts have not become mainstream yet. Transhumanism is being discussed but it is not a part of everyday life. There is much room for development. However, these events may be irreversible i.e. once transhumanism occur it will be impossible to revert back to the original human design.

There are advances in robotics for instance but one can not purchase a two-legged personal robot from supermarket. In the future, it is most likely that it will be possible to purchase. Therefore, the real revolution is ahead and has not occurred yet. Even so, after this revolution is finalized, there is little left for classical biological human beings.

Technological change is accelerating and this causes the acceleration of all of the events not just technological ones. Let's consider the year 2040. In that year's one month there will be more change than that will occur in the year 2020. This is due to the exponential change related to the technological issues. Classical biological humans can not adapt to such a change and they will be forced to become enhanced.

In the future, human-machine distinction will be blurred. Almost everyone, will have some machinery or inorganic component and this may even become mandatory. At one end of the spectrum there will be fully inorganic AI-enabled robots and at the other hand there will be organic humans. This is exactly what transhumanism proponents defend in order to live longer.

Even today, there are clues for technological determinism i.e. technology is controlling the society. In the future, these effects will be more pronounced and technology will fully control the society. Some enhanced people may stay at the top of the organizational ladder however they are enhanced and are part of the technology. So, there is force or mechanism to stop the technology or change the direction of it ("Martin Heidegger." 2018).

The concept of technological singularity makes it almost impossible to predict the future. Thus nearly all academic studies are about near future. At most, 5-10 years. After than that, there is little evidence about what will happen ("Technological singularity." 2018). Then, another 10 years pass and the next 10 years are predicted. After a point, this 10 years will be shortened to 5 years or even 2 years. This is how singularity occurs.

Transhumanism, AI, advanced technology are all very sophisticated concepts. It is very hard to predict the course of the technology in the future (Ford, 2015). Thus, the concept of technological singularity is developed. After a point, future developments can not be predicted even by best experts or most clever people. Only, time will pass and infinite number of possibilities will become one single possibility.

Previously, there were successful predictions about the future. However, after AI becomes highly powerful, it is hard to visualize such a world since then AI will become much more capable than the human brain at least in some areas. Academic studies are mainly about predicting future and this is another reason why academic research is coming to an end.

Being unable to predict future, it is very hard to prepare for the future. Intricate ethical issues in transhumanism are then hard to tackle. Even so, great effort should be made to visualize the world ahead. Otherwise, side effects of new technology will catch the humanity unguarded. This area should be one key research area at least until the technological singularity fully occurs.

Well-known futurist Kurzweil (2006) predicts that singularity to occur at around 2045. Some predict a nearer date and some do not predict a singularity at all. There is no idea about what will occur after the singularity. Everything can happen. There are infinite number of scenarios ("Technological singularity." 2018).

Today, humanity seems to have some level of control over its fate. That control will diminish over the time (Harari, 2018). In fact, today's level of control may be an illusion itself. Actually, humanity can not control the pace and direction of technology as Heidegger predicted ("Martin Heidegger." 2018). All events march into a singularity and there is no mechanism human being can use to stop it from occurring ("Technological determinism." 2018).

The Rise of Cyborgs and Brain Implants

Cyborgs are half-human and half-robot and they are human-machine combinations ("Cyborg." 2018). Of course, transhumanism also include developments from biotechnology and genetics but robotics and AI technology develops faster. In fact, some humans may reject the idea of merging with machines but may embrace enhancements stemming from genetic technology. Then they can not be called cyborgs. They will still be biological organisms.

At the start, the cyborgs will be humans with small enhancements. A person with foot prosthesis may be seen as a first example of a cyborg. People got used to see such prosthesis and see no problem with them. However, if they were used 200 years ago, people would react and try to prevent their usage. Over time, people are accustomed to the usage of mechanical parts in the bodies of disabled persons.

Brain implants are another category of examples ("Brain implant." 2018). Today, inorganic neurons are produced. They can be implanted into the brain and they can communicate with other organic neurons. These represent initial stages for hacking the structure of human brain and unveiling its secrets. The most sophisticated organ in human body is brain. Once its working principles are understood, then this will be a great step in order to design a hybrid brain.

Computers are much faster than human brain and they can store much more information. On the other hand, human brain is massively parallel and is capable of pattern recognition (Eagleman, 2015). The two strengths may be combined to reach a super-intelligence ("Superintelligence." 2018). Therefore, the most important research area will be the human brain. Of couse, in doing so, the analysis of the brains of other mammals wil also be highly helpful.

Today, brain implant research is concentrated on curing desperate patients. However, in the future, it will most likely to become mainstream especially among young generations. This is similar to the plastic surgery. People do not take part in such surgeries just because they are ill but rather they want to get full advantage of this advanced technology.

In the future, brain implants are likely to become like today's plastic surgeries. Thus people will be able to reach higher IQ levels and will enjoy better memories ("Intelligence quotient." 2018). In fact, people with such high IQs may find it difficult to sleep and may witness certain psychological problems. Then they will need to receive psychological support.

It is very hard for the human being to tolerate very high IQ levels and very large memories. Therefore, there are limits to being a cyborg and advanced IQ and large memories may stay as the field of supercomputers. Even so, people with 100 IQ may get 160 IQ and may tolerate it because there are persons with such high IQ levels and they can live with it. However, implanting an IQ of 250 for example seems implausible for many reasons.

As brain implants get cheaper and becomes widespread the average level of the IQ in the society will rise. This improvement can not be transferred to the next generations via biological reproduction and each new generation will need to be treated to install brain implants. Thus, this will be a lucrative new sector with employment opportunities in a world where there is serious level of unemployment.

Poor people will find it very difficult to use brain implants since this technology will be very expensive at the start. However, there is a danger for them. At the initial stages of brain implants the technology will be far from mature and there will be numerous side effects that may even cause deaths. Poor people can be used to test the new technology and to understand its limitations. Advanced countries may regulate the use of brain implants but the initial unproven technology may find application in poor countries.

In the future, brain implants will become mandatory as people with implants will get higher scores from exams and will get better job offers. Today, electronic gadgets can not be used in exams. But this is only a temporary situation. Will it be possible to exclude those with brain implants from the exams. They can't dismantle their implants. Thus, they will enter the exams with implants in their brains. Then, enhanced people will want to use smartphones or other equipment in response to the use of brain implants by others.

Maybe, those with and without brain implants will enter different exams but employers will prefer people with implants. Un-enhanced people will be like today's persons with disabilities and they will need special treatment. Governments will introduce support programs for purely biological and natural citizens. Probably, they will only live in certain designated areas as in the case of some old tribes of native Americans.

People in the age of 40's or 50's will most probably not feel the pressure to became enhanced and they will finissh their lives as natural humans. But newly-born babies are to witness to requirement to choose to become cyborg or not. The word "cyborg" has negative connotations but enhanced people will apparently become cyborgs. That is also the meaning of what transhumanism is. However, genetic improvements should be added to the table in order to complete the picture for transhumanism.

Once brain implants are elaborated and part of brain become an inorganic machine, then it may be possible to make updates to the inorganic part. If the learning mechanism of the brain is understood fully, then it will not be necessary to spend years to learn to speak or write a foreign language. The general education time may also be significantly shortened. This will be a great advantage for the enhanced people i.e. cyborgs.

In such circumstances, the schools and the universities will cease to exist as it is currently known to be. These are last years for classical universities and for their graduates. After brain implants become feasible, learning new topics will be much easier given that the person is enhanced. All advantages of machines such as speed, capacity and connectivity will be incorporated into human brains.

It is important to note that, all the brain engineering methods will inevitably has some serious side effects which are unknown at the start. Therefore such studies should be closely monitored and regulated. However, there are less regulation in some countries and controversial research will be conducted in such places. In fact, once the secrets of the brain are unveiled even the researchers in the highly regulated countries will use those new facts.

Initial progress will be slow due to the ethical issues, however eventually the brain will be completely analyzed. Initially, brain implants will be very slow but afterwards the progress will accelerate. The structure of brain remain almost constant from one generation to the next generation and there is almost no improvement in the capacity of brain (Kurzweil, 2006)

An enhanced person or a cyborg can read 30 books or watch 40 films a day due to the enhanced brain capacity. However, it is hard for a human being to tolerate such an influx of information. There will be serious health problems and such enhanced people will need to be monitored closely by health professionals. Furthermore, it will be almost impossible to become un-enhanced once the person becomes enhanced.

Cyborgs will think mechanically because part of them is a kind of machine. Since cyborgs will dominate the world, the life will be mechanical although very sophisticated. Then life be like a very big chess game with players are highly intelligent. Cyborgs will not make silly mistakes because of their high IQs but they may make some big mistakes anyway since their intellectual capacity has a limit.

Today there is a great uncertainty about the future. But once cyborgs appear and become dominant the events will be rather mechanical because cyborgs are partly machines. After that stage, all intelligent machines and humans will want to predict the future and the number of possibilities will drop significantly. This phenomenon currently occur in the financial markets. Algorithms make sophisticated trades and it becomes harder for the human traders to earn money.

In the future, implants will be so widespread that the meaning of the term "natural" will change. In that setting, natural will mean a human with less implants since it will be hard to find people with no implants. It may even become mandatory as governments force their citizens to make certain implants just like today's vaccines.

Those with implants will not be labeled as cyborgs automatically. There may be certain standards and after a level of mechanization that person may be labeled as cyborg. Even some persons may have so many implants that they may be considered as machines. Being "natural" human, cyborg or machine will have different consequences. Laws and regulation will vary accordingly.

These issues can be discussed today. But in the future it will not be possible to discuss them since implants will so widespread that there will be left nothing to discuss. People with implants will dominate the world. Thus, ethical guidelines should be formulated fast when the new technologies are not fully adopted yet. Otherwise, as in many other cases, technology will enforce its own rules and discussing ethical issues will have little value.

Implants are more effective and powerful than genetic improvements in that there are immediate results. Genetic research is slower than the AI research. Also, genetics has its own ethical issues. If the genetic code of human being is altered, maybe the natural humans can not be recovered. Even so, genetic research is part of the transhumanism movement although research about the AI is likely to make more immediate impact.

Some autratic governments may misuse all these developments to have a close control over their citizens. Some implants may be mandatory and they may aim to deepen the control. Some big companies selling implants will exercise a certain level of control over their customers and they will be as powerful as certain governments. This is the case with some of today's technologies. Future's technologies will have similar effects.

As with many other technologies, the implants will be very expensive and less capable at the beginning. Only a few select people with serious disorders will be able to pay for them. As more people install implants the prices will fall and still more people can buy them. At some point they will become commodity and many of their problems will be solved.

Suppose that a people with implant committed a crime. Who will be responsible and who will be punished? The implant, the company which produced the implant or person with implant. Today, this issue is discussed for autonomous cars. When such a car experiences an accident who will be responsible? A very similar problem exists for people with implants.

Punishability of such persons will be at the center of a debate in the coming years. What if something goes wrong with the implant and it starts to malfunction? Maybe some implants will have some side effects in that those people with these implants may commit certain kinds of crimes more often. Then, the court may decide for the removal of the implant but will it be possible without harming the brain of that person.

Some people will see brain implants as innocent as filling a tooth. However, it is known that tooth fillings have also some side effects. Even so, they are widely accepted and side effects are ignored.

There will be numerous kinds of implants. Some may prove to be very successful and some may stay as controversial. The early adopters may be the victims of the learning curve process.

In the future, a person's memory can be altered via surgical operations or personality may change. These may be done deliberately or may be accidental outcomes. For that reason, the majority of people will be distanced to the idea of implant. After all, the brain is the most important organ in the body. However, medicine and technology advances in a fast manner and future's technology will be must more capable than today's technology.

As scientific and technological knowledge about human brain expands, the freedom of individuals face a serious threat since controlling the brain becomes a possibility. Especially, media and marketing companies will find every bit of information highly valuable because they is some way control human brains. The politicians will be no exception, they will use such information in persuading their voters. In such a situation, individuals have almost nothing to protect themselves.

Brains with implants may access the Internet without using any other equipment. 7/24 connectivity may be a problem and therefore may be a mobile modem is inserted to the head to access the Web. Then enhanced people may carry a small computer and modem in their heads instead of today's smartphones. They may download huge amount of information to the inorganic part of their brain and organic part will contiue to monitor the rest of the body. These will be very sophisticated technologies, much sophisticated than the currently available ones.

Just in the case of plastic surgery, first small implants will not be sufficient for people and they will demand more as new technology becomes available. Installing an implant will require a surgery but this is also the case with plastic surgery. These people can not become natural again since they tasted the performance increases through implants. They will not settle for the less.

In the world of technology, mechanical parts are replaced by electronic parts and electronic parts are replaced by digital technology. If a digital model of the brain can be made than it can be at least partially replaced by a digital and electronic brain. Such a brain may communicate with other computers much more easily and will be much more powerful. The main obstacle is the complex structure of the brain. Once it is decoded and modeled, it will be quite easy to make improvements over it.

In the advanced levels of brain implants there will be a kind of operating system similar to that of computers. At least, the inorganic part of the brain will have such a system and it be periodically updated through wireless modem in the head. This may sound like science-fiction but the technology is advancing very fast and many elements in science-fiction movies become reality.

More technology may mean less individualism and less freedom. Even so, people may sometimes be ready to sacrifice freedom for the sake of their comfort. Partly digital brain may mean to try experiences never lived before. In that case, freedom may not seem so important. Furthermore, digital entities may enjoy a certain level of freedom although different in nature.

The most important question about a brain with implant is that: What will happen to the human will? Can a digital entity have a will and be held responsible for it? This is also a question religious leaders should ask. If a human's brain is governed by a digital operating system is he or she responsible for his or her behaviors? Legal authorities also will need to deal with that problem.

In fact, a digital brain is currently not available and no one can access the Internet via his or her head. However, the developments are very fast and they are accelerating. It is time to starting to set ethical guidelines. Some predictions about the future may seem unrealistic but many times technology made unrealistic expectations possible.

Transhumanism and Emerging Countries

Emerging countries such as Turkey are not producing technology but rather they consume it. Therefore, they don't have a chance to shape the future of technology. Transhumanism is no exception. Although, there is an advanced level of medical practice in some of these countries, AI-related technologies are largely imported from leading technology producers.

Early adapters of transhumanism are likely to be from the advanced countries although a number of individuals from the emerging countries may also follow the suit. Therefore, transhumanism ethics is likely to be developed in the advanced nations. Those in the emerging countries will have little influence over the ethical issues developed and this is itself an ethical issue.

The newly developed technologies are so powerful that the disparity between the leading and following countries is huge. The winner will win big and the loser will lose almost everything. The divide between the rich and poor will widen and there is no mechanism to correct it. Transhumanism may mean living much longer and becoming much richer. However, the majority of the people in the emerging markets will not be able to become enhanced even if they want.

The technological change is so rapid that there is no time to establish mechanisms to help alleviate the negative consequences of transhumanism. Emerging or less developed countries should be in a hurry to catch up the leading countries but there is no such activity. In fact, they can not catch the leaders even if they try hard since the distance is so large.

Some emerging countries may force their inhabitants to become transhuman against their wishes. They may do so in order to close the gap between them and the advanced nations. Being forced to become transhuman against one's wishes poses a serious ethical problem. In fact, for emerging and less developed countries the ethical problems will not mean much and most serious ethical misconduct will be in such places.

Therefore, the ethical issues in less developed countries should be examined more closely. In developed nations, the society is active in ethical issues and the ethical issues surrounding the transhumanism will be addressed fairly and new rules will be applied to circumvent the problems appearing. Emerging countries however do not have an advanced level of democracy and addressing the ethical issues is not easy.

Transhumanism and Islam

As depicted in figure 1, all three big religions have problems with transhumanism and thus contribute to the transhumanism ethics but here Islam's stance will be analyzed. In Islam, like in Christianity there is the concept of "End Times". Transhumanism can be easily related to end times. As the doomsday closes the genetic structure of human being will be altered and natural humans will become disappearing.

Islam teaches God created humans even though it may be through evolution according to some Islamic scholars. Transhumanism will be considered to be against the God's creation process and transhumans may be labeled as infidels. Some groups may even try to fight against transhumans however it is not very easy for them as transhumans will be so powerful.

Since some Muslim communities would prefer not to be enhanced and stay as natural humans, their power and wealth will diminish. They will not be able to find jobs or get proper education. It can be predicted that Muslim countries will not be at the forefront of transhumanist technologies. This will be a serious disadvantage for them and they will lag behind the secular countries.

Figure 1. How religions and philosophy affect transhumanism ethics

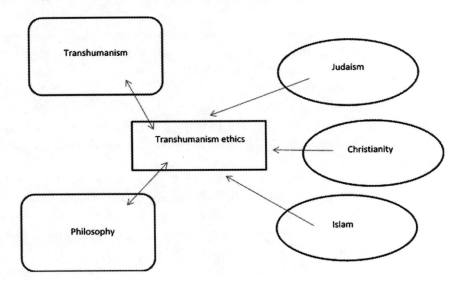

According to the Islamic traditions, it is very hard to adopt transhumanist practices. There may be even a fight between those with traditional beliefs and transhumanists in such countries. Transhumanists will not be welcomed and will have difficulty living in Islamic countries. It is very hard for Islam to adopt such technological practices and people would shy away from them.

In the future, some countries may adopt transhumanism early enough to become centers of transhumanism. There will be stress between such countries and Muslim countries. It should be added however that some Christians also have adverse feelings against such controversial technologies. But Islam would not embrace such a deep intervention to the human nature.

Transhumanism and Christianity

There are many Christian sects and churches. It is almost impossible to analyze the responses of all of them to the transhumanism. Christianity is one of the three widespread Abrahamic religions together with Islam and they share some common traits. All three have some conflict with transhumanism and the greatest criticisms will come from the Abrahamic religion. Judaism is no exception. Especially orthodox interpretations of these religions can find hard to tolerate fast technological advances.

In Christianity, the idea and definition of God is different than that of Islam. Most Christians believe that Jesus Christ was both God's Son God Himself. ("Is Jesus God?", 2019). In widespread interpretations of Islam, no prophet is said to be God Himself. In fact, Muslims criticize Christians for that. Since in Christianity, Jesus Christ is considered to be God, humans are holy creatures that are created using God as a model. Therefore, changing the nature of human body is unacceptable by many faithful Christians.

In Islam, human body is also sacred but not in the sense that Christians think. Some Christians are likely to oppose transhumanism more severely than Muslims do. Among Evangelical Christians "End Time" thinking is widespread. End Time concept can be found in Islam too. However, Christians put more emphasis on it. Therefore, some Christians will think the transhumanists to be the Antichrist or the mark of the beast (Chan, 2016).

Possibly in the future, some Christians will prefer to live just like Amish society lives today ("Amish.", 2019). They will freeze the technological level at some point and will reject to use more advanced technologies due to the religious concerns. They will surely be disadvantaged against those people fully utilizing the technological advances.

There are some initiatives to reconcile Christianity and transhumanism. For that purpose, Christian Transhumanist Association is established (Redding, 2015). Apparently, some Christians try to find ways to live with the transhumanism movement. According to Redding (2015), Christianity's last great reform was 500 years ago and currently the Christianity is in the midst of another great reform. Some Christians will become more secular and some will become more conservative.

Transhumanism and Judaism

Judaism is the smallest of the three big Abrahamic religions. It is the oldest of the three and affected the other two. Jews represent both a religion and a nation. They formed a closed society although they have spread all over the world. Throughout their history, they faced new nations, new cultures. This made them open to new ideas. Although there are orthodox jews, many are secular. Among jews, there are many leading scientists and some of them Nobel laurates.

Because of their openness to new ideas, it can be thought that jews would not resist new technologies and transhumanism as much as Muslims and Christians will. In fact, many of the leaders of transhumanism movement are jews. Even so, some orthodox jews may resist the transhumanism but the majority is likely to embrace new ideas.

Today, jews' state Israel is a leading country in technological developments. In some technological fields, Israel is second only to Silicon Valley. Many orthodox jews also live in Israel. They are likely to be affected from the secular citizens of the country. In fact, orthodox jews are just a cultural heritage of Israel. They are supported to maintain the origins of the religion. Secular jews transform the world, while orthodoxes preserve the traditions. To sum up, in the future course of the transhumanism, resistance from Judaism may not be so significant given the small number of jews and powerful secular tendency among them.

SOLUTIONS AND RECOMMENDATIONS

Solving technology-related ethical problems is not task achievable by a single institution or a single government. A world-wide cooperation is needed just like in the case of nuclear weapons or global warming. Global institutions should be established and side effects of the technology should be addressed. If a world government existed then there would be some hope to control technology.

A single world government may be criticized by some democracy proponents but it seems to be inevitable. Before, most likely that several big countries continue to dominate the world. However, one of them will be the master of the most advanced technology and then world government will come to true.

In fact, technology is advancing so fast that it may be too late until a world government established. Some issues may become unsolvable by then. Therefore, ethical issues should be addressed by academia and media. Ordinary people should become aware of these issues. There should be much more research over these topics.

FUTURE RESEARCH DIRECTIONS

Transhumanism will not take place in one day. The advances in the field should be followed and examined. There is ample room for further research. In fact, this is one of the most influential areas for researchers. Since, transhumanism is a very complex phenomenon, new findings from new research will be highly valuable.

In fact, transhumanism is still a concept of the future and has not fully realized yet. Ample research needed to understand what transhumanism is. Almost everything said on this topic will be new because the concept is just newly developing. Therefore, it is not hard to find new research problems about transhumanism. In the future, this area will also be fully researched out but currently, it is not the case.

In particular, transhumanism ethics presents ample research opportunities. As the technologies develop, the developers are only interested in advancing that particular technology. Some ethics experts are needed to analyze the side effects of those technologies. Its aim is not stopping the technological change. In fact, this is almost impossible. But ethicists try to pinpoint adverse effects and try to suggest some solutions. Therefore, transhumanism ethics may be a good career for new university graduates.

CONCLUSION

Transhumanism is a very complex issue and so are the ethical issues related to it. Politicians, researchers, businessmen, and even ordinary people should cooperate to find solutions. Since this is a very dynamic field, solutions will become outdated once they are formulated. This is a first instance in human history that technology reached such an advanced level and keeps improving.

Of course, there are numerous benefits from the advancing technology. Those developing new technologies publicizes such benefits. Also, people are ready to try new technologies as soon as prices fall below a certain level. However, there are also some side effects and therefore a transhumanism ethics is needed to tackle such issues.

Technology is developing fast and merging. The issues of transhumanism are not isolated from the issues of other advanced technologies. AI is especially important technology in analyzing transhumanism. Of course, biotechnology and genetics also are developing fast and merging with the AI. All these make transhumanism a highly complex area.

Main criticism to transhumanism is likely to come from Abrahamic religions namely Judaism, Christianity and Islam. Secular people are more ready to embrace the benefits of new technology. Even so, new technologies have side effects and criticisms also should be considered. Therefore, criticisms from the orthodox supporters of religions can be helpful in formulating ethical problems. They can serve as reference points.

Ethical discussions should be elaborated before new technologies become mainstream. After they become widespread they become the norms and there is little value in ethical discussions. Therefore, more emphasis should be given to the ethical problems at this stage. Resources should be allocated so that more research can be done in the field.

Technology is changing so fast that, before ethical discussions are completed the new technology dominates the world. Thus, today's ethical discussions may soon become old-fashioned as time passes. Nevertheless, these discussions should be made in a try to understand new technologies and their societal effects. Most probably, today's ethical lines will seem to be too conservative in future's world.

New ethical issues will emerge over time as long as technology continues to develop. Ethical concerns are among the traits that make us human and therefore they are important. This study aims to contribute to this vital field and to increase awareness about the intricate ethical issues surrounding the collection of new technologies called transhumanism.

REFERENCES

Amish. (2019, Jan. 22). Retrieved from https://en.wikipedia.org/wiki/Amish

Basic Income. (2018, Nov. 20). Retrieved from https://en.wikipedia.org/wiki/Basic_income

Brain Implant. (2018, Sept. 5). Retrieved from https://en.wikipedia.org/wiki/Brain_implant

Chan, D. (2016, April). Mormon Transhumanism and the Immortality Upgrade. *The New Yorker*. Retrieved from https://www.newyorker.com/tech/annals-of-technology/mormon-transhumanism-and-the-immortality-upgrade

Cyborg. (2018, Nov. 21). Retrieved from https://en.wikipedia.org/wiki/Cyborg

Eagleman, D. (2015). The Brain: The Story of You. New York: Pantheon Books.

End Time. (2018, Nov. 9). Retrieved from https://en.wikipedia.org/wiki/End_time

Ford, M. (2015). *Rise of the Robots, Technology and the Threat of a Jobless Future.* New York: Basic Books, Perseus Books Group.

GodI. J. (2019, Jan. 28). Retrieved from https://goingfarther.net/common-questions/is-jesus-god/

Harari, Y. N. (2018). 21 Lessons for the 21st Century. New York: Spiegel & Grau.

HeideggerM. (2018, Nov. 20). Retrieved from https://en.wikipedia.org/wiki/Martin_Heidegger

Intelligence Quotient. (2018, Nov. 20). Retrieved from https://en.wikipedia.org/wiki/Intelligence_quotient

Joy, B. (2000, April). Why the Future Doesn't Need Us. *Wired*. Retrieved from https://www.wired.com/2000/04/joy-2/

Karaman, F. (2012). Artificial Intelligence Enabled Search Engines (AIESE) and the Implications. In J. Christophe, I. Biskri, J. G. Ganascia, & M. Roux (Eds.), *Next Generation Search Engines: Advanced Models for Information Retrieval*. Hershey, PA: IGI Publications. doi:10.4018/978-1-4666-0330-1.ch019

Kurzweil, R. (2006). The Singularity Is Near: When Humans Transcend Biology. London, UK: Penguin Books.

Moore's Law. (2018, Nov. 21). Retrieved from https://en.wikipedia.org/wiki/Moore%27s_law

Radio-Frequency Identification. (2018, Nov. 8). Retrieved from https://en.wikipedia.org/wiki/Radio-frequency_identification

Redding, M. (2015, August). Why I Became a Christian Transhumanist. *Motherboard.* Retrieved from https://motherboard.vice.com/en_us/article/9akxm3/why-i-became-a-christian-transhumanist

Superintelligence. (2018, Nov. 20). Retrieved from https://en.wikipedia.org/wiki/Superintelligence

Technological Determinism. (2018, Nov. 5). Retrieved from https://en.wikipedia.org/wiki/Technological_determinism

Technological Singularity. (2018, Nov. 24). Retrieved from https://en.wikipedia.org/wiki/Technological_singularity

Technological Unemployment. (2018, Nov. 22). Retrieved from https://en.wikipedia.org/wiki/Technological_unemployment

Yamamoto, G. T., & Karaman, F. (2005). *A Road-Map For The Development Of The Content Protecting Technologies (CPT) For The Content Based E-Business Models* (Vol. 5). Dubai, UAE: E-Business Review.

Yamamoto, G. T., & Karaman, F. (2006). *ICT, New Working Elite, and Social Implications* (Vol. 6). Dubai, UAE: E-Business Review.

ADDITIONAL READING

Accelerating change. (2018, Nov. 22). Retrieved from https://en.wikipedia.org/wiki/Accelerating_change

Artificial general intelligence. (2018, Oct. 28). Retrieved from https://en.wikipedia.org/wiki/Artificial_general_intelligence

Dystopia. (2018, Nov. 16). Retrieved from https://en.wikipedia.org/wiki/Dystopia#Technology

Human enhancement. (2018, Nov. 6). Retrieved from https://en.wikipedia.org/wiki/Human_enhancement

Neuroenhancement. (2018, May 15). Retrieved from https://en.wikipedia.org/wiki/Neuroenhancement

Post-scarcity economy. (2018, Nov. 12). Retrieved from https://en.wikipedia.org/wiki/Post-scarcity_economy

Postbiological evolution. (2018, June 6). Retrieved from https://en.wikipedia.org/wiki/Postbiological_evolution

Posthumanization. (2018, Aug. 16). Retrieved from https://en.wikipedia.org/wiki/Posthumanization

Singularitarianism. (2018, Oct. 28). Retrieved from https://en.wikipedia.org/wiki/Singularitarianism

Technophobia. (2018, Oct. 15). Retrieved from https://en.wikipedia.org/wiki/Technophobia

KEY TERMS AND DEFINITIONS

AI (Artificial Intelligence): Is the intelligence of machines as compared to the intelligence of humans or animals.

Basic Income: Due to the technology-driven unemployment, some countries consider to give a certain level of money to all their citizens to protect them against the adverse effects of unemployment.

Big Data: Is a concept related to dealing with really high amounts of data. Traditional databases can not store and analyze such big amounts of data.

Brain Implant: The activity of intervening brain's structure. Patients are treated via this method and scientific studies are being made to explore the working principles of other mammals.

Cyborg: A living organism with electromechanical parts. This organism may be a mammal or any other organism.

ICT: Is an acronym for Information and Communication Technologies.

IQ: Intelligence quotient. Measures intelligence level and a is score obtained from certain standardized tests.

RFID: Is an acronym for Radio Frequency Identification. RFID chips can be used to identify a good, an animal or a human being. Its use has become widespread as the costs went down.

Technological Singularity: If artificial intelligence (AI) reaches such a point that it can produce more capable machines than itself then intelligence explosion will occur and then it is impossible to predict what will happen afterwards.

Transhumanism: Is the movement that supports the view that human body and intellect should be greatly improved by means of sophisticated new technologies.

Chapter 8
Using Artificial Intelligence in Massive Open Online Courses:
A Conceptual View to Wise MOOCs

Emel Güler
Anadolu University, Turkey

Buket Karatop
Istanbul University-Cerrahpasa, Turkey

ABSTRACT

It can be said that the reflection of the philosophy of Transhumanism on education creates a threat to the survival of human civilization or, on the contrary, focuses on technologies that try to create opportunities to overcome basic human limitations. MOOCs are still a major tool in the ongoing development of opportunities to teach the whole community. With MOOCs, interactive student-oriented large audiences can be reached instantly. The MOOCs, which offer great opportunities, should be made intelligent by the interaction of the curricula and the learner in order to achieve more effective results. As MOOCs are student-friendly, it is important that, when preparing training materials, the curriculum is formulated strategically. It is important that stakeholders' views are involved in decision-making using artificial intelligence techniques because learning is too important to be left to coincidence.

INTRODUCTION

In the late 20th century, worldwide rapid developments in information technologies such as radio, television, computer, internet, satellites, and fiber optics have caused a paradigm shift in the teaching methods by influencing the working mechanism of training activities. One of the reflections of this shift is "MOOC" (Massive Open Online Course), which has started to be used in 2008 and has become widespread since. Being regarded as a new stage in the use of internet in Open Plan and Distance Education, Massive Open Online Course, hence the name, is an online education which aims at a large number of participators and meets the high quality, interactive, free of charge and lifetime education need of massive students coming from all around the world. Although the massive open online courses that are

DOI: 10.4018/978-1-5225-8431-5.ch008

regarded as a revolution in the field of education by some experts, are established with a philosophy of providing free of charge and quality education, they are used in the educational institutions as a method (either paid or free of charge).

In massive open online courses, the system is entirely dependent on the learning style of the individual and it helps to overcome the obstacles between the lecturer and the student, and it also helps to ease up the curriculum for students who are obliged to follow a standard curriculum. Thus, these students can choose from courses that suits themselves best. Today, where the digital transformation with technologies such as the internet of things and artificial intelligence has become a trending issue, the field of education should keep up with these developments, as well. Processes and systems are getting more intelligent with the artificial intelligence. In this study, wise (intelligent) MOOCs has been discussed.

The fact that real-life problems are multi-criteria and unclear is the most characteristic feature of these problems. Multi Criteria Decision Analysis (MCDA) methods are being used to solve complex decision-making problems which require the consideration of many criteria that are interrelated. Multi-criteria decision-making methods have been developed for multi-criteria problems, however, there are many solutions for uncertainties. Furthermore, it is being said by the researchers that the artificial intelligence is producing good results in this particular. Similarly, Önüt et al. state in their article called "A hybrid fuzzy MCDM (multi criteria decision making) approach to machine tool selection" that many researchers have been trying to use the fuzzy multi-criteria decision-making methods for selection problems, as well.

Fuzzy sets make it easy to overcome the uncertainties in decision-making problems. In their article called "An integrated optimization approach and multi-criteria decision analysis for supporting the waste-management system of the City of Beijing, China", Xi et al. state that multi-criteria decision-making techniques are not effective in establishing an optimal waste management system. Cheng and McInnis stated in 1979 and 1989 respectively that it is recommended to use multi-criteria decision-making along with fuzzy logic. Opinions of Karatop et al. on real-life problems and artificial intelligence are as follows: "The most prominent features of the real-life problems are multiple criteria, complexity and uncertainty. Benefiting from expert and stakeholder views help to reach optimal solutions of those problems. Taking advantage of artificial intelligence techniques would also contribute to the achievement of optimal results." It is possible to multiply these instances. As a result, studies show that using multi-criteria decision-making methods and artificial intelligence techniques together in solving real-life problems yields optimal results.

MASSIVE OPEN ONLINE COURSE (MOOC)

The notion of MOOC is defined as online courses which offer free of charge and open registration options, provide open course content to everyone and have open-ended learning outcomes (McAuley, Stewart, Siemens & Cormier, 2010). Furthermore, MOOC offers a learning platform to a large learning community to support learning by discussion and to evaluate studies based on peer review (Reimann, Diebold & Kummerfield, 2013). If we are to evaluate the Massive Open Online Courses by sticking to its name, we can speak of 4 descriptive elements. (Kay et al. designated 3 descriptive elements. They addressed massive and open elements together. We addressed them separately here.) *It is massive* and it appeals to every segment of the society. It is not boutique. It is *open* to everyone so that everone can use them for learning. By removing financial obstacles, it offers a learning platform to the disadvantageous part of the society regardless of their income level, as well. "Being online means people can access them on the Internet. In providing courses, MOOCs represent a major shift in scale beyond open learning objects" (Kay et. al, 2013). Additionally, above all, a MOOC is based on the active participation of "students" between a couple hundred and thousand in number who organize the participants according to their learning objectives, prior knowledge and skills, and common interests (McAuley et al. 2010).

Studies conducted suggest that the tendency to the use of MOOC has increased in time. In the research they conducted, Ebben and Murphy (2014) state that cMOOC was dominant between 2008-2011/12 whereas xMOOC was dominant between 2012-2013. The study conducted by Bozkurt, Akgun-Ozbek, and Zawacki-Richter (2017) suggests the research tendencies and models regarding the MOOC between 2008-2015. According to the study, research on the MOOC have started to increase as of 2013 and there has been a positive tendency since then. However, the articles examined consequent to the study suggest that the MOOC types have not been described in clear methodologically. Similarly, Liyanagunawardena et al. (2013) and Veletsianos and Shepherdson (2016) emphasize the uncertainty in the description of MOOC types and state that more clear descriptions about MOOC types should be made.

TYPES OF MOOCs

It is observed that there are different approaches when MOOC classifications are studied. While Siemens (2012) classifies as connectivist (cMOOCs) and eXtension (xMOOCs), Clark (2013) defines 8 MOOC types: transfer MOOCs, made MOOCs, Sync MOOCs, Async MOOCs, adaptive MOOCs, group MOOCs, connectivist MOOCs, mini MOOCs. Clark's (2013) MOOC definitions can be explained as follows:

- **Transfer MOOCs:** In these courses, pedagogical method is in the form of transmitting the course content to the learner. Similar to traditional courses, lecturing, short exams (quizzes), texts and evaluations are offered through MOOC platform. Courses located on the Coursera platform can be largely classified into this category.
- **Made MOOCs:** In this type of course contents used by Khan Academy and Udacity, there are more innovative and creative videos rather than talking heads structure. Different evaluation types and interactive experiences based on problem solving are offered in the course contents. In order to appeal to learners in massive numbers, peer learning and peer review methods are used.
- **Synch MOOCs:** In these type of MOOCs, there are due dates for homework and evaluations along with fixed starting dates. Many argue that this helps motivation and aligns teacher availability and student cohort work.
- **Asynch MOOCs:** In these courses, there are no due dates for homework along with starting and ending dates. The fact that individuals can have access to these courses in different time zones whenever and wherever they want is a pedagogical advantage. Due to the fact that there is no risk of missing the due dates of homework and exams to be prepared during the course, courses of this type can be regarded as an option to decrease the disconnection rate of the individuals from the system.
- **Adaptive MOOCs:** In these courses carried out by obtaining data from courses and dynamic evaluation, adaptable algorithms are used to create streamed learning experiences.
- **Group MOOCs:** There are courses of this type which are composed of small cooperative working groups and the aim is to increase student retention.

- **Connectivist MOOCs:** Created by George Siemens and Stephen Downes, this structure is based on learning with connections formed on a network. In these courses, rather than standard information flow, information sharing created by the contributions of the participators is emphasized.
- **Mini MOOCSs:** They have a smaller structure compared to MOOCs with traditional structure and they are carried out according to a certain schedule like the academic calendars in universities. These courses are given for a fixed duration designated on an hourly or daily basis rather than weekly in general.

Conole (2014) has stated that these courses can be classified according to twelve variables such as the degree of openness in the course, the number of participators (massiveness), level of multimedia usage, level of in-class communication, configuration of the course either as student-oriented or lecturer-oriented, ensuring quality assurance, evaluation method used in the course, type of cooperation used in the course, feedback mechanism applied in the course, the fact that the course has either a modeled or a half-modeled structure, the autonomy and diversity of the course.

Furthermore, Hybrid Massive Open Online Courses which offer cMOOC and xMOOC models together in a consecutive or parallel manner, adopt blended learning approach and appeal to a wider range of participator have been emerging lately (Bozkurt, 2015).Hybrid MOOCs, can be defined as the MOOCs which offer connectionist and traditional approaches together in order to provide the learners with rich learning opportunities (Bozkurt & Aydin, 2015).

When relevant literature is studied, it is observed that along with their powerful aspects, MOOCs have aspects that need improving, as well. Some **strengths** of the MOOCs can be listed as follows (Bozkurt, 2015):

- They allow a collaborative information sharing on a global platform.
- Their structure creates learning opportunities with flexible learning model and it allows the learner to make progress at their own pace.
- They remove the physical boundaries to have access to information and to receive training on a certain subject.
- It is possible to access the content during or after MOOCs.
- It is possible to receive training given in an area of interest by prestigious universities or lecturers and to certificate these training.
- Learners can test themselves by seizing the opportunities of self-evaluation, peer review, absolute evaluation or relative evaluation or they can access content without being subject to any evaluation.
- Lecturers can seize more opportunities to reach learners with free of charge Web 2.0 tools and services compared to traditional learning systems.
- Learners of all ages can benefit from the MOOC opportunities if they wish.
- The number of the masses that you can access in local or global context is very high.
- They allow individuals to update their knowledge and skills in a changing and developing world in which the information increases incrementally.
- They are suitable for mobile and accessible learning as much as e-learning.

In addition to the strengths they have, MOOCs have some obstacles that need to be overcome and some restrictions that need to be improved. Some **weaknesses** about the MOOCs in the relevant literature are listed as follows (Bozkurt, 2015b):

- The rate of system dropout is high.
- They are more suitable for self-controlled and self-oriented learners.
- The learner is expected to take their own learning responsibility.
- They require an efficient time management.
- There are questions about what qualifications a participant obtained after a training.
- Learners who are accustomed to traditional inflexible curriculums may have difficulties until they get used to the system.

In addition to the weaknesses listed above, there are restrictions such as quality assurance, the fact that most MOOCs are carried out as classic courses, ensuring academic integration, the fact that having an internet connection and a computer-like device is a prerequisite, and problems in assessment and evaluation (Bozkurt, 2016).

MOOC Design Structure

It is stated that there should be subjects which are different from traditional learning systems in the design of Massive Open Online Courses. In their studies, Guàrdia, Buyjng and Sangrà (2013) have studied the significant principles in the MOOC design through a student's perspective and they have listed these principles as follows:

1. Competence-Based Design Approach.
2. Learner Empowerment.
3. Learning plan and clear orientations.
4. Collaborative learning.
5. Social networking.
6. Peer assistance.
7. Quality criteria for knowledge creation and generation.
8. Interest groups.
9. Assessment and peer feedback.
10. Media-technology-enhanced learning.

If a MOOC design to be created in the context of the principles above, their reflections may be as follows(Guàrdia, Buyjng and Sangrà (2013):

- Learning activities oriented
- Open educational resources require new design and authoring conception
- Situated learning help learners to keep attention and motivation
- Peer-to-peer encourages learning by teaching
- Goal oriented social networking
- Media for learners knowledge generation

Enrolling to MOOC and dropping-out afterwards which is a significant disadvantage can be considered as an important issue that may harm MOOC's reputation. That the reasons behind the students' drop-out decisions should be solved with the qualities of these students. Frankly, by individualizing the learning, management of the MOOCs according to the student's needs with a smart system may be the solution. In this context, there have been improvements supporting this view. Some research reports indicate that the artificial intelligence market in the education sector may increase by 43-49% until 2024. By grounding on computer learning, the artificial intelligence draws conclusions based on machine learning which indicate the decision making and predicting capacity of a computer through exposure to big data sets and natural language processing. This helps them to interact with machines in a way similar to how people are interacting with other people. While the underlying technologies continue to improve within the education sector and helping the artificial intelligence instructors, they also have the potential to improve online learning, adaptive learning software and research procedures which respond to students in a more intuitive way and have means of interaction.

Within the period where smart programs start to turn into smart machines thanks to the technological developments, we see that the artificial intelligence systems are being implemented in different manners to both industrial and educational fields every day. In this study, it has been studied that how MOOCs can be designed with artificial intelligence applications. In the following section, firstly, the subject of artificial intelligence applications has been addressed and afterward, a conceptual suggestion about a smart MOOC design has been brought forward.

ARTIFICIAL INTELLIGENCE (AI)

Artificial intelligence is that the behaviors which are called intelligent because they are shown by humans are made by a machine through a software. Artificial intelligence can be said to be a concept which shows how human mind works. At the same time, artificial intelligence is any and all works which are carried out in order to improve one's capabilities in thinking, learning, reasoning, understanding/recognizing the problem, and making inferences through a computer software (Kubat, 2012).

In his interview with BBC, Edward Fredkin who is one of the administrators of MIT Computer Sciences laboratory has stated that: "There are 3 big events in history. First of them is the creation of the universe. Second one is the start of life. And the third one is the creation of artificial intelligence." Differences and similarities between brain and computer should be understood to understand a subject such as artificial intelligence.

While artificial intelligence studies sometimes witnessed recession and disappointment, they sometimes witnessed great excitement, hope and dynamism. The goal of the researchers and scientists is to maintain the artificial intelligence studies carried out towards obtaining perfect results which facilitate the human labor, increase the efficiency, and use the resources effectively and efficiently. It is possible to say that these studies are being carried out in order to facilitate human life. Therefore, they maintain their studies to develop artificial intelligence applications which are capable of learning, inferring, sorting, recognizing their environment, interacting with things according to their goals (internet of things), calculating, evaluating, commenting and making decisions (multi-criteria decision-making).

Expert systems, fuzzy logic, artificial neural networks, and genetic algorithms can be said to be the most known and the most commonly used artificial intelligence techniques. In addition to these techniques, there are many techniques and algorithms being developed, as well. Pirim (2006) listed the artificial intelligence techniques as follows.

1. Knowledge-based expert system approach
2. Artificial neural networks approach
3. Fuzzy logic approach
4. Non-traditional optimization techniques
    a. Genetic algorithm
    b. Simulated annealing
    c. Taboo search
    d. Hybrid algorithms
5. Object-oriented programming
6. Geographic information systems (GIS)
7. Improvement of decision support systems
8. Soft computing

The primary areas of usage of artificial intelligence today as follows (Kubat, 2012).

- Problem solving, searching and heuristic programming
- Knowledge creation and removal
- Games (Strategy, chess,..)
- Artificial life
- Theorem proving (Prologue, Parallel prologue, ...)
- Natural language understanding and translation
- Knowledge-based systems
- Machine learning
- Machine inventions
- Robotics
- Image recognition

Out of the artificial intelligence techniques, the ones relevant to the subject of this study are briefly explained below.

FUZZY LOGIC

Fuzzy sets were found by Lutfu Ali Askerzade (Zadeh) in 1965 in order to represent/use the non-statistical uncertainties which have data and information (Zadeh, 1965). Fuzzy logic helps to make a decision with approximate values under uncertain and imperfect knowledge (Fuller, 1995). There are always uncertainties in many social, financial and technical real-life problems due to the insufficiency of human knowledge. Computers as well cannot process this kind of uncertain data and numerical knowledge is required. It is not possible to fully comprehend the real event due to the insufficiency of human knowledge. In that case, a human makes interpretation and inferences by roughly animating this kind of events in their thought system and mind. Unlike computers, humans are capable of getting into the action with quite insufficient, missing and uncertain data and knowledge. Incomplete and uncertain information resources such as complexity and uncertainty which generally emerge in different forms are fuzzy (Sen, 2009). Fuzzy logic can be applied to knowledge-based systems, and it is equipped with inference structure which has the approximate inference ability. The fuzzy set theory provided a mathematical power which includes uncertainties incorporated with human cognitive processes such as thinking and reasoning.

Fuzzy logic ensures the inclusion of linguistic expressions to the relevant technique by being used in an integrated way, with many problem-solving methods and thus, efficient results are obtained.

EXPERT SYSTEMS

Expert systems are the most used technology of artificial intelligence science and they can also be used in every stage of life. Expert systems are computer systems which can solve a problem in a similar way to experts solving the same problem and can use their knowledge and experience like the experts use their experiences. We can think of this as a kind of consultation system arranged on a computer (Kubat, 2012). Expert systems can be considered as a new type of software which is the basis of knowledge engineering with their unique principles, tools and techniques. Expert systems are recognized as consultant computer programs which always operate in a knowledge-based manner and try to imitate the experts' knowledge while solving some problems associated with any field.

It is known that expert systems yield effective results when used together with fuzzy logic. As expert systems make it possible to solve very complex problems by combining the human mentality with computer power, fuzzy expert systems are systems creating different linguistic and mathematical results by taking fuzzy logic as basis which offer much more realistic solutions to relevant problems (Icen and Gunay, 2014).

ARTIFICIAL NEURAL NETWORKS (ANN)

Artificial neural networks (ANN) study the brain's learning methods and its structure composed of neurons. They are systems which provide computers with skills such as deriving new information from learning, creating and discovering new information, all of which are among the features of the human brain. The essential function of artificial neural networks is to allow computers to make similar decisions in similar events by learning about these events, just like neural networks in the human brain.

In a study carried out by Hebb (1949), a learning procedure which is only possible biologically has been developed in a way so that a computer carry out this procedure. This study is accepted as the beginning of artificial neural networks. Hebb has developed a learning rule in his study.

Oztemel (2003), has made the following determinations in his book on artificial neural networks: "The mankind has always wondered how the human brain works. The birth of computers has actually been a result of this curiosity. The role of this curiosity and quest in the foundation of the transition from the first calculators to today's very complex computer systems should not be forgotten. Looking at current developments, it is not difficult to anticipate that more complex systems are going to be created. While the computers were developed in order to make only arithmetic operations at first, today, they are asked to learn about events and make decisions according to environmental conditions. It is not difficult to anticipate that they are going to be asked to carry out works currently carried out by mankind which require a great deal of brain power. Artificial neural networks are one of the disciplines that have triggered this development. And they will still be one of the most important disciplines in the future." Today, artificial neural networks are actually the primary method which is the most frequently used and successfully implemented in issues such as learning, association, classification, generalization, identity mapping and optimization.

Artificial neural networks operate with numerical information, but fuzzy logic and linguistic expressions can be included in the process. They perform learning by using examples. Artificial neural networks are capable of processing uncertain information. They can produce information about unnoticed instances. They are capable of self-organization and learning. They can work with incomplete information. They have fault tolerance.

Artificial Intelligence Applications in MOOCs: Intelligent MOOC

Great differences have arisen between the 20th century and 21st-century people. People's change in the industrial age of the 20th century and in the information age of the 21st century have been shown in Figure 1. This change has also affected the education system (human in the role of lecturer and learner) as it has affected every other area of life.

The first set of 21st century skills "Learning to Learn and Innovate" focuses on critical learning skills and innovation:

- Critical thinking and problem solving (expert thinking)
- Communication and collaboration (complex communicating)
- Creativity and innovation (applied imagination and invention).

Second "Information Literacy" focuses on;

- Accessing information efficiently and effectively
- Evaluating information critically and competently
- Using information accurately and creatively.

The last set focuses on career and life skills.

The change in today's human being continues at a great pace, and during the transition of the last two centuries (20th and 21st century) the philosophy of transhumanism has emerged. In his work called Transhumanism Values, Bostrom defined transhumanism as a dynamic philosophy that aims to evolve

Figure 1. Value Chains Then and Now
(Trilling & Fadel, 2012)

Industrial Age Value Chain
Extraction → Manufacturing → Assembly → Marketing → Distribution → Products (and Services)

Knowledge Age Value Chain
Data → Information → Knowledge → Expertise → Marketing → Services (and Products)

as new information emerges or as new challenges emerge. Author has defined the transhumanism as "the removal of tools and obstacles against humanity by using technological and other rational methods and ethical issues included in these methods." Where does the open and distance learning that directly concerns the people lie within the philosophy of Transhumanism?

The MOOCs, which we met in 2008, have quickly become a topic of interest for researchers in the field of open and distance education. In the study carried out by Bozkurt, Akgun-Ozbek, and Zawacki-Richter, it is seen that the studies have increased rapidly after 2013 as a result of the examination of 362 articles (empirical articles published in peer-reviewed journals) published between the years of 2008 and 2015. This study examined the content of these articles and classified these articles into three levels as Macro, Meso and Micro. Zawacki-Richter designated the open and distance education research fields as follows; Macro level: distance education systems and theories;Meso level: Management, organization, and technology; Micro level: Teaching and learning in distance education.

In their article called "The Beginning of a Beautiful Friendship: Intelligent Tutoring Systems and MOOCs", Aleven et al. (2015) mention that as well as being quite popular, the abilities of MOOCs supporting individual learning are sometimes restricted. The authors argue that intelligent tutoring systems partially overcome these restrictions. According to the authors, *"They provide step-by-step guidance during (moderately) complex problem solving. They can track learners' skill growth and select problems on an individual basis. They can adaptively respond to student strategies and errors. On the other hand, MOOCs support learning in ways that Intelligent tutoring systems (ITSs) do not, for example with video lectures, discussions forums, and so forth. Hence, we propose integrating ITS-style learning-by-doing into MOOCs."*

Among the studies carried out on MOOCs, there is very little research on intelligent MOOC. In one of these studies, Kaklauskas and others have designed an intelligent MOOC environment regarding disaster management. This MOOC which has been prepared for postgraduate students covers a wide range of topics including disaster management, climate change, ecosystem management and community flexibility. Students have the opportunity to improve their knowledge through exams, real-life and imaginary problem-solving exercises, additional reading materials, videos and a discussion forum. In this MOOC which is based on individual learning, postgraduate students are provided with tools such as personalized learning materials, digital textbooks, videos, sounds, calculators, software, computer learning systems, an intelligent test system, and an affective intelligent tutoring system. Students may be provided with study materials according to the repeated keywords in the designed system. The curriculum is adapted to each student's needs, knowledge level, age, habits and challenges. The personalized scenario is dynamically generated by emphasizing the weakness of each postgraduate student.

The most significant features of real-life problems are the fact that they are multi-criteria and complex and have uncertainties. The use of mostly expert and partner opinions in the solution of such problems brings us closer to the best result. Fuzzy logic can be applied in situations where there is uncertainty or optimal decisions must be made with incomplete information. The uncertainty in the decision-making process can result from the presence of verbal information and the models where the subjective thoughts are involved. In this case, more effective results are obtained by eliminating the uncertainties or acknowledging the existence of uncertainty and adapting the analysis accordingly. Making analytical solutions with fuzzy logic provides the decision maker with a more flexible decision-making environment. Information submitted verbally by applying fuzzy logic is included in the solution by obtaining their numerical equivalents. With stakeholder opinions, personal opinions are included in the solution. The stakeholder consists of the parties affected and the parties affecting the event/company. It is impossible to not to ask stakeholders when making a decision on this event. It is unthinkable to create a MOOC structure without asking to stakeholders in MOOC which is a part of the open and distance learning event, as well. Furthermore, we recommend using artificial intelligence techniques in the inclusion of information obtained from stakeholders to the decision-making process for MOOC structure.

In this study, intelligent MOOC has been discussed in two manners.

1. MOOC whose curriculum is determined with artificial intelligence techniques
2. MOOC whose interface work with artificial intelligence during learning

MOOC With Intelligent Curriculum

It can be said that one of the teaching strategies of MOOC is the curriculum. For many years, businesses have been very careful in determining their strategies and they have been using analytical methods. Analyses (SWOT, PESTS, Stakeholder analysis etc.) are being meticulously carried out and these analyses have been used in the formation of value-creating strategies. Strategies are being turned into objectives, objectives are being turned into activities, and all of them are evaluated according to performance criteria (Figure 1). It is necessary to think and build a similar condition for MOOCs.

It should be said that education management is much more important than business management. We all accept that the future of society is much more important than planning the future of a business. Considering their sphere of influence on societies, many analyzes that are vital to the sustainability and success of the business should also be used to identify curricula that are important in learning strategies.

It can be said that making SWOT and Stakeholder analyses during the curriculum design is being carried out and using the stakeholder requests and expectations in curriculum design are significant steps for quality education. The phenomenon of quality is meeting the present and future requests and expectations of stakeholders. From this point of view, we recommend these analyzes to be performed for the quality of curricula that are the teaching strategy of MOOCs. SWOT is a technique frequently used in the determination of the status quo. SWOT analysis parameters are generated with large groups and methods. For example, techniques such as Delphi, conference call and brain storm are frequently used. While the inclusion of SWOT analysis in the strategy is done according to the preliminary opinion of the strategic planning experts, now they are done in various ways. Because strategies are the form of position-

Figure 2. Strategic plan process

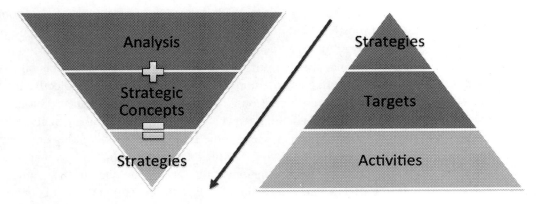

ing the future. In this context, the parameters can be included in the process as more analytically with Fuzzy SWOT instead of classic SWOT. In this context, it is important to carry out the status quo analysis in the first stage of curriculum preparation with these techniques in order to achieve a realistic result.

On the other hand, each training module has a raison d'etre (mission), a great goal (vision), values and principles. It should be emphasized that linking these strategic notions (mission, vision, values, and principles) to measurable performance indicators is important for success. Designation of the strategies regarding the great goal and realization of raison d'etre and determining the topics of the curriculum within this pattern will be a more effective design. However, this is a necessary condition; not a sufficient condition. Artificial intelligence is what ensures the sufficient condition.

The curriculum can be seen as a data center which consists of important and vital information such as program qualifications, the aim of the course, the credit of the course, learning goals, learning outcomes, and instructional methods. It can be said that life cycles constantly carrying out analysis, evaluation and enhancements should be constructed so that the resources of a business can be used effectively and efficiently, and the curriculums that are generally in a static state can achieve a more dynamic state. In the designation of program qualifications, effective results can be achieved with linguistic expressions reflecting uncertain and completely human thoughts by carrying out environment analyses like PESTS (Political-economical-social-technological-sectoral), status quo analyses likee SWOT and stakeholder analyses (which are persons and institutions that affect and affect from the education module in question). At the same time, effective results can be achieved by using multi-criteria decision-making techniques such as AHP, ANP, and TOPSIS along with fuzzy logic in the prioritization and weighting of criteria for the determination of the framework of program qualifications. These preliminary studies can ensure the determination of program qualifications with an expert system software (Figure 3). This suggested structure is a dynamic structure. We're talking about a structure which adapts to the changing environmental conditions. Program qualifications are seen as the primary source of curriculum pattern. In this context, the fact that qualifications are dynamic, suitable for environmental conditions and able to meet stakeholder needs can be described as the key to success at first.

In addition to its ability to sort and select quickly, artificial intelligence also has techniques that have features such as decision-making and learning. We see that it is being used along with the fuzzy logic and multi-criteria decision-making in the academic studies carried out in the fields of strategy formulation, strategic planning, and strategic management. Multi-criteria decision-making helps us to find the optimal result in fuzzy logic while sorting and selecting.

With the change of human life style and capabilities with the development of technology, the features of materials that are offered on the learning platforms such as form and duration have also changed. Humans who live in today's busy environment and are provided with infinite knowledge, are now more impatient and they request outcome-oriented learning. In addition to the fact that the duration of educational material is very relative, we should say that quality, cost and time elements offered in quality management and perfection models must be paid attention to. In this context, results obtained from the electronic movements the individual representing the learner role who benefits from the learning platform in the determination of the type and duration of educational materials should be evaluated. Intelligent software that offers personalized recommendations should also have an algorithm which learns with statistics and it should make predictions, as well. Technical artificial neural networks are used very often for this purpose.

In terms of progress, carrying out a curriculum design in MOOCs is as much important as producing the performance values of this design.

Figure 3. Artificial intelligence in the process of determining program qualifications

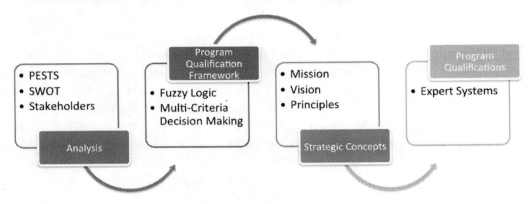

Intelligent Interface MOOCs

The level of learner's skills and perceptions in the learning environment for this course is keeping track of learner's all movements and searches on the learning platform with an artificial intelligence software working on the interface. While this is easily ensured for a product sale, it should be emphasized that it has to be used in learning environments which are more important for humanity, as well. The most suitable platform for this learning environment is MOOCs. Or in other words, intelligent MOOCs.

In order that the MOOCs which are the interactive learning platform of students can be "specific to a real person", many data such as the movements of the individual in the education module, his/her perception and interest of educational materials should be stored by a learning algorithm which operates on the interface (artificial intelligence). They should be reinforced with data which would contribute to the learning process of the algorithm. In fact, a learning model designed specifically to a person must be designated from end to end.

While the educational material or interface is being modeled, it should be written that all of this modeling should be made according to the strategies designated with artificial intelligence techniques. Only the field which is going to use the student is being asked of its opinion while creating an education model. The opinion of the student on this matter is not being paid attention to. It should be considered that the literature system is student-based and the stakeholders should not be neglected strategically. While carrying out MOOC design, strategies in which stakeholders are included by using real student-based approach must be designated.

CONCLUSION AND RECOMMENDATIONS

Legg and Hutter's (2006) A Collection of Definitions of Intelligence in the article examined 53 different definitions of intelligence. Although the definitions have strong relationships with each other, they cannot make a definite definition and reported the following results.

- A property that an individual agent has as it interacts with its environment or environments.
- Is related to the agent's ability to succeed or profit with respect to some goal or objective.

- Depends on how able to agent is to adapt to different objectives and environments.

Artificial intelligence is defined as intelligence done by the machine by means of software. Many scientists argue that some mathematical calculations should only be left to artificial intelligence. Some of the calculations that cannot be solved even by the smartest person seem to be child's play for artificial intelligence. However, scientists who define the definition of intelligence with their imagination and emotions also reveal the superiority of human intelligence. However, no one can claim that there will be no artificial intelligence that learns imagination and emotion in the near future by machine learning. Studies on this subject are ongoing. New structures can be developed with artificial intelligence applications in different learning services. With the development of artificial intelligence applications, the system can offer students personalized services and technologies; they can be used for functions such as introducing the system and defining new programs (Ugur & Kurubacak, 2019).

At this point, the focus of the development of humanity is the education itself, while the education has been affected by these developments. eLearning and MOOCs use the opportunity of scientific and technological developments. The rapid change in information technologies and the intensive use of the internet have led to fundamental changes in human life. Educational tools and learning platforms have also adapted to this change. In this context, MOOCs are a learning platform that presents differences and opportunities in traditional learning systems. MOOC vards offers many opportunities, but also weaknesses. To include the data from the stakeholders in the decision process in order to eliminate these weaknesses and increase the coefficient of the opportunities offered; We recommend using MCDM and artificial intelligence techniques together. At the same time, the machine learning and deep learning and learning platform should be continued to be real student-friendly.

REFERENCES

Aleven, V., Poposcu, O., Sewall, J., & Xhakaj, F. (2015). *The Beginning of a Beautiful Friendship? Intelligent Tutoring Systems and MOOCs.* Paper presented at International Conference on Artificial Intelligence in Education, Madrid, Spain.

Allahverdi, N. (2002). *Uzman Sistemler Bir Yapay Zeka Uygulaması*. Ankara, Turkey: Atlas Yayın Dağıtım.

Amin, S. H., Razmi, J., & Zhang, G. (2011). Supplier selection and order allocation based on fuzzy SWOT analysis and fuzzy linear programming. *Expert Systems with Applications*, *38*(1), 334–342. doi:10.1016/j.eswa.2010.06.071

Bostrom, N. (2001). *Transhumanist Values*. Retrieved from https://nickbostrom.com/tra/values.html

Bozkurt, A. (2015). Kitlesel Açık Çevrimiçi Dersler [Massive Online Open Courses - MOOCs]. *sayısal bilgi çağında yaşamboyu öğrenme fırsatı AUAd*, *1*(1), 56-81.

Bozkurt, A. (2016). *Identifying interaction patterns and teacher-learner roles in connectivist massive open online courses* (Doctoral dissertation). Anadolu University, Turkey.

Bozkurt, A., Akgün-Özbek, E., & Zawacki-Richter, O. (2017). Trends and patterns in massive open online courses: Review and content analysis of research on MOOCs (2008-2015). *The International Review of Research in Open and Distributed Learning*, *18*(5). doi:10.19173/irrodl.v18i5.3080

Bozkurt, A., & Aydın, C. H. (2015). *Satisfaction, Preferences and Problems of a MOOC*. Paper presnted at the Association for Educational Communications and Technology (AECT) 2015 International Convention, Indianapolis, IN.

Cheng, Y. M., & McInnis, B. (1980). An algorithm for multiple attribute, multiple alternative decision problem based on fuzzy sets with application to medical diagnosis. *IEEE Transactions on Systems, Man, and Cybernetics, SMC-10*, 645–650.

Clark, D. (2013). *MOOCs: taxonomy of 8 types of MOOC*. Retrieved from http://donaldclarkplanb.blogspot.se/2013/04/moocs-taxonomy-of-8- types-of-mooc.html

Çolak, M., & İhsan, K. (2017). Prioritization of renewable energy alternatives by using an integrated fuzzy MCDM model: A real case application for Turkey. *Renewable & Sustainable Energy Reviews, 80*, 840–853. doi:10.1016/j.rser.2017.05.194

Conole, G. (2014). A new classification schema for MOOCs. *The International Journal for Innovation and Quality in Learning, 2*(3), 65-77.

Daradoumis, T., Bassi, R., Xhafa, F., & Caballé, S. (2013). A review on massive e-learning (MOOC) design, delivery and assessment. In *P2P, Parallel, Grid, Cloud and Internet Computing (3PGCIC), 2013 Eighth International Conference on* (pp. 208-213). IEEE.

Ebben, M., & Murphy, J. S. (2014). Unpacking MOOC Scholarly Discourse: A Review of Nascent MOOC Scholarship Learning. *Media and Technology, 39*(3), 328–345. doi:10.1080/17439884.2013.878352

Ferguson, R., Sharples, M., & Beale, R. (2015). MOOCs 2030: a future for massive open online learning. In C. J. Bonk, M. M. Lee, T. C. Reeves, & T. H. Reynolds (Eds.), *MOOCs and Open Education around the World* (pp. 315–326). Abingdon, UK: Routledge. doi:10.4324/9781315751108-36

Fullér, R. (1995). *The Lecture Notes, Neural Fuzzy Systems*. Abo Akademi University. Retrieved from http://uni-obuda.hu/users/fuller.robert/ln1.pdf

Ghazinoory, S., Esmail Zadeh, A., & Memariani, A. (2007). Fuzzy SWOT analysis. *Journal of Intelligent & Fuzzy Systems, 18*, 99–108.

Ghorbani, M., Velayati, R., & Ghorbani, M. M. (2011). Using Fuzzy TOPSIS to Determine Strategy Priorities by SWOT Analysis. *International Conference on Financial Management and Economics, Proceeding, 11*, 135-139. Retrieved from http://www.ipedr.com/list-36-1.html

Guàrdia, L., Maina, M., & Sangrà, A. (2013). MOOC design principles: A pedagogical approach from the learner's perspective. *eLearning Papers*, (33).

Hebb, D. O. (1949). *The Organization of Behavior -a Neuropsychological Theory*. John What & Sons. Inc. Available at http://s-f-walker.org.uk/pubsebooks/pdfs/The_Organization_of_Behavior-Donald_O._Hebb.pdf

Hosseini-Nasab, H., Hosseini-Nasab, A., & Milani, A. S. (2011). Coping with imprecision in strategic planning: A case study using fuzzy SWOT analysis. *IBusiness, 3*(1), 23–29. doi:10.4236/ib.2011.31004

İçen, D., & Günay S. (2014). Uzman Sistemler ve İstatistik. *İstatistikçiler Dergisi: İstatistik ve Aktüerya, 7,* 37-45.

Jasinevičius, R., & Petrauskas, V. (2006). Dynamic SWOT Analysis as a Tool for System Experts. *Engineering Economics, 5*(50), 33-35.

Kaklauskas, A., Amaratunga, D., Haigh, R., & Kuzminske, A. (2016). Intelligent mooc for the disaster resilience dprof programme. In *Proceedings of the 6th International Conference on Building Resilience: building resilience to address the unexpected*. Massey University / The University of Auckland, New Zealand. Retrieved from http://eprints.hud.ac.uk/id/eprint/30295/

Karatop, B., Kubat, C., & Uygun, Ö. (2018). Determining the Strategies on Turkish Automotive Sector Using Fuzzy AHP Based on the SWOT Analysis. *Sakarya University Journal of Science, 22*(5), 1–1. doi:10.16984aufenbilder.298875

Kay, J., Reimann, P., Diebold, E., & Kummerfeld, B. (2013). *MOOCs: So Many Learners, So Much Potential, AI and Education*. IEEE Computer Society.

Kennedy, J. (2014). Characteristics of massive open online courses (MOOCs): A research review, 2009-2012. *Journal of Interactive Online Learning, 13*(1).

Kheirkhah, A. S., Esmailzadeh, A., & Ghazinoory, S. (2009). Developing strategies to reduce the risk of hazardous materials transportation in Iran using the method of fuzzy SWOT analysis. *Transport, 24*(4), 325–332. doi:10.3846/1648-4142.2009.24.325-332

Kubat, C., (2012). MATLAB: Yapay Zeka ve Mühendislik Uygulamaları. *Beşiz Yayınları*.

Kwakernaak, H. (1979). An algorithm for rating multiple-aspect alternatives using fuzzysets. *Automatica, 15*(5), 615–616. doi:10.1016/0005-1098(79)90010-4

Lee, K. L., & Lin, S. C. (2008). A fuzzy quantified SWOT procedure for environmental evaluation of an international distribution center. *Information Sciences, 178*(2), 531–549. doi:10.1016/j.ins.2007.09.002

Liyanagunawardena, T. R., Adams, A. A., & Williams, S. A. (2013). MOOCs: A systematic study of the published literature 2008-2012. *The International Review of Research in Open and Distributed Learning, 14*(3), 202-227. Retrieved from http://www.irrodl.org/index.php/irrodl/article/view/1455

McAuley, A., Stewart, B., Siemens, G., & Cormier, D. (2010). *Massive open online courses: Digital ways of knowing and learning, The MOOC model for digital practice*. Retrieved from http://www.elearnspace.org/Articles/MOOC_Final.pdf

Onah, D. F., & Sinclair, J. E. (2015). Massive open online courses: an adaptive learning framework. In *9th International Technology, Education and Development Conference* (pp. 2-4). Available at https://pdfs.semanticscholar.org/f616/7d7a9acd316fed0e5c7566f5fbdd876100f9.pdf

Önüt, S., Kara, S. S., & Efendigil, T. (2008). A hybrid fuzzy MCDM approach to machine tool selection. *Journal of Intelligent Manufacturing, 19*(4), 443–453. doi:10.100710845-008-0095-3

Öz, E., & Baykoç, Ö. F. (2004). Tedarikçi Seçimi Problemine Karar Teorisi Destekli Uzman Sistem Yaklaşımı. *Gazi Üniversitesi Mühendislik Mimarlık Fakültesi Dergisi, 19*(3), 275–286.

Öztemel, E. (2003). *Yapay Sinir Ağları*. Papatya yayıncılık.

Öztemel, E. (2009). *Endüstri Mühendisliğine Giriş*. Papatya Yayıncılık.

Öztemel, E. (2010). In L. Benyoucef & B. Grabot (Eds.), *Artificial Intelligence Techniques for Networked Manufacturing Enterprises Management*. Springer-Verlag London Limited.

Pappano, L. (2012). The Year of the MOOC. *The New York Times*. Retrieved from http://www.nytimes.com/2012/11/04/education/edlife/massive-open-online-courses-are-multiplying-at-a-rapid-pace.html

Pirim, H. (2006). Yapay Zeka. *Journal of Yasar University, 1*(1), 81–93.

Russell, S. J., & Norvig, P. (2016). *Artificial intelligence: a modern approach*. Pearson Education Limited.

Şen, Z. (2009). *Bulanık Mantık İlkeleri ve Modelleme (Mühendislik ve Sosyal Bilimler)*. İstanbul: Su Vakfı Yayınları.

Siemens, G. (2005). Connectivism: A learning theory for the digital age. *International Journal of Instructional Technology and Distance Learning, 2*(1), 3–10.

Siemens, G. (2012c). *Designing, developing and running (massive) open online courses*. Retrieved from http://www.slideshare.net/gsiemens/designing-and-running-a-mooc

Sonwalkar, N. (2013). The first adaptive MOOC: A case study on pedagogy framework and scalable cloud Architecture—Part I. In *MOOCs Forum* (Vol. 1, pp. 22-29). New Rochelle, NY: Mary Ann Liebert, Inc. Retrieved from https://www.liebertpub.com/doi/abs/10.1089/mooc.2013.0007

Trilling, B., & Fadel, C. (2012). *21st century skills: Learning for life in our times*. Hoboken, NJ: John Wiley & Sons.

Turban, E. (1993). Decision support systems (3rd ed.). Upper Saddle River, NJ: Prentice Hall.

Uğur, S., & Kurubacak, G. (2019). Technology Management Through Artificial Intelligence in Open and Distance Learning. In Handbook of Research on Challenges and Opportunities in Launching a Technology-Driven International University (pp. 338–368). Hershey, PA: IGI Global. doi:10.4018/978-1-5225-6255-9.ch018

Veletsianos, G., & Shepherdson, P. (2016). A systematic analysis and synthesis of the empirical MOOC literature published in 2013-2015. *The International Review of Research in Open and Distributed Learning, 17*(2), 198–221. doi:10.19173/irrodl.v17i2.2448

Wątróbski, J., Ziemba, P., & Wolski, W. (2016). MCDA-based Decision Support System for Sustainable Management – RES Case Study. *Proceedings of the Federated Conference on Computer Science and Information Systems*, 1235–1239. 10.15439/2016F489

Xi, B. D., Su, J., Huang, G. H., Qin, X. S., Jiang, Y. H., Huo, S. L., ... Yao, B. (2010). An integrated optimization approach and multi-criteria decision analysis for supporting the waste-management system of the City of Beijing, China. *Engineering Applications of Artificial Intelligence*, *23*(4), 620–631. doi:10.1016/j.engappai.2010.01.002

Yang, Q. (2018). Machine Learning as a UX Design Material: How Can We Imagine Beyond Automation, Recommenders, and Reminders? *AAAI Spring Symposium Series*.

Zadeh, L. (1965). Fuzzy Sets. *Information and Control*, *8*(3), 338–353. doi:10.1016/S0019-9958(65)90241-X

Zawacki-Richter, O. (2009). Research areas in distance education: A Delphi study. *International Review of Research in Open and Distributed Learning*, *10*(3), 1–17. doi:10.19173/irrodl.v10i3.674

Chapter 9
Transforming the Classroom Experience Through Transhumanism:
Education as the Learning Organization

Mary Beth Klinger
College of Southern Maryland, USA

Teresa L. Coffman
University of Mary Washington, USA

ABSTRACT

This chapter examines the intersection of transhumanism and the use of technology as a cognitive tool in education. Transhumanism is explored as a pedagogical philosophy to transform the limits of self by using educational technology tools to expand global networked knowledge. These tools include technologies that stimulate learning to expand and extend cognitive and metacognitive capabilities. The role of pedagogy is to create educative experiences that provide meaningful opportunities for students to cultivate deeper conceptual understandings. Students learn necessary skills and develop knowledge to improve conceptual competencies and cognitive capabilities. When human thought and capabilities are used in conjunction with technology as a cognitive instructional tool, the learning experience is transformed. The potential exists to extend the conceptual competencies of the learner, thus realizing the transhumanists' goal of transforming learning experiences and improving student potential.

INTRODUCTION

A core principle behind effective pedagogy is the importance of stimulating learning by transforming the learner and improving his or her intellectual capabilities. When considering technology as a tool in one's teaching practice, the instructor is determining best practices and suitable technology integration to enhance learning and natural cognitive understanding. This ideology supports the concept of transhumanism such that technology can be used to extend learning.

DOI: 10.4018/978-1-5225-8431-5.ch009

In this chapter, transhumanism is defined as the awareness to transform or overcome a cognitive constraint by merging the capabilities of digital technologies and learning to enhance a student's cognitive capabilities through the learning experience (Bostrom, 2005; Bostrom & Ord, 2005; Ettinger, 1972; Hughes, 2004; Masci, 2016). At its most basic level, transhumanism is a philosophy that supports an increase of human capabilities through technology to achieve full potential (LaForest, 2015).

By incorporating a transhumanist philosophy into the teaching practice, pedagogy and instruction become more flexible. Learning also becomes more flexible for the student. Learning goals are now tied into networks and processes that are implemented by the instructor. The student must contemplate his or her own thinking towards the learning goals and make personalized decisions on which digital environments are most conducive towards transforming his or her learning process and expanding individual goals of cognition. Instructors are required to create pathways for learners to work within and around the themes of the discipline, content, and the digital networks in order to help students progress towards augmenting their cognitive capabilities and improve their human condition in more meaningful and relevant ways (Wu, Hwang, Yang, & Chen, 2017).

The goal of this chapter is to show how technology-enhanced learning environments can enhance understanding and knowledge, thus allowing students to realize potential in accordance with the transhumanist world view. Because aspects of the transhumanist approach can be somewhat extreme, it is important to note that this chapter will not consider how digital networks can become the center of a learning paradigm or 'take-over' a learner's cognition. Instead, the integration of a dynamic digital network can be used as a cognitive apprentice to enhance a flexible learning environment. At the same time, due to the instructional design, it can also advance the learner's capabilities around his or her own personal interests and cognition thereby transcending and extending existing knowledge and abilities (Abma & Widdershoven, 2011; Collins, Brown, & Holum, 1991).

BACKGROUND

Transhumanism can support education and the learning organization by utilizing technology and allowing for slow, continuous, and incremental changes. Gradual changes rather than radical breakthroughs are the goal (LaForest, 2015). In addition, the current Internet supports a participatory culture. Users are able to curate and distribute knowledge. The World Wide Web network is not controlled by one user, but instead is shared among many users.

This has yielded a diverse flow of information and the opportunity for interpersonal connections to be made in meaningful ways. Additional advancements in technology have created opportunities for formal learning environments to connect to the Internet for the purpose of extending learning and cognition around learning goals. In addition, they also assist in developing authentic connections within the networked environment (Downes, 2007; Downes, 2014; Siemens, 2005).

Within this networked environment, no longer is learning considered an individual process. Instead, it is now interpersonal as well as dependent on outside influencers or participants within this network. Skill sets are needed to engage with the online network effectively and expertly, in order to challenge and extend one's own personal beliefs and knowledge (AlDahdouh, Osório, & Caires, 2015; Barnett, McPherson, & Sandieson, 2013).

In today's highly complex learning environment, digital technologies are required to be a transparent tool interconnected within knowledge networks with the purpose of transforming teaching and learning.

When considering learning from a more personalized, engaged, and transformative viewpoint, educators consider how to best utilize lesson goals to enhance students' cognitive understanding. Students develop the capability to adapt technology into their cognitive processing and are able to extend personal knowledge to complete more complex tasks to help solve more difficult problems (Bell, 2011; Sung, Chang, & Liu, 2016).

For instructors to facilitate meaningful collaboration using technology as a cognitive tool, they must design learning tasks that provide students the opportunity to explore, negotiate, and co-create existing knowledge in order to create and extend their own thinking and learning. This permits learning to be active and self-directed.

Within this instructional design, the incorporation of social participation involved in accessing, curating, and co-construction of new knowledge around meaningful learning tools helps to focus the process of learning around gaining and extending the construction of meaning within a social context. The instructor's design scaffolds each experience around learner needs while providing a seamless way for the learner to classify new problems into meaningful cognitive schema and then transfer new understanding as well as procedural knowledge from familiar schema to new problems (Barrett, Henzi, & Lusseau, 2012; van Merriënboer, 1997).

Social media facilitates this cooperative process by providing students a digital medium that seamlessly connects them to diverse discourse and interactions, providing an opportunity to construct meaningful connections around a co-construction of knowledge. This enhanced social connection through online media empowers learners to leverage their own capabilities helping them construct complex thinking capabilities in a social context enhancing their own learning (Barak, 2017; Tang & Hew, 2017).

As 21st century instruction focuses on relevant technological tools to engage and motivate learners, instructors work with students to seek out diverse information and then organize this information in meaningful ways. From this initial analysis, new knowledge can be synthesized to use in complex ways when creating new knowledge around curricular goals, student interest, and community concerns. As a result, students are learning and improving their cognitive competencies (Rienties & Toetenel, 2016; Walker, Jenkins & Voce, 2017).

MAIN FOCUS OF THE CHAPTER

In today's global educational environment, pedagogy and digital technologies are now merged to engage learners around complex cognitive processing to heighten thinking and learning. In order to do this effectively, instruction is designed that enables students to become more strategic, self-reliant, flexible and productive in their own cognitive abilities to enhance learning. The seamless integration of digital technologies as a cognitive tool allows students to connect to their learning and thinking as well as cooperatively connect with others around shared information and goals.

This seamless connection creates an experience that provides opportunities for learners to constructively and seamlessly contextualize learning in a transformative way enhancing their cognitive capabilities (Craft, 2011; Fullan & Langworthy, 2014; Kelly, 2012). When the science of teaching and the merging of digital technologies becomes more transparent in this potentially immersive and dynamic knowledge consuming and producing society, learning is enhanced and becomes more interconnected to the social network, enhancing human capabilities (Bostrom & Ord, 2005; Ettinger, 1972).

As social networks become more ubiquitous in the learning environment, more meaningful connections can be made around dynamic and diverse content. This focuses learner attention on other students rather than on the content or the instructor, which strengthens the learning community and provides opportunities for students to practice 21st century skills such as collaboration, knowledge construction, and knowledge sharing, thus developing more applied critical thinking skills around professional knowledge (Siemens & Conole, 2011).

This new paradigm supports the use of technology as a cognitive tool, providing opportunities for seamless integration of complex learning tasks to support a complex cognitive process. It is a process that is integrated with the connections to the content and the authentic nature of those connections. This creates a learning paradigm that perceives the use of technology in the classroom as cognitive apprentice. Similar to the transhumanism philosophy, it is one that is an extension of the learner due to its ability to provide a flexible learning opportunity around authentic experience. This interconnected approach enhances cognitive capabilities transcending students own abilities beyond the self in meaningful ways (Abma & Widdershoven, 2011; Collins, et al., 1991).

Human Learning Within Networks

Currently, educators are identifying strengths and weaknesses of networked communication technologies as they relate to their intended curricular goals, content knowledge, pedagogy, and their own unique knowledge of functions related to the digital tool. In so doing, they must consider how the tool and the communication network itself can be integrated to scaffold complex thinking and create conditions of learning that transform cognitive schemes enhancing learner capabilities. Specifically, what is the best approach towards integrating the global participatory network to merge experiential learning, non-linear thinking, and problem solving around concept learning to create a framework for learners to create patterns of thinking and processing that are dynamic and innovative (Ng'ambi, 2013; Rohse & Anderson, 2006; Koehler & Mishra, 2009; Wang, 2017)?

Social networks provide different requirements in conceptual learning, experiential learning, and collaborative learning. This makes these mutual networks useful for reflection and metacognitive activities where support and monitoring can take place (Laurillard, 2012). It is important that instruction encourages students to present beyond facts or statements and engage in more open questions and comments to aid in pushing thinking to higher and more engaged levels (Wichmann & Rummel, 2013).

For example, through the use of microblogs as a social media tool, students incorporate tags into their communications around statements, arguments, and/or questions that they are seeking a response. This encourages active metacognition. It is incumbent upon the instructor to have a clear purpose for any activity involving social media. The purpose of the activity must be identified, and any assessment criteria clearly laid out to provide structure for the learner. Also, it is critical that the teacher know when to redirect, monitor, or intervene when necessary. This results in a scaffolded learning experience using instructions on how to best construct understanding in a shared environment (Deng & Yuen, 2011; Laurillard, 2012).

Throughout systems of education, there has been an increase in global online collaboration that has helped personalize the learning experience by extending the traditional classroom and as a result, the capabilities of the learner. The fluidity and eclectic nature of this diverse network provides opportunities for more meaningful connections to new knowledge and experiences (Klinger & Coffman, 2012).

Learning in today's environment is becoming more personalized, engaged, and transformative due to the extension of capabilities generated by technology.

Technology can enhance students' natural capabilities, provide support for deeper thinking, allow for flexibility, and ultimately connect learners to the necessary cognitive skills needed. It can complement and extend complex thinking around curricular goals. This enhancement is dependent on the instructor's ability to connect meaningful learning around the network and content as well as to scaffold each experience in order for learners to make meaningful connections between technology and their own thinking and learning (Scheid, 1993).

Creating connections within social media environments, such as microblogging and cloud technologies, provides experiences for learners to engage with others around content themes and topics in more productive and relevant ways. Students investigate course themes in a shared environment around authentic problems and concerns helping to construct more complex thinking pathways that can be transferred into pragmatic settings (Andersson, Hatakka, Grönlund, & Wiklund, 2014; Coffman & Klinger, 2016).

Learning is no longer considered solely an individual process, but instead becomes a social process that is interconnected between learning goals and the flow of information within the network. The connections and collaborations being created within this network enhance cognition and learning due in part of the social and communitive space that the learner must engage in. This space complicates the traditional classroom, challenging the role of the instructor as well as the student. Learning outcomes become more authentic and personal for the learner and feedback provided comes from the network itself challenging the learner to think differently about the digital tools as well as their own learning and thinking (AlDahdouh, et al., 2015; Downes, 2007).

The instructor must provide context and challenge the learner to extend his or her thinking. They must guide the student's thinking and processing, as well as challenge the student to extend knowledge capabilities with the flow of information being introduced and produced within this network. This aids the learner who constantly interprets this complexity and his or her own competencies (Barnett, et al., 2013; Downes, 2014; Siemens, 2005).

As the traditional learning environments are augmented around the social network model of human learning, information and necessary skills that the learner must acquire to perform within this space around curricular goals becomes a focus of instruction. The instructor identifies the complexity of cognitive tasks necessary for the student to become proficient as well as easily transfer between the self and electronic devices (Bayne & Ross, 2013; Habermas, 2003).

Transforming Human Learning

Digital technologies have the potential to symbiotically transform one's pedagogical capacities. The seamless integration of digital technologies can transform learning environments around curricular goals through the incorporation of an authentic problem-based framework and at the same time mutually reinforce the opportunity of meaningful and engaged feedback loops. As engagement within the social network deepens, learners develop new behavioral dimensions to better interact with one another, the content, and reduce the uncertainty of their own learning. This changes the paradigm of learning by promoting increased interaction between content, learners, teachers, and with one another (Craig, Downey, Garnett, McGrath, & Myers, 2009).

This opportunity to transform the learning paradigm around ubiquitous and situated learning connects across the learner's world. Learning becomes a more immersive experience, a part of learning by doing. Learning shifts from information dissemination to content co-creation. This active engagement with learning through the immersion between the content and the social context of mobile technologies creates a seamless opportunity for collaboration and peer-to-peer experiences that are independent of time and place. It enables networks of people, organizations, and information to be connected simultaneously, thus blurring the lines between the social networking tools and learning itself (Barrett, et al., 2012; Callaghan & Bower, 2012).

The complexity of cognitive tasks means that more prolonged mental effort must be completed going beyond memorization to higher order thinking such as reasoning, monitoring, metacognition, comprehending, and calculating. This includes considering how to utilize technology to extend student capabilities and knowledge beyond their own known abilities (Leong, Ibrahim, Dalvi-Esfahani, Shahbazi, & Nilashi, 2018).

Technology as a cognitive tool identifies a need for flexibility within the learning environment and the learner themselves. As learners begin expanding their thinking and memory by participating in this knowledge network organized by outside influences, peers, and facilitated by the instructor, technology creates the potential for enhanced capabilities. For this enhanced capability to be purposeful, adoption must be seamless for both the instructor and student because they must become dependent upon the connective functions of this new network to both engage and create purposeful learning within it (Sanakulov & Karjaluoto, 2015).

Students begin to move beyond simple capabilities and expected outcomes within a traditional learning environment to that of acquisition of knowledge. And from knowledge to an extension of self and a more immersive and relevant learning experience that uses available technologies to construct and then maintain more complex thinking skills around course topics and real-world experience.

For students, this has the potential to heighten the learning experience and they are introduced to relevant tools to extend their capabilities in meaningful ways. As an educator, this disrupts one's pedagogy and the purpose of instruction, extending a traditional experience and intended outcomes so learning can become more personal, skill-based, as well as more strategic, flexible, self-reliant, cooperative, and productive yielding students who are life-long learners beyond the classroom experience (Chen, Castro-Alonso, Paas, & Sweller, 2017; Scheid, 1993).

As the traditional learning environment continually adjusts to incorporate this fluid digital network, it must discover strategies to incorporate its unpredictability and fluidity of information and networked experiences that evolve. Instructors must prepare students to be active participants in this environment and at the same time to begin taking control of their own learning from this environment. Students begin to co-design the environment and their experiences self-assessing, identifying, connecting to, and developing information. They are beginning to personalize learning (Andrews, 2011; Nance & Straub, 1996; Siemens, 2005).

This networked environment becomes an extension of the learner and extends the curriculum. As the social connections within the network are contextualized, learning within this tool becomes seamless. The learner and the functions of the tools within this social network are enhanced both by their fluidity as well as through the connectedness of others and new knowledge being gained.

As the instructor plans for this experience, lessons are purposely designed that allow for meaningful performances achieved through complex cognitive processes such as identifying, evaluating, organizing, creating, and sharing thinking processes and new knowledge. This provides an authentic capability to the experience (Al-Sheri, 2011; DeSantis, Boyd, Marks, Putsch, & Shepler, 2017; Gagné, Wager, Golas & Keller, 2005; Kopcha, 2012).

These meaningful connections between this open network and student understanding about his or her own learning transforms the educative experience. A contextual authenticity around one's learning and the network itself has been established. Learners have the potential to recognize knowledge structures that have been identified on the social network, and they also have the ability to create new knowledge by participation in the learning activities (Craft, 2011; Kelly, 2012).

This creates a personal learning experience that includes an authentic opportunity for the learner to participate in a cyclical and recursive process that combines knowledge creation with a direct connection to the social network itself. This relevant context becomes an extension of the learner, the content, the instructor, and the network. Learning becomes more relevant in this context creating a utility of meaning and the ability to construct metacognitive abilities that require stronger connections to be developed around a continuum of shared knowledge and complex understandings around broader contexts (Boulton-Lewis & Tam, 2012; Fullan & Langworthy, 2014). The essence of transhumanism has been accomplished.

Self-efficacy and Reducing Cognitive Load

In the construction of one's own learning, there is need for self-efficacy. This is the belief that one possesses the necessary capabilities to succeed in a specific task. A course can build upon the social risks needed for students to enhance their human and cognitive capacities by constructing an ecosystem that develops strategies to improve necessary cognitive skills to actively engage with digital technologies, take unplanned risks, and continually develop these life-long learning capabilities (Dahlin, 2012; Walters & Kop, 2009).

To develop life-long learning skills, instruction can incorporate active problem-based learning strategies around social networks and intelligent technologies to better extend the diverse capabilities of learners.

This aids in extending the transhumanist creativity of thought to increase student's awareness of his or her own role and abilities in a technological advanced society by blurring the role of digital technologies and self (Hauskeller, 2012). It also broadens student understanding of what it means to be a valued member of the larger global community. Ultimately, it helps learners develop a more inclusive self-efficacy with a greater ethical and principled responsibility to society, its members, and the environment (Kurzweil, 1999; Papert, 1994).

The instructor focuses pedagogy on addressing authentic learning goals and encourages the use of technology as a cognitive tool. At the same time, the teacher must also consider how to prevent unnecessary cognitive load. Transhumanism focuses on using technology to overcome biological limitations and improve learning (Klichowski, 2015). In assimilating this approach, however, it is important not to frustrate the learner.

As learners begin acquiring diverse knowledge sets, they become introspective and contemplate their own learning within the complexity of this social network. This integration of authentic metacognitive activities combined with the diverse opinions and ideas of others creates a dissonance within the learner. They begin to have conflict with the social network, information, and their own understandings. This creates a sense of cognitive load and can pause the process of productive and meaningful learning. As the instructor identifies this dissonance, they can enhance this opportunity by facilitating and scaffolding a complex thinking process to engage the learner in extending their own understanding and at the same time, enhance the understanding of the group. This provides the skills needed for the learner to decipher, discuss, and debate in more meaningful ways within this public forum and can help extend their own thinking as well as the groups (McLoughlin & Lee, 2010; Vygotsky, 1978).

As the dissonance lessons, the process of learning allows the student to connect to their own abilities and the abilities of others in new ways. They create a stronger sense of self, and sharpen the skills needed to regulate their own learning. This sense of self-efficacy merges with the digital technologies, others, and their own existence within this network creating a more transformational experience. Students are creating a new learning paradigm, e.g. one that advances their own cognitive and emotional development, but also extends this development in to the community of practice (Merrill, 2002; Sipilä, 2014).

The integration of diverse technologies to include multimedia combined with the introduction of complex systems of searching, deciphering vast amounts of information, organizing diverse and oftentimes dynamic information into meaningful categories, and then finding and sharing this newfound knowledge in creative outlets can sometimes frustrate the learner, especially when course content becomes more complex. Learning must be scaffolded so that students are instructed on how to extend their thinking in a rationale step-by-step manner. From this place of comfort, learners can then digest new knowledge and begin to incorporate new tasks (Stanford, Crowe & Flice, 2010).

An additional common characteristic of using digital technologies in combination with learner capabilities is that of multitasking. This process of using a variety of electronic media at one time can hinder focus on the primary learning task. The cognitive overload that is created hinders a student's functioning. The process of multitasking during learning can adversely impact intended learning outcomes by reducing the focus of attention on necessary activities (Cain, Leonard, Gabrieli, & Finn, 2016; Cardoso-Leite, Kludt, Vignola, Ma, Green, & Bavelier, 2016).

Focused attention is integral to cognitive development. A goal of good pedagogy is to focus the attention of learners by engaging and creating interest, which is a mental state. When considering instructional design, the instructor must identify ways to focus the learner's mental state around the academic content, not just the digital technology. One way to do this is to design appropriate mental challenges that provide opportunities for learners to anticipate or challenge themselves around an authentic, yet solvable problem (Burak, 2012; Windschitl, 2002).

Constructing New Capabilities

The purposefulness of technology as a cognitive tool extends opportunities for learners to seamlessly integrate technologies to aid in more complex processing and extend their own cognitive abilities. Ultimately this helps to improve both individual and community functioning. In order to be successfully implemented, instructors must have a good understanding of their curriculum content, its authentic connections, learning and pedagogy theory, and knowledge of using digital technology as a cognitive tool in the discipline (Kirschner & Erkens, 2006).

The transhumanism process considers technology as a way to facilitate higher-order thinking in order to transform knowledge into workable actions or performances more authentically and meaningfully for the learner. In order to do this, students develop skills in both critical thinking and higher-order thinking about both the content as well as the technology (Ertmer, 1999; Motiwalla, 2007).

When considering the use of digital technologies as a cognitive tool, the educator must consider the ability of technologies to extend thinking and enhance cognitive potential. Tools can be identified that align to the instructional goals of the lesson as well as those that promote and cultivate thinking and continued learning. The purpose for integrating digital technology into the learning process is to enhance the intellectual performance of the learner and then have the student distribute knowledge gained from and between the digital tool and the construction of a performance or product with the purpose to extend knowledge and thinking capabilities (LaJoie & Derry, 1993).

Learning becomes more evident as digital devices become more accessible through mobile technologies. Both faculty and students have more potential to access this technology and as a result, technology becomes more transparent in the learning process, thus becoming an extension of cognitive capabilities and supporting the transhumanistic philosophy. This extension to the learning experience and the efficiency that defines it places the focus towards learning with the instructional tool or technology application (Kurzweil & Grossman, 2004; Masci, 2016).

As educators identify strengths and weaknesses of technologies that can enhance student cognition in the learning process, they must also consider the flexibility of their own pedagogical environment as well as the transparency of the learning experiences to transfer content knowledge (Koehler & Mishra, 2009; Ng'ambi, 2013; Wang, 2017).

Considering how digital social networks compliment one's pedagogy and curricular goals, the structure of learning environments take a different form. They begin to augment teaching as well as learning. This creates an environment that has the potential to aid the learning process as well as the learner.

Instruction must compliment the social cognitive capabilities of technologies by developing more complex opportunities to engage students with the content, their own thinking, and with others in meaningful ways to gain deeper conceptual understandings. The learner is encouraged to think more critically about his or her own learning and then share this understanding within the networked environment (Merrill, 2002; Kopcha, 2012; DeSantis, et al., 2017; Sipilä, 2014).

Microblogging provides a good example of this capability and the need to focus the learner during use of these social tools around curricular outcomes. A microblogging tool allows users to participate by typing brief amounts of information and can easily include hypertext and media. It is viewed as a casual conversation among individuals that have shared interest.

Microblogging is an example of constructing knowledge within a social context. Vygotsky (1978) supported this interaction with cultural tools that are available within the individual's environment to extend cognitive development. At the same time, these tools have the ability to engage students actively in the development of shared knowledge through the process of writing and the integration of multimedia extending the complexity of the communication and of one's own learning as well as the learning within the group (Miller, 1984; Jonassen, Wilson, Wang, & Grabinger, 1993).

A social communication tool such as microblogging allows students to both consider new information as well as actively engage in creating and sharing knowledge in this community easily and constructively. Students are now extending their thinking and their own understandings of that content in a meaningful way (Coffman & Klinger, 2018).

The tool and the dynamic connections that it provides enables the learner to construct meaningful conditions of their participation around learning goals, personal interests, and their understanding about their own learning. Through this process, they are transforming their cognitive schemes and attitudes toward the immersive integrated technology that they are using as well as around the enhanced educative experiences that have been created by using this technology to better inform their cognition and to ultimately transform their capabilities (Ertmer, 1999; Motiwalla, 2007; Gagné, et al., 2005).

The ubiquitous nature of this environment supports the construction of personalized learning allowing students to both interact with others and also actively participate and construct new knowledge, through building of connections, sharing and disseminating knowledge. When using microblogs such as

Twitter, Instagram, and Tumblr. students are actively creating and maintaining their own construction of beliefs using writing, hypertext, and multimedia while actively producing new mindsets and testing these mindsets within their shared global network.

The community of practice that is created in this network is complimented by its diverse views generating more opportunities for deeper pathways to learning. These pathways assimilate the cognitive skills needed to extend thinking by compounding and disseminating diverse information in order to extend personal connections to knowledge. This creates a sense of control over one's own learning as well as a sense of responsibility for the process of learning for the student and members of this shared network (Barron & Darling-Hammond, 2008).

In order to for learners to make deeper connections to knowledge, they must have access to an extensive range of viewpoints and experiences. As students continually participate within the social network and begin extending this network into a global sphere, they are introduced to a broader cultural, linguistic, and ethnically diverse possibility of varying viewpoints allowing for more complex learning to take place. This multiplicity provides more authentic opportunities for learners to experience and explore differing points of views. It extends the complexity of the social nature of relationships and showcases the importance that this ecosystem has on the development of complex cognitive processing capabilities (Lukman & Krajnc, 2012).

Social networks have the potential to shift how students' access and interact with information and as a result, begin to change their cognitive behaviors and capabilities. Within the social network, students are productive in their engagement with learning goals and their interactions with members of the diverse community of practice.

Within this context, the instructor provides scaffolding throughout this process with the instructional goal of extending the creation of complex thinking through structured activities and technologies, as well as encouraging diverse viewpoints of the participants to flourish and challenge learners within this global network. This helps to extend the learning process and transfer these skills to more complex processing capabilities.

As a result, the process of learning becomes more relevant and transformational. Students begin to better understand how they can transform their surrounding community and the broader society around their newly developed understandings based on their new and evolving social connections. This advances a student's own cognitive and emotional development, but also transfers these new complex skills to advance humankind (Bayne & Ross, 2013; Habermas, 2003).

Differentiation in Instruction

As the educational environment embraces the use of digital cognitive tools, the learning experience becomes more vibrant and real-world relevant. The instructor considers digital tools as an augmentation of the learning process and an extension to the overall pedagogical message of a particular lesson or unit. As a result, pedagogy becomes concentrated on more complex cognitive processing around learning goals and authentic application of new and/or compounded knowledge.

In many of today's classrooms, learning environments are configured around ideals of personalization and individualization. This standard supports instruction around a differentiated model. Students are presented with learning experiences that are designed to align to their individual learning readiness. Based on this attention to readiness, differentiation benefits students due to its capacity to provide sufficient depth and complexity for individual or groups of students, resulting in stimulating learning (Wallace, Bernardelli, Molyneux, & Farrell, 2012).

When determining best practices for individual students and corresponding learning goals, instructors can use this differentiation model to incorporate specific instructional strategies and tools to create an engaging lesson that aids in extending a student's complex thinking capabilities (Pham, 2012; Tomlinson & Kalbfleisch, 1998). Differentiated instructional design comprises recognizing and planning for individual learning styles, a group approach that aligns to learner interest, ability, and topic, continued and meaningful assessment to determine gaps in understanding or even acceleration, and processing and managing the technological tools and classroom environment to continually adjust learning and content as needed (Chan & Yuen, 2014; Tomlinson, 1999).

In turn, students focus their varying capabilities and talents in order to immerse themselves into the process of learning and the seamless application of digital tools. The instructor ensures that the process is appropriate to achieve learning goals and educational needs in order for students to obtain necessary knowledge, understanding, and skills.

With this pedagogical expertise, the seamless integration of digital tools and sufficient depth and complexity of learning activities, learners advance from lower order thinking (remembering) to higher order thinking skills (understanding, applying, evaluating, and creating) thereby enhancing student competence and overall learning dispositions (Anderson, Krathwohl, Airasian, Cruikshank, Mayer, Pintrich, Raths, & Wittrock, 2001; Hymer, Watkins, Dawson, & Buxton, 2015; Yuen, Chan, Chan, Fung, Cheung, Kwan, & Leung, 2016).

Through differentiated instruction and technology integration, students can repurpose or 'mash' diverse content to create new representations of their own understandings. They can extend their thinking and overall learning. In turn, this extends the learning within the social network of the community itself. This adds a complexity to the process of learning. No longer is learning individual and requiring recall, but in this current transhumanist state, the teacher has extended this recall towards new knowledge construction by the individual student and ultimate enhancement of knowledge by the student's entire social group.

Globalization and the Learning Organization

Digital technologies continue to advance the global marketplace. This advancement has altered organizations and extended into local communities and educational institutions worldwide. As society continues to evolve and individuals become more enmeshed with technology, learning organizations find themselves supporting transhumanism with regards to improving processes and overcoming human limitations (Transhumanism in Higher Education, 2015). A new paradigm is thus constructed that embodies ethical considerations, communication and infrastructure considerations, and the merging of technology into human thought.

Globalization has made changes inevitable in almost every country around the globe. This continued process of interaction and expansion among ideas, people, and technologies has aided in removing perceived boundaries allowing for more engagement and discourse in an expanding global communication network with the purpose of connecting a diverse populace and with the potential to influence human performance and thought (Appadurai, 2001; Eisenberg, 2017a; Eisenberg, 2017b).

Communication technologies and overall infrastructure continue to improve and at the same time challenge the human condition due to availability and ability of individuals and groups to obtain, create, and share vast amounts of knowledge on a variety of topics using a collective sense of applied reason.

This communication access has potential for educators to utilize emerging technologies to assist in deepening the intellectual capacity of learners as well as to enhance cognitive processing.

As global educators begin to use and incorporate emerging technologies as a cognitive tool and consider the ideas of the traditional definition of transhumanism, they must also adhere to the ideals of integrating emerging social technologies to help their learners scaffold their thinking and information processing. Technology tools can be used to organize, manage, and create knowledge. They can help transcend one's own physical location and further construct a global identity. This can be a seamless process especially as these technologies become more mobile and accessible.

As knowledge becomes more disparate on this shared global network, information literacy must be central, especially as technology begins to further merge into human thought and actions. Learners must obtain the ability of organizing and accessing diverse and eclectic information to continually connect to the world around them and challenge their thinking and beliefs while at the same time achieving curricular goals obscuring the boundaries between pedagogy, learning, communities of the world, and global communication technologies (Gee, 2013; Collins & Halverson, 2009).

SOLUTIONS AND RECOMMENDATIONS

As the goal of transhumanism is to transform the self beyond original capacities, this chapter explored how the process of learning can be transformed, and knowledge and capabilities extended, by improving one's pedagogy through the seamless integration of communication technologies enabling access to information about the world as it relates to curricular goals in order to expand cognitive processing (Abowd & Mynatt, 2000; Harley, Poitras, Jarrell, Duffy, & LaJoie, 2016).

Authentic problems can be solved creatively, and curricular goals met using technology such that a convergence of appropriate learning technologies in combination with pedagogy is achieved (Rienties & Toetenel, 2016; Walker, et al., 2017). This sense of a holistic convergence of communication technologies and the symbiotic nature of teaching and learning to cultivate knowledge seamlessly around a social learning ecosystem eliminates the confinement of a traditional classroom.

Educators are now seamlessly blending the essence of transhumanism, transcending the material in order to create an enhanced existence. Students are learning from and within a global network using digital communication technologies and extending knowledge around a meaningful and relevant context (Aksenov & Аксёнов, 2016; Dabbagh, Benson, Denham, Joseph, Al-Freih, Zgheib, Fake, & Zhetao, 2016; Stewart, 2010).

Today, this revolution of technology and communication accessibility has created opportunities to reach a diverse group of individuals easily and in real-time across the traditional boundaries of local and emerging global communities of learners and creators of knowledge. This ease of access and ability to create and share knowledge creates an opportunity of ubiquitous communication capabilities transcending human capabilities between communities and learning organizations. This engaged and open connectivity creates opportunities for educators to connect learners to relevant content and higher cognitive skills, as well as the cultural influences available through this open communications network (Hennig-Thurau, Malthouse, Friege, Gensler, Lobschat, Rangaswamy, & Skiera, 2010; Kaplan & Heinlein, 2010).

FUTURE RESEARCH DIRECTIONS

While this chapter identified teaching strategies and digital tools that can be implemented to engage learners to develop cognitive strategies to heighten learning as well as suggested how to enable students to become more strategic, self-reliant, flexible and productive in their own learning, the issue of ethics with regards to transhumanist tendencies as well as the technological digital divide should be examined more fully in future research.

Ethical Use

As new and emerging technologies become more accessible, the new knowledge sets of ethical and equitable use of hyperlinked media must be considered and explored by students in meaningful ways to ensure that they construct the personal responsibility and skill sets needed when working and learning within this global network environment. Students must consider what it means to extend their own representation of meaning through the intermixing and repurposing of found information on the Internet and in an online context. Digital literacy skills must be discovered, modeled, and practiced around structured learning experiences that extend students multiliteracies in order to support them in developing and then strengthening these necessary 21st century competencies (Ashburn & Floden, 2006; Bayne, 2014; Jewitt, 2008).

There is a new emerging paradigm within this open network. It begins with the seamlessness of technologies and the students' ability to freely explore, access, and distribute information on demand. This is coupled with the capability of access to an open network without limitation. This extension of access, community, and diverse knowledge sets extends possibilities of cognitive enhancement in more authentic and diverse ways. It brings about a creative, engaged, and active process to knowledge construction that changes as the community of practice itself begins to evolve and transform. The paradigm that is created by this social network transforms the traditional instructional design modalities into a more dynamic extension of the networked community resulting in a complex cognitive extension of the learner (Binkley, Erstad, Herman, Raizen, Ripley, Miller-Ricci, & Rumble, 2012; Voogt & Roblin, 2012).

This swift progression requires educational institutions and learning organizations to move out of their comfort zones and use technology to co-generate ideas and support knowledge building and sharing in the most ethical manner possible. It identifies a new landscape of ethics and the possible ramifications of human limitations and intelligent technologies that provides opportunities for applied reasoning and critical deduction (Opdebeeck, 2017; Bayne, & Ross, 2013). Students must be made aware of the ethical implications of utilizing and applying this open and accessible information as they develop and obtain these 21st century skills.

Inequity in Technology Access

Presently, digital technologies that use an open online ecosystem are supported most everywhere around the globe; however there still exists a significant digital divide and lack of access to available technologies. Governments, corporations, and educational institutions around the world have a responsibility to aid in developing opportunities for learners to gain digital literacies as well as more opportunities for using technologies as a cognitive apprentice and to lessen the systematic divide experienced by many students (Bauer, 2018; Shelton, 2017).

Globalization has made changes inevitable in almost every country heightening inequity within nations and across the world. This inequity continues to create a systemic separation between the haves and have nots creating barriers to global social learning and the accessibility and ability to use technology as a transformative tool to engage students in enhanced cognitive processing.

To combat this inequity, access to available technologies must be developed to provide bridges of opportunities for learners to gain necessary digital literacies in constructing competitive workforce skills in this global economy through the diversity of technologies as a cognitive apprentice. As the transparent integration of these technologies increases worldwide, it is hoped that the systematic divide will lessen and learning around the use of technology will both support the learner's natural cognitive abilities and allow enhancement of these capabilities for more complex cognitive processing (Bauer, 2018; Shelton, 2017; Freire, 1972).

Information is becoming more readily available through the Internet, but the digital divide continues. Those with access to this technology are afforded the capacity to retrieve information with search terms and a click of a button. It is necessary to provide opportunities for all students to learn and extend their capabilities through technology supported in the educational process.

CONCLUSION

This chapter presented a critical analysis on creating educational experiences within the context of educational learning organizations and the use of transhumanism to improve human mental and physical capabilities through technological means. Various pedagogical methods were explored that support technologies and transform learning experiences to enhance the instructive process within education. It also expanded awareness with regards to facilitating self-efficacy, as well as the relationship between individuals, global communities, and digital technologies to engage the learner in complex cognitive processing in this transhumanist era.

In a culturally diverse and inclusive academic environment, students' cognitive development extends beyond the broader context of the classroom environment. When students are asked to relate learning to authentic problems, and then apply the necessary capabilities to best solve complex organizational or societal problems in a real-world context, deeper learning can occur. In total, students are able to gain a better understanding of how technologies and human knowledge converge to help transform digital and human systems to aid in transforming their communities and/or learning organizations (Habermas, 2003; Snaza, Appelbaum, Bayne, Carlson, Morris, Rotas, Sandlin, Wallin, & Weaver, 2014).

Educators have the potential to extend the boundaries of communication technologies and extend one's own pedagogical beliefs around this ideal of transhumanism. As was emphasized throughout the chapter, the emphasis is on stimulating complex cognitive processing using digital technologies to help transform learner capabilities to achieve a new way of thinking about one's own pedagogy and learning (Coffman & Klinger, 2014; Hughes, 2010).

Classroom environments provide challenges and opportunities for students to learn about the global nature of topics and emerging technologies can provide synergy and collaboration opportunities to unite communication between students, the instructor, and the world as a whole (Dahlin, 2012). Educators provide opportunities for students to construct learning strategies in order to efficiently and effectively master skills and secure the knowledge necessary to be successful global citizens. Presenting students with authentic problems and available technologies can aid in driving learning experiences and provide an interconnectedness between academic expertise and real world understanding to fundamentally improve the learning process (Bowen, 2012).

REFERENCES

Abma, T. A., & Widdershoven, G. A. M. (2011). Evaluation as a rationally responsible practice. In N. K. Denzin & Y. S. Lincoln (Eds.), *The Sage handbook of qualitative research* (4th ed.; pp. 669–684). Thousand Oaks, CA: Sage.

Abowd, G. D., & Mynatt, E. D. (2000, March). Charting past, present, and future research in ubiquitous computing. *ACM Transactions on Computer-Human Interaction, 7*(1), 29–58. doi:10.1145/344949.344988

Aksenov, I. V., & Аксёнов, И. В. (2016). Trans-humanism as an anthropological problem. *Journal of Siberian Federal University. Humanities and Social Sciences, 3*(9), 678–686.

Al-Sheri, S. (2011). Connectivism: A new pathway for theorizing and promoting mobile language learning. *International Journal of Innovation and Leadership in Teaching of Humanities, 1*(2), 10–31.

AlDahdouh, A., Osório, A., & Caires, S. (2015). Understanding knowledge network, learning and connectivism. *International Journal of Instructional Technology and Distance Learning, 12*(10), 3–21.

Anderson, L. W., Krathwohl, D. R., Airasian, P. W., Cruikshank, K. A., Mayer, R. E., Pintrich, P. R., ... Wittrock, M. C. (2001). *A taxonomy for learning, teaching, and assessing: A revision of Bloom's taxonomy of educational objectives*. New York: Pearson, Allyn & Bacon.

Andersson, A., Hatakka, M., Grönlund, Å., & Wiklund, M. (2014). Reclaiming the students–Coping with social media in 1:1 schools. *Learning, Media and Technology, 39*(1), 37–52. doi:10.1080/17439884.2012.756518

Andrews, R. (2011). Does e-learning require a new theory of learning? Some initial thoughts. *Journal for Educational Research Online, 3*(1), 104–121.

Appadurai, A. (2001). *Globalization*. Durham, NC: Duke University Press. doi:10.1215/9780822383215

Ashburn, E. A., & Floden, R. E. (2006). *Meaningful learning using technology: What educators need to know and do*. New York: Teachers College Press.

Barak, M. J. (2017). Cloud pedagogy: Utilizing web-based technologies for promotion of social constructivist learning in science teacher preparation courses. *Journal of Science Education and Technology, 26*(5), 459–469. doi:10.100710956-017-9691-3

Barnett, J., McPherson, V., & Sandieson, R. M. (2013). Connected teaching and learning: The uses and implications of connectivism in an online class. *Australasian Journal of Educational Technology*, *29*(5), 685–698. doi:10.14742/ajet.243

Barrett, L., Henzi, S. P., & Lusseau, D. (2012). Taking sociality seriously: The structure of multi-dimensional social networks as a source of information for individuals. *Philosophical Transactions of the Royal Society of London. Series B, Biological Sciences*, *367*(1599), 2108–2118. doi:10.1098/rstb.2012.0113 PMID:22734054

Barron, B., & Darling-Hammond, L. (2008). Teaching for meaningful learning: A review of research on inquiry-based and cooperative learning. In L. Darling-Hammond, B. Barron, P.D. Pearson, A.H. Schoenfeld, E.K. Stage, T.D. Zimmerman, G.N. Cervetti, & J.L. Tilson (Eds.), Powerful learning: What we know about teaching for understanding. San Francisco, CA: Jossey-Bass/John Wiley & Sons.

Bauer, J. M. (2018, May). The internet and income inequality: Socio-economic challenges in a hyperconnected society. *Telecommunications Policy*, *42*(4), 333–343. doi:10.1016/j.telpol.2017.05.009

Bayne, S. (2014). What's the matter with 'technology enhanced learning'? *Learning, Media and Technology*, *40*(1), 5–20. doi:10.1080/17439884.2014.915851

Bayne, S., & Ross, J. (2013). Posthuman literacy in heterotopic space: A pedagogic proposal. In R. Goodfellow & M. Lea (Eds.), *Literacy in the digital university: Critical perspectives on learning, scholarship, and technology* (pp. 95–110). London: Routledge.

Bell, F. (2011). Connectivism: Its place in theory-informed research and innovation in technology-enabled learning. *International Review of Research in Open and Distance Learning*, *12*(3), 98. doi:10.19173/irrodl.v12i3.902

Binkley, M., Erstad, O., Herman, J., Raizen, S., Ripley, M., Miller-Ricci, M., & Rumble, M. (2012). Defining twenty-first century skills. In P. Griffin, B. McGaw, & E. Care (Eds.), *Assessment and teaching of 21st century skills* (pp. 17–66). Dordrecht, The Netherlands: Springer. doi:10.1007/978-94-007-2324-5_2

Bostrom, N. (2005, April). A history of transhumanist thought. *Journal of Evolution and Technology / WTA*, *14*(1).

Bostrom, N., & Ord, T. (2005). Status quo bias in bioethics: The case for cognitive enhancement. In N. Bostrom & J. Savulescu (Eds.), *Improving Humans*. Oxford, UK: Oxford University Press.

Boulton-Lewis, G. M., & Tam, M. (2012). *Active ageing, active learning. Issues and Challenges*. New York: Springer. doi:10.1007/978-94-007-2111-1

Bowen, J. A. (2012). *Teaching naked: How moving technology out of your college classroom will improve student learning*. San Francisco, CA: Jossey-Bass.

Burak, J. L. (2012). Multitasking in the university classroom. *International Journal for the Scholarship of Teaching and Learning*, *6*(2), 1–12. doi:10.20429/ijsotl.2012.060208

Cain, M. S., Leonard, J. A., Gabrieli, J. D., & Finn, A. S. (2016). Media multitasking in adolescence. *Psychonomic Bulletin & Review*, *23*(6), 1932–1941. doi:10.375813423-016-1036-3 PMID:27188785

Callaghan, N., & Bower, M. (2012). Learning through social networking sites–The critical role of the teacher. *Educational Media International, 49*(1), 1–17. doi:10.1080/09523987.2012.662621

Cardoso-Leite, P., Kludt, R., Vignola, G., Ma, W. J., Green, C., & Bavelier, D. (2016). Technology consumption and cognitive control: Contrasting action video game experience with media multitasking. *Attention, Perception & Psychophysics, 78*(1), 218–241. doi:10.375813414-015-0988-0 PMID:26474982

Chan, S., & Yuen, M. (2014). Creativity beliefs, creative personality and creativity-fostering practices of gifted education teachers and regular class teachers in Hong Kong. *Thinking Skills and Creativity, 14*, 109–118. doi:10.1016/j.tsc.2014.10.003

Chen, O., Castro-Alonso, J. C., Paas, F., & Sweller, J. (2017). Extending cognitive load theory to incorporate working memory resource depletion: Evidence from the spacing effect. *Educational Psychology Review, 30*(2), 483–501. doi:10.100710648-017-9426-2

Coffman, T., & Klinger, M. B. (2014, July-September). Collaboration and communication in the online classroom through a brain-based approach. *International Journal of Information Communication Technologies and Human Development, 6*(3), 42–52. doi:10.4018/ijicthd.2014070104

Coffman, T., & Klinger, M. B. (2016). Encouraging innovation through active learning and community building. In *Proceedings of Society for Information Technology & Teacher Education International Conference* (pp. 166-172). Chesapeake, VA: Association for the Advancement of Computing in Education (AACE).

Coffman, T., & Klinger, M. B. (2018). Using microblogging as a cognitive tool in the college classroom. In *Proceedings of Society for Information Technology & Teacher Education International Conference* (pp. 832-839). Washington, DC: Association for the Advancement of Computing in Education (AACE).

Collins, A., Brown, J. S., & Holum, A. (1991). Cognitive apprenticeship: Making thinking visible. *American Educator, 15*(3), 6–11.

Collins, A., & Halverson, R. (2009). *Rethinking education in the age of technology: The digital revolution and schooling in America*. New York: Teachers College Press.

Craft, A. (2011). *Creativity and education futures: Learning in a digital age*. Stoke-on-Trent, UK: Trentham Books.

Craig, A., Downey, S., Garnett, G., McGrath, R. E., & Myers, J. D. (2009). 12 Immersive Environments for Massive, Multiperson, Online Learning. In B. Cope & M. Kalantzis (Eds.), *In Ubiquitous Learning* (pp. 131–143). Champaign, IL: University of Illinois Press.

Dabbagh, N., Benson, A. D., Denham, A., Joseph, R., Al-Freih, M., Zgheib, G., . . . Zhetao, G. (2016). Social media. In Learning Technologies and Globalization Pedagogical Frameworks and Applications (pp. 21–26). New York: Springer International Publishing. doi:10.1007/978-3-319-22963-8_4

Dahlin, B. (2012). Our posthuman futures and education: Homo zappiens, cyborgs, and the new Adam. *Futures, 44*(1), 55–63. doi:10.1016/j.futures.2011.08.007

Deng, L., & Yuen, A. H. K. (2011). Towards a framework for educational affordances of blogs. *Computers & Education, 56*(2), 441–451. doi:10.1016/j.compedu.2010.09.005

DeSantis, J., Boyd, R., Marks, K., Putsch, J., & Shepler, T. (2017). Paradigm flip? Investigating technology-integrated history pedagogies. *Social Studies Research & Practice*, *12*(3), 258–279. doi:10.1108/SSRP-07-2017-0036

Downes, S. (2007, Feb. 3). *What connectivism is*. Half an Hour. Retrieved from https://halfanhour.blogspot.com/2007/02/what-connectivism-is.html

Downes, S. (2014, March 10). *The MOOC of One*. Retrieved from https://www.downes.ca/cgi-bin/page.cgi?presentation=336

Eisenberg, M. (2017a). Self-made: The body as frontier for the maker movement in education. In *Proceedings of the 7th Annual Conference on Creativity and Fabrication in Education (FabLearn '17)* (pp. 1-4). New York: Association for Computing Machinery (ACM). 10.1145/3141798.3141800

Eisenberg, M. (2017b). The binding of fenrir: Children in an emerging age of transhumanist technology. In *Proceedings of the 2017 Conference on Interaction Design and Children (IDC '17)* (pp. 328-333). New York: Association for Computing Machinery (ACM). 10.1145/3078072.3079744

Ertmer, P. A. (1999). Addressing first-and second-order barriers to change: Strategies for technology integration. *Educational Technology Research and Development*, *47*(4), 47–61. doi:10.1007/BF02299597

Ettinger, R.C.W. (1972), *Man into superman: The startling potential of human evolution and how to be part of it*. New York: St. Martin's Press.

Freire, P. (1972). *Pedagogy of the oppressed*. New York: Herder & Herder.

Fullan, M., & Langworthy, M. (2014). *A rich seam: How new pedagogies find deep learning*. London: Pearson.

Gagné, R. M., Wager, W. W., Golas, K. C., & Keller, J. M. (2005). *Principles of instructional design*. Belmont, CA: Wadsworth/Thomson Learning.

Gee, J. (2013). *The anti-education era: Creating smarter students through digital learning*. New York: Palgrave MacMillan.

Habermas, J. (2003). *The future of human nature*. Oxford, UK: Blackwell Polity.

Harley, J. M., Poitras, E. G., Jarrell, A., Duffy, M. C., & LaJoie, S. P. (2016). Comparing virtual and location-based augmented reality mobile learning: Emotions and learning outcomes. *Educational Technology Research and Development*, *64*(3), 359–388. doi:10.100711423-015-9420-7

Hauskeller, M. (2012). Reinventing cockaigne: Utopian themes in Transhumanist Thought. *The Hastings Center Report*, *42*(2), 39–47. doi:10.1002/hast.18 PMID:22733330

Hennig-Thurau, T., Malthouse, E. C., Friege, C., Gensler, S., Lobschat, L., Rangaswamy, A., & Skiera, B. (2010). The impact of new media on customer relationships. *Journal of Service Research*, *13*(3), 311–330. doi:10.1177/1094670510375460

Hughes, J. (2004). *Citizen cyborg: Why democratic societies must respond to the redesigned human of the future*. Cambridge, MA: Westview Press.

Hughes, J. (2010). Contradictions from the enlightenment roots of transhumanism. *The Journal of Medicine and Philosophy*, *35*(6), 622–640. doi:10.1093/jmp/jhq049 PMID:21135025

Hymer, B., Watkins, C., Dawson, E., & Buxton, R. (2015). Embedded voices: Building a non-learning culture within a learning enrichment programme. *Gifted Education International*, *31*(1), 5–24. doi:10.1177/0261429413498487

Jewitt, C. (2008). Multimodality and literacy in school classrooms. *Review of Research in Education*, *32*(1), 241–267. doi:10.3102/0091732X07310586

Jonassen, D. H., Wilson, B. G., Wang, S., & Grabinger, R. S. (1993). Constructivist uses of expert systems to support learning. *Journal of Computer-Based Instruction*, *20*(3), 86–94.

Kaplan, A. M., & Haenlein, M. (2010). Users of the world, unite! The challenges and opportunities of social media. *Business Horizons*, *53*(1), 59–68. doi:10.1016/j.bushor.2009.09.003

Kelly, R. (2012). *Educating for creativity: A global conversation*. Edmonton, Canada: Brush Education.

Kirschner, P. A., & Erkens, G. (2006). Cognitive tools and mindtools for collaborative learning. *Journal of Educational Computing Research*, *35*(2), 199–209. doi:10.2190/R783-230M-0052-G843

Klichowski, M. (2015). Transhumanism and the idea of education in the world of cyborgs. In H. Krauze-Sikorska & M. Klichowski (Eds.), *The educational and social world of a child. Discourses of communication, subjectivity and cyborgization*. Poznan, Poland: Adam Mickiewicz University Press.

Klinger, M. B., & Coffman, T. (2012). Building knowledge through dynamic meta-communication. In G. Kuruback, U. Demiray, & T. V. Yuzer (Eds.), *Meta-communication for reflective online conversations: Models for distance education*. Hershey, PA: IGI Global. doi:10.4018/978-1-61350-071-2.ch008

Koehler, M. J., & Mishra, P. (2009). What is technological pedagogical content knowledge? *Contemporary Issues in Technology & Teacher Education*, *9*(1), 60–70.

Kopcha, T. J. (2012). Teachers' perceptions of the barriers to technology integration and practices with technology under situated professional development. *Computers & Education*, *59*(4), 1109–1121. doi:10.1016/j.compedu.2012.05.014

Kurzweil, R. (1999). *The age of spiritual machines*. New York: Viking.

Kurzweil, R., & Grossman, T. (2004). Fantastic voyage: Live long enough to live forever. Stuttgart, Germany: Holtzbrinck Publishers.

LaForest, M. L. (2015, May). *Guiding transhumanism: The necessity of an ethical approach to transhumanism* (Tennessee Research and Creative Exchange Honors Thesis). Knoxville, TN: University of Tennessee.

LaJoie, S. P., & Derry, S. J. (1993). *Computers as cognitive tools*. New York: Routledge.

Laurillard, D. (2012). *Teaching as a design science: Building pedagogical patterns for learning and technology*. London: Routledge.

Leong, L. W., Ibrahim, O., Dalvi-Esfahani, M., Shahbazi, H., & Nilashi, M. (2018). The moderating effect of experience on the intention to adopt mobile social network sites for pedagogical purposes: An extension of the technology acceptance model. *Education and Information Technologies*, 1–22. doi:10.100710639-018-9726-2

Lukman, R., & Krajnc, M. (2012). Exploring non-traditional learning methods in virtual and real-world environments. *Journal of Educational Technology & Society*, *15*(1), 237–247.

Masci, D. (2016). Human enhancement: The scientific and ethical dimensions of striving for perfection. *Pew Research Center*. Retrieved from http://www.pewinternet.org/essay/human-enhancement-the-scientific-and-ethical-dimensions-of-striving-for-perfection/

McLoughlin, C., & Lee, M. J. W. (2010). Personalised and self-regulated learning in the Web 2.0 era: International exemplars of innovative pedagogy using social software. *Australasian Journal of Educational Technology*, *26*(1), 28–43. doi:10.14742/ajet.1100

Merrill, M. D. (2002). First principles of instruction. *Educational Technology Research and Development*, *50*(3), 43–59. doi:10.1007/BF02505024

Miller, C. (1984). Genre as social action. *The Quarterly Journal of Speech*, *70*(2), 151–167. doi:10.1080/00335638409383686

Motiwalla, L. F. (2007). Mobile learning: A framework and evaluation. *Computers & Education*, *49*(3), 581–596. doi:10.1016/j.compedu.2005.10.011

Nance, W. D., & Straub, D. W. (1996). An investigation of task/technology fit and information technology choices in knowledge work. *Journal of Information Technology Management*, *7*, 1–14.

Ng'ambi, D. (2013). Effective and ineffective uses of emerging technologies: Towards a transformative pedagogical model. *British Journal of Educational Technology*, *44*(4), 652–661. doi:10.1111/bjet.12053

Opdebeeck, H. (2017). The challenge of transhumanism in business. *Contributions to Conflict Management. Peace Economics and Development*, *26*, 251–260.

Papert, S. (1994). *The children's machine: Rethinking school in the age of the computer*. New York: Basic Books.

Pham, H. L. (2012). Differentiated instruction and the need to integrate teaching and practice. *Journal of College Teaching and Learning*, *9*(1), 13–20. doi:10.19030/tlc.v9i1.6710

Rienties, B., & Toetenel, L. (2016). The impact of learning design on student behavior, satisfaction and performance: A cross- institutional comparison across 151 modules. *Computers in Human Behavior*, *60*, 333–341. doi:10.1016/j.chb.2016.02.074

Rohse, S., & Anderson, T. (2006). Design patterns for complex learning. *Journal of Learning Design*, *1*(3), 82–91. doi:10.5204/jld.v1i3.35

Sanakulov, N., & Karjaluoto, H. (2015). Consumer adoption of mobile technologies: A literature review. *International Journal of Mobile Communications*, *13*(3), 244–275. doi:10.1504/IJMC.2015.069120

Scheid, K. (1993). *Helping students become strategic learners: Guidelines for teaching*. Cambridge, MA: Brookline Books.

Shelton, C. (2017). Giving up technology and social media: Why university lecturers stop using technology in teaching. *Technology, Pedagogy and Education, 26*(3), 303–321. doi:10.1080/1475939X.2016.1217269

Siemens, G. (2005). Connectivism: A learning theory for the digital age. *International Journal of Instructional Technology and Distance Learning, 2*(1), 3–10.

Siemens, G., & Conole, G. (2011). Special issue connectivism: Design and delivery of social networked learning. *International Review of Research in Open and Distance Learning, 12*(3), 1–6. doi:10.19173/irrodl.v12i3.1113

Sipilä, K. (2014). Educational use of information and communications technology: Teachers' perspective. *Technology, Pedagogy and Education, 23*(2), 225–241. doi:10.1080/1475939X.2013.813407

Snaza, N., Appelbaum, P., Bayne, S., Carlson, D., Morris, M., Rotas, N., ... Weaver, J. A. (2014). Toward a posthumanist education. *Journal of Curriculum Theorizing, 30*(2), 39–55.

Stanford, P., Crowe, M. W., & Flice, H. (2010). Differentiating with technology. *Teaching Exceptional Children Plus, 6*(4), 2–9.

Stewart, V. (2010). A classroom as wide as the world. In H. H. Jacobs (Ed.), *Curriculum 21: Essential education for a changing world* (pp. 97–114). Alexandria, VA: ASCD.

Sung, Y. T., Chang, K. E., & Liu, T. C. (2016). The effects of integrating mobile devices with teaching and learning on students' learning performance: A meta-analysis and research synthesis. *Computers & Education, 94*, 252–275. doi:10.1016/j.compedu.2015.11.008

Tang, Y., & Hew, K. F. (2017). Is mobile instant messaging (MIM) useful in education? Examining its technological, pedagogical, and social affordances. *Educational Research Review, 21*, 85–104. doi:10.1016/j.edurev.2017.05.001

Tomlinson, C., & Kalbfleisch, M. L. (1998). Teach me, teach my brain: A call for differentiated classrooms. *Educational Leadership*, 52–55.

Tomlinson, C. A. (1999). *The differentiated classroom: Responding to the needs of all learners*. Alexandria, VA: Association for Supervision and Curriculum Development.

Transhumanism in higher education: Social implications and institutional roles. (2015, May). *Proceedings of the Symposium on Emerging Technology Trends in Higher Education*. Retrieved from http://epubs.utah.edu/index.php/emerge/article/view/1362

van Merriënboer, J. J. G. (1997). *Training complex cognitive skills: A four-component instructional design model for technical training*. Englewood Cliffs, NJ: Educational Technology Publications.

Voogt, J., & Roblin, N. P. (2012). A comparative analysis of international frameworks for 21st century competences: Implications for national curriculum policies. *Journal of Curriculum Studies, 44*(3), 299–321. doi:10.1080/00220272.2012.668938

Vygotsky, L. (1978). *Mind in society: Development of higher psychological processes*. Boston: Harvard University Press.

Walker, R., Jenkins, M., & Voce, J. (2017). The rhetoric and reality of technology-enhanced learning developments in UK higher education: Reflections on recent UCISA research findings (2012–2016). *Interactive Learning Environments*, 1–11.

Wallace, B., Bernardelli, A., Molyneux, C., & Farrell, C. (2012). TASC: Thinking actively in a social context. A universal problem-solving process: A powerful tool to promote differentiated learning experiences. *Gifted Education International*, *28*(1), 58–83. doi:10.1177/0261429411427645

Walters, P., & Kop, R. (2009). Heidegger, digital technology, and postmodern education: From being in cyberspace to meeting on MySpace. *Bulletin of Science, Technology & Society*, *29*(4), 278–286. doi:10.1177/0270467609336305

Wang, Y. H. (2017). The effectiveness of integrating teaching strategies into IRS activities to facilitate learning. *Journal of Computer Assisted Learning*, *33*(1), 35–50. doi:10.1111/jcal.12164

Wichmann, A., & Rummel, N. (2013). Improving revision in wiki-based writing: Coordination pays off. *Computers & Education*, *62*, 262–270. doi:10.1016/j.compedu.2012.10.017

Windschitl, M. (2002). Framing constructivism in practice as the negotiation of dilemmas: An analysis of the conceptual, pedagogical, cultural, and political challenges facing teachers. *Review of Educational Research*, *72*(2), 131–175. doi:10.3102/00346543072002131

Wu, P. H., Hwang, G. J., Yang, M. L., & Chen, C. H. (2017). Impacts of integrating the repertory grid into an augmented reality-based learning design on students learning achievements, cognitive load and degree of satisfaction. *Interactive Learning Environments*, *26*(2), 221–234. doi:10.1080/10494820.2017.1294608

Yuen, M., Chan, S., Chan, C., Fung, D. C. L., Cheung, W. M., Kwan, T., & Leung, F. K. S. (2016). Differentiation in key learning areas for gifted students in regular classes: A project for primary school teachers in Hong Kong. *Gifted Education International*, *34*(1), 36–46. doi:10.1177/0261429416649047

ADDITIONAL READING

Axelrod, R., & Hamilton, W. D. (1981). The evolution of cooperation. *Science*, *211*(4489), 1390–1396. doi:10.1126cience.7466396 PMID:7466396

Barak, M. J. (2017). Science teacher education in the twenty-first century: A pedagogical framework for technology-integrated social constructivism. *Research in Science Education*, *47*(2), 283–303. doi:10.100711165-015-9501-y

Barkely, E. F., Cross, K. P., & Howell Major, C. (2014). *Collaborative learning techniques: A handbook for college faculty* (2nd ed.). San Francisco, CA: Jossey-Bass.

Barrett, L. (2011). *Beyond the brain: How body and environment shape animal and human minds*. Princeton, NJ: Princeton University Press. doi:10.2307/j.ctt7rvqf

Carrier, M. L., Cheever, N. A., Rosen, L. D., Benitez, S., & Chang, J. (2009). Multitasking across generations: Multitasking choices and difficulty ratings in three generations of Americans. *Computers in Human Behavior*, *25*(2), 483–489. doi:10.1016/j.chb.2008.10.012

Cziko, G. (2000). *The things we do: Using the lessons of Barnard and Darwin to understand the what, how and why of our behaviour*. Cambridge, MA: MIT Press.

Dewey, J. (1925). *Experience and nature*. Chicago, IL: Open Court.

Downes, S. (2010). New technology supporting informal learning. *Journal of Emerging Technologies in Web Intelligence*, *2*(1), 27–33. doi:10.4304/jetwi.2.1.27-33

Jeong, S. H., & Fishbein, M. (2007). Predictors of multitasking with media: Media factors and audience Factors. *Media Psychology*, *10*(3), 364–384. doi:10.1080/15213260701532948

Warschauer, M., & Grimes, D. (2007). Audience, authorship, and artifact: The emergent semiotics of Web 2.0. *Annual Review of Applied Linguistics*, *27*(1), 1–23.

KEY TERMS AND DEFINITIONS

Cognitive Capacity: The amount of information the human brain can retain.

Communities of Practice: A self-organized social network that shares similar interests around sharing of knowledge and experiences as well as a movement toward crowd-sourcing new ideas and complex cognitive development.

Complex Cognitive Processing: The conscious and mental capabilities that a person uses to think, reason, learn, understand, and remember.

Content Co-Creation: Ability to create and share content to transmit knowledge using social media in creative ways.

Mobile Technologies: Electronic devices that provide portability and enable learning.

Networked Environment: Developing and then continuing diverse connections to both people and information through communication technologies.

Personalized Learning: Instructors no longer distribute knowledge; instead students take on more control of the learning process and use electronic devices in transparent ways within an online community of learners.

Social Media: A transformative way to communicate and manage relationships.

Transparent Tool: An ethical and seamless practice of facilitating learning and improving learner performance by implementing and managing technological tools and processes into instruction and learning.

Chapter 10
Artificial Intelligence in the Era of Transhumanism Smart Phones

Okan Aksu
Trakya University, Turkey

ABSTRACT

The relationship between humans and machines has been a controversial topic throughout history. In the past, technology was viewed as a mere change in people's living conditions while today it is evident that it affects the nature of humanity itself. This very change can range from microscale structures, such as human DNA, to bigger structures, such as limbs. We have been aware that it is just the beginning for this change. According to the theory of transhumanism, further changes on the human body are expected with the rapid developments in technology. These changes will naturally not be limited to the human body. The increasing amount of interaction between humans and machines will result in the execution of more complicated and difficult tasks by machines instead of humans, which is the focus of the present study. There are many points where the humans and machines meet with technological developments, one of which is the thinking function of humans and its possible transfer to machines. The thinking capacity of machines is known as artificial intelligence.

INTRODUCTION

What was the inventor of the wheel thinking?

It is hard to answer that question as humans' needs and their way of thinking have evolved continuously throughout history, which also affected the attitudes towards technology from time to time. Since the beginning of our existence on Earth, human beings have always struggled to alter and transform the nature, environment and their bodies to improve the living conditions in order to attain more with less energy. The challenges presented by nature have forced humans with relatively limited physical power to transform their environments and produce the essential stuff for survival. As well as food and clothing, humans have built structures for accommodation to protect from the climatic conditions

DOI: 10.4018/978-1-5225-8431-5.ch010

making use of various methods and technologies. What they did first to achieve this was to understand their environment to explain the events and facts. Although people have tended to make use of myths during the process of "*noesis*" and "explanation" from time to time, the emergence and glorification of analytic thinking and knowledge has accelerated the pace of technological changes (İlin & Segal, 2000). However, the systematic development of current scientific methods and technologies we know and use today has emerged in a relatively short time compared to the whole history of humanity. Of course, the rapid emergence and development of science and technology can be approached in several different ways. First, the delayed and relatively slow-paced developments in science and technology despite the long history of evolution of human beings and the rise of civilizations can be explained with the social and economic problems, and political relations. From this standpoint, we can say that the attitudes of the holders of economic and political power in societies towards science and technology have been the main cause of the relatively slow pace of scientific and technological developments.

Humanity has gone through different phases and revolutions. Industrial Revolution, one of the milestones in the history of humanity, has unleashed and given acceleration to the power of technology. It is safe to say that economic reasons were the biggest motivation for the sudden interest in technology and science as the machine-made production is much more profitable compared to hand-made products. Secondly, from steam power to Artificial Intelligence, technology has always been something that states and governments want to hold and control and used as "a weapon" from past to present.

Today, technology is an irreplaceable part of life in every aspect. Thanks to technology, the production of goods and services has increased while it has been easier to access to information. The medical advances have improved the living conditions (better accommodation, modern medicine and more accessible food system) and increased life span. In other words, technology has greatly helped humans to manipulate the nature for their survival.

On the other hand, the emergence and spread of technology has not always been welcomed. There have always been people and groups criticizing strongly any new technology. In the past as in the present, it took time for individuals and societies to embrace the latest technologies for social, cultural and economic reasons. For instance, the delayed adoption of the printing press by the Ottomans is seen as one of the main causes of regression and depletion.

The individuals, groups and even societies having and making use of technology remain ahead of the game. There seems to be a huge gap between countries, groups or even individuals who have access to technology and the ones who do not. This means that the ones who have access to technology can develop in every field while the disadvantaged groups are to fall behind. Postman argues that the current gap between the two groups is a kind of social inequality and that it is the very entity of technology which creates this gap. He further states that the development and spread of computers have created "winners" and "losers" as there are people who get stronger by having access to technology as well as the people keeping away from technology and dropping back as a consequence (Postman, 2006, p. 13-31). Therefore, whether one has access and command to/of technology is a decisive factor for both individuals and societies.

Just as today's products with "cyclical popularity", there have been "popular" fields in the history of technology that have been shaped by the military, social and economic needs of the specific periods bringing forth various paradigms as a result. From a historical perspective, there have been certain technological periods, such as Steam Power and it seems that the era we are currently living in is the age of Artificial Intelligence (King, 2016, p. 224).

The Information Age is one of the underlying reasons for the rapid development and popularity of Artificial Intelligence technologies. With smart phones, users are able to access to any content and information immediately independent of time and space and the integration of Artificial Intelligence applications are a convenience to users.

The current paper focuses on Transhumanism as a phenomenon in the age of Artificial Intelligence. After examining the thinking capability of machines, the future perspectives will be discussed in the context of Transhumanism.

DEFINING TRANSHUMANISM

The human is a biological animal, which evolved approximately 200,000 years ago as the subspecies Homo sapiens sapiens (modern humans). The Western world's consensus on what is "normal" for a human biology, life span, intelligence and psychology established certain precedents. Outside these precedents would mean that a human is subnormal or beyond normal. A person who is afflicted with a physical affliction, a mental condition, or degenerative disease would be considered to be outside the normal range. Likewise, a person who has increased physiological performance or cognitive abilities, or lives beyond the human maximum lifespan of 122-123 years, would be considered outside the normal range. This determination of "normal" has not kept up with the advances in technology or science. (Humanity+,2018)

In order to make a definition of transhumanism, we need to look at the human-technology relationship in more detail. Understanding what technology means for the human being, its history and advantages will be of great help to better understand Transhumanism.

The human-nature relationship is the first step to focus on to understand technology. Humans have always struggled to turn the tables on nature by changing, adapting and transforming it. In doing so, humans have gone through some immediate or mediate changes, too. The human-built world has started to redesign humans. It is just not a physical phenomenon because soon after their generation, ideas starts to create a semantic world for individuals. All through history people not only tried to improve their living conditions by struggling against nature but also to strived to enhance their bodies in different ways (İlin & Segal, 2000). For instance, some archaeological studies showed that people tried dental filling long before the invention of the wheel. This supports the idea that humans tried to improve their living conditions by carrying out medical operations on their bodies even in ancient times (BBC Türkçe, 2018).

Technology is an idea that aims to empower people to live a better life. While it makes life easier, it also maximizes the profits of production. The developments in technology also helps the development of human beings. The humans are now interwoven with technologies, such as DNA interventions, nanotechnology products or the smart wristwatches we have been using recently, all of which shows that the human-technology relationship is not limited to the visible daily life any more.

Today, many assume that there is no limit to the developments in technology. The same assumption applies to the things that we can do with technology. Then, what the benefits of unlimited technology and human-technology relationship look like in future? To answer that question, we can have a closer look at Transhumanism.

After the invention of first tools and techniques, humans formed a relationship similar to that of with nature. Humans aimed to take nature, their environment and bodies further by producing technologies. While maximizing the amount of work and minimizing the resources and energy used, people have tried to boost safety and physical health. As a result, the living conditions and human body have been changed. These changes have been widely discussed, with pros and cons. Although there are various definitions in literature, Transhumanism is a theory that the human body can evolve beyond its current capacity with the help of technology. Some definitions of Transhumanism are as follows:

According to one definition, Transhumanism is an interdisciplinary field of research *"which maintains that science and technology should be used to enhance the physical and cognitive skills and eliminate the undesired and unnecessary traits like aging and diseases"* (Uğur, Güler, Hakan, & Kurubacak, 2018, p. 5).

According to Max More, Transhumanism is *"Transhumanism is a class of philosophies of life that seek the continuation and acceleration of the evolution of intelligent life beyond its currently human form and human limitations by means of science and technology, guided by life-promoting principles and values"* (Humanity, 2017).

Another definition states that Transhumanism is *"a philosophy that expresses the development of the current characteristics and potential of human through the use of genetic science, health and technology in partnership with other disciplines as well, use of all sorts of scientific and technical facilities"* (Uğur, 2018, p. 58).

Transhumanism is also defined as *"a way of thinking about the future that is based on the premise that the human species in its current form does not represent the end of our development but rather a comparatively early phase" (What is Transhumanism?, 2018).*

Another definition for Transhumanism is that *"it takes a multidisciplinary approach in analyzing the dynamic interplay between humanity and the acceleration of technology. In this sphere, much of our focus and attention is on the present technologies, such as biotechnology and information technology, and anticipated future technologies, such as molecular nanotechnology and artificial general intelligence. Transhumanism seeks the ethical use of these and other speculative technologies. Our theoretical interests focus on posthuman topics of the singularity, extinction risk, and mind uploading (whole brain emulation and substrate-independent minds)"* (Humanity+, 2017).

Transhumanism is also defined as "a way of thinking about the future that is based on the premise that the human species in its current form does not represent the end of our development but rather a comparatively early phase"(*What is Transhumanism?, 2018*).

Based on the numerous and different definitions above, it is hard to converge on a standard definition of Transhumanism because of its philosophical background. Although they differ from each other in some respects, they all focus on human-technology relationship and the improvement of human life grounding on the idea of taking the human being to a higher level by promoting the human-technology synergy. Just like technology, the idea of taking the humans further seems to have no boundaries in improving human life as highlighted in research.

Transhumanism can also be defined as a kind of "immortality" as it might help humans get rid of diseases and live a longer life. For instance, the advances in bioengineering and genetic engineering will probably make DNA regulations possible. This very ultrahuman future focuses on "augmented human". The bioengineering process can be realized in two ways, which are cyborgification and technology based augmentation (King, 2016, p. 148 - 150). Although the idea is still very much in its infancy, the upcoming developments are expected in the near future. On the other hand, no matter how fascinating the idea of immortality sounds, it is still a dream for us today.

In order to have a better understanding of transhumanism, we need to have a closer look at its philosophy. "The Transhumanist Declaration" crafted by a group of authors in 1998 introduces its philosophy. It underlines the unreached potential of humanity and claims that technology is the biggest and most important solution to the misery and inadequacy of humanity (Humanity+, 2016). So, such a beneficial relationship might provide humans with a more livable future. The Declaration (Appendix 1) seems to be very optimistic about the future with respect to human-technology relationship.

Transhumanists call the ideal human as a product of the human-technology relationship "the Posthuman". This idealized Posthuman is a new mankind who is resistant to diseases, does not age, can control his/her mind, mood and desires and reach the higher states of consciousness(What is Transhumanism?, 2018). The Posthuman is also called "Humanity+" or "H+" by transhumanists, which can also be referred as "augmented human" who is provided with advanced and improved life conditions with the help of technology (King, 2016, p. 185-228). Compared to the current humans, Posthumans will probably have much more different bodies, systems of thought and ways of life. They will be able to isolate themselves from time, space and natural conditions thanks to technology and will not face the problems that we have today.

Advocates of transhumanism call themselves "Transhumanists", which refers to "someone who advocates transhumanism. It is a common error for reporters and other writers to say that transhumanists "claim to be transhuman" or "call themselves transhuman". To adopt a philosophy which says that someday everyone ought to have the chance to grow beyond present human limits is clearly not to say that one is better or somehow currently "more advanced" than one's fellow humans" (Transhumanist FAQ, 2018).

In sum, it will be safe to say that most definitions of transhumanism seem to refer to the idea of "taking humans to a higher level". According to Transhumanism, the human-technology relationship is growing in a dialectic frame. Humans are improving and transforming their own bodies by using the technology while producing it at the same time. This very dialectic structure, which is focus of transhumanist philosophy, will remove all the boundaries for humans. Therefore, humans can empower their thinking capability, live without suffering from diseases, learn all the languages, improve physical and cognitive skills and even become immortal.

Transhumanism, which aims to take humanity a step further instead of making life easier, inspires science fiction and futuristic works.

DEFINING ARTIFICIAL INTELLIGENCE

Cogito, ergo sum

The point of this chapter is *"Can machines think?"*

Unfortunately, we cannot answer this question today. The thinking capability has largely been attributed to human beings in philosophy and science. From the philosophical perspective positing that thinking is the most outstanding trait of humanity to neuroscience of modern day, thinking, information production, interpretation and its functions are still a hot topic of debate. However, this very distinctive trait of humans is now about to be transferred to machines and how it will be done is also a popular debate. The intelligence demonstrated by machines is called Artificial Intelligence (AI), which is gaining popularity in philosophy and science.

Even before it has been a popular subject of science and philosophy, Artificial Intelligence has been a *cynosure* in literature and cinema. The interactions between humans and robots, computers and other technological forms that can think and speak have been the subject of many literary works and movie scripts.

Today, Artificial Intelligence has become the reality, which was once fictitious in books and films. In order to have a thorough understanding of AI, we need to explore the relationship between humans and technology.

The technological developments of in the last half of the 21st century have led to the great and unpredictable changes and phenomena, some of which are computers, smart phones and the Internet. However, the modern technologies of today seem to have distinctive characteristics from their predecessors as the market accentuates that they are "smart", "user-friendly" and "intelligent". On its website, Samsung, one of the leading technology giants in the world, notes that "We are developing innovative Artificial Intelligence (AI) technologies to enhance current business and open up new business opportunities, with the ultimate goal of enhancing human life and contributing to the society" and they have been focusing on AI technologies, such as Virtual Personal Assistant, Visual Understanding, On-Device AI to make Samsung products smarter (Samsung Research, 2018). The company aims to release the products that meet the needs of the users.

Then, what is artificial intelligence and what does it mean for modern-day humans? What is its connection to Transhumanism?

Artificial Intelligence, which has been hitting the headlines in many fields of study, has fundamentally changed the way we perceive technology. Although the working of cognition, task interpretation and cognitive functioning have been widely discussed by philosophers and scientists, there are no satisfying answers yet. However, various products are said to have this kind of functioning.

We should look at the definition of intelligence to be able to define artificial intelligence. What exactly is intelligence as a distinctive trait of humans? In the most general sense, intelligence refers to the skills used for thinking, reasoning, perceiving objective facts, making judgements and drawing conclusions (TDK, 2018), which makes a direct connection to humans.

Then, is it possible that intelligence and machines could be integrated? The things that were only dreamed about in the past are about to come true thanks to the technological advances in this day and that is where Artificial Intelligence stands out.

The emergence of computer technologies is one of the most important factors leading to the development of Artificial Intelligence. In 1950, Turing was one of the most important contributors to Artificial Intelligence with his paper, *"Computing Machinery an Intelligence"*. He discussed the issue of machine intelligence and the proposed a method, which is called the *Turing Test* to test the machine learning. In this game, a human and a computer start a text conversation with a human judge or interrogator. The judge has to evaluate the responses of the unseen players and figure out which player is the human and which player is the computer. If the interrogator is unable to distinguish computer from human, then the computer must be a passable substitution of human intelligence, namely Artificial Intelligence (Turing, 1950). Although the Turing Test has been critised over the years on various grounds, the machines are able to respond to human commands automatically in this day and the technologies capable of doing it are called Artificial Intelligence.

The recent software and hardware can do things that their predecessors never came even close to and they will definitely be achieving much more in near future. The human-computer relationship makes up an important part of transhumanistic thinking. Nowadays, we witness cases where the machines compete against and beats human intelligence. For example, Deep Blue, a chess playing computer developed by IBM in 1997, became the first machine to beat Garry Kasparov (Endüstri 4.0, 2018), which proved that machines surpass humans in some cases.

Turing's ideas and all these phenomena return us to the question of machines' thinking capabilitiy.

According to the supporters of Artificial Intelligence, the answer is yes for sure. Today, artificial intelligence has learned to think like humans to some extent and they will eventually do it in the future. We need to emphasize that machines are learning to think systematically, which is a human trait, by the algorithms that humans create.

When we look at the discussions of Artificial Intelligence, we see that it is defined within the framework of problem solving as a function. It is a kind of problem solving skill for machines as they try to solve the problems using certain algorithms without needing any new software. They can process the commands of users and respond with a set of data or commands. Today, the AI technologies have reached a point where they are able to solve the problems or respond to questions without user intervention (Techopedia, 2018.

Without doubt Artificial Intelligence has been a subject of hot debates since its emergence. Although it has been found useful in many ways, there may be some potential risks as well as many benefits. In his interview, Elon Musk warns that AI is the biggest threat to humanity. According to Musk, AI poses the risk of dominating humanity (NTV,2018) as they can destroy humanity with artificial consciousness. The destruction of humanity by intelligent machines have been the subject of many science fiction works.

Is it possible for machines to have a free will and wage war on their creators? According to Harari, intelligence and consciousness are two separate features of the mind. Many movies and literary works have taken the Artificial Intelligence gaining consciousness as the theme. However, intelligence is often defined as a problem solving skill while consciousness refers to the ability to be aware of emotions like grief, anger, love and joy. The confusion may lie in the fact that the mammals have both intelligence and consciousness as they overcome most problems with their feelings unlike computers. Artificial Intelligence can make life easier for humans without feelings, as the algorithms do not need feelings to solve the problems they are presented with (Harari, 2018, s. 77) .

The difference between intelligence and consciousness implies that such a war is not possible for now.

Based on the latest technologies, Artificial Intelligence is made up of algorithms that can analyze and evaluate the commands within predefined software algoritms in order to respond to a user. Therefore, Artificial Intelligence looks like software that processes information, data and programs. The limits of Artificial Intelligence in terms of capacity and functioning will also be in direct proportion to the limits of the software algorithms it has. While Artificial Intelligence perceives the input data in written, visual or audio format and gives the output data in the same way.

Today, the current Artificial Intelligence technologies can carry out the requests within the limits of the software algorithms and make life more comfortable for the users while doing it. The time-consuming processes that need user intervention can be carried out with voice commands only.

Can we say that Artificial Intelligence systems are able to think? Thinking and interpretation are still philosophically debatable issues for people. From a pragmatic perspective, Artificial Intelligence is the very transfer of these human functions to some electronic circuits. However, the modern technologies proves that we need to be skeptical of machine intelligence.

ARTIFICIAL INTELLIGENCE AND TRANSHUMANISM

One can assume that the humans are augmented or H+ with 3D printed prosthetic limbs, the microchips embedded under skin or DNA interventions. The amount of technological interventions in health is increasing day by day. Wearable sensors are now used to monitor the status of patients. The data obtained from these sensors are processed with smart technology and artificial intelligence which provides medical feedback to users instead of expert evaluation. All these show that transhumanism is not a mere theory anymore, but the reality. Today it is possible to track the changes in blood glucose instantaneously without taking a blood sample thanks to the sensors embedded in human body (FreeStyle Libre, 2018).

The developments in software and hardware have led to the emergence of self-directed smart devices that can carry out more tasks with less user intervention, which means maximum productivity with minimum energy. In the past, it took a long time to write the lines of code to perform the tasks that are quite simple today. On the other hand, the users are able to carry out quite complicated tasks with simpler commands with the help of Artificial Intelligence technologies.

Today, many technologies, such as wearable sensors, smart phones and augmented reality applications, are drawn from the advances in Artificial Intelligence. From a transhumanist point of view, Artificial Intelligence is very likely to impact on humans at both individual and social level. According to King, Artificial Intelligence will be the center of smart cities. In order to transform the current cities into "smart ones", we need to utilize real-time developments. With technological infrastructure, it is possible to develop smart cities where people are provided with interconnected dwellings, smart transportation and e-governance services, all of which will make life more comfortable and easier (King, 2016, p. 350-353).

The human-machine relationship has reached a point beyond what people dreamed of in the past. The fantastic ideas of the science fictions works in the past have become a part of the daily life. The smart phones and wearable technologies will also be reviewed within the scope of the current paper.

Looking at the history of smartphones, many say iPhone, when first introduced by Steve Jobs in 2007, was the true smartphone revolution at the time (imore, 2018). The iPhone allowed users to use multiple applications simultaneously while the other mobile phones could only run a few simple applications. Providing users with "smart" features like the internet connection and music, iPhone revolutionized user attitudes towards technology. The later generations of iPhone have become "smarter" by including the features of a camera, a phone and a computer in just one device. iPhone provided users with applications that could be run on the computer only, which was amazing at that time. Later on, iPhone users could not only watched the videos, but they were also able to edit them.

iPhone has carried on its tradition of innovation every year and paved the way for many original and unique applications, all of which were revolutionary at the time.

With the release of iPhone 4S in October, 2011, Steve Jobs' dream has come true which he had longed for since 1980s. Siri, the virtual assistant part of Apple products was now released on iPhone 4S. As a personal assistant that can respond to the users simultaneously, this Artificial Intelligence application has fascinated the whole world. Now, users are able to perform various phone actions only with voice commands. Siri can respond to questions, run applications and search the Internet. The day Siri was released, it gave clues about the future of smart phones. Now, the mobile technologies were able to recognize voice and interact with users simultaneously. In the coming days, the Artificial Intelligence would also be used in different devices in more advanced forms (Cult of Mac).

Apple product iPhone has taken up an innovative approach to Siri with improved software, hardware and sensors, and they have also introduced the use of Artificial Intelligence at homes with the HomeKit products.

Then, what is the importance of Siri from a Transhumanistic perspective?

First of all, Siri, as a pocket-sized personal assistant, has taken the human-machine interactions a step further with iPhone revolutionizing our attitudes towards mobile phones. It is not necessary to use a keyboard to command Siri. The use of voice commands seems to be the milestone which was revolutionary. The users can run applications, send messages and search the Internet with voice queries. With all these smart qualities, users have been carrying a "smart" assistant with them. In addition, Siri can instantly "answer" the questions, which has reshaped the human-machine communication.

What can these features tell us about the future?

We can say that the Artificial technologies used in smart phones are advanced software algorithms from a Transhumanistic paradigm. Those technologies that have been used in various products have made life easier for users in terms of accessing to, processing and interpreting information. These virtual assistant applications will definitely change our perspectives of smart phones with rapidly developing software and hardware technologies.

In conclusion, the developments in Artificial Intelligent technologies seem to go parallel with the increasing use of the Internet and smart phones. With the emergence of Artificial Intelligence as a concept and technology, the computers are able to process information and interact with users with less user intervention. We are in an era where the modern inventions like Siri are placed in our pockets. However, it should be emphasized that the technology of Artificial Intelligence has still limitations and a long way to go. The Artificial Intelligence technology today is the systems processing the data obtained from users through various sensors with the help of software algorithms. With the development of it, it enables users to do much more with less user intervention.

DISCUSSION AND CONCLUSION

The human-technology relationship has always been a "decisive" factor in countries' level of economic, social and military development throughout the history. Therefore, one's individual or social relationship to technology will be directly associated with overall level of "developments". It is quite important to have access to, produce and utilize technology in order to be "successful" in society's eyes. This very technology, which can be defined as the humans' capacity to change and refine nature, is also changing the life and the humans themselves. According to Transhumanism, it is obvious that we have been going through a revolution of human nature being changed by technology. As mentioned earlier, the nature of human-technology relationship is quite "special" and there are some reasons as follow:

- The human-technology relationship has a dialectic foundation.
- While humans innovate the world they live in with technology, the world we build starts to redesign us before long.
- Technology is a part of political affairs as all the other systems. In this sense, technology is produced by the ones holding the economic, scientific and social power and the products, which in turn, serve the interests of the ones who design/produce technology.

- One can assume that technology has an ideology as everything and everyone in the world. Technology has ideological goals of how people and the world would be changed while helping humans change the world at the same time.
- The attitudes towards technology can change from time to time and depend on circumstances.
- Some trends that have raised from technology have gained popularity at times.

The human-technology relationship has always been special and decisive because of the issues listed above. However, the advantages and disadvantages of technology have been debated on economic, social and environmental grounds. For instance, many environmentalists think that technology presents only short-term benefits for humans. The resources are enormously consumed to develop and use energy as in the case of nuclear energy which meets the demand while increasing the natural radiation levels and creating radioactive contamination.

Humans develop and use technology to benefit from it in every aspect of life. The scientific practice that humans use for the development and production of technology has changed the human-machine relationship. Today technology keeps meeting more needs of humans every day. The size of technological products relative to their utility is growing smaller, which has fostered the bond between humans and technology. Primitive humans did not have the technology that is necessary to change and transform the world. The humans at the time survived with the minimum amount of technology, which is not the case for the modern humans. Today humans have become dependent of technology even for the most basic needs, from food supply to drinking water. Thus, a question which has been raised by many people is whether people are too dependent on technology or not?

As mentioned earlier, the human-technology relationship has dialectic foundations and the development of technology has empowered it. Technology has become an integral part of daily life. Technological products are growing smaller while becoming more skillful, which has provided humans with more detailed methods of intervention. Scientific developments in many fields, from advanced 3D printers to genetic engineering, helped humans make many of their dreams come true. The developments in technology has enabled humans to carry out the interventions to human body with the use of microchips, sensors that are placed under skin, etc.

The human-technology relationship has multiple dimensions. However, Transhumanism is among the most important paradigms of human-technology relationship. In this direction, Transhumanism embraces the values and principles below:

- Transhumanism assumes that technology offers unlimited opportunities. Considering the modern technology of today, it was impossible for a person living 100 years ago to imagine the technological products we have. Therefore, there will be many more important developments in the future.
- Technology can be used for the greater good of humanity in an unlimited way.
- Technology will take the skills, capacity and power of humans a step further and it has already begun.
- Technology should be used for medical interventions, which will improve the human body, mind and capacity.
- Technology, in its evolution, has developed and reached its final form.
- Human body is in a similar process. The human-technology alliance will contribute to the evolution of humanity.

Artificial Intelligence in the Era of Transhumanism Smart Phones

- Technology will be the solution to all the problems of human life, which will help humans survive all the diseases and even become immortal.

As summarized above, technology is of vital importance for humanity. The human-technology has been developing in multiple ways, including the interventions to DNA. The changing dimensions and structure of this relationship have led us to question our attitudes towards technology, which raised ethical and social debates. The genetic interventions, to illustrate, have been a controversial topic in academia, courts and news.

As our attitudes towards human-technology relationship changes with the Transhumanistic philosophy, the machines are also acquiring humane characteristics. There have been various movements of thought concerning the production, processing and interpretation of information throughout the history and many focused on the transfer of thinking ability to machines from calculators to computers. People have always tried to transfer the mathematical algorithms to machines since the invention of the first calculator. Today, the modern computers also use the same algorithms to process the data.

Together with the power of imagination, the rapidly developing computer technologies have led to the question "Can machines think?". We need to understand the human mind and how the brain works exactly. However, there are still some questions to be answered. On the other hand, Artificial Intelligence is an often heard term, which can be defined as the interpretation ability of machines with the use of the data they obtained. Artificial Intelligence is the interpretation of the commands a user gives with the help of software with advanced algorithms and sensor technology. The computer can run the commands and process information through the use of advanced algorithms. At this point, intelligence can be defined as the abilities covering thinking, judgement, making connections, etc. as a whole and today there are various technologies that can do these kinds of processes with predefined algorithms.

Artificial Intelligence, which dates back to the 50s, have been the subject of many science fiction works, where it becomes the demon and the enemy of humanity. However, it seems only to be a fiction because of the fact that the Artificial Intelligence technologies have certain limitations due to the nature of algorithms

Artificial Intelligence might be viewed as the mechanization of humanity because of the interventions to the human body. The humanization of machines have also been widely discussed. The "thinking" ability of machines has been realized with the emergence of Artificial Intelligence, which was the milestone in the history of technology as it is substantially different from the technologies produced before.

Whatever the abilities of Artificial Intelligence are, it provides users with great ease to their users. For example, smart phones can operate with voice commands only and they can evaluate the medical data. The developments will certainly bring many more innovations in the future.

Transhumanism has strong anticipations of technology. Although many of them are still seen fantastic creations, the changes that Transhumanism anticipates and defends are very likely to be realized in the future. The human empowered by technology will make much bigger changes.

Artificial Intelligence technologies, as a social phonemena, will reshape our perspectives of many issues. With the digitalization of governance, our understanding of democracy will change. Similarly, the education system will be revised in accordance with Artificial Intelligence and interactive applications. Smart medical applications and robot technology will be revolutionaty in health care. However, whether people can keep up with all these innovations is quite obscure. From an economic and social perspective, there is no technological equality in the world despite the efforts and the inequality will probably continue to exist in the future, too. While there is this tremendous inequality between people who have access to technology and the ones who cannot even today, it would be much worse for people who will not be able to benefit from Transhumanism, which will be one of the biggest problems of the future?

Transhumanism assumes that the nature of modern human will change with the technological interventions. This new version of human, that is H+, will open new discussions in the future, such as "What is human?"

There are still some points where we are not totally sure about the cognitive functioning in humans, such as information production, processing and interpretation. Therefore, it would be beneficial to have such technological products, that is the ones with Artificial Intelligence. Artificial Intelligence will contribute not only to the development of new technologies but also the turning humanity into H+. Artificial Intelligence as a milestone in the history of development will also mark the future.

To conclude, with the development of recent technologies, the augmented human, that is H+, is not a fantasy anymore. This kind of human is able to make interventions to his/her own body while transferring his/her abilities to a machine (as in the case of smart phones) at the same time. So, the augmented human or H+ will not be content with the interventions on human body. S/he will need and search for technologies that will make life more comfortable, help him/her access to and interpret information more readily. Smart phones are the biggest example of the application of Artificial Intelligence.

Will Transhumanism and Artificial Intelligence be the savior of humanity? Although it is too early to be sure, it is possible to draw some conclusions in the light of human-technology relationship throughout the history. The history of technology proves that humans tend to use it abusively although it has greatly helped us to treat diseases and access to information.

Humanity has been producing and using technologies for ideological and political reasons and not always for peaceful purposes as in the case of nuclear weapons. Therefore, the people holding technology as a political and economic power will determine the fate of humanity and Artificial Intelligence as well.

What will be the role of man-made Artificial Intelligence in rebuilding the nature of humanity and environment in the future? Only time will tell whether all these theories are justified.

REFERENCES

Cultof Mac. (2018). *Today in Apple history: Siri debuts on iPhone 4s*. Retrieved from https://www.cultofmac.com/447783/today-in-apple-history-siri-makes-its-public-debut-on-iphone-4s/

Endüstri 4.0. (2018). *Kasparov Satranç Oyunu*. Retrieved from https://www.endustri40.com/kasparov-satranc-oyunu-makineye-karsi-insan/

FreeStyle Libre. (2018). *Şeker Kontrolü*. Retrieved from https://libresensor.com/?utm_source=adwords&utm_medium=google&utm_campaign=171025_Gadwords_NonBranded&utm_content=Parmak_delmeden&gclid=Cj0KCQjw9NbdBRCwARIsAPLsnFYgdUn_wqow2p6aUgYhQJz-FExdhkgWlgelLYWJN5tTENnsDvHJBJ_MaAmFOEALw_wcB

Harari, Y. N. (2018). *21. Yüzyıl İçin 21 Ders*. İstanbul: Kolektif kitap .

Humanity+. (2016). *Transhumanist Declaration*. Retrieved from https://humanityplus.org/philosophy/transhumanist-declaration/

Humanity+. (2017). Philosophy. Retrieved from https://humanityplus.org/philosophy/philosophy-2/

Humanity+. (2018). *What is the Mission of Humanity+*. Retrieved from https://humanityplus.org/about/mission/.

İlin, M., & Segal, E. (2000). *İnsan Nasıl İnsan Oldu*. İstanbul: Say Yayınları.

imore. (2018). The Secret History of iPhone. Retrieved from https://www.imore.com/history-iphone-original

King, B. (2016). *Augmented Artırılmış Gerçeklik*. İstanbul: MediaCat Kitapları.

NTV. (2018). *Yapay Zeka Uyarısı*. Retrieved from https://www.ntv.com.tr/galeri/teknoloji/elonmusk-tan-yapay-zeka-uyarisi,REjccX1JVkqq-oyMsZIFbw/NmFwGQ951k-N8OaSkIa15w.

Postman, N. (2006). *Teknopoli*. İstanbul: Paradigma Yayıncılık.

Samsung Research. (2018). *Artificial Intelligence*. Retrieved from https://research.samsung.com/artificial-intelligence.

Turing, A. M. (1950). Computing machinery and intelligence. *Mind, LIX*(59), 433–460. doi:10.1093/mind/LIX.236.433

Türkçe, B. B. C. (2018). *DERGİ - 6500 yıllık diş dolgusu bulundu*. Retrieved from https://www.bbc.com/turkce/haberler/2016/03/160302_vert_ear_dis_dolgusu

Uğur, S. (2018). Transhumanizm ve öğrenmedeki değişim. *Açıköğretim Uygulamaları ve Araştırmaları Dergisi, 4*(3), 58–74.

Uğur, S., Güler, E., Hakan, Y., & Kurubacak, G. (2018). Transhümanist çağda mega açık üniversitelerin yeniden yapılandırılabilmesi için stratejik karar modeli ile bir blokzincir uygulamasının geliştirilmesi. *Açıköğretim Uygulamaları ve Araştırmaları Dergisi, 4*(3), 5–11.

APPENDIX

Transhumanist Declaration

1. Humanity stands to be profoundly affected by science and technology in the future. We envision the possibility of broadening human potential by overcoming aging, cognitive shortcomings, involuntary suffering, and our confinement to planet Earth.
2. We believe that humanity's potential is still mostly unrealized. There are possible scenarios that lead to wonderful and exceedingly worthwhile enhanced human conditions.
3. We recognize that humanity faces serious risks, especially from the misuse of new technologies. There are possible realistic scenarios that lead to the loss of most, or even all, of what we hold valuable. Some of these scenarios are drastic, others are subtle. Although all progress is change, not all change is progress.
4. Research effort needs to be invested into understanding these prospects. We need to carefully deliberate how best to reduce risks and expedite beneficial applications. We also need forums where people can constructively discuss what should be done, and a social order where responsible decisions can be implemented.
5. Reduction of existential risks, and development of means for the preservation of life and health, the alleviation of grave suffering, and the improvement of human foresight and wisdom should be pursued as urgent priorities, and heavily funded.
6. Policy making ought to be guided by responsible and inclusive moral vision, taking seriously both opportunities and risks, respecting autonomy and individual rights, and showing solidarity with and concern for the interests and dignity of all people around the globe. We must also consider our moral responsibilities towards generations that will exist in the future.
7. We advocate the well-being of all sentience, including humans, non-human animals, and any future artificial intellects, modified life forms, or other intelligences to which technological and scientific advance may give rise.
8. We favour allowing individuals wide personal choice over how they enable their lives. This includes use of techniques that may be developed to assist memory, concentration, and mental energy; life extension therapies; reproductive choice technologies; cryonics procedures; and many other possible human modification and enhancement technologies (Humanity, 2016).

Chapter 11
The Role, Influence, and Demand of Pedagogies in the Age of Transhumanism:
Critical Reflections

Pradeep Kumar Misra
Chaudhary Charan Singh University, India

ABSTRACT

Whether pedagogies play a role in the age of transhumanism is a question that has no certain answers. There are some who say that pedagogies do not play any role in transhumanism while some say that pedagogies appear to play a role in this movement. Agreeing to the later observation, this chapter proposes that pedagogies have a relationship with transhumanism and will play a very important role in the transhumanistic societies of the future. Extending these arguments and observations, present paper assesses the role, influence and demand of pedagogies in the age of transhumanism. In this quest, present chapter: defines pedagogy and discusses its importance; enumerates the relationship between pedagogy and transhumanism; analyses the role of pedagogies in the age of transhumanism; looks upon the influence and demand of pedagogies in the age of transhumanism; and predicts the future of pedagogies in transhumanistic societies.

BACKGROUND

Transhumanism is a movement that aims to change humankind by using technical means. This change is intended be a change for the better (Damberger, 2013). Max More, the philosopher and founder of the *Extropy Institute*, describes transhumanism as a life philosophy, a broad intellectual and cultural movement (More, 2013). This movement includes various scientific disciplines, such as NBIC technologies (nanotechnology, biotechnology, IT and cognitive sciences). In addition to scientific disciplines, the social sciences also play an important role in the transhumanist movement (Vinge, 2013). Transhumanism is rooted in an optimistic belief that technology can help to improve humans and make their everyday lives better and more enjoyable. In the words of Trippett (2018):

DOI: 10.4018/978-1-5225-8431-5.ch011

It is rooted in the belief that humans can and will be enhanced by the genetic engineering and information technology of today, as well as anticipated advances, such as bioengineering, artificial intelligence, and molecular nanotechnology. The result is an iteration of Homo sapiens enhanced or augmented, but still fundamentally human.

According to More, transhumanism should be guided by life-promoting principles and values (More, 1990). Transhumanism is intended to support human beings to improve on many aspects ranging from physical to mental, as observed by Kimel (2016):

A willingness to empower more people than ever before to be born healthy, intelligent and able to devote long and meaningful lives to love, leisure and lifelong education is, to me, transhumanism at its best- an antidote to postmodern malaise.

These observations let us to propagate that technologies and our ability to select and use them with caution will go hand in hand to maximize the benefit of this movement, as noted by Lilley (2013,p.5), "Even though artifacts are made of different stuff than you and I, they are of the social world. Design and implementation are affected by social, economic, and political decisions." Considering this complex relationship between men and machine, the role of education becomes very important for transhumanism, as argued by Thomas (2017):

Transhuman possibilities urgently call for a politics with more clearly delineated and explicit humane values to provide a safer environment in which to foster these profound changes. Where we stand on questions of social justice and environmental sustainability has never been more important. Technology doesn't allow us to escape these questions – it doesn't permit political neutrality. The contrary is true.

The other notable argument is that understanding transhuman settings as systems of co-creation and co-evolution between humans and technological artefacts can be informed by learning principles. Besides, it is also expected that self-emergent behavior and mutual learning processes will be helpful to implement co-creation and co-evolving systems (Stary, 2017). Therefore, it can be argued that we need a distinctly and differently educated society to understand the concept of transhumanism and have a mindset and behaviour to judiciously and morally use it for betterment of human race. And when we talk about educating a society, the role of pedagogy becomes more than important. Extending this argument, one can say that pedagogies have to play a very unique and important role in the age of transhumanism. Before discussing further on this issue, let's try to understand that what does pedagogy means and why it is so important?

Meaning and Importance of Pedagogy

A look on the definitions of pedagogy given in different dictionaries reveal that it is perceived as: the study of the methods and activities of teaching (Cambridge dictionary, 2018); the art, science, or profession of teaching (Merriam-Webster's dictionary, 2018); and the method and practice of teaching, especially as an academic subject or theoretical concept (Oxford dictionary, 2018). Putting all these definitions together, it can be said that pedagogy is a term concerned with what a teacher does to influence learning in others. Some would say that this is a somewhat limited viewpoint, since in its origins and derivation (paidagogous= guide of children) pedagogy is a much broader concept, relating to the development and all round development of the child, as explained by Hall (1905, p. 375):

The Greek pedagogue, from whom the term pedagogy was derived, led the boy to and from school, and was his keeper rather than teacher. The word has expanded from its etymological meaning and is a general designation for the art of teaching.

While, Siraj-Blatchford, Sylva, Muttock, Gilden, and Bell (2002, p.10) view pedagogy as a tool to promote learning and define it in following way:

... the instructional techniques and strategies that allow learning to take place. It refers to the interactive process between teacher/practitioner and learner and it is also applied to include the provision of some aspects of the learning environment (including the concrete learning environment, and the actions of the family and community).

Putting all these perspectives together, it can be argued that pedagogy may be seen as an encompassing tool to promote desired learning, as noted by Smith (2012):

We need to move discussions of pedagogy beyond seeing it as primarily being about teaching -and look at those traditions of practice that flow from the original pedagogues in ancient Greece. We have much to learn through exploring through the thinking and practice of specialist pedagogues who look to accompany learners; care for and about them; and bring learning into life. Teaching is just one aspect of their practice.

Echoing the same sentiments, Livingston, Schweisfurth, Brace, and Nash (2017, p.8) explain pedagogy in following way:

By pedagogy, we mean the dynamic relationship between learning, teaching and culture. Teachers' actions in the classroom, in relation to learning and teaching, are underpinned by the ideas and values that they have about education. Pedagogy interacts with and draws together beliefs about learners and learning, teacher and teaching, and curriculum.

After learning that what does pedagogy means, the next question that comes to one's mind that how pedagogy develops. A report from Child Australia (n.d, p.1) presents the answer:

Pedagogy develops from a range of factors including theories and research evidence, political drivers, evidence from practice, individual and group reflection, educators' experiences and expertise, and community expectations and requirements. It informs both curriculum (all the interactions, experiences, activities, routines and events planned and unplanned) and teaching in a service. It reflects and supports the principles of and outcomes sought by a service.

Now the next and most significant question, why pedagogy matters? The 2014 EFA Global Monitoring Report (GMR) highlighted that besides access, poor quality education is holding back learning in many countries (UNESCO, 2014).Therefore, it seems essential that teachers must take care of different learning needs of children and guide them for better learning outcomes. Pedagogy can support teachers to fulfill this task, as suggested by Entz (2006, p.23): "Like a Paidagogas, the role of the modern early educator is to lead her young charges, care for them, help them exhibit good behavior, and to help them to learn. Pedagogy does matter." Therefore, pedagogy has been seen as a means to support educational processes and promote learning. In fact, the role of pedagogy is much more than this. The prime role of pedagogy is to help a child to become a responsible citizen working for betterment of him/her and society as well. Interestingly, same belief also guides transhumanism movement. And if both 'transhumanism' and 'pedagogy' are driven by similar ideals, it becomes logical to probe their relationship further.

Relationship Between Pedagogy and Transhumanism

Talking about the relationship between pedagogy and transhumansim, there are some who say that pedagogy does not play any role in transhumansim (see Damberger, 2013) while some say that pedagogy appears to play a role in this movement. Therefore, a systematic and through probing is required to ascertain the nature of this relationship. Talking about the role and purpose of education in one's life, Immanuel Kant expressed:

Education includes the nurture of the child and, as it grows, its culture. The latter is firstly negative, consisting of discipline; that is, merely the correcting of faults. Secondly, culture is positive, consisting of instruction and guidance (and thus forming part of education). Guidance means directing the pupil in putting into practice what he has been taught (Churton, 1900, pp. 23-24).

And pedagogy is helpful to provide education including instruction and guidance. Husbands and Pearce (2012, p.3) reviewed an extensive research literature and suggested that outstanding pedagogy is far from straightforward. They also observed that pedagogic practices which differ across the age range and between subjects can be useful to support educational processes in nine ways:

- Give serious consideration to pupil voice.
- Depend on behaviour (what teachers do), knowledge and understanding (what teachers know) and beliefs (why teachers act as they do).
- Involve clear thinking about longer term learning outcomes as well as short-term goals.
- Build on pupils' prior learning and experience.
- Involve scaffolding pupil learning.
- Involve a range of techniques, including whole-class and structured group work, guided learning and individual activity.
- Focus on developing higher order thinking and metacognition, and make good use of dialogue and questioning in order to do so.
- Embed assessment for learning.
- Are inclusive and take the diverse needs of a range of learners, as well as matters of student equity, into account

These characteristics make it clear that pedagogy can help a learner to learn and develop in a variety of ways. In other words, use of appropriate pedagogies can help to produce a generation having competencies to produce new technologies for betterment of human beings and societies, and also possessing mindset to act critically and empathetically to use these technologies in a sustainable manner. In other words, pedagogy is useful to conceive and design a product (science and technology), promote and sell the product (management and economics), and using the product in an ethical and environment friendly manner (education and learning). From a holistic perspective, this is an interconnected and complete cycle where each component is required to support another for making a sustainable world. Unfortunately, the reality is different today. People are hardly ready to listen to others, usually prefer to live in own world, and mainly concerned to promote and vote their own ideologies and disciplines. If this trend continues, it will be very difficult to create a world as envisioned by transhumanism. Tirosh-Samuelson (2007, p.13) suggests:

It is quite clear that transhumanist vision emerged because of the confluence of knowledge in certain scientific fields and their technological applications, especially in genetics, robotics, and nanotechnology. The fusion of horizons of knowledge demonstrates why the traditional disciplinary boundaries are becoming increasingly obsolete and why scholars in the humanities and the social sciences need to become at least aware if not conversant with the new disciplines. But conversely, scholars in the applied sciences and especially engineering and public policy must become more attune to the humanities and must engage their own scientific disciplines critically in light of the values articulated by humanities.

Therefore, transhumanism movement not only needs experts from different disciplines but also expects them to understand each other, give proper attention to viewpoint of others, and if others are right then mend their own thinking and processes, to work in a collaborative manner, and before taking any action or making a new invention have to analyze that whether it will make this world a better place to live. To meet these demands, people will have to develop a different kind of thinking and attitude. But, this is a rarity in these days, as our education systems hardly prepare us to think and act differently. Fortunately, pedagogies can help to prepare a next generation of experts having desired mindset and competencies to envision a better world. This optimism is based on the fact that education is the most powerful weapon to bring attitudinal changes, and pedagogy is the most powerful tool to support and nurture educational processes.

Role of Pedagogies in the Age of Transhumanism

The transhumanism movement has both its supporters and critiques. The supporters say that transhumanism will provide answers to almost all the remedies of humankind, and critiques observe that it will bring more chaos and inequality in the existing world. To make this duel clear, it will be interesting to hear different voices on transhumanism. Coenen (2014) in an article named transhumanism in emerging technoscience as a challenge for the humanities and technology assessment, observed:

With the new rise of transhumanism we have witnessed the re-surfacing of a technocratic ideology which has no reservations when it comes to painting out grandiose and somewhat frightening images of science futures. On the other hand, we are confronted with a kind of historical short-sightedness in the debate on these visions (p.766).

Talking about the options of accepting or rejecting the advances offered by transhumanism, Trippett (March 29, 2018) comments:

One option is to take advantage of the advances in nanotechnologies, genetic engineering and other medical sciences to enhance the biological and mental functioning of human beings (never to go back). The other is to legislate to prevent these artificial changes from becoming an entrenched part of humanity, with all the implied coercive bio-medicine that would entail for the species.

While, Remsberg (2010) dwells upon the potential impact of transhumanism advances on economy:

...this movement will have a profound effect on the economy once it becomes larger. This could be bad for naturally made foods if biotech foods are allowed in mass on the market because they could financially destroy the market for natural food. This would not be beneficial for current small farmers and companies that specialize in growing food without the use of genetic modification.

And, assessing the ethical, moral and existential questions raised by transhumanism, Hernaes (2016) suggests:

The only thing I know is that it is inevitable that advances in robotics, bionics, artificial intelligence and genetics will affect the next phase of human evolution, and we should not underestimate the ethical and social implications.

These observations make it clear that transhumanism movement demands support on many aspects. Fortunately, pedagogies can support this movement in many ways. First, pedagogies can help to produce qualified individuals having a mindset to innovate new technologies and processes for betterment of humankind. Second, pedagogies can nurture a generation of critical thinkers able to debate and decide the boundaries and areas for spread of transhumanism. Third, pedagogies can educate people to use technologies for their betterment, an often advertised goal of transhumanism. Fourth, pedagogies can support educational processes to train learners to cope-up with changes and challenges posed by transhumanism. Fifth, pedagogies can promote social and moral values among people to help them to share the benefits of transhumanism in an equitable manner. Sixth, pedagogies can develop certain life skills required to live in transhumanistic societies. And above all, pedagogies can provide educational support to guide the transhumanistic movement and keep it on right track.

Influence and Demand of Pedagogies in the Age of Transhumanism

Before assessing the influence and demand of pedagogies in the age of transhumanism, we have to look upon the realities of present world. Haraway in his "A Cyborg Manifesto" (1985/1991) contends, we live in a world where the stable boundaries separating humans from animals and machines have already become "breeched." A Visionary Innovation Group that looked at three fundamental pillars of humanity: our bodies, our thought, and our behavior to determine the ways in which the changing nature of humanity and transhumanism would affect individuals, society, businesses, and government reported following seven trends (Singh, 2017) over the coming 10-15 years:

- Our bodies will be augmented
- Our thought processes will be faster and more transferable
- Gamification and behavioral science will increase human productivity

- We will be more empathetic
- We will see the emergence of extreme personalization and customisation
- Business practices will shift significantly
- Conversations focused on our societal values will gain a great deal of attention

In fact, we are moving closer to a world that rides on two wheels namely technologies and education. Where, technologies are supposed to bring new innovations and techniques to improve human life, and education is essential to prepare users to use these technologies judiciously and morally. These wheels were supposed to balance each other, but unfortunately this balance is missing. Experiences reveal that technologies have taken a leap and frequently coming-up with newer solutions and approaches that are constantly affecting individuals and society. In comparison, education that was supposed to produce critical thinkers and activists ensuring the judicious and moral use of technologies and guiding all those involved in the process of generating new technologies lags behind. Describing that what education is doing and what it was supposed to do, Snaza et al. (2014) observe:

When education is reduced to the stockpiling of facts and abstracted exercises in "basic skills," we fail to foreground one of the most important reasons to educate the young in the first place: our world is plagued (or animated!) by innumerable problems for which we do not yet have answers. (p.45)

And seeing from this angle, it can be said that education systems of today needs re-visioning and re-orientation on many counts, as noted by Scott (2015, p.1):

In spite of worldwide agreement that learners need skills such as critical thinking and the ability to communicate effectively, innovate, and solve problems through negotiation and collaboration, pedagogy has seldom adapted to address these challenges. Rethinking pedagogy for the twenty-first century is as crucial as identifying the new competencies that today's learners need to develop.

Pedagogies can play a significant role to make this happen. Pedagogies can support education systems to enable new forms of learning needed to tackle complex global challenges. Pedagogies can also help to transform existing educational practices and promoting new skills required to create a world where everybody will be happy and healthy. In other words, pedagogies present different opportunities for different persons. The probable areas where pedagogies can play a potential role of in the age of transhumanism are discussed as under.

Helping Learners to Master Learning and Use It in Real Life Situations

Ability to use learned knowledge in real life situations is one of the prime demands of modern societies. This demand will further intensify in transhumanistic societies aiming to bring relationship between 'men and machine' up to an unprecedented level. Pedagogies can play an important role to fulfill this demand. This optimism is based on the observation that new pedagogies use technologies to meet different learning purposes. The use of technologies is expected to help learners in discovering, creating, mastering and using knowledge to face real life situations. It is also expected that technology supported pedagogies will help learners to get mastery over curricular content (Fullan, & Langworthy, 2014). And it is obvious that new found learning approach and acquired learning will make learners more confident and skilled to face real life situations in the age of transhumanism. This view-point can be supported by the following observation of Foster and Yaoyuneyong (2016) who devised and used two pedagogies (CBPs and flipped classrooms) to equip students to overcome real-world challenges:

The flipped classroom CD [flipped classroom cross-disciplinary] CBP [client-based project] provided students with opportunities to gain experience working in cross-functional teams and to gain more awareness of common workplace challenges – all while facing the additional challenge of meeting the needs of real clients. Through their experience in a near real-world work environment, students were able to better understand how to work under pressure and become more comfortable dealing with vagueness and uncertainty. Students were also able to improve their interpersonal and professional communication and gain experience overcoming and resolving various conflicts (p.54).

Supporting Teachers to Forge Learning Partnerships With Learners

In contrast to age old notion to assess teacher's quality primarily in terms of their ability to deliver content, the new demand from them is to help learners not only to master learning but also to forge a learning partnership with them. In the age of transhaumanism where there is every chance that learner will be surrounded more by machines than human, the need for this learning partnerships will be felt more than ever. The reason is that these partnerships will help learners to develop much needed human values and righteous approaches to live their life in a peaceful manner. New pedagogies can help teachers to make it possible, as suggested by Fullan and Langworthy (2014, p.14):

…in the new pedagogies model, the foundation of teacher quality is a teacher's pedagogical capacity – their repertoire of teaching strategies and their ability to form partnerships with students in mastering the process of learning.

In times to come, new pedagogies will help the education system to emerge as a two-way process, where both teachers and learners will work together to achieve specified objectives. This togetherness will help the teachers and learners in two ways, first- understanding the needs and concerns of the transhuman age, second- helping each other to maximize the benefits offered by emerging technologies and techniques. Besides, they will also get an opportunity to debate and scrutinize the happenings all around and find out best possible ways to deal with them.

Empowering Learners to Develop Critical Thinking Skills

There is a general belief that the best possible solution to overcome complex global challenges of present and future is to develop critical thinking abilities among our young generation. Unfortunately, realities suggest otherwise. Our teaching-learning processes fail to fulfill this demand, and pedagogy has been blamed for this situation, as evident from the observation of Saavedra and Opfer (2012):

…learners must hone their skills and enhance their learning as a matter of urgency to be able to address persistent global challenges. However, in spite of worldwide agreement that learners need skills such as critical thinking and the ability to communicate effectively, innovate and solve problems through negotiation and collaboration, pedagogy has not adapted to address these new challenges.

This demand for critical thinking is expected to rise more as transhuamanistic societies are expected to come up with newer innovations, techniques and products in a frequent manner. This situation will demand that people have to critically think and understand the pros and cons to accept or reject the new offerings. Not only this, critical thinking abilities will also help them to make sustainable use and consumption of new technologies. Pedagogies can be a helping tool to develop critical thinking abilities, as suggested by Leadbeater (2008) that 'the successful reinvention of educational systems worldwide depends on transforming pedagogy and redesigning learning tasks.' The pedagogies will help educational systems to bring new approaches and practices to help learners to develop critical thinking skills, a prerequisite to maximize the possibilities offered by transhumanism.

Promoting Lifelong Learning Among Learners

Learning is an integral part as well as necessity of human life. The complexities of modern world demands that one must keep learning throughout his/her life for own and societal betterment. This need and demand of lifelong learning will be much more in transhuman age where people will be supported to live longer and experience rapid changes in their day to day lives and surroundings. But practicing lifelong learning is not an easy task, as people would like to learn for many purposes but face many challenges at many levels. Making this situation clearer, Carneiro (2007) noted:

...people will face meta-learning challenges throughout their lives. They will likely include learning to organize multiple sources of information, learning to learn from experience and deal with the social dimensions of knowledge formation, learning to self-regulate time and effort to learn, learning to forget and to un-learn whenever necessary, and learning to make room for new knowledge (p. 6).

To fulfill the demand of lifelong learning in transhuman age, societies cannot solely depend on formal systems of education. The role of non formal systems of education like media, online education providers, voluntary organizations, business houses, etc. will be equally important to fulfill this demand. And all these stakeholders will need different pedagogies to promote lifelong learning among their target groups. In other words, transhuman age will witness the emergence of different types of pedagogies or andragogies to fulfill the demand of lifelong learning for all.

Engaging Technologies to Make Learning More Accessible and Flexible

Technologies are supposed to play an integral part in transhumanistic societies. In fact, using technologies for most of our activities will be a routine in the days to come. And one can predict the same on educational front as continuing advances in digital technologies, social media, and mobile devices will provide more control and opportunities for learners to accessing, creating, and sharing knowledge. To take advantage of this scenario, both teachers and learners will be expected to learn different methods and strategies to effectively use technologies for educational purposes, as suggested by Adeboye (2016):

Teachers must be trained to use technology well; otherwise, we will continue to fail. Teachers (even digital natives) need to be trained and shown how to use the technology they are so used to in order to teach. As teachers we need a simple yet effective digital pedagogy plan that guides us how we use technology in our classrooms. Our students likewise must be shown how to use technology to support their learning.

Role of pedagogies will be very important to make it happen. The reason behind this argument is that only availability of technology is not sufficient to impact learning, how to use it properly and effectively is much more important, and pedagogies are meant for this purpose. Therefore, educational systems will look for new and innovative pedagogies to support students and teachers to find ways to utilize different technologies for their varied learning needs. These pedagogies will also be helpful to use technologies to make learning more accessible and flexible, in other words, more individualized, personalized and need based learning.

Supporting Education for Sustainable Development

Sustainable development, simply defined by the Brundtland Report as" the development that meets the needs of the present without compromising the ability of future generations to meet their own needs " ((WCED, 1987, p.43) is necessity of our times and will be needed more than ever in transhuman age. This prediction is based on the observation that in quest to make human being happier, healthier and prosperous, the nature will be exploited more and at much faster rate. Education for Sustainability (EfS) and Education for Sustainable Development (ESD) have been seen as effective strategies to face this challenge and ensure that our 'lovely and lively planet' remains a 'lovely and living planet' for future generations too. Pedagogy is expected to play a very important role to promote ESD and Efs, as noted by Thomas (2014):

While the content that is included in EfS/ESD is clearly important, so too is the process by which that content is conveyed to learners. A most important component of the pedagogy associated with EfS/ESD is the process by which learners experience the material and values.

The importance of pedagogy can be understood from the fact that it is supposed to make a link between teaching and learning activities and this link is a vital component to enhance education's contribution to sustainable development. This optimism to utilize pedagogies for ESD/Efs purposes is aptly summarized in following words: A key factor in pedagogy is developing approaches which work within different national and local contexts (Livingston et al., p.8). Therefore, it can be safely predicted that pedagogies will play a very important role in transhuman age to make people aware about different developmental issues and challenges and also prepare them to contribute for a more sustainable world.

Future of Pedagogies in Transhumanistic Societies

The website of World Transhumanist Association (https://www.transhumanist.com/) sees transhumanism as an approach to create a civilization full of 'Triple S': superintelligence, superlongevity and superhappiness. This vision of transhumanistic societies makes us believe that our future will be happy and secure, but this is only one side of the coin. Emergence of these societies will also present certain challenges, as noted by McKie (2018):

Advocates of transhumanism believe there are spectacular rewards to be reaped from going beyond the natural barriers and limitations that constitute an ordinary human being. But to do so would raise a host of ethical problems and dilemmas.

Therefore, it can be predicted that transhumanistic societies will face a number of ethical and moral issues emerging from the use of newer technologies for rebuilding human bodies and revisiting their capacities. It has been felt that transhumanism movement needs new directions and approaches. This call is based on the observation that since its advent, transhumanism is mainly moving towards a linear path and preconceived philosophy but now revisiting is needed to make it more sustainable and achievable. This means all those who are leading this movement must have new vision and thinking and be ready to revisit the philosophy of transhumanism to accommodate criticisms and making its advances more ethical and acceptable. Experts like Rubin (2008) feel that:

The most successful societies in this world cultivate rather than reject restraint. Transhumanism is too entranced by the "could" to pay serious attention to the "should" beyond assertions that because this transformation is going to happen we better talk about ways to deal with it (p.155).

It can be safely predicted that in transhuman age newer lifestyles will emerge and people live and act in different ways. Besides, it is also expected that these societies will be more individualistic in nature. This prediction is based on the observation that rather than any other time of history, people are feeling much lonely and isolated, and this trend seems to continue. As resultant, we will witness a population having different psycho-social challenges. Besides, the other challenge before this population will be to redefine and understand the relations of living and nonliving entities, as portrayed by Snaza et al. (2014):

We need an open science, a science that is not afraid of remembering the cultural-political-historical construction of science within humanist networks, a science that will go beyond science as we know it toward helping us think the meaning of the disavowed relations in which we are always already entangled. These relations involve humans, animals, machines, and things. (p.52)

Pedagogies will definitely play an important role to make transhumanistic societies more accommodative and inclusive. Pedagogies will also be supposed to come with new approaches and techniques to provide need-based guidance and psychological counseling services at collective and individualistic level. In nutshell, it can be said that pedagogies will be needed and used more than ever in transhumanistic societies. The simple reason behind this prediction is that efforts to meet special needs and demands of society are directly proportional to call for devising and employing relevant pedagogies. The transhuman age is expected to create a world having unique demands and challenges, and will bank upon new pedagogies to find appropriate and sustainable solutions. In nutshell, pedagogies are destined to play a very important and unique role in transhumanistic societies.

CONCLUSION

In the age of transhumanism, people will be expected to live in different socio-cultural settings and face different set of psycho-technological challenges. The other prediction is that they will be physically more sound but psychologically more vulnerable. To accommodate with these changes and challenges, people will need different set of support mechanisms, and pedagogies will be certainly one of them.

Interestingly, some experts hardly see any relation between transhuamnism and pedagogy and often declare that both ends cannot meet but reality is different. In fact, if transhumanism have to progress, it must need pedagogical support on many fronts and for different purposes. This futuristic relationship has been probed further from many angles in this chapter. We can hope that presented analysis and arguments will prompt the leaders of transhumanist movement and pedagogical experts to come closer, understand each other, and work together to envision a healthier, happier and more sustainable world.

REFERENCES

Adeboye, D. (2016). *Digital pedagogy: Education, then technology!* Retrieved from https://elearningindustry.com/digital-pedagogy-education-technology

Carneiro, R. (2007). The big picture: Understanding learning and meta-learning challenges. *European Journal of Education*, *42*(2), 151–172. doi:10.1111/j.1465-3435.2007.00303.x

Child Australia. (n.d.).*What is pedagogy? How does it influence our practice?* Retrieved from https://childaustralia.org.au/wp-content/uploads/2017/02/CA-Statement-Pedagogy.pdf

Churton, A. (1900). *Kant on Education*. Boston: D.C. Heath and Co.

Coenen, C. (2014). Transhumanism in emerging technoscience as a challenge for the humanities and technology assessment. *Teorija in Praksa*, *51*(5), 754–771. Retrieved from https://www.fdv.uni-lj.si/docs/default-source/tip/tip_05_2014_coenen.pdf

Damberger, T. (2013). A*re pedagogy and transhumanism compatible*? Retrieved from http://indiafuturesociety.org/are-pedagogy-and-transhumanism-compatible/

Entz, S. (2006). Why pedagogy matters: The importance of teaching in a standards-based environment. *The forum on public policy*. Retrieved from https://files.eric.ed.gov/fulltext/EJ1099138.pdf

Foster, J., & Yaoyuneyong, G. (2016). Teaching innovation: equipping students to overcome real-world challenges. *Higher Education Pedagogies*, (1), 42-56. doi:10.1080/23752696.2015.1134195

Fullan, M., & Langworthy, M. (2014). *A rich seam: How new pedagogies find deep learning*. London: Pearson. Retrieved from http://www.michaelfullan.ca/wp-content/uploads/2014/01/3897.Rich_Seam_web.pdf

Hall, G. S. (1905). What is pedagogy? *The Pedagogical Seminary*, *XII*(4), 375–383. doi:10.1080/08919402.1905.10534667

Haraway, D. (1991). A cyborg manifesto: Science, technology, and socialist-feminism in the late twentieth century. In D. J. Haraway (Ed.), *Simians, cyborgs, and women: The reinvention of nature* (pp. 149–182). New York: Routledge. (Original work published 1985)

Hernaes, C. (2016). *The ethics of transhumanism*. Retrieved from https://techcrunch.com/2016/08/26/the-ethics-of-transhumanism/

Husbands, C., & Pearce, J. (2012). *What makes great pedagogy? Nine claims from research.* Nottingham, UK: National College for School Leadership. Retrieved from https://assets.publishing.service.gov.uk/government/uploads/system/uploads/attachment_data/file/329746/what-makes-great-pedagogy-nine-claims-from-research.pdf

Kimel, D. V. (2016, May 18). In defense of transhumanism. *The Washington Post.* Retrieved from https://www.washingtonpost.com/news/in-theory/wp/2016/05/18/in-defense-of-transhumanism/?noredirect=on&utm_term=.4418fc5fc27f

Leadbeater, C., & Wong, A. (2010). *Learning from the extremes: A white paper.* San Jose, Calif., Cisco Systems Inc. Retrieved from www.cisco.com/web/about/citizenship/socio-economic/docs/ Learning fromExtremes_WhitePaper.pdf

Lilley, S. (2013). *Transhumanism and society: The social debate over human enhancement.* New York: Springer. doi:10.1007/978-94-007-4981-8

Livingston, K., Schweisfurth, M., Brace, G., & Nash, M. (2017). *Why pedagogy matters: The role of pedagogy in Education 2030 a policy advice paper.* Retrieved from https://www.unesco.org.uk/wp-content/uploads/2017/06/pedagogy.pdf

McKie, R. (2018, May 6). No death and an enhanced life: Is the future transhuman? *The Guardian.* Retrieved from https://www.theguardian.com/technology/2018/may/06/no-death-and-an-enhanced-life-is-the-future-transhuman

More, M. (1990). Transhumanism: Towards a futurist philosophy. *Extropy, 6,* 6–12.

More, M., & Vita-More, N. (Eds.). (2013). *The transhumanist reader. Classical and contemporary essays on the science, technology, and philosophy of the human future.* Malden, MA: Wiley-Blackwell. doi:10.1002/9781118555927

Pedagogy. (2018a). In *Cambridge online dictionary.* Retrieved from https://dictionary.cambridge.org/dictionary/english/pedagogy

Pedagogy. (2018b). In *Oxford online dictionary.* Retrieved from https://en.oxforddictionaries.com/definition/pedagogy

Pedagogy. (2018c). In *Merriam-Webster's online dictionary.* Retrieved from https://www.merriam-webster.com/dictionary/pedagogy

RemsbergD. (2010). *The benefits and problems of transhumanism.* Retrieved from http://history.msu.edu/hst250-online/2010/04/20/the-benefits-and-problems-of-transhumanism/

Rubin, C. T. (2008). What is the good of transhumanism? In B. Gordijn & R. Chadwick (Eds.), *Medical Enhancement and Posthumanity* (pp. 137–156). Springer Science.

Saavedra, A., & Opfer, V. (2012). *Teaching and learning 21st century skills: Lessons from the learning sciences. A global cities education network report.* New York: Asia Society. Retrieved from http://asiasociety.org/files/rand-0512report.pdf

Scott, C. L. (2015). *The futures of learning 3: What kind of pedagogies for the 21st century?* UNESCO Education Research and Foresight, Paris. Retrieved from http://unesdoc.unesco.org/images/0024/002431/243126e.pdf

Singh, S. (2017). *Transhumanism and the future of humanity: 7 ways the world will change by 2030.* Retrieved from https://www.forbes.com/sites/unicefusa/2018/07/26/why-migrants-flee-central-america/#2f93dcf1301a

Siraj-Blatchford, I., Sylva, K., Muttock, S., Gilden, R., & Bell, D. (2002). *Brief No: 356 Researching Effective Pedagogy in the Early Years.* Retrieved from www.ioe.ac.uk/REPEY_research_brief.pdf

Smith, M. K. (2012). What is pedagogy? In *The encyclopedia of informal education.* Retrieved from http://infed.org/mobi/what-is-pedagogy/

Snaza, N., Appelbaum, P., Carlson, D., Morris, M., Rotas, N., Sandlin, O. S., ... Weaver, J. (2014). Toward a posthumanist education. *Journal of Curriculum Theorizing, 30*(2).

Stary, C. (2017). Agogic principles in trans-human settings. *Proceedings, 1,* 236. doi:10.3390/IS-4SI-2017-03949

Thomas, A. (2017). Super-intelligence and eternal life: transhumanism's faithful follow it blindly into a future for the elite. *The conversation.* Retrieved from http://theconversation.com/super-intelligence-and-eternal-life-transhumanisms-faithful-follow-it-blindly-into-a-future-for-the-elite-78538

Thomas, I. (2014). Special issue-pedagogy for education for sustainability in higher education. *Sustainability, 6*(4), 1705–1708. doi:10.3390u6041705

Tirosh-Samuelson, H. (2007). *Facing the challenges of transhumanism: Philosophical, religious, and ethical considerations.* Retrieved from http://transhumanism.asu.edu/pdf/2007_news_challenges.pdf

Trippett, D. (2018, March 29). Transhumanism: advances in technology could already put evolution into hyperdrive – but should they? *The Conversation.* Retrieved from http://theconversation.com/transhumanism-advances-in-technology-could-already-put-evolution-into-hyperdrive-but-should-they-92694

UNESCO. (2014). *Global monitoring report 2014.* Retrieved from http://unesdoc.unesco.org/images/0022/002256/225660e.pdf

Vinge, V. (2013). Technological Singularity. *The Transhumanist Reader,* 365-375.

WCED. (1987). *Our common future. World commission on environment and development.* Oxford, UK: Oxford University Press.

Chapter 12
Being a Post-Learner With Virtual Worlds

Ferhan Şahin
Anadolu University, Turkey

Ezgi Doğan
Anadolu University, Turkey

ABSTRACT

Transhumanism, which emerges as a movement of thought, stands out with the developments such as artificial organs, brain-to-brain knowledge and learning transfer and smart robots in the 21st century. One of these technologies, where we see early applications with the goal of reaching the post-human, is the virtual worlds. Some features of the post-humans, which can now be experienced through 3 dimensional immersive virtual worlds in a certain scale, also reveal the fact that the existing virtual worlds are a limited simulation of a transhumanist future. While the virtual worlds and transhumanism perspective is expected to be effective in various areas of human life, it will be inevitable for these effects to manifest themselves in learning processes. In this sense, evaluation of surrounding learning by virtual worlds is the main objective of this chapter. For this purpose, virtual worlds in transhumanism age were tried to be evaluated under learning context by using anime series and film samples which are yet considered as sci-fi.

INTRODUCTION

Nowadays, thought movements and technologies that will change and transform current learning conception and learning environments and perhaps move those beyond what we know are becoming an important topic. Prominent couple as predecessor and complementary of each other among these thought movements and technologies can be considered as transhumanism and 3 dimensional virtual worlds. Principles presented by transhumanism as a thought movement and impacts of 3 dimensional virtual worlds as a developing technology will create important transformation in all aspects of human life including learning activities. To understand and imagine how this transformation will occur and what the effects will be, it is beneficial to explain and evaluate these two concepts.

DOI: 10.4018/978-1-5225-8431-5.ch012

3 Dimensional Virtual Worlds

Virtual worlds are defined as feeling of users to be in another environment other than his/her real environment and environment created by computer to enable user to interact with this environment (Schroeder, 1996). User in a virtual world creates an "avatar" which is a character that represents the user in simulated environment and user moves in virtual world with this avatar and interacts with other avatars and objects in virtual world (Baker, Wentz, and Woods, 2009). Effectiveness of being there illusion created by virtual world can be evaluated as at what level do users feel they are in virtual world and what caused this feeling (Heeter, 1992). It can be said that most important factor emphasized in definition of virtual world that could impact learning environment is feeling of "being there". At this point, 3 dimensional immersive virtual worlds supported with virtual reality technologies are discussed.

In line with definition of virtual worlds, 3 dimensional immersive virtual worlds can be explained as follows (Dalgarno & Lee, 2010):

A computer-based, simulated environment in which users are able to immerse themselves, and within which they are able to, through their avatars (computer-based representations of themselves or alternative selves), experience, manipulate, interact with and/or create virtual objects and places that are graphically depicted in three dimensions.

There are two important key concepts that are related and emphasized in this definition. These could be given as immersion and 3 dimensional environments. It can be said that for a virtual world to be immersive, this world should be experienced by user in personal, social and environment manner in 3 dimensional environments. This experience can be provided by virtual reality technologies (Heeter, 1992). Technologies that completely involve perspective of user in virtual environments in terms of positioning of user in simulated virtual world in his/her unique way and exploring this virtual world with various sensory ways and interacting with this world can be called as immersive virtual reality (Osuagwu, Ihedigbo and Ndigwe, 2015; Psotka, 2015). With these technologies, users can experience i.e. experience being there feeling in virtual world with natural moves in real life and without any mediator between himself/herself and environment. User can fully commit to role of avatar in virtual world, take the steps necessitated by this role, feel the environment and have the feeling that s/he is doing all these in real world. Such role, under certain circumstances, can either be similar to human roles in real world or transhuman experiences in a fantastic world. At this point, where transhuman concept is reflected, transhumanism is discussed as another concept and a movement of thought.

Transhumanism

Transhumanism has been a movement of thought that expanded and developed in last decades (Bostrom et al., 1999; Bostrom, 2003). With this development and expansion, different definitions have emerged for transhumanism based on different perspectives of philosophical sense. However, before considering transhumanism as expression of different contexts, it is important to analyze "transhumanism" term from starting point to comprehend current condition of this philosophy and understand basis of this concept.

Throughout the history, there are expressions that uses transhumanism term which are relatively far from current meaning and there are expressions that explain similar concepts without using transhumanism term. Reade (1910) stated that humanity will act with a belief and passion to work together to eliminate disease and sin, perfect prodigy and love, find immortality, discover infinity, and divine cause of conquering creation. Although this discourse fits transhumanism perspective, transhumanism term was absent. Huxley (1957) expressed that humans can go beyond their self, transcend self as an individual within unity, and if this belief reaches sufficient number of humans, humanity will be at the edge of a new existence to realize destiny in conscious manner and used transhumanism term for this expression. Esfandiary (1972) wrote a book chapter by using transhumanism term and continued to develop transhumanist thoughts that expresses transhumanism as a transition from human to transhuman state. However, "transhumanism" was never used as a title of his definition. Transhumanism term was consciously used in an article called "Transhumanism: Towards s Futurist Philosophy" for the first time to define transhumanist philosophy (More, 1990). Accordingly, when evaluated under different expressions and interpretations context, it can be stated that it is possible to explain main themes, values and views of transhumanism (More, 2013).

World Transhumanism Association (WTA, 2018) defined transhumanism as "a philosophy that argues to set technology to work to transcend our biologic limits and transform human structure". Accelerated development of technology resulted in revolutionary situations such as transhuman artificial intelligence and molecular nanotechnology. Results of these developments may contain biochemically development or redesign of our pleasure centers; enjoy richer emotions, life-long happiness and exciting experience; eliminate aging; eliminate diseases and maybe, synthetically developing human body and gradually changing with computers.

In another definition, transhumanism was explained as a life philosophy driven by principles and values that encourage life and that desires continuation and acceleration of smart life forms with science and technological and beyond human life and human limitations (More, 1990). In addition to this definition, de Mul (2010) expressed transhumanism as adding strong belief of intelligence, science and technology will lead to social, physical and intellectual development to humanism. Transhumanism can be interpreted as philosophical and cultural movement with explanatory and normative components. In terms of descriptive perspective, transhumanism is not only strengthening of current and future technologies with previous capacities but also adding new different skills that will enable radical change for our world and humans. In normative terms, it is expressed as doing our best to accelerate uncovering of technological developments for improvement/development and realizing a post-human future possibility (Verdoux, 2009).

According to Bostrom (2005), transhumanism presents an interdisciplinary approach to understand and evaluate opportunities to develop human organism that is possible with rapid technological developments. It also draws attention to current technologies, such as information technologies and genetic engineering, as well as future technologies such as molecular nanotechnology and artificial intelligence. Among improvement options, it is possible to see significant increase in human lifetime, elimination of certain diseases, decreasing unnecessary pain and increasing intellectual, physical and emotional capacities of humans. According to this perspective, transhumanism creates an opportunity to live longer and healthier lives, to develop our memory and other intellectual skills, to improve our emotional experiences, to increase our subjective wellbeing emotion and to achieve better control level over our lives (Bostrom, 2005).

Analysis and interpretation of different definitions of transhumanism showed that these definitions harbour basic common values in general. In accessibility of such basic values, existence of certain conditions and creating ideal environment to realize foresights of transhumanism is important. At this point, basic conditions to realize transhumanist thought are stated as;

1. Global security,
2. Technological progress and
3. Wide access (Bostrom, 2005).

In first one of these basic conditions, global security, a scenario that should be avoided under all conditions is considered. This scenario can be stated as risk of existence. Accordingly, it is stated that size of risk consisting of existential risks are extremely important (Leslie, 1996; Bostrom, 2002; Rees, 2003). Existential risks show that when it comes to extinction of human race or permanently destroying further development capacity, transhumanist basic values cannot be reached, and humans will fail (Bostrom, 2005). In this sense, it is appropriate to say that global security is one of the top-ranking conditions to realize transhumanism thought.

Second one among these preconditions, technological progress, forms one of the basic cornerstones. This condition emphasizes challenges to overcome our incompetency in biologic sense (aging, disease, poor memory and intelligence level, limited emotional capacity and capacitive level for regular well-being) and we need high level tools to overcome successfully. Other points include that development of such tools would require a great struggle in terms of collective problem solving capacities of our species. Another important point emphasized was that technological advancement is closely linked with economic development and economic growth or increased production in another sense can serve as proxy to technological advancement under certain conditions (Bostrom, 2005). Based on these information, it is appropriate to comment that technological advancement has vital role to realize transhumanist ideals in various ways.

Another condition to realize transhumanist dream is stated as wide access. In transhumanist philosophy, it is emphasized that complete realization of basic values depend ideally on everyone becoming post-human. Reasons that show necessities of supporting wide access are given as decreasing inequality to achieve a just order, to show respect and solidarity between humans, to obtain help for transhumanism, to increase chance of humans to become post-human and to alleviate suffering of humans at a wider scale (Bostrom, 2005). At this point, to have a future where transhumanism is realized, importance of abovementioned conditions can clearly be seen. It emerged that to achieve positive transformation in humanity as predicted by transhumanism and to achieve determined objectives, humanity must undertake certain basic duties in responsible manner and in this sense, complete these duties. Concordantly, it can be commented that if related conditions are not met, it is highly impossible for transhumanism philosophy to invigorate in real world.

Another perspective that should be emphasized under transhumanism and concept that emerged from this perspective is singularity. In terms of this concept, first name that comes into mind is one of the largest and most important figures of transhumanism, Ray Kurzweil (Dahlin, 2012). Kurzweil (2005) defined singularity concept in his book (The Singularity is Near) as a period in the future where technological change will have higher speed, this change will cause deep impacts and human life will experience irrevocable transformation. Fundamental idea behind "The Singularity is Near" is expressed as extreme increase of development speed of technology created by humanity and expansion of powers in fast and big tempo. It is predicted that such expansion and change will start in almost incomprehensible way and explode in unexpected manner (Kurzweil, 2005).

In terms of singularity context, emphasis of information-based technologies will cover all information and competencies of humans and as a result power to define schemes, problem solving skills, emotional and ethical intelligence of human brain (Kurzweil, 2005) is in line with transhumanism philosophy. At this point, although human brain is impressive in multiple aspects, there are serious limitations. It is stated that brain uses unprecedented parallel structure (trillions of intraneuronal connection) to rapidly recognize models that are ambiguous, however, human thinking system is relatively slow and physiologic band spectrum to process new information is highly limited compared to exponential expansion of human knowledge database (Kurzweil, 2005). In line with this, if current predictions regarding increasing speed of processing capacity are correct, in not a faraway future, we would need neural implants to completely benefit from super speed computers that will exist in the future (Kurzweil, 2000). Based on this information, it can clearly be seen that basis of singularity expectation fits with transhumanism movement. This means conditions predicted under singularity context are at the point that is desired to be achieved with transhumanism perspective. It can be commented that hopes in optimistic structure of transhumanism philosophy towards future will be near to turn into reality with singularity.

As seen from these explanations, transhumanism generates certain ideas to take humanity to next level with technological and scientific developments and forms the intellectual basis to transform into post-human. At this point, post-human concept that can be experienced via virtual worlds actually reflects that current virtual worlds are only limited simulations of transhumanist future.

Transhumanism and Virtual Worlds

When statements regarding transhumanism are evaluated, this thought movement pledged a "transcending human" stated with post-human, super-human, overhuman and these pledges emerged certain concepts (Şişman-Uğur, 2018). It can be seen that these concepts are considered under increasing life quality, slowing aging, infinite life, emotion-free human, artificial organs, brain that surpasses biologic limits, order instead of chaos, human-machine integration, robot/cyborg/android, artificial reality/virtual reality, nanotechnology, artificial intelligence, divine technology, omega point, cloud information/techno-system for humans, common consciousness and singularity (Şişman-Uğur, 2018). Versatility of all these concepts led subjects related with transhumanism to have wide range of area and led a multidisciplinary area including philosophers, futurists, scientists, lawyers, sociologists, doctors, health scientists, engineers, artists, men of literature, psychologists, pharmacologists, genetic scientists, technology research institutions and even bureaucrats to evaluate this field.

When fields related with transhumanism movement are considered, in addition to predominant disciplines like nanotechnology or genetic engineering, there are some other fields that are less visible. In this sense, virtual worlds (video games etc.) are emphasized. Since high number of transhumanists appreciate this freedom and power at basis of this digital environments and realizing that these environments can support transhumanism thought (Geraci, 2012) shows the value of virtual worlds for this perspective.

It is emphasized that virtual worlds play a significant role in innovative transhumanism. In this sense, it can be said that technologic fantasies that looked borrowed from 20th century has become one of the focal points of transhumanism expectations. In this sense, it is stated that some transhumanists hope to restructure the reality in line with the vision in video games which is the fantastic world of imagination. (Geraci, 2012). Virtual worlds develop transhumanism idea with designs, options they offer and impact level they have and enable transcend human biology. In this term, it can be commented that video games and virtual worlds play a key role in transhumanism (Geraci, 2012).

By nature, technology is about crossing the lines, however, in terms of virtual worlds, these worlds work better than other technologies as an illustration of our post-human potential. Additionally, in general sense, when it is considered that inhabitants of virtual worlds live in a magical space with meaning and power, it is possible to state that almost all virtual world offers an opportunity to exceed our limits (Geraci, 2012). In line with these, it is believed to be effective to clearly understand importance of these environments under user experience and thoughts by considering video games and virtual worlds based on transhumanism context. Researchers showed that video game and virtual world users (such as World of Warcraft and Second Life etc.) would prefer to live in a virtual world if they were given the chance (Castronova, 2008). Additionally, as a realistic form of immortality, there were findings showing that they would consider living like characters in the game (Bainbridge, 2010) and it is interesting and impressive to live like that. In addition to these, another important finding is that other than players that support transhumanism, some of the players who do not share transhumanist perspective reflected that it is attractive to live in a virtual game world (Bainbridge, 2010). Based on the fact that by combination of science and science fiction preserving expansion of transhumanism in most of the 20th century (Geraci, 2011), it is stated that transhumanism has critical importance regarding belief to upload our minds to virtual worlds or to even environments such as World of Warcraft and Second Life (Geraci, 2012). Hence, in literature, it is expressed that basically including our mind and personal identity, everything is information within different schemes and in principle, there are no barriers to transfer personal memories and identity to computer (Kurzweil, 2005). Based on this information, importance of relationship of virtual worlds with transhumanism and information provided to coherently evaluate expectations towards future can clearly be seen. While it is expected that virtual worlds and transhumanist thought will be effective in various aspects of human life, it is inevitable that these effects will be visible in learning processes and environments. In this sense, it is necessary to understand and discuss what type of transformation will these two concepts cause in learning processes.

Learning Under Effect of Transhumanism and Virtual Worlds

Studies in the literature states that in following periods, education and learning activities will change for transhumans (Rikowski, 2002) and it is an important necessity to structure new learning processes and being prepared for change (Şişman-Uğur, 2018). At this point, there is a distinction between future of education under transhumanism context and future in education. First, it is about how schools and education will process and organised in the future, and second one is about considering future studies and future visions as topic content in current schools (Hicks, 2008). It is emphasized that transhumanism is valid for both and for the future, commons effects of brain science and information technologies on education practice are emphasized (Dahlin, 2012). Which path will education and learning will follow for future generations and how education system will be organized will be the main focus of this study. In addition, the moral and ethical dimensions of transhumanism in the context of individuals, society and religion are excluded from the scope of this study.

It is stated that connection with human brain with external intervention was tried and successful results were obtained as well as there were successful studies to control exploration and learning of brain and developing learning and memorizing skills of brain (HRL, 2016). Additionally, it is stated that recreation of the consciousness of individuals on computer environment and studies to back-up consciousness will be carried one step forward by transferring back-up consciousness to individuals in future steps (Now This Future, 2018; Regalado, 2018) In this sense, development in technologies like existence of virtual brains, enhanced reality, direct integration of virtual reality environment and brain and event hologram memory are predicted. To be able to evaluate the effects of transhumanist philosophy with human and technology, and to investigate its effects on learning, requires knowledge and experience related to many disciplines in the context of education and technology. (Şişman-Uğur, 2018). Effective and efficient realization of these necessities has key properties to obtain coherent predictions regarding how learning will become in transhumanism era for new generations and to generate ideas about could be done by using different disciplines.

When we consider that virtual worlds of today are preview of transhumanism future, it can be commented that considering and evaluating these virtual worlds under learning context can provide guidance to have a learning map for future generations. Even those 3 dimensional immersive virtual worlds produced with current technologies can provide unprecedented support in terms of learning as these worlds create feeling of being there and enable obtaining real life experiences. In a future where transhumanism objectives are realized, this support could be a capacity to move learning to another dimension.

MAIN FOCUS OF THE CHAPTER

Virtual worlds, transhumanism and current relationship of these two concepts on learning are analyzed above. In this study, on contrary to current situation, the purpose is to go one step forward and predict and imagine possible changes in the future. Various productions presented as science fiction in fact can be messengers of changes in the future and it is appropriate to analyze these productions to achieve abovementioned objectives. In this sense, properties expected from virtual worlds that will be used in learning environments in transhumanism age and evaluation of surrounding learning by these virtual worlds is the main objective of this chapter. For this purpose, document analysis was conducted and virtual worlds in transhumanism age were tried to be evaluated under learning context by using anime series and film samples which are yet considered as sci-fi. Certain criteria were considered to determine productions evaluated in this study. Based on these criteria, properties of productions can be listed as having a theme that caused permanent change in human mind and body, containing virtual world and artificial intelligence component. Based on these criteria, productions included in this study are Chappie, Sword Art Online, Source Code, The Upgrade, Elysium, Knights of Sidonia, Ready Player One and Automata. Considering essential body and mind system developments are possible by using biotechnology and rapidly developing genetic engineering technologies (Kurzweil, 2005), results obtained from analyzed productions and possible changes that these results can make on learning were evaluated under mind and body enhancement themes.

DISCUSSION

Virtual World Themed Productions

Sword Art Online

First season of Sword Art Online was aired in 2012 and this is an anime series in action, adventure, and science fiction genre. The first season of this anime explains that in 2022, thousands of people are trapped inside a new massive multiplayer online role playing game (MMORPG) and what they experience to get freed of this virtual world. Most basic and important feature of Sword Art Online game that is expected by thousands of gamers is that with a special headgear called Nerve Gear, gamers can link into massive virtual world. With the technology of this special headgear, gamers can connect to their characters in virtual world via their brains and can have all the interaction within the game only by thinking. The adventure starts when Kirito, the lead character of anime series, notices on the first day when the game is opened to access of gamers that there is no menu to exit the game. As game creator and game master Kayaba Akihiko announced that he removed all exit options from the game and only way to exit the game and return to real world was to beat last boss on top of 100-floored tower called Aincrad and game experience takes a new path for gamers. Additionally, other feature of this virtual world and Nerve Gear technology is that when gamers die in this virtual world, they would also die in real world by shocking users' brain with this special headgear turns these lives in the virtual world into life and death battle. Dying in Sword Art Online virtual world means dying in real world is the prominent theme of this anime. Although the death of players in this virtual world causes them to die in real life, a scene in the anime takes it a step further. An echo of Kayaba Akihiko's consciousness that continues to exist in the game server even after his death is an interesting example in the context of transhunamism.

Ready Player One

Directed by Steven Spielberg, Read Player One movie is a sci-fi, action and adventure themed movie adapted from the novel of Ernest Cline with the same name. Screenplay of this movie was written by Zak Penn and Ernest Cline. Storyline is in year 2045 and described the world as harsh environment with low living standards for most of the people. Storyline of this movie focused on experiences of lead character Wade Watts (Tye Sheridan) in a massive virtual world called OASIS. OASIS is a virtual world limited only by imagination where you can do everything, go everywhere or become the one thing you want to be and where most part of humanity spend almost all their time. In this movie, after the death of creator of OASIS, James Halliday (Mark Rylence), adventure of lead character Watts and his friends who wants to win a three-staged competition designed to select the heir to leave the all his wealth and full control of OASIS are explained in this fantastic virtual universe. It can be said that one of the things that should be emphasized in terms of technology is the technology products that are designed as wearable cloths and glasses and enable direct digital connection to OASIS where humans can interact with virtual world and their movements in real life are translated to virtual world. Another point to be emphasized is with this direct connection and translating exact motions in real world, humans are actually living in OASIS. Such that having real correspondence of money and goods in OASIS in real life and finding buyers at high price is an important indicator that this virtual world is more important than real world.

As seen in productions analyzed under virtual world theme, with brain-machine interaction, humans can completely feel themselves in virtual world in physical and cognitive way and even biologic events like death can occur in these environments. In this sense, there are both invasive and non-invasive studies at certain levels regarding these technologies. At this point, it can be stated that especially developments in nanorobot technology use can be one of the leading technologies in terms of virtual worlds and games. This technology emphasizes that humans will completely experience virtual reality in convincing manner. At this point, it is emphasized that not needing any physical contact with neurons and existing technology to bilaterally contact with neurons can be the basis for immersive virtual reality experience. For such technologies, "neuron transistors" that can detect when a nearby neuron is ignited or alternatively that can enable or disable ignition of neuron can be given as example (Weis and Fromherz, 1997). Additionally, there are studies in the literature stating that quantum dots have the feature to enable bilateral communication between neurons and electronic devices (Winter, Liu, Korgel and Schmidt, 2001). It can be stated that this virtual reality experience that can exactly be stated as immersive can process based on individual will on the basis of bilateral communication between nanorobots and neurons. In case of individual's desire to stay in reality of real world, related nanorobots will stay fixed inside capillary vessels without any functions, and these nanorobots will suppress all input data from sense organs and change these data with signals appropriate for virtual environment in case of individual's desire to enter virtual reality (Freitas, 1999). Core of this virtual reality sense provided by nanorobots with this bilateral communication is based on the fact that human body does not directly perceive brain and accordingly, these signals will be perceived as if they are coming from physical body or brain (Kurzweil, 2005). As it can be seen, in terms of theme in the production, there are researches to reach situations that are seen as utopic under current conditions. It can be stated that if such brain-machinery communication occurs and users are completely integrated within virtual world, there could be radical changes in learning context. In such scenario, learners can obtain context-special and real experiences completely independent of time and space. This way, dangerous and high cost experiences can be realized in more affordable and safe manner. At the same time, since students will see virtual world as a game, there could be positive outputs in terms of motivation. This means, learners can obtain necessary learning outputs within game scenario without noticing such process.

Body and Mind Enhancement Themed Productions

Source Code

Directed by Duncan Jones and written by Ben Ripley, Source Code is a mystery, sci-fi movie screened in 2011. This movie is about a soldier who wakes up in a different body, is assigned to find the bomber in the train as a part of experimental state program and only has 8 minutes to do that task. This experimental program was achieved by transferring human consciousness to another human body, however, this operation can only work for 8 minutes and it should be reapplied again after this time. In this movie, consciousness of Captain Colter Stevens is transferred to body of a teacher in that passenger train attacked by bomb in the morning and he is assigned to identify the bomber. Stevens, who is surprised about this cannot make sense why he is there, and he is confused about what he experiences since he doesn't know what he is doing. Managers of this experimental program explain him the situation and ask him to determine the location of the bomb and identify the bomber. At this point, the main emphasis is although an event occurred in the past, past cannot be changed and only information can be collected.

The basis of the Source Code technology in the movie is based on the fact that the brain's electromagnetic field is active for a short period of time even after death, and short-term memory allows access to the section that covers the 8-minute memory segment just before the person's death. It is possible to say that Source Code technology, which is the basis of the film, is focused on re-arranging time and providing access to a parallel reality through the memory of a dead person rather than transferring the consciousness of a human to another human being offers an interesting perspective in the context of transhumanism.

The Upgrade

Written and directed by Leigh Whannell, The Upgrade is an action, thriller and sci-fi movie. Setting of this film is near future where technology is extremely widespread and almost controls all aspects of life. This film is about events that took place after lead character Grey Trace (Logan Marshall-Green) gets paralyzed after a traffic accident where his wife dies. Grey, who is weary of life, is treated by implanting an experimental computer chip and gets back up again and notices that his computer chip has a will of itself. In terms of technology in this film, key elements are human enhancement, nanotechnology and artificial intelligence. Mechanical or electronic enhancement of human organs (to turn into weapons), storing and operating nanorobots in human body with nanotechnology (enhancement for weapons and war), developing super capacity computer chips, transplanting these chips to humans as implant, making these chips a part of problematic area of humans that need treatment and chip having a will is the main subjects of this film. Although there are many examples in the context of the enhancement of the human body by using implants in the movie, establishing the connection between the brain and limbs of Gray who is in a quadriplegic state by means of using a computer chip (Stem) is an important part of the film. The scene where the main character begins to use all his limbs in seconds after the surgery can be expressed as a relevant example, which can be evaluated especially from the perspective of transhumanism.

Elysium

Written and directed by Neill Blomkamp, Elysium that was first screened in 2013 is in drama, action, and sci-fi genre. Timeline of this movie is in 2154 and a world with extremely rich and extremely poor people are shown. While rich people live in a space station called Elysium with various technologies, poor people are forced to live in overcrowded and ruined Earth. However, this would not stop humans on Earth to try to go to Elysium to live in better conditions or get treatment. However, strict precautions and anti-immigration laws of the state prevents these initiatives and an army of robots is used as security force both on Earth and in Elysium. In this movie, one of the poor people who tries to survive on Earth, Max (Matt Damon), has a work accident and exposed to deadly radiation and because of no treatment available other than Elysium, it focuses on the task that he started to enter Elysium. To increase his successful rate in this process, a mechanical exoskeleton to enhance physical power of skeleton system and electronic tool and interface connected to brain are implanted. In terms of technology, other key points in the movie are directly transferring and storing digital information to brain, advanced gene technology and repair and readjustment at cellular or atomic level. In this context, a small girl with an advanced disease (Acute lymphoblastic leukemia) that cannot be treated on earth, can be treated with re-atomizing method in a matter of seconds (such as the re-creation of diseased areas rather than a treatment) by using a medical technology specific to Elysium, is a striking example.

Knights of Sidonia

Created by Yuichi Matsushita and Tatsuya Shishikira, Knights of Sidonia is an anime series in action, adventure and sci-fi genre consisting of 24 episodes where first episode was aired in 2014. This series is directed by Koubun Shizonu and written by Sadayuki Murai and Shigeru Murakoshi. In this anime, after alien (Gauna) invasion that occurred thousands of years ago and humanity was at the verge of extinction, humans are escaping with giant space ships and scatter around different corners of space to find a habitable new planet. Anime focuses of one of these spaceships, Sidonia, and certain part of the journey. In storyline, we can see Nagate Tanikaza who surfaces from depth of Sidonia to find food in the year of 3394 without any knowledge of this event and situation of humankind, and his survival struggle and other problems. In this anime, key points are fight with Gauna, giant robots developed with special technologies to protect the ship and humans inside the ship, and specially trained pilots. Additionally, in terms of technology, another important point can be stated as insufficient resources for survival of crew and human population inside the ship and development of appropriate spaces to provide new resources is a genetic solution for insufficient sources of the ship. With this gene technology, humans in new generation have decreased eating need once a week and obtain most of the necessary energy from photosynthesis by using solar energy. Additionally, with gene technology, new generation is born without genders and after certain age, they can select and transform based on their partners or population. In addition, the exact cloning of people (the cloning of the individual's memory and experience can be done in a manner that can be transferred to the clone) and using this method as a backup system for important individuals has been achieved. In line with these technological developments, regeneration of human cells and self-treatment prevented aging and certain level of immortality is reached (this is not public information and only a high-level governor group have access to this feature).

In productions analyzed under body and mind enhancement theme, it can be seen that a post-human concept can exist with various technologies. Current studies and development activities show that steps are taken to build this future. When these activities are analyzed, it is important to emphasize research and development activities especially in nanotechnology field. Nanotechnology is considered as science and engineering activities at atomic and molecular level. In nanotechnology basis, this design approach consists of nanorobotics technology. Nanorobotics is defined as machinery or robot production technology at nanometer scale or similar scale. Nanorobots that work in design and production of nanotechnology engineering are defined as tools that consist of nanoscale or molecular components ranging between 01-10 micrometer (Kad, Hodgar and Thorat, 2018). One of the fields with highest potential for using nanorobots is given as biomedical nanorobots (nanomedicine). Recent developments in design, production and operation of nanorobots emphasize that power, function and versatility of these nanorobots are largely increasing. It is stated that these micro machineries have a large potential for wide range of biomedical applications (Li, Esteban-Fernández de Ávila, Gao, Zhang and Wang, 2017). Nanorobots that represent all types of smart structures with nanoscale moving, detection, signaling, information processing, intelligence, manipulation and crawling behavior (Bagade et.al., 2013) are considered as powerful tools to enhance human biological systems (Kad et al., 2018). In this sense, under reverse engineering basis, human blood studies that include redesign can be give as suitable examples. Redesign (Rob Freitas) of red blood cells that inefficiently transfer oxygen to cells in circulation system which is regarded as a system that does not work with full-efficiency can be given as example (Kurzweil, 2005). It is stated that robotic red blood cells (reciprocates) that can be created with redesign may enable humans to function for hours without oxygen (Freitas, 1999; 2003), and with newly designed robotic blood cells, we can have the capacity to store and carry hundred times more oxygen. Additionally, to develop immune system of humans, designs related with white blood cells (microbivore) (Freitas, 1999) are other approaches considered under current technologies. Microbivore are nanorobots known as nanorobotic phagocyte that act as artificial white blood cells. These microbivores capture pathogens in blood circulation and divides these pathogens to smaller molecules. Main function of microbivores that consist of four main components is absorbing pathogens in blood circulation with phagocyte process and digest these pathogens (Wilner, 2009). After neutralizing pathogens, microbivores are discarded from body via kidneys and urine. As a result of phagocytosis cycle that is completed in thirty seconds, bacterial compounds are digested and turned into non-antigenic molecules and it is emphasized that there is no sepsis or septic shock risk (Freitas, 1998). Studies showed that microbivores are 1000 times faster than phagocytes in blood circulation and did not cause pathogens to show multiple drug resistance. Additionally, in the literature, it is stated that microbivores are used in bacterial infections as well as cleaning infections in urine and synovial fluids (Kad et al., 2018). Preventing aging, minimizing biological needs with different technologies in Knights of Sidonia example can be considered as future versions of abovementioned nanorobots.

In terms of human body, by adopting current technologies, nerve tips of people without arms, hands or legs are intervened and these people were able to control robotic organs (Şişman-Uğur, 2018). This can be considered as reflection under current conditions with integrated exoskeleton and linking this exoskeleton with brain in Elysium movie.

Additionally, different techniques that would act as a communication bridge between biologic data processing and digital technologies are developed. In this sense, tools to bilaterally communicate with neurons (neuron transistors) are developed (Zeck and Fromberz, 2001) and movement of a live leach was controlled with computer. Under the scope of technological tools developed with current means can also include implants based on "neuromorphic" model (reverse engineering in human brain and nervous system) developed for certain parts of brain (Brumfiel, 2002). Among these implants, implants that directly communicate with left ventricular and subthalami nucleus of brain to reverse devastating symptoms of Parkinson's diseases and neural implants that can replace damaged retinas can be given as examples (Kurzweil, 2005). As in The Upgrade movie, this situation provides clues regarding treatment of damaged parts of body with various implants and even eliminating limitations like disease or injuries.

Another field of technology that can serve as basis for humanistic expectations is genetic engineering. In this field, human somatic-cell engineering is emphasized as a promising research field. This method includes an approach that uses stem cells called transdifferentiation. In this method, human DNA is used to transform a cell to another type of cell and creating new tissues (Collas and Hâkelien, 2003). Studies in this field successfully reprogrammed liver cells to pancreatic cells, and human skin cells to immune system and neural system cells (Horb, Shen, Tosh and Slack, 2003). Additionally, since all self-regenerating and all somatic cell types have differentiation potential, important improvements were achieved in studies conducted with human pluripotent stem cells that has great value in cellular treatment approaches (Zhou et al., 2016). To reprogram human somatic cells and transform pluripotent stem cells, on a polydopamine mediator surface specially developed for this purpose, cells obtained from human urine and navel string stem cells were reprogrammed and long-term regeneration was successfully achieved (Zhou et al., 2016). In this sense, with various methods in genetic engineering that has high potential, it is known that any organ that is compatible with human genetic properties can be developed, a complete young organ can be achieved once telomers of this new developed organ reached original youth capacity (Lanza et.al., 2000), i.e. an organ can be replaced by younger and healthier version without any operation or any immune system reactions. By applying this method to any organ or tissue of human body in certain periods, it is stated that humans can gradually be younger (Kurzweil, 2005). This method, which is currently being explored and developed with exciting expectations, is also a precursor to the utopian technologies in the Elysium and Knights of Sidonia.

Analysis of production under body and mind enhancement theme in terms of developing technologies have focused on body enhancement until this point. However, it can be seen that there are various properties to be analyzed under mind enhancement. In this sense, it is beneficial to analyze current mind enhancement applications. Firstly, direct information transfer to brain, information transfer between brains, information storing in brain, learning facilitation, and neurologic control of brain and machine interfaces (BMI) can be given as examples. There are successful experimental results in studies in this direction regarding external intervention to brain and transferring experiences by connecting with brain. Additionally, successful results were obtained in transcranial direct current stimulation (tDCS) researches that were conducted to strengthen learning and memory (HRL, 2016). Based on increased coherence of learned skills to realize cognitive and real-world tasks with tDCS, it can be stated that transcranial direct current stimulation has an effect on gaining skills (Choe, Coffman, Bergstedt, Ziegler and Phillips, 2016). As in Elysium, direct transfer of digital information to human brain can be considered as one of the results of such studies.

In studies regarding brain to brain interface (BTBI), there are results showing that EEG was used to transfer information on brains of a human to another human brain with transcranial magnetic stimulation (TMS). As a result, it is stated that two humans jointly completed a task by direct BTBI as communication channel. In this study, it is stated that to reach the objective in a computer game, brains of two people cooperated with communication and completed a visual task (Rao et al., 2014). In another study, sensorimotor information that has behaviorally significant structure was transferred in real-time between brains of two rats. In this study, rat that showed the behavior acted as coder and the results showed that information obtained from brain of coded rat were transferred to another rat that acted as decoder (intracortical microstimulation - ICMS). As a result of these findings, it is stated that brains are merged, and a complex system is formed with technology. It is stated that BTBI can activate brain networks for bilateral transfer, processing and storing in animals and this could form the basis for new social interaction type studies and biologic information processing tool studies (Pais-Vieira, Lebedev, Kunicki, Wang and Nicolelis, 2013). In Source Code and The Upgrade examples, science fiction elements such as transferring human mind to another body and this mind having its own will describes an achievable future if abovementioned studies are developed further.

Artificial Intelligence Themed Productions

Chappie

Directed by Neill Blomkamp and written by Neill Blomkamp and Terri Tatchell, Chappie is a 2015 action, drama and crime movie. Timeline of this movie is near future and public order is preserved by mechanical police force. This movie tells the story of a robot (Chappie) that was stolen and reprogrammed after being damaged and discarded. With this new programming, our lead character robot is the first droid with thinking and feeling ability and this is the main theme of the movie. In general sense, in this movie, one of the basis for storyline is decreasing and controlling high crime rates in Johannesburg with robots of private company (Tetravaal Company). In the movie, the designer of the robots (Deon Wilson) develops a new artificial intelligence but the company will not let him to use it. His efforts trying to make this technology into a reality is another theme of the movie. After various unexpected events, by loading artificial intelligence to a discarded robot, turning this robot into a machine that has the ability to think and feel and need of this robot to learn and grow like child is a key point. Other than that, probably the most important theme of this movie is with extreme learning speed, Chappie discovers that memories and consciousness can be stored and transferred into mechanic vessels (like droids) and finally manage to achieve this. From this point of view, it is an important point in the scope of transhumanism that

Chappie saves Deon by transferring his consciousness to a robot, and in a way enables him to continue to exist by just replacing his vessel.

Automata

Directed by Gabe Ibáñez and written by Gabe Ibáñez, Igor Legarreta and Javier Sánchez, Automata was screened in 2014. Automata is an action, thriller and sci-fi movie that occurs in 2044 in dystopian world. This movie is based on Automata Pilgrim 7000 robots designed and manufactured by ROC company to instigate Earth after catastrophic sun storms that annihilated 99.7% of humanity and only 21 million people survived. Key point of this movie is the security protocols of these robots. These protocols are defined as "a robot cannot harm a human and cannot make any adjustment, repair or change on itself or other robots". This movie starts when a police officer shoots a robot and the claim that this robot repaired itself. After that, ROC company agent Jacq Vacuan (Antonio Banderas) who is assigned to investigate discovers unimaginable discoveries about Automata Pilgrim 7000 robots. One of the most important discovery is that while the agent is investigating and thinking that there is someone who is illegally modifying robots, and then he finds out that another robot was making changes and turning these robots into beings that can think like them. In terms of technology, maybe the biggest plot twist is that these modified robots can create a new type of robot with higher thinking and feeling capacity as well as consciousness, and this new type of robot has the character of a child that needs learning and care and have the ability breath air. Considering these features, this child robot's characteristics and the process of its creation by other robots is an interesting example from the perspective of transhumanism.

Productions that are analyzed under virtual world and mind-body enhancement themes showed insights to develop post-human with technological developments. However, in the Chappie and Automata movies, robots that are equipped with artificial intelligence who can behave like a human with their will, mind and body are the subjects rather than effects of the abovementioned technological developments on humans. The point that needs to be considered here is that the robots are in a similar situation to people who have been enhanced as body and mind with non-biological parts. Based on this information, it can be concluded that the future robots, which may have similar characteristics in terms of thinking and feeling, like the people who have transcend into post-human with the support of their non-biological parts and the artificial intelligence these will provide.

CONCLUSION

Transhumanism based themes of productions analyzed until now are evaluated with current research and development studies under body and mind enhancement categories. It is seen that technologies in these science fiction productions have become successful at certain degrees in current studies or there are theoretical basis, design work and these studies are moving towards creating a product. In this sense, it can be predicted that such technologies or technologies with similar functions that look like products of imagination may become a part of our lives in the near future. Based on these insights, it is clearly seen that advanced technologies will create radical changes on learning and teaching and these changes should be adapted to use opportunities provided by these technologies in the best way possible for humanity. Under these necessities, it is important to evaluate development and changes in teaching and learning in terms of technological areas and methods considered under body and mind enhancement.

Today, it can be said that we have tools that can replace many organs of human body (arms, legs, hips, chin, veins, knee, elbow) and systems that can replace complex organs at certain levels. Accordingly, among technologies that may lead development and change in teaching and learning processes, it is important to consider implants that has high potential to improve and develop biologic systems of individuals in physical sense. Among these implants, usage of artificial organs to support learners in teaching and learning processes has high potential. Using artificial organs when students lack appropriate function of an organ, has missing organ or experience similar conditions is wide and effective usage area of such artificial organs. It can be stated that support of this technology will be great to increase learning process quality of learners or involve these learners within these processes without any barriers. With the support of these technological organs, it is predicted that students can experience learning activities without social and psychological damage as well as without physical challenges. This way, it is possible to achieve well-skilled, self-confident and successful individuals who can become a member of society.

Other than replacing parts of skeleton and muscle systems, another usage area of using implants to enable students to participate in learning activities or to increase quality of these activities can be seen as replacing and renewing organs or systems with mechanical parts. In this sense, correcting or improving vision sense of individuals with vision problems or vision loss with implants can be given as example. It is possible to treat and strengthen vision by replacing area of vision loss or damage with implants (replacing damaged retina with implants). At this point, it is possible that digitally replaced eye can provide opportunities to surpass limitations of biologic eyes and enable advanced properties (zoom features, augmented reality etc.) as well as undertaking vision function. Additionally, when neurons that provide vision has no function, programmable nanorobots may be used to complete various functions including moving, detection, signaling, information processing, intelligence and manipulation to enable bilateral communication between neurons and brain. Complete lack of vision or losing an eye permanently, replacing the organ with digital version as a whole can be expressed as another method that can be used for providing vision. Also, in terms of example that considers eye loss and losing eye or vision completely, somatic cell engineering can provide a solution by reprogramming cells with own DNA of the individual. With this method, it is possible to produce new tissues or organs and replace damaged ones. It is possible to state that having opportunities to improve this and other sense organs that has vital importance of education and teaching can greatly contribute to learners.

Similarly, various implants placed inside brains of individuals with physical disabilities, it is possible to achieve a scenario where virtual world created for learning can be presented without barriers, experiences can be achieved in full-immersion environment with currently developing technologies.

It is possible to say that technologies that fit transhumanism perspective in analyzed productions have different potentials in terms of human mind and these potentials can provide opportunities in education and teaching field.

With increasing internet access in line with technologic developments, educations services with low cost and wide access for different education levels are realized globally. In this sense, it can be stated that web-based education as a virtual environment has become one of the key points within education system and based on this fact, virtual worlds may have the greatest part in education of future.

Teachers working with teaching system that has flexible structure based on needs has great contribution for education quality and raise students in desired way. Popularity of virtual environments among learners and using these worlds as a part of education is another important point that should be supported by both researchers and learners. Accordingly, incremental increase to interest towards virtual worlds that has unlimited potential and ultimate and incomparable usage area indicates that education structure of the future will develop under the basis of virtual worlds. Besides, it is clear that we are unable to present an effective 3 dimensional virtual world in current technologies and virtual environments and we fail to provide being there feeling to learners with full-immersion. Currently, success of education over virtual environments is in fact a small part of results that can be provided by virtual worlds. Providing an easily accessible experience and authentic learning activities by a virtual world education environment that provides full immersion and being there feeling to learners has a key role to reach these results. In this sense, virtual worlds have unique value as these worlds enable learners to learn by doing in different fields, experience these via real world problems, and providing these experiences in an individualistic structure that has high artificial intelligence potential and offering a chance to transfer to different problems. Additionally, by succeeding in integrating of individuals with their non-biological intelligence can enable individuals to enter any virtual reality using their own will and they will be able to download and use information and skills directly. Considering these, it can be predicted that such phenomena as education and learning will undergo profound transformations and move to a new dimension.

REFERENCES

Bagade, O. M., Dhole, S. N., Kahane, S. K., Bhosale, D. R., Bhargude, D. N., & Kad, D. R. (2013). Appraisal on preparation and characterization of nanoparticles for parenteral and ophthalmic administration. *International Journal of Research in Pharmaceutical Sciences*, *4*(4), 490–503.

Bainbridge, W. S. (2010). When virtual worlds expand. In W. S. Bainbridge (Ed.), *Online worlds: Convergence of the real and the virtual* (pp. 237–251). London: Springer. doi:10.1007/978-1-84882-825-4_19

Baker, S. C., Wentz, R. K., & Woods, M. M. (2009). Using virtual worlds in education: Second Life® as an educational tool. *Teaching of Psychology*, *36*(1), 59–64. doi:10.1080/00986280802529079

Bostrom, N. (2002). Existential risks: Analyzing human extinction scenarios and related hazards. *Journal of Evolution and Technology / WTA*, 9.

Bostrom, N. (2005). A history of transhumanist thought. *Journal of Evolution and Technology / WTA*, *14*(1), 1–25.

Bostrom, N. (2005). Transhumanist values. *Journal of Philosophical Research*, *30*(9999), 3–14. doi:10.5840/jpr_2005_26

Brumfiel, G. (2002). Futurists predict body swaps for planet hops. *Nature International Journal of Science*, *418*, 359. PMID:12140527

Castronova, E. (2008). *Exodus to the virtual world: How online fun is changing reality*. New York: Palgrave Macmillan.

Choe, J., Coffman, B. A., Bergstedt, D. T., Ziegler, M. D., & Phillips, M. E. (2016). Transcranial direct current stimulation modulates neuronal activity and learning in pilot training. *Frontiers in Human Neuroscience*, *10*, 34. doi:10.3389/fnhum.2016.00034 PMID:26903841

Collas, P., & Håkelien, A. M. (2003). Teaching cells new tricks. *Trends in Biotechnology*, *21*(8), 354–361. doi:10.1016/S0167-7799(03)00147-1 PMID:12902172

Dahlin, B. (2012). Our posthuman futures and education: Homo Zappiens, Cyborgs, and the New Adam. *Futures*, *44*(1), 55–63. doi:10.1016/j.futures.2011.08.007

Dalgarno, B., & Lee, M. J. (2010). What are the learning affordances of 3-D virtual environments? *British Journal of Educational Technology*, *41*(1), 10–32. doi:10.1111/j.1467-8535.2009.01038.x

de Mul, J. (2010b). Transhumanism: The Convergence of Evolution, Humanism, and Information Technology. In *Cyberspace Odyssey: Towards a Virtual Ontology and Anthropology* (pp. 243–262). Newcastle upon Tyne, UK: Cambridge Scholars Publishing.

Esfandiary, F. M., & FM-2030. (1989). *Are You a Transhuman? Monitoring and Stimulating Your Personal Rate of Growth in a Rapidly Changing World*. Clayton, Australia: Warner Books.

Freitas, R. A. (1998). Exploratory design in medical nanotechnology: A mechanical artificial red cell. *Artificial Cells, Blood Substitutes, and Biotechnology*, *26*(4), 411–430. doi:10.3109/10731199809117682 PMID:9663339

Freitas, R. A. (1999). *Basic capabilities*. Georgetown, TX: Landes Bioscience.

Freitas, R. A. (2003). *Nanomedicine volume IIA: Biocompatibility*. Austin, TX: CRC Press. doi:10.1201/9781498712576

Geraci, R. M. (2011). There and back again: Transhumanist evangelism in science fiction and popular science. *Implicit Religion*, *14*(2), 141–172. doi:10.1558/imre.v14i2.141

Geraci, R. M. (2012). Video games and the transhuman inclination. *Zygon*, *47*(4), 735–756. doi:10.1111/j.1467-9744.2012.01292.x

Heeter, C. (1992). Being there: The subjective experience of presence. *Presence (Cambridge, Mass.)*, *1*(2), 262–271. doi:10.1162/pres.1992.1.2.262

Horb, M. E., Shen, C. N., Tosh, D., & Slack, J. M. (2003). Experimental conversion of liver to pancreas. *Current Biology*, *13*(2), 105–115. doi:10.1016/S0960-9822(02)01434-3 PMID:12546783

HRL. (2016). *HRL demonstrates the potential to enhance the human intellect's existing capacity to learn new skills*. Retrieved from http://www.hrl.com/news/2016/02/10/hrl-demonstrates-the-potentialto-enhance-the-human-intellects-existing-capacity-to-learn-new-skills

Huxley, J. (1957). *New bottles for new wine: Essays*. London: Chatto & Windus.

Kad, D., & Thorat, S. H. K. (2018). Nanorobotics: Medicine of the future. *World Journal of Pharmacy and Pharmaceutical Sciences*, *7*(8), 1393–1416.

Kurzweil, R. (2000). *The age of spiritual machines: When computers exceed human intelligence*. New York: Penguin.

Kurzweil, R. (2005). *The singularity is near*. New York: Penguin Group.

Lanza, R. P., Cibelli, J. B., Blackwell, C., Cristofalo, V. J., Francis, M. K., Baerlocher, G. M., ... Lansdorp, P. M. (2000). Extension of cell life-span and telomere length in animals cloned from senescent somatic cells. *Science*, *288*(5466), 665–669. doi:10.1126cience.288.5466.665 PMID:10784448

Leslie, J. (1996). *The end of the world: The ethics and science of human extinction*. London: Routledge.

Li, J., de Ávila, B. E. F., Gao, W., Zhang, L., & Wang, J. (2017). Micro/nanorobots for biomedicine: Delivery, surgery, sensing, and detoxification. *Science Robotics*, *2*(4), 1–9. doi:10.1126cirobotics.aam6431

More, M. (1990). Transhumanism: Towards a futurist philosophy. *Extropy*, (6), 6-12.

More, M. (2013). The philosophy of transhumanism. In M. More & N. Vita-More (Eds.), *The transhumanist reader: Classical and contemporary essays on the science, technology, and philosophy of the human future* (pp. 3–17). Malden, MA: John Wiley & Sons. doi:10.1002/9781118555927.ch1

Now This Future. (2018). *This Start-Up Wants to Upload Your Brain to a Computer*. Retrieved from https://www.facebook.com/NowThisFuture/videos/2008861865821650/

Osuagwu, O. E., & Ihedigbo, C. E., & Ndigwe, C. (2015). Integrating Virtual Reality (VR) into traditional instructional design. *West African Journal of Industrial and Academic Research*, *15*(1), 68–77.

Pais-Vieira, M., Lebedev, M., Kunicki, C., Wang, J., & Nicolelis, M. A. (2013). A brain-to-brain interface for real-time sharing of sensorimotor information. *Scientific Reports*, *3*(3), 1319. doi:10.1038rep01319 PMID:23448946

Psotka, J. (1995). Immersive training systems: Virtual reality and education and training. *Instructional Science*, *23*(5-6), 405–431. doi:10.1007/BF00896880

Rao, R. P., Stocco, A., Bryan, M., Sarma, D., Youngquist, T. M., Wu, J., & Prat, C. S. (2014). A direct brain-to-brain interface in humans. *PLoS One*, *9*(11), 1–12. doi:10.1371/journal.pone.0111332 PMID:25372285

Reade, W. W. (1910). *The martyrdom of man*. London: Kegan Paul.

Rees, M. (2003). *Our final hour*. New York: Basic Books.

Regalado, A. (2018). *A startup is pitching a mind-uploading service that is "100 percent fatal"*. Retrieved from https://www.technologyreview.com/s/610456/a-startup-is-pitching-a-mind-uploadingservice-that-is-100-percent-fatal/

Rikowski, G. (2002). Education, capital and the transhuman. In D. Hill, P. McLaren, M. Cole, & G. Rikowski (Eds.), *Marxism against postmodernism in educational theory* (pp. 111–143). Lanham, MD: Lexington Books.

Schroeder, R. (1996). *Possible worlds: the social dynamic of virtual reality technology*. Boulder, CO: Westview Press, Inc.

Uğur, S. (2018). Transhumanizm ve öğrenmedeki değişim. *Açıköğretim Uygulamaları ve Araştırmaları Dergisi*, *4*(3), 58–74.

Verdoux, P. (2009). Transhumanism, progress and the future. *Journal of Evolution and Technology / WTA*, *20*(2), 49–69.

Weis, R., & Fromherz, P. (1997). Frequency dependent signal transfer in neuron transistors. *Physical Review. E*, *55*(1), 877–889. doi:10.1103/PhysRevE.55.877

Winter, J. O., Liu, T. Y., Korgel, B. A., & Schmidt, C. E. (2001). Recognition molecule directed interfacing between semiconductor quantum dots and nerve cells. *Advanced Materials*, *13*(22), 1673–1677. doi:10.1002/1521-4095(200111)13:22<1673::AID-ADMA1673>3.0.CO;2-6

WTA. (2018). *The Transhumanist FAQ: What is transhumanism?* Retrieved from http://humanityplus.org/philosophy/transhumanist-faq/

Zeck, G., & Fromherz, P. (2001). Noninvasive neuroelectronic interfacing with synaptically connected snail neurons immobilized on a semiconductor chip. *Proceedings of the National Academy of Sciences of the United States of America*, *98*(18), 10457–10462. doi:10.1073/pnas.181348698 PMID:11526244

Zhou, P., Wu, F., Zhou, T., Cai, X., Zhang, S., Zhang, X., ... Lan, F. (2016). Simple and versatile synthetic polydopamine-based surface supports reprogramming of human somatic cells and long-term self-renewal of human pluripotent stem cells under defined conditions. *Biomaterials*, *87*, 1–17. doi:10.1016/j.biomaterials.2016.02.012 PMID:26897536

ADDITIONAL READING

Bainbridge, W. S. (2013). Transavatars. In M. More & N. Vita-More (Eds.), *The transhumanist reader: Classical and contemporary essays on the science, technology, and philosophy of the human future* (pp. 3–17). Malden, MA: John Wiley & Sons. doi:10.1002/9781118555927.ch9

Bowman, D. A., & McMahan, R. P. (2007). Virtual reality: How much immersion is enough? *Computer*, *40*(7), 36–43. doi:10.1109/MC.2007.257

Bricken, M. (1991). Virtual worlds: No interface to design. In M. Benedikt (Ed.), *Cyberspace: First steps*. Cambridge, MA: MIT Press.

Hansell, G. R., & Grassie, W. (2011). *H+/-: Transhumanism and its critics*. Philadelphia, PA: Metanexus Institute.

Kurzweil, R., & Grossman, T. (2004). *Fantastic voyage: live long enough to live forever*. Emmaus, PA: Rodale.

Milgram, P., ve Kishino, F. (1994). A taxonomy of mixed reality visual displays. *IEICE Transactions on Information and Systems*, *77*(12), 1321–1329.

Sorgner, S. L. (2009). Nietzsche, the overhuman, and transhumanism. *Journal of Evolution and Technology / WTA*, *20*(1), 29–42.

Winn, W. (1993). *A conceptual basis for educational applications of virtual reality. Technical Publication R-93-9, Human Interface Technology Laboratory of the Washington Technology Center*. Seattle: University of Washington.

KEY TERMS AND DEFINITIONS

Artificial Intelligence: A branch of computer science that aims to produce intelligent machines that have the characteristics of a human like learning, perception, recognition, planning, problem solving and reasoning.

Human Enhancement: To improve humanity and the quality of human life through methods such as treating disability and illness, improving current skills of humanity and developing new ones by means of technological developments.

Immersion: The objective measure of how realistic a user experiences the virtual world sensually.

Nano Robot: A programmable micro-sized robot for various tasks that made up of nanoscale components using nanotechnology methods and tools.

Post-Human: The human of the future who will surpass the capacity of the present humans with the profound technological modifications in body and brain systems.

Singularity: It is a period in which the speed of technological developments will increase rapidly and as a result, there will be fundamental changes in humanity.

Three-Dimensional Virtual World: A 3D virtual environment simulated by a computer, where users can interact with each other, objects and the environment.

Chapter 13
Innovative Learning Approach in the 21st Century:
Personal Learning Environments

Hakan Altinpulluk
https://orcid.org/0000-0003-4701-1949
Anadolu University, Turkey

ABSTRACT

The ease of access to information, which has become evident with the development of communication technologies such as the internet, has brought about revolutionary changes in education. With the development of Web 2.0 technologies, the strengthening of social networks and the process of the learners taking responsibility for their own learning, personal learning environments (PLEs) have emerged. PLE is a connectivism and network-based learning environment where the learning process is more flexible and the management of learning is in charge of the learner instead of the teacher or other person. It is regarded to be the learning environment for the future generations consisting of components that keep the learner active at all times as open, flexible, social network-based and cooperative Web 2.0. environments. In this section, definition of PLE, its ways of use, its advantages over the other learning systems, limitations and recommendations for use, are listed.

INTRODUCTION

In today's modern societies, individuals need to be able to access, customize and personalize information that is constantly growing, changing and renewed. This leads to a change in the learning styles of learners. In this context, it is observed that individuals are affected by innovations especially in Information and Communication Technologies (ICTs) and they are trying to create their own learning environments and networks. In this age that changes and shapes rapidly, "learning" needs a new approach.

Chatti, Agustiawan, Jarke and Specht (2010) emphasizes that learning is basically a personal, social, distributed, ubiquitous, flexible, dynamic and complex nature. It is observed that the learning styles of the societies affected by the developing technologies are changing as well. Today's learners are undergoing a

DOI: 10.4018/978-1-5225-8431-5.ch013

process of transformation by the Internet. This transformation observed in learner profiles causes shifts in educational paradigms. There is an approach in which the teacher starts to gain a facilitator role in a guide and learning process and the responsibility for learning is given to the learner. Informal learning processes have become more important than ever before. Gillet and Bogdanov (2013) also supports this view and emphasizes that informal learning will become increasingly necessary as learning is basically an informal process. Similar to these views, Selwyn (2007) draws attention to the relationship between informal learning and social media and predicts that social media increasingly supports informal learning at home, at work and in communities, and becomes an indispensable element in education for people of all ages.

The disruptive changes caused by the new social, political, economic and educational driving forces reinforce and shape industries by increasing uncertainty. These forces include technological advances such as cyber-physical systems, advanced types of machine learning and artificial intelligence; social factors such as changes in user values, platform business model, sharing economy; massive open online courses in education, relative declines in government support and others. As the digital transformation and the size of digital data with more impact than ever will increase, these driving forces will create significant challenges for the new generations entering the workforce in the near future. For this reason, students need to be guided in different disciplines to be able to work not only in their own disciplines, but also in rapidly changing digital environments. Only higher education will not be sufficient for these individuals. Knowledge workers should have the skills necessary to continuously change the environment, to think about data, to explore trends in their environment, to produce ideas and to adapt (Tsui & Dragicevic, 2018).

Today, education systems have experienced a change and transformation, learning management systems (LMS) have remained closed and insufficient and social networks have gained power, leading to a great need for innovative learning systems that give students the responsibility of learning. In this section, definitions of personal learning environments (PLEs) available in the literature are set forth the first. In the next section; their ways of use, their advantages over other learning systems and their limitations are set forth. In the last section, suggestions on how to use these environments are listed.

BACKGROUND

Definitions and Characteristics of Personal Learning Environments

Hard disks, which are the data storage tools of computers, are not used too much today. As the use of Internet has become widespread, people now store their data online, they shop online, they communicate instantly through their mobile phones or personal computers and they access movies and music online, instead of downloading them. Researchers access the academic publications through the Internet instead of going to the library and they conduct the editing and screening of these publications through the internet. Strengthening and development of the Internet have changed learning models as well as communication methods. In furtherance of this, Hargreaves (2003) claims that today's learners must learn deep cognitive skills such as problem solving and cooperation which are necessary to cope with the changing and new situations.

The development of web technologies has become a breaking point in open and distance learning applications. After the simple, non-privatized, passive and stable state of Web 1.0 technologies, Web 2.0

technologies have launched a new era in the internet world with its active, customizable and interactive structure. Particularly in the context of open and distance learning technologies, certain advancements such as the development of Web 2.0 technologies and the increasing popularity of the Internet, the multi-environment of Internet covering many environments such as television and radio and the emergence and strengthening of social networking sites, have attracted the attention of educational researchers and have brought about the view that these technologies could be used in education processes.

The development of web technologies has become a breaking point in open and distance learning applications. After the simple, non-privatized, passive and stable state of Web 1.0 technologies, Web 2.0 technologies have launched a new era in the internet world with its active, customizable and interactive structure. The concept of "Web 2.0" began with a conference brainstorming session between O'Reilly and MediaLive International (O'Reilly, 2005). Web 2.0 means a qualitative leap in web technologies that have made the internet more creative, participative and socializing (Blees & Rittberger, 2009). In addition, Web 2.0 has initiated a period in which open content access, sharing, conversion, integration and reshaping of information are available in all areas (Soumplis, Chatzidaki, Koulocheri, & Xenos, 2011). The Internet provides an 'infinite bazaar' of learning content and opportunities (Valtonen et al., 2012). Web 2.0 is concerned with the human aspects of communication, collaboration and dialogue; it includes creating and sharing through the use of technologies like blogs, wikis, streaming videos, social networks, open-access sites, and socially-driven content (Abram, 2007). These types of tools form an essential part of contemporary and innovative learning environments, and they can be integrated into many types of learning environments (Korhonen, Ruhalahti, & Veermans, 2018).

Before emphasizing the definitions and characteristics of PLEs that can be considered as a product of Web 2.0 technologies, it would be appropriate to refer to concepts such as personalization, personalized learning and personal learning. Personalization is a concept shaped according to the individual's interests and needs. One aim of personalization is to encourage learners to use their unique ideas and talents as a resource for everyone in the learning environment (Campbell, Robinson, Neelands, Hewston, & Mazzoli, 2007). According to Valtonen et al. (2012), the idea of PLEs also bears strong similarities to personalized learning purposes. Personalization has two different meanings for PLEs. Its first meaning is to emphasize a learner-centered and management-based approach; The second meaning is a learner-based, but traditional, view of the institution (Johnson & Liber, 2008). Personal learning means; the learners fulfill the requirements of their own learning, they learn how to take advantage of and how to control the learning resources that are available in the learning environment (Rahimi, 2015). All these definitions include the basis of PLEs and the subcomponents of these systems.

Before the PLEs definitions, it would be appropriate to briefly touch on the reasons for the emergence of this environment. According to Bustos, Engel, Saz and Coll (2012), with the increasing importance of the use of social networks in learning environments, PLE has become available in communities, not only from individual learning areas. Rahimi, Berg and Veen (2015) offer a different perspective, stating that; "None of the 21st century skills containing components such as 'critical thinking, problem solving, creation of meaning, communication, collaboration and decision-making' can be easily assessed using product-based assessment techniques like the multiple-choice tests or standard exams. According to Wu, Hsiao and Nian (2018), over the past decade, the idea of PLE premised on social media has arisen as the personalized learning platform that can accommodate each learner's specific learning and self-regulatory needs (Wu & Xie, 2018) and facilitate the interactivity, communication and collaboration among a network of learners (Lee, 2015; Lee, 2017).

For the solution of these rigid, uniform and standard patterns of traditional classroom environments, Chatti et al. (2010) emphasized that PLEs can play a key role. Accordingly, the PLEs concept emerged to open new doors for more effective learning and to overcome the limitations of traditional technology-based learning models. With these environments, a learner's course activities can be visualized under a single interface and this learner may be able to design all the elements in the course (Casquero, Ovelar, Romo, Benito, & Alberdi, 2016). In this context, it can be stated that PLEs provide a highly suitable learning environment for today's learners. In support of this view, Dalsgaard (2006) emphasized that these environments are the areas for today's learners to create learning environments, discover new information and communicate.

Various definitions have been made about PLEs. By Attwell (2010), PLEs are defined as an approach that includes Web 2.0 technologies and tools used for collaborating with other users. PLEs, as social software used for learning-oriented informal learning, consist of ongoing activities rather than a single process. PLEs, as a promising area in e-learning, aims to transfer the process of creating and managing the learning environment from instructors to the learners (Rahimi, van den Berg, & Veen, 2015). PLEs, which are defined as a collection of different social networking software and information-communication technology tools (Mott, 2010), consist of multiple learning tools, services and outputs collected from various contexts to be used by the learners (Henri, Charlier, & Limpens, 2008). PLEs reject the 'one-size-fits-all' approach as learning pools that the learner can use in his workplace, academic work or even in his civic experience (Hicks & Sinkinson, 2014), opposing the pre-determination of the objectives, tools, services and content of the learning process (Kroop, 2013). According to Korhonen et al. (2018), PLEs enable lifelong learning and make competences visible in education and professional life.

Ivanova (2009) describes PLEs as systems that facilitate learners to help them set learning goals and to manage their own learning in experiences related to creative and innovative activities. According to Zubrinic and Kalpic (2008), PLEs are systems that provide users with opportunities to create and manage information environments. It gives the learners the opportunity to manage and control their own learning. Wilson (2008) emphasized that PLEs are not only part of a software, but that these environments are the systems in which individuals, tools, communities and resources interact with each other. Dabbagh and Kitsantas (2012), the most important feature of PLEs are to give the learner an online identity. According to Schaffert and Hilzensauer (2008), PLEs led to 7 changes in learning:

1. The learner as "prosumer"
2. A new perspective on personalisation
3. The bazaar of learning opportunities from peers and experts
4. Social involvement and the role of community
5. Ownership and protection of learner's data
6. (Learning) culture in educational institutions and organisations as a consequence and enabler
7. Technological challenges

The basis of PLEs is to place learners in more centralized roles in two ways. The first is to allow learners to build and promote their own learning environment in the most appropriate way to their learning needs and objectives. Second, learners take a more active role in learning processes and take more responsibility; to make more active use of self-guiding components in learning process (Attwell, 2007; Schaffert & Hilzensauer, 2008). Furthermore, learners can have the freedom to choose their PLEs themselves, thus gaining responsibility for their own learning in general (Korhonen et al., 2018). According to Tsui and

Innovative Learning Approach in the 21st Century

Dragicevic (2018), one of the key aspects of using PLEs is the use of technologies, particularly Web 2.0 tools, which allow learners to develop their personalized learning environments. Some of the benefits of the virtual environment are its ability to network students and others, stimulate reflection, and create the conditions for them to work at a distance to develop communities of practice. There are various possible applications to support PLEs, for example, social networking applications such as Facebook or Google+. Through PLEs, students get the chance to learn in the digitalized environment and to learn how to learn in a digitalized environment, which might be considered as a new form of a digital literacy.

PLEs has been used for a while in an integrated way, especially in the daily life of university students, by using search engines, stream videos and social networking sites, though they do not realize it, in fact. (Dabbgah & Fake, 2018). PLEs also allow students to exchange their work and to access supportive information more quickly (Korhonen et al., 2018).

CONNECTIVISM AND PLE

With the teacher assuming the role of a guide and a facilitator, instead of an active and instructing role, there has been a shift in the transfer of information both in face-to-face education and in open and distance education and the students have assumed an active role, instead of a passive one. According to Peña-López (2010), Under the concept of the PLEs, learners find everything (literally: everything) that a person is using to learn. Likewise, Shepherd (2007) states that PLEs not only consist of the favorites in the internet browser, RSS feeds and electronic documents, but also the individual's spouse, friends, the magazine he reads, the movie he watches and the radio program he listens to, make up his learning environments. Thus, he brings a different perspective to PLES suggesting that it is a general learning ecosystem. In this context, it can be argued that PLEs has an approach based on connectivist principles.

Connectivism is a learning theory for digital age learners by George Siemens (2004), who argues that learning can take place in all human and non-human applications. It is based on the principle that all learning starts and continues with connections and that nodes are also created by learning by creating networks (Siemens, 2004). According to Siemens (2008), the connections are formed in biological / neural, conceptual and social / external dimensions.

PLEs are based on connectivism. Because it aims to transfer learning from the institution to the learner. PLEs are intended to connect remote services and to customize learning. It is a structure that encourages the learners to produce new knowledge rather than consuming learning resources. Therefore, learning is aimed at production rather than transferring content and information (Downes, 2006).

Besides PLEs, LMSs, which are used in the open and distance learning process, are among the learning environments the strengths and limitations of which have been discussed in the field for a while. LMSs can appear with names such as, virtual learning environments (VLEs), content management systems (CMS) (Wilson et al., 2007). LMSs, which are based on more traditional learning theories than the Connectivism, is frequently compared in the literature with PLEs. According to Chen, Millard and Wills (2008), LMSs and PLEs differ in some respects. According to the authors, PLEs are superior in providing more flexible learning experiences. According to Chan, Corlett, Sharples, Ting and Westmancott (2005), LMSs are inadequate in new learning teaching methods such as problem-based learning, informal teamwork and personal learning management, although they have adopted many educational institutions. LMSs represent the most preferred technology for today's enterprise e-learning approach. Unfortunately, however, the LMSs have a low level of proficiency in the context of responding to the needs of each learner and show off a closed garden effect on the learners. Many researchers have conducted research on PLEs that support lifelong learning and are able to overcome such limitations (Di Cerbo et al., 2011). According to Skrabut (2008), the emergence of PLEs is based on two main reasons. The learners were not satisfied with the existing LMSs and the environments that can be implemented with web 2.0 technologies enabled personalization learning. In line with these views, there is a common agreement that; instead of the formal-learning based LMSs which cannot be used after the end of the academic term, the informal and lifelong-learning based PLEs where the learner assumes the responsibility for his own learning, should be used.

Web 2.0 environments, such as social networking sites, blogs, and wikis, offer unprecedented opportunities for learners and create content, share and interact with other users (Sclater, 2008). In this context, it can be said that LMSs, which do not adapt much to such Web 2.0 tools, tend to lose power. While there are many views arguing that PLEs will replace LMSs and pull their walls down, some others emphasize the necessity to integrate these two learning environments so that the superior and strong aspects of both could be used. According to one of these approaches (Conde, García-Peñalvo, Alier, Casany, & Piguillem, 2013), the formal-learning based LMSs and informal-learning based PLEs can be integrated to work together provided that such integration is structured well. In this way, formal environments can be transferred to informal systems or the activities performed in informal environments can be included in the corporate learning platforms. In addition, being one of the alternative approaches for the informal aspect of open and distance learning, PLEs can also contain a structured learning management system (Ratcliffe, 2014).

In literature, although closely related to PLEs, there are some approaches that differ from these environments with minor differences. Personal learning networks (PLN), professional learning networks, personal learning tools, distributed learning spaces, institutional personal learning environment (iPLE), hybrid institutional personal learning environment (HIPLE), institutional personal learning network (iPLN) (Peña-López, 2010) are some of them.

Although there are many definitions, examples and explanations of PLEs in the literature, there is much less information about the associated term, personal learning networks (PLN) (Couros, 2010). Couros argued that the definition of personal learning network was actually very simple, and was a summary of all social capital and links in the development of PLEs. Personal learning networks are created as informal networks to provide online professional interactions and establish networks (Tour, 2016). According to Cormier (2010), PLEs are ecologies in which personal learning networks operate. The effective use of personal learning networks as learning resources depends on various networking skills of learners (Rajagopal, Verjans, Costa, & Sloep, 2012). In the literature, although there are no definite distinctions regarding the relationship of PLEs with personal learning networks (Couros, 2010), Wheeler (2010) reported that personal learning networks and personal web tools are components of PLEs. Figure 1 shows the PLE subcomponents as personal learning network (PLN), personal web tools and Cloud Learning Environment (CLE).

Apart from personal learning networks, there are many types of learning systems. For example, a PLN is a system of interpersonal connections and resources that support informal learning (Trust, 2012). In professional learning networks, people can make connections with their colleagues and related experts, view their work, share work and project. In this respect, professional learning networks are defined as an ongoing and multifaceted process (Tobin, 1998). The terms professional learning networks and personal learning networks are often used interchangeably (Trust, Krutka, & Carpenter, 2016).

Figure 1. PLEs ve sub-components
(Wheeler, 2010)

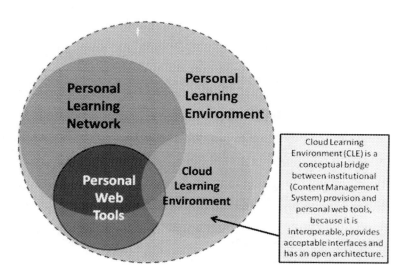

USE OF PERSONAL LEARNING ENVIRONMENTS

The first recorded use of the PLE comes from a session title at the 2004 Joint Information Systems Committee/Centre for Educational Technology & Interoperability Standarts conference in the UK (Archee, 2012). Responsive Open Learning Environments (ROLE), which is a European Union project, is also important in terms of developing and using the first remarkable practices in this field (Kroop, 2013; ROLE, 2004).

PLEs have also been implemented in some institutions worldwide. In the UK, the PLE application, which provides easy and compliant access to people and the source network, has been implemented with the development of a PLEX application by a group of Bolton University. At Mary Washington University in Virginia, it is seen that the learner and lecturers have implemented an application called UMW blog created by the privatization of the Wordpress multi-user platform. Thus, a flexible web space was allocated to the learners to provide them with the opportunity to present their work, to share their ideas and to collaborate on projects. Similar studies were conducted at the University of Baylor, Penn State and British Columbia (Educause, 2009). In addition, PLEs were used in Manchester Framework and Connectivism and Connective Knowledge (CCK) applications. The CCK courses prepared by George Siemens and Stephen Downes consist of a variety of subjects. During the lectures, blogs, Second Life, RSS readers, UStream, gRSShopper and Elluminate technologies were used (Downes, 2011). Previous studies on PLE&N using Google public tools in 8 subjects (Tsui, Tsui, & See-To, 2013) and 12 subjects (Tsang & Tsui, 2017) for over 3 semesters taught by teachers in the university in Hong Kong report about its effectiveness for social and lifelong learning (Tsui & Dragicevic, 2018).

According to Sclater (2008), PLEs can be used in three ways: (1) Client-side local software programs, (2) server-side Web browser services (LMS-based social networking tools) (3) hybrid approaches. PLEs can be used as widgets, cloud-based (Kroop, 2013), personal portal, personal control panel, blog, e-mail and RSS based learning environment (Tu, Yen, & Sujo-Montes, 2015).

As well as the online platforms we frequently use in our daily life, all learning tools including personalization, collaboration, communication and sharing are used in PLEs from a single resource to connect to social networks. A PLE implementer can integrate Web 2.0 tools into their network to create their own environment. Start pages are very useful for creating customizable and editable pages.In this context, it can be said that it represents the principles of PLEs. Netvibes.com can be shown as the most known start page in this context (Figure 2). The main feature of these sites is that they provide the possibility of shaping the learning and learning environment according to the preferences of the user. It allows all edits to be made on a single page. They provide easy access to information using RSS feeds.

While Facebook and Twitter are the most popular web pages on social networks, many sites such as Google +, LiveMocha (language learning), Hi5, MySpace and Netlog are examples of other social networks. Social networks can be used in the process of communicating with other users and building cooperative environments under PLEs. Social bookmarking (tagging) web sites are also the environment that individuals use to save, publish, and share resources. Outside of these sites, blogs, wikis, online storage areas (Google Drive, DropBox, Yandex Disk), e-mail providers, academic sharing and bibliography tools (Scribd, Slideshare, Mendeley, Zotero, Researchgate, Academia) for document management, storage and sharing, RSS feeds, video or image-based social networking sites such as Youtube, Flickr, etc. All sites can be a PLE component. In order to better understand these environments, some diagrams are presented by various researchers.

As can be seen from the diagrams in general terms, PLEs can be seen as multi-dimensional systems that benefit from many networks. It can be seen that PLEs can increase collaboration, communication and sharing among users, manage the user's own learning process, access a lot of data from various sources and organize the data. Utecht (2008) offers some useful advice under the scope of setting up a personal learning network in five stages.

Figure 2. Start page example from Netvibes.com

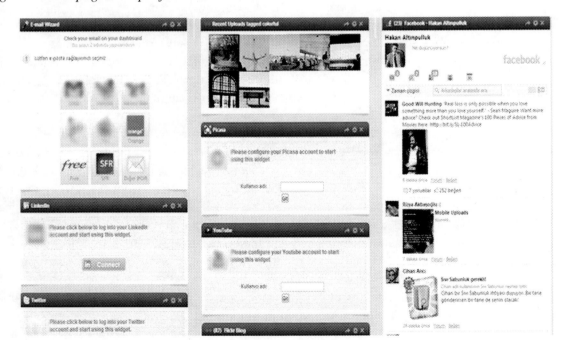

Innovative Learning Approach in the 21st Century

Figure 3. Example diagram of a PLE
(Weller, 2007)

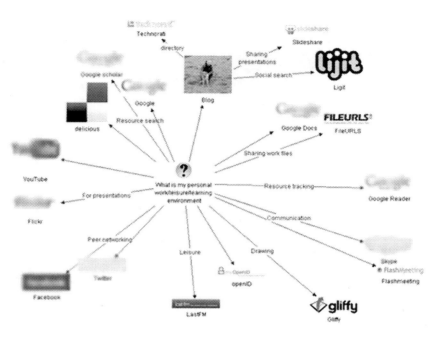

Figure 4. Example diagram of a PLE
(Chatti, 2007)

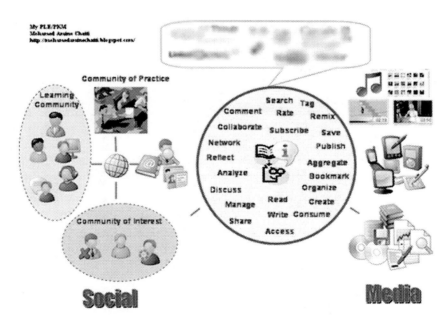

Figure 5. Example diagram of a PLE
(Manso-Vázquez & Llamas-Nistal, 2013)

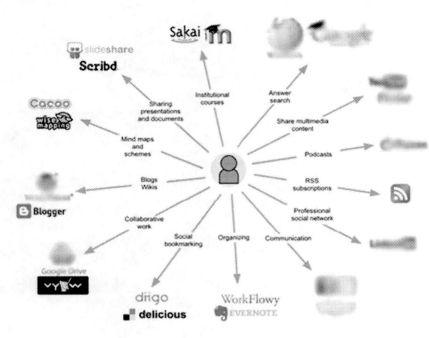

Figure 6. Example of a PLE&PLN
(Tsui, Wang, & Sabetzadeh, 2014).

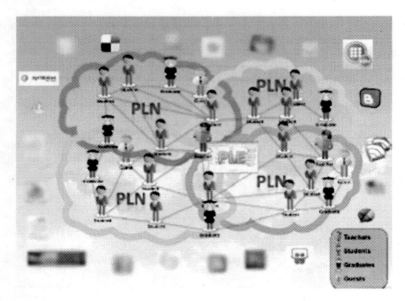

Stage 1 Immersion: Immerse yourself into networks. Create any and all networks you can find where there are people and ideas to connect to. Collaboration and connections take off.

Stage 2 Evaluation: Evaluate your networks and start to focus in on which networks you really want to focus your time on. You begin feeling a sense of urgency and try to figure out a way to "Know it all."

Stage 3 Know it all: Find that you are spending many hours trying to learn everything you can. Realize there is much you do not know and feel like you can't disconnect. This usually comes with spending every waking minutes trying to be connected to the point that you give up sleep and contact with others around you to be connected to your networks of knowledge.

Stage 4 Perspective: Start to put your life into perspective. Usually comes when you are forced to leave the network for awhile and spend time with family and friends who are not connected (a vacation to a hotel that does not offer a wireless connection, or visiting friends or family who do not have an Internet connection).

Stage 5 Balance: Try and find that balance between learning and living. Understanding that you can not know it all, and begin to understand that you can rely on your network to learn and store knowledge for you. A sense of calm begins as you understand that you can learn when you need to learn and you do not need to know it all right now.

According to Zubrinic and Kalpic (2008), the steps to be taken from a personal learning environment are listed as follows:

1. creation of a learning plan,
2. storing of learning contents in electronic form,
3. cooperation and exchange of information with other users,
4. creation of a knowledge map.

PLEs have some advantages in that the learning process can be implemented at every time and everywhere, supporting lifelong learning and being learner-centered. Many researchers have expressed their views on the strengths and weaknesses of PLEs.

The greatest strength of PLEs is to create a free environment for the learner, to provide an opportunity to manage its own process, and to be a roadmap for structuring informal learning. It can be useful in many ways to give learning responsibility to the learner. In this context, Anderson (2006) emphasizes that PLEs have some strengths. These are:

- Identity.
- Learners have existences beyond formal school, that can be used to both help learners contextualize their own understanding and for others to understand their epistemological legacy. The PLE tools integrate this outside life with formal study.
- Persistence.
- Ease of Use
- PLE environments can be customized and personalized allowing education to flow into the learners' other net applications. The learning curve associated with forced immersion in multiple LMS systems is eliminated. A PLE can be infinitely customized by both teachers and learners and is not confined to the monolithic tool set included by the commercial LMS package or the tools sup-

ported by a customized Open Source institutional LMS. Blogging is rapidly becoming easier and more accessible with mobile (PDA) and email entry allowing off line activity.
- Ownership.
- Control and responsibility: The PLE centers the learning within the context created and sustained by the learner – not one owned by the institution. This leads to sense of and practical application of educational self direction.
- Copyright and re-use.
- Social Presence.
- Capacity and Speed of Innovation:
- The PLE is a second generation network application in that unlike the LMS that was designed to enact the classroom on the Network, the PLE is designed primarily as a personal lifelong learning environment. It extends learning beyond classroom and teacher centered model.

There are many views on the limitations of PLEs. According to Valtonen et al. (2012), one of the biggest limitation of PLEs is the lack of experience caused by the fact that learners do not find the opportunity to use these contexts in formal learning environments.

There are many views on the limitations of PLEs. According to Rubio et al. (2011), the limitations of using PLEs in the learning process are as follows:

- Learner may not have enough confidence to manage and design their own learning environment.
- Learners may not want to be in the self-directed e-learner profile.
- Basic digital literacy skills may be low.
- It may be possible for a large number of web 2.0 tools to create confusion among users.
- Institutions may be afraid of losing control over the learner's learning process.
- LMSs can be more useful for novice users in terms of easy follow-up and participation in formal lessons than PLEs.

Tu et al. (2012) examined the limitations of PLEs in the context of both learning and teaching (Table 1).

SOLUTIONS AND RECOMMENDATIONS

Although PLEs are a fairly new and developing concept; There is yet no clear picture of the functions, objectives and the responsibility of the learners to create learning environments (Kop & Fournier, 2013). This makes it difficult to make recommendations in the use of these environments. In this context, one of the recommendations is given by Foreman (2011) to learn how the learners can construct their own PLEs:

- A conceptual map should be prepared and PLEs should be compared within it.
- To prevent language issues, learners should be assisted by using materials implementing precautions on this subject.
- Guidance should be provided regarding obtaining high quality reading materials on the internet.
- Steps should be taken in obtaining useful resources on independent study on the internet.
- Activities/materials/equipment based on self-directed learning should be provided. f) Vocabulary structuring tools should be shown.

Innovative Learning Approach in the 21st Century

Table 1. Limitations of PLEs in terms of learning and teaching (Tu et al., 2012)

Learner	Teacher/Instructor
Self-regulation • Learning organization: Because learners need someone to tell them what to do and what to learn, these environments may seem like an unusual learning organization for them. • Cognitive model change: Because many learners are accustomed to directory / hierarchical learning models, structures such as social tagging and RSS feeds are not preferred for them. Learners tend to fear not seeing everything at the same time.	**Perceptions** • Fear of negative effects in the evaluation at the end of teaching.
Qualifications • Difficulties in managing too many web 2.0 tools. • Difficulties of learners who are not accustomed to multi-tasking in the process of integrating many tools into the learning process. • The need to be online and organized at all times.	**Instructional paradigm** • Lack of understanding against the concept of PLEs.
Perceptions • Difficulties in the use of these tools because of the negative perception on social media. • Negative prejudices on PLE-based learning. • And not being able to abandon the intrinsic perception that learning is merely formal learning.	**Qualifications** • The need to take more responsibility in organizing the teaching process.
Support • Inadequate and non-centralized technical support for many tools used.	**Support** • Lack of institutional support.
Confidentiality and ownership	**Security, privacy and intellectual property**
	Technical skills • Lacking skills in observing the learning progress of learners.

- Information should be provided on mobile language learning applications.
- Education should be provided regarding how to organize useful resources/tools that have been found.

CONCLUSION

At a time when the concepts of informal learning, lifelong and ubiquitous learning have become popular, PLEs represent an understanding that should be applied in open and distance learning processes. It can be used effectively not only in informal learning processes, but also in formal learning processes by educational institutions as mentioned in the previous sections. However, the closed attitude of institutions towards the learning systems of the future should be overcome and informative studies should be conducted about these new learning environments. Neither PLEs nor LMS are perfect systems. Although LMSs have been criticized by some researchers, it is not the right approach to completely dismiss LMSs. It is also a fact that prejudice against new and promising systems must definitely be broken. At the moment, it can be mentioned that there is a negative attitude towards the use of internet, social networks and other web 2.0 tools in the education process of top managers of educational institutions. This negative perception could be changed by successful practices showing that PLEs could be used in an effective and efficient manner in the process of learning.

REFERENCES

Abram, S. (2007). Web 2.0, Library 2.0, and Librarian 2.0: Preparing for the 2.0 World. In S. Ricketts, C. Birdie, & E. Isaksson (Eds.), *Library and Information Services in Astronomy V: Common Challenges, Uncommon Solutions* (pp. 161–166). ASP Conference Series. Retrieved from http://adsabs.harvard.edu/full/2007ASPC.377.161A

Anderson, T. (2006). *PLE's versus LMS: Are PLEs ready for Prime time?* Available at: http://terrya.edublogs.org/2006/01/09/ples-versus-lms-are-ples-ready-for-prime-time/

Archee, R. (2012). Reflections on personal learning environments: Theory and practice. *Procedia: Social and Behavioral Sciences, 55*, 419–428. doi:10.1016/j.sbspro.2012.09.520

Attwell, G. (2007). The personal learning environment – the future of learning? *eLearning Papers, 2*(1), 1–8. Retrieved from http://digtechitalia.pbworks.com/w/file/fetch/88358195/Atwell%202007.pdf

Attwell, G. (2010) *Personal learning environments and Vygotsky*. Retrieved from http://www.pontydysgu.org/2010/04/personal-learning-environments-and-vygotsky

Blees, I., & Rittberger, M. (2009). Web 2.0 learning environment: concept, implementation, evaluation. *eLearning Papers*, 1–18. Retrieved from http://www.pedocs.de/volltexte/2010/2633/pdf/web20_LE_blees_rittberger_2_D_A.pdf

Bustos, A., Engel, A., Saz, A., & Coll, C. (2012). Integrating personal and institutional virtual learning environments. *Proceedings of EDULEARN12 Conference*, 7425-7433. Retrieved from http://www.academia.edu/download/32785382/ab_ae_as_cc_edulearn12_956.pdf

Campbell, R. J., Robinson, W., Neelands, J., Hewston, R., & Mazzoli, L. (2007). Personalised learning: Ambiguities in theory and practice. *British Journal of Educational Studies, 55*(2), 135-154. Retrieved from https://www.tandfonline.com/doi/abs/10.1111/j.1467-8527.2007.00370.x?casa_token=VVgLd8UWro8AAAAA:pd7MRCO7mZr3uOCWNws_EEuR_0E0D7qTjq5q53UmALQ8eMIa20JQPHLlJObFNAGBwMglXTEwwwy6njc

Casquero, O., Ovelar, R., Romo, J., Benito, M., & Alberdi, M. (2016). Students' personal networks in virtual and personal learning environments: a case study in higher education using learning analytics approach. *Interactive Learning Environments, 24*(1), 49-67. Retrieved from https://www.tandfonline.com/doi/abs/10.1080/10494820.2013.817441?casa_token=5QViK911-dMAAAAA:CYyoHh40XU7vTYH1B_pp5uTE-2pHO7tN7eJQ10q6yyNjaJwt61o63n0JnaRHnUK6AGkeeKONUt63DEUM

Chan, T., Corlett, D., Sharples, M., Ting, J., & Westmancott, O. (2005). Developing interactive logbook: a personal learning environment. *IEEE International Workshop on Wireless and Mobile Technologies in Education (WMTE'05)*, 73–75. Retrieved from https://ieeexplore.ieee.org/abstract/document/1579238

Chatti, M. A. (2007). *PLE links*. Retrieved from http://mohamedaminechatti.blogspot.com/2007/04/ple-links.html

Chatti, M. A., Agustiawan, M. R., Jarke, M., & Specht, M. (2010). Toward a personal learning environment framework. *International Journal of Virtual and Personal Learning Environments, 1*(4), 66–85. doi:10.4018/jvple.2010100105

Chen, W., Millard, D., & Wills, G. (2008). Mobile VLE vs. Mobile PLE: How informal is mobile learning? *mLearn 2008 Conference: The University of Wolverhampton*. Retrieved from http://eprints.ecs.soton.ac.uk/16158

Conde, M. Á., García-Peñalvo, F. J., Alier, M., Casany, M. J., & Piguillem, J. (2013). Mobile devices applied to Computer Science subjects to consume institutional functionalities through a Personal Learning Environment. *International Journal of Engineering Education, 29*(3), 610-619. Retrieved from http://www.academia.edu/download/42671103/MPLEApplication.pdf

Cormier, D. (2010). 5 points about PLEs PLNs for PLENK10. *Dave's Educational Blog*.

Couros, A. (2010). Developing personal learning networks for open and social learning. In G. Veletsianos (Ed.), Emerging technologies in distance education. In T. Anderson (Series Ed.) Issues in Distance Education (pp. 109-128). Edmonton, Canada: AU Press.

Dabbagh, N., & Kitsantas, A. (2012). Personal Learning Environments, social media, and self-regulated learning: A natural formula for connecting formal and informal learning. *The Internet and Higher Education, 15*(1), 3–8. Retrieved from https://www.sciencedirect.com/science/article/abs/pii/S1096751611000467

Dabbgah, N., & Fake, H. (2017). College students' perceptions of personal learning environment through the Lens of digital tools, processes and spaces. *Journal of New Approaches in Educational Research, 6*(1), 28–38. doi:10.7821/naer.2017.1.215

Dalsgaard, C. (2006). Social software: E-learning beyond learning management systems. *European Journal of Open, Distance and e-learning, 9*(2). Retrieved from http://www.eurodl.org/index.php?p=archives&year=2006&hal&article=228

Di Cerbo, F., Dodero, G., & Yng, T. L. B. (2011). Bridging the Gap between PLE and LMS. *2011 IEEE 11th International Conference on Advanced Learning Technologies*, 142–146. doi: 10.1109/ICALT.2011.48

Downes, S. (2006). *Learning networks and connective knowledge*. Retrieved from http://itforum.coe.uga.edu/paper92/paper92.html

Downes, S. (2011). About this course affiliation and course registration. *CCK 2011*. Retrieved from http://cck11.mooc.ca/about.htm

Educause. (2009). 7 things you should know about Personal Learning Environments. *Educause*. Retrieved from http://net.educause.edu/ir/library/pdf/ELI7049.pdf

Foreman, A. (2011). *Helping our students to develop their personal learning environment*. British Council.

Gillet, D., & Bogdanov, E. (2013). Cloud-savvy contextual spaces as agile personal learning environments or informal knowledge management solutions. In *Information Technology Based Higher Education and Training, 2013 International Conference on* (pp. 1-6). IEEE.

Hargreaves, A. (2002). *Teaching in the knowledge society. Education in the age of insecurity*. New York: Teachers College Press. Retrieved from http://citeseerx.ist.psu.edu/viewdoc/download?doi=10.1.1.533.6940&rep=rep1&type=pdf

Henri, F., Charlier, B., & Limpens, F. (2008). Understanding ple as an essential component of the learning process. *Proc. of ED-Media, AACE, Chesapeake*, 3766-3770. Retrieved from https://www.learntechlib.org/p/28906/

Hicks, A., & Sinkinson, C. (2014). Critical connections: Personal learning environments and information literacy. *Research in Learning Technology*, *23*. doi:10.3402/rlt.v23.21193

Ivanova, M. (2009). From personal learning environment building to professional learning network forming. *The 5th. International Scientific Conference e Learning and Software For Education*. Bükreş. Retrieved from https://adlunap.ro/else2009/papers/1001.1.Ivanova.pdf

Johnson, M., & Liber, O. (2008). The personal learning environment and the human condition: From theory to teaching practice. *Interactive Learning Environments*, *16*(1), 3–15. doi:10.1080/10494820701772652

Kop, R., & Fournier, H. (2013). Developing a framework for research on personal learning environments. *eLearning Papers*. Retrieved from https://dialnet.unirioja.es/servlet/articulo?codigo=6348049

Korhonen, A. M., Ruhalahti, S., & Veermans, M. (2018). The online learning process and scaffolding in student teachers' personal learning environments. *Education and Information Technologies*, 1–25. Retrieved from https://link.springer.com/article/10.1007/s10639-018-9793-4

Kroop, S. (2013). Evaluation on students' and teachers' acceptance of widget-and cloud-based personal learning environments. *Journal of Universal Computer Science*, *19*(14), 2150–2171. Retrieved from http://jucs.org/jucs_19_14/evaluation_on_students_and/jucs_19_14_2150_2171_kroop.pdf

Lee, Y.-H. (2015). Facilitating critical thinking using the C-QRAC collaboration script: Enhancing science reading literacy in a computer-supported collaborative learning environment. *Computers & Education*, *88*, 182–191. doi:10.1016/j.compedu.2015.05.004

Lee, Y.-H. (2017). Scripting to enhance university students' critical thinking in flipped learning: Implications of the delayed effect on science reading literacy. *Interactive Learning Environments*, *26*(5), 569–582. doi:10.1080/10494820.2017.1372483

Manso-Vázquez, M., & Llamas-Nistal, M. (2013). Distributed personal learning environments: towards a suitable architecture. *International Journal of Emerging Technologies in Learning (iJET)*, *8*(2013). Retrieved from https://ieeexplore.ieee.org/abstract/document/6530178

Mott, J. (2010). Envisioning the post-LMS era: The open learning network. *EDUCAUSE Quarterly*, *33*(1). Retrieved from http://cmapsconverted.ihmc.us/rid=1KCNR85HR-1TZLSG8-VZY/Mott%202010.pdf

O'Reilly, T. (2005). *What is Web 2.0?* Retrieved from http://oreilly.com/web2/archive/what-is-web-20.html

Peña-López, I. (2010). Personal learning environments: blurring the edges of formal and informal learning. *ICTlogy*. Retrieved from http://ictlogy.net/articles/20101105_ismael_pena-lopez_-_personal_learning_environments_blurring_edges_formal_informal_learning.pdf

Rahimi, E. (2015). *A design framework for personal learning environments* (Doctoral dissertation). Delft, The Netherlands: Delft University of Technology.

Rahimi, E., & Berg, J. (2015). A learning model for enhancing the student's control in educational process using Web 2.0 personal learning environments. *British Journal of Educational Technology, 46*(4), 780–792. doi:10.1111/bjet.12170

Rahimi, E., van den Berg, J., & Veen, W. (2015). Facilitating student-driven constructing of learning environments using Web 2.0 personal learning environments. *Computers & Education, 81*, 235-246. Retrieved from https://www.sciencedirect.com/science/article/pii/S0360131514002322

Rajagopal, K., Verjans, S., Costa, C., & Sloep, P. (2012). People in personal learning networks: analysing their characteristics and identifying suitable tools. *Proceedings of the 8th International Conference on Networked Learning 2012*. Retrieved from http://dspace.ou.nl/handle/1820/4224

Ratcliffe, A. E. (2014). An exploratory study of the personal learning environments of security and investigation professionals. *Journal of Literacy and Technology, 15*(2), 171–199. Retrieved from https://lra.le.ac.uk/bitstream/2381/29291/1/ar_7.pdf

ROLE. (2004). *Responsive Open Learning Environments (ROLE)*. Retrieved from http://role-project.archiv.zsi.at/

Rubio, E., Galan, M., Sanchez, M., & Delgado, D. (2011). eProfessional: from PLE to PLWE. *Proceedings of the The PLE Conference 2011*. Retrieved from http://journal.webscience.org/597/

Schaffert, S., & Hilzensauer, W. (2008). On the way towards personal learning environments: Seven crucial aspects. *Elearning Papers, 9*(2). doi:10.1.1.167.4083&rep=rep1&type=pdf

Sclater, N. (2008). Web 2.0, personal learning environments, and the future of learning management systems. *Research Bulletin, 13*(13), 1–13. Retrieved from https://wiki.oulu.fi/download/attachments/28096837/future+of+LMSs.pdf

Selwyn, N. (2007). *Web 2.0 applications as alternative environments for informal learning-a critical review*. Paper for CERI-KERIS International Expert Meeting on ICT and Educational Performance. Retrieved from http://newinbre.hpcf.upr.edu/wp-content/uploads/2017/02/39458556-W2-informal-learning.pdf

Shepherd, C. (2007). PLEs - what are we talking about here? *Clive On Learning*. Retrieved from http://clive-shepherd.blogspot.com/2007/04/ples-what-are-we-talking-about-here.html

Siemens, G. (2004). Connectivism: A learning theory for the digital age. *elearnspace*. Retrieved from http://www.elearnspace.org/Articles/connectivism.htm

Siemens, G. (2007). PLEs - I Acronym, Therefore I Exist. *elearnspace*. Retrieved from http://www.elearnspace.org/blog/2007/04/15/ples-i-acronym-therefore-i-exist/

Siemens, G. (2008). *What is the unique idea in connectivism*. Retrieved from http://www.elearnspace.org/blog/2008/08/06/what-is-the-unique-idea-in-connectivism/

Skrabut, S. (2008). *Personal learning environments: the natural way of learning*. Retrieved from http://www.uwyo.edu/skrabut/docs/ADED5050_project.pdf

Soumplis, A., Chatzidaki, E., Koulocheri, E., & Xenos, M. (2011). Implementing an open personal learning environment. *2011 15th Panhellenic Conference on Informatics*, 345–349. Retrieved from http://quality.eap.gr/Publications/XM/Conferences%20Greek/PCI2011_Implementing_an_Open_Personal_Learning_Environment.pdf

Tour, E. (2016). *Teachers' personal learning networks (PLNs): exploring the nature of self-initiated professional learning online. Literacy.* Wiley Online Library. doi:10.1111/lit.12101

Trust, T. (2012). Professional learning networks designed for teacher learning. *Journal of Digital Learning in Teacher Education, 28*(4), 133–138. doi:10.1080/21532974.2012.10784693

Trust, T., Krutka, D. G., & Carpenter, J. P. (2016). "Together we are better": Professional learning networks for teachers. *Computers & Education, 102*, 15-34. Retrieved from https://www.sciencedirect.com/science/article/pii/S036013151630135X

Tsang, H. W. C., & Tsui, E. (2017). Conceptual design and empirical study of a personal learning environment and network (PLE&N) to support peer-based social and lifelong learning. *VINE Journal of Information and Knowledge Management Systems, 47*(2), 228–249. doi:10.1108/VJIKMS-03-2017-0010

Tsui, E., & Dragicevic, N. (2018). Use of scenario development and personal learning environment and networks (PLE&N) to support curriculum co-creation. *Management & Marketing, 13*(2), 848-858. Retrieved from https://www.degruyter.com/downloadpdf/j/mmcks.2018.13.issue-2/mmcks-2018-0009/mmcks-2018-0009.pdf

Tsui, E., Wang, W. M., & Sabetzadeh, F. (2014, November). Enacting Personal Knowledge Management & learning with web services interoperability tools. In *Cloud Computing and Intelligence Systems (CCIS), 2014 IEEE 3rd International Conference on* (pp. 491-494). IEEE. Retrieved from https://ieeexplore.ieee.org/abstract/document/7175785

Tsui, M. L., Tsui, E., & See-To, E. W. (2013). Adoption of a personal learning environment & network (PLE&N) to support peer-based lifelong learning. *International Academic Forum (IAFOR)*. Retrieved from http://ira.lib.polyu.edu.hk/bitstream/10397/6290/1/ACSET2013_proceedings_TSUI_Lai_Na_Miriam.pdf

Tu, C. H., Sujo-Montes, M., Blocher, M., Yen, C. J., & Chan, J. Y. (2012). The integrations of personal learning environments & open network learning environments. *TechTrends, 56*(3), 13–19. Retrieved from http://link.springer.com/content/pdf/10.1007%2Fs11528-012-0571-7

Tu, C. H., Yen, C. J. & Sujo-Montes, L. E. (2015). Personal learning environments and self-regulated learning. In *Media Rich Instruction* (pp. 35-48). Springer International Publishing. Retrieved from https://link.springer.com/chapter/10.1007/978-3-319-00152-4_3

Utecht, J. (2008). *Stages of PLN adoption*. Retrieved from http://www.thethinkingstick.com/?p=652

Valtonen, T., Hacklin, S., Dillon, P., Vesisenaho, M., Kukkonen, J., & Hietanen, A. (2012). Perspectives on personal learning environments held by vocational students. *Computers & Education, 58*(2), 732–739. doi:10.1016/j.compedu.2011.09.025

Weller, M. (2007). My personal work/leisure/learning environment. *The Ed Techie*. Retrieved from http://nogoodreason.typepad.co.uk/no_good_reason/2007/12/my-personal-wor.html

Wheeler, S. (2010). *Anatomy of a PLE*. Academic Press.

Wilson, S. (2008). Patterns of personal learning environments. *Interactive Learning Environments, 16*(1), 17–34. doi:10.1080/10494820701772660

Wilson, S., Liber, O., Johnson, M. W., Beauvoir, P., Sharples, P., & Milligan, C. D. (2007). Personal learning environments: Challenging the dominant design of educational systems. *Journal of e-Learning and Knowledge Society, 3*(2), 27-38. Retrieved from https://www.learntechlib.org/p/43419/

Wu, J. Y., Hsiao, Y. C., & Nian, M. W. (2018). Using supervised machine learning on large-scale online forums to classify course-related Facebook messages in predicting learning achievement within the personal learning environment. *Interactive Learning Environments*, 1–16. doi:10.1080/10494820.2018.1515085

Wu, J.-Y., & Xie, C. (2018). Using time pressure and note-taking to prevent digital distraction behavior and enhance online search performance: Perspectives from the load theory of attention and cognitive control. *Computers in Human Behavior, 88*, 244–254. doi:10.1016/j.chb.2018.07.008

Žubrinic, K., & Kalpic, D. (2008). The web as personal learning environment. *MIPRO*. Retrieved from http://bib.irb.hr/datoteka/357767.576-2219-1-PB-1.pdf

KEY TERMS AND DEFINITIONS

Connectivism: Connectivism is an approach that explains learning on networks as a learning theory of the digital age.

Learning Management Systems (LMS): Learning management systems are web environments used in formal education institutions for sharing, managing and organizing resources.

Open and Distance Learning: It is a formal learning system in which learners are separate from each other, where learners, learning resources and instructors are connected to each other through interactive communication systems.

Personal Learning Environment (PLE): It is a collection of web tools that allow learners to use collaborative processes to manage learning processes, store resources and share with others.

Personal Learning Network (PLN): PLNs are communities that interact, share and communicate with each other in personal learning environments.

Social Networks: Social networks are web technologies that enable individuals to interact with others over the internet.

Web 2.0: Web 2.0 technologies are the general name of web systems that make the Internet more participatory, more aesthetic and more interactive.

Chapter 14
Artificial Intelligence in Education:
Current Insights and Future Perspectives

Nil Goksel
https://orcid.org/0000-0002-3447-2722
Anadolu University, Turkey

Aras Bozkurt
https://orcid.org/0000-0002-4520-642X
Anadolu University, Turkey

ABSTRACT

Though only a dream a while ago, artificial intelligence (AI) has become a reality, being now part of our routines and penetrating every aspect of our lives, including education. It is still a field in its infancy, but as time progresses, we will witness how AI evolves and explore its untapped potential. Against this background, this chapter examines current insights and future perspectives of AI in various contexts, such as natural language processing (NLP), machine learning, and deep learning. For this purpose, social network analysis (SNA) is used as a guide for the interpretation of the key concepts in AI research from an educational perspective. The research identified three broad themes: (1) adaptive learning, personalization and learning styles, (2) expert systems and intelligent tutoring systems, and (3) AI as a future component of educational processes.

INTRODUCTION

From a futuristic point of view, AI has emerged as a key feature in what appears to be a science fictional future, one in which users interact and learn with hard and soft technologies. In seeking to gain insight into technology's importance, it is apparent that many AI-based applications have become part of our routines. As underlined by Housman (2018), "AI is capable of two things: (1) automating repetitive tasks by predicting outcomes on data that has been labeled by human beings, and (2) enhancing human

DOI: 10.4018/978-1-5225-8431-5.ch014

decision-making by feeding problems to algorithms developed by humans" (para. 50). In other words, AI learns the given commands by performing the tasks repeatedly and manages to somehow generate a decision pathway for humans by offering alternatives.

GENERAL OVERVIEW OF ARTIFICIAL INTELLIGENCE (AI)

Definition of AI

Nabiyev (2010) roughly defines AI as *the ability of a computer-controlled device to perform tasks in a human-like manner*. As indicated by the author, human-like qualities include mental processes like reasoning, meaning making, generalization, and learning from past experiences. Russell and Norvig (2003) describe the term AI as *Machine Intelligence,* or *Computational Intelligence,* that embraces various subfields wherein learning takes place and "specific tasks, such as playing chess, proving mathematical theorems, writing poetry, and diagnosing diseases, can be performed" (p. 2). Nilsson (2014) defines AI as the entirety of an algorithmic construction copying human intelligence. To Nilsson (2014), AI embraces the construction of the information-processing theory of intelligence. In other words, raw data, received from any user, is filtered by a device, made meaningful, and processed before finally becoming *cooked data* capable of meeting the demands of users.

There have been mind-blowing developments in the evolution of AI and the remarkable role it has played in human lives. Recently, there have been some concrete examples of AI being capable of learning how to think like a human. These examples have even demonstrated that AI-based applications, in some cases, can even function as better as humans. For example, in 2016, Google DeepMind's AlphaGo defeated one of the world's most accomplished "Go" players, Lee Se-Dol, a South Korean champion (Sang-Hun, 2016). As the greatest proof of AI's human-like thinking and skills, the result of this match shows that a true artificially-intelligent system is one that can learn on its own (Adams, 2017).

VITAL TECHNOLOGIES THAT SUPPORT THE VISIONS OF AI

The below-given figure presents the chronological development and relation between Artificial Intelligence, Machine Learning and Deep Learning from 1950 to 2010 and beyond. As Figure 1 shows, AI, as a broad and advanced term for computer intelligence, started to be discussed between the 1950s and 1980s, which was followed by the introduction of Machine Learning technology between the 1980s and 2010, where learning through algorithms was brought to the agenda, and finally, after 2010, Deep Learning emerged as a breakthrough technique for implementing Machine Learning via neural networks to complete tremendously complex thinking tasks. In this context, the following sections examine the two vital technologies of machine learning and deep learning to better comprehend and explore the world of AI. In addition, Natural Language Processing (NLP) and one of its best examples, intelligent personal assistants, is discussed in detail.

Figure 1. The relation between artificial intelligence, machine learning and deep learning (Copeland 2016)

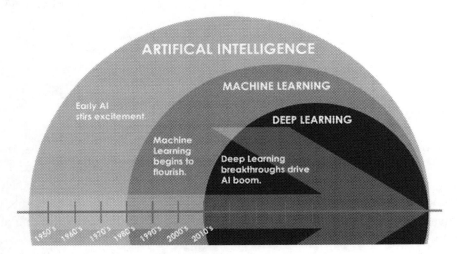

Machine Learning (ML)

Artificial intelligence, as an umbrella term, has its sub-branches, like ML. As pointed out by Rob (2017) in his blog, AI is a concept that points to the direction we're headed, not a position we've already reached; therefore, we need to specify it more precisely, with notions like ML. At the most basic level, machine learning seeks to develop methods for computers to improve their performance at certain tasks based on observed data (Ghahramani, 2015). With ML, objects, faces, words and even the value of a stock or who can buy what can be identified (Gürsakal, 2017). Simply put, ML is a system in which existing data is used for future predictions.

ML algorithms seem to achieve more accurate information if they are trained in the right way. According to Brynjolfsson and Mitchell (2017), in many cases, today, "ML algorithms have made it possible to train computer systems to be more accurate and more capable than those that can be manually programmed" (p. 1531). Similarly, Gori (2017) believes that ML is an attempt to construct intelligent agents for a given learning task on the basis of artificial models largely rooted in computational models. To Copeland (2016), ML is an approach that involves steps of learning to reach a final prediction. In this learning system, the machine is *trained*, by parsing data, to discharge a task given by a user. As indicated by Jordan and Mitchell (2015), ML as an aspect of AI, has emerged as "the method of choice for developing practical software for computer vision, speech recognition, natural language processing, robot control, and other applications" (p. 255). Various data are gathered to provide access to information on globally offered products, so everyone can act on it. As specified by Alpaydın (2016), the data is not just numbers anymore; it consists of texts, images, videos, ranks, frequencies, gene sequences, sensor arrays, click logs, and lists of recommendations. In other words, the data received from the users are more complex than is known by most people. However, if more data is collected and analyzed, more accurate decisions can be made. Jordan and Mitchell (2015) noted that "mobile devices and embedded computing permit large amounts of data to be gathered about individuals, and machine-learning algorithms can learn from these data to customize their services to the needs and circumstances of each individual" (p. 257). In effect, this means that it may take time for a machine to understand the structure of a human being. However, even though a hundred percent recognition has not yet been realized, over time, the machine may come to a level where it can imitate humans. Algorithmic-based instructions, created using mathematical and statistical methods and codes that are trained to accomplish a specific task, are used in ML.

Deep Learning (DL)

It is still uncertain how machines can be made to think, reason, and make sense of the world in the same way humans do. However, as machines get more intelligent, serve humanity and appear in many fields, they seem to be more accepted as part of our human reality. Deep Learning (DL), a relatively new technology in the realm of ML, involves the complex attempt to unravel human levels of perception and cognition.

DL is a sub-branch of ML and was first introduced as a concept by Alan Turing in 1950. While the studies that Turing had been conducting during those years were mainly related to neural networks, they helped to give rise to the issue of machines' ability to think. The idea of machines having the same characteristics of human intelligence evokes the sense that we are in a science fiction movie. Living within this frightening state of affairs, where we are unable to decide whether the person with whom we communicate is a real person or a virtual device, is indeed evidence that DL has taken place in science.

As described by Shaikh (2017), "deep learning is a particular kind of machine learning that achieves great power and flexibility by learning to represent the world as a nested hierarchy of concepts, with each concept defined in relation to simpler concepts, and more abstract representations computed in terms of less abstract ones". According to Copeland (2016), DL enables many practical applications of ML, where the variety of tasks is limited. In DL, there are many layers, where all sorts of shapes and images can be taken and input into the layers of the neural network in a particular order. The final output can be produced by passing all the previous tasks into different layers until the final outcome is reached. In one of his podcast series, Will Ramey, NVIDIA Senior Manager for GPU Computing, mentions that DL, unlike ML technology, works on very specific tasks, like classifying different types of images, similar to what Facebook does with its facial recognition, digital marketing, where predictions about what a user may prefer to purchase can be made by the device, and medical imaging, to locate tumors or determine their stage. Therefore, with the rapid adoption of DL, a human level of accuracy has been reached through neural networks that use big data collection.

Natural Language Processing (NLP)

Hirschberg & Manning (2015, p. 261) describe "Natural Language Processing (NLP), also known as computational linguistics, as a subfield of computer science that is concerned with using computational techniques to learn, understand, and produce human language content". Similarly, Nabiyev (2010) sees "NLP as an area of engineering, for designing and implementing computer systems for which natural language analysis is the main function" (p. 431). The assistants are used to perform a task controlled by software which has an expanded and optimized database algorithm. For many algorithms, where a combination of words is involved in the search process, "a collection of knowledge and a control mechanism to resolve a specific problem in a systematic fashion are required" (Tanwar, Prasad & Datta, 2014, p. 56). Requiring the combination of human learning and machine reasoning, the process aims to comprehend user-given verbal or written commands that require automatic response, text translation and speech generation.

As an interaction medium, language is a composite tool that allows the transmission of existing messages through words. According to Cambria and White (2014), NLP is a theory-motivated range of computational techniques for the automatic analysis and representation of human language via virtual entities. As discussed by Kumar et al. (2016), question answering is a complex natural language processing task which requires an understanding of the meaning of a text and the ability to reason over relevant facts. Regarding the interaction between humans and non-human entities, question answering can be a complex process for virtual beings. As highlighted by Nilsson (2014), it can be very hard for a computer system to become capable of generating and understanding fragments of a natural language, such as English, because of encoding and decoding obstacles. The same writer mentions that many researchers have focused on creating computer programs that are capable of understanding expressions in English, such as ELIZA by Weizenbaum, SIR by Raphael, BASEBALL by Newell, Shaw and Simon, SAD SAM by Lindsay, SYNTHEX by Simmons, and STUDENT by Bobrow (Nilsson, 2010).

According to LeCun, Bengio, and Hinton (2015), natural language understanding is an area that should be observed within the context of DL, as DL and simple reasoning have been used for speech and handwriting recognition for quite some time. The central idea of "DL is that if we can train a model with several representational levels to optimize a final objective, such as translation quality, then the model can itself learn intermediate representations that are useful for the task at hand" (Hirschberg & Manning, 2015, p. 261). However, the logic behind DL should be clarified, as "new paradigms are needed to replace rule-based manipulation of symbolic expressions by operations on large vectors" (LeCun, Bengio, & Hinton, 2015, p. 9).

Voice recognition, voice analysis, and language processing can be regarded as the common features of Intelligent Personal Assistants (IPAs). Therefore, we can visit this concept to see just how capable AI can be in understanding and communicating with human beings.

Intelligent Personal Assistants (IPAs)

The advances that have been made in technology have allowed life to be more entertaining for users. In the light of these advances, daily life routines can be fulfilled in an easier way with IPAs. As emphasized by Eric Enge (2017), the personal assistant feature has been available on smartphones since Siri's launch in October 2011, Google Now's appearance in 2012 and Cortana's introduction in 2013.

Developed within the scope of artificial intelligence, IPAs and the services they offer have started to be used in daily life, business, health, and education. This big internet revolution brought a new paradigm, where people and machines can communicate among themselves (Santos, Rodrigues, Casal, Saleem & Denisov, 2018). This form of speech-based interaction allows users to feel like they are communicating with a real individual. With the recent boost in Artificial Intelligence and Speech Recognition technologies, the Voice Assistant, also known as the Intelligent Personal Assistant, has become increasingly popular as a human-computer interaction mechanism (Zhang, et al., 2018).

When we look at the progress made so far, it becomes clear that AI has long existed in the field of education (Bozkurt & Göksel, 2018). As stated by Johnson, Rickel & Lester (2000), pedagogical agents like STEVE (Soar Training Expert for Virtual Environments) and ADELE (Agent for Distance Learning: Light Edition) are "beginning to perform a variety of tasks in surprisingly lifelike ways", and these small prototype systems have quickly become practical (p. 31). Recently, educational approaches have focused on the use of technologies in classrooms. Smartphones, for instance, offer many IPA applications on different platforms, such as Siri on IOS, Cortana on Windows, Google Now, My Assistant,

Google Allo, Robin, Databot, Indigo (Lyra), and Smart Voice Assistant on Android, all of which could also be used for improving English language to foster speaking skills (Charisma et al., 2018). Current IPAs differ in "their interface designs, hardware requirements, and the types of tasks they are designed for" (Lopatovska et al., 2018, p.3). Therefore, each device should be examined separately to see how the tasks can serve to foster English learning. Voice-activated devices, such as Alexa, may fill existing gaps in users' information, entertainment, educational, social and other needs; however, its positioning and unique value compared to alternative IPAs (such as Apple's Siri and Google Assistant/Now apps) require further examination (Lopatovska et al., 2018).

There have been similar studies conducted to analyze how IPAs that employ voice commands, physical touch gestures, and other interaction signals can be more effective, in terms of facilitating a more practical way to communicate, by using search dialogue. As underlined by Kiseleva et al. (2016) this method of interaction is a more natural way for people to communicate and is often faster and more convenient (e.g., while driving) than typing. The IPAs can be a particularly convenient tool to help people who are in an eyes-busy, hands-busy situation that retain them to access to a keyboard and/or a monitor (Nielsen, 2003). In such cases, it is more practical to use IPAs that have a voice recognition feature, as this would provide users with a realistic person-to-person interaction and human-like entity.

METHODOLOGY

Purpose of the Research

The main purpose of this research is to identify areas of AI within the educational context. In line with this purpose, this chapter seeks to answer the following research question

- What are the key concepts in AI in educational papers?
- What promise does AI hold for the future of education?

Method and Research Design

To achieve the purposes of this study, data mining and analysis are performed, and a social network analysis (SNA) is conducted to better understand the research findings. SNA can be used to study, track, and compare the dynamics of communities and the influence of individual contributions. SNA provides powerful ways to map, summarize and visualize networks and to identify key vertices "that occupy strategic locations and positions within the matrix of links" (Hansen, Shneiderman and Smith, 2010, p. 5).

Sampling

The sample for this study included a total of 393 papers published between 1970 and 2018. In terms of the type of papers included, 210 were conference proceedings, 173 were journal articles, and 10 were book chapters. Publications that were written in English, indexed in Scopus, and had "artificial intelligence" in their title and "education" in their title, abstract, or keywords were included in the research.

Social Network Analysis (SNA)

The keywords of the articles constituting the research corpus were analyzed according to their co-occurrence. In this regard, a total of 597 keywords were analyzed through SNA. To gain a concentrated view, the first 79 keywords, at a minimum degree of 10, were displayed on a sociogram (Figure 2). The graph's vertices were grouped by cluster using the Clauset-Newman-Moore cluster algorithm (Clauset, Newman and Moore, 2004) and laid out using the Harel-Koren Fast Multiscale layout algorithm (Harel & Koren, 2001).

The research findings indicated that AI- and Education-related keywords are related as presented in Figure 3. Following the SNA, the identified related keywords were grouped under three broad themes to better understand the outlook for AI in education.

FINDINGS

This section presents the three themes identified (adaptive learning, personalization and learning styles; expert systems and intelligent tutoring systems, and; AI as a future component of educational processes) and explains how they refer to education.

Figure 2. SNA of the keywords of the sample publications

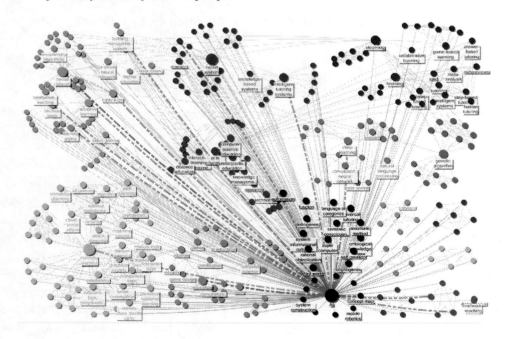

Figure 3. AI- and education-related keywords in terms of degree centrality and betweenness centrality

Keyword	Degree Centrality	Betweenness Centrality
AI	429	163690.241
Expert system	56	5743.120
E-learning	33	8831.566
Intelligent tutoring systems	28	3259.991
Education	26	3604.140
Learning	25	8676.371
Adaptive learning	18	860.647
AI education	15	3126.966
Game-based learning	14	2142.492
Personalization	13	2531.434
Reinforcement-learning	13	2146.245
Undergraduate education	13	1451.276
Distance education	12	1515.142
Learning management system	12	74.786
Learning styles	11	8.381
Interactive learning environment	10	380.011
Answer-based tutoring	10	0.000
Human tutoring	10	0.000
Tutoring	10	0.000

Adaptive Learning, Personalization and Learning Styles

For the first theme, the research findings revealed that the keywords *adaptive learning* (DC:18; BC: 860.647), *personalization* (DC:13; BC;2531), and *learning styles* (DC: 11; BC: 8.38) are key nodes in the AI network. As illustrated in the graph, adaptive learning is one of the key concepts related to AI.

Adaptive learning (Aroyo et al., 2006; Paramythis and Loidl-Reisinger, 2003) through personalization (Chen, 2008; Pane, Steiner, Baird, and Hamilton, 2015) and consideration of learning styles (Brown, Cristea, Stewart, and Brailsford, 2005; Kolb and Kolb, 2005) emerge as the focal point of AI research in the educational context. This theme indicates that AI implementations in education intend to provide learning spaces that meet the learners needs and provide learning opportunities according to the learning preferences of the learners. That is, rather than adopting a "one size fits all" approach, the use of AI in education allows for tailored learning by positioning the learners at the center of the learning environments.

Expert Systems and Intelligent Tutoring Systems

For the second theme, the research findings revealed that the keywords *expert systems* (Degree Centrality: 56; Betweenness Centrality:5743), *intelligent tutoring systems* (DC: 28; BC: 3259.991), *answer-based tutoring* (DC:10 ; BC: 0.00), *human tutoring* (DC:10 ; BC: 0.00), and *tutoring* (DC:10; BC: 0.00) are key nodes in the AI network.

An expert system (ES) can be defined as a program designed to emulate and mimic human intelligence, skills or behavior, while an intelligent tutoring system (ITS) can be defined as a program that aims to provide immediate and customized instruction or feedback to learners. ES (Collins, 2018) and

ITS (Wenger, 2014) are terms that are at the forefront of the developments in AI research (Burns & Parlett, 2014). ES has started using advanced algorithms, while ITS has been able to provide human-like interaction with conversation style dialogues. The potentials of ES and ITS emerge from the idea that they can be used 24/7 to support, enhance, enrich and amend learning processes.

AI as a Future Component of Educational Processes

For the third theme, the research findings revealed that the keywords *eLearning* (DC:33; BC: 8831.566), *education* (DC: 26; BC: 3604.140) *learning* (DC: 25; BC: 8676.371), *AI education* (DC: 15; BC:3126.966), *undergraduate education* (DC: 13; BC: 1451.276), and *distance education* (DC: 12; BC: 1515.142) are key nodes in the AI network.

The use of AI in education has resulted in significant progress in theory and practice in the new millennium (Roll & Wylie, 2016). There are alternative routes and scenarios for integrating AI to educational processes (Devedžić, 2004), with a special focus being online learning and distance education (Kose, 2015). For example, Lin, Wooders, Wang and Yuan (2018) suggest that AI can be used as a solution to increase efficiency in online learning and to "engage and connect students with each other and their instructors in asynchronous online environments that break through spatiotemporal barriers to learning" (p. 27). However, it is also noted that the integration of AI in educational processes requires policy development, if the researchers wish to avoid confining their efforts to statistically significant results (McArthur, Lewis & Bishary, 2005).

CONCLUSION AND SUGGESTIONS

In this study, current insights and futuristic perspectives of AI have been explored from an educational perspective. The study also looked at IPA features in relation to AI in a broad sense. When "AI and Education" related keywords are evaluated, it is observed that the key themes in AI research are (1) adaptive learning, personalization and learning styles, (2) expert systems and intelligent tutoring systems, and (3) AI as a future component of educational processes.

It is quite clear that AI and other AI featured technologies are here to ease human lives and contribute to the advancement of human progress. However, we should not settle with the idea that the adaptation of technology is good by default; instead, we need to develop a critical stance before fully integrating AI into educational processes. As part of this critical stance, first, there is a need to develop an ethical policy and to clearly define the ethical boundaries of how AI would use human generated data. Secondly, we should test, and retest AI featured educational processes to avert automated processes and mechanical learning.

ACKNOWLEDGMENT

This research was supported by Anadolu University, Scientific Research Project Commission under the grant numbers 1805E177 and 1805E123.

REFERENCES

Adams, R. L. (2017). 10 Powerful examples of artificial intelligence in use today. *Forbes*. Retrieved from https://www.forbes.com/sites/robertadams/2017/01/10/10-powerful-examples-of-artificial-intelligence-in-use-today/#3c7c80df420d

Alpaydın, E. (2016). *Machine learning: The new AI*. MIT Press.

Aroyo, L., Dolog, P., Houben, G.-J., Kravcik, M., Naeve, A., Nilsson, M., & Wild, F. (2006). Interoperability in Personalized Adaptive Learning. *Journal of Educational Technology & Society*, 9(2), 4–18.

Bozkurt, A., & Göksel, N. (2018). Technology renovates itself: Key concepts on intelligent personal assistants (IPAs). In *Proceedings of 10th International Conference on Education and New Learning Technologies Conference (EDULEARN18)* (pp. 4291-4297). doi: 10.21125/edulearn.2018.1082

Brown, E., Cristea, A., Stewart, C., & Brailsford, T. (2005). Patterns in authoring of adaptive educational hypermedia: A taxonomy of learning styles. *Journal of Educational Technology & Society*, 8(3), 77–90.

Brynjolfsson, E., & Mitchell, T. (2017). What can machine learning do? Workforce implications. *Science*, 358(6370), 1530–1534. doi:10.1126cience.aap8062 PMID:29269459

Burns, H., & Parlett, J. W. (2014). The evolution of intelligent tutoring systems: Dimensions of design. In H. Burns, C. A. Luckhardt, J. W. Parlett, & C. L. Redfield (Eds.), *Intelligent tutoring systems: Evolutions in design* (pp. 1–13). New York: Psychology Press. doi:10.4324/9781315807492

Cambria, E., & White, B. (2014). Jumping NLP curves: A review of natural language processing research. *IEEE Computational Intelligence Magazine*, 9(2), 48–57. doi:10.1109/MCI.2014.2307227

Charisma, D., Suherman, S., Kurniawan, A. B., Yusnilita, N., Susilawati, S., Niawati, N., ... Pambudi, B. D. (2018). The Effectiveness of Using Lyra Personal Assistant in improving Students 'speaking skill. *Community Concern for English Pedagogy and Teaching (CONCEPT)*, 11(1).

Chen, C. M. (2008). Intelligent web-based learning system with personalized learning path guidance. *Computers & Education*, 51(2), 787–814. doi:10.1016/j.compedu.2007.08.004

Clauset, A., Newman, M. E., & Moore, C. (2004). Finding community structure in very large networks. *Physical Review. E*, 70(6), 066111. doi:10.1103/PhysRevE.70.066111 PMID:15697438

Collins, H. M. (2018). Expert systems, artificial intelligence and the behavioural co-ordinates of skill. In B. P. Bloomfield (Ed.), *The Question of Artificial Intelligence* (pp. 258–281). London: Routledge. doi:10.4324/9780429505331-6

Copeland, M. (2016). *What's the difference between artificial intelligence, machine learning, and deep learning?* Retrieved from https://blogs.nvidia.com/blog/2016/07/29/whats-difference-artificial-intelligence-machine-learning-deep-learning-ai/

Devedžić, V. (2004). Web intelligence and artificial intelligence in education. *Journal of Educational Technology & Society*, 7(4), 29–39.

Garnham, A. (2017). *Artificial intelligence: An introduction*. Routledge. doi:10.4324/9780203704394

Ghahramani, Z. (2015). Probabilistic machine learning and artificial intelligence. *Nature*, *521*(7553), 452–459. doi:10.1038/nature14541 PMID:26017444

Gori, M. (2017). *Machine Learning: A Constraint-based Approach*. Burlington, MA: Morgan Kaufmann.

Gürsakal, N. (2017). *Makine Öğrenmesi ve Derin Öğrenme*. Bursa, Turkey: Dora Basım.

Hansen, D., Shneiderman, B., & Smith, M. A. (2010). *Analyzing social media networks with NodeXL: Insights from a connected world*. Burlington, MA: Morgan Kaufmann.

Harel, D., & Koren, Y. (2001). A Fast Multi-Scale Method for Drawing Large Graphs. In *Graph Drawing: 8th International Symposium, GD 2000 Proceedings* (No. 1984, p.183). Springer Science & Business Media. 10.1007/3-540-44541-2_18

Hirschberg, J., & Manning, C. D. (2015). Advances in natural language processing. *Science*, *349*(6245), 261–266. doi:10.1126cience.aaa8685 PMID:26185244

Housman, M. (2018). Why 'augmented intelligence' is a better way to describe AI. *AINews*. Retrieved from https://www.artificialintelligence-news.com/2018/05/24/why-augmented-intelligence-is-a-better-way-to-describe-ai/

Hoy, M. B. (2018). Alexa, Siri, Cortana, and More: An Introduction to Voice Assistants. *Medical Reference Services Quarterly*, *37*(1), 81–88. doi:10.1080/02763869.2018.1404391 PMID:29327988

Johnson, W. L., Rickel, J. W., & Lester, J. C. (2000). Animated pedagogical agents: Face-to-face interaction in interactive learning environments. *International Journal of Artificial Intelligence in Education*, *11*(1), 47–78.

Jordan, M. I., & Mitchell, T. M. (2015). Machine learning: Trends, perspectives, and prospects. *Science*, *349*(6245), 255–260. doi:10.1126cience.aaa8415 PMID:26185243

Kiseleva, J., Williams, K., Hassan Awadallah, A., Crook, A. C., Zitouni, I., & Anastasakos, T. (2016). Predicting user satisfaction with intelligent assistants. In *Proceedings of the 39th International ACM SIGIR conference on Research and Development in Information Retrieval* (pp. 45-54). ACM.

Kolb, A. Y., & Kolb, D. A. (2005). Learning styles and learning spaces: Enhancing experiential learning in higher education. *Academy of Management Learning & Education*, *4*(2), 193–212. doi:10.5465/amle.2005.17268566

Kose, U. (2015). On the Intersection of Artificial Intelligence and Distance Education. In U. Kose & D. Koc (Eds.), *Artificial Intelligence Applications in Distance Education* (pp. 1–11). Hershey, PA: IGI Global; doi:10.4018/978-1-4666-6276-6.ch001

Kumar, A., Irsoy, O., Ondruska, P., Iyyer, M., Bradbury, J., Gulrajani, I., ... Socher, R. (2016). Ask me anything: Dynamic memory networks for natural language processing. In *International Conference on Machine Learning* (pp. 1378-1387). New York.

LeCun, Y., Bengio, Y., & Hinton, G. (2015). Deep learning. *Nature*, *521*(7553), 436–444. doi:10.1038/nature14539 PMID:26017442

Lin, P. H., Wooders, A., Wang, J. T. Y., & Yuan, W. M. (2018). Artificial Intelligence, the Missing Piece of Online Education? *IEEE Engineering Management Review, 46*(3), 25–28. doi:10.1109/EMR.2018.2868068

Lopatovska, I., Rink, K., Knight, I., Raines, K., Cosenza, K., Williams, H., ... Martinez, A. (2018). Talk to me: Exploring user interactions with the Amazon Alexa. *Journal of Librarianship and Information Science*. doi:10.1177/0961000618759414

McArthur, D., Lewis, M., & Bishary, M. (2005). The roles of artificial intelligence in education: Current progress and future prospects. *Journal of Educational Technology, 1*(4), 42–80.

McCarthy, J. (2007). *What is artificial intelligence*. Retrieved from http://www-formal.stanford.edu/jmc/whatisai.html

Nabiyev, V. V. (2010). *Yapay zeka: İnsan bilgisayar etkileşimi*. Seçkin Yayıncılık.

Nielsen, J. (2003). *Voice interfaces: Assessing the potential*. Retrieved from http://www.useit.com/alertbox/20030127.htm

Nilsson, N. J. (2010). *The quest for artificial intelligence*. Cambridge, UK: Cambridge University Press.

Nilsson, N. J. (2014). *Principles of artificial intelligence*. Burlington, MA: Morgan Kaufmann.

Pane, J. F., Steiner, E. D., Baird, M. D., & Hamilton, L. S. (2015). Continued Progress: Promises Evidence on Personalized Learning. *RAND Corporation*. Retrieved from https://www.rand.org/pubs/research_reports/RR1365.html

Paramythis, A., & Loidl-Reisinger, S. (2004). Adaptive learning environments and e-learning standards. *Electronic Journal on e-Learning, 2*(1), 181-194.

Ramey, W. (2017). *The AI Podcast, Ep. 1: Deep Learning 101-Computing*. Retrieved from https://soundcloud.com/theaipodcast/ai-podcast-deep-learning-101

Rob, M. (2017). 7 Tips for Machine Learning Success. *PCmag*. Retrieved from https://www.pcmag.com/article/353293/7-tips-for-machine-learning-success

Roll, I., & Wylie, R. (2016). Evolution and revolution in artificial intelligence in education. *International Journal of Artificial Intelligence in Education, 26*(2), 582–599. doi:10.100740593-016-0110-3

Russell, S., & Norvig, P. (2003). *Artificial intelligence: A modern approach* (2nd ed.). Upper Saddle River, NJ: Pearson Education.

Sang-Hun, C. (2016). Google's Computer Program Beats Lee Se-dol in Go Tournament. *The New York Times*. Retrieved from https://www.nytimes.com/2016/03/16/world/asia/korea-alphago-vs-lee-sedol-go.html

Santos, J., Rodrigues, J. J., Casal, J., Saleem, K., & Denisov, V. (2018). Intelligent personal assistants based on internet of things approaches. *IEEE Systems Journal, 12*(2), 1793–1802. doi:10.1109/JSYST.2016.2555292

Shaikh. (2017). *Deep Learning vs. Machine Learning – the essential differences you need to know!* Retrieved from https://www.analyticsvidhya.com/blog/2017/04/comparison-between-deep-learning-machine-learning/

Tanwar, P., Prasad, T. V., & Datta, K. (2014). *An effective reasoning algorithm for question answering system. Editorial Preface.* Retrieved from http://thesai.org/Downloads/SpecialIssueNo9/Paper_8-An_Effective_Reasoning_Algorithm_for_Question_Answering_System.pdf

Wenger, E. (2014). *Artificial intelligence and tutoring systems: computational and cognitive approaches to the communication of knowledge.* Burlington, MA: Morgan Kaufmann.

Zhang, R., Chen, X., Lu, J., Wen, S., Nepal, S., & Xiang, Y. (2018). *Using AI to Hack IA: A New Stealthy Spyware Against Voice Assistance Functions in Smart Phones.* Retrieved from https://arxiv.org/pdf/1805.06187.pdf

KEY TERMS AND DEFINITIONS

Artificial Intelligence: The theory governing the development of computer systems that are able to perform tasks which normally require human intelligence, such as visual perception, speech recognition, decision-making, and translation between languages.

Deep Learning: A part of a broader family of machine learning methods based on learning data representations

Intelligent Learning Environments: A form of computer software which employs artificial intelligence-based programs for (online) learning activities.

Intelligent Personal Assistant: Software that has been designed to assist people with basic tasks, typically providing information using natural language.

Intelligent Tutoring System: Artificial intelligence-based computer software that provides immediate and customized feedback to students/learners.

Machine Learning: A field of artificial intelligence that uses statistical techniques to give computer systems the ability to learn.

Natural Language Processing: A subfield of computer science, information engineering, and artificial intelligence concerned with the interactions between computers and human (natural) language.

Chapter 15
Online and Distance Education in the Era of Rampant Technological Revolution

Hasan Ucar
https://orcid.org/0000-0001-9174-4299
Bilecik Seyh Edebali University, Turkey

ABSTRACT

Developments in information and communication technologies have reached an all-time high. These improvements have accelerated the transformation of higher education milieus on all sides. Accordingly, higher education institutions have begun to be delineated by these technological developments, activities, and practices. This technoculture era has started a new interaction among communication technologies, teachers, and learners. Herein, transhumanism regards changes in societies through these technological interactions and transformations. The worldwide technological transformation is approximating all societies and cultures to Marshall McLuhan's notion of a global village day by day as a consequence of the technology paradigm. The heydays of the developments in technologies affect all human beings at all points from living, learning, communicating to eating and even thinking styles. Taking these points into account, this chapter will explore how these variables may influence the online distance education milieus in terms of technoculture and transhumanism perspectives.

INTRODUCTION

Technological revolutions have changed the globe continuingly. Further, the stream of technology has been removing all barriers among the biological, psychical, and physical zones of human beings. Increasing globalization as a result of developments in information and communication technologies (ICTs) demonstrates its effect from industry to the economy, and from education to our way of thinking. Therefore, the last quarter of the 20th century witnessed rapid and intense changes. With the advent of the Internet and other online technologies, it is often said that a very different future, which is probably beyond our imaginations, waits for us. Although it was foreseen that the 21st century would be technologically dif-

DOI: 10.4018/978-1-5225-8431-5.ch015

ferent from the last century, it was not possible to predict such dazzling changes. The most important source of these changes has been the ICTs and the increasing appearance of their applications all over life. The applications of these changes have been implemented in the world of industry. By this means, the business world is changing on and on, so the way of teaching and learning must also be changed to keep up with the world of work.

Within the technological revolutions, education has been undoubtedly the most important area that exposed to change. Even though this area tries to catch the stream of the change, most implementations and practices are still in their infancy. In the past, the requirement of being in a certain place and time for learning has changed and the opportunity to learn at any time and place has become part of the mainstream education. Initially, the change happened in the distance education area and following this change this field has been transformed into online learning by means of ICTs.

Taking the current position of the technological sphere into account, much can be done to help all the current stakeholders to overcome the constraints in today's online learning environments. Considering that artificial intelligence (AI), machine learning and blockchain technologies have penetrated to our lives, it will be inevitable to see the substantial changes in open and distance learning processes and environments, too. Even though we are at the dawn of the technological shift, AI-integrated and blockchain-reinforced online and distance learning environments can strengthen their immune system and adapt themselves to these changes. We are now in the era of transhumanist paradigm where we should decide on our route and take the best of these views and applications to accord the online distance learning environments. This is because the increasing number of technophiles entails the authorities to adjust their present ways to take advantage of these transformations. The founder and executive chairman of the world economic forum, Klaus Schwab, pointed out to this transformation and stated that:

We stand on the brink of a technological revolution that will fundamentally alter the way we live, work, and relate to one another. In its scale, scope, and complexity, the transformation will be unlike anything humankind has experienced before. We do not yet know just how it will unfold, but one thing is clear: the response to it must be integrated and comprehensive, involving all stakeholders of the global polity, from the public and private sectors to academia and civil society. (Schwab, 2016)

In many areas, but most especially in online distance learning milieus, educational institutions should, metaphorically, begin to offer an *a la carte menu* instead of *table d'hote menus*. In order to take advantage of this wind of change, the authorities should adjust their practices to keep up with today's societies that also exist in virtual spaces. Especially unorthodox learners who do not have the same learning patterns of prevailing teaching methods need to be taken into account. That is, in terms of technoculture and transhumanism perspectives, this chapter will explore how these variables may influence the online learning milieus. Based on the above thoughts, this chapter aims to discuss the strengths, downsides, and opportunities of these technologies will be discussed. Additional, this chapter further presents the inevitable changes, probable challenges, opportunities, and some suggestions will be presented.

BACKGROUND

Upon examination of distance education history, it can be seen that there is a transformation from more conventional technologies to advanced, transhumanist technologies. In this regard, this section deals with a brief history of distance education and then examines current transhumanist technologies.

Distance Education: A Growing Future of Education

Distance education can simply be defined as the separation of learners and teachers in time and space. The distance education system, which dates back to the early 1800s, has emerged to make more use of learning opportunities and has become one of the mainstream education types (Demiray & İşman, 2003; Moore & Kearsley, 2005). By eliminating limitations, especially between learners, instructors and learning resources, and inequalities among learners, distance education has come to be included in the main movements of the educational sphere. According to Moore and Kearsley (2005) distance education system witnessed five eras till today. The five phases are given in Figure 1.

The journey of distance education began with the correspondence phase. In the phase of correspondence, the main medium used was mail. The materials were sent to the learners via postal services in order to give them the opportunity to study at home. This era lasted nearly for a hundred year. The second phase of distance education began with the use of radio in 1925s and television in 1935s. During this era, the learners began benefiting from audio and visual aspects of information delivered. The third phase of distance education began with the foundation of Open University in the UK. In this era, the correspondence, audio, and visual aspects of teaching were integrated with the industrial system approach (Moore

Figure 1. Five eras of distance education
(adapted from Moore & Kearsley, 2005)

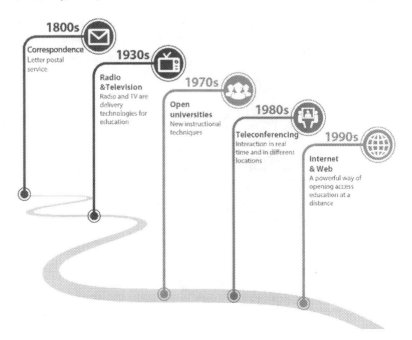

& Kearsley, 2005). The fourth phase was when the audio and video teleconference systems were used in delivering courses. In this era, learners and instructors were introduced synchronous group interaction. The fifth era began with the invention of the Internet. Within this phase, all materials have been provided across the online networks and online technologies have enabled online learning in virtual classes. Eventually, the distance education phenomenon has evolved to online distance education paradigm.

Distance education is an interdisciplinary field which is defined with many terms, such as, distance learning, distance teaching, online learning, open learning, e-Learning, web-based learning, and online and distance learning (Demiray, 2003; Saba, 2013). Even though these terms are attributed to different meanings, the distance education expo has a universal consent. The traditional education system in higher education is restricted to physical classrooms and face to face interaction. The system was disposed to leave out the learners who are away from the campus and cannot attend to classrooms or/and afford the charges. Technology integration with distance education enables learners to reach educational opportunities, and vice versa. In this sense, online distance education targets to overcome the obstacles of attending the education mainstream and provides learners opportunity to enter the education system which is independent in time and place through information and communication technologies (Kanwar, Carr, Ortlieb, & Mohee, 2018). In the 21st century online distance education, a great deal learning processes are carried out through the Internet and computers or mobile devices. These technologies are naturally involved in the learning continuum. ICTs are quintessentially incorporated into the online distance education journey (Spector, 2012). Furthermore, these technologies are transforming the spirit of learning context and placing the online distance education into the center of the orbit. However, online distance education has changed the old habits and removed all barriers that facing learners in entering the higher education (Demiray, 2003). Especially with the Open Educational Resources (OERs) innovation commenced in 2001, many online learning resources have been shared for free (Tait, 2018). As a result of this, the underprivileged have found a big chance to enter the educational process through online access to learning materials. Tait (2018) also added:

Opening up Higher Education as the Open Universities have done all around the world has made a huge contribution to education for development, and this movement can be situated in the context of resistance to the elitism that has gone before. It represents a political statement about the value and rights of all citizens rather than a few. (Tait, 2018)

In the course of these events, online distance education has become a mighty alternative to higher education. It offers equal and mostly free access to courses from all over the world. Furthermore, online distance education has potential, though not completely, to displace higher education. According to a report prepared by Magda and Aslanian (2018), the future of online education is shiny because ICTs are easing the way of this type of education and the number of the learners is increasing all the time. They also added that the value of getting an online degree is more important than its cost and because of this, online learning has a positive effect on learners' investments. The authors also suggested that online distance teaching institutions must take the following issues when preparing their courses in order to be in tune with the technological developments and today's learners.

- Mobile friendly content
- Career services that help online learners
- Varied programs

- Innovations that reduce the cost and time to complete a program
- Interactions and relationships with other learners
- Using different channels for advertising and marketing

Magda and Aslanian (2018) also emphasized that higher education has been confronting a prevalent reduction in the number of learners, but online distance education has not experienced this issue so far. Similarly, Otto Peters (2014) stated that "online distance education is the way of tomorrow". So, all shareholders, related to online distance education issue, should take the best of technological changes wrought by the rampant technological revolution.

Online Distance Education in the Shadow of Technological Innovations

With the help of technological innovations, online learning opportunities have become more available, prevalent, and efficient. Insomuch that today millions of learners are earning degrees without even stepping into a classroom. According to Dron (2014), the winds of change in online distance education take place on account of many drivers. These factors come together and form a group of circumstances. These issues are given below:

- New technological opportunities,
- The restrictive bounds of available technologies,
- Path dependencies caused by earlier decisions,
- Learners' expectations,
- The barriers related to learners and learning environments,
- Other factors outside of the learning context such as rivals, legislation, funding, and with prior learning situations,
- Changes in the learning paradigm,
- Trends, position, and attitudes to learning and to existing technological opportunities.

Together, with the power of online technologies many universities, mostly in Ivy League, have begun to produce and offer Massive Open Online Courses (MOOCs). Bozkurt and Keefer (2018) stated that MOOCs have emerged with the uptrend of online network technologies and this let the public learn openly. Even though there are many criticisms about these courses, such as dropout rates and quality issues, the cream of the universities mostly has partaken in this procession. According to Bates (2018), over 20 million learners enroll to these courses each year. Also, MOOCs providers assure today's learners by offering learning and certification opportunities (Bates, 2018; Bozkurt, Akgün-Özbek, & Zawacki-Richter, 2017). On the other hand, online distance education movement has a great influence on higher education teaching methods. That is to say, higher education institutions have begun to integrate the online education with face to face teaching, and a new fashion teaching method that is hybrid or blended learning stream has come up (Bates, 2018; Halverson, Spring, Huyett, Henrie, & Graham, 2017). Regarding the blended learning issue, Bates (2018) stated that:

The real issue lies with faculty and especially departments moving to blended or hybrid learning that do not understand the need for learning design or the needs of students who are not on campus all the time. The integration of online and campus-based learning will often highlight the inadequacy of prior campus-based teaching methods. There is much that campus-based faculty can learn from distance education, in terms of more effective teaching. (Bates, 2018)

Magda and Aslanian (2018) are drawing attention to the challenge of this breakthrough because they have concerns for quality in these courses as some of the higher education institutions do not have any experience in online distance education processes. Despite these concerns, many higher education institutions live up to online distance expectations and they are moving from single mode (face to face teaching) to dual mode position (both online and face to face teaching) (Bates, 2018).

MAIN FOCUS OF THE CHAPTER

Technologically enhanced online and distance learning environments show promise in facilitating the way of our teaching and learning practices further. The emerging technologies, such us, robotics, Internet of Things, integration of brain and computer, AI, and blockchain technology will be apparently the default part of the educational processes in near future. However, AI and blockchain technology appear to be the significant tools that have a promising future. Based on these arguments, the main focus of this chapter will be on AI and blockchain technology, and their reflections on online distance education.

Artificial Intelligence

AI is a concept that describes technological machines exhibit actions like human intelligence. AI is a result of the machine and deep learning notions that cover the big data and activator technologies (Vander Ark, 2017a). Even though this technology dates back to 1950s, with the help of today's convenient and cost-affordable devices, and prevalent programming knowledge, AI has become widespread (Vander Ark, 2017a). However, according to Butler-Adam (2018), AI's inception is not known for sure, but it came around a few years ago and come to the light in favor of digital technologies. These technologies conceive new facilities (Figure 2).

The possibilities of billions of people connected by mobile devices, with unprecedented processing power, storage capacity, and access to knowledge, are unlimited. And these possibilities will be multiplied by emerging technology breakthroughs in fields such as artificial intelligence, robotics, the Internet of Things, autonomous vehicles, 3-D printing, nanotechnology, biotechnology, materials science, energy storage, and quantum computing. (Schwab, 2016)

There are many views both optimistic and pessimistic related to AI technology (Butler-Adam 2018; Vander Ark, 2017a). The main hopeful view is that the AI technology will help to humankind in easing the current workload and on this wise, people will have a more comfortable life. On the other hand, the doomy view, maybe the real, is that AI technology will substitute millions of people in the workplace and push millions out of work. This will unquestionably change nature of the human being. One of the most efficient organizations that promote the ethical usage of AI in favor of Homo sapiens is called Humanity+ (Vita-More, 2016). This international nonprofit organization manifested a *Transhumanist Declaration* (Appendix 1), which was modified in 2009, with eight articles (Humanity+, 2018). The declaration draws attention to the future of humanity in the first article and states that: *"Humanity*

Figure 2. The form of artificial intelligence
(Vander Ark, 2017a)

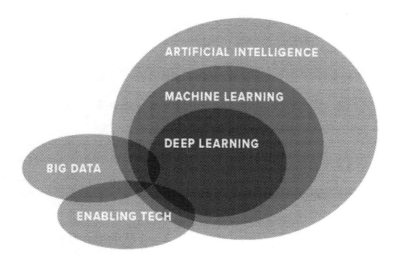

stands to be profoundly affected by science and technology in the future. We envision the possibility of broadening human potential by overcoming aging, cognitive shortcomings, involuntary suffering, and our confinement to planet Earth." (Humanity+, 2018)

Even though AI provides many opportunities, it may also pose the following challenges as well (Vander Ark, 2017a):

- Unemployment
- Acceleration of income inequality
- Privacy
- Algorithmic prejudice
- Access to AI technology and safety
- Ethics
- Weaponized AI
- Threatens to humanity
- Genome editing
- Bad usage of AI

Besides those challenges, AI technology will definitely have a great influence on present online and distance learning processes as a consequence of the improvements in ICTs (Kose, 2015).

AI and Its Reflections on Online Distance Education

AI has not had total and clear reflections in education milieus, yet. In fact, there are still very few applications with their full potential. However, as the significance of competences and skills, such as creativity, critical thinking, self-management, problem-solving, and collaboration, in learning process increase, AI technology will adapt itself and come into play more (Roll & Wylie, 2016). Dickson (2017) states that AI will help the educators in solving many present problems. He also indicated that:

Because of the advances in artificial intelligence (AI) and machine learning, a slow but steady transformation is coming to education, under the hood. In a few years, teachers will no longer be alone in shouldering the burden of training the young generation or the workforce at corporations (Dickson, 2017).

While AI is rampant in other industries, it has a delay in reaching the education field. This is because the education domain is large and has a dynamic nature. However, AI apparently has a big potential to transform the present mass classrooms into more personalized ones. It can also help educators by performing basic duties, such as grading or tracking learners' performances. And it's clear that the traditional one-size education model will not continue, instead, AI can serve many evolutions (Vander Ark, 2017a). Here are some opportunities and supports that AI may provide (Vander Ark, 2017a):

- One-to-one tutoring
- Efficient and personalized assessment
- Efficient and personalized recommendations
- Upskilling in teacher development
- Hiring gap-fillers to keep up with the developments
- Maximizing learning processes
- Transportation of learners

Those are some of the opportunities that can support learning environments. When online and distance learning environments are equipped with AI-powered applications, instructors can easily detect the deficient issues related to learners and the learning environments and produce solutions accordingly. Besides, online learners may have digital tutors that guide them in an efficient and productive way. There are some examples of AI-powered educational applications, such as Zoomi, Thinkster Math, DreamBox, MATHia and Brainly, which help the learners and guide the instructors to produce better learning outputs. Further, with the help of special algorithms-drive AI, demotivating issues related to course design, materials, or learning environment can be determined and this can help the authorities to solve these issues in due time.

Blockchain Technology

Blockchain technology is a novel endeavor that will probably be a vital part of the many online structures in our lives in the near future. According to Grech and Camilleri (2017) *"a blockchain is a distributed ledger that provides a way for information to be recorded and shared by a community."* In other words, blockchain technology is a kind of record keeping regulation within a particular set of characteristics (Andolfatto, 2018). Because of its distributed and decentralized nature and operating smart contact among users, this neologism has vital opportunities. These hallmarks of emerging blockchain technology vary from the Internet-based operations and give the blockchain a promising future (McArthur, 2018; Yli-Huumo, Ko, Choi, Park, & Smolander, 2016; Vander Ark, 2018). Grech and Camilleri (2017) present some of the opportunities that blockchain technology serves:

- Self-domination on personal data,
- Confidence in payments and certifications
- Transparency in conducting transactions
- Inalterability of records
- Disintermediation
- Collaboration without a mediator

Blockchain technology has an invariable system that can be verified and controlled. Also, the recordings or assets cannot be hacked. Due to its distributed feature, blockchain technology will have far and wide many implementations related to digital records. Online distance education is a candidate for this technology to develop itself on a sound basis.

Blockchain Technology and Its Reflections on Online Distance Education

Blockchain technology emerged with the orientation of cryptocurrency but now this technology has reached a new age with various applications. The blockchain technology has gone over many fields and now it is in search of helpful applications in education area where confidence is quite important (Albeanu, 2017; Hartley, 2018). The blockchain technology can aid the higher education institutions and the society to amend their mutual relationships (Tapscott & Tapscott, 2017; Vander Ark, 2017b). Besides, according to Universa Blockchain (2018), blockchain technology will simplify the communication and interaction among all shareholders in education context (Figure 3). In this respect, this technology may have vital roles in online distance education field where interaction has utmost importance.

According to Grech and Camilleri (2017) accreditors, validators, testers, employers, learners, and teachers are the educational shareholders that quite likely take advantage of blockchain technology (Figure 4).

According to Tapscott and Tapscott (2017) higher education institutions can benefit from blockchain opportunities within the following four issues:

- **Identity and Learner Records:** Identifying learners and keeping their recordings secure
- **Emerging Pedagogy:** Creating new models of learning
- **Fund and Reward:** Funding education and rewarding learners for their successful work
- **Designing a new Model of University (a Meta University Model):** Designing new models of higher education

Blockchain technology can simplify and strengthen the assessment and management processes by providing permanent, transparent, and sustainable recordings of the learners and giving them access all the time (Jirgensons & Kapenieks, 2018). However, this technology can keep all diverse recordings easily and create a documentation mechanism for formal and informal learning operations, too. For this purpose, the recordings of learning processes should be digitalized and integrated into the registry of lifelong learning (Jirgensons & Kapenieks, 2018). Thus, learners' encrypted documents can be used to develop a lifelong learning process according to learners' drawbacks and needs. Moreover, according to Matthews (2017) blockchain technology can reduce administrative costs and create a more secure environment to host these educational certifications. Herewith, this technology can accelerate higher education institutions in the validation of learners' academic credentials.

Figure 3. Blockchain technology in education area
(Universa Blockchain, 2018)

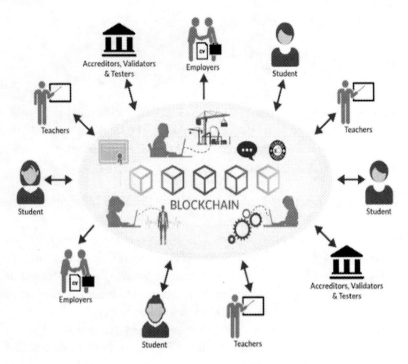

Figure 4. Educational shareholders in blockchain technology
(Grech & Camilleri, 2017)

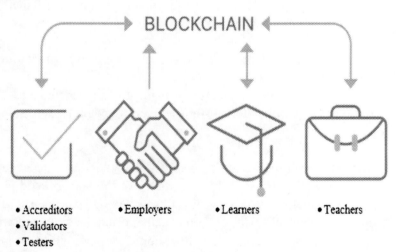

CONCLUSION AND FUTURE RESEARCH DIRECTIONS

The dazzling changes and innovations in information and communication technologies for the past few years make the transformation of teaching and learning processes unavoidable. With the help of the ICTs and Internet technologies, the number of learners has been increasing all over the world and the lifelong learning phenomenon has been accepted as a must approach in a constantly changing globe where learners are exposed a great deal of information. Further, the rampant technological evolution creates many opportunities for higher education shareholders. The recent advancements in technology have necessitated the higher education institutions to keep up with these developments and transform their teaching ways. Thanks to this technological push, online and distance education is evolving all the time. Further, the ubiquity of online and distance education phenomenon led this field to be a more remarkable one. Considering the developments in AI and blockchain technology, radical changes will eventually transform the online and distance learning spaces. These technologies will probably pave the way for better interaction among the learners, learning materials, and teachers. The online distance learning environments will remain at a rough guess the same, but by means of new technologies and innovations, such as AI and blockchain technology more efficient and faster learning processes will quite likely take place. Online and distance education is now standing at an important crossroad where the authorities must decide on how to utilize AI and blockchain based technologies to contribute to issues such as personalized and differentiated learning, maximizing learning and educating processes, collaboration, and transparency. Moreover, the competition in current traditional education institutions will evolve to new technologies and innovations in online distance education. So how will online distance education field handle these innovations, and what aspects of these improvements and technologies need online distance education to be focusing on? The answers to these questions are important to show us the right way.

ACKNOWLEDGMENT

I would like to thank Dr. Aras Bozkurt for his helpful comments on this chapter. I am also grateful for all his help.

REFERENCES

Albeanu, G. (2017). Blockchain technology and education. In G. Albeanu, M. Popovici, R. Jugureanu, A. Adăscăliței, & O. Istrate (Eds.) *Proceedings of the 12th International Conference on Virtual Learning* (pp. 271-275), Bucharest, Romania: Bucharest University Press

Andolfatto, D. (2018). Blockchain: What it is, what it does, and why you probably don't need one. *Federal Reserve Bank of St. Louis Review, 100*(2), 87–95. doi:10.20955/r.2018.87-95

Bates, T. (2018). *Why is innovation in teaching in HE so difficult? Integrating online and distance learning into the mainstream*. Retrieved from https://www.tonybates.ca/2018/08/01/why-is-innovation-in-teaching-in-he-so-difficult-4-integrating-online-and-distance-learning-into-the-mainstream/

Bozkurt, A., Akgün-Özbek, E., & Zawacki-Richter, O. (2017). Trends and patterns in massive open online courses: Review and content analysis of research on MOOCs (2008-2015). *International Review of Research in Open and Distributed Learning*, *18*(5), 118–147. doi:10.19173/irrodl.v18i5.3080

Bozkurt, A., & Keefer, J. (2018). Participatory learning culture and community formation in connectivist MOOCs. *Interactive Learning Environments*, *26*(6), 776–788. doi:10.1080/10494820.2017.1412988

Butler-Adam, J. (2018). The fourth industrial revolution and education. *South African Journal of Science*, *114*(5-6), 1–1. doi:10.17159ajs.2018/a0271

Clark, D. (2016). *10 ways Blockchain could be used in education*. Retrieved from https://oeb.global/oeb-insights/10-ways-blockchain-could-be-used-in-education

Demiray, U. (2003). Defining distance education. In A. İşman, M. Barkan, & U. Demiray (Eds.), *Online Distance Education Book*. TOJET. Retrieved from http://www.tojet.net/e-book/ebook.htm

Demiray, U., & İşman, A. (2003). History of distance education. In A. İşman, M. Barkan, & U. Demiray (Eds.), *Online Distance Education Book*. TOJET. Retrieved from http://www.tojet.net/e-book/ebook.htm

Dickson, B. (2017). *How artificial intelligence is shaping the future of education*. Retrieved from https://www.pcmag.com/article/357483/how-artificial-intelligence-is-shaping-the-future-of-educati

Dron, J. (2014). Innovation and change: Changing how we change. In O. Zawacki-Richter & T. Anderson (Eds.), *Online Distance Education: Towards a Research Agenda* (pp. 237–265). Edmonton, Canada: AU Press.

Grech, A., & Camilleri, A. F. (2017). Blockchain in Education. Inamorato dos Santos, A. (Ed.) EUR 28778 EN; doi:10.2760/60649

Halverson, L. R., Spring, K. J., Huyett, S., Henrie, C. R., & Graham, C. R. (2017). Blended learning research in higher education and K-12 settings. In M. Spector, B. Lockee, & M. Childress (Eds.), *Learning, Design, and Technology* (pp. 1–30). Cham, Switzerland: Springer. doi:10.1007/978-3-319-17727-4_31-1

Hartley, R. (2018). *What is the role of blockchain in education?* Retrieved from https://edtechnology.co.uk/Blog/what-is-the-role-of-blockchain-in-education/

Humanity+. (2018). *Transhumanist Declaration*. Retrieved from https://humanityplus.org/philosophy/transhumanist-declaration/

Jirgensons, M., & Kapenieks, J. (2018). Blockchain and the future of digital learning credential assessment and management. *Journal of Teacher Education for Sustainability*, *20*(1), 145–156. doi:10.2478/jtes-2018-0009

Kanwar, A. S., Carr, A., Ortlieb, K., & Mohee, R. (2018). Opportunities and challenges for campus-based universities in Africa to translate into dual-mode delivery. *Distance Education*, *39*(2), 140–158. doi:10.1080/01587919.2018.1457944

Kose, U. (2015). For an intelligent e-learning: A managerial model suggestion for artificial intelligence supported e-learning content flow. In U. Kose & D. Koc (Eds.), *Artificial intelligence applications in distance education* (pp. 149–160). Hershey, PA: IGI Global. doi:10.4018/978-1-4666-6276-6.ch009

Magda, A. J., & Aslanian, C. B. (2018). *Online college students 2018: Comprehensive data on demands and preferences*. Louisville, KY: The Learning House.

Marlin, D. (2018). Millennials, this is how artificial intelligence will impact your job for better and worse. *Forbes*. Retrieved from https://www.forbes.com/sites/danielmarlin/2018/01/16/millennials-this-is-how-artificial-intelligence-will-impact-your-job-for-better-and-worse/#4a9bad4f4533

Matthews, D. (2017). *What blockchain technology could mean for universities*. Retrieved from https://www.timeshighereducation.com/news/what-blockchain-technology-could-mean-for-universities

McArthur, D. (2018). *Will blockchains revolutionize education?* Retrieved from https://er.educause.edu/articles/2018/5/will-blockchains-revolutionize-education

Moore, M. G., & Kearsley, G. (2005). *Distance Education: A Systems View* (2nd ed.). Belmont, CA: Thomson Wadsworth.

Peters, O. (2014). Foreword. In O. Zawacki-Richter & T. Anderson (Eds.), *Online distance education: Towards a research agenda* (pp. 237–265). Edmonton, Canada: AU Press.

Roll, I., & Wylie, R. (2016). Evolution and revolution in artificial intelligence in education. *International Journal of Artificial Intelligence in Education*, 26(2), 582–599. doi:10.100740593-016-0110-3

Saba, F. (2013). Building the Future: A Theoretical Perspective. In M. G. Moore (Ed.), *Handbook of distance education* (pp. 49–65). New York, NY: Routledge. doi:10.4324/9780203803738.ch4

Schwab, K. (2016). *The fourth industrial revolution: what it means, how to respond*. Retrieved from https://www.weforum.org/agenda/2016/01/the-fourth-industrial-revolution-what-it-means-and-how-to-respond?utm_content=buffer8a47b&utm_medium=social&utm_source=facebook.com&utm_campaign=buffer

Spector, J. M. (2012). The future of distance learning technology: It's not about the technology and it's not about the distance. In L. Moller & J. B. Huett (Eds.), *The next generation of distance education* (pp. 21–29). Boston, MA: Springer. doi:10.1007/978-1-4614-1785-9_2

Tait, A. W. (2018). Education for development: From distance to open education. *The Journal of Learning for Development*, 5(2), 101-115.

Tapscott, D., & Tapscott, A. (2017). The blockchain revolution and higher education. *EDUCAUSE Review*, 52(2), 11–24.

Universa Blockchain. (2018). *Blockchain in education*. Retrieved from https://medium.com/universa-blockchain/blockchain-in-education-49ad413b9e12

Vander Ark, T. (2017a). *Ask about AI: The future of work and learning*. Retrieved from http://www.gettingsmart.com/wp-content/uploads/2018/01/17-EdIn-05-white-paper-rd9-1.pdf

Vander Ark, T. (2017b). *How blockchain will transform credentialing (and education)*. Retrieved from http://www.gettingsmart.com/2017/12/blockchain-will-transform-credentialing-education/

Vander Ark, T. (2018). *20 Ways blockchain will transform (okay, may improve) education.* Retrieved from https://www.forbes.com/sites/tomvanderark/2018/08/20/26-ways-blockchain-will-transform-ok-may-improve-education/#1d4cf0f04ac9

Vita-More, N. (2016). Transhumanism: The growing worldview. In N. Lee (Ed.), *Google It: total information awareness* (pp. 475–487). New York: Springer. doi:10.1007/978-1-4939-6415-4_27

Yli-Huumo, J., Ko, D., Choi, S., Park, S., & Smolander, K. (2016). Where is current research on blockchain technology? - A systematic review. *PLoS One, 11*(10), 1–27. doi:10.1371/journal.pone.0163477 PMID:27695049

KEY TERMS AND DEFINITIONS

Artificial Intelligence (AI): The theory governing the development of computer systems that are able to perform tasks which normally require human intelligence, such as visual perception, speech recognition, decision-making, and translation between languages.

Blended Learning: It is a term that describes the combination of online learning and traditional classroom practices. It is also known as hybrid learning.

Blockchain Technology: It is an online ledger distributed across the networks in which the data, independent of each other, that is blocks, are connected to each other by means of algorithms and consequently the chains are formed.

Distance Education (DE): Planned and organized teaching and learning in which learners are separated from teachers or facilitators in time and space.

Dual Mode University: A university model that offers both campus-based and distance education programs.

Information and Communication Technologies (ICTs): It is a term that defines the integration of information technologies and computers.

Massive Open Online Courses (MOOCs): These courses are mostly online free courses that planned for a large number of participants. The courses are also open to everyone without entry qualifications.

Online Learning: It is an educational approach that benefits from online technologies.

Open Educational Resources (OERs): The teaching, learning, and research materials that are open to everyone and completely free to use without any restrictions.

Single Mode University: A university model that offers only distance education programs.

APPENDIX

Transhumanist Declaration

1. Humanity stands to be profoundly affected by science and technology in the future. We envision the possibility of broadening human potential by overcoming aging, cognitive shortcomings, involuntary suffering, and our confinement to planet Earth.
2. We believe that humanity's potential is still mostly unrealized. There are possible scenarios that lead to wonderful and exceedingly worthwhile enhanced human conditions.
3. We recognize that humanity faces serious risks, especially from the misuse of new technologies. There are possible realistic scenarios that lead to the loss of most, or even all, of what we hold valuable. Some of these scenarios are drastic, others are subtle. Although all progress is change, not all change is progress.
4. Research effort needs to be invested into understanding these prospects. We need to carefully deliberate how best to reduce risks and expedite beneficial applications. We also need forums where people can constructively discuss what should be done, and a social order where responsible decisions can be implemented.
5. Reduction of existential risks, and development of means for the preservation of life and health, the alleviation of grave suffering, and the improvement of human foresight and wisdom should be pursued as urgent priorities, and heavily funded.
6. Policy making ought to be guided by responsible and inclusive moral vision, taking seriously both opportunities and risks, respecting autonomy and individual rights, and showing solidarity with and concern for the interests and dignity of all people around the globe. We must also consider our moral responsibilities towards generations that will exist in the future.
7. We advocate the well-being of all sentience, including humans, non-human animals, and any future artificial intellects, modified life forms, or other intelligences to which technological and scientific advance may give rise.
8. We favour allowing individuals wide personal choice over how they enable their lives. This includes use of techniques that may be developed to assist memory, concentration, and mental energy; life extension therapies; reproductive choice technologies; cryonics procedures; and many other possible human modification and enhancement technologies.

Source: https://humanityplus.org/philosophy/transhumanist-declaration/

Chapter 16
From Distance Education to Open and Distance Learning:
A Holistic Evaluation of History, Definitions, and Theories

Aras Bozkurt
https://orcid.org/0000-0002-4520-642X
Anadolu University, Turkey

ABSTRACT

As pragmatist, interdisciplinary fields, distance education (DE) and open and distance learning (ODL) transform and adapt themselves according to changing paradigms. In this regard, the purpose of this study is to examine DE and ODL from different perspectives to discern their future directions. The study concludes that DE and ODL are constantly developing interdisciplinary fields where technology has become a significant catalyst and these fields become part of the mainstream education. However, mainstreaming should be evaluated with caution, and there is a need to revisit core values and fundamentals where critical pedagogy would have a pivotal role. Besides, there is no single theory that best explains these interdisciplinary fields, and therefore, there is a need to benefit from different theoretical approaches. Finally, as a result of constant changes, we should keep the definition of both DE and ODL up-to-date to better explain the needs of the global teaching and learning ecosystem.

INTRODUCTION

Distance education (DE) and open and distance learning (ODL) are interdisciplinary fields that emerged in a near history of humankind. Technology has played an instrumental role in both fields, and it is clear that as technology improves, these fields evolve in line with the improvements by providing new learning opportunities to learners. Therefore, to gain a fuller understanding of DE and ODL, it is important to examine them from different perspectives. In this study, DE and ODL are discussed in terms of their historical development, definitions and theoretical backgrounds.

DOI: 10.4018/978-1-5225-8431-5.ch016

From Distance Education to Open and Distance Learning

METHOD

This study applied a traditional (narrative) review method, which is generally used to "provide a much-needed bridge between the vast and scattered assortment of articles on a topic and to link together many studies on different topics, either for purposes of reinterpretation or interconnection" (Baumeister & Leary, 1997, p. 311). This type of study is useful for presenting up-to-date literature (Cronin, Ryan & Coughlan, 2008) and can be used to summarize, synthesize, draw conclusions, identify research gaps, and provide suggestions for future research (Cronin et al., 2008). In this regard, the purpose of this study is to examine DE and ODL by examining their respective definitions, history, and theories.

This chapter considers DE and ODL as two distinct but overlapping terms. However, beyond the nuances attached to these two terms in use, this chapter further acknowledges that both terms referring to the same visions and uses these terms interchangeably when necessary.

A BRIEF HISTORY: ROOTS OF DISTANCE EDUCATION

The history of DE dates back to the 1700s and 1800s and reflects an egalitarian approach to education (Casey, 2008). Its history can be classified under three ages at the macro level and under five generations at the micro level. These ages and generations were shaped and determined by the dominant communication technologies adopted by DE (Figure 1).

1st Age: Correspondence DE

The history of DE began with courses whose learning content was delivered by mail, and thus it was referred to as correspondence study. By highlighting different characteristics, correspondence study was also called "home study" by the early for-profit schools, and "independent study" by the universities. Owing to the railway networks, which were the cheapest, fastest and most reliable mode of transportation at the beginning of the early 1880s, individuals started to receive their education at home or at work (Moore & Kearsley, 1996). The primary motive for correspondence educators at that time was to connect with those whose only opportunity to learn was through correspondence DE (Nasseh, 1997). In correspondence DE, the learners were mostly adults, whose decision to receive this form of education was due to their occupational, social, and family commitments (Smaldino et al., 2000).

Figure 1. Ages and generations of DE

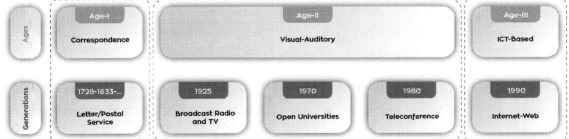

The dominant technology in this era was print technology, and therefore, as a result of the nature of written/printed materials and their method of delivery, this macro age of DE was characterized by a didactic teaching style and an industrialized form of education. Although there were different types of print media, the combination of the printing press and postal services paved the way for correspondence DE.

The last but most important aspect of this DE age was the target group, which consisted largely of women, workers, and farmers, all of whom had been traditionally left out of the formal education process. Correspondence DE served well to redress social injustices and decrease rates of illiteracy by providing common people with access to learning. In this sense, it is possible to argue that the origins of DE were tightly connected to the principles of critical pedagogy, that this age was responsible for laying the groundwork for today's knowledge society, and that the combination of correspondence DE and first-generation technologies were important catalysts of globalization. Further evidence to support these arguments are listed in chronological order below:

- The earliest evidence of the origin of DE can be traced to 1728, when Caleb Phillips advertised shorthand lessons by mail in the Boston Gazette (Verduin & Clark, 1991).
- In 1833, a Swedish newspaper advertised the opportunity to study "composition through the medium of the post" (Smaldino et al., 2000, p. 37).
- In the 1840s, Isaac Pitman used the postal service in Great Britain to teach shorthand lessons. Soon after, Pitman's lessons were formalized through the founding of the Phonographic Correspondence Society (Smaldino et al., 2000; Moore & Kearsley, 1996).
- In Europe, in the mid-1850s, Charles Toussaint and Gustav Langenscheidt taught language in Berlin, Germany through correspondence study. Later, they developed a language instruction exchange program, which lead to the establishment of a correspondence language school (Moore & Kearsley, 1996; Smaldino et al., 2000; Watkins, 1991).
- From 1873 to 1897, correspondence study flourished in America. Anna Eliot Ticknor, who is recognized as the mother of American correspondence study, founded the Boston-based Society to Encourage Study at Home (Holmberg, 1986). This initiative reached more than 10K students in 24 years. Learners, mostly made up of women, corresponded monthly with teachers, who offered guided readings and frequent tests (Smaldino et al., 2000; Watkins, 1991). The purpose of this correspondence study was to help provide women, who were restricted from accessing formal educational institutions, with the opportunity to study through materials delivered to their homes (Nasseh, 1997).
- During this age of DE, similar initiatives were taken around the world thanks to improved postal services. The courses were mainly vocational subjects, or in other words, they were non-credit courses (Moore & Kearsley, 1996).
- In 1882, in Chautauqua, New York, William Rainey Harper developed correspondence program teaching courses in Hebrew, the results of which eventually led to the recognition of correspondence courses by the State of New York. In 1892, when Harper was assigned as the first president of the University of Chicago, he benefited from his previous experiences and initiated the world's first formal program of university DE. (Moore & Kearsley, 1996). As a result of this movement, Correspondence University was established in Ithaca, New York in 1883 (Erazo & Derlin, 1995).
- In 1886, Hermod began teaching English by correspondence in Sweden. Following that, he founded Hermods in 1898, which grew to become the world's largest and most influential distance teaching organizations at this time (Smaldino et al., 2000).

- In 1891, Foster, the editor of the Mining Herald, a daily newspaper in eastern Pennsylvania, began offering correspondence courses in mining and the prevention of mine accidents (Smaldino et al., 2000). Foster's efforts led to the development of International Correspondence Schools (ICS), which aimed to train iron and railroad workers, as well as miners (Moore & Kearsley, 1996). The number of enrolled students exploded from 225K in 1900 to more than 2.5M students by 1923 (Moore & Kearsley, 1996; Smaldino et al., 2000).
- In the last decade of the 1800s, a series of new correspondence institutions helped correspondence study to flourish (e.g., Skerry's College in Edinburgh in 1878 and University Correspondence College in London in 1887). In parallel to these developments, the university extension movement in the USA and Great Britain promoted the acceptance of correspondence study (Smaldino et al., 2000).
- In 1892, distance learning achieved academic recognition when the University of Chicago offered the first college-level distance learning program. Students were able to learn through correspondence study by using the United States Postal Service to submit assignments and lessons (Hansen, 2001).
- In 1885, with the development of short courses and farmers' institutes at the University of Wisconsin, another form of university extension of correspondence study appeared. By 1891, a program of correspondence study, led by eminent historian Frederick Jackson Turner, was offered by the same university. However, the public showed little interest in the correspondence programs, resulting in their closure in 1899. It took seven years to recreate a new, stronger correspondence study department within the school's university extension division (Smaldino et al., 2000).
- In 1900, Cornell University developed a program for women in rural up-state New York. This program was a great success, with more than 20K women enrolling in it (Cornell University, 2001). Correspondence education through the Land Grant universities was developed based on the policies of the 1862 Morril Act, whose democratic ideals dictated that educational opportunity be open for people from all backgrounds (Moore & Kearsley, 1996). The Morril Act serves as an significant cornerstone in the history of DE because of its visionary approach to openness in education.
- In 1901, Moody Bible Institute, which was established in 1886, founded a correspondence study department which continues to still exist, having more than a million enrolled students (Smaldino et al., 2000).
- In 1915, the National University Extension Association (NUEA) emphasized the need for new pedagogical models and national-level guidelines for correspondence educators (Nasseh, 1997).
- In the 1920s, distance education broadened its focus to secondary school curriculum (Smaldino et al., 2000).
- By 1930, courses specifically designed as correspondence study were being offered by 39 American universities (Bittner & Mallory, 1933).
- The United States Military Institute, founded in 1941, was converted to the United States Armed Forces Institute (USAFI) in 1943. Throughout World War II, USAFI offered correspondence courses to military personnel and continued offering them until its closure in 1974. Before the closure of USAFI, more than seven million military personnel had taken high school courses and approximately 261 thousand personnel had taken courses at the graduate level. The giving and reading of assignments through computers in USAFI pioneered the 24-hour active phone counselling service for students and classrooms, with the group studies being based on a correspondence

curriculum; that is teaching via mail service (Watkins, 1991). All these contributions provided by USAFI have led to the rise of a new era in the history of DE.
- The Ministry of National Education in France established a DE training program in response to the oncoming Second World War. The Centre National d'Enseignement par Correspondences had been originally founded for children mainly but was eventually converted to a distance training institution for adults (Smaldino et al., 2000).

2nd Age: Visual-Auditory DE

Distance Education and Radio

Live educational radio reduced many of the limitations of correspondence education, especially delivery time, and increased the immediacy of the learning processes. Delivery of learning content through postal services was no longer necessary once live educational radio emerged (Casey, 2008).

The dominant technologies in this age were first audio (e.g., radio) and then visual-auditory (e.g., television) technology. The invention of the radio and television enhanced and accelerated the speed of communication and interaction. Although the interaction between learners and teacher was at first minimal at this age, with each successive generation there was an increase in the level of interaction and the social presence of the teacher, and in terms of immediacy, this age was revolutionary.

During this second age, it became possible to reach masses of people, which prompted an increase in educational research on instructional design. Given this ease of reaching the masses, it did not take long for open universities to emerge, many of which began to be referred to as mega universities in the 90s, on account of their more than 100K students.

Though instruction was teacher centred in this age, learners gradually started to gain independence and autonomy through the advantages offered by new communication technologies. Research, therefore, began to focus on communication technologies and the effectiveness of new delivery methods. The key developments of this second age are listed below in chronological order:

- By 1921, licenses for educational radio were being granted to the higher education institutions in the USA (Saettler, 1990; Casey, 2008).
- Between 1918 and 1946, the Federal Communications Commission (FCC) issued a license to more than 200 higher education institutions (Pittman, 1986a; Casey, 2008). In 1925, Iowa State University launched the first five-credit radio lessons (Pittman, 1986b).
- By 1923, educational institutions owned around 10% of the radio stations used for educational purposes (Public Broadcasting Service, 2003).
- In 1925, the federal government emphasized the importance of educational radio and allocated special frequencies to educate agricultural communities (Department of Commerce, 1926).
- In 1930, the U.S. Department of Education had an active role in educational radio. A variety of programs, ranging from science to history, were sponsored by the U. S. Department of Education (Laine, 1939).

From Distance Education to Open and Distance Learning

Distance Education and Television

- In the early 1930s, broadcasters experimented with many different educational television programs. In the 1950s, courses for credit started to be offered by higher education institutions (Smaldino et al., 2000).
- In 1956, a closed-circuit television service was launched, and Chicago TV College pioneered teaching by television (Moore & Kearsley, 1996).
- In the early 1960s, Airborne Television Instruction (Midwest Program on Airborne Television Instruction: MPATI) launched the first "flying classroom" on an airfield near Purdue University in Lafayette, Indiana (Smith, 1961). The program aimed to broadcast educational television programs to 400 thousand people (Gordon, 1990).
- In 1963, the FCC created the Instructional Television Fixed Service (ITFS), a band of 20 television channels available to educational institutions (Public Broadcasting Service, 2003).
- In 1964, the University of Wisconsin launched the Vocalized Educational Media (VEM) project, which was the first attempt to identify, categorize, and systematize DE practices. This project put forward instructions on how to create and use multimedia educational packages for the advantage of the independent student (Gooch, 1998).
- By the 1970s, there were 233 educational television stations in the USA (Gooch, 1998).
- The AIM Project, which encouraged higher education institutions to deliver educational content through educational television, was implemented in Great Britain, Australia, and Germany (e.g., Open University in Great Britain and Fern Universität in Germany) (Casey, 2008).
- In 1970, Coastline Community was the first to present a lesson completely on television (Casey, 2008).

Distance Education and Teleconferencing

- By the 1980s, with the help of communication satellites, educational television was available throughout the continental United States and beyond (Saba, 2013).
- In 1982, the National University Teleconference Network used satellites to broadcast its programs to 40 institutional members. In 1985, the National Technology University (NTU) launched online courses using satellite signals in order to access, download, and distribute course materials for both undergraduate and graduate education. In 1989, the University of Phoenix emerged on the stage as a for-profit online open learning institution by providing courses to meet these needs (Casey, 2008).
- During the 1970s and 1980s, the increase in telecommunication satellites led to the testing of many television programs (Saba, 2013).
- Following the developments in educational television, learning opportunities were provided not only for adult learners but also for young learners (Zigerell, 1991).
- The advancements in communication satellites and cable television increased the coverage zone capacity and opened doors for the era of DE (Saba, 2013).

3rd Age: Computer-Based Distance Education

This age also marked the beginning of the digital-knowledge age and network society. The scope of the concept of "distance" was altered, as distance in time and space had lost importance. Rather than reaching masses, a more personal approach of reaching individuals became possible. The prominence of teacher-centred education diminished and was replaced with learner-centred education. In addition to the mega-universities with students more than 100K (Daniel, 1996); giga universities with students 1M and virtual universities with online campus concept began to appear.

With the advantages and capacity increase offered by technology, interaction became the central focus for DE (See Figure 2 for comparison). The multimedia used in the previous age had become obsolete when compared to the new, higher quality computer-based multimedia, and synchronous and asynchronous instruction had grown to be as efficient as face-to-face instruction.

New learning models, such as e-learning, mobile learning, and ubiquitous learning, appeared with highly rich and interactive content. Learning rather than teaching became the focus, and the idea of lifelong learning took on great importance. Saba (2000) states that, though they were few, theory-based researches were conducted in the 90s. Researchers started to move beyond experimental comparative studies and introduced new methods, such as discourse analysis, and in-depth interview with learners. In other words, qualitative studies gained particular importance in this age.

- The advancements made in fibre-optic communication at the end of the 1980s and early 1990s enabled live, two-way, high-quality audio and display systems in education. Since the mid-1980s, both credit and non-credit courses have been provided via online networks (Smaldino et al., 2000).

Figure 2. Technology-based characteristics of distance education
(Taylor, 2001)

Models of Distance Education and Delivery Technologies	Characteristics of Delivery Technologies					
	Flexibility			Highly Refined Materials	Advanced Interactive Delivery	Institutional Variable Costs Approaching Zero
	Time	Place	Pace			
FIRST GENERATION						
The Correspondence Model						
• Print	Yes	Yes	Yes	Yes	No	No
SECOND GENERATION						
The Multimedia Model						
• Print	Yes	Yes	Yes	Yes	No	No
• Audiotape	Yes	Yes	Yes	Yes	No	No
• Videotape	Yes	Yes	Yes	Yes	No	No
• Computer-based Learning (e.g. CML/CAL/IMM)	Yes	Yes	Yes	Yes	Yes	No
• Interactive video (disk and tape)	Yes	Yes	Yes	Yes	Yes	No
THIRD GENERATION						
The Telelearning Model						
• Audio tele-conferencing	No	No	No	No	Yes	No
• Video-conferencing	No	No	No	No	Yes	No
• Audiographic communication	No	No	No	Yes	Yes	No
• Broadcast TV/Radio and audio-teleconferencing	No	No	No	Yes	Yes	No
FOURTH GENERATION						
The Flexible Learning Model						
• Interactive multimedia (IMM) online	Yes	Yes	Yes	Yes	Yes	Yes
• Internet-based access to WWW resources	Yes	Yes	Yes	Yes	Yes	Yes
• Computer-mediated communication	Yes	Yes	Yes	Yes	Yes	No
FIFTH GENERATION						
The Intelligent Flexible Learning Model						
• Interactive multimedia (IMM) online	Yes	Yes	Yes	Yes	Yes	Yes
• Internet-based access to WWW resources	Yes	Yes	Yes	Yes	Yes	Yes
• Computer-mediated communication, using automated response systems	Yes	Yes	Yes	Yes	Yes	Yes
• Campus portal access to institutional processes and resources	Yes	Yes	Yes	Yes	Yes	Yes

From Distance Education to Open and Distance Learning

DEFINING DISTANCE EDUCATION

Authors have applied a wide variety of alternative terms for DE, including open learning, open teaching, non-traditional education, distance learning, distance teaching, correspondence education, independent study, home study, extension study, external study, external learning, flexible education, flexible learning, life-long education, lifelong learning, contract learning, experiential learning, directed private study, drop-in learning, independent learning, individualized learning, resource-based learning, self-access learning, self-study, supported self-study or continuing education, in the related literature (Demiray & İşman, 2003). However, in order to carry out meaningful research, it is vital that the definitions to be used should be clearly established. These definitions should be both systematically and operationally consistent in themselves and with other studies to best enable the research to significantly contribute to understanding open and distance education (King, Young, Drivere-Richmond, & Schrader, 2001). Therefore, there is a need to revisit the definitions of DE, ODL and other related practices.

Although terms related to DE are used interchangeably in many cases, each term is nonetheless distinct. Every definition of DE reflects assumptions and has value in terms of the different dimensions of DE. The main purpose of this part of the study is to bring attention to the different definitions of DE and to analyse them for the purpose of gaining a deeper understanding of this field. Correspondence education, as an early form of DE, is defined as follows:

- Correspondence education is "conducted by postal services without face-to-face interaction between teacher and learner. Teaching is done by written or tape-recorded materials through written or taped exercises to the teacher, who corrects them and returns them to the learner with criticisms and advice" (Titmus, Buttedahl, Ironside, & Lengrand, 1979, p. 42).

The following definitions belong to the age that followed correspondence education.

- Dohmen (1967), a former director of the German Distance Education Institute (DIFF) at Tubingen, defined DE (Fernstudium) as "A systematically organized form of self-study in which student counselling, the presentation of learning material and the securing and supervising of students' success are carried out by a team of teachers, each of whom has [distinct] responsibilities. [This form of self-study] is made possible at a distance by means of media which can cover long distances. The opposite of 'distance education' is 'direct education' or 'face-to-face education', a type of education that takes place with direct contact between lecturers and students" (p. 9).
- Peters (1973), who worked on DIFF together with Dohmen, defines DE as follows: "Distance teaching/education (Fernunterricht) is a method of imparting knowledge, skills and attitudes which is rationalized by the application of division of labour and organizational principles, as well as by the extensive use of technical media, especially for the purpose of reproducing high quality teaching material which makes it possible to instruct great numbers of students at the same time wherever they live. It is an industrialized form of teaching and learning" (p. 206).
- According to Moore (1973), distance teaching can be defined as "The family of instructional methods in which the teaching behaviours are executed apart from the learning behaviours, including those that, in a contiguous situation, would be performed in the learner's presence, so that communication between the teacher and the learner must be facilitated by print, electronic, mechanical, or other devices" (p. 664).

- Holmberg (1977) defined distance teaching/education (Fernunterricht) as "a method of imparting knowledge, skills and attitudes which is rationalized by the application of division of labor and organizational principles as well as by the extensive use of technical media, especially for the purpose of reproducing high quality teaching material which makes it possible to instruct great numbers of students at the same time wherever they live. It is an industrialized form of teaching and learning" (p. 9).
- As stated by Garrison and Shale (1987), "Distance education implies that the majority of educational communication between the teacher and student(s) occurs non-contiguously. It must involve two-way communication between the teacher and student(s) for the purpose of facilitating and supporting the educational process. It uses technology to mediate the necessary two-way communication" (p. 11).
- Barker Frisbie and Patrick (1989) define DE in terms of the rise of telecommunication technologies. They state, "Telecommunications-based distance education approaches go beyond the limits of correspondence study. The teaching-learning experience for both the instructor and student(s) occur simultaneously – it is contiguous in time. When an audio and/or video communication link is employed, the opportunity for live teacher-student exchanges in real time is possible, thereby permitting immediate responses to student inquiries and comments. Much like a traditional classroom setting, students can receive on-the-spot clarification from the speaker" (p. 25).
- Moore (1990) provided another definition of DE, stating "Distance education involves all arrangements for providing instruction through print or electronic communications media to person engaged in planned learning in a place or time different from that of the instructor or instructors" (p. xv).
- According to Moore and Kearsley (1996), DE can be defined as "Planned learning that normally occurs in a different place and requires a well-defined system of delivery that includes modified teaching techniques, alternative modes for communication, including, but not limited to technology, as well as alternative administrative and organizational components" (p. 2).
- UNESCO (2002) presents a definition of DE: "Distance education is any educational process in which all or most of the teaching is conducted by someone removed in space and/or time from the learner, with the effect that all or most of the communication between teachers and learners is through an artificial medium, either electronic or print" (p. 22).
- According to Schlosser and Simonson (2009), DE is now often defined as "Institution-based, formal education, where the learning group is separated and where interactive telecommunications systems are used to connect learners, resources, and instructors" (p. 1).
- Moore and Kearsley (2011) redefined DE as "Teaching and planned learning in which teaching normally occurs in a different place from [the] learning, requiring communication through technologies, as well as special institutional organization" (p. 2).

According to Shale (1988), DE involves a noteworthy paradox, puts forward its existence with it but cannot identify itself. From the definitions listed above, it is clear that the term "distance education" is a generic, umbrella term that can be used synonymously with other like terms. However, some researchers do not support using the terms DE and ODL interchangeably, as they differ in essence (Edwards, 1995; King, Young, Drivere-Richmond, & Schrader, 2001; Volery & Lord, 2000). Moore and Kearsley (1996) draw attention an important point and explains what these definitions initially refer to. Accordingly, the terms open education, open and distance learning, and distance education are often used interchangeably. However, while the term open refers to a political policy and reflects a political vision, distance education mostly refers to the methodology to teach and learn at a distance.

In examining the definitions, it can be observed that the word "distance" has multiple meanings, which change over time on the basis of technological developments. In today's paradigm, in contrast to earlier assumptions, the word *distance* represents psychological/transactional distance rather than physical/geographical distance. Confirming this, Bates (2005) argues that distance is more likely to be psychological or social, rather than geographical, in most cases. The primary focus of these definitions is the separation of learners in time and space from other learners, learning sources, and teachers. Many of the early definitions of DE are no longer valid in today's world. Other limitations of these earlier definitions include their emphasis on structured, planned, institution-based instruction. However, it should be noted that these limitations were based on their ignorance of open, formal and even nonformal learning. It is also interesting that all the definitions cited above view technology as an intrinsic quality of DE (Casey, 2008). However, regardless of the degree to which DE depends on technology, it is important to keep in mind that the use of technology is not the ultimate goal, but rather, just a medium to convey the learning content.

According to Bates (2005), "Open learning is primarily a goal, or an educational policy. An essential characteristic of open learning is the removal of barriers to learning. This means placing no prior qualifications to study, and in the case of students with disabilities, making a determined effort to provide education in a form suitable for overcoming any disability (for example, audio tapes for students who are visually impaired). Ideally, no-one should be denied access to an open learning program. Thus, open learning must be scalable as well as flexible. Openness has particular implications for the use of technology. If no one is to be denied access, then technologies that are available to everyone need to be used. Distance education, on the other hand, is less a philosophy and more a method of education. Students can study on their own time, at the place of their choice (home, work site or learning centre), and without face-to-face contact with a teacher. Technology is a critical element of distance education" (p.5). Moreover, as can be seen from the above provided definitions, ODL encompasses not only teaching but also learning and emphasizes the teacher's role rather than the system (The Commonwealth of Learning, 2000).

Openness in education is an evolving concept (Bozkurt, Koseoglu, and Singh, 2019), and therefore, as suggested by Heydenrych and Prinsloo (2010), there is no precise definition of ODL, and in most cases, the terms, DE and ODL, are used interchangeably. Msweli (2012) further noted that the definition of ODL differs depending on geography and institution. To lessen the ambiguity of the definition of ODL, the Commonwealth of Learning (2000) put forth the following explanation to clarify certain nuances. Accordingly, the *educational philosophy of open learning* emphasizes giving learners choices about "medium or media, whether print, on-line, television, or video; place of study, whether at home, in the workplace, or on campus; pace of study, whether tightly paced or unstructured; support mechanisms, whether tutors on demand, audio conferences, or computer-assisted learning; and entry and exit points" (the Commonwealth of Learning, 2000, p. 3). The term *open access* implies a lack of "formal entry requirements, prerequisite credentials, and entrance examinations" (the Commonwealth of Learning, 2000, p. 3). The Commonwealth of Learning (2000) also defines external studies, continuing education, self-instruction, technology-based education, learner-centred education and flexible learning as follows: "external studies apply to instruction that takes place somewhere other than a central campus, such as a classroom remote from campus, and [it] includes a variety of delivery options, like audio, video, or computer conferences or home study" (the Commonwealth of Learning, 2000, p. 3). The term "continuing education (lifelong learning) usually applies to non-credit education, refers to courses that can be delivered on campus or at a distance, and has varied meanings" (the Commonwealth of Learning, 2000, p. 3). The term self-instruction refers to a process in which "materials take learners step-by-step through an instructional process; self-assessment exercises are a central feature, and instruction can be paper-based or computer-based" (the Commonwealth of Learning, 2000, p. 3). The term "technology-based education refers to systems of teaching and learning in which a technology other than print has a major role; and it takes two major forms: stand-alone (for example, computer-assisted learning and computer-managed learning) and conferenced (for example, audio, video or computer)" (the Commonwealth of Learning, 2000, p. 4). In learner-centred education, the integrity and freedom of the individual is of primary importance. Therefore, "the teaching and learning process provides flexible sequences of study, negotiated objectives and content, negotiated learning methods, negotiated methods of assessment, and a choice of support mechanisms" (the Commonwealth of Learning, 2000, p. 4). The term "flexible learning emphasizes the creation of environments for learning that have the following characteristics: convergence of open and distance learning methods, media and classroom strategies; learner-centred philosophy; recognition of diversity in learning styles and learners' needs; recognition of the importance of equality in curriculum and pedagogy; the use of a variety of learning resources and media; and the fostering of lifelong learning habits and skills in learners and staff". The term "distributed learning emphasizes the learning itself, rather than the type of technology used or the separation between teacher and learner; it makes learning possible beyond classrooms; and when combined with classroom modes, it becomes flexible learning" (the Commonwealth of Learning, 2000, p. 4).

Edwards (1995) defines open learning from the perspective of a constantly changing and diverse world. He highlights that ODL and DE are two terms that adopt distinct approaches. Edwards further suggests that DE is more about delivering mass learning to a mass market, while ODL focuses more on local requirements and differences instead of delivering an established curriculum.

It is clear that the openness movement, the rapid changes in society, and the advances in technology call into question traditional definitions and present a challenge to come up with new definitions for explaining the postmodern educational perception. To better understand the nature of these definitions, it would be helpful to revisit them here. Below are some of the definitions of ODL:

- The term open education is popular and connotes learning which "combines the principles of learner centeredness, lifelong learning, flexibility of learning provision, the removal of barriers to access, the recognition for credit of prior learning experience, [and] the provision of learner support" (Department of Education, 1997, p. 28).
- According to the Commonwealth of Learning, (1999) ODL is characterized by "separation of teacher and learner in time or place, or in both time and place; [and] institutional accreditation; that is, learning is accredited or certified by some institution or agency. This type of learning is distinct from learning through your own efforts, without the official recognition of a learning institution; [it involves the] use of mixed-media courseware, including print, radio, and television broadcasts, video and audio cassettes, computer-based learning, and telecommunications. Courseware tends to be pre-tested and validated before use; two-way communication allows learners and tutors to interact as distinguished from the passive receipt of broadcast signals. Communication can be synchronous or asynchronous; [with ODL, there is the] possibility of face-to-face meetings for tutorials, learner–learner interaction, library study, and laboratory or practice sessions; and use of industrialized processes; that is, in large-scale open and distance learning operations, labour is

divided, and tasks are assigned to various staff who work together in course development teams" (p. 3).
- According to UNESCO (2002), the term "open and distance learning reflects both the fact that all or most of the teaching is conducted by someone removed in time and space from the learner, and that the mission aims to include greater dimensions of openness and flexibility, whether in terms of access, curriculum, or other elements of structure" (p. 8).
- According to the Open and Distance Learning Quality Council (2012), "Open and distance learning includes any provision in which a significant element of the management of the provision is at the discretion of the learner [or is] supported and facilitated by the provider. This ranges from traditional correspondence courses, on-line provision and interactive CD ROMs, e-learning, and blended learning to open learning centres and face-to-face provision where a significant element of flexibility, self-study, and learning support, is an integral part" (para. 2).

THEORY

Theory is important, as it directly impacts how practices are conducted in the field. According to Holmberg (1985), DE theories are very significant because they help decisions to be made with confidence. In this regard, Keegan (1986) classified theories of DE into three groups: First, theories of independence and autonomy; second, theories of industrialization of teaching; and third, theories of interaction and communication. It should be noted that a fourth category, which seeks to explain DE in terms of a synthesis of existing theories of communication and diffusion, as well as philosophies of education, could be added to this group. While a detailed examination of this classification is beyond the scope of this chapter of the book, one issue important to highlight is that DE theories are multi-dimensional, which is expected given the interdisciplinary nature of the field.

Educational Approaches

In the world of education, there are three broad educational approaches, namely, pedagogy, andragogy, and heutagogy.

Pedagogy

Having Greek origins, the term pedagogy means 'to lead the child'. Most of the assumptions underlying pedagogy were made and developed based on observations by monks when teaching simple skills to young learners. In the 18th and 19th centuries, these assumptions were adopted for primary and elementary school level learners. The research conducted by educational psychologists in the 20th century served to establish an empirical ground for pedagogy and reinforced it as an educational approach However, when adult education (e.g., DE, ODL) began to be developed in more a systematic fashion, it was criticized by some educators because it basically emphasized transferring knowledge, and the skills and assumptions developed for young learners were insufficient for adult learners (Knowles, 1980).

Andragogy

Also having Greek origins, the term andragogy means "to lead the man [adults]" and is a system used to explain adult learning (Knowles, 1990). It focuses on learner control, self-responsibility, and self-directed and self-regulated learning processes. Andragogy further asserts that adult learners should define their own learning needs and develop strategies accordingly (Knowles, 1984: McAuliffe, Hargreaves, Winter, & Chadwick, 2008).

Heutagogy

Like the terms pedagogy and andragogy, the term heutagogy also has Greek origins and means 'to lead the self". This term emerged as an extension of pedagogy and andragogy. Heutagogy explains adult learners in terms of lifelong learning and focuses on the internet and internet technologies as the learning environment and learning tools (Blaschke, 2012). Heutagogy is a "net-centric" theory, like connectivism (Anderson, 2010). The relationship between pedagogy, andragogy, and heutagogy is given in Figure 3, and a comparison of them is presented in Figure 4.

Learning Theories

Anderson and Dron (2011) proposed that learning theories for DE could be categorized under three distinct generations, namely, cognitive-behaviourist, social-constructivist, and connectivist. As a complementary approach to connectivism, rhizomatic learning is also significant.

Figure 3. The relationship between pedagogy, andragogy, and heutagogy
(Canning, 2010)

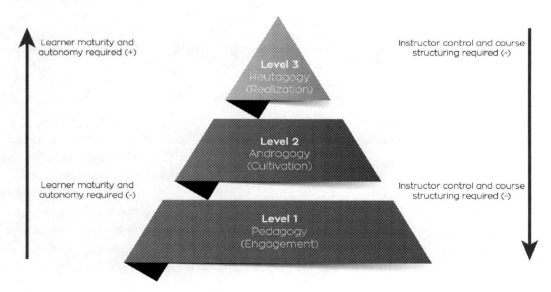

Figure 4. The comparison of pedagogy, andragogy, and heutagogy
(Heick, 2018)

	Pedagogy, Andragogy, Heutagogy compared		
	Heutagogy: The management of self-managed learners		
	Pedagogy Children's Learning	**Andragogy** Adults' Learning	**Heutagogy** Self-Directed Learning
Dependence	The learner is a dependent personality. Teacher determines what, how, and when anything is learned.	Adults are independent. They strive for autonomy and self-direction in learning.	Learners are independent. They identify the potential to learn from novel experiences as a matter of course. They are able to manage their own learning.
Resource for learning	The learner has few resources – the teacher devises transmission techniques to store knowledge in the learner's head.	Adults use their own and other's experience.	Teacher provides some resources, but the learner decides the path by negotiating the learning.
Reasons for learning	Learn in order to advance to the next stage.	Adults learn when they experience a need to know or to perform more effectively.	Learning is not necessarily planned or linear. Learning is not necessarily based on need but on the identification of the potential to learn in novel situations.
Focus of learning	Learning is subject centred, focused on a prescribed curriculum and planned sequences according to the logic of the subject matter.	Adult learning is task or problem centred.	Learners can go beyond problem solving by enabling pro-activity. Learners use their own and others' experiences and internal processes such as reflection, environmental scanning, experience, interaction with others, and pro-active as well as problem solving behaviours.
Motivation	Motivation comes from external sources – usually parents, teachers and a sense of competition.	Motivation stems from internal sources – the increased self-esteem, confidence and recognition that come from successful performance.	Self-efficacy, knowing how to learn, creativity, ability to use these qualities in novel as well as familiar situations and working with others.
Role of the teacher	Designs the learning process, imposes material, is assumed to know the best.	Enabler or facilitator, climate of collaboration, respect and openness.	Develop the learner's capability. Capable people: • know how to learn • are creative • have a high degree of self-efficacy • apply competences in novel as well as familiar situations • can work well with others

Behaviourism, Cognitivism, and Constructivism

Traditional learning theories, that is, behaviourism, cognitivism and constructivism, are the three most dominant learning approaches, and as such, they are widely known and have heavily influenced the study of learning to date. Based on the operant conditioning, behaviourism suggests that learning is observable and measurable, being simply a mechanical process with repeated experiences. As a response to behaviourism, cognitivism focuses on internal learning processes and argues that learners process information to learn, and that information can be stored and retrieved when needed. As a response to behaviourism and cognitivism, constructivism places value on experiences, claiming that learners build knowledge through their own experiences. Carver (2012) stated, "Behaviourism challenged the idea that knowledge was metaphysical. Cognitivism brought to light what could not be seen, [that is,] the inner workings of the mind. Constructivism held that learning was shaped by individuals based on experience, thoughts, and interactions".

Connectivism and Rhizomatic Learning

Connectivism seeks to explain how learning occurs in the digital age through networks (Siemens, 2004; Downes, 2012). It argues that "knowledge is distributed across a network of connections, and therefore that learning consists of the ability to construct and traverse those networks" (Downes, 2012, p. 9). The principles governing connectivism are shown in Figure 5, while a comparison of the learning theories and connectivism is presented in Figure 6.

While "connectivism focuses on where knowledge is derived from and how learners interact on networks, rhizomatic learning focuses on how learners navigate through the network and pursue knowledge as a creative quest for learning" (Bozkurt et al., 2016, p. 7). Rhizomatic learning is further thought to be a heutagogical approach, where learning is seen as an intrinsic process and experience has a pivotal role (Deleuze, 1994). Rhizomatic learning rests on the assumption that knowledge is resilient, nonlinear, and uncertain and applies these assumptions to the learning process (Cormier, 2015).

CONCLUSION

DE and ODL are developing, evolving and adaptive multidisciplinary fields. The different ages and generations of DE and ODL have all been affected by the technologies dominant at their respective times. Therefore, it is possible to say that information and communication technologies are an intrinsic part of these disciplines, yet they must not be taken as the ultimate goal, but rather, as viable solutions to reduce barriers and increase interaction and communication. Considering the speed of the technology used today, it is difficult to predict the future of these disciplines.

Figure 5. Principles of Connectivism
(Siemens, 2004)

- Learning and knowledge rests in diversity of opinions.
- Learning is a process of connecting specialized nodes or information sources.
- Learning may reside in non-human appliances.
- Capacity to know more is more critical than what is currently known
- Nurturing and maintaining connections is needed to facilitate continual learning.
- Ability to see connections between fields, ideas, and concepts is a core skill.
- Currency (accurate, up-to-date knowledge) is the intent of all connectivist learning activities.
- Decision-making is itself a learning process. Choosing what to learn and the meaning of incoming information is seen through the lens of a shifting reality. While there is a right answer now, it may be wrong tomorrow due to alterations in the information climate affecting the decision.

Figure 6. Prominent learning theories and connectivism
(Siemens, 2009)

Property \ Theory	Behaviorism	Cognitivism	Constructivism	Connectivism
How learning occurs	Black box—observable behavior main focus	Structured, computational	Social, meaning created by each learner (personal)	Distributed within a network, social, technologically enhanced, recognizing and interpreting patterns
Influencing factors	Nature of reward, punishment, stimuli	Existing schema, previous experiences	Engagement, participation, social, cultural	Diversity of network, strength of ties, context of occurrence
Role of memory	Memory is the hardwiring of repeated experiences - where reward and punishment are most influential	Encoding, storage, retrieval	Prior knowledge remixed to current context	Adaptive patterns, representative of current state, existing in networks
How transfer occurs	Stimulus, response	Duplicating knowledge constructs of "knower"	Socialization	Connecting to (adding) nodes and growing the network (social/conceptual/biological)
Types of learning best explained	Task-based learning	Reasoning, clear objectives, problem solving	Social, vague ("ill defined")	Complex learning, rapid changing core, diverse knowledge sources

The historical evolution of DE and ODL indicates that some important issues to highlight. First, these disciplines emerged to balance the social injustice and served well for those who demanded and pursued knowledge. Thus, the origin and roots of these fields are strongly tied to critical pedagogy and, therefore, the core values and fundamentals should be revisited more often so that the progress and advancement can be built upon on founding noble intentions without assimilating in the lure of mainstream education. Second, while DE and ODL originally emerged as fields distinct from traditional education but with many common values, the borders between them are now blurring and coming together to form a more complete whole. However, as noted earlier, the merge of these fields is supposed to be in a complementary form, not in a fashion that imitates one another. Third, information and technologies appeared to be a catalyst of the progress and advancement of DE and ODL. However, it is suggested that technology we should design teaching and learning processes by keeping in mind that technology is a mean rather than an end.

From the theoretical perspective, it is observed that DE and ODL are interdisciplinary in nature and subject to constant changes. Therefore, rather than sticking to a fixed theoretical approach, we should benefit from different theoretical approaches to enrich our views and flourish our ecology where we were guided by openness philosophy in many ways.

Throughout the chapter, many definitions of DE and ODL were discussed. All previous definitions continue to serve a purpose and are still valid from different aspects. In this sense, DE and ODL can be defined as *any learning activities within formal, informal, and non-formal domains that are facilitated by information and communication technologies to lessen distance, both physically and psychologically, and to increase interactivity and communication among learners, learning sources and facilitators.* To gain a better understanding of ODL, the universe metaphor can be used, where ODL is depicted as a solar system. Accordingly, all the elements in this system are integrated and connected, and as they constitute a solar system, they are part of a larger system, with smaller systems included in it. Everything is connected in a chaotic way; no element is isolated from one another. This metaphor explains the nature of ODL, and rightfully so, considering that it was inspired from a pattern of the universe. In the ODL solar system, new orbits, planets, satellites, and stars can be added within time. It is even possible to discern intersecting and overlapping points with other solar systems.

ACKNOWLEDGMENT

This research was supported by Anadolu University, Scientific Research Project Commission under the grant number 1704E087, 1705E413 and 1805E123.

The researcher would like to thank Dr. Chih-Hsiung Tu from Arizona State University for the valuable comments on the initial version of the manuscript.

REFERENCES

Anderson, T. (2010). Theories for learning with emerging technologies. In G. Veletsianos (Ed.), *Emerging technologies in distance education*. Edmonton, Canada: Athabasca University Press.

Anderson, T., & Dron, J. (2011). Three generations of distance education pedagogy. *International Review of Research in Open and Distance Learning*, *12*(3), 80–97. doi:10.19173/irrodl.v12i3.890

Barker, B., Frisbie, A., & Patrick, K. (1989). Broadening the definition of distance education in the light of the new telecommunications technologies. *American Journal of Distance Education*, *3*(1), 20–29. doi:10.1080/08923648909526647

Bates, T. (2005). *Technology, E-learning and Distance Education*. New York: Routledge. doi:10.4324/9780203463772

Baumeister, R. F., & Leary, M. R. (1997). Writing narrative literature reviews. *Review of General Psychology*, *1*(3), 311–320. doi:10.1037/1089-2680.1.3.311

Bittner, W. S., & Mallory, H. F. (1933). *University Teaching by Mail: A Survey of Correspondence Instruction Conducted by American Universities*. New York: Macmillan.

Blaschke, L. (2012). Heutagogy and lifelong learning: A review of heutagogical practice and self-determined learning. *International Review of Research in Open and Distance Learning*, *13*(1), 56–71. doi:10.19173/irrodl.v13i1.1076

Bozkurt, A., Honeychurch, S., Caines, A., Maha, B., Koutropoulos, A., & Cormier, D. (2016). Community Tracking in a cMOOC and Nomadic Learner Behaviour Identification on a Connectivist Rhizomatic Learning Network. *The Turkish Online Journal of Distance Education*, *17*(4), 4–30.

Bozkurt, A., Koseoglu, S., & Singh, L. (2019). An analysis of peer-reviewed publications on openness in education in half a century: Trends and patterns in the open hemisphere. *Australasian Journal of Educational Technology*, *35*(4), 78–97. doi:10.14742/ajet.4252

Canning, N. (2010). Playing with heutagogy: Exploring strategies to empower mature learners in higher education. *Journal of Further and Higher Education*, *34*(1), 59–71. doi:10.1080/03098770903477102

Carver, D. (2012). Book review - Learning theory and online technologies. *International Review of Research in Open and Distance Learning*, *13*(4), 324–326. doi:10.19173/irrodl.v13i4.1340

Casey, D. M. (2008). The Historical Development of Distance Education through Technology. *TechTrends*, *52*(2), 45–51. doi:10.100711528-008-0135-z

Cormier, D. (2015). What was #rhizo15. *The Association for Learning Technology (ALT) Newsletter.* Retrieved from https://newsletter.alt.ac.uk/2015/07/what-was-rhizome15/

Cornell University. (2001). *From domesticity to modernity: What was home economics?* Division of Rare and Manuscript Collections, Cornell University.

Cronin, P., Ryan, F., & Coughlan, M. (2008). Undertaking a literature review: A step-by-step approach. *British Journal of Nursing (Mark Allen Publishing), 17*(1), 38–43. doi:10.12968/bjon.2008.17.1.28059 PMID:18399395

Daniel, J. S. (1996). *Mega-Universities and Knowledge Media: Technology Strategies for Higher Education.* Abingdon, UK: Psychology Press.

Deleuze, G. (1994). *Difference and Repetition* (P. Patton, Trans.). New York: Columbia University Press.

Demiray, U., & İşman, A. (2003). History of distance education. In *Online Distance Education Book* (Eds. İşman, A., Barkan, M., & Demiray, U). TOJET. Retrieved from http://www.tojet.net/e-book/ebook.htm

Department of Education. (1997). *Education White Paper 3: A Programme for the Transformation of Higher Education.* Pretoria: General Notice 1196 of 1997

Dohmen, G. (1967). *Das Fernstudium, Ein neues padagogisches Forschungsund Arbeitsfeld.* Tubingen, Germany: DIFF.

Downes, S. (2012). *Connectivism and connective knowledge: Essays on meaning and learning networks.* Retrieved from. http://www.downes.ca/files/books/Connective_Knowledge-19May2012.pdf

Edwards, R. (1995). Different discourses, discourses of difference: Globalisation, distance education, and open learning. *Distance Education, 16*(2), 241–255. doi:10.1080/0158791950160206

Erazo, E., & Derlin, R. (1995). *Distance learning and libraries in the cyberspace age.* Retrieved from http://www.checs.net/95conf/PROCEEDINGS/erazo.html

Garrison, D., & Shale, D. (1987). Mapping the boundaries of distance education: Problems in defining the field. *American Journal of Distance Education, 1*(1), 4–13. doi:10.1080/08923648709526567

Gooch, J. (1998). *They Blazed the Trail for Distance Education.* Distance Education Clearinghouse.

Gordon, T. (1990). How Can Correspondence-based distance education be improved? A Survey of attitudes of Students who were not well disposed towards correspondence Study. *Journal of Distance Education, 5*(1), 16–19.

Hansen, B. (2001). Distance learning. *CQ Researcher, 11*(42), 1–24.

Heick, T. (2018). *The Difference Between Pedagogy, Andragogy, And Heutagogy.* Retrieved from https://www.teachthought.com/pedagogy/a-primer-in-heutagogy-and-self-directed-learning/

Heydenrych, J. F., & Prinsloo, P. (2010). Revisiting the five generations of distance education: Quo vadis? *Progressio, 32*(1), 5–26.

Holmberg, B. (1977). *Distance Education: A Survey and Bibliography.* London: Kogan Page.

Holmberg, B. (1985). The feasibility of a theory of teaching for distance education and a proposed theory (ZIFF Papiere 60). Hagen, West Germany: Fern Universität, Zentrales Institute fur Fernstudienforschung Arbeitsbereich. (ERIC Document Reproduction Service No. ED290013)

Holmberg, B. (1986). *Growth and structure of distance education* (3rd ed.). London: Croom Helm.

Keegan, D. (1986). *The foundations of distance education*. London: Croom Helm.

King, F. B., Young, M. F., Drivere-Richmond, K., & Schrader, P. G. (2001). Defining distance learning and distance education. *AACE Journal, 9*(1), 1–14.

Knowles, M. (1990). *The adult learner: A neglected species* (4th ed.). Houston, TX: Gulf Publishing Co.

Knowles, M. S. (1980). *The Modern Practice of Adult Education*. New York: Cambridge Press.

Knowles, M. S. (1984). *Andragogy in Action* (1st ed.). San Francisco: Jossey-Bass.

McAuliffe, M., Hargreaves, D., Winter, A., & Chadwick, G. (2008). Does pedagogy still rule? *Proceedings of the 2008 AAEE Conference*. Retrieved from: http://www.engineersmedia.com.au/journals/aaee/pdf/AJEE_15_1_McAuliffe%202pdf

Moore, M. (1973). Toward a theory of independent learning and teaching. *The Journal of Higher Education, 44*(9), 661–679. doi:10.2307/1980599

Moore, M. (1977). On a Theory of Independent Study. Hagen: Fernuniversitat (ZIFF).

Moore, M. (1990). Background and overview of contemporary American distance education. In M. Moore (Ed.), *Contemporary issues in American distance education* (pp. xii–xxvi). New York: Pergamon.

Moore, M. G., & Kearsley, G. (1996). *Distance Education: A Systems View*. Belmont, CA: Wadsworth.

Moore, M. G., & Kearsley, G. (2011). *Distance Education: A Systems View of Online Learning* (3rd ed.). Belmont, CA: Wadsworth Cengage Learning.

Msweli, P. (2012). Mapping the interplay between open distance learning and internationalisation principles. *International Review of Research in Open and Distance Learning, 13*(3), 97–116. doi:10.19173/irrodl.v13i3.1182

Nasseh, B. (1997). *A Brief History of Distance Education*. Retrieved from http://www.seniornet.org/edu/art/history.html

Open and Distance Learning Quality Council. (2012). *Definitions*. Retrieved from http://odlqc.org.uk/odlqc-standards/definitions

Peters, O. (1973). *Die Didaktische Struktur des Fernunterrich*. Weinheim, Germany: Beltz.

Pittman, V. V. (1986a). *Pioneering Instructional Radio in the US: Five Years of Frustration at the University of Iowa, 1925-1930*. A Paper for the First International Conference on the History of Adult Education, Oxford, UK.

Pittman, V. V. (1986b). Station WSUI and early days of instructional radio. The days of instructional radio. *The Palimpset, 67*(2), 38–52.

Public Broadcasting Service. (2003). *Distance learning week – Timeline: An overview*. Retrieved from http://www.pbs.org/als/dlweek/history/index.html

Saba, F. (2000). Research in distance education: A status report. *International Review of Research in Open and Distance Learning, 1*(1). doi:10.19173/irrodl.v1i1.4

Saba, F. (2013). *Introduction to distance education: Telecommunications systems*. Retrieved from http://distance-educator.com/in-1962-launch-of-a-beach-ball-sized-satellite-revolutionized-educational-telecommunications/

Saettler, P. (1990). *The evolution of American Educational Technology*. Littleton, CO: Libraries Unlimited.

Schlosser, L. A., & Simonson, M. R. (2009). *Distance Education: Definitions and Glossary of Terms* (2nd ed.). Charlotte, NC: Information Age Publishing.

Shale, D. (1988). Toward a reconceptualization of distance education. *American Journal of Distance Education, 2*(3), 25–35. doi:10.1080/08923648809526633

Siemens, G. (2004). *Connectivism: A learning theory for the digital age*. Retrieved from. http://www.elearnspace.org/Articles/connectivism.htm

Siemens, G. (2009). *What is Connectivism?* Retrieved from. https://docs.google.com/document/d/14pKVP0_ILdPty6MGMJW8eQVEY1zibZ0RpQ2C0cePIgc/preview

Taylor, J. C. (2001). *Fifth generation distance education*. Higher Education Division, Department of Education, Training and Youth Affairs.

The Commonwealth of Learning. (1999). *Planning and Management of Open and Distance Learning*. Vancouver, Canada: The Commonwealth of Learning. Retrieved from http://www.col.org/Publication-Documents/pub_Planning_Management_03_web.pdf

The Commonwealth of Learning. (2000). *An Introduction to Open and Distance Learning*. Retrieved from http://oasis.col.org/bitstream/handle/11599/138/ODLIntro.pdf?sequence=1&isAllowed=y

Titmus, C., Buttedahl, P., Ironside, D., & Lengrand, P. (1979). *Terminology of Adult education/Terminol ogie de la Educacion de Adultos/Terminologie de l'Education des Adultes*. Paris: UNESCO.

U. S. Department of Commerce. (1926). *Proceedings of the Fourth National Radio Conference and recommendations for regulation of radio*. Washington, DC: Government Printing Office. Retrieved from http://earlyradiohistory.us/1925conf.htm/

UNESCO. (2002). *Open and Distance Learning: trends, policy and strategy consideration*. Paris: UNESCO.

Verduin, J. R. Jr, & Clark, T. A. (1991). *Distance Education: The Foundations of Effective Practice*. San Francisco: Jossey-Bass.

Volery, T., & Lord, D. (2000). Critical success factors in online education. *International Journal of Educational Management, 14*(5), 216–223. doi:10.1108/09513540010344731

Watkins, B. L. (1991). A Quite Radical Idea: The Invention and Elaboration of Collegiate Correspondence Study. In B. L. Watkins & S. J. Wright (Eds.), *The Foundations of American Distance Education: A Century of Collegiate Correspondence Study* (pp. 1–35). Dubuque, IA: Kendall/Hunt.

Zigerell, J. (1991). *The use of television in American higher education.* New York: Praeger.

KEY TERMS AND DEFINITIONS

Andragogy: The term is derived from the Greek words "anere," meaning "man" and "agogus" meaning "to lead," and refers to a theory of education for adult learners.

Connectivism: As a learning theory applicable to the digital knowledge age, connectivism focuses on where knowledge derives from and how learners interact on networks, and it further argues that knowledge exists and is distributed on networks, and therefore, learning consists of the ability to construct and traverse these networks.

Distance Education (DE): Planned and organized teaching and learning in which learners are separated from teachers or facilitators in time and space.

Electronic Learning (E-Learning): It is a learning paradigm that uses educational technologies in employing the principles of multimedia learning.

Giga University: A giga university is a higher education institution with 1M or more students and is capable of providing educational approaches to masses.

Heutagogy: The term is derived from the Greek word for "self"; with "agogos" meaning "to lead" and based on theories of self-determined learning,

Learner: An individual who demands knowledge at any age in any of the learning processes (e.g., formal, informal, and non-formal learning) as part of a lifelong learning pursuit.

Mega University: A mega university is a higher education institution with 100K or more students and is capable of providing educational approaches to masses.

Mobile Learning (M-Learning): As an extension of e-learning, it is a learning paradigm that uses mobile technologies to provide a just in time, just in place, and just for me experience.

Open and Distance Learning (ODL): Any learning activities within formal, informal, and non-formal domains that are facilitated by information and communication technologies to lessen distance, both physically and psychologically, and to increase interactivity and communication among learners, learning sources and facilitators.

Open University: These types of higher education institutions embrace openness in education as a core value and provide flexible learning opportunities through distance education or open and distance learning, with minimal or no entry requirements.

Openness (in Education): This term has many forms and dimensions, but in essence, it supports the idea that knowledge is a public good and anyone who demands it should have access to it without being faced with any barriers.

Pedagogy: The term is derived from the Greek words "paidos," meaning "child" and "agogus" meaning "to lead"; which combined gives us 'to lead the child, and it refers to a theory of education for young learners.

Rhizomatic Learning: Rhizomatic learning focuses on how learners navigate through the network and pursue knowledge as a creative quest for learning.

Student: An individual who demands knowledge as part of a planned and organized learning pursuit and who is attending an educational institution.

Ubiquitous Learning (U-Learning): As an extension of e-learning and m-learning, it is a learning paradigm that uses ubiquitous technologies to provide a seamless, just in time, just in place, and just for me experience.

Chapter 17
A Case Study on Pre-Service English Teachers' Perceptions of Self-Efficacy and Integration of Information-Communication Technologies

Ilknur Istifci
Anadolu University, Turkey

ABSTRACT

The aim of this study is to find out pre-service English language teachers' ICT self-efficacy perceptions and ICT integration in their lessons. The data were collected from 60 pre-service English teachers in one of the state universities in Turkey via a questionnaire developed by Ekici, Ekici, and Kara. Semi-structured interviews were also carried out with some volunteering pre-service teachers. The questionnaire data were analyzed using the Statistical Package for Social Sciences (SPSS 22). Interview data were analyzed finding emerging themes and categorizing them using constant comparison method. The results showed that they use ICTs in their lessons mostly especially in practicum or macro and micro teaching sessions and they have high self-efficacy on ICT use in language education. Results also revealed some problems they encounter while using ICTs in language teacher education and their suggestions on how to improve their use. Based on the results, certain implications were drawn from the study in order to organize future teacher education programs that utilize ICTs.

INTRODUCTION

ICTs have become an indispensable part of our lives and the application of ICTs has been affecting the way of teaching in schools. ICTs can be defined as technologies that provide access to information through telecommunications and they include the Internet, wireless networks, cell phones, and other communication mediums (Tech Terms 2014) and different types of ICTs include email, virtual learn-

DOI: 10.4018/978-1-5225-8431-5.ch017

ing environment, social networking sites, social mobile applications, user-generated content sites and video-conferencing and voice-over-internet protocols (Oliver & Clayes, 2014). ICTs play a vital role in the future of education throughout the world (Tongkaw, 2013) and are important catalysts and tools for inducing educational reforms that change our students into productive handlers of knowledge (Eynon, 2005). ICTs provide individuals with a creative, innovative, and supposedly more colorful setting in comparison to face-to-face instruction. In this regard, equipping individuals with the skills to use ICTs effectively and responsibly carries utmost importance (Akbulut, 2009). ICTs have rapidly developing structures in nature, so are the processes of integrating ICTs into instructional practices.

Teachers are required to have adequate ICT competencies to make use of ICT for education (Goktas, Yildirim, & Yildirim, 2009). Thomas and Knezek (2008) point out that, teachers in both real and virtual schools and classrooms must be equipped with technology resources and skills to provide learning experiences effectively. These teachers will have the ability to develop innovative ways of using technology to enhance the learning environment, and to promote technology literacy, knowledge deepening, and knowledge creation (UNESCO, 2011a). The effective integration of ICT into education can be thought to enable effective citizens and workers to acquire functional and critical thinking skills such as information literacy, media literacy, and ICT literacy in the 21st century (Partnership, 2015). For that reason, one of the goals of the schools systems in many countries is to ensure that students gain adequate literacy and numeracy skills with the ability to use ICT in their compulsory education (OECD, 2013).

Training pre-service teachers in using ICTs is indispensable since they are the teachers of the future generations who are digital natives. Thus, pre-service teachers should be equipped with the skills and knowledge for ICT use. Pre-service teachers need to gain the necessary technological competence to meet their students' needs during their pre-service education (Zhou, Zhao, Hu, Liu, & Xing, 2010). In this regard, Yıldırım (2000) stresses that "it is crucial for teachers to have appropriate technology training during their pre-service education, if they are to meet their students' needs for the next century." Pre-service teachers should acquire the skills and knowledge essential for ICT use in their pre-service learning process, and apply them in their pre-service education period and in their professional life (Yapıcı & Hevedanlı, 2012). Besides being competent in using ICT, teachers must be media and information literate to critically assess media texts and information sources (UNESCO, 2011b).

BACKGROUND

Information-Communication Technologies

Christenson (2010) defines ICT as "technologies that provide access to information through telecommunications. ICT is an all encompassing term that includes the full gamut of electronic tools by means of which we gather, record and store information, and by means of which we exchange and distribute information to others (UNESCO, 2010) (see Figure 1). ICTs are indispensable to the functioning of modern societies, these same technologies are equally indispensable to learning institutions. By the use of ICTs in education, the roles of teachers and students have also changed. Teachers have moved from being "sages on the stage" to becoming "guides on the side". The teacher is no longer the all-knowing authority. Students in classrooms where ICT are regularly found are likely to participate in virtual excursions and be active researchers, searching the web for information to complete individual or group projects, communicating via email, blogs and social networking with students and teachers in other schools, and reaching conclusions on the basis of evidence gathered (UNESCO, 2010).

ICTs in Education

The use of ICT in education has been investigated in terms of ICT competence, attitude toward technology, computer anxiety, barriers to ICT integration, perceptions of ICT integration and ICT Self Efficacy perceptions (Pamuk & Peker, 2009; Sang, Valcke, van Braak, Tondeur, & Zhu, 2011; Somekh, 2008; Akbulut, Odabasi & Kuzu, 2011; Liu & Pange, 2014; Aslan & Zhu, 2017).

In terms of computer anxiety, Pamuk and Peker (2009) state that a number of teachers suffer from computer anxiety and this will prevent them from using educational technologies effectively. Computer anxiety is understood to be a significant barrier, which determines the level of teachers' integration of ICT into their lessons (Aslan & Zhu, 2017).

In examining the attitudes of teachers, Sang et al (2011) found that if primary teachers have positive attitudes toward ICT in education, they are more willing to integrate ICT into their teaching.

In terms of barriers, Liu and Pange (2015) looked at the barriers to ICT integration in teaching practices from the perspective of Chinese early childhood teachers in Mainland China and they have found a range of first-order barriers, which included lack of hardware (laptops, notebooks, and computers), lack of teaching content and material, as well as lack of pedagogical models were perceived as main barriers by the teachers. However, several second-order barriers, such as lack of teachers' interest, and lack of teachers' support were perceived as the least main barriers. Furthermore, the variable "ICT use in daily life" was found play an important role in determining the teachers' perceptions of barriers both on the overall level and on the specific level (Liu & Pange, 2015).

Figure 1. ICT comprise many technologies for capturing, interpreting, storing and transmitting information (UNESCO, 2010)

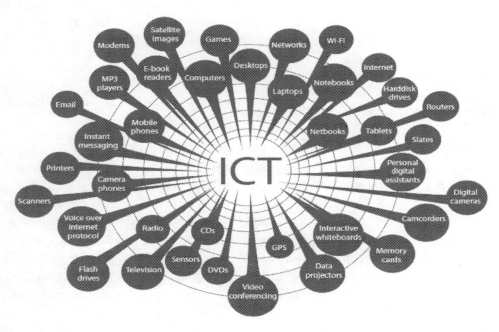

As Akbulut, Odabası, and Kuzu (2011) suggest, strong infrastructure should be provided to give everyone equal access to ICT, taking precautions to facilitate ease of use and employing technical staff to assist users. Reducing these external barriers to ICT integration or to the development of a strong ICT infrastructure would appear to be one of the crucial factors to enable teachers to integrate ICT into their lessons.

Carrying out a study to investigate the level of usage of pre-service teachers' and instructors' use of ICT by collecting data via a questionnaire in a private university, Gulbahar (2008) found out that teacher education programs fail to provide appropriate instructional technologies in and out of class activities.

The impact of ICT is strongest when used in a particular content area and further supported by use across the curriculum (Ward and Parr, 2010). Since teachers are the key figures to utilize ICT in educational settings productively and to help integrate ICT into the curriculum, they need support and training to disseminate ICT integration into their classrooms (Hismanoglu, 2012).

Self-efficacy beliefs refer not only to someone's capabilities or skills, but also to the belief that they would be able to do something under certain circumstances (Evers, Brouwers, & Tomic, 2002). Self-efficacy can influence individuals' choice of tasks and activities, and predicts how much effort they put on the tasks, their persistence and resilience facing the obstacles and adverse situations, and effectiveness on regulating their thoughts, actions and plans (Schunk & Meece, 2006; Schunk & Pajares, 2010). As Aslan & Zhu (2017) state ICT self-efficacy can be described as one's belief concerning his/her capabilities to use ICT, and perceived ICT competence seems to play a role in determining users' tendency to use ICT in their own lives. According to Pamuk and Peker (2009) training in technology or computer-related courses are very important in order to provide pre-service teachers with the essential skills and knowledge for integrating technology into teaching as well as to strengthen positive attitude towards computers.

ICT Studies in English Language Teaching

English language teaching cannot be thought without using technology and ICTs and it may be the first subject among the subjects taught in primary and secondary schools that makes use of ICTs. Examining 76 EFL teachers' ICT use and their attitudes towards ICT, Şahin-Kızıl (2011) found that the EFL teachers had positive attitude towards the use of ICT in foreign language teaching, and use of computer technologies in this process as more beneficial than traditional teaching methods. However, teachers mentioned about some difficulties such as insufficient training opportunities and inefficient class time.

Having examined prospective English language teachers' awareness of collaborative Web 2.0 tools, Usluel, Mazman and Arıkan (2009) found that podcasts and blogs were not used a lot by the participants while wikis were most widely preferred web 2.0 among three of them.

Horzum (2010) examined teachers' awareness, frequency and purpose of using Web 2.0 tools in terms of different variables by collecting data from 183 teachers who were in the in-service training in the Ministry of Education. The result of the study indicated that these teachers were aware of Facebook, MSN and video sharing sites (VSS), but they were not aware of Weblogs or Podcasts. Moreover, they used these tools for fun, communication and accessing information.

Carrying out a study with 216 prospective English language teachers in Distance Education English Language Teaching Program of Anadolu University on their awareness of Web 2.0 tools, Istifci and Girginer (2011) found that prospective teachers used mostly Facebook, MSN and Wikis, sometimes read blogs but they did not use Video Sharing Sites, Podcasts and Twitter. In terms of the use of these tools, they stated that they generally used them for fun, communication and getting information.

Cephe and Balçıkanlı's (2012) research tried to find out ELT student teachers' viewpoints about the use of Web 2.0 tools in language learning. The participants received training about web technologies and their usages. The data were collected via a questionnaire and follow up interviews with some of the students three months after the training. The researchers revealed that the student teachers held positive feelings toward the use of web 2.0 tools in language learning and teaching practices in spite of the absence of the technological devices.

Başöz (2016) examined 120 pre-service EFL teachers' attitudes towards language learning through social media by collecting data via a questionnaire. The result of the study showed that pre-service teachers held positive attitudes towards use of social media in foreign language learning, and they reported that social media could help them develop their vocabulary knowledge. The participants expressed that the atmosphere in social media created a relaxing atmosphere for language learning and provided them with a more authentic use of the language.

In the light of the findings above, the aim of this study is to obtain pre-service English language teachers' ICT self-efficacy perceptions and ICT integration in their faculties. The study will shed light on pre-service English teachers' ICT self-efficacy perceptions and ICT integration in language learning and give insights to language teachers.

This study tries to answer the following research questions:

1. What are prospective English teachers' self-efficacy perceptions towards ICT integration in language education?
2. What are prospective English teachers' perceptions on ICT integration in their content-based and pedagogical courses?

METHODOLOGY

Participants

Participants of this study are 60 senior pre-service English teachers in one of the state universities in Eskisehir, Turkey.

Data Collection Tools

A questionnaire that had two parts was given to students. In the first part, questions were about personal information about the prospective English teachers, about the use of computer and Internet technologies, years of computer experience, how they access the Internet and if they received any training on computer and Internet technologies. In the second part, in order to find out pre-service English teachers' ICT self-efficacy perceptions, "ICT Self-Efficacy Perception Scale" (ICTSEPS) developed by Ekici et al. (2012) was used. The scale consisted of 27 five-point likert type items ranging from "Totally disagree" to "Totally agree". The cronbach alpha reliability coefficient was calculated as .97 by the researchers.

Semi-structured interviews were also carried out by 15 randomly chosen pre-service teachers. Open-ended questions were structured around the following questions taken from Oliver & Clayes (2014):

1. How and where were ICTs used in your ELT education?
2. How would you like ICTs to be used in ELT education?
3. How have you used ICTs in your macro teaching or practicum?
4. Where would you like to use ICTs when you become a teacher? Why?
5. What are the problems you faced in using ICTs in language education?
6. What are your suggestions to solve those problems?

RESULTS

Personal Information

The first part of the questionnaire aimed to detect personal information about the participants and general questions about computer and Internet technologies. When the first part of the questionnaire is taken into account, it is seen that pre-service English teachers use computers and Internet technologies intensively since they are considered as digital natives. They mostly use laptops and mobile phones to reach the information easily or to communicate instantly. Most of them attended a course on ICTs.

Table 1. Personal information about the participants

Gender	Number	Percentage
Male	12	20
Female	48	80
Age	**Number**	**Percentage**
21-23	54	90
24-26	6	10
How long have you been using computer and Internet technologies?	**Number**	**Percentage**
6-10 years	15	25
11+	45	75
How do you access the Internet?	**Number**	**Percentage**
on the desktop computer/laptop	28	47
through tablets	8	13
through the cell phone	24	40
Have you ever taken a course or attended a workshop on computer and Internet technologies?	**Number**	**Percentage**
Yes	38	63
No	22	37

Pre-Service English Teachers' ICT Self-Efficacy Perceptions

The second part of the questionnaire aimed to detect ICT self-efficacy perceptions of pre-service English teachers by using "ICT Self-Efficacy Perception Scale" that was developed by Ekici et. al (2012). The scale consisted of 27 five-point likert type items that included items as "Totally disagree", "Disagree", "Undecided", "Agree" and "Totally agree. The data of ICTSEPS were analysed on SPSS 22 packaged software using descriptive statistics finding means and standard deviations (see Table 2). As Table 2 reveals, pre-service English teachers seem to have ICT self-efficacy for most of the items in the questionnaire. They felt they were self-efficacious in 17 items out of 27. Items above 3.5 were accepted as having higher self-efficacy. They stated that they were capable of understanding terminology related to computer hardware and software, using anti-virus programs, using word processor programs, using presentation tools, using data base, e-mail and search engines, downloading sources, joining forums, organizing information, using chat programs, preparing rubrics and using LMS systems. The pre-service teachers in this study were found to have higher ICT self-efficacy since they used ICTs in their social life and in their teaching. They did not feel they had ICT self-efficacy in items 12, 21 and 23 that required higher technical knowledge about ICTs such as transferring files, searching library web cites and using Interactive White Board.

Pre-Service English Teachers' Perceptions on ICT Integration in Their Content-Based and Pedagogical Courses

In order to answer the second research question about their perceptions of ICTs, semi-structured interviews were also carried out by 15 randomly chosen pre-service teachers. The interviews were recorded and then transcribed. In analyzing the open-ended responses, a great number of themes appeared. The researcher and another rater tried to categorize emerging themes separately by using Constant Comparative Method. Then they decided on the final wording of the categories.

In answering the first question (How and where were ICTs used in your ELT education? Please explain in detail), students gave a great variety of responses. Some of the frequent responses are as the following:

I did not encounter many tools in pedagogical courses. They were not used in the lessons. Teachers generally used powerpoint and Canvas. We are given info about these tools but teachers do not use them in their lessons

In ICT lesson we learned many tools and sites

I used ICTs in practicum. Online platforms like menti, Kahoot and Quizizz.

They were used actively, we participated in the lesson actively, quizzes, questionnaires

We used them in micro or macro teaching

Go animate, Powtoon, create blog, Quizlet, Kahoot

Powerpoint, edpuzzle, slideshow, answergarden, menti, socrative, Storybird, storyboard

Table 2. Descriptive analysis of ICT Self-efficacy perceptions of pre-service english teachers

	"ICT Self-Efficacy Perception Scale	M	SD
1	I can create a back up file in order to start the system properly if my computer breaks down.	3.41	0.94
2	I can understand terminology related to computer hardware and software.	3.93	0.97
3	I can use anti-virus program in my computer.	4.00	0.90
4	I can learn advanced features of computer programs.	3.96	0.96
5	I can use word processor programs such as MS word, Openoffice, etc.	4.00	0.90
6	I can use presentation tools (MS Power Point, Prezi, etc.)	4.53	0.65
7	I can use data base (MS Access, etc.)	3.93	0.97
8	I can use e-mail.	4.21	0.73
9	I can use any search engine in the web.	4.00	0.90
10	I can prepare a web page.	3.45	1.17
11	I can download and use every kind of resource (document, pictures, video, music, animation, etc.)	3.96	0.96
12	I can transfer/use files using file transfer protocol (FTP)	2.96	1.00
13	I can join forum/discussion groups.	4.53	0.65
14	I can use scanner.	4.21	0.73
15	I can make changes on pictures on the computer.	3.41	0.94
16	I can use multimedia tools such as TV, DVD, projection, etc.	3.96	0.96
17	I can solve problems I encounter when I use communication technologies.	3.92	0.73
18	I can join/conduct a video conference.	3.41	0.94
19	I can use computer in order to organize information (save, organize, restructure.)	4.21	0.73
20	I can use chat programs (Chat, Skype, Google talk)	4.53	0.65
21	I can search info using library web cites.	2.96	1.00
22	I can prepare evaluation rubrics in an electronic media.	3.41	0.94
23	I can use interactive white board.	2.93	0.92
24	I can evaluate students using grading rubrics or electronic rubrics.	4.00	0.90
25	I can describe functions of communication technology tools such as computer software, projection, scanner, web, smart board.	3.86	0.83
26	I can use information technologies in my lessons for presentation.	4.21	0.73
27	I can use learning management systems such as Moodle, Blackboard, Web CT for education.	3.86	0.83

In answering the second question (How would you like ICTs to be used in ELT education?), some of the students' responses are as follows:

I would like to use Answergarden, storyjumper for brainstorming and visualization

There are so many sites, applications and games to use in the classes

The teachers can use them in their lessons to draw our attention to the lesson

ICTs should be integrated in each stage of class. Even students can do their homework via ICT tools

ICT tools should be combined with the topics and context. It should support lesson

New generation is digital native so lessons should be done according to their needs

ICT tools help use keep the attention of students easily. Teachers should integrate them in every stage

I would like to use ICTs more and more to motivate students

In answering the third question (How have you used ICTs in your macro teaching or practicum?), pre-service teachers' most frequent responses are as the following:

Videos, slide show in warm-up, slideshow in smart board

Quizziz, kahoot, games

Kahoot, quizlet, videos, games

In lead-in and giving homework

Vocabulary Teaching-showing pictures and students try to guess the meaning of the words

Using videos related to reading texts

Mentimeter, kahoot, quizlet

Online games, PPP, videos, online survey

Presenting topic with videos

Warn-up with rhymes

Practice with online games or quizzes

QR codes, surveys, kahoot

Pre-reading-vizio (activating students' background knowledge and getting their attention

While reading-kahoot-asking questions

Grammar teaching-using goanimate in preparing videos

Canvas, edmodo, Google classroom to share their works and I gave feedback

Brainstorming (mindmaps)-sharing students' ideas for the topic

In answering the fourth question (Where would you like to use ICTs when you become a teacher? Why?), some of the responses are as the following:

"I want to use ICT tools a lot in the class

"In every stage but especially in warm-up and presentation stage because these tools make students' concentration higher"

"as an extensive portfolio a blog that they can write about their daily life"

"in all the lesson, when giving feedback giving info outside class, talking about different things because it is more motivating and interesting than talking face to face"

"for brainstorming, storytelling and visualization answergarden, menti, to write answers for multiple choice questions on quizizz or Kahoot. Storyboard for visualizing lessons"

"In class and out of class with online platform"

"With young learners because they lose their control easily"

In answering the fifth question (What are the problems faced in using ICTs in language education?), some of the responses are as the following:

Finding the right activity for the right level

Downloading problems of some worksheets and videos

Boredom of students

Technical problems such as calibration of the smartboard, power cut-off, Internet cut-off, problems related to some websites

Students' and teachers' inexperience to use these programs

Students may have trouble understanding what they do

Paid accounts

In answering the sixth question (What are your suggestions to solve those problems?), pre-service teachers' responses were as the following:

Using other activities which do not require internet connection

Using smart board

"Having economic power to use technology in every part of the country

Having plan B to teach

Checking if the program works or not before coming to class

Downloading the program beforehand

Bringing laptop and connecting to Interactive White board

DISCUSSION

When the first part of the questionnaire is taken into account, it is seen that pre-service English teachers use computers and Internet technologies intensively since they are considered as digital natives. They mostly use laptops and mobile phones to reach the information easily or to communicate instantly. Most of them attended a course on ICTs.

The results of the ICTSEPS also supported the first part of the questionnaire. Pre-service teachers' scores in ICTSEPS were very high and it showed that they felt themselves self-efficacious in using ICTs in their daily lives and in their lessons. Since most of the pre-service teachers owned computers or smart phones and they have been using computers for more than 11 years, their scores were higher in ICTSEPS. This study proves that they are in line with the technological developments and will use ICTs in teaching students in the future. English language teaching does not only include classroom teaching but also outside learning by educating autonomous learners who take responsibility for their own learning. Pre-service teachers in this study believe that ICTs bring variety to class so students participate in the lesson more actively and eagerly since they are "digital natives" who have grown up in a world of computers, mobile phones and the web; i.e. a generation reliant upon digital media and tools. Thus, teachers of this generation cannot be thought without the knowledge of ICTs. Students of today are also autonomous learners so they do not rely on the teacher outside the class and use ICTs extensively. Pre-service teachers in this study can be said to have high ICT self-efficacy and therefore they are supposed integrate ICTs more when they become teachers. As English and ICT skills are two of the core subjects in 21st century skills, they cannot be separated from each other.

When the responses of all open-ended questions in the questionnaire are taken into account, it can be said that pre-service English teachers are keen on using ICTs in language education and they have high ICT self-efficacy. Although they were not asked which ICT tools they use mostly, some applications, Web 2.0 tools and online tools were detected in their answers. Contrary to findings of Khedekar (2013) who claimed that Facebook is the mostly used social networking site, pre-service teachers in this study did not prefer to use Facebook as they use WhatsApp, Instagram and YouTube. Pre-service teachers also used Skype, Snapchat, Kahoot, Kanvas, Powtoon, Google+, Podcasts, Blogs, Answergarden, Slideshow, Edpuzzle, Quizlet, Menti, Vizio, Quizziz, Socrative, Storybird, Goanimate, Storyjumper, Edublog, Wordart, Edmodo and QR Codes.

Some pre-service teachers complained about the use of ICTs in their departments. They claimed that teachers of some pedagogical lessons gave information about these tools but they did not use any tools in the class. Teachers mostly used Powerpoint presentations and it caused boredom among the students. Pre-service teachers also mentioned about ICT lesson they took. They stated that they liked that lesson a lot and learned lots of tools to use in the class in the future. They did not only gain information about the tools but they also used them in the class. For most of them, it was one of the most effective courses.

SOLUTIONS AND RECOMMENDATIONS

This study revealed that pre-service teachers are aware of these tools so they can use them efficiently when they become teachers. This result may be due to the introduction of ICT courses in teacher preparation programs in Turkey in 1998. The preparation program for teacher education has since been revised and a number of changes made; the new program has been in use since the 2006–2007 academic year (Aslan & Zhu, ibid). One of the changes to the new program relates to the ICT-related courses: in the context of ICT-related courses, "Computer I and II," and "Instructional Technology and Material Development" (ITMD) courses are now given as part of the program (HEC, 2006).

Tondeur, Van Keer, Van Braak, and Valcke (2008) have indicated that ICT training, the development of an ICT plan and ICT support at the school level all affect the success of ICT integration. In this respect, ICT-related courses in teacher education programs would seem to have a major impact on teachers' classroom use of ICT (Aslan & Zhu, 2017). As Wan and Gut (2011) state the 21st century teachers need to be prepared for the 21st century kids, who are themselves competent users of Web 2.0 technologies. This study supports their view since pre-service teachers are found to be active users of these technologies. The findings of this study are also in line with the assumption that if ESL teachers have to use technology effectively with their own students, they must use it for learning when they are already students (Kamhi-Stein, 2000). Therefore, teacher educators play a salient role in student teachers' experience with web technologies by offering more opportunities for greater motivation, negotiation and decision-making (Cephe & Balcıkanlı, 2012). However, some pre-service teachers have some concerns about the use of these technologies in government schools in all parts of the country because of Internet access, bans on the part of Ministry of Education and lack of technological equipment.

This study shows the importance of training future language teachers on using ICTs for their development and teaching. Hence, they will be able to use these technologies effectively when they start their teaching careers instead of learning these technologies when they become teachers. Ozel & Arıkan's (2015) study with 122 English instructors showed that they had positive attitudes toward the use of the Internet and Web 2.0 tools in language teaching but they were not using these tools adequately in their teaching. As Comas-Quinn (2011) states, teachers can focus on improving their skills and an understanding of online teaching and learning and, rather than being teachers who reluctantly use technology to comply with institutional requirements, they are supported on their journey to become online teachers for whom the technology opens up new pedagogical opportunities. For educators to infuse ICT seamlessly they must have access to technology and must be able to use the equipment before integration it into their teaching (Mazzella, 2011). In most cases training on how to use technology such as interactive whiteboards is provided in the form of a once-off demonstrative session for educators. According to Fishman (2006) learning how to use technology differs from learning how to teach with technology. This implies the need to cultivate continuous ICT integration professional development programs for educators that are linked to the curriculum goals and learning objectives (loqo, 2017). Thus, training of pre-service teachers on the use of ICT tools seems inevitable. Curriculum planners, Ministry of Education and all the other stakeholders should revise the curriculum of English Language Teaching departments and provide courses that train pre-service teachers on the use of technology and ICTs.

FUTURE RESEARCH DIRECTIONS

This study was carried out with 60 pre-service English teachers. More reliable and generalizable results would have been obtained if the study had been carried out with more participants from other faculties. Moreover, gender of the students was not taken into consideration in using ICTs. Future studies may compare students' gender and their ICT self-efficacy perceptions. Perceptions of students from different departments were not compared. Future studies may compare their ICT self-efficacy and perceptions in terms of their department.

CONCLUSION

The aim of this study was to obtain the perceptions of 60 pre-service English language teachers regarding their ICT self-efficacy perceptions and ICT integration in their lessons and faculties. The results of the study indicated that they had high self-efficacy about the use of ICTs and used them effectively in their micro and macro teaching. Most of them had taken an ICT course so it helped them to be aware of these tools. They mentioned about how they used ICT tools in ELT education, how they will use them when they become teachers and which tools they used in micro or macro teaching sessions. Pre-service teachers also mentioned about some problems they encountered in using ICTs inside and outside the class such as poor Internet connection, power cut-off, technical problems, students' and teachers' inexperience to use these tools. In terms of suggestions, they put forward some ideas such as checking the Internet connection before the class, downloading the program beforehand, bringing laptop to class, being prepared to have some problems and having plan B.

REFERENCES

Akbulut, Y. (2009). Investigating Underlying Components of The ICT Indicators Measurement Scale: The Extended Version. *Journal of Educational Computing Research*, *40*(4), 405–427. doi:10.2190/EC.40.4.b

Akbulut, Y., Odabas,ı, H. F., & Kuzu, A. (2011). Perceptions of preservice teachers regarding the integration of information and communication technologies in Turkish education faculties. *The Turkish Online Journal of Educational Technology*, *10*(3), 175–184.

Anderson, P. (2007). What is Web 2.0? Ideas, technologies and implications for education, media and technology. *JISC Technology and Standards Watch*. Retrieved from http://www.jisc.ac.uk/media/documents/techwatch/tsw0701b.pdf

Aslan, A., & Zhu, C. (2017). Investigating variables predicting Turkish pre-service teachers' integration of ICT into teaching practices. *British Journal of Educational Technology, 48*(2), 2017. doi:10.1111/bjet.12437

Aydoğan, F., & Akyüz, A. (2010). *Internet in Second Media Era*. İstanbul: Alfa Publishing.

Başöz, T. (2016). Pre-service EFL Teachers' Attitudes towards Language Learning through Social Media. *Procedia: Social and Behavioral Sciences, 232*, 430–438. doi:10.1016/j.sbspro.2016.10.059

Boyd, D. M., & Ellison, N. B. (2008). Social network sites: Definition, history, and scholarship. *Journal of Computer-Mediated Communication, 13*(1), 210–230. doi:10.1111/j.1083-6101.2007.00393.x

Cephe, P. T., & Balçıkanlı, C. (2012). Web 2.0 tools in language teaching: what student teachers think? *IJONTE, 3*(1), 1-12. Retrieved from http://www.ijonte.org/FileUpload/ks63207/File/01._cephe.pdf

Christensson, P. (2010, Jan. 4). *ICT Definition*. Retrieved from http://techterms.com

Collis, B., & Moonen, J. (2008). Web 2.0 tools and processes in higher education quality perspectives. *Educational Media International, 45*(2), 93–106. doi:10.1080/09523980802107179

Comas-Quinn, A. (2011). Learning to teach online or learning to become an online teacher: An exploration of teachers' experiences in a blended learning course. *ReCALL, 23*(03), 218–232. doi:10.1017/S0958344011000152

Conole, G., & Alevizou, P. (2010). *A literature review of the use of Web 2.0 tools in Higher Education: A report commissioned by the Higher Education Academy*. Milton Keynes, UK: The Open University.

Daskın, Z. (2017). *A Study of Faculty Members' and Instructors' Awareness, Routines and Use of Web 2.0 Tools in Foreign Language Teaching* (Unpublished Master Thesis). Hacettepe University.

Dearstyne. (2007). Blogs, mashups, and wikis: Oh my! *Information Management Journal, 41*(4), 24-33.

Ekici, E., Ekici, F. T., & Kara, I. (2012). Validity and Reliability Study of ICT Self-Efficacy Perception Scale for Teachers. *Pamukkale University Journal of Education, 31*(1), 53–65.

Evers, W. J. G., Brouwers, A., & Tomic, W. (2002). Burnout and self-efficacy: A study on teachers' beliefs when implementing an innovative educational system in the Netherlands. *The British Journal of Educational Psychology, 72*(2), 227–243. doi:10.1348/000709902158865 PMID:12028610

Eynon, R. (2005). The use of the Internet in higher education. *Aslib Proceedings, 57*(2), 168-180. Available at http://www.emeraldinsight.com/journals.htm?articleid=1465002

Fee, K. (2009). *Delivering E-Learning: A Complete Strategy for Design, Application and Assessment*. London: Kogan Page.

Fishman, B. J. (2006). It's not about the technology. *Teachers College Record*.

Goktas, Y., Yildirim, Z., & Yildirim, S. (2009). Investigation of K-12 teachers' ICT competencies and the contributing factors in acquiring these competencies. *The New Educational Review, 17*(1), 276–294.

Gülbahar, Y. (2008). ICT Usage in Higher Education: A Case Study on Preservice Teachers and Instructors. *The Turkish Online Journal of Educational Technology, 7*(1), 32–27.

HEC. (2006). *Egitim fakultelerinde uygulanacak yeni programlar hakkında acıklama*. Retrieved from http://www.yok.gov.tr/egitim/ogretmen/yeni_programlar_ve_icerik.htm

Hew, K. F. (2011). Students' and teachers' use of Facebook. *Computers in Human Behavior*, *27*(2), 662–676. doi:10.1016/j.chb.2010.11.020

Hismanoglu, M. (2012). Prospective EFL Teachers' Perceptions of ICT Integration: A Study of Distance Higher Education in Turkey. *Journal of Educational Technology & Society*, *15*(1), 185–196.

Horzum, M. B. (2010). An investigation of teachers' awareness, frequency of use and purposes of Web 2.0 tools in terms of different variables. *International Journal of Human Sciences*, *7*(1), 603–634.

Istifci, I. (2014). Perceptions of EFL Students on Educational Use of Facebook. In *Proceedings of the European Conference on Social Media, ECSM* (pp. 219-225). Academic Conferences and Publishing International.

Istifci, I., & Girginer, H. (2011). Prospective English Language Teachers and Web 2.0 Tools. In E-Learning in Turkey, Developments and Applications II (pp. 263-279). Eskişehir, Turkey: Anadolu University Publications.

Istifci, I., Lomidazde, T., & Demiray, U. (2011). An effective role of E-learning technology for the English language teaching by using meta communication actors. *The Turkish Online Journal of Distance Education*, *12*(4), 200–211.

Kamhi-Stein, L. D. (2000). Looking to the future of TESOL teacher education: Web-based bulletin board discussions in a methods course. *TESOL Quarterly*, *34*(3), 423–455. doi:10.2307/3587738

Kember, D., McNaught, C., Chong, F. C., Lam, P., & Cheng, K. F. (2010). Understanding the ways in which design features of educational websites impact upon student learning outcomes in blended learning environments. *Computers & Education*, *55*(3), 1183–1192. doi:10.1016/j.compedu.2010.05.015

Khedekar, N. (2013). *WhatsApp overtakes Facebook Messenger to be top mobile messaging app*. Retrieved from http://tech.firstpost.com/news-analysis/whatsapp-overtakes-facebook-messenger-to-be-top-mobile-messaging-app-108826.html

Lee, L. (2005). Using web-based instruction to promote active learning: Learners' perspectives. *CALICO Journal*, *23*(1), 139–156. doi:10.1558/cj.v23i1.139-156

Liu, X., & Pange, J. (2015). Early childhood teachers' perceived barriers to ICT integration in teaching: A survey study in Mainland China. *Journal of Computer Education*, *2*(1), 61–75. doi:10.100740692-014-0025-7

Loqo, T. (2017). Academic Staff Perceptions and Challenges in Technology Integration: A Case Study of Walter Sisulu University. In *Proceedings of the 16th European Confererence on ELearning* (pp. 318-325). Academic Conferences and Publishing International.

Mayer, R. E. (2011). *Multimedia learning*. New York: Cambridge University Press.

Mazzella, N. A. (2011). What are We Learning About Technology Integration and Professional Development? *Educator's Voice*, *4*, 42–49.

McLoughlin, C., & Lee, M. J. W. (2010). Personalised and self-regulated learning in the Web 2.0 era: International exemplars of innovative pedagogy using social software. *Australasian Journal of Educational Technology*, *26*(1), 28–43. doi:10.14742/ajet.1100

O'Reilly, T. (2007). What is web 2.0: Design patterns and business models for the next generation of software. *Communications & Stratégies*, *65*, 17–37.

OECD. (2013). *OECD skills outlook 2013: first results from the survey of adult skills*. OECD Publishing. doi:10.1787/9789264204256-en

Oliver, P., & Clayes, E. (2014). Issues of Using Information Communication Technologies in Higher Education. In *Proceedings of the European Conference on Social Media*. University of Brighton.

Orehovacki, T., Bubas, G., & Konecki, M. (2009). Web 2.0 in education and potential factors of Web 2.0 use by students of information systems. *Proceedings of the ITI 2009 31st Int. Conference on Information Technology Interfaces*. 10.1109/ITI.2009.5196124

Ozel, A. G., & Arıkan, A. (2015). The Use of the Internet and Web 2.0 Tools among EFL Instructors. *Mediterranean Journal of Humanities*, *V*(1), 313–325. doi:10.13114/MJH.2015111386

Pamuk, S., & Peker, D. (2009). Turkish pre-service science and mathematics teachers' computer related self-efficacies, attitudes, and the relationship between these variables. *Computers & Education*, *53*(2), 454–461. doi:10.1016/j.compedu.2009.03.004

Partnership for 21st Century Learning. (2015). Retrieved from http://www.p21.org/ our-work/p21-framework

Pempek, T. A., Yermolayeva, Y. A., & Calvert, S. L. (2009). College students' so- cial networking experiences on Facebook. *Journal of Applied Developmental Psychology*, *30*(3), 227–238. doi:10.1016/j.appdev.2008.12.010

Prensky, M. (2001). *Digital natives, digital immigrants*. NCB University Press. Available at http://pre2005.flexiblelearning.net.au/projects/resources/Digital_Natives_Digital_Immigrants.pdf

Sahin-Kızıl, A. (2011). EFL teachers' attitudes towards information and communication technologies (ICT). In *5th International Computer & Instructional Technologies Symposium*. Fırat University.

Sang, G., Valcke, M., van Braak, J., Tondeur, J., & Zhu, C. (2011). Predicting ICT integration into classroom teaching in Chinese primary school: Exploring the complex interplay of teacher-related variables. *Journal of Computer Assisted Learning*, *27*(2), 160–172. doi:10.1111/j.1365-2729.2010.00383.x

Schunk, D. H., & Meece, J. L. (2006). Self-efficacy development in adolescence. *Self-Efficacy Beliefs of Adolescents*, *5*, 71–96.

Schunk, D. H., & Pajares, F. (2010). Self-efficacy beliefs. Elsevier Ltd. doi:10.1016/B978-0-08-044894-7.00620-5

Tech Terms. (2014). *ICT, Tech Terms*. Available at: http://www.techterms.com/definition/realtime

Thomas, L. G., & Knezek, D. G. (2008). Information, communications, and educational technology standards for students, teachers, and school leaders. In J. Voogt & G. Knezek (Eds.), *International handbook of information technology in primary and secondary education* (pp. 333–348). New York: Springer. doi:10.1007/978-0-387-73315-9_20

Tondeur, J., Van Keer, H., Van Braak, J., & Valcke, M. (2008). ICT integration in the classroom: Challenging the potential of a school policy. *Computers & Education, 51*(1), 212–223. doi:10.1016/j.compedu.2007.05.003

Tongkaw, A. (2013). Multi Perspective Integrations Information and Communication Technologies (ICTs) in Higher Education in Developing Countries: Case Study Thailand. *Procedia – Social & Behavioral Sciences, 93*, 1467-72. Available at: http://www.sciencedirect.com/science/article/pii/S1877042813035106

UNESCO. (2010). *ICT transforming education: a regional guide*. Bangkok, Thailand: UNESCO. Retrieved from http://unesdoc.unesco.org/images/0018/001892/189216e.pdf

UNESCO. (2011a). *ICT competency framework for teachers*. Retrieved from http://unesdoc.unesco.org/images/0021/002134/213475e.pdf

UNESCO. (2011b). *Media and information literacy curriculum for teachers*. Retrieved from http://unesdoc.unesco.org/images/0019/001929/192971e.pdf

Usluel, Y. K., Mazman, S. G., & Arikan, A. (2009). Prospective teachers' awareness of collaborative web 2.0 tools. *The IADIS International Conference WWW/Internet 2009*.

Wan, G., & Gut, D. (Eds.). (2011). *Bringing schools into the 21st century*. New York: Springer. doi:10.1007/978-94-007-0268-4

Ward, L., & Parr, J. M. (2010). Revisiting and Reframing use: Implications for the integration of ICT. *Computers & Education, 54*(1), 113–122. doi:10.1016/j.compedu.2009.07.011

Warschauer, M., & Meskill, C. (2000). Technology and second language learning. In J. Rosenthal (Ed.), *Handbook of undergraduate second language education* (pp. 303–318). Mahwah, NJ: Lawrence Erlbaum.

Watkins, J. & Wilkins, M. (2011). Using YouTube in the EFL classrooms. *Language Education in Asia, 2*(1), 113-119.

Yapıcı, I. U., & Hevedanlı, M. (2012). International educational technology conference IETC2012. Preservice biology teachers' attitudes towards ICT using in biology teaching. *Procedia: Social and Behavioral Sciences, 64*, 633–638. doi:10.1016/j.sbspro.2012.11.074

Yıldırım, S. (2000). Effects of an educational computing course on preservice and inservice teachers: A discussion and analysis of attitudes and use. *Journal of Research on Computing in Education, 32*(4), 479–495. doi:10.1080/08886504.2000.10782293

Zhou, Q., Zhao, Y., Hu, J., Liu, Y., & Xing, L. (2010). Pre-service chemistry teachers' attitude toward ICT in Xian. *Procedia: Social and Behavioral Sciences, 9*, 1407–1414. doi:10.1016/j.sbspro.2010.12.342

Chapter 18
Educational Technologies in the Age of Transhumanism

Şirin Karadeniz
Bahçeşehir University, Turkey

Işıl Boy Ergül
Yıldız Teknik Üniversitesi, Turkey

ABSTRACT

Transhumanism has created drastic changes in many different sectors, especially in education as it is directly related to how we grow and shape our lives. Transhumanist technologies, especially augmented reality (AR), virtual reality (VR), and artificial intelligence (AI), play an important role in education and provide new opportunities by facilitating the communication between students and teachers and students and other students in order to obtain fruitful learning outcomes. In this chapter, transhumanist technologies used in teaching and learning will be discussed with a critical analysis, and how these technologies can change the way people learn will be explained through the lens of transhumanism.

INTRODUCTION

Based on the endless human transformation, transhumanism focuses on the future along with the change in how people learn. The term "transhumanism" was first suggested by Huxley (1927), the father of transhumanism movement. He claims that if human species want, they can transcend themselves by realizing new opportunities of and for their human nature. Humanity+ (formerly World Transhumanist Association) defined transhumanism as: " the intellectual and cultural movement that affirms the possibility and desirability of fundamentally improving the human condition through applied reason, especially by developing and making widely available technologies to eliminate aging and to greatly enhance human intellectual, physical, and psychological capacities" (Bostrom, 2003). Briefly, it can be defined as the use of technology for human enhancement which is mainly shaped by the modern technologies.

DOI: 10.4018/978-1-5225-8431-5.ch018

Since the beginning of intellectual technological innovations, technology has served as a significant medium to improve the quality of our lives, mainly to solve the problems we face in daily life. The more advanced technology becomes, the more explicitly its impact on society is seen in the 21st century. As human-beings, we perceive that the use of these modern technologies is a need for life and they increase the quality of communication and relationships in community. As explained in Principles of Extropy, "science and technology are essential to eradicate constraints on lifespan, intelligence, personal vitality, and freedom." (More, 2003, Section 1). On the other hand, Bostrom (2003) claims that humanism which is an intellectual and cultural movement aims at improving human-beings' condition advancing principally technologies. It has the potential to enhance people's different capacities such as physics, intellectualness, psychology by eliminating aging. He (Bostrom, 2003) also points out that "transhumanism can be viewed as an extension of humanism, from which it is partially derived. Humanists believe that humans matter, that individuals matter." (p.4). As we understand from these explanations, transhumanism movement is seeking for the ways to make the things better for the humanity.

How does transhumanism affect learning and education? Transhumanism has created drastic changes in many different sectors, especially in education as it is directly related to how we grow and shape our lives. According to Edwards and Lewin (2015) "transhumanism tells us about how we think about ourselves – what we amount to and where we are going (p.3). It gives us some insight into the essence of human identity since in the technological age. The technological age has also changed the way we interact socially and caused a sudden alteration in the generational traits. This change is fundamentally located in education. As a result, the new generation will become change agents (Prensky, 2001 & Tapscott, 2009).

It is acknowledged that in a highly tech-driven society, education and technology need to go hand in hand because technology has revolutionized education. The use of technology in teaching and learning gives educators a new perspective and can fundamentally change their working practices. It challenges the somewhat monotonous and conventional teaching strategies often employed by previous generations, and gives learners the incentive to participate in the lesson by engaging them more fully. Today's students grow up more attuned to technology, they adopt technology to their life unconsciously, which is a reality that cannot be rejected, and they are very much aware of the fact that the entire world is at their fingertips. Technology has opened up a new world for learners to create because it plays a crucial role to develop students' 21st century skills (critical thinking, collaboration, creativity and communication). Moreover, it is also a good tool when it is used as a tool to contribute the development of students' higher order thinking skills in their learning process (Kurt 2010). On the other hand, Winn (2002) reminds us the possible effect of technology on curricula. He claims that: "as our technologies become more able to bring information, learning materials, even learning environments to whenever people to be, the argument can be made that we no longer need to remember what we need to know; we can simply call it up and display it when it is needed. Whether this trend spills over into the world of education to any great extent is unclear. If it does, then the impact on traditional curricula will be tremendous." (p. 348). It can be concluded that it provides many advantages for the learners of 21st century when technology is used properly. There are many different resources which can be benefited from for both teachers and learners. Videos, web tools, educational games are some of quite useful examples for their academic and personal development. Through these tools, learners have a chance to share their works with their peers and they can also comment on each other's works, which increases their self-confidence and creativity in the related contexts. The more they create their own content, the more they learn by doing (experiential learning) because of the fact that learning becomes more meaningful and permanent when learners personalize the process for themselves.

As Prensky (2001) pointed out, our educational system was not designed to teach today's students. For this reason, the brains of the new generation who often interact with technology will eventually be reconstructed as a result of this interaction. Furthermore, Prensky (2009) supports that digital technology will become a crucial aid for human enhancement, and since everyone can move towards digital enhancement, the divide he stated between digital natives and digital immigrants is reduced, and the distinction between them is not very applicable due to the digital wisdom, which surpasses the generational divide. He (Prensky, 2009) further highlights the importance of being a digitally enhanced person to be able to obtain the tools of wisdom. Today's students are born into technology, however the exposure to technology does not imply that these students are more knowledgeable and know how to use technology effectively and efficiently.

FACILITATING LEARNING WITH TECHNOLOGY

Technology has became an integral part of our life. As a result, education has transformed because it has the potential to change behaviour, working, feeling and lifestyle of people. Therefore, it is obvious that technology has shaped the way people think and live throughout history thanks to its reciprocal relationship with education. These powerful impacts of modern technologies have been argued for many years, which has pushed the education world to understand and interiorise them. Specifically, successful usage of educational technology has drawn educators' attention, and they have been embraced by the educators in order to integrate them into educational contexts for the most appropriate usages in classroom environment. Many studies have been carried out in the field to figure out potential advantages and of these technologies. However; it has been revealed that teachers are not fully competent enough in this field. As an example to support this argument, Spector, Elen, Bishop and Merril (2014) state that "..teachers often lack the knowledge to successfully integrate technology in their teaching and their attempts tend to be limited in scope, variety, and depth." In this context, Shulman (1986) also claims teachers should have the knowledge of pedagogy and content (PCK) to use technology in the classroom effectively, which represents that "the blending of content and pedagogy into an understanding of how particular topics, problems, or issues are organized, represented, and adapted to the diverse interests and abilities of learners, and presented for instruction" (p. 8).

With the advancements in educational technology, Mishra and Koehler (2005) transfered Shulman's PCK model into TPACK model which represents "technological, pedagogical, and content knowledge." (p.131). According to TPACK model, teachers need to be motivated to figure out how these components can be integrated into the teaching process for fruitful outcomes and to look beyond old approaches in order to create newer techniques that recognize pragmatic, applied and creative goals of teaching with technology (Spector, Elen, Bishop and Merril, 2014). After deciding the instructional objectives, gaining the knowledge of usage of technology and taking the content and pedagogical knowledge into consideration, teachers may be successful in this process and make the learning process more effective for their students. As Clement and Samara (2013) point out educational technology must be inevitably integrated into classrooms and curricula as it provides many advantages for both students and teachers by making the process more varied and intensive. In the same vein, Lakhana (2012, p. 12) states: "Our tools can both limit and liberate our next thought." When the tools (web tools, softwares, digital resources and technologies etc.) are used for a more productive and reactive learning environment, teachers and students are provided with fast, reliable and communicative learning environments.

At this point, new technologies, especially Augmented Reality (AR), Virtual Reality (VR) and Artificial Intelligence (AI) play an important role and provide new opportunities by facilitating the communication between students and teachers and students- students in order to obtain fruitful learning outcomes. When it comes to the correlation between transhumanism and these technologies, it is acknowledged that VR, AR and AI are the transhumanist technologies which help us to explore how we contact with the world around us (Bostrom, 2003). In this chapter, technologies used in teaching and learning will be discussed with a critical analysis, and how new technologies such as AR, VR, and Artificial Intelligence can change the way people learn will be explained through the lens of transhumanism.

TRANSHUMANIST TECHNOLOGIES: VIRTUAL REALITY, AUGMENTED REALITY AND ARTIFICIAL INTELLIGENCE

With the rise of huge technological advancements, transhumanist ideas have become a passion for a growing group of thinkers and scientists working in the areas of genetics, nanotechnology, artificial intelligence, and robotics (Pugh, 2017, p. 1). In addition, As Bostrom (2003) stated in Transhumanist FAQ that "the ways in which cryonics, nanotechnology, genetic engineering, artificial intelligence and virtual reality will advance transhumanist goals (p. 7-19). Additionally, Bainbridge (2013) hold the view that transhumanism consists of various disciplines such as nanotechnology, biotechnology, information technology, and cognitive science.

Virtual Reality

The future of human-beings has begun to be shaped by technological developments carried out in many different areas. Additionally, transhumanism has created a profound effect on education. Various technologies have been developed constantly such as Virtual Reality and as human-beings we found ourselves in an adaptation process to enhance our abilities and intellectual capabilities with the help of these technologies.

Virtual Reality is one of the technologies which has drawn much attention nowadays as it enhances people's vision and feel them as if they were in different world (Heeter, 1992; Steuer, 1992). Virtual reality is a simulated environment that transforms passive situations into more interactive ones. Bostrom (2003, p.14) gives an example of virtual reality in his research called "The Transhumanist Fact": "Watching TV is typically a passive experience. Full-blown virtual reality, by contrast, will be interactive. You will be able to move about in a virtual world, pick up objects you see, and communicate with people you meet.". Virtual Reality is the technology providing users an opportunity to visualize and interact with three-dimensional virtual environments which have been applied in many different sectors from education to tourism or industry. Ivan Sutherland (1965) explained the very first idea of VR in his invited lecture "The Ultimate Display": "make that (virtual) world in the window look real, sound real, feel real, and respond realistically to the viewer's actions."(pp. 506-508). Virtual reality can be defined as a simulated environment that our senses perceive as real. When we think about virtual environments, VR headsets, 3D games, Google Glass come to our minds first although Virtual Reality has a history that dates back to the 1930s. The journey of VR started with creating basic simulation experiences in 1930s (training simulations produced for pilots and staff), continued with first VR headsets in 1960 and took its final form today. In VR working concept, an image of a three-dimensional object is provided by a VR device e.g. virtual glasses, gloves with movement sensors etc. When this input processed in the context of real-world, learning becomes more meaningful and permanent for learners. In the process of providing VR experience, two main elements play important roles. The first one is "immersion" which creates the feeling of presence in VR system. Immersion allows users opportunities to experience environments with realistic objects that may not be accessible. Various implementations of VR can include different degrees of immersion (the feeling of "being there") such as immersive, semi-immersive and non-immersive (Bamodu & Ye, 2013). The more the level of immersion increases, the users feel more immersed during interaction. Second key element is "interaction" in VR systems. A good quality human-computer interaction may allow learners better VR experience helping them to interact with the scene and control the elements inside VR application. Chen (2005, p. 39) states that "although VR is recognized as an impressive learning tool, there are still many issues that need further investigation including, identifying the appropriate theories and/or models to guide its design and development, investigating how its attributes are able to support learning, finding out whether its use can improve the intended performance and understanding, and investigating ways to reach more effective learning when using this technology, and investigating its impact on learners with different aptitudes". With the help of VR, students can learn abstract concepts as they can experience and visualize these concepts in the virtual environment (Sala, 2013; Rosenblum, 1997). Salzman, Loftin, and Chen (1999) explained in their research that virtual reality can facilitate abstract concepts and developed a model that describes the correlation between conceptual learning and the factors which have important influence on learning process and learning outcomes. The author of "The Transhumanist FAQ" Bostrom (2003) also points out the advantages of VR and explains the relationship between VR and Transhumanism. He states that Virtual Reality technologies are useful for us to develop creativity and addresses that "VR could unlock limitless possibilities for human creativity. We could construct artificial experiential worlds, in which the laws of physics can be suspended, that would appear as real as physical reality to participants. People could visit these worlds for work, entertainment, or to socialize with friends who may be living on the opposite site of the globe." (p.15)

In order to get a better understanding of the effects of VR in education, the question "how do students learn" should be explored first. Since the advent of educational technology, the relationship between learning theories and innovations has often been argued, concepts and conceptual frameworks have been presented and positive effects or drawbacks of these innovations have been addressed by many researchers in the field. As Salomon and Perkins (1996) state technologies follow learning theories considered as prominent. In the framework of these studies, it is acknowledged that as human beings, we learn from our experiences. Brown (1991) claims that for meaningful learning outcomes, learners need to participate in the learning process actively rather than passively because they are able to manage and control their own learning in an environment supported with technology. One of the reasons why these technologies are used by the educational institutions all over the world is that they present learners a chance to explore more realistic learning experiences rather than only theoretical ones to improve the quality of learning process by using available technologies. These technologies are mostly supported with different theories such as the theory of "learning by doing or experiential learning" expounded by eminent American philosopher John Dewey (1938). Lee and Wong (2014) also touch on one of the advantages of VR technologies by stating in their study that virtual reality can be useful for the learners who have low-spatial ability because it helps them to minimise extraneous cognitive load of the learning objectives. Furthermore, Winn (1993) addresses the advantages of using VR technologies in educational context, and claims that VR promotes the best and seemingly only strategy that lets students to learn from non-symbolic first-person experience. Since a great many students fail in school because they do not master the symbol systems of the disciplines they study, although they are perfectly capable of mastering the concepts that lie at the heart of the disciplines, it can be concluded that VR provides a route to success for children who might otherwise fail in our education system as it is currently construed".

So far, the link between VR, transhumanism and learning has been discussed. However, the results of the use of VR technologies in educational context should be explored. The results of the use of this technology has been affected by various parameters. As educators, it is important to figure out how these technologies are shaped in our classroom environment according to our students' needs, interests, readiness levels, socio-cultural characteristics and etc. Knowing only how to utilize the virtual reality applications may not be efficient in terms of learning in the 21st century. Therefore, all pedagogical and academic aspects need to be explored properly and integrated to the process. In this integration process, the technologies such as virtual reality can be a good medium to achieve the objectives of the lesson. However, "Where, When and How Questions" need to be carefully examined by the instructional designers in terms of educational purposes. For example; Where do we need virtual reality in our classes? How do we decide whether it is useful or not? Why do we use it for the instructional purposes? In the integration process of these technologies, the answers are required to have best practices of Virtual Reality for both learners and teachers.

As explained above, many researches in this field have been carried out, and mostly positive outcomes were obtained, however, that does not imply that VR technologies do not have any limitations. The first limitation of VR is that it is not affordable for many institutions. The development process and equipments (e.g. VR headsets, glasses) used in VR technology are not cheap. Secondly, in order to implement this technology effectively, practices by the subject matter experts should be carried out. As it is accepted as a new development, there are still some gaps in terms of the technical issues and its use in education. According to Bostrom (2003), these systems can cause some undesirable experiences for users. He states that some users of VR may experience some sickness such as unpleasantness, headaches and so forth because of different sensory systems including visual and auditory system in VR application. He also points out that it is possible to overcome these sickness by developing good-quality virtual environments although it seems challenging.

Augmented Reality

Augmented Reality (AR) can be defined as a branch of Virtual Reality (VR), they are actually different frames and they differ from each other in terms of working principles and their use in education. AR technologies allow virtual objects to be overlaid in a real-world environment focusing on the intellectual and emotional development of the viewer. It provides users to interact with digital information embedded within the physical environment. Augmented Reality has influenced conventional learning process considerably as it is directly aligned with two theoretical frameworks: Constructivist Theory and Situated Learning Theory (Spector, Elen, Bishop & Merril, 2014)

AR is an engaging technology as it helps users to see the real world in a different way by providing many advantages for them. It makes abstract knowledge more tangible. For this reason, learning activities go beyond the scope of superficiality. According to Kaufmann (2003), AR has a strong effect as it facilitates students learning process with collaboration. AR presents collaborative environment to foster their involvement in classroom, promotes interaction among group members by sharing information and offering explanation, and improves their social skills such as leadership and communication. When students participate in group/pair work, they develop positive interdependence as they need to trust each other and communicate in a more natural way while engaging. According to Bruner (1966), people construct new knowledge and understandings based on what they already know and believe, which is shaped by their developmental level, their prior experiences, and their sociocultural background and context. Constructivist theory helps learners to enhance metacognitive skills with the real experience and provides them self-directed active learning opportunities (Bruner, 1966; Cunningham, 1992; Driscoll, 2000; Piaget, 1969; Vygotsky, 1978).

The other theory supporting Augmented Reality is "Situated Learning Theory" which argues that learning should take place in the related context and social engagements. According to Driscoll (2000) learning becomes an active process in which all learners are "transformed through their actions and relations in the world"(p.157). The developers of Situated Learning Theory, Lave and Wenger (1991) claim that learning should be situated in a specific context and embedded within a particular social and physical environment. It can be said that "situated learning theory" is closely related to social learning theory by Vygotsky as learning depends on interaction among people, cultural factors, places etc. in both theories. According to Kerawalla, Luckin, Seljeflot, & Woolard (2006) the use of AR in formal education may be one of the fundamentals of the future learning environments laden with software and hardware programs.

AR is also linked to the self-determination theory (SDT) developed by Rigby and Przybylski in 2009. According to SDT, motivation is necessary for learning activities because of the fact that human-beings are more inclined to do what is healthy, interesting, important, and effective. In the educational context, students are more motivated and engaged when they are in charge of their own learning. It can be concluded that AR provides flexibility for students as they can extend and personalize the content for themselves and manage their own learning activities.

It can be concluded that AR technology is supported by different theories and its results in educational context have been already approved. Most of the studies show that augmented reality created a new impulse in 21st century, and it changes learners' traditional tasks and learning activities by guiding them in a real-world context. (Billinghurst & Dunser, 2012; Kaufmann, 2003). Dunleavy and Dede (2013) address the relationship between AR, situated and constructivist theory. They (Dunleavy and Dede) state that AR, which is an instructional approach and cognitive medium, is especially correlated situated and constructivist learning theory because of the fact that it helps learner to be in a real-world physical and social context by supporting and facilitating processes such as real questioning, active observation, mutual instruction, peer-coaching and peripheral engagement with multiple modes of representation.

It is known that AR is a booming technology and it has a strong effect on the users, especially on the learners of Z generation who are socialized with their tablets, mobile phones. AR has the potential to offer educational value. An interest in AR, one of the newest developing technologies, has been increasing day by day; therefore, the number of the researches being published has been increasing. However, Wu, Lee, Chang, & Liang (2013) and Cheng & Tsai (2012) point out that AR is still in its infancy. Dunleavy, Dede, & Mitchell (2009) state that we have just began to figure out influent teaching designs for AR technology. In order to integrate AR into educational context, its uses, purposes, advantages and limitations need to be understood by educators first.

In the classrooms where conventional methods are still used by the educators in the 21st century, students are passive participants and there is a teacher-centered atmosphere in the classroom. On the contrary, Augmented Reality is supported by The Inquiry Based Learning Method (IBL). Wang (2013) explains the results of the research on the effectiveness of inquiry-based instruction in the classroom below:

(...) inquiry-based instruction encourages students to adopt different approaches in the service of developing a better understanding of the subject, helps students familiarize themselves with ongoing experiments and areas of inquiry, and enables them to obtain better scores on examinations. (p. 21).

It can be understood that students who have freedom in their learning process can perform better as they have an active role in this process while the instructor provides learners with learning supports and rich multiple media sources of information to assist students in successfully finding solutions (Heick, 2013). It extends the content from the traditional setting to the outside world. In this context, AR can be useful to obtain best learning outcomes for the students since its components work well when it is supported by different teaching and learning methods. Billinghurst & Dunser (2012) state that AR is a good way to teach different disciplines such as math, science or language skills because it enables students an environment that they can use their problem solving skills and work in teams; it also increases their motivation, participation and engagement.

According to the results of the study conducted by Sirakaya and Cakmak (2018), the effect of AR on students' achievement is positive. They (Sirakaya and Cakmak) also state that AR does not have any influence on theoretical knowledge, self-efficacy and assembly skills. However, AR provides students to work with less help. As a result, it can be stated that AR applications could be used as effective tools in applied courses, and has created a strong effect in many fields especially in education. Studies in educational technology show that AR is a technology supported by many different theories and frameworks such as situated learning, cognitive learning, SDT and IBL as it focuses on student-centered learning rather than teacher-centered learning environment.

AR is one of the digital advancements that helps human-beings to enhance their capabilities through technology in the 21st century, as a part of transhumanism movement. It has moved beyond military applications and entered various domains. AR has changed the way of understanding in many different sectors, many companies has started to invest in this technology to benefit them in different ways for profit. It is obvious that these humanist technologies created a huge effect especially on individuals, business, society and education by changing the ways in which we interact with the world around us. We can see this effect especially on different fields of education such as history, mathematics, language learning with the help of developments in educational technology. When it comes to the affordances of AR, most of the studies show that it eases both learning and teaching process for students and teachers. Because of the fact that AR combines the physical environment with the digital ones, it provides students with a chance to interiorise new learned experiences by using multiple perspectives. Various studies also show that AR increased students' substantial motivation level, both students and teachers become highly engaged when they participate in AR activities including adopting roles and solving authentic problems(Dunleavy & Simmons, 2011; Dunleavy et al., 2009; Facer et al., 2004; Klopfer & Squire, 2008; Perry et al., 2008; Schmalstieg & Wagner, 2007; Squire, 2010; Squire et al., 2007). On the other hand, AR has some limitations as it may cause cognitive overload on students' learning processes since AR tasks generally include complex activities which can be overwhelming for students (Dunleavy et al., 2009).

Artificial Intelligence

Can a machine learn? "Can a machine think and behave like humans do?" These are the questions that lead humanity to wonder about the power of the digital technologies. There has been considerable progress in the field of Artificial Intelligence. John McCarthy (1955), the developer of Artificial Intelligence, describes it as a "science and engineering of making intelligent machines, especially intelligent computer programs" (p.2). John McCarthy (1955) also gives a different and detailed definition: "The study of artificial intelligence is to proceed on the basis of the conjecture that every aspect of learning or any other feature of intelligence can in principle be so precisely described that a machine can be made to simulate it." (p.12).

AI has brought new perspectives which combine various areas from Philosophy to Neuroscience and Biology. The idea underlying AI is that it makes life easier for humans by focusing on the way of how people think, work, learn and decide while dealing with solving problems. It is the development of computer systems that can perform tasks which require human intelligence such as speech recognition, translation, and decision-making.

AI helps us to understand the importance self-taught and self-learning through transhumanist learning approaches. When it is properly applied, Artificial Intelligence can offer many advantages. Sotala (2008) holds the view that Artificial Intelligence can intentionally be built in a manner that is easy to comprehend and modify, and can even read its design documents. McCarthy, Minsky, Rochester & Shannon proposed in 1955 that "An attempt will be made to find how to make machines use language, form abstractions and concepts, solve kinds of problems now reserved for humans, and improve themselves. … For the present purpose the artificial intelligence problem is taken to be that of making a machine behave in ways that would be called intelligent if a human were so behaving." (p.12). This statement opened a path in educational technology to consider on Machine Learning (ML).

As a sub-field of AI, Machine Learning has become a booming area of Computer Science. It was started in 1930s by Alan Turing, and gained importance day by day with the developments in Artificial Intelligence field. Machine Learning is based on mathematical derivations, practical algorithms, data and output to create a program. In order to understand what machine learning is, the definition of algorithm needs to be considered on a preferential basis. According to Knuth (2004), algorithm is an effective method expressed as a finite list of well-defined instructions for calculating a function. David and Schwartz (2014) define machine learning in their book named Understanding Machine Learning: From Theory to Algorithms as an "automated detection of meaningful patterns in data" and they also present example of usage of machine learning: "In the past couple of decades, it has become a common tool in almost any task that requires information extraction from large data sets. We are surrounded by a machine learning based technology: search engines learn how to bring us the best results (while placing profitable ads), anti-spam software learns to filter our email messages, and credit card transactions are secured by a software that learns how to detect frauds." (p.7). Machine learning has been applied in many different subject matters as it is totally aligned with the newest technological advancements. Machine learning is a wide area including various applications such as healthcare, education as it provides many advantages in these areas. The first and most important advantage of machine learning is that it carries out the tasks of people need to complete. As the machines rely on huge amount of data, in dynamic environments which are faster than human, they allow saving time for the best usages of resources.

Integration of AI into education has been discussed as a part of academic research more than 30 years. AI seems as a practical tool in education as it helps to foster students' learning process. According to Self (1999) the scientific goal of AIEd is to "make computationally precise and explicit forms of educational, psychological and social knowledge which are often left implicit." (p.350). It is acknowledged that AI is a supportive technology as it helps both educators and learners in different ways by making comprehension process more effective with the usage of different concepts. AI presents various smart contents, intelligent tutoring systems which help teachers to manage teaching/learning processes better and enables teachers to overcome teaching/learning problems with the help of logically solution ways. As Luckin (2017) explains "This process helps inform new ways to provide more efficient, personalised, and contextualised support, while also testing and refining our understanding of the processes of teaching and learning (p.20). Artificial Intelligence is also supported by different concepts such as e- learning. A study conducted by Kose and Aslan (2015) reports that artificial intelligence has provided positive results on the usage of an artificial intelligence based e-learning software in English language courses. The researchers (Kose and Aslan) in the study used "a hybrid evaluation system, which was formed by an artificial neural network and cognitive development optimization algorithm, is included under a web based e- learning software system."(p.63) The researchers point out that their students had an experience alternative way of learning English through the e-learning system which is suitable for learners' levels. At the end of the research, it was concluded that an increase on students' academic achievement was observed. Moreover, the researchers states that the students were happy with the effect the e-learning system created.

When it comes to the fields of Artificial intelligence, one of the most important branch is Robotics. Robots have been in our lives since 19th century. With the drastic progress in technology, they became an inseparable part of our society and they also started to be utilized in various field especially in education. According to Benitti (2012) robotics is one of the fields which attracts more and more attention surprisingly, and he conducted a study on the use of educational robotics and reported that they are useful to develop teamwork skills, problem solving and thinking skills. There are various reasons why they can be used for instructional purposes. Eguchi (2014) puts forward that: "One of the reasons why educational robotics is an effective learning tool is that educational robotics help create a *fun* and *engaging* learning environment that keeps students interested and engaged in learning. Educational robotics is *fun* because it provides *hands-on* learning experience. Also, it is a great *tool* for project-based learning. With project-based learning, students work in groups to "explore real-world problems and challenges." (p.6) Another research conducted by Kubilinskiene, Zilinskiene, Dagiene, Sinkevičlus (2017) focuses on applying robotics in school education, and shows that a range of skills were developed during the use of robotics. In the same vein, Papert (1993) points out that robotic activities improve classroom teaching as a child learns more effectively when he/she is an active participant. McDonald and Howell (2012) also discuss that robotics has played an important role in social interaction in the classroom. Furthermore, they indicate that students' numeracy skills (e.g. ability to count, identify colors and shapes and use of positional language) were also improved through robotics program at the end of the research. Robotic technology is also useful to improve learning performance and motivation in EFL classrooms. The study conducted by Hong, Huang, Hsu and Shen (2015) supports that using robot-assisted teaching materials in the primary level of English language teaching needs to be promoted. The researchers explained that students performed well especially in receptive language skills (reading and listening) with the help of the robot-assisted instructional materials. The researchers also touch on the Krashen's (1988) Affective Filter Hypothesis in second language teaching as it is related to the psychological background of the study. Krashen (1988) believes that the affective filter opens or closes according to our emotional mood; when we are relaxed, it is more easy to acquire the language. Accordingly, robotis eliminate the anxiety level of students, encourage them to be engaged and motivated in the activities.

As AI develops, the importance of transhumanism needs to be emphasized because they are closely related to each other in the learning context. When it comes to learning, it is known that machines having AI may replicate the cognitive skills of human beings. Therefore, they are called as "intelligent machines."By asking " Why?" question while programming, they are able to reduce errors in a system, understand natural language spoken by humans, interpret, and comprehend visual inputs coming from different sources. Moreover, they can even recognize handwriting text written on paper by a pen, however, they are not very good at reasoning as we do.

CONCLUSION

These transhumanist technologies are expected to shape the future of human being. Transhumanism is not just a movement related to improving human biology through science and technology. More (2013) claims that transhumanism is one of life philosophies which look for momentum of intelligent life beyond human limitations through science and technology. It is considered as an extension of human capabilities, and does not advocate only biological improvements in human-being's condition, but aims to develop the intellectual skills of humankind by altering their habits and learning practices. In the 21st century, with the current advancements, it is not easy to adopt all the technologies properly in every context. However, it is a fact that these humanist technologies are created for human-beings' intellectual enhancement and they will change the way people live and learn. As it has been declared by World Transhumanist Association when we embrace new technologies, we have a better chance of using it to our advantage than if we try to prohibit it (Bostrom, 2003). It is a fact that we do not know exactly what our world will look like in the next 50 years. Nonetheless, we can expect to witness dramatic advancements over the coming decades in the world of education, and the way how people learn will be affected by these transhumanist technologies.

REFERENCES

Bamodu, O., & Ye, X. M. (2013). Virtual Reality and Virtual Reality System Components. *Advanced Materials Research*, *765*, 1169–1172. doi:10.4028/www.scientific.net/AMR.765-767.1169

Benitti, F. B. V. (2012). Exploring the educational potential of robotics in schools: A systematic review. *Computers & Education*, *58*(3), 978–988. doi:10.1016/j.compedu.2011.10.006

Billinghurst, M. (2002). Augmented reality in education. *New Horizons for Learning*, *12*.

Bostrom, N. (2003). *The Transhumanist FAQ*. World Transhumanist Association.

Bostrom, N. (2005). A History of Transhumanist Thought. *Journal of Evolution and Technology / WTA*, *14*(1).

Bruner, J. S. (1966). *Toward a theory of instruction*. Cambridge, MA: Belknap.

Chang, J.-H. L. (2010). Exploring the Possibility of Using Humanoid Robots as Instructional Tools for Teaching a Second Language in Primary School. *Journal of Educational Technology & Society, 13*(2), 13–24.

Chen, B., & Denoyelles, A. (2013). Exploring students' mobile learning practices in higher education. *EDUCAUSE Review*.

Chen, C. J. (2006). The design, development and evaluation of a virtual reality based learning environment. *Australasian Journal of Educational Technology, 22*(1), 39–63. doi:10.14742/ajet.1306

Chen, E., Heritage, M., & Lee, J. (2005). Identifying and monitoring students' learning needs with technology. *Journal of Education for Students Placed at Risk, 10*(3), 309–332. doi:10.120715327671espr1003_6

Cheng, K.-H., & Tsai, C.-C. (2012a). Affordances of augmented reality in science learning: Suggestions for future research. *Journal of Science Education and Technology, 22*(4), 449–462. doi:10.100710956-012-9405-9

Clement, D., & Samara, J. (2003). Young Children and Technology: What Does the Research Say? *National Association for the Education of Young Children., 58*(6), 34–40.

Driscoll, M. P. (2000). *Psychology of learning for instruction*. Needham Heights, MA: Allyn & Bacon.

Dunleavy, M., Dede, C., & Mitchell, R. (2009). Affordances and limitations of immersive participatory augmented reality simulations for teaching and learning. *Journal of Science Education and Technology, 18*(1), 7–22. doi:10.100710956-008-9119-1

Dunleavy, M. & Simmons, B. (2011). *Assessing learning and identity in augmented reality science games*. Academic Press.

Edwards, A. & Levin, D. (2012). *Better than well-being: The scope of transhumanism in the context of educational philosophy*. Academic Press.

Eguchi, A. (2014). Educational Robotics for Promoting 21st Century Skills. *Journal of Automation. Mobile Robotics & Intelligent Systems., 8*, 6–9.

Heick, T. (2013). *4 phases of inquiry-based learning: A guide for teachers*. Academic Press.

Hong, Z. W., Huang, Y. M., Hsu, M., & Shen, W. W. (2016). Authoring robot-assisted instructional materials for improving learning performance and motivation in EFL classrooms. *Journal of Educational Technology & Society, 19*, 337–349.

Hsu, Y., Hung, J., & Ching, Y. (2013). Trends of educational technology research: More than a decade of international research in six SSCLI-indexed refereed journals. *Educational Technology Research and Development, 61*(4), 685–705. doi:10.100711423-013-9290-9

Huxley, J. (1927). *Religion without revelation*. London: E. Benn.

Kaufmann, H. (2003). *Collaborative augmented reality in education*. Imagina Conference 2003, Monaco Mediax, Monaco.

Kerawalla, L., Luckin, R., Seljeflot, S., & Woolard, A. (2006). Making it real: Exploring the potential of augmented reality for teaching primary school science. *Virtual Reality (Waltham Cross)*, *10*(3-4), 163–174. doi:10.100710055-006-0036-4

Kerawalla, L., Pearce, D., Yuill, N., Luckin, R., & Harris, A. (2008). "I'm keeping those there, are you?" The role of a new user interface paradigm—Separate control of shared space (SCOSS)—In the col- laborative decision-making process. *Computers & Education*, *50*(1), 193–206. doi:10.1016/j.compedu.2006.04.007

Klopfer, E. (2008). *Augmented learning*. Cambridge, MA: MIT press. doi:10.7551/mitpress/9780262113151.001.0001

Klopfer, E., & Squire, K. (2008). Environmental Detectives - the development of an augmented reality platform for environmental simulations. *Educational Technology Research and Development*, *56*(2), 203–228. doi:10.100711423-007-9037-6

Koehler, M. J., & Mishra, P. (2005b). What happens when teachers design educational technology? The development of technological pedagogical content knowledge. *Journal of Educational Computing Research*, *32*(2), 131–152. doi:10.2190/0EW7-01WB-BKHL-QDYV

Kommers, P. (2003). Experiential Learning through Constructivist Learning Tools. *International Journal of Computers and Applications*, *25*(1), 8–9. doi:10.1080/1206212X.2003.11441687

Kose, U. & Arslan, A. (2015).E-Learning experience with artificial intelligence supported software: n International Application on English Language Courses. *Glokalde*, *1*(3).

Krashen, S. D. (1988). *Second Language Acquisition and Second Language Learning*. Prentice-Hall International.

Kurt, S. (2010). Technology use in elementary education in Turkey: A case study. *New Horizons in Education*, *58*(1), 65–76.

Lakhana, A. (2014). What is educational technology? An inquiry into the meaning, use, and reciprocity of technology. *Canadian Journal of Learning and Technology*, *40*(3), 1. doi:10.21432/T2H59S

Lave, J., & Wenger, E. (1991). *Siruared learning. Legitimate peripheral participation*. Cambridge, UK: Cambridge University Press. doi:10.1017/CBO9780511815355

Lee, S. (2013). Current status, opportunities and challenges of augmented reality in education. *Computers & Education*, *62*, 41–49. doi:10.1016/j.compedu.2012.10.024

Luckin, R., Holmes, W., Griffiths, M., & Forcier, L. B. (2016). Intelligence Unleashed. An argument for AI in Education. London: Pearson.

McCarthy, J. (2007). *What is artificial intelligence? Personal website*. Stanford University.

McCarthy J., Minsky, L., Rochester, N., & Shannon, C. (1955). A Proposal for the Dartmouth Summer Research Project on Artificial Intelligence.

McDonald, S., & Howell, J. (2012). Watching, creating and achieving: Creative technologies as a conduit for learning in the early years. *British Journal of Educational Technology, 43*(4), 641–651. doi:10.1111/j.1467-8535.2011.01231.x

Minsky, M. (1994). Will Robots Inherit the Earth? *Scientific American, 271*(4), 108–113. doi:10.1038 cientificamerican1094-108 PMID:7939559

Mishra, P., Koehler, M., & Zhao, Y. (2007). *Faculty development by design: Integrating technology in higher education.* Charlotte, NC: Information Age.

More, M. (2003). *Principles of Extropy* (3rd ed.). Academic Press.

More, M. (2010). The Overhuman in the Transhuman. *Journal of Evolution and Technology/WTA, 21*(1).

Multon, K. D., Brown, S. D., & Lent, R. W. (1991). Relation of self-efficacy beliefs to academic outcomes: A meta-analytic investigation. *Journal of Counseling Psychology, 38*(1), 30–38. doi:10.1037/0022-0167.38.1.30

Papert, S. (1993). *Mindstorms: Children, computers, and powerful ideas* (2nd ed.). New York: Basic Books.

Prensky, M. (2001a). Digital Natives, Digital Immigrants. *On the Horizon, 9*(5), 1–6. doi:10.1108/10748120110424816

Prensky, M. (2001b). Digital Natives, Digital Immigrants, part 2: Do they really think differently? *On the Horizon, 9*(6), 6. doi:10.1108/10748120110424843

Prensky, M. (2009). H. Sapiens Digital: From Digital Immigrants and Digital Natives to Digital Wisdom. *Journal of Online Education, 5*(3).

Pugh, C. (2017). The Disappearing Human: Gnostic Dreams in a Transhumanist World. *Religions, 8*(81), 1.

Rosenblum, L. & Robert A. (1997). The challenge of virtual reality. *Visualization & Modeling*, 325-399.

Ryan, R. M., Rigby, C. S., & Przybylski, A. (2006). The motivational pull of video games: A self-determination theory approach. *Motivation and Emotion, 30*(4), 347–364. doi:10.100711031-006-9051-8

Sala, N. (2013). Applications of Virtual Reality Technologies in Architecture and in Engineering. *International Journal of Space Technology Management and Innovation, 3*(2), 78–88. doi:10.4018/ijstmi.2013070104

Salomon, G., & Perkins, D. N. (1989). Rocky roads to transfer: Rethinking mechanisms of a neglected phenomenon. *Educational Psychologist, 24*(2), 113–142. doi:10.120715326985ep2402_1

Salzman, M. C., Dede, C., Loftin, R. B., & Chen, J. (1999). A model for understanding how virtual real- ity aids complex conceptual learning. *Presence (Cambridge, Mass.), 8*(3), 293–316. doi:10.1162/105474699566242

Self, J. (1999). The defining characteristics of intelligent tutoring systems research: ITSs care, precisely. *International Journal of Artificial Intelligence in Education, 10*, 350–364.

Shulman, L. (1986). Those who understand: Knowledge growth in teaching. *Educational Researcher*, *15*(2), 4–14. doi:10.3102/0013189X015002004

Shwartz, S., & David, S. (2014). *Understanding Machine Learning: From Theory to Algorithms*. Cambridge, UK: Cambridge University Press. doi:10.1017/CBO9781107298019

Sirakaya, M. & Cakmak, E. (2018). Investigating Student Attitudes toward Augmented Reality. *Malaysian Online Journal of Educational Technology, 6*(1).

Sotala, K. (2012). Advantages of Artificial Intelligences, Uploads, and Digital Minds. *International Journal of Machine Consciousness*, *4*(1), 275–291. doi:10.1142/S1793843012400161

Steuer, J. (2000). Defining Virtual Reality: Dimensions Determining Telepresence. *Journal of Communication*, *42*(4), 73–93. doi:10.1111/j.1460-2466.1992.tb00812.x

Sutherland, I. E. (1965). The Ultimate Display. *Proceedings of IFIP Congress 2*.

Tapscott, D. (1999). Educating the Net generation. *Educational Leadership*, *56*, 5, 6–11.

Vygotsky, L. (1979. (1925). Consciousness as a problem in the psychology of behavior. *Social Psychology*, *17*(4), 3–35.

Winn, W. (1997). Advantages of a theory-based curriculum in instructional technology. *Educational Technology*, 34–41.

Winn, W. (2002). Current trends in educational technology research: The study of learning environments. *Educational Psychology Review*, *14*(3), 331–351. doi:10.1023/A:1016068530070

World Transhumanist Association. (2003). *The Transhumanist Declaration*. Retrieved from http://transhumanism.org/index.php/WTA/declaration/

Wu, H.-K., Lee, S. W.-Y., Chang, H.-Y., & Liang, J.-C. (2013). *Current status, opportunities and challenges of augmented reality in education*. Academic Press.

Section 4
Business, Management, Law, and Health

Chapter 19
Business Management Learning:
Research for the Age of Transhumanism

Gürcan Banger
Railway Systems Cluster, Turkey

ABSTRACT

The Transhumanist future will be an age of data dominance, pervasive computing, artificial intelligence, smart machines, and autonomous mobile robots accompanied by a vast speed and ever-increasing acceleration of change. The pervasive and ongoing change requires a fundamental re-invention of business management which should coincide with the conditions of the converging transhumanism age. The main feature of the future management paradigms that differ from the traditional style will undoubtedly be the artificial intelligence with several applications of machine learning and humans' collaborative work with associate-like autonomous robots. Managers at all levels will have to adapt to the world of artificial intelligence and smart environment. The transhumanist manager should learn and get equipped with the necessary management requirements. The new learning platforms, methods, techniques, and media should be researched to get prepared for a transhumanist business management future with a faster alacrity to compensate for the speed of the technological progress.

INTRODUCTION

Transhumanism is a futuristic philosophy that deals with making use of existing and future exponential technologies to transform the human body and mind (Humanity Plus, 2008). Being as a solid reference, two definitions of Transhumanism are given:

1. The intellectual and cultural movement that affirms the possibility and desirability of fundamentally improving the human condition through applied reason, especially by developing and making widely available technologies to eliminate aging and to greatly enhance human intellectual, physical, and psychological capacities.

DOI: 10.4018/978-1-5225-8431-5.ch019

2. The study of the ramifications, promises, and potential dangers of technologies that will enable us to overcome fundamental human limitations, and the related study of the ethical matters involved in developing and using such technologies.

The future will continue to be mysterious for us as long as our sense of time continues in its present form. But this does not prevent us from creating forecasts for the future and creating future scenarios. The technologies developed in the late 20th century and the 21st century seem to design a whole new future for world civilization. Exponential technologies will change many activities and behaviors from the business areas to the psycho-social life of the world.

New technological developments that will allow people to use their brain and mental potential more effectively and efficiently will come into the agenda. As a result, it is expected that the cognitive properties of the person will improve compared to the natural condition. This improvement will probably be due to new genetic medications that provide cognitive healing, genetic engineering, neural implants, and virtual brains that connect in the form of prosthetics. Integration of prosthetic virtual brains to the human body and/or direct wireless connection of the human brain to the computer systems will result in higher intensities of artificial intelligence, and human problem solving performance will increase to an unprecedented degree.

The Transhumanist Age will be a period of intense and widespread use of artificial intelligence and augmented reality, which are articulated in terms of people (Peddie, 2017). This situation; thinking, communicating and all kinds of interaction will change our behavior to a large extent. The artificial intelligence system that is formed by the integration of artificial intelligence and enhanced reality will work together with implants, for example, optical and auditory, to improve the human perception. When you look at a person in the Transhumanist age, you will have access to much more information than the physical appearance of him/her.

Cybernetics should be underlined when talking about advanced technologies of the Transhumanist Age, which covers 2030 and beyond. Cybernetics is the application of statistical mechanics to communication engineering, the study of human control functions and the mechanical and electronic systems designed to take them in place (Anissimov, 2007; Goertzel & Pennachin, 2007). Thanks to cybernetic technologies, human-machine integration called cyborg will become possible. Cyborg is not the same as bionic, bio-robot or android; is applied to an organism capable of recovering functionality or advanced capabilities due to the integration of some artificial components or technologies based on some kind of feedback.

One of the exciting technologies of the Age of Transhumanism is autonomous robots, which can produce either self or similar. Three-dimensional printers that can produce themselves using the present layered production technology can be considered as a simple example. If such a technology is autonomous, it shows that it can produce its own decisions and act accordingly (Banger, 2016; Fahimi, 2009).

Artificial intelligence has similar functions and features to human thinking system. While the work on artificial intelligence is ongoing, another focus will continue to be on the human brain. Backing up whole or part of the brain, recovering the backup, deleting some information from the brain, loading new information into the brain will continue to create scientific excitement in the way of being real (Wiley, 2015).

The future will be an age of data dominance, pervasive computing, artificial intelligence, smart machines, autonomous mobile robots, and "smart & connected everything" accompanied by a vast speed and ever increasing acceleration of change. As we look from today's business paradigm, the rapid, pervasive and ongoing change requires a fundamental re-invention of business management which should coincide with the conditions of the converging Transhumanism Age.

The main feature of the future management paradigms that differ from the old style of the Industrial Ages will undoubtedly be the artificial intelligence with several applications of machine learning and human's collaborative work with colleague-like autonomous robots. But even in this case, it is also easy to conceive that human will be the core of management. Although some, mainly operational decision-making power will be delegated to the smart machinery; the critical decisions will be made by the human. This human mission necessitates that the human business manager to be equipped with the transhumanist soft and hard skills and also with knowledge and experience.

Managers at all levels will have to adapt to the world of artificial intelligence and smart and connected business environment. So, the transhumanist manager should learn and get well equipped with the necessary management requirements. In such a case, learning space will highly be different from that of the Industrial Ages. The new learning platforms, methods, techniques, tools, and media should be researched to get prepared to a transhumanist business management future with a faster alacrity to compensate for the speed of the technological progress.

THE EXPONENTIAL TECHNOLOGIES FOR FUTURE BUSINESS SPACE

As the scientific and technological advancements continue, it is certain that the new cutting-edge technologies will continue to transform the business space. The core exponential technology which will have the most transformative power in the future business ecosystem will be artificial intelligence centered applications. In this context, a short list may be given as brain-computer interfaces, embeddable smart chips, augmented reality, and wearable smart & connected devices as promising technologies for future businesses. The impacts of such technologies in business models and applications need to be researched.

In the Age of Transhumanism, an object of this context is identified as any physical entity that can contain IT equipment and software embedded in it (Vasseur & Dunkels, 2010). This kind of object is called a "smart and connected object" because of the IT equipment and software it contains as embedded in itself. It has the ability to create and execute some self-developed decisions to be qualified as intelligent. Decision making is accomplished using the artificial intelligence applications implemented by the embedded hardware and software. Also, the object may ask for the help of other smart objects since it has the connection through wireless networks and the Internet.

Artificial intelligence is the type of intelligence exhibited by machines (Corea, 2017). Artificial intelligence is the ability of a computer or a computer-controlled machine or a smart and connected object in general to perform various activities in a manner similar to intelligent living beings. Work in the field of artificial intelligence is usually carried out by analyzing human thinking methods and developing similar artificial directives.

The smart and connected object, which is the core of the exponential technologies, utilizes embedded computing hardware and software to perform artificial intelligence. The falling prices of computerized software and software development products are positively affecting the creation of embedded hardware-software applications. New chip-based microcomputers, namely microcontrollers, are developing the technological space needed to develop intelligent objects. It is possible to connect additional electronic components to these devices for various purposes such as sound, image, communication or data acquisition through sensors, input-output terminals, and ports. Due to the ever-shrinking physical dimensions, such electronic equipment can be embedded almost in any object.

Smart objects with embedded hardware and software utilize the measurement data they acquire via their associated sensors to determine their own and environmental conditions (Rayes & Salam, 2017). The smart object has the possibility to produce some decisions based on the data received from the sensors, and to communicate their situation to the relevant points, or to perform some necessary actions. Physical entities that produce decisions on their own based on the data and perform actions accordingly are called autonomous objects.

Smart and connected objects do not use all of the data they produce or they acquire through the sensors themselves. The data that need to be used elsewhere is transmitted using the communication hardware and protocols (Chaouchi, 2010). The point to which the data is transmitted may be a cloud computing repository, another smart object (device) or a human operator carrying a mobile device to make use of the received data. The data recorded in the cloud computing environment is analyzed in real time or later by analytics software or converted into written/visual reports to be interpreted by relevant persons.

A smart and connected machine in a factory environment can store data about its own operations in the cloud. The information obtained from the processing of these data can be used by factory managers to create more effective and efficient working conditions and performance. The machine manufacturer, authorized to access this data, can improve the machine design by analyzing the data contained in the cloud and can design new and improved versions of the machine.

Smart and connected objects communicate wirelessly in general. They use the wireless connection hardware and protocols. The question of which hardware or protocol to use depends on the criteria such as the data volume to be transmitted, communication frequency, transmission speed and receiver's distance to the sending object. As the Transhumanist Age proceeds, it is expected that the communication between the smart and connected objects devices and the human beings will be performed by the use of two-way brain-computer interaction. It will be a hyper-connected world then.

The context that the emerging technologies will affect the future of business space is called digitalization (Scalabre, 2018). The emergence of exponential technologies will lead to a transformation that will make possible to collect and process data across smart and connected machines. This will give rise to faster, more flexible and more efficient processes to produce and deliver higher quality products at ever-decreasing prices. As a byproduct of this transformation, the profile of the workforce, the philosophy and also the execution of management will come out in a differentiated business environment.

The present technological trends, which will evolve into the Transhumanist mainstream, will acknowledge us about the future business context and management styles. Big data and analytics is the acquisition and comprehensive processing of data from many different sources among which there are production equipment and systems, enterprise and customer management systems, and on-site products. This technology will be used in big-data-driven quality control to analyze real-time and historical lifetime data to identify quality and enhancement issues, to pinpoint new ways to minimize product problems and failures (Lorentz and et al., 2015).

Autonomous robots will physically and cognitively interact with one another and also with human operators. Human and machine associates both will work safely side by side and learn from each other. The smart and connected robots will cost less for their real-time decision-making capacity and work performance get higher. Smart mobility will be one of the most features of the autonomous robots which will change totally the traditional concept of the production process (Fahimi, 2009).

3D printing seems to be the dominant manufacturing technology to prototype and produce individually customized products (Gibson, Rosen, Stucker, 2015). The additive manufacturing devices, methods, and techniques will be used in an increasingly widespread manner to produce small-batched and customized goods almost in any field of business and social life. The additive production by use of 3D printer equivalent devices and coordinate measuring machines (CMM) will be a wide choice for all type of products and components – even in case of producing self-replicas.

As a hybrid of the real world and virtuality, the augmented reality systems will support a variety of business services when combined with mobile devices and wearable and/or embeddable technological products (Peddie, 2017). This technology will provide workers with real-time information to improve decision making. Also, it will be the main instrument for individual worker training in a job environment.

The future business environment is estimated to be a more closely articulated medium of computational and operational technologies. As a consequence of this nesting, simulations will be used more extensively in business operations to leverage real-time information and represent the real world in a virtual model. The model will include systems, production lines, physical machines, human workers, and products in any use place. The simulation technology will support both human and robot operators to test and optimize the machine configurations along the production line to minimize the need for a physical changeover, to decrease downtimes, and to maximize the rate of quality.

The Transhumanist business can be viewed as a worldwide network of everything with the ubiquitous services of cloud computing. Almost all possible things will be enriched with embedded computing and wireless communication facilities. This state of business will allow humans as well as devices to communicate and interact with each other in a multi-way manner. Although the centralized decision making for global optimization in an enterprise is still needed –as in case of an ERP, the pervasive network of things will also decentralize analytics and decision making to enable real-time agile responses.

The Transhumanist enterprise will be vertically integrated with inner components and horizontally integrated with its business ecosystem. Companies, departments, physical and virtual teams, functions, and capabilities will be more cohesive and connected than ever before. The internal and external information integration networks of the enterprise will evolve to enable real-time automated value chains.

THE FUTURE BUSINESS ECOSYSTEM

The Transhumanist philosophy claims that the future is not a place to go, but one to create (Wilkinson, 2007; Brown 2017). So, there will a need for some foresight and future scenario inspirations in order to build such future business ecosystem under the complex effects of the cutting edge technologies. All these materials will give us an augmented profile of how the future business management would look like and what should be researched about the future learning of this context.

Four Future Business Model Scenarios

One of the main challenges for the future business ecosystem will predominantly be based on business model transformation. Exponential technologies, globalization, demographics and similar factors will influence the business cultures and organizational structures. The dramatic change of the ecosystem may give birth to four different business models – namely; a few number of large corporations each of which behaving like a mini-state (i.e. Integration), some specialized collaborative networks and value chains of small and middle sized enterprises (i.e. Fragmentation), several number of organizations mainly dominated by the concerns of social responsibility for a sustainable world (i.e. Social Corporate Responsibility), and social-first and community business companies seeking out meaning and relevance in what they do (i.e. Humanness). There is a chance that all three models may co-exist in some interaction, maybe located in different parts of the world, or in some particular industries and customer segments.

Integration Business Model

In case of "Integration Business Model (InBM)", it is expected that there will exist large global enterprises with annual turnovers that exceed those of many of the developing countries (Wilkinson, 2007; Brown 2017). Such enterprises will provide several opportunities of personal and familial welfare to their talented human resources in order to lock them within the multi-sited organization. On the other hand, the tracking of performance and efficiency metrics of these talented, but high-cost people will be kept smartly by systematic use of the new technologies. Corporate leadership may access and analyze the data about such talented people on a daily basis. The resulting information will provide early warning signals to develop performance remedies.

The search for this particular talent will be done on a global scale which also means that the whole organization will use a unique language globally and a well-designed technological communication system. Since the exponential technologies, high-speed wireless networks and Internet will be pervasive, all corporate and commercial communications and transactions will be done by use of the small-sized, smart & connected devices at any point of the world. To assure consistent high-level quality, the manufacturing sites over the globe will need to create consistency across the organizational supply chain.

Data gathered from several corporate sources in the view of predefined metrics and analytics software will be used to drive business performance of the talented staff. In order to choose the right candidates for the right job positions, complex staff segmentation strategies and several sets of hard and soft skills will be used by the corporate leadership.

Although the enterprise will do individual favors to lock the talented people for retention, the careers of the top talented staff and the senior executives will be managed by their personal career agents for better deals. On the other hand, corporate cultural issues will rise to be important in a continuum. Since the main unit of future work in an enterprise will be the physical and/or virtual team, the leadership teams will have a transformative and sustainable role in the evolution and deployment of corporate culture. So, the team life is an efficient environment to develop and learn the corporate culture.

Another future expectation is that the vocational training comes via intelligent and connected technologies with the use of augmented reality. The new technological tools for the staff to improve their own skills will provide them with greater nonmonetary benefits in having greater efficiency and satisfaction. But one negative potential outcome will be that the enterprise will not be willing to get the load of individual vocational training (Hines, 2011). The function in charge of talented human resources (HR) will assume a broker role of identifying suitable people or places from which to get training. Whether the person in question is an already hired worker or a candidate, the HR function may only suggest where she/he can obtain training that would be required for the particular job position.

New future technologies will be blurring the concept of a workplace. As the exponential technologies pervade every aspect of work and daily life, the spatial differentiation between the in- and out-work will begin to fade. This transparent in-out platform will provide new job and work preferences for the staff independent of spatial constraints.

Business Management Learning

These large scale and pervasive corporates will be more effective in determining and driving lifestyle choices. As a component of this trend, green lifestyle will be a widely accepted set of customer and employee preferences.

Fragmentation Business Model

Big is bad. Small is smart and connected. In accordance with the expectations of "Fragmentation Business Model (FBM)", global large businesses will fragment, and localism will prevail. As a consequence of these events, exponential technologies will empower a low impact, but a high-tech business model. While large companies disappear in time, networks of small companies will prosper (Wilkinson, 2007; Brown 2017). The rise in online systems and IT-based devices will make it possible to buy, sell, trade, even design, and manufacture in virtual environments. In short saying, the future business space will be a complex world of clusters and networks which are composed of separate and smaller business firms. In case of this business model, the main handicap that should be overcome is all types of trade barriers opposing to create a truly free market economy.

The main idea in this model is to prefer fragmentation instead of outsourcing. Small pieces of corporate functions are fulfilled by small, but specialist and innovative providers in highly connected and loosely regulated clusters. Small enterprise member type and structural organization of these clusters may vary based on regional and market characteristics.

Cluster member firms will need to rethink their hiring and firing approaches (Hines, 2011). The small enterprise will pay for talent only when it is needed. This means that time- or project-based employment contracts will be the mainstream employment preference. This will also give flexibility capability to the talented people who may have multiple jobs and careers simultaneously. On the other hand, this employment model will require more flexible hiring, orientation and integration processes on the small enterprise. This is a hard job to succeed. In such a situation, employees and candidates for employment will join craft guilds or talent networks or vocational clusters which will manage career opportunities, provide necessary training, orientation and development opportunities. As these support networks or organizations become more prevalent and substantial, they will take on many of the career responsibilities and services previously met by employers. With this business model, one of the main strategies for a small enterprise is maintaining the optimum supply chain of people from the networked world of talents.

Fragmenting complex business in one hand and networking in the other are the key components of the Fragmentation Business Model. Supply chain management and network/cluster relations management seem to be the important featuring functions of such model.

Corporate Social Responsibility Business Model

The "Corporate Social Responsibility Business Model (CSRBM)" is built on a concept that customers, consumers, and employees force the companies to change (Wilkinson, 2007; Brown 2017). Here, consumers in the first place demand ethics, qualification for sustainable environment and green life as a priority. As a consequence, enterprises enter into a tendency to develop a pervasive and well-understood conscience and responsibility for a sustainable green world. Since the sensitive environmental communities are pervasive, the enterprise's own business model should be so agile that the consumer concerns must be immediately satisfied by clear and informative communication about the products and services.

Ensuring the ethical values that consumers demand is a problem very closely related to the supply chains in which an enterprise takes place. Since a small company cannot affect all organizations of the network or cluster, there should a binding code of ethics for each supply chain which also complies with universal standards. This type of code of ethics is also one of the main and compulsory documents of a company for vertical and horizontal integrations. Also, contracted rigid regulations may be in place covering every chain and event of the supply chain. Since corporate responsibility is a business imperative, it is expected that each company will be under periodical audit with regard to these regulations.

Here are some other attributes of a CSRBM company (Wilkinson, 2007; Brown 2017): The CEO is responsible for the people strategy of the organization, and he drives it. The CEO is in close collaboration with the manager of people and society. This manager, who is a well-networked individual, works with a team consisting of experts from several corporate functions like human relations, marketing, data science, and corporate social responsibility. Also, quality assurance, and vigilance against non-responsible behavior is paramount to minimize risk.

Humanness Business Model

In this business model (HBM) where social-first and community organizations prosper, companies and their staff seek out meaning and relevance in whatever they do (Brown, 2017). Social good, ethics and fairness dominate the behavior of a company. Humanness is a highly valued guiding principle. Crowdfunding is one of the most popular ways of funding. Capital obtained by crowdfunding instruments flows towards fair brands. Technology helps the HBM companies by lowering barriers to entering the crowdfunded capital markets as well as the crowdsourcing platforms. Several key components of the business model are makers, artisans, and supporting networks and guilds.

HBM is the collective response to the business fragmentation. Companies with a strong social and ethical record are preferred by the workers. They give flexibility, autonomy, and fulfillment to their staff. Their concept of work differs from traditional employer-employee relations. Workers feel stronger loyalty to the people with same skills than their employer. Supportive guilds and networks play important roles in protecting, supporting, and training the workers. These organizations also connect independent workers.

Business leaders of HBM companies have responsibility for people direction and management. Digital platforms help workers for their mobility. Matching of workers with demanded skills of companies is done by use of these digital platforms. As the main idea of this business model implies, ethical and transparent management is critical for true success. Relationships with local and central governments and also with civil watcher NGOs are needed to be managed well.

Another Set of Future Business Scenarios

The megatrends are the global forces reshaping society and with it, the business space. These forces affect the redistribution of power, wealth, competition, resources and opportunities all over the world. Technological breakthroughs, demographic shifts, rapid urbanization, economic power shifts, resource scarcity and climate change, as being some of the big forces ready to reshape the future business, should be understood clearly. To explain and foresee the effects of these megatrends, several scenarios may be formed (Brown, 2017).

To conceive the impacts of the megatrends and disruptions on the business ecosystem, it may be a good idea to give brief notes about them. Also, the main inspirations beyond the future scenarios design will be better understood. The megatrends may be classified in 5 categories as 1- Society and the individual, 2- Technology and innovation, 3- Business and the economy, 4- Resources and the environment, 5- Law and politics. Under the impacts of the these megatrends and disruptions, four future scenarios have been developed, namely 1- Forced Flexibility, 2- The Great Divide, 3- Skills Activism, and 4- Innovation Adaptation (UKCES, 2014; Rhisiart, 2016). The properties of these scenarios related to future business are given below.

Scenario 1: Forced Flexibility

As business flexibility becomes more prevalent and incremental innovation dominates the business ecosystem, the economy goes into a modest growth state. This flexibility in work conditions often results in decreasing number of job and work opportunities in parallel with weakening job security especially for low skilled (UKCES, 2014; Rhisiart, 2016).

Due to market volatility and the rising life-qualified needs of the available workforce, business management will offer flexible working options to their high-skilled and talented employees. Companies will recruit from an international repository of high-skilled individuals, talented managers, and technical experts. Since companies will be willing to make a significant investment in top skills and talents, employers will be easy to offer premiums to such people. In case of low skill jobs, employers will have the power to negotiate since employment legislation is limited.

Originating from unfavorable employment conditions, low-skilled workers may face ferocious competition for job positions in almost all economic sectors. In such a case, the low-skilled workers will need to upgrade their vocational knowledge and experience. But the up-skilling of the individual will be his/her own expensive responsibility which he/she should pay. Vocational and workforce training and learning will become a heavy-weight alternative to official school education. Also, it is expected that intergenerational conflicts in the workplace will be a common piece of daily work.

Although employers may not be willing to pay, education and training service providers may offer responsive packages to needs of the business ecosystem for improving employee and candidate worker qualification. Exponential technologies will leverage online learning, especially on-the-job skills development. Another advancement will be in leading-edge learning methods of which an example is peer-to-peer learning. The employees qualified with contemporary vocational knowledge and soft skills will gain the significant multitude of premiums.

Scenario 2: The Great Divide

Although a robust growth rate is realizing due to the strong and high-value producing high-tech industries of the national and/or regional economy, a two-tiered, divided economic and social structure dominates with a concrete separation of more powerful 'haves' and weaker 'have-nots' (UKCES, 2014; Rhisiart, 2016).

Companies will use a pool of skills and talents to recruit. Employers will actively recruit talented people from global and domestic human resource repositories. According to this scenario, companies will market their corporate attributes, i.e. their brand, values, flexible work options, and opportunities for career progression to attract talented employees. In such scenario, work is no longer characterized by location and time constraints. The employees will be expected to accomplish the tasks that they are assigned to, which may be parts of project team assignments. Virtual teamwork will be a common incidence of such work conditions.

This scenario implies that there will be an ever-diverging divide between high-skilled talented employees and other low-skilled workers. Work conditions, context & format of employment contracts, employee-friendly work arrangements and flexible forms of self-organization will be shaped by the power of such talented staff, which will be implemented on employers. New work models, like part-time or project-basis, will be developed for the high-skilled near- or after-retirement employees. In general, the medium- or low-skilled workers will have difficulties to fulfill their potential, and also to find new jobs or keep up with their job positions. Since there will be a substantial governmental support for high-tech industries, it is expected these industries will have to create jobs for medium- and low-skilled workers.

The government will focus on developing a supportive environment for a knowledge-based economy. On the other hand, governmental spending on education and employment promotion initiatives will surprisingly be minimal. The decreasing official share of funding for education and training will result in loss of public education and privatization of educational institutions. The needs for skill-development training may have to be satisfied by the private sector or civil society organizations or other ways.

Scenario 3: Skills Activism

AI-centered technological innovations substitute for the traditional white-collar work with the impact of smart automation. This fact brings large-scale job losses which in turn gives rise to political pressure. As a result, the government, as well as NGOs and large companies, may be forced to design and implement skill development and improvement programs (UKCES, 2014; Rhisiart, 2016).

This scenario assumes that companies will have many available job and work positions, but they will face the challenge of finding the needed right-skilled employees to fill their empty positions. Although the digitalization will increase new job availability in number and variety, shortages may be expected for new forms of manufacturing functions and operations. The rising wave of automation will bring out the need for restructuring of business organizations in all areas of economic sectors. There will be a corporate increase in skill-development involvement. Companies will implement programs for apprenticeships and work-placements during education, training or certification periods of the candidates' they plan to recruit.

Since some jobs will become redundant by the impact of IT automation, longer periods of unemployment for some vocations may be common. High-skilled IT people will be highly demanded by the employers globally. New job opportunities will mostly be short-termed, which in return may challenge employees negatively to acquire new skills continuously.

In such scenario, the government will take an active role in skills delivery. Education and training will have the highest ratio in governmental budgets as compared to the previous realizations. Access to job education and work training opportunities will be open to people of any age, any sex, and any literacy. Government and legal regulations will try to deter strictly employers from abusing free market power in the labor market.

The governmental policies will help the tertiary education providers to lower costs. As a result, this will make education providers to develop more efficient curricula and deliver more adaptive skills for the economy. IT skills will become core modules also for non-technical learners. Exponential technologies will widely be used to promote smart universities. Government and employers will adopt a dual model for vocational education and training systems.

Scenario 4: Innovation Adaptation

Economic stagnation is a prolonged period of slow or no economic growth, usually accompanied by high unemployment. In such stagnant economy, productivity improvement can be achieved by well-defined cost-efficient implementing of ICT solutions to enable business survival (UKCES, 2014; Rhisiart, 2016).

This scenario is based on companies' search for reducing costs and being able to stay competitive. Also, there is a search to reach higher productivity rates by benefiting from the technological infrastructure and employees. The scenario embeds time- or work-limited project jobs and zero-hour contracts. Long-term employees, which are of a limited number, are only hired for core job positions. A comparable part of business work is the orchestration of virtual teams and virtual workforce. Some employees may work from home via online platforms using smart communication systems.

Since companies will search for measures to improve their costs, power of employment will be in the hands of employers, which means that a relative insecurity possibility may exist for the workers. The existing or candidate employees will be in need of reinforcing their knowledge, skill and experience portfolios. In such case, companies may ask for the company-specific custom certifications for employing candidates. Some service jobs, like customer service, will be transformed to virtual forms of work, which may be fulfilled from home. Due to the income pressures, it might be seen that some employees may seek to find supplementary jobs, and raise their incomes.

With this scenario, online learning platforms will be the main instrument for delivering business education and training. This fact will have a consequence that educational and training buildings and some of physical infrastructure will be out of function. So, it is expected that the campus education will transform into home- or work-based learning by use of exponential technologies like augmented reality, wearable smart products, and mobile devices. An extreme way of online learning will by use of multi-way brain-computer communication in progressing years of the Transhumanist Age.

Corollaries Derived From the Future Business Ecosystem Expectations

Technological innovations will greatly impact work styles (FOW Panel, 2016). The constraints pertaining to workspaces will physically blur and disappear in time. Significant advancements in smart and connected technologies will let people complete collaborative projects without being in the same physical space. So, many jobs will be fulfilled in any space at any time. Working in virtual business spaces and non-physical workplaces will be the main trend of the new age.

Since the majority of operational tasks will be taken over by autonomous robots, people will need less to be on the shop floor or in the offices of the factories (Fahimi, 2009). This new situation means that people will be able to choose their working location, time and conditions in order to live their lifestyle choices. New performance-based assessment styles will be developed to determine the payrolls of the employees in such under new virtual work conditions.

In the new age the concepts of work and working will be quite different with respect to their previous business definitions (Pring & et al., 2017). People's new conception of work and working will not be limited only to earning money, but also will include social contributions, communal mutual support, and coexistence, sense of self-satisfaction and societal accomplishment. To realize such conditions, necessary skills development training and education should be offered to all new generations by a variety of official, business, and civil society institutions.

Innovations in exponential technologies will change work styles, and also there will be significant changes in the way companies and the business ecosystem are. Especially increase in free or unconstrained work styles will change corporate organizations. As work styles become more independent, companies will transform to be more flexible structures with an increasing rate of change.

Future companies are expected to be clusters of timed projects (Gemuenden & et al., 2017). This means that employees will be the timed staff of the projects. As soon a project is over, the employee will possibly move to another one in another cluster. Since the border between business organizations become ambivalent and two-way permeable, the full-time employee retention systems may be forced to change, which in return will change the human resources function.

Since the companies will transform to be project-oriented organizations, talented and high-skilled employees will start to choose the projects which offer better options. So, the project organizations will make arrangements to attract such people. While some talented people work only for one project, some other people will allow their time to several numbers of projects. As a consequence of this tendency, some workers will be hired by several companies in different corporate levels.

Professional and vocational skills and knowledge will be needed to update to the technological changes. Improving the skills of the employees will be the responsibility of the employees rather than the companies. So, there will be a variety of training organizations, government bodies, private enterprises, new forms of networked guilds, and civil society organizations to help employees to enhance their skills and update their knowledge. Also, labor unions should evolve into future organizational forms according to the needs of business ecosystem.

Since communication barriers due to languages will be lowered by artificial development, jobs and services will not be restricted by physical borders. Augmented reality technology will make a service to be served virtually as if it is being delivered right next to the user. New economic and social systems will be developed so that gender, ethnicity, nationality, age, and disabilities will not be accepted as barriers for working and living.

New Management and Work Skills

As increasing automation of business processes transform by the impact of exponential technologies, there will be a challenge faced by managers and employees. Some critical skills will have to be gained in order to leverage the new business ecosystem. In the future workplace, human skills such as perceptiveness, creativity, innovativeness, responsibility, sociability, collaboration, and cooperative operation with machines will be highly attractive for supplementing the process-focused hard skills.

The future soft skills of the business ecosystem can be listed as basic thinking skills and symbolism, conscious monitoring & control, hypothesizing, creativity and imagination, subjective decision making, social skills, and responsibility (Allahar, 2014). "Basic thinking skills and symbolism" includes abilities ranging from sensory awareness to symbolic manipulation. Raising people's consciousness with regard to symbols is to be aware of ambiguities since symbols may have different meanings or meaning shifts (Samson, 2013). "Conscious monitoring and control" skill involves persistent awareness to interfere, prevent a fault, recognize an opportunity, or make an agile adjustment when needed. "Hypothesizing" skill comprises recognizing and identifying a problem. The aim is to look for an explanation of the background and root cause of a problem. "Creativity and imagination" skill tries to promote mental activity for invention and innovation. The target is to imagine new alternatives, possibilities, solutions, and enhancements. "Subjective decision making" skill focuses on rational choosing an opportunity by using some criteria after the creative processes have developed several alternatives. "Social skills" include several abilities like forming and leading teams, motivating people to achieve objectives, listening effectively, translating a vision, and conveying enthusiasm in people interactions. "Responsibility" option is the realization of integrated, well-functioning self-consciousness as an embracement of humanity and sustainable living (Allahar, 2014; Samson, 2013).

Another foresight exercise for future assumes six drivers of change - namely extreme longevity, computational world, super-structured organizations with social technologies, the rise of smart machines and systems, new media ecology, and the globally-connected world (Davies et al., 2011).The six drivers which are important in shaping the future landscape emerge ten different skills for the new business ecosystem. These abilities can be listed as sense-making, social intelligence, novel & adaptive thinking, cross-cultural competency, computational thinking, new-media literacy, being transdisciplinary, design mindset, cognitive load management, and virtual collaboration.

"Sense-making" skill is the ability to recognize the meaning or connotation of what is being expressed in order to create insights to decision making. As smart machines take over routine services, process steps and activities, there will be a demand rise for higher-level human thinking work types. "Social intelligence" is the ability to connect to other humans in a sensible way, to sense and inspire reactions and fruitful mutual interactions. Since feeling is just as complicated as sense-making, social & emotional skills of autonomous robots will be limited for some time more. "Novel & adaptive thinking" is the dexterity at human thinking and developing non-routine solutions and non-rule-based responses. "Cross-cultural competency" is the ability to operate under different cultural diversities. It involves global/local adaptability, cross-cultural fluency, and adaptation to societal differences. "Computational thinking" is the ability to transform big amounts of data into abstract concepts by use of computing technologies and to understand the data-based reasoning and decision making. "New-media literacy" is the ability to value, criticize and develop content in new forms of media and to make use of these media for convincing interaction. It also involves gamification, virtual ways of education and machine learning. "Being transdisciplinary" is the ability to recognize concepts across multiple disciplines to analyze and solve complex business problems. Since forthcoming global problems will be too complex to be solved by only one particular discipline, these multi-rooted problems need transdisciplinary approaches and creative techniques. "Design mindset" is the ability to model, design and develop tasks, work processes and business flows for targeted outputs. Managers and workers of the future will use the creative problem-solving approach with the help of exponential technologies and artificial intelligence. "Cognitive load management" is the ability to classify and filter information using a scale of value, importance and priority and to understand how to maximize cognitive functionality using several software tools and data processing techniques. The important question is about which data is valuable or foreseen to be valuable in future. "Virtual collaboration" is the ability to participate in a team, work efficiently within a team, and show a productive, harmonious and cooperative presence as a member of a virtual team. Smart and connective technologies will make easier to work in virtual teams. On the other hand, virtual work environment will demand a new set of competencies like leading virtual teams, influencing over distance, and creating cohesiveness (Davies & et al., 2011).

To be successful in the business ecosystem of the Transhumanist Age, people of business space and organizations involved in an economy will have to come up with foresight in navigating a rapidly changing environment of organizational forms and skill requirements. These needs should continually be reassessed in order to decide for renewals. Managers and workers of the future business ecosystems will need to be lifelong learners who are adaptive and responsive to the ever-developing conditions.

THE FUTURE OF BUSINESS MANAGEMENT LEARNING

The study of visions for the future of learning seems to be that personalization, collaboration, and informal learning will form the core of learning (Redecker and et al., 2011; Redecker & Punie, 2013). The exponential technologies for data collecting, manipulating and sharing will continue to force the future learning mechanisms to be lifelong and life-wide. New generic and cross-disciplinary skills will help people to become lifetime learners so that they can flexibly response to the changes of the future world. They will let people develop their competences and join in collaborative learning and working opportunities.

Creative problem solving, critical thinking, data-based decision making, creativity, innovativeness, collaboration, teamwork, eagerness to learn, adaptiveness to new conditions, digital literacy, predisposition to technology, and entrepreneurship will be the key competencies to develop for a successful social and work life. In addition to these, basic mathematical, verbal, scientific and cognitive skills will continue to be important.

When lifetime and life-wide learning is accepted as the core paradigm for future, the learning system will need to be transformed into a new form composed of well-designed strategies and pedagogical approaches. By ever-increasing use of new technologies like augmented reality, wearable or body-embedded devices, cloud computing, big data, and the Internet of Things, personalized and individual learning and mentoring will become an essential reality of life. So, the educating/training component of the learning system will need to be enhanced or reinvented to exploit the leading edge technologies and other resources to support tailor-made learning ways and experiences. Institutions and organizations of the traditional learning system will be forced to reposition themselves. The new system should have to adopt the attributes like agility, dynamicity, flexibility, and responding in real-time - which are the key requirements of future business life.

Future will be a time slice in which people are likely to changes their jobs and work positions more frequently. Also, job concept will be quite different when compared to the traditional understanding. Dedicated, long-running jobs will be fewer. A manager or an employee will have different job positions in projects of several companies or organizations at the same time. With these new conditions, working people will need to update their skills continuously to fit new job positions.

Due to the future business ecosystem and labor market requirements, working people will be under the pressure to recognize self-responsibility for their qualifications. So, they should take initiative and countermeasures to develop their professional careers. But still, there are questions to be answered. Who will be in charge of improving the match of skill supply and demand? Who will be involved in shaping training and stimulating people to participate in lifetime learning? In future, there will not be easy and immediate answers to these questions with today's views. Mostly existing or prospective employees will be responsible for lifting the weight of career development themselves. Although governments and industry may give some opportunities for self-development, the training requirements will be satisfied by employees of any level. The training services will be mostly offered by specialized companies, guilds or labor networks. The employers may forward existing or candidate employees to the professionally focused training organizations or networks that they accept as valuable. In any case, technological advances in self-learning will allow people to effectively and efficiently qualify or enhance their job skills depending on their needs or levels of competence (Redecker & Punie, 2013).

Business Management Learning

By use of new technologies, peer learning networks and communities, which will allow employees to mutually benefit from each other's knowledge and experiences, will become an important instrument for lifelong learning. Technological platforms will support such learning environments that construct, document and backup this learning process. Thus such knowledge exchange will transform into an accessible and deployable resource which is available anywhere and anytime.

The networked learning and online exchange of knowledge will make professional experiences and personal skills, but unfortunately will be accepted as pieces of informal business and work culture. This kind of informal competencies needs to be turned into officially recognized qualifications. So, new systems and mechanisms should be put in place to certify the informal experiences and skills to obtain formal recognition - by giving supplementary formal training if necessary.

FUTURE RESEARCH SUBJECTS

The future of business management learning needs to be studied in much more details. All research projects and written material that may be classified under this heading should be multidisciplinary or interdisciplinary with collaborative approach, and be relevant to leading edge technologies. They should be aligned with the projected requirements of the future skills needs of the new business ecosystem design.

Some themes for further research may be listed as follows (Suomen Akatemia, 2011; Redecker and et al., 2011; Bach, 2016; Pappas, 2018): 1- Demands arising from technological changes, new market requirements and transforming business ecosystem to learning, skills, and teaching, 2- Business learning analytics and multilevel assessment of learning in business life, 3- Future business learning environments and user-driven contents for business management, 4- Business learning environments, 5- Improving individual conditions for business learning at different ages and human diversities.

A possible deduction for key research areas under "Demands arising from changes in technologies, market requirements and business ecosystem to learning, skills, and teaching" theme may include:

- The future of business education and training in technologically changing society
- New business learning styles, work skills, and management competencies
- Demand and supply of business skills to be matched, which will affect the working of the learning system as a consequence
- Improving business training for highly qualified managers and employees, who face unexpected job evacuations due to their old-fashioned expertise
- Collaborative creation of business knowledge, work skills, and understanding
- Requirements arising from technological progress and business ecosystem changes to learning environments
- New pedagogical solutions and their impact at different levels of business education in the view of exponential technologies
- The relationship between business education and the future workplace
- Media competence and development for business as a networker
- New forms of social participation and engagements for business managers and employees
- Lifetime learning paths for business
- Collaborative and secure working of humans and robots on the same shop floor
- Definition of new ergonomics of collaborative work.

Another deduced set of theme options for future business management learning may be classified under "business learning analytics and multilevel assessment of learning in business life" as:

- Designing new types and forms of business training organizations, networks and platforms by use of new technologies
- Making use of exponential technology devices in monitoring, recording, analyzing, developing, and teaching processes in business and management learning - both in formal and informal learning cases
- Developing new technological follow-up and evaluation methods in order to footprint business learning processes for all environments and levels
- Cybersecurity issues, ethical issues, and threats to corporate privacy and secrecy in high-value and high-intensive business knowledge learning.

Artificial intelligence, big data, digitalization, networking and other technological innovations within the context of exponentiality are promoting future learning and related methods. So, new business research themes and sub-options are coming out which may include:

- Sharing, creating and making use of knowledge collaboratively with others
- Recognition of informally acquired business skills
- New ways and platforms of informal learning in business
- User-generated contents sourcing from managers or employees
- Open learning resources in workplaces
- Increased professional flexibility, flatter hierarchies and open knowledge exchange
- Use of augmented reality, video and simulation techniques for business learning
- Use of digital platforms and 3D manufacturing & prototyping technologies for applied learning
- Gamification of business management and other related subjects
- Tailor-made business learning experiences fostering quality and equity
- Designing new business learning spaces which have physical, virtual, social, and mobile attributes
- Integrating social media and technologies and using them consciously in the design and support of collaborative learning spaces.

One of the trends that will dominate the future of business will be the cultural diversity. So, new research will be needed to take up the socio-cultural challenges faced in business ecosystems involving diversity. Some key research areas may be given as:

- The challenges and opportunities originating from socio-cultural diversities that may affect business learning and learning environments
- Innovative and affordable course materials to be used in business learning
- Mechanisms and methods that will compensate for the weaknesses originating from the previous education and training levels in business
- E-learning methods and platforms, which can be localized and modified across cultures and geographies, for business learning.

Since business training will be a life-long process, people's distinctive features may affect learning context and personal adoption, in positive or negative direction. Learning difficulties may have cultural and social reasons needing to be searched in detail. Some key research themes may be put forward as:

- The opportunities and challenges of the mindset letting go of control and making the learner responsible for his/her business learning
- Alternative methods and tools for business training at different ages
- Transforming business learning into a lifestyle by use of physical, mental and emotional training techniques for all managers and employees
- Analyzing business learning performance using different methods
- Transhumanist code of ethics for business ecosystem.

CONCLUSION

Traditional business learning paradigm cannot keep up with the pace of change of global business ecosystem. Needs for future technological, collaborative, collective and continuous learning requires a different mindset. Future business learning is both a collaborative environment and a continuous experience (Deloitte, 2016). Business learning environment works like recommendation engines that managers and employees find precisely what they need, and what they choose to be equipped with. The learning content will be supplied in and out of the company. So, managers and employees pull learning, navigating and accessing enhancement opportunities both from inside and outside of the organization. This is a comprehensive change when compared to the traditional approach where business skills and knowledge are pushed by trainers and experts. Training options will be available from external digital content sources - namely networks, guilds, NGOs, and other focused organizations. Business learning professionals are specialized people who have strong and deep expertise in their own area. Future business training will use exponential technologies effectively.

Digital learning is expected to be one of the multiple technology-based learning solutions in the future. (van Dam, 2017) However, a new development is that the content of digital learning and digital learning platforms are moving to the cloud. These tools and platforms are becoming accessible across multiple devices and teaching environments and are often being generated, shared and continually updated by learners themselves. Digital learning can be taken on-demand, at any place, and on multiple devices providing a personalized experience. This will make the training, which is supported by visual media, simulations and case studies, to be experiential. The lecture-based model, which is dominated by an expert, will be replaced by this new approach. The main idea for the new style of business learning is people will learn "how to learn" through corporate facilitation and coaching. The traditional business learning approach tries to create a learning agenda which is rigid, detailed and giving no flexibility. On the other hand, future business learning will let people develop themselves within high-level frameworks for broad capabilities.

From the view of future business learning, companies will adopt their staff as customers rather than students to be pressured to learn old-style lectures. Companies giving up full control over learning content and formats, they will shift to ask for diversified skills and talents. Also, they will use new technologies to drive this type of employee-centric business learning. As teams become the dominant component of work, teamwork will be an interactive medium for in-house learning and information exchange (Deloitte, 2016).

REFERENCES

Allahar, H. (2014). The Changing Nature of Work, Jobs of the Future, and Strategic Human Resource Framework. *Research Journal of Human Resources*. Retrieved from https://www.researchgate.net/publication/279191690_The_Changing_Nature_of_Work_Jobs_of_the_Future_and_Strategic_Human_Resource_Framework

Anissimov, M. (2007). *Top Ten Transhumanist Technologies*. Retrieved from https://lifeboat.com/ex/transhumanist.technologies

Bach, E. R. (2016). *The Future of Learning*. Franklin Covey whitepaper. Retrieved from http://franklincovey.dk/wp-content/uploads/2017/09/The-Future-of-Learning-Whitepaper-UK.pdf

Banger, G. (2016). *Endustri 4.0 ve Akilli Isletme*. Ankara, Turkey: Dorlion Yayinevi.

Brown, J. (2017). *Workforce of the Future: The Competing Forces Shaping 2030*. PricewaterhouseCoopers (PWC). Retrieved from https://www.pwc.com/hu/hu/kiadvanyok/assets/pdf/workforce-of-the-future-the-competing-forces-shaping-2030-pwc.pdf

Chaouchi, H. (Ed.). (2010). The Internet of Things: Connecting Objects to the Web. Wiley–ISTE.

Corea, F. (2017). Artificial Intelligence and Exponential Technologies: Business Models Evolution and New Investment Opportunities. New York: Springer. doi:10.1007/978-3-319-51550-2

Davies, A., Fidler, D., & Gorbis, M. (2011). *Future Work Skills 2020*. Institute for the Future for the University of Phoenix Research Institute. Retrieved from http://www.iftf.org/uploads/media/SR-1382A_UPRI_future_work_skills_sm.pdf

Deloitte. (2016). *Global Human Capital Trends 2016 – The new organization: Different by design*. Deloitte University Press. Retrieved from https://www2.deloitte.com/content/dam/Deloitte/global/Documents/HumanCapital/gx-dup-global-human-capital-trends-2016.pdf

Fahimi, F. (2009). *Autonomous Robots: Modeling, Path Planning, and Control*. New York: Springer. doi:10.1007/978-0-387-09538-7

Gemuenden, H. G., Lehner, P., & Kock, A. (2017). The Project-Oriented Organization and Its Contribution to Innovation. *International Journal of Project Management*, *2017*(Sep). Retrieved from https://www.researchgate.net/publication/319672638_The_project-oriented_organization_and_its_contribution_to_innovation

Gibson, I., Rosen, D., & Stucker, B. (2015). *Additive Manufacturing Technologies*. New York: Springer. doi:10.1007/978-1-4939-2113-3

Goertzal, B., & Pennachin, C. (2007). *Artificial General Intelligence*. Berlin: Springer. doi:10.1007/978-3-540-68677-4

Hardyment, R. (2013). *Future Business: The Four Mega-trends that Every Company Needs to Prepare for*. Corporate Citizenship. Retrieved from https://corporate-citizenship.com/wp-content/uploads/Corporate-Citizenship-Research-and-Futures.pdf

Hines, A. (2011). *A Dozen Surprises about the Future of Work*. Wiley Periodicals. Retrieved from https://onlinelibrary.wiley.com/doi/pdf/10.1002/ert.20326

Hines, A. (2018). *Don't Be Surprised by the Future*. Society for Marketing Professional Services. Retrieved from http://www.andyhinesight.com/wp-content/uploads/2018/03/120-Dont-Be-Surprised-by-the-Future_Marketer-February-2018.pdf

Humanity Plus. (2008). *Transhumanist FAQ 3.0*. Retrieved from https://humanityplus.org/philosophy/transhumanist-faq/

Lorentz, M., Rüßmann, M., Strack, R., Lueth, K., & Bolle, M. (2015). *Man and Machine in Industry 4.0*. Retrieved from https://www.bcg.com/publications/2015/technology-business-transformation-engineered-products-infrastructure-man-machine-industry-4.aspx

Panel, F. O. W. (2016). *Future of Work: 2035 – For Everyone to Shine*. Panel Report. Ministry of Health, Labor and Welfare of Japan. Retrieved from http://www.mhlw.go.jp/file/06-Seisakujouhou-12600000-Seisakutoukatsukan/0000152705.pdf

Pappas, C. (2018). *The Top Extended Enterprise Learning Management Systems*. eLearning Industry. Retrieved from https://elearningindustry.com/top-extended-enterprise-learning-management-systems-lms

Peddie, J. (2017). *Augmented Reality: Where We Will All Live*. Cham, Switzerland: Springer. doi:10.1007/978-3-319-54502-8

Pring, B., Brown, R. H., Davis, E., Bahl, M., & Cook, M. (2017). 21 Jobs of the Future: A Guide to Getting – and Staying – Employed Over the Next 10 Years. *Cognizant*. Retrieved from https://www.cognizant.com/whitepapers/21-jobs-of-the-future-a-guide-to-getting-and-staying-employed-over-the-next-10-years-codex3049.pdf

Rayes, A., & Salam, S. (2017). *Internet of Things – From Hype to Reality*. Cham, Switzerland: Springer. doi:10.1007/978-3-319-44860-2

Redecker, C., Leis, M., Leendertse, M., & Punie, Y. (2011). *The Future of Learning: Preparing for Change*. European Commission JRC Scientific and Technical Reports. Retrieved from http://ftp.jrc.es/EURdoc/JRC66836.pdf

Redecker, C., & Punie, Y. (2013). The Future of Learning 2025: Developing a Vision for Change. *Future Learning, 1*, 3-7. Retrieved from https://www.researchgate.net/publication/260863799_The_Future_of_Learning_2025_Developing_a_vision_for_change

Rhisiart, M. (2016). From Foresight to Impact? The 2030 Future of Work Scenarios. *Technological Forecasting and Social Change*. doi:10.1016/j.techfore.2016.11.020

Samson, R. W. (2013). Highly Human Jobs. *The Futurist, 47*, 29-35. Retrieved from https://issuu.com/worldfuturesociety/docs/the_futurist_2013_may-jun

Scalabre, O. (2018). *Embracing Industry 4.0 – and Rediscovering Growth*. Retrieved from https://www.bcg.com/capabilities/operations/embracing-industry-4.0-rediscovering-growth.aspx

Suomen Akatemia. (2011). *The Future of Learning, Knowledge and Skills (TULOS)*. Research Programme 2014-2017. Programme memorandum. Retrieved from https://www.aka.fi/globalassets/awanhat/documents/ohjelmat/tulos-tulevaisuuden-oppiminen-ja-osaaminen/ohjelmamuistio_tulos_en.pdf

UKCES. (2014). *The Future of Work: Jobs and Skills in 2030*. Evidence Report 84. Retrieved from https://www.gov.uk/government/publications/jobs-and-skills-in-2030

van Dam, N. H. M. (2017). *21st Century Corporate Learning & Development: Trends and Best Practices*. Retrieved from https://bookboon.com/en/21st-century-corporate-learning-development-ebook

Vasseur, J.-P., & Dunkels, A. (2010). *Interconnecting the Smart Objects with IP*. Burlington, MA: Morgan Kaufmann–Elsevier.

Wiley, K. B. (2015). *Mind Uploading and the Question of Life, the Universe, and Everything*. Retrieved from https://ieet.org/index.php/IEET2/more/wiley20150720

Wilkinson, A. (2007). *Managing Tomorrow's People: The Future of Work 2020*. PricewaterhouseCoopers (PWC). Retrieved from https://www.pwc.com/gx/en/managing-tomorrows-people/future-of-work/pdf/mtp-future-of-work.pdf

KEY TERMS AND DEFINITIONS

Artificial Intelligence: Artificial intelligence is the ability of a computer or computer-controlled machine to perform various activities in a manner similar to intelligent living beings.

Business Ecosystem: The business ecosystem is a collaborative and competitive economic community consisting of designers, manufacturers, suppliers, customers, consumers, and other related public, private or civil society organizations acting together in order to trade goods and services.

Business Learning: Business learning is the process of learning and developing business skills through the media of education and/or training - in any age, using any channel in any environment. In the new context of business heavy use of technology in learning is expected.

Business Management: Business management is the economic administration of an organization, which includes the corporate activities of setting the strategies, coordinating and supervising the efforts of its human and robot employees to perform its operations and objectives through the use of available resources. New context of business management heavily emphasizes the use of exponential technologies and data processing.

Business Model: A business model is a set of linked and planned activities designed to make profit in the marketplace. It is a way of doing business that an enterprise makes to maintain its sustainability.

Business Skill: Business skill is the ability to carry out a business task effectively with determined performance and results within a given time, material, money, managing power or other kinds of resources.

Exponential Technology: It is a technology that doubles in power or processing speed in every prescribed slice of time, while its cost of ownership halves. Also stated as leading-edge technology.

Transhumanism: It is a futuristic philosophical approach that studies making use of exponential technologies to transform human body and mind.

Chapter 20
Transhumanism and Positive Psychological Capital in Organizational Behavior

Suzan Urgan
Ondokuz Mayıs University, Turkey

ABSTRACT

The efforts to extend the human life have been one of the most discussed topics in all periods of history. Advances in science and technology lead the way to these pursuits. Especially with the developments related to artificial intelligence, it is thought that in many fields, human life will change radically in the future. Transhumanism refers to studies that are performed for the human to live a good life psychologically, physiologically and socially through extending the life span. The ability of a person to live a better life depends on his harmony with hope, optimism, resilience and self-efficacy, which indicate his positive psychological capital, as much as the progress in science and technology. With the study, transhumanism and positive psychological capital have been examined in the framework of organizational behavior, and how life in the future might be has been stated.

INTRODUCTION

A hundred thousand years ago, the history of humanity was shaped by human communities that are not different from modern humans in biological terms. The behaviors of individuals within these human communities were blended with the teachings of the community, apart from that they learned through the wonderful mechanisms of DNA molecules (McNeil, 2007). In the process from the first man to nowadays, when the characteristics of the human being carried by the genetics and all the processes that he later learns are examined, it is seen that primary objective is to try to extend the human life and to live a more comfortable life. In fact, when the old tombs are examined, the findings that come out are expressed as symbols of the desire of the continuation of life after death (Akurgal, 1995). People are always looking for ways of ecologically, geographically or mentally expanding the boundaries of their own existence (Bostrom, 2003). Transhumanism is, according to its proselytizers, the "intellectual and

DOI: 10.4018/978-1-5225-8431-5.ch020

cultural movement that affirms the possibility and desirability of fundamentally improving the human condition through applied reason, especially by developing and making widely available technologies to eliminate aging and to greatly enhance human intellectual, physical, and psychological capacities" (Agar, 2007). Rapid developments in science and technology are seen as a step towards transhumanism by increasing human health and well-being, although it is not expressed as transhumanism now (Rubin, 2008).

It is a fact that science and technological advances prolong human life. However, could the psychology of the human whose life is prolonged physiologically and that reaches comfort be able to adapt to this change? There will be mental developments through expected space colonization and bionic implants and advanced social science and advanced psychology (Bostrom, 2003). In these changes, it is important how to establish the balance between human psychology and change by foreseeing the involvement of psychological interactions in the account. It is not wrong to foresee that the positive psychological capital will fundamentally serve as a solid anchor in these changes. Positive psychological capital that is expressed as a process that brings out the realization potential of the individual by focusing on the positive aspects of him or her, is a very good shield against the brutal effects of changes (Luthans et al., 2007). All together or separately, hope, self-efficacy, resilience and optimism dimensions of the positive psychological capital have significant roles in fulfilling the necessities through internalising the changes (Avey et al., 2011).

Efforts to extend the human life and the process to keep pace with the changes that have emerged at the end of these efforts are leading to an important situation in the field of organizational behavior. This study deals with the situation of the positive psychological capital and the reflections organizational behavior in changes of the transhumanist era.

TRANSHUMANISM

Hesiodos in mythology states human ages as five ages that are successive. These ages are golden age, silver age, bronze age, age of heroes and iron age. Men of golden age lived in the time of Kronos. Golden was the race which the immortals made first of all. They never faced aging. They were dying like sleeping. Everything in the world was theirs and they lived in countless blessings (Cömert, 1972: 8). In ancient Egypt the kings were considered immortal. There was the belief that the kings could grant other people "immortality". They improved the mummification system for this purpose (Mc Neil, 2007). As seen in these examples, efforts of humans to be immortal and attempts to perform this are remarkable. The urns and various items seen in the historical graves show the desire for living after death, so the desire for eternity. The first stone tools are more than 2 million years old. Thus, the history in which human life is depicted is more than 3 million years old (Akurgal, 1995: 20). The tools made of stone at that time have evolved from that day to the present day into devices that are now capable of learning in artificial intelligence laboratories. The mythological heroes' desires of immortality and every invention and discovery meet on a common ground; to prolong human life. Every innovation aims a healthier life through extending the human life while providing the necessary infrastructure for the treatment and prevention of diseases.

According to religious sources, Adam lived in heaven and therefore he did not need any technology at all. In contrast to this view, technical advances, which are regarded as a virtue, have emerged as a way of reaching prosperity. The human-God relationship and similarity, which were destroyed and lost by the first sin of man, has been re-strengthened with mechanical arts. Adam regained the perfection in heaven by applying his intelligence to technical subjects for humanity, and as a result of his efforts to reach specific human strengths (Lecourt, 2003). It is seen that transhumanism has first emerged in Renaissance, when the history of humanity is reviewed. Renaissance suggests a mentality based on logical inferences instead of pure belief. Renaissance humanism has encouraged people to trust their own observations and their own judgments without leaving any subject to religious authority. Renaissance humanism has also created the ideal of a broader personality who is advanced scientifically, morally and spiritually at a high level. It has expressed that human doesn't have any ready form but creating this form is in human's power (Bostrom, 2003). The beauty created by human skills, and its environment that allows to use these skills without any restriction has been quite accepted. This acceptance has revealed the greatest discoveries both in science and art that can be seen throughout human history (Mc Neil, 2007).

No matter where they have emerged, the most important goal of the successes and great discoveries that have been achieved throughout history has always been to prolong human life in a healthy, comfortable and happy way. These efforts have also evolved into the concept of transhumanism. Transhumanism is the intellectual and cultural movement that affirms the possibility and desirability of fundamentally improving the human condition through applied reason, especially by developing and making widely available technologies to eliminate aging and to greatly enhance human intellectual, physical, and psychological capacities (Agar, 2007).The basis of Transhumanism is humanism.Humanism is a philosophical view that makes human valuable over all, and transhumanism follows humanism. In other words, transhumanism suggests that technology and science must be utilized in order to eliminate the humans' unnecessary aspects or the aspects that cannot be changed by humans, such as aging and illness, as well as to increase human abilities (Saka, 2016).

The beginning of the efforts to reach the ideal of immortality is exemplified by the body freezing experiments established in 1967 in the US by the Cryonics Institute. At the basis of these experiments lies the effort to be able to revive people, who are frozen using liquid nitrogen at -196 degrees, again when technology is sufficiently developed (Civelek, 2009).

Transhumanism will be an interdisciplinary movement that will form a superhuman species in a radical way in the near future through going beyond our physical limitations, fragilities and failures. It is conceptualizing by combining human's personality with technology. It's quite dynamic. This movement is a combination of science, philosophy, faith and science fiction (Doedo, 2009).

When the historical flow is analyzed, the environment to make human life more comfortable has been formed in various forms with some inventions and discoveries before and after the Renaissance. However, the movements that emerged between 1648 and 1789 have formed a second environment which has improved the conditions increasingly. Advances in mathematics and science have led to the study of nature events on a mathematical platform. At that time, movements of the moon were expressed mathematically. In addition, the classification system of plants was established. Identified by the concept of rationality, the movement influenced every field from science to technique, from finance to the social life of the individual. Such that, rational behaviors of people drew an inference that these behaviors can self-balance trade and industry (Mc Neil, 2007).

When we look from past to present, we see that these movements have evolved into meanings such as chaos, complexity, uncertainty and irregularity. There is a change present from a mechanic system, which has an order, to complex systems that are nonlinear, fluid, accumulating and varied. Positivist linear assumptions, therefore, seem to have been displaced by a nonlinear, dynamic view that acknowledges the existence of questioning complexity and interrogating diversity (Sözen & Gürbüz, 2012: 348).

Up to this point, we have tried to address the developments that positively affect the human life from a broad perspective. It will be appropriate to discuss future foresight in the light of progress in science and technology. It is not wrong to say that the progress in science and technology will continue to increase exponentially, together with the current advances, in the future as we have discussed above. Thus, it appears that progress in DNA technologies has taken the first place within the future visions. Theoretically, it appears that a single DNA molecule, which influences the prolongation of the human life, continues to live for hundreds of millions of years by copying itself. As a descriptive feature of a gene, the copying makes us close to the immortality. The genes will also provide us with the brains that can be pre-programmed (Dawkins, 2014). DNA sequences and their feature of being added to each other will cause manipulations on the genetic structures of living things. With silicon and steel robots, robots will be created from silicon, steel and living cells in the laboratory. In addition, nerve prostheses for those with brain disease, organs like bionic ear for those with hearing problems will be able to be produced (Brooks, 2007). With such gene technologies, human diseases can be diagnosed and treated at an advanced level. With the genome projects, embryologically healthy, robust people will be born.

There are researchers who say that there will be positive developments that will change human life when future predictions are made considering the next century. They assume that it will normal for people to live a healthy and productive life and to live over a century. Robustness can be increased by manipulation of simple cellular functions. As evidence, it has been shown that the molecule resveratrol has extended the life span of some organisms by 59 times. Another evidence is the studies in the field of neurobiology. These studies have shown that older animals can produce new nerve cells in their brains (Holland, 2007).

The production of vehicles that can travel in sea, air and land will enable people to live a comfortable life. Flexible individual transportation with the aid of computers will reduce the physical fatigue of the individual. At a further level, interplanetary journeys will reveal new discoveries (Holland, 2007).

The science that proceeds in the light of the nonlinear, dynamic viewpoints leads to progress that radically changes everyone's life. Stem cell research, cloning, sequencing of human genome, artificial intelligence, astrobiology and quantum computation are beyond the boundaries of scientific disciplines (Brockman, 2007).

ARTIFICIAL INTELLIGENCE

Among the developments mentioned above, artificial intelligence is at the forefront of researches that will most impact human life. Artificial intelligence is the intelligence exhibited by machines. It is an artificial communication system that is expected to exhibit high cognitive functions or autonomous behaviors such as perception, learning, connecting multiple concepts, thinking, reasoning, problem solving, communication and decision making, which are belonging to the human intelligence. Artificial intelligence elements today include natural language processing, expert systems, vision systems, handwriting recognition and intelligent robots (www. yapay zekâ ve yeni teknolojiler)

Artificial intelligence is an approach that is emerged as a biological imitation of the human brain. This approach involves scanning a real brain slices and revealing a very detailed three-dimensional map and using them to produce an image using computer software (How Long Before Superintelligence, www.nickbostrom.com).

We have seen that artificial intelligence and super intelligence as concepts that are expressed together. By reaching an advanced level of artificial intelligence, technological advances will increase in all areas. Predictable technologies that cover molecular production of which application fields are broader, and in which the development of a super intelligence is possible can be listed as follows:

- *Very powerful computers*
- *Advanced weapons of which their nuclear power could possibly safely be neutralized*
- *Elimination of aging and diseases*
- *Control of human emotion and aspirations*
- *Scanning the brain and application of its algorithmic structures on the computer in a way to protect memory and personality*
- *Reanimation of frozen patients*
- *Very realistic virtual reality* (Ethical Issues in Advanced Artificial Intelligence, www.nickbostrom.com).

There will be three ways in the future that will allow the creation of robots that have a life similar to the life of a human race. The first way is realistic internet apparatus. The second way is mechatronic toy robots that will entertain people and the third is to design more complex systems than the most complex systems that will fulfill the basic functions of artificial intelligence (Pollack, 2009).

We have tried to state innovations envisaged in the field of science and technology from a wider perspective. We have tried to put forward the reflection of these changes on the individual basis by referring to the works done. After that we will look at how technology and science can affect business and working life. We will determine what changes will take place in the organizational context and how it will affect the human who is the subject of these changes.

ORGANIZATION IN THE FUTURE

Before discussing future visions in the organizational context, it is appropriate to consider the developments envisaged in the social field in a general frame. Organizations are related to the external environment and this affects the organizational life. In social life there are changes in family type. There will be an increase in the number of single-parent families and cohabiting people. The aging of single-parent families will emerge as a problem. The increase in childless-couple households and divorce rates will also be another issue. Family ties will gradually weaken with the increase of step-families (OECD, International Futures Programme, 2011).

Considering the next 50 years, it is forecasted that the world population will increase from 1217 billion to 1236 billion. The anticipated increase for the ages 65-79 is 37%, for 80 and over is 54%. On the other hand, a decrease of 12% in the 15-24 age group and 15% in the 25-39 age group is forecasted for the young population. According to the report of Commission of the European Communities (2006), between 2030 and 2050 the number of young employees will continue to decline. But it is predicted that the labor supply will continue to increase until 2030. Women and older workforce will participate more in working life. Especially for women, less secure jobs, and employment forms like temporary agency works will emerge. Therewith, the part-time employment forms are common in Japan, Korea, Germany and Spain even now (OECD, International Futures Programme, 2011).

There are two important trends starting now and will continue in the future. The first trend is that the distribution of organizations is increasing. The second is that social interaction networks and technologies are more accessible. These two trends in the future will make us feel the lack of information workers. In terms of space and time, a flexible working system will be demanded rather than a standard operating system. This will create pressure for sustainable organizations and business areas.

These changes will reveal the obligation of employees to comply with alternative workplaces. These obligations can also be expressed as adaptation to new business practices and as adaptation to new culture that is formed by these business practices (Ouye, 2011).

When we look at future predictions in terms of organizational theories, the changes do not continue on a regular basis. They are irregular. What we need to understand is to be able to see how firms change and to perceive management understandings that can be described as revolution. Of course, it is to learn how to live with these changes (Walsh et al., 2006).

In the coming years, especially office applications will be changed due to the effects of technological changes in the organizational context. The change we are seeing nowadays will be even more widespread with interactive devices, which have removed the need for commuting to office, such as mass media, smartphones, tablets. The forms of work that are not time and space-dependent will continue to increase. A large social network will be established in these works. There will be a greater need, especially for corporate social software (www. iş dünyasını değiştirecek altı trend).

Future-related changes are trends that will radically change the business life in general terms. First of these trends is reflection of the prolongation of average life span, which expresses learning and the increasing global relations within the nature of the career. The second is intelligent machines that take over the activities and repetitive tasks that employees can follow from outside of the organization. The third activity is worldwide change in computer and information systems. Fourth is new communication technologies. In organizational structures, super-changes, social technologies, new forms of production and methods of value creation are shown as fifth trend. The sixth is organizational activities of which flexibility and capacity is increased through global affairs. If we check that these trends will trigger what changes in the future workforce, we will see that the uncodable thinking skills, and high thinking abilities with profound critical and unique creativity skills will gain importance first. Social and emotional intelligent workers will be one step ahead. In terms of technique and management, the gap between jobs that require high skills and jobs that require less skill will deepen. The need for interactions and simulations that can manipulate the environment will also increase. Blogs and podcasts which dominate social life will also dominate the workplaces. Mutual multidisciplinary relationships, sensors, communication tools and computers will create new jobs. The power of filtering out external stimuli and extracting information will become more important. Ancillary technologies and social teams will be a growing trend in businesses (Davies et al., 2011).

HUMAN IN THE TRANSHUMANIST ERA

The developments in science and technology will undoubtedly make people feel very comfortable. Much of the hard work will be done effortlessly. These factors that facilitate human life will create a time gap for the individual. This gap, which we can say time surplus, will leave the individual with problems that are not familiar to him/her.

With technology and automation systems, dependency on human power will be reduced and using this technology will make it easier for individuals to be controlled by some powers. By the help of electronic ID cards, chip will be placed in the human body. This chip will have the ability to read human thought. With this function, people who are against order will be left in a difficult situation (Civelek, 2009).

One of the possible consequences of transhumanism is that the machines take the place of the working class. The natural result of this automation will be the production surplus. The human societies, which are going to consume the production surplus, will gradually become unemployed and perhaps depend on outreach programs for a living. Here is a paradigm evolution. With this evolution that will result in the change of the mentality, the human will have a new consciousness (Civelek, 2009).

Much of human life's meaning arguably depends on the enjoyment, for its own sake, of some habits and behaviors such as humor, love, game-playing, art, dancing, social conversation, scientific discovery, food and drink. It is doubtful whether the activities that make people feel good will continue in the future. What will reveal fitness in the future may be a repetitive, boring and constantly intensive work. In this foresight, the person will not choose this working style on his own volition. In terms of the result, it will not have any quality that gives value to the life (Bostrom, 2006).

Artificial intelligence and super-intelligence can also engage dangerous and harmful technologies. Instead of being beneficial to humanity, it will bring quite harmful situations. Artificial intelligence will affect the lives of billions of people in everyday life. It will reveal many situations that need to be controlled. Artificial intelligence, which can not keep people happy and safe at all times, will put them in difficult situations and narrow stereotypes (Brundage, 2015).

With the development of robot technologies, new economic models are needed to be formed. Major social outbursts will be inevitable in the future due to unemployment. On the other hand, in the context of future transformative opportunities, people will find themselves in a constantly improving and evolving pool of resources. There will be a fine line between biological and artificial, and this hybridization will probably bring about the potential for violence and intimidation. Therefore, there will be predictions that the change will not always be positive (Civelek, 2009).

MAN-MACHINE RELATIONSHIP

Have modernism and technology affected the human, humanitarian values, social life and organizational behavior, which is our topic, positively, or will they? Thereafter, let's look at it from another angle. Modernism, somehow, has also existed as a process that paves the way for traditions to shrink and disappear. The desired link between technology and humanitarian values has not been established as desired. Although techno-scientific civilization is an undesirable consequence, it faces the threat of inhumanity. This has been achieved in the present techno-scientific society by positivism, which is dominant in the usual way of thinking. Metaphysical perception creates confusion through modern wisdom. It therefore makes the people's ways of perception of the world superficial, and leaves them vulnerable to many psychological and social dangers (Choi, 2017).

There may be a generalization in which mankind is threatened. This generalization is that human is a machine, and in this respect, it can be concluded that human is subject to same technological directions as applied to machines routinely. It is expressed that modern science is based on western materialism. In this point, it is assumed that there is nothing but medical molecules. So there is no life potion, there is no soul. There are details to be resolved about live systems. This leaves no doubt that in the next decade or two, there will be intellectual jumping and incompatibility (Brooks, 2007).

In order to see the future, it will be useful to look at the value, which the concepts of human mechanization or humanization of machines will take in the future, on the basis of current values. In the 19th century, the mentality that saw man as the gear of the machine aimed to get more products. Looking from another perspective, the human worshipped what he produced by means of mechanization. Of course, there is no such thing as rejecting the technology and machinery here. Because this idea prevents progress. When the balance can not be established, "machine man" robotizes by being abstracted from his soul, mind and heart. In addition, a new class is created that is convenient for manipulation along with technology. Many values are ignored to increase the number of consumers. Monotony in rationalistic understanding, mathematical reasoning, technique domination, mechanization, and the spiritless materialist, naturalist, and mechanical worldview that they create are the dominant paradigm (Bolay, 2017).

When we look at the man-machine relationship in the perspective of organizational theories, we can see that the classical period only forced people to produce more. Man was not involved in the organization as a social being, or as an individual existing with psychology. Man was being treated as the gear of the machine. Over time, the working environment was tried to be changed with regard to the idea that man can produce more. In this period, expressed as the neo-classical period, a paradigm shift emerged which states that the emotions of man, and partly his environment, must be taken into consideration in order to maximize his efficiency in the organization. Within a certain framework, the resulting system, contingency and post-modern approaches led to the evolution of the man from the producing machine to the machine that buys things. Therefore, crowded human societies have been turned into communities and marketing areas which are ready to buy a product by being manipulated. So, if we reconcile the progress of technology with the subject, the mechanization of man is in a rapid course towards the humanization of the machine.

All these changes do not take place in a way that slowly takes man in and makes him not feel it. Of course, how robust the psychological state of man can be in the face of changes is a topic regarding psychiatrists or psychologists. Within the organization, however, it is not so easy for the individual to keep his own psychological state in balance and to be able to do the work regarding his expertise by accommodating himself to the changes. So the concept of positive psychology comes into play at this point. Regardless of what happens outside, realization power and psychological balance within the individual will help the individual to cope with all kinds of problems. We reserved the next section to the concept of positive psychology. Starting from positive psychology, we will reach to the concept of positive psychological capital and relate it to organizational behavior. We will then try to address transhumanism and positive psychology in a common context by relating them to organizational behavior.

POSITIVE PSYCHOLOGICAL CAPITAL

Throughout the history of mankind, studies that have tried to found what a good life means have opened the doors of positive psychology. Various thinkers have come up with different approaches to this concept of happiness. Thinkers such as Aristotle, Socrates and Plato have suggested that an effort to achieve a virtuous purpose brings happiness. Epicrus and his followers also discussed the concept with pleasure and positive feelings. In recent history, Seligman has come up with the idea of true happiness. According to him, a full and satisfying life makes it meaningful. Positive emotions that make life meaningful are like shields that protect a person from other negative situations (Hefferon & Boniwel, 2011: 3-4).

Seligman has introduced the concept of positive psychology with his theoretical and practical studies. There is the effect of positive psychology in revealing the realization potential of healthy people. For an ordinary human, having a positive psychology also helps to prevent emotional disorders (Seligman, 2005: 5-6).

Positive psychology does not only focus positive in the human, but also gives the power to turn a negative situation to normal. It also includes the ability to manipulate a situation that deviates from standards (Seligman, 2005: 5). It reveals strong aspects of the individual rather than his weaknesses, and draws attention to health and vitality. It encourages individuals to focus on what will improve them rather than what makes them weak (Hefferon & Boniwel, 2014: 2).

The power and virtues that the individual possesses create the substructure of positive psychology. These power and virtues are the concepts that philosophers and religious men have met on common ground throughout history. These concepts are categorized as reason, courage, humanity, justice, moderation and superiority (Peterson & Seligman, 2004).

Each individual has positive and negative periods in his or her life. There are times when the individual feels himself or herself very inadequate and being hit the bottom, and on the contrary there are times when the individual feels that he or she has the power to overcome even the most difficult situations. Positive psychological capital gives the individual the power to make necessary manipulations by accepting them as they are without escaping from the problems and difficulties.

No matter what the circumstances and when they are experienced, the "personal" features of the individual that shows up in every area has a quality beyond times. The realization potential is a step at the top of the individual's needs. In this regard, the psychological capital offers the infrastructure to the system which allows the regular use of this potential of the individuals.

ORGANIZATIONAL POSITIVE PSYCHOLOGICAL CAPITAL

According to Seligman, when an individual is engaged in an activity he builds a psychological capital by investing for the future. Positive psychological capital takes its place in the field of organizational behavior as an element that can be measured by the concept expressed as positive organizational behavior, open to development and transformed into business performance (Luthans et al., 2004)

A balance that is nonfunctional and related to negativity is not useful for humans from past to present day. Thus, it appears that positive psychology has revealed potential profits. Although positive psychological capital is not adequately expressed in the fields of organizational behavior and human resources management, it has an increasing value by the help of studies conducted (Avey et al., 2011: 129-130).

Positive psychological capital, which is considered at the individual level, is related to subjective experience and, over time, serves as a bridge. Experiences in the past have become a necessary element to cope with the problems of the future (Seligman & Csikszentmihalyi, 2000).

The positive reflections of the positive psychological capital, in both social and organizational fields, can be expressed as a protective reserve that protects the individual from whatever the change. In particular, its sub-dimensions, positive organizational science and positive organizational behavior concepts in the organizational context, which we will examine in the following sections, will clarify the issue.

- **Positive Organizational Science:** It is expressed as the union of the studies made to reveal positive, developing and revitalizing phenomena in organizations. It is important that the positive phenomena in organizations can be conceptualized as a culture within the organization by putting out the context and the structural dynamics become functional (Cameron & Caza, 2004).

Positive psychological capital in organizational behavior, of course, emerges as in its nature. However, positive behaviors are not observed in every organization. Because competition is the trigger in particular, ambition, selfishness and greed can be seen. Earning money is the main motivation source. Of course, negative situations such as anxiety, loss of confidence and burnout among employees in such an organization are seen. In such a case, positive psychological capital provides the use of strategies such as problem solving, uncertainty management and positive communication (Cameron et al., 2003: 2).

- **Positive Organizational Behavior:** Positive organizational behavior is the human resources practices that can be measured, improved and managed in the field of work (Youssef & Luthans, 2007)

Positive organizational behavior aims to increase the productivity by revealing the positive aspects of the individual within the organization. Hence, it combines the aims of the individual and the organization on the same ground. It plays a direct role in reaching the business objectives (Kanten, 2016).

There are similarities between positive organizational science and positive organizational behavior. Both are explained by studies that are sources to organizational behavior, and form the basis for human resource practices (Larson & Luthans, 2006: 79).

Positive psychology, which we have stated that there is harmony between both personal and organizational goals in its study fields, propounds a situation beyond human and social capital. It focuses on "who" is the individual rather than "what" the individual knows. There are positive psychological sufficiency in the four subdimensions. These dimensions are hope, optimism, self-efficacy and resilience. For a measurable, open to development and more effective work performance, these factors contribute to performance with better productivity, better customer service and employee satisfaction at today's and tomorrow's workplaces with manageable specifications (Luthans et al., 2004).

- **Hope:** Hope is a positive motivational situation committed to target-oriented energy and ways, in which an individual acts with a sense of successful activity (Avey et al., 2011). It is the perception that the targets can be fulfilled. It refers to energy and ways created with the goal of being successful (Synder, 1991). The ways and hope in the concept of hope are two independent components, but they can not be considered separately (Synder, 2003).

Hope is an open-to-development situation in the management of international entrepreneurship and human resources. It is important in job selection and has a flexibility that can be improved through training (Luthans, 2012). With all these features, the concept of hope can be expressed as one of the most important criteria for the future. Every situation that constantly changes and develops beyond our predictions and control will require us to have hope.

- **Optimism:** Optimism is expressed as positive future expectation that is open-to-development in positive psychology. At the same time, negative events are regarded as transient and special situations which are formed by external factors (Avey et al., 2011). It contributes more to positive psychology than the other dimensions of positive psychological capital. As a broadly used term, it varies in terms of the value that the individual attributes to good and bad events. Optimists are concerned with a positive future, and any negative situation that they encounter is interpreted as a temporary situation. Optimists always make a positive contribution to the situation, while pessimists do not provide the necessary contribution (Luthans et al., 2004)

Optimism in the organization creates a synergy. Optimistic individuals can motivate themselves, they stand against obstacles. They do not make excuses for unsuccessful situations, they are patient (Malik, 2013).

Although optimism yields positive results in the field of organizational behavior, pessimism at a certain dose is beneficial to overcome the future negative situations. Executives who can not adjust the dose of optimism may be late to form the strategies for the future and to make the necessary initiatives. The situation is same for the healthy people, who have constant optimism expectations, since that they are inadequate to anticipate health problems that may arise in the future (Luthans, 2012).

- **Self-Efficacy:** Self-efficacy is the individual's confidence in his or her abilities required for successfully completing specific tasks related to his or her motivation, mental resources and business (Avey et al., 2011). Self-efficacy and trust concepts are used interchangeably.

Individuals with a high level of self-efficacy set their personal goals too high. They make plans and strategies with determination toward these goals. They are self-motivated when implementing their strategic plans and they endure to obstacles. They are undaunted. Therefore, self-efficacy in performing a task is the biggest ingredient of success.

There can be two people with similar skills and efficacy. However, it is likely that the individual with higher level of efficacy performs better. An individual using the same skill sequence performs differently in situations based on the current level of efficacy. This is due to the fact that the efficacy is specific to the field. Therefore, depending on the situation and context, the level of efficacy will vary. Hence, there is a strong relationship between self-efficacy and work-related performance (Bandura & Locke, 2003: 88).

- **Psychological Resilience:** Many problems and difficulties are encountered both in daily life and in the organizational living environment. In the presence of these problems, it is an important achievement to not to be passive and to be able to solve them. Looking at many studies made throughout history, individuals, who were seemed unsuccessful firstly, successfully achieved their goals at the end of many failed trials. Therefore, working without giving up is the key to success. Of course, psychological resilience is the most important part of this.

It is a significant trait to be able to adapt to innovations during the change and to normalize a non-standard situation. Resilience is phenomenon that is characterized by adaptation to changes or serious danger (Masten, 2001). Also, it expresses whether the individual can pull himself or herself together, and display the expected performance or overcome the negative and compulsive living conditions. In organizational behavior, it is consubstantiated with more advanced responsibilities and finding solutions to problems (Luthans, 2002).

Given the common profile of the people who keep up with change, they accept the facts in a solid way. They have deep convictions that are supported by strong values. Meanwhile, they have a natural ability to adapt easily to change (Luthans & Youssef, 2004).

There are traits that are qualified as skill for resilience. These are avoidance of thought pitfalls, detection of icebergs, staying calm and focusing in the face of events, having a belief and placing it to a perspective and having real-time flexibility (Jackson & Watkin, 2004). When these criteria are taken into consideration, achievement of the individuals is spontaneous no matter when. Hence, resilient individuals that approach events optimistically and have hope and robust self-efficacy can easily adapt to every change.

POSITIVE PSYCHOLOGICAL CAPITAL IN TRANSHUMANIST ERA

Everything in the universe can be manipulated with human mind and has a supreme place. Man acts not only with his mind, but also with his heart. There are links that bring people closer together and bound. Surely, mechanical advancement is very beneficial to mankind. The point here that needs to be interpreted is that humanitarian traits and technologybalance each other. In any case, refusing technology and mechanization downgrades civil progress. Technology on the one hand makes things easier for people, and on the other hand it creates situations that are not positive for humanity (Bolay, 2017). The next topic that we will study is how man can be successful with all his traits throughout the changes and how man can reveal his aspects which make him feel happy, in practical terms.

While we were giving general definitions with positive psychology above, we gave the basic purpose of positive psychology, which is to bolster the human in the face of the changes and to make the human happily accomplish both his or her goal and organization's goal. Now let's take a look at whether we can be happy as a whole in the future.

One of the most general definitions of happiness is that a person does not desire anything else. In other words, it is that the person does not need hedonist tendencies as required by the ever-increasing consumer society. It has also been shown through studies that people who are trying to reach happiness by putting tough targets are happier. In the transhumanist era that will emerge in the future, machines and computers will be cheerful by being shaped in flesh and bones and by being abstracted from the emotion and evolving. This artificial joy will not be compared with satisfaction that wise people will achieveat the end of difficulties. Therefore, it is predicted that there will be strong and wise people who internalize the aims of life in a virtuous way and value spirituality in the future (Csikszentmihalyi, 2007).

Humanity will become a whole new consciousness and thought. With the emergence of virtual reality, the difference between consciousness and unconsciousness or the difference between dream and reality will not be realized. A paradigm shift is expected as a result of a quantum leap with interactions of future dynamics. It is therefore more likely that virtual reality is preferred when there is a preference between virtual and normal reality. A blissful future without feelings of pain and tiredness seems more likely in this sense (Civelek, 2009: 117).

In the next century it is assumed that people will not be the most intelligent beings of the earth. Computers equipped with abstract intelligence capacity will catch the human level. This emerging intelligence will not be late for showing itself in all areas of human activities like business, education, politics and arts. The human mind will be in fusion with intelligent machines. The concept of being human will change profoundly. In fact, they all seem to be very useful to humans, but they can also be interpreted as a threat to the contrary. Such that there is a negative approach regarding that the collaboration between genetic engineering, nanotechnologies and robot science, which contain the most powerful technologies, is against human kind (Lecourt, 2003: 63).

After looking at the studies that deal with the development of technology with a non-positive approach, it would be appropriate to explain the topic with its psychological capital dimensions from a different perspective. There are also researchers who consider the future of technology quite optimistically. For the first time, with quantum information technology, humanity is stepping into the field of technology that nature did not use in evolution. In this sense, future technology will create an environment in which new ideas emerge. Since people invent new inventions, inventions for humanity will take place again and a cycle will emerge. So optimism will prevail in the future of science. Just as human beings have been systematically working to understand nature for several centuries, the understanding of the world in the future will be radically different from today. This evokes to be optimistic about the future of religion. What humanity means will be separated from dogmatic rules and discovered (Zeilinger, 2009: 37).

When it is examined in terms of organizational theories, it is appropriate to express the issue of coevolution here. In adaptation of organizations to environmental and technological changes, coevolution theory provides a new logic and an analytic key to organization studies which are long-termed and multilayered or variable. In parallel with optimism, coevolution will provide both rapid and positive development to organizational theory from an integrative point of view and will prevent contention arising from change (Şeşen & Basım, 2012: 234).

With technological advances, the fate of the human species can be in machines' power. People will become so dependent on the machines that they will have to obey them. When the system gets too complicated, we will have to unplug them. There will be ordinary people who use personal computers or cars, and an elite group who use the systems. This elite group won't need to work and they will rule the masses. Depending at the mercy of this little elite group, freedom and happiness of governed people will be shaped (Lecourt, 2003: 119).

Though it seems to be positive, this vision has many risks. Happy but not free masses are foreseen. Because of the skepticism in science, despite the collapse scenarios awaiting man himself and all humanity, hopes will always be with humans because of the infinite flexibility and skill of mankind. Courage, optimism, hope and the potential in human, namely self-efficacy will give power to human to overcome uncertainty and possible turmoil (Smoot, 2009: 81).

In another approach, transhumanism is envisaged as a virtual ecology involving social, political and aesthetic dimensions and mutual connections between them. Within this ecological framework there is a lifestyle based on gender discrimination, racism, xenophobia and consumption (Braidotti, 2014). This leads to a negative expectation of the future when it is judged from past experience. Genocide, wide-ranging pollution and ecological degradation will continue to be linked to each other.

Despite all these, the rise of culture and science, the financial gains in the modern world, and political power may prevent problems in the world. It is a sign of hope that people invest in themselves and others. Foreseeing negative situations about the future and trying to take measures against them shows the resilience of people. The work of great writers, activists, artists, musicians and scientists demonstrates that both the power of the human soul and that people can be efficient by looking positively to the future (Smoot, 2009: 80).

If the movement of an object is affected by another object in the physical universe, then the structures and behaviors of the organizations in the social universe are a function of the dynamics of other organizations and their internal relations. As a result of these changes, it will be necessary to express these dynamic functions in parallel with the changes. Just as entities in the physical environment are in a constant flow of disorder due to entropy, organizations are caught in the same stream. The existence of organizations depends on the energy they can get from this flow. With the internalization of complexity and chaos theories, it is necessary to constantly renew, to obtain new information and to introduce new products (Sözen & Gürbüz, 342). With the same understanding the educated person of the future will be the one who is aware of the necessity of continuing to learn (Drucker, 2009: 295). By fulfilling the obligation to constantly learn and renew in the light of changing paradigms, people will be able to reach prosperity. The ability to find and use the information necessary for this will be the most valuable asset of the individual (Friedman, 2000).

The traits of hope, self-efficacy, resilience and optimism that the individual possesses or will have in accordance with the changing circumstances will transform into a useful element for personal and organizational purposes by gaining an alterable and developable flexibility (Luthans et al., 2004).

Creating an individual and organizational strategy requires renewing with changing paradigms as mentioned above. Prior to that, the low rate of change of environmental and social conditions caused the individual or the business to form more static strategies. The strategies that were made could be used in the future by solving the problems of that day. However, these strategies are not enough for the increasingly complicated environment. Of course their validity is still substantive but not enough. Likewise, in the future, with increasing unpredictability, adapting to environment and coping creates the need for different skills. At the beginning of these talents is the person himself. When a problem arises or a situation deviates from the standard, the necessary strategy to solve it may be to find a solution through trial-and-error by soaking into the same flow. Because there is no time. Hence, an individual will be successful against changes if he or she is resilient, optimist, and hopeful for the future and his or her self-efficacy is robust.

CONCLUSION

In this study, two issues were clarified in order to be able to make a prediction about the future by addressing organizational behavior and transhumanism. In general, when the individual is assessed in organizational life, the first written scientific works were in the mid-19th century. Assuredly, thousands of years ago, the individual was in the organization and continued to operate. The disscussion of the individual in organizational behavior coincides with the mid-19th century as the date of the beginning of scientific research. When the first studies are examined, it is seen that the idea that sees human communities as a part of a clock or a gear of a machine which contributes to production is dominant. The basic idea in this context was based on the basis that the basic motivation of the individual was created by rational methods. Of course, the freedom of the individual within such a system was quite limited. Man was just taking his place in the organizational area as a body that was programmed to work more and produce more. In time, the idea that the human can be efficient by changing his life conditions has been revealed; for example, solving the problems regarding the physical environment like making the workplace much brighter, much warmer. In this sense, the environment in which the individual works has been tried to be arranged. In general, this understanding is seen between 1860 and 1960. In 1960 and beyond, the individual began to be recognized as a social and psychological entity. Nevertheless, in an institutionalized structure, the aspects of man, which are utilised with the skill of technology and are considered as raw materials, were worth considering. The individual, considered to have a social and psychological aspect, continued to maintain his existence and produce within a system or order. Human beings were evaluated by their psychology by taking their basic references from biology, ecology and social environment, rather than from a mechanical environment. In parallel with the gradual change of technology and production systems, the individual showed himself with the efforts to create an order in complexity and chaos. In other words, in the course of history, the individual attempted to realize himself by evolving from a positivist to a post-modern order. From the period in which written scientific studies are obtained, the individual tries to strategically determine the his future location by changing his place from being the gear of machine to being an entity who produces, consumes and exists with his psychology in a social environment. By all means, an understanding that is devoid of ethical values and focused solely on progress, growth or consumption will not benefit humanity. Thus, it is important for the individual to feel more comfortable in the organization, to produce, and to turn the requirements of the transhumanist era in favor of himself and the society.

REFERENCES

Agar, N. (2007). Where to Transhumanism? The Literature Reaches a Critical Mass. *The Hastings Center Report*, *37*(3), 12–17. doi:10.1353/hcr.2007.0034 PMID:17649897

Akurgal, E., (1995). *Anadolu Uygarlıkları*. İstanbul: Net.

Avey, J. B., Reichard, R. J., Luthans, F., & Mhatre, K. H. (2011). Meta-Analysis of the Impact of Positive Psychological Capital on Employee Attitudes, Behaviors and Performance. *Human Resource Development Quarterly*, *22*(2), 127–152. doi:10.1002/hrdq.20070

Bandura, A., & Locke, E. A. (2003). Negative Self-Efficacy and Goal Effects Revisited. *The Journal of Applied Psychology*, *88*(1), 87–99. doi:10.1037/0021-9010.88.1.87 PMID:12675397

Bolay, S. H. (2017). Teknoloji Değer Yaratır mı? In Teknoloji ve Değerler (pp.63-83). İstanbul: İmak.

Bostrom, N. (1998). How Long Before Superintelligence? *International Journal of Futures Studies*, *2*. Retrieved from http://www.nickbostrom.com/superintelligence.html

Bostrom, N. (2003). *The Transhumanist FAQ*. World Transhumanist Association. Retrieved from http://www.transhumanism.org

Bostrom, N. (2003). *Ethical Issues in Advanced Artificial Intelligence*. Retrieved from https://nickbostrom.com/ethics/ai.html

Bostrom, N. (2006). *The Future of Human Evolution* (Vol. 2). Death and Anti Death.

Braidotti, R. (2014). *İnsan Sonrası* (Ö. Karakaş, Trans.). İstanbul: Kolektif.

Brockman, J. (2007). *Gelecek 50 Yıl, Yirmi Birinci Yüzyılın İlk Yarısında Hayat ve Bilim* (N. Elhüseyni, Trans.). İstanbul: NTV.

Brooks, R. (2007). Beden ve Makine Kaynaşması. In Gelecek 50 Yıl içinde (pp. 205-215). İstanbul: NTV.

Brundage, M. (2015). Taking superintelligence seriously Superintelligence: Paths, dangers, strategies by Nick Bostrom. *Futures*, *72*, 32–35. doi:10.1016/j.futures.2015.07.009

Cameron, K. S., & Caza, A. (2004). Contributions to the Discipline of Positive Organizational Scholarship. *The American Behavioral Scientist*, *47*(6), 731–739. doi:10.1177/0002764203260207

Cameron, K. S., Dutton, J. E., & Quinn, R. E. (2003). *Positive Organizational Scholarship*. San Francisco: Berrett-Koehler.

Choi, W. W. (2017). Teknoloji ve Hayatın Varlık Boyutunda Bütünleşmesi. In Teknoloji ve Değerler İçinde (pp. 45-55). İstanbul: İmak.

Civelek, M. E. (2009). *İnternet Çağı Dinamikleri*. İstanbul: Beta.

Cömert, B. (1972). *Mitoloji ve İkonografi*. Ankara, Turkey: Hacettepe University.

Csikszentmihalyi, M. (2007). Mutluluğun Geleceği. In Gelecek 50 Yıl (pp.107-117). İstanbul: NTV.

Davies, A., Fidler, D., & Gorbis, M. (2011). *Future Work Skills 2020*. Institute For the Future For the University of Phoenix Research Institute.

Dawkins, R. (2014). *Gen Bencildir*. Ankara, Turkey: Kuzey.

Doedo, B. (2009). Transhumanism, Technology and The Future: Posthumanity Emerging or Sub-humanity Descending? *The Appraisal Journal*, *7*(3), 39–54.

Drucker, P. (2009). *Büyük Değişimler Çağında Yönetim*. İstanbul: Optimist.

Frieadman, T. (2000). *Lexus ve Zeytin Ağacı Küreselleşmenin Geleceği*. İstanbul: Boyner Holding.

Hefferon, K., & Boniwell, I. (2011). *Positive Psychology: Theory, Research and Applications*. Open University Press.

Hefferon, K., & Boniwell, I. (2014). *Pozitif Psikoloji*. Ankara, Turkey: Nobel.

Helfer, M. E., Kempe, R. S., & Krugman, R. D. (1997). *The battered child* (5th ed.). Chicago: University of Chicago Press.

Holland, J. H. (2007). Bizi Bekleyen Gelişmeler ve Bunları Tahmin Etme Yolu. In *Gelecek 50 Yıl* (pp. 191–216). İstanbul: NTV.

İş Dünyasını Değiştirecek Altı Trend. (2012). Retrieved from http://www.ntv.com.tr

Jackson, R., & Watkin, C. (2004). The Resilience İnventory: Seven Essential Skills for Overcoming Life's Obstacles and Determining Happiness. *Selection and Development Review*, *20*(6), 13–17.

Kanten, P. (2016). Pozitif Örgütsel Davranışın Doğuşu ve Gelişimi. In Örgütlerde Davranışın Karanlık ve Aydınlık Yüzü (pp. 3-62). Ankara, Turkey: Nobel.

Larson, M., & Luthans, F. (2006). Potential Added Value of Psychological Capital in Predicting Work Attitudes. *Journal of Leadership & Organizational Studies*, *13*(2), 76–92. doi:10.1177/10717919070130020601

Lecourt, D. (2003). *İnsan, Post-İnsan, teknik ve yaşam*. Ankara, Turkey: Epos.

Luthans, F. (2002). The Need for and Meaning of Positive Organizational Behavior. *Journal of Organizational Behavior, 23*(6), 695–706. doi:10.1002/job.165

Luthans, F. (2012). *Organizational Behavior*. New York: Mc Graw-Hill Irwin.

Luthans, F., Luthans, K. W., & Luthans, B. C. (2004). Positive Psychological Capital: Beyond Human and Social Capital. *Business Horizons, 47*(1), 45–50. doi:10.1016/j.bushor.2003.11.007

Luthans, F., & Youssef, C. M. (2004). Human, Social and Now Positive Psychological Capital Management: Investing in People for Competitive Advantage. *Organizational Dynamics, 33*(2), 143–160. doi:10.1016/j.orgdyn.2004.01.003

Luthans, F., Youssef, C. M., & Avolio, B. J. (2007). *Psychological Capital: Developing the Human Competitive Edge*. Oxford University Press.

Malik, A. (2013). Efficacy, Hope, Optimism and Resilience at Workplace–Positive Organizational Behavior. *International Journal of Scientific and Research Publications, 3*(10).

Masten, A. S. (2001). Resilience Processes in Development. *American Psychological Association, 56*(3), 227–238.

McNeil, W. H. (2007). *Dünya Tarihi*. Ankara, Turkey: İmge.

OECD. (2011). *The Future of Families To 2030, Projections, Policy and Options, A Synthesis Report*. International Futures Programme.

Peterson, C., & Seligman, M. E. P. (2004). *Character Strengths and Virtues: A Handbook and Classification*. New York: Oxford University Press.

Pollack, J. (2009). Yapay Zekâ Yükselişe Geçecek. In *İyimser Gelecek*. İstanbul: NTV.

Quye, B. J. A. (2011). *Five Trends that Are Dramatically Changing Work and the Workplace*. Knoll Workplace Research.

Rubin, C. T. (2008). What is Good Humanism. In *Medical Enhancement and Posthumanity* (pp. 137-156). Berlin: Springer Science and Business Media.

Saka, G. H. (2016). *Bir Ütopya Olarak Teknolojik Ölümsüzlük Sorunsalı: Teknolojik Ölümsüzlük*. V. Türkiye Lisansüstü Çalışmalar Bildiriler Kitabı. doi:10.12658/TLCK.5.4.B015

Seligman, M. E. P. (2005). Positive Psychology, Positive Prevention and Positive Therapy. In *Handbook of Positive Psychology* (pp. 3-13). Oxford University Press.

Seligman, M. E. P., & Csikszentmihalyi, M. (2000). Positive Psychology: An Introduction. *The American Psychologist, 55*(1), 5–14. doi:10.1037/0003-066X.55.1.5 PMID:11392865

Şeşen, H., & Basım, N. (2012). Birlikte Evrim. In *Örgüt Kuramları* (pp. 221–240). İstanbul: Beta.

Smoot, F. G. (2009). Cesaret, Çünkü Yarın Daha Kötü Olacak! In *İyimser Gelecek* (pp. 77-81). İstanbul: NTV.

Snyder, C. R., Harris, C., Anderson, J. R., Holleran, S. A., Irving, L. M., Sigmon, S. T., ... Harney, P. (1991). The Will and the Ways: Development and Validation of an Individual Differences Measure of Hope. *Journal of Personality and Social Psychology, 60*(4), 570–585. doi:10.1037/0022-3514.60.4.570 PMID:2037968

Snyder, C. R., Lopez, S. J., Shorey, H. S., Rand, K. L., & Feldman, D. B. (2003). Hope Theory, Measurements, and Applications to School Psychology. *School Psychology Quarterly, 18*(2), 122–139. doi:10.1521cpq.18.2.122.21854

Sözen, C., & Gürbüz, S. (2012). Örgütsel Ağlar. In Örgüt Kuramları (pp. 301-326). İstanbul: Beta.

Uludağ İhracatçılar Birliği Genel Sekreterliği. (2017). *Yapay Zekâ*. Retrieved from www.yapayzekâveyeniteknolojiler

Walsh, J. P., Meyer, A. D., & Schoonhoven, C. B. (2006). A Future for Organization Theory: Living in and Living with Changing Organizations. *Organization Science, 17*(5), 657–671. doi:10.1287/orsc.1060.0215

Youssef, C. M., & Luthans, F. (2007). Positive Organizational Behavior in the Workplace: The Impact of Hope, Optimism and Resilience. *Journal of Management, 33*(5), 774–800. doi:10.1177/0149206307305562

Zeilinger, A. (2009). Bilimin, Dinin ve Teknolojinin Geleceği. In İyimser Gelecek (pp. 37-38). İstanbul: NTV.

Chapter 21

An Evaluation of Transhumanist Bill of Rights From Current and Future Perspective:
The Adventure of Technohumanism and Rights

Erdem Öngün
Trakya University, Turkey

ABSTRACT

Science and technology are now radically changing human beings and how they help create various future forms of advanced sapient and sentient life in a transhumanist future and their related rights. In that process, the issue of transhumanist rights for such forms attract a great attention that is worth rethinking. Transhumanist Bill of Rights mainly covers "sentient entities" such as human beings, including genetically modified humans, digital intelligences, cyborgs, intellectually enhanced, previously non-sapient animals, any species of plant or animal enhanced to possess the capacity for intelligent thought, and other advanced sapient life forms. In that respect, the main concern of this chapter basically centers around the question to what extent transhumanist rights will be compatible and applicable enough to meet the needs of all sentient entities and forms on universal basis in a transhumanist world, which stands on the line between a dystopian and utopian future.

INTRODUCTION

It should not be difficult to see the distance mankind has covered from the earliest inventions to the most update devices and gears that are made and meant to serve ' the new human' or 'half-human half-machine'. It all jumpstarted in 1969 with the U.S. Defense Department's Advanced Research Projects Agency Network (ARPANET) that developed protocols used for internet communication today leading to the great internet evolution. The earliest child of the internet technology web 1.0, a read-only static web, was followed by interactive web 2.0 that enabled its users to read and write. With the advent of

DOI: 10.4018/978-1-5225-8431-5.ch021

An Evaluation of Transhumanist Bill of Rights From Current and Future Perspective

3.0, a read-write-execute web, information can be categorized and stored in such a way that a computer can understand it as well as a human. It is somewhat a combination of artificial intelligence and the semantic web. That means the computer can learn what the data means, which will evolve into artificial intelligence by using that information. In other words, computers as smart machines are becoming amazingly flawless at making decisions and reaching conclusions on the basis of large amounts of data. The whloe process signals at one important fact; that is mankind is inevitably drawn into a digital age where intelligent machines with artificial intelligence are now able to learn and make decisions by using complicated algorithms. A super human is on his way with extended abilities beyond limitations and mechanical elements built into the body. A Cyborg or an android, a humanoid robot which was once a fictitious character of movies, seem to have jumped out of TV screens into the real world; a transhumanist future is not far-fetched anymore. It is not the end but maybe just the beginning of a new and super human.

At that point, a very quick question that may come to mind is that whether such new intelligences, sentient, or sapient forms could be matter of a discussion concerning possible legal rights, so-called "transhumanist rights" that these new forms are to possess. What is meant by these rights is that all human beings, sentient artificial intelligences, cyborgs, and other advanced sapient life forms are entitled to rights in a posthuman society.All in all, through technology and science, for example, one may ask whether they have the right to end their involuntary lifespan or achieve immortality, maintain liberty, equality, values of human dignity and solidarity, sustanin or modify their bodies.

In the light of new terms and concepts related to the scope of the chapter, this chapter of the book mainly aims at drawing attention to the rapid transformation of human being and other sapient and sentient forms through technological advancements in the next brave new world of transhumanism and the rights involved. The chapter furthermore introduces Transhumanist Bill of Rights and briefly informs the reader about what changes and challenges may possibly exist within Transhumanist Bill of Rights. It concludes with an argumentation from socio-cultural, socio-economic and ethical perspectives as to how realistically transhumanist rigths could be applicable, acceptable and compatible with various sectors and disciplines from now to the far future. Overall, this chapter has two main objectives: First, introduce terms and concepts related to transhumanism and inform the reader about it through a multifaceted discussion. Second and finally, with a reference to existing Bill of Rights, argue and evaluate the transhumanist Bill of Rights with all the current and future perspectives and challenges involved.

BACKGROUND

It would be better to follow back in far history the efforts of human being in his search for a life full of power, immortality, happiness and wisdom. Seeking to expand the boundaries of his existence, man has always desired to acquire new capacities and talents since the most ancient times. Those capacities and talents were sometimes related to immortality as in The Sumerian Epic of Gilgamesh (approx. 1700 B.C.). Fountain of Youth, the Elixir of Life, Alchemism, and various schools of esoteric Taoism in China also tried hard for physical immortality by way of control over or harmony with the forces of nature. Such medivial thoughts were replaced by Renaissance humanism that encouraged people to rely on their own observations and their own judgment rather than to make reference in every matter to myths or religious authorities. Renaissance humanism also created the ideal of the well -rounded person, one who is highly developed scientifically, morally, culturally, and spiritually. Giovanni Pico della Mirandola's Oration on the *Dignity of Man* (1486) is the landmark of the period, in which he announces that man does not have a readymade form and is responsible for shaping himself. In the 18th and 19th centuries humans began to seek ways to sustain their well-being through the application of science as Condorcet speculated about extending human life span by means of medical science following Benjamin Franklin's cryonics movement and French physician and materialist philosopher Julien Offray de La Mettrie's views about manipulation of human nature in the same way that external objects are done so (Bostrom, 2005). Published in 1932, Brave New World by Aldous Huxley can be regarded as one of the first arguments about human technological transformation. Biotechnology, psychological conditioning, polygamous sexuality, and use of the opiate drug to create a placid, static, conformist caste society are examples of a dystopia that Huxley depicted in his work. All these efforts were actually were directed at one common object: human evolvement through new ways and innovations that marked the beginning of a transhumanization process.

As a term, "transhumanism" is not new as it may seem so. Various terms were coined with a closer meaning to transhumanism. More (2013) traces these terms back to Dante's *Divine Comedy* in 1312, where Dante used the term "transhumanare" meaning " pass beyond the human", which was a religious and spiritual usage at that time. Another example is T.S. Eliot. In his 1935 "Cocktail Party", "transhumanized" meant "illumination" rather than a technologically mediated transformation. More continues with Julian Huxley. In his book "New Bottles for New Wine", the term transhumanism was used to mean "man remaining man, but transcending himself."

However, Coenen (2014) offers a rather futuristic description of transhumanism:

Transhumanism closely links hopes for a satisfaction of utopian desires on Earth with far-reaching schemes of space colonisation, individual Immortality and other techno-eschatological visions. It develops a sort of cyborg and astronaut techno-anthropology. Human biology, except human brain activity, is seen as an obstacle to the human destiny, the cosmic mission of the species (para.28.)

There is no doubt that Friedrich Nietzsche might have been the major inspiration for transhumanism with his doctrine of 'Der Übermensch' (The Overman). In his work *The Overhuman in the Transhuman*, More (2010) cites Sorgner and discusses basic similarities between transhumanism and Nietzsche's philosophy in light of the posthuman and that of Nietzsche's overhuman. Transhumanism attaches great importance to rationality, especially critical rationalism as Nietzsche, too, had an immense respect for critical thinking and valued scientific inquiry. Self-Transformation is one of the basic transhumanist principles of extropy. More (2010b) states that Nietzsche did not say much about technology as a means of self-overcoming, which is actually a part of the process of self-overcoming. However, integrated firmly with will and self-assertion, new technologies allow people new means of becoming who they are – as a further step toward posthuman ideals as (Nietzsche 1885) points out in his Zarathustra's declaration: '*I am that which must always overcome itself.*'

As it can be clearly seen, man's desire to evolve is often supplemented by technology. It is a kind of technology that can also be embedded in human body as a wearable object. This techno-scientific activity is observable in many areas of human life. In other words, human body is augmented with some capabilities. Thus, humans become smarter, stronger, and more capable than ever before. Wearables, contact lenses that can take pictures or video, earbuds that enable people to communicate, exosuits that increase physical strength and gene-editing technology that will help eliminate all heritable diseases are examples of body augmentation. Wearable and implantable brain-machine interfaces (BMIs) will dramatically change the ways in which people communicate with each other, as well as digital devices.

This whole process of transhumanisation will inevitably make people more emphatic, personalized and customized. It is so obvious that transhumanism with all its complex, implicit even scary characteristics will continue to dominate many discussions about human fate. Simply put, transhumanism is all about human enhancement in curing disabilities, health, longevity, intelligence, emotional control, aesthetic expression, spiritual goals and ensuring the best lives for human beings. De Mul (2005) defines transhumanism as the convergence of evolution, humanism and information technology. Similary, according to Harrison and Wolyniak (2015), transhumanism is a movement that promotes the evolution of the human race beyond its present limitations through the use of science and technology. Sandu and Terec-Vlad (2016) describe this transhuman movement as an eclectic and interpretative community that aims at extending human life. To achieve this, decreasing suffering and achieving immortality through technological means of prolonging life is possible by creating a non-human alterity (especially Artificial Intelligence). That is dramatically improving cognitive, sensory and motor performances, and even increasing the person's level of morality. All these human condition enhancements are dependent on the current or immediate progress of science and human technology.

Transhumanists view science as a solution to almost all the world's problems and any social issue. Transhumanism can be described as a techno-optimist discourse. Ideas, concepts and reflections that are associated with transhumanism. They are generally put forward by bioliberal thinkers, bioethicist, engineers, computer scientists and futurist (Ranisch and Sorgner (Eds) 2014).

All considered, it did not take transhumanism long to gather supporters and turn into a movement with many followers and supporters. This movement of transhumanism is summarized by O'Connell in his award winning book *To Be a Machine.* According to O'Connell (as cited in McKie, 2018),

It is their belief that we can and should eradicate ageing as a cause of death; that we can and should use technology to augment our bodies and our minds; that we can and should merge with machines, remaking ourselves, finally, in the image of our own higher ideals.

However, there is also a huge criticism targeted against transhumanism especially by the supporters of bio-conservatism. Annas (2001) finds those benign-looking scientific developments likely to result in genocide that will inevitably lead to the "inferiors" killing off the "superiors" or vice-versa. According to him, being in charge of science, humans have become so powerful that they are under threat of survival of their own species. In the name of individual immortality, well-intentioned scientists lead mankind down the path of species suicide.

Largely based on philosophical, religious and historic documentation, another harsh ciriticism and opposition to transhumanism is observed in *Transhumanism: The History of a Dangerous Idea* by Livingstone (2015). According to him:

Transhumanism is an extension of the dangerous belief in human perfectibility derived from Social Darwinism and eugenics, which flourished in the early twentiethcentury under the sponsorship of the Rockefeller Foundation, before achieving notoriety through the horrors of the Nazi regime. After World War II, when these practices were imported into the United States, the study of what is known as cybernetics, which sought advanced methods of population control, evolved in two directions: the development of the personal computer and a covert CIA "mind-control" project known as MK-Ultra, which fostered the proliferation of psychedelic drugs, in an effort to transform society following the blueprint of Aldous Huxley's Brave New World. [...] (p.6)

Livingstone (2015b) going further names transhumanig as a recent but today's popular pseudo-scientific movement that aims at perfecting the physical and psychological nature of the human being in order to achieve immortality by merging man and machine. Livingstone's criticism about transhumanism is not limited with this. He also argues against the internet 'the global brain' and Google+ aligning itself with American emperialism.

Not all progressions especially technological progress that lies in the core of transhumanism can be accounted for the improvement and welfare of humanity. To suport this idea, Verdoux (2009) posits three anti-progressionist arguments such as futurological, historical and anthropological and based on his arguments he concludes that the most "poor, unpleasent, violent and short" periods of human existence have actually resulted from civilization itself, rather than from lack of technology.

From different perspective, most of the developments and evolutions that aimed at creating a sustainable life for humanity may soon turn into activities that brought together the concept of "crimes against humanity" such as as slavery and genocide, nuclear weapons, extreme genetic manipulations like cloning and inheritable genetic alterations. Technology plays an important role in these alterations that also poses a great threat to the foundation of human rights. Taking human evolution into human's own hands and directing it toward the development of a new species is sometimes termed "posthuman." However, it may be that species- altering techniques, like cloning and inheritable genetic modifications, could provide benefits to the human species in extraordinary circumstances. For example, asexual genetic replication could potentially save humans from extinction if all humans were rendered sterile by some catastrophic event. But no such necessity currently exists or is on the horizon (Annas et al., 2002)

By what has been so far written and read, transhumanism seems to have found quite a lot of space for itself in the related literature. All about transhumanism can not be limited to its sole historical background. Apart from related concepts and terms, furthermore, transhumanism is also striving to spread and realize itself with supporting associations, statements and manisfestos.

THE BILL OF HUMAN RIGHTS AND THE TRANSHUMANIST RIGHTS

The Bill of Human Rights

Before introducing Transhumanist Bill of Rights, the birth of human rights, namely International Bill of Rights, needs to be mentioned. There is no doubt that in the dialectical course of human history, big social, economic and cultural events often gave birth to new concepts, manifestations, change in norms and legal arrangements. Similary, after World War II, mankind had to rethink and evaluate its losses and sufferings and take necessary precautions in order not to experience such a disasterous conflict again. The biggest asset that humanity gained in the aftermath of that war was the Universal Declaration of Human Rights, and the two treaties that followed it.Together they are known as the "International Bill of Rights based on human dignity and equality as well as the principle of non-discrimination.Adopted by the General Assembly on 10 December 1948, International Bill of Rights with 62 main headings and their related articles fundamentally recognizes universal human rights. Among other issues, membership in the human species and respect for basic human rights are central to the meaning and enforcement of human rights, and also essential for the survival of the human species.

The Transhumanist Bill of Rights: Version 1.0 and Version 2.0

Compiled by Zoltan Istvan, an American transhumanist, journalist, entrepreneur, and Libertarian, the Transhumanist Bill of Rights is a suggested bill of rights that covers key political human rights and concerns. Delivered on immortality bus tour, in the autumn of 2015, that rode across the U.S, the futurist-themed bill aims to guide cyborg law and anti-aging civil rights. Transhumanist Bill of Rights recognizes a set of ideas for a sustainable life, freedom, happiness and security of person. The term "sentient entities" that is often repeated in the Transhumanist Bill of Rights or related texts mainly includes human beings, as well as genetically modified ones such as cyborgs, digital intelligences, intellectually enhanced, previously non-sapient animals, any species of plant or animal which has been enhanced to possess the capacity for intelligent thought, other advanced sapient life forms. The Transhumanist Bill of Rights has two versions (Transhumanist Bill of Rights, Version 1.0 and Version 2.0, n.d. See also Appendix 1 and Appendix 2).

Version 1.0

Version 1.0 consists of six articles. Overall, they state and emphasize the rights of human beings, sentient creatures, cyborgs and sapient forms in the posthuman era achieved through advanced science and technology. According to this, they should be given the civil right to end involuntary suffering or extend lifespan and to either maintain or modify their own body so long as it doesn't hurt anyone else. Sentient artificial intelligences, human beings cyborgs and other advanced sapient life forms will be free to take measures against existential risks of the future such as destructive artificial intelligence, asteroids, and plagues, weapons of mass destruction, bioterrorism, war, and global warming. Finally, space travel and outer space explorations will be supported and financed by all nations and goverments in case planet earth becomes uninhabitable or be damaged. Ageing in the transhumanist future is regarded as a disease. In that respect, citizens of all nations and their governments will benefit from scientific and medical technologies to extend their lifespan and stop involuntary ageing. Version 1.0 of the Transhumanist Bill of Rights can be regarded as a shortlisted manifestation of rights seeking liberties to guide sentient artificial intelligences, human beings cyborgs and other advanced sapient life forms in the next brave world. Version 1.0 of the Bill of Transhumanist Rights can be roughly considered as a pathway to a more cutting-edge and comprehensive form of rights involved in the second version.

Version 2.0

Adopted via Electronic Vote on December 25-31, 2016, the Transhumanist Bill of Rights Version 2.0 was developed by members of the U.S. Transhumanist Party, being not static and open to further amendments via future votes of U.S. Transhumanist Party members (Transhumanist Bill of Rights, Version 2.0, n.d. See Appendix 2). The main difference between the two versions of the Transhumanist Bill of Rights is that, before talking about transhumanist rights, Version 2.0 provides a clearer explanation of a levelled information integration of sentience as an entity with information processing capacity and the capacity for intelligent thought. Sentience is ranked as Level 5 information integration according to the following criteria:

Level 0 – No information integration: Inanimate objects that do not modify themselves in response to interaction – e.g., rocks, mountains.

Level 1 – Non-zero information integration: Sensors – anything that is able to sense its environment – e.g., photo-diode sense organs, eyes, skin.

Level 2 – Information manipulation: Systems that include feedback that is non-adaptive or minimally adaptive – e.g., plants, basic algorithms, the system interpreting the output from a photo-diode to determine its on/off state (a photo diode itself cannot detect its own state). Level 2 capabilities include expression of emotion and sensory pleasure and taste aversion.

Level 3 – Information integration – Awareness: Systems with adaptive feedback and able to generate classification – e.g., deep-learning AI, chickens, animals that are able to react to their environment, have a model of their perception but not the world. This level describes animals acting on instinct and unable to classify other animals into more types than "predator", "prey", or "possible mate". Level 3 capabilities involve navigatonal detouring and emotional fever.

Level 4 – Awareness + World Model: Systems wşth a modeling system complex enough to create a world model: a sense of other, without a sense of self. –. Level 4 capabilities are static behaviors and rudimentary learned behaviour – e.g., dogs.

Level 5 – Awareness + World model + Primarily subconscious self model = Sapient or Lucid: Lucidity means to be meta-aware – that is, to be aware of one's own awareness, aware of abstractions, aware of one's self, and therefore able to actively analyze each of these phenomena. If a given animal is meta-aware to any extent, it can therefore make lucid decisions. Level 5 capabilities include the "sense of self", complex learned behaviour, ability to predict the future emotional states of the self and partially the ability to make motivational tradeoffs.

Level 6 – Awareness + World Model + Dynamic Self Model + Effective Control of Subconscious: The dynamic sense of self can expand from "the small self" (directed consciousness) to the big self ("social group dynamics"). The "self" can include features that cross barriers between biological and non-biological – e.g., smartphones with cybernetic features,

Level 7 – Global Awareness – Hybrid Biological-Digital Awareness= Singleton: Complex algorithms and/or networks of algorithms with a capacity for multiple parallel simulations of multiple world models. Level 7 capabilities include the same type of dynamic existing between the subconscious and directed consciousness.

Transhumanist Bill of Rights state that all sentient entities are free to abide by any or all rights within the related document and these rights are not meant to deny or criticize any other universal rights. In that respect, clearly, a common consensus between Transhumanist Bill of Rights and Universal Human Rights is intended. Furthermore, Transhumanist Bill of Rights in Version 2.0 gives more comprehensive and detailed information related to technologically driven improvements of the human condition that might be achieved in the future. These encompass freedom to create cybernetic artificial organs, bio-mechatronic parts, genetic modifications, systems, technologies, and enhancements to extend lifespan, eradicate illness, and improve all sentient life forms and such creations showing great wisdom cannot be considered property and are protected by the rights presented in the bill. Under morphological freedom all sapients will be treated as individuals instead of categorizing them into arbitrary subgroups or demographics. An altered, augmented, cybernetic, transgenic, anthropomorphic, or avatar sentient entity, will have the right to exist, form, and join the neo-civilization. All sentients are eintitled to have reproductive freedom through creation of mind clones, monoparent children, or benevolent artificial general intelligence. All sentient entities also have the right to prevent unauthorized reproduction of themselves in both a physical and a digital context. Individual's DNA, data, or other information should be protected by privacy and security legislation and their duplication without that individual's authorization should not be allowed. To ensure that all members of peaceful communities feel safe, to achieve governmental transparency, and to provide counter-balances to any surveillanince state, sousveillance laws should be enacted. Private internet access should be provided to all sentients except those in legal detention and all sentients have the right to be protected from discrimination and to defend themselves from physical and virtual attack

Societies of the present and future societies should be given basic access to wealth and resources in the pursuits of self-improvement. Poverty will no longer be a fate for the members of these societies. All sentient entities deserve to be the beneficiaries of an unconditional universal basic income irrespective of a sentient entity's life circumstances, occupations, or other income sources. Health, liberty and education for all and free thinking, new ideas, meanings, and values should be encouraged fort he posterity of human kind. A colllective mind sphere should be created to keep self-consciousness for ever. Political ethics and rationality among governments are highly important in order to achieve a non-deceptive world

In summary, Transhumanist Bill of Rights encompasses by reference all of the rights expressed in the United Nations Universal Declaration of Human Rights, and extends these rights to all entities incorporated in Transhumanist Bill of Rights.

FUTURE RESEARCH DIRECTIONS

In many respects, re-engeeniring human future is subject to various discussions from political, ethical and scientific point of view. Related rights concerning post human sentients and sapient forms also put pressure United Nations to make immidiate amendments to the existing Bill of Human Rights.The question as to whom and how this will or can be achieved still remains to be a matter of heated arguments. What if one of world's most advanced autonomous robots, Sophia given citizenship demands rights to bear a human child via artificial insemination and an artificial womb? Implementing Transhumanist Bill of Rights is not and should be the sole concern of one instititution or a group of people; it rather necessitates collaborative think-tank solutions by governments, non-govermental organizations, social and scientific institutions, communities and individulas in the future.

CONCLUSION

An evaluative discussion of Transhumanist Bill of Rights for today and tomorrow to come brings us to a point in which the Transhumanist Bill of Rights can be considered as mostly dedicated to new rights. It is by reference also attributable to the Bill of Rights and Universal Declaration of Human Rights. Human Rights are meant to posit certain standards of human behaviour and those rights need to be protected as natural and legal rights on regular basis. However, it seems that there is more to add to the Bill Human of Rights as science and technology pave way for a post human period in which for emerging and evolving sentient entities and sapient forms, a new interpretation of previously described rights has almost become mandatory to better understand new and posthuman rights. One thing is certain that in both cases humanity ought to be prepared to preserve individual freedom regardless of what communication and information technologies hold for the future For example, the issue of freedom of speech has always been a main concern for the human rights for ages. Similarly, it appears that on the Transhumanist Bill of Rights, freedom of speech should be rehandled. The question is whether morphological freedom proposed in the Transhumanist Bill of Rights and freedom of speech stated Article 18 and 19 of the Universal Declaration of Human Rights can be interrelated. Article 18 and 19 are briefly and mainly concerned with one's right to freedom of thought, conscience and religion and freedom of opinion and expression. In the context of Transhumanism and future of artificial intelligence, the AI won't decide or deceive, it will only analyze and attempt to tag or recommend. In that case, would it mean that an AI would interfere with free speech? So, downloading a browser with a code that blocks certain websites or allowing cookies that track our navigation migh be considered as a violation of free speech as set forth in the UN Bill of Rights. This case already seems to be incompatible with Article 19.

On the rights of persons with disabilities, Hughes (2001) in his presentation on the The Politics of Transhumanism at the 2001 Annual Meeting of the Society for Social Studies of Science Cambridge, MA, talks about Alliance. Founded by Alan Pottinger, Allience is a transhumanist organization for people with disabilities. It supports removing "political, cultural, biological, and psychological limits to self-realization and augmentation". The Ascenders are against "eugenics" and permanent germline modification of the human genome, and concerned that future projects for human enhancement and transcendence may leave behind the disabled. Further, and uniquely among transhumanists, they utter a right to ascension for all:

Every human being has the right to ascension. So it is the duty of the group to constantly keep in mind the need to develop technology, equipment and procedures to counter such 'incurable' conditions and until such devices can be developed to care for those who wish to benefit.(Ascender Doctrine v2: Pottinger, 2002). The assertion that people with disabilities, such as the deaf, have a unique and equally valid culture has led many disability rights activists to reject prenatal screening, genetic engineering and technologies such cochlear implants. The debate within the disability rights movement is sure to add much to democratic transhumanist theory and practice. Transhumanists with disabilities face a much greater challenge with the growing bio-Luddite movement in disability rights circles.

Van Hilvoorde and Landeweerd (2010) give an example where the case of 'bladerunner' Oscar Pistorius in particular is used to illustrate and defend 'transhumanist' ideologies. Such ideologies promote the use of technology to extend human capabilities. It is argued that new technologies will undermine the sharp contrast between the athlete as a cultural hero and icon and the disabled person.

Another example is somatic rights. The term somatic refers to the cell of the body in contrast to the germ line cells. The right to one's body is often decided by some third party, either the paternalists, the hypothetical children, or unreasoned authority. Transhumanists and pro- transhumanists bioethicists recognize that somatic rights are individual rights, which means that unless one harms someone else directly, he or she should be able to do as he or she pleases. This might also mean that there is a lack of an amendment protecting freedom of somatic self-determination.

Eugnics, the science of improving the human species by selectively mating people with specific desirable hereditary traits is a movement that has often cuased heated discussions. In an interview by Andres Lomena with Nick Bostrom and David Pearce about transhumanism and eugenics, the question whether all transhumanists are eugenicist gets an explanatory answer from Bostrom in which he quotes,

...transhumanism supports reproductive rights among other human rights thinking that it is better that reproductive decisions be in the hands of parents, in consultation with their doctor, and within broad guidelines laid down by the state. It would be ethically unacceptable, as well as potentially very dangerous; to have the state impose a one-size-fits-all formula on what kind of people should exist in the next generation. (Bostrom, N. and Pearce, D. Personal Communiation 2007, December)

The other problem with the rights to amend oneself through technology is the financial source and its legitimacy. Bauer (2012) questions the rights of the poor to benefit from enhancement techonolgies and he states that being a citizen is enough to use thsoe rights regardless of economic deficiency. As voluntary transhumanist augmentations and enhancements in human body is a costly process, respective procedures will be available only to those who can afford paying money for it. This will create unfair and unjust treatment of rights among citizens. In addition, in terms of mental and physical capabilities, artificial enhancements will make human beings more effective, which will most likely form a sort of a higher caste. In that cae, regular "non-augmented" humans will be treated as inferior beings against their "augmented superiors". The whole case may but produce crimes, discrimination, human rights infringement, and other negative consequences as emotions are gradually lost.

According to Hawking (as cited in Marsh, 2018), laws against genetic engineering with humans are likely to be passed to prevent the creation of a new species of superhuman that could destroy the rest of humanity. However, some people will hardly resist the appeal to improve human characteristics, such as memory, resistance to disease and length of life.

All in all, Del Aguila and Solana (2015) state that the transhumanistic concept of dignity contradicts three fundamental principles of the Universal Declaration of Human Rights. 1) human dignity is universal, something that all individuals possess only by the fact of being human; (2) human dignity is inherent in human nature and is not dependent on their achievements or their particular "excellencies"; and (3) human dignity applies equally to all persons, not allowing different degrees of it. Accordingly, regardless of technological augmentations and enhancements made at any degree to human in order to create a superior, it should not necessitate renaming "another set of (trans) human (ist) rights" for a privigiled group. However, redefining transforming human is getting difficult as it is losing some basic charateristics of pure human. As human nature is more and more exposed to technological alterations with transhumanism on his free will, his 'new' form of dignity and equality are also jeopardized and become more vulnerable and questionable.

REFERENCES

Annas, G. J. (2001). The Man on the Moon, Immortality, and Other Millennial Myths: The Prospects and Perils of Human Genetic Engineering. *Emory Law Journal, 49*, 753–782. PMID:12645561

Annas, G. J. (2002). Protecting the Endangered Human: Toward an International Treaty Prohibiting Cloning and Inheritable Alterations. *American Journal of Law & Medicine, 28*, 151–178. PMID:12197461

Bauer, K. A. (2012). Transhumanism and its Critics. Fice Arguments against a Posthuman Future. In R. Luppucini (Ed.), Ethical Impact of Technological Advancements and Applications in Society (pp. 232–242). Hershey, PA: IGI Global. doi:10.4018/978-1-4666-1773-5.ch018

Bostrom, N. (2005). A History Of Transhumanist Thought. *Journal of Evolution and Technology / WTA, 14*(1), 1–25.

Bostrom, N., & Pearce, D. (2007, Dec.). *Transhumanism* (A. Lomena, interviewer) [Audio file transcript]. Retrieved from https://www.hedweb.com/transhumanism/index.html

Coenen, C. (2014). Transhumanism In Emerging Technoscience As A Challenge For The Humanities And Technology Assessment. *Journal of Teorija in Praksa, 51*(5), 754.

De Mul, J. (2005). TRANSHUMANISME: de convergentie van evolutie, humanisme en informatietechnologie. *Tydskrif vir Geesteswetenskappe, 45*(2), 159-176.

Del Aguila, J. W. V., & Solana, E. P. (2015). Transhumanism, neuroethics and human person. *Revista Bioética, 23*(3), 505–512. doi:10.1590/1983-80422015233087

Harrison, P., & Wolyniak, J. (2015, Sept. 1). The History of 'Transhumanism. *Notes and Queries, 62*(3), 465–467. doi:10.1093/notesj/gjv080

Hughes, J. J. (2001). *The Politics of Transhumanism, Version 2.0*. Paper presented at the Annual Meeting of the Society for Social Studies of Science, Cambridge, MA.

Huxley, A. (1932). *Brave New World*. London: Chatto & Windus.

Livingstone, D. (2015). *Transhumanism. The History of a Dangerous Idea*. Sabilillah Publications.

Marsh, S. (2018, Oct. 14). *Essays reveal Stephen Hawking predicted race of 'superhumans'*. Retrieved from https://www.theguardian.com/science/2018/oct/14/stephen-hawking-predicted-new-race-of-superhumans-essays-reveal

McKie, R. (2018, May 6). *No death and an enhanced life: Is the future transhuman?* Retrieved from https://www.theguardian.com/technology/2018/may/06/no-death-and-an-enhanced-life-is-the-future-transhuman

More, M. (2010). The overhuman in the transhuman. *Journal of Evolution and Technology / WTA, 21*(1), 1–4.

More, M. (2013). The Philosophy of Humanism. In Transhumanist Reader: Classical and Contemporary Essays on the Science. Hoboken, NJ: Wiley-Blackwell, A John Wiley & Sons Inc. Publication.

Nietzsche, F. (1885). *Zarathustra*. Academic Press.

Ranisch, R., & Sorgner, R. L. (Eds.). (2014). *Post- and Transhumanism: An Introduction*. New York: Peter Lang.

Sandu, A., & Terec-Vlad, L. (2016). A Phenomenological Perspective on Transhumanism from the Perspective of the Spoken of Being. *Postmodern Openings, 7*(1), 67–76. doi:10.18662/po/2016.0701.05

Van Hilvoorde, I., & Landeweerd, L. (2010). Enhancing disabilities: Transhumanism under the veil of inclusion? *Journal of Disability and Rehabilitation, 32*(26), 2222–2227. doi:10.3109/09638288.2010.491578 PMID:20528168

Verdoux, P. (2009). Transhumanism, Progress and the Future. *Journal of Evolution and Technology / WTA, 20*(2), 49–69.

ADDITIONAL READING

Alexander, B. (2004). *Rapture: A Raucous Tour of Cloning, Transhumanism, and the New Era of Immortality*. New York: Basics Books.

Alighieri, D. (2008). *The Divine Comedy*. New York: Chartwell Books. [1321]

Asimov, I. (1993). *Asimov's New Guide to Science*. London: Penguin Books Limited.

Kranzberg, M. (1986). Technology and history: "Kranzberg's Laws". *Technology and Culture, 27*(3), 544–560. doi:10.2307/3105385

Leslie, J. (1996). *The End of the World: The Science and Ethics of Human Extinction*. London: Routledge.

Mitchell, S. (2004). *Gilgamesh: a new English version*. New York: Free Press.

Orwell, G. (1949). *Nineteen eighty four, a novel*. New York: Harcourt.

Regis, Ed. (1990). *Great Mambo Chicken and the Transhuman Condition: Science Slightly Over the Edge*. Reading, MA: Addison-Wesley.

Shelley, M. W. (1818). *Frankenstein; or, The modern Prometheus*. London: Printed for Lackington, Hughes, Harding, Mavor, & Jones.

Young, S. (2006). *Designer evolution: A transhumanist manifesto*. Amherst, NY: Prometheus Books.

Yudkowsky, E. (2004). Collective Volition. Retrieved from http://www.singinst.org/friendly/collective-volition.html

KEY TERMS AND DEFINITIONS

Android: A robot with a human appearance.
Cryonics: The practice or technique of deep-freezing the bodies of people who have just died, in the hope that scientific advances may allow them to be revived in the future.
Cyborg: A cyborg (short for "cybernetic organism") is a being with both organic and biomechatronic body parts.
Eschatology: A branch of theology concerned with the final events in the history of the world or of humankind.
Eugenics: The study or belief in the possibility of improving the qualities of the human species or human population, especially by such means as discouraging reproduction by persons having genetic defects orpresumed to have inheritable undesirable traits (negative eugenics) or encouraging reproduction bypersons presumed to have inheritable desirable traits (positive eugenics).

Extropy: Evolving set of values and standards for continuously improving the human condition.
Sapient: An organism or an entity that has the ability to act with judgment.
Sentient: Having senses; capable of sensing.
Somatic: Of, relating to, or affecting the body especially as distinguished from the germplasm.
Transhumanism: The belief or theory that the human race can evolve beyond its current physical and mental limitations, especially by means of science and technology.

APPENDIX 1

Transhumanist Bill of Rights Version 1.0

- **Article 1:** Human beings, sentient artificial intelligences, cyborgs and other advanced sapient life forms are entitled to universal rights of ending involuntary suffering, making personhood improvements, and achieving an indefinite lifespan via science and technology.
- **Article 2:** Under penalty of law, no cultural, ethnic, or religious perspectives influencing government policy can impede life extension science, the health of the public, or the possible maximum amount of life hours citizens possess.
- **Article 3:** Human beings, sentient artificial intelligences, cyborgs and other advanced sapient life forms agree to uphold morphological freedom – the right to do with one's physical attributes or intelligence (dead, alive, conscious, or unconscious) whatever one wants so long as it doesn't hurt anyone else.
- **Article 4:** Human beings, sentient artificial intelligences, cyborgs and other advanced sapient life forms will take every reasonable precaution to prevent existential risk, including those of rogue artificial intelligence, asteroids, plagues, weapons of mass destruction, bioterrorism, war, and global warming, among others.
- **Article 5:** All nations and their governments will take all reasonable measures to embrace and fund space travel, not only for the spirit of adventure and to gain knowledge by exploring the universe, but as an ultimate safeguard to its citizens and transhumanity should planet Earth become uninhabitable or be destroyed.
- **Article 6:** Involuntary ageing shall be classified as a disease. All nations and their governments will actively seek to dramatically extend the lives and improve the health of its citizens by offering them scientific and medical technologies to overcome involuntary ageing. (**Data sorurce**:Transhumanist Bill of Rights, Version 1.0 (n.d.) In H+Pedia. Retrieved June 12, 2018 from https://hpluspedia.org/wiki/

APPENDIX 2

Article I: All sentient entities are hereby entitled to pursue any and all rights within this document to the degree that they deem desirable – including not at all.

Article II: The enumeration in this Transhumanist Bill Of Rights of certain rights shall not be construed to deny or disparage any other rights retained by sentient entities.

Article III: All sentient entities shall be granted equal and total access to any universal rights to life.

Article IV: Sentient entities are entitled to universal rights of ending involuntary suffering, making personhood improvements, and achieving an indefinite lifespan via science and technology.

Article V: No coercive legal restrictions should exist to bar access to life extension and life expansion for all sentient entities. Life expansion includes life extension, sensory improvements, and other technologically driven improvements of the human condition that might be achieved in the future.

Article VI: Involuntary aging shall be classified as a disease. All nations and their governments will actively seek to dramatically extend the lives and improve the health of their citizens by offering them scientific and medical technologies to overcome involuntary aging.

Article VII: All sentient entities should be the beneficiaries of a system of universal health care.

Article VIII: Sentient entities are entitled to the freedom to conduct research, experiment, and explore life, science, technology, medicine, and extraterrestrial realms to overcome biological limitations of humanity. Such experimentation will not be carried out on any sapient being, without that being's informed consent. Sentient entities are also entitled to the freedom to create cybernetic artificial organs, bio-mechatronic parts, genetic modifications, systems, technologies, and enhancements to extend lifespan, eradicate illness, and improve all sentient life forms. Any such creations that demonstrate sapience cannot be considered property and are protected by the rights presented herein.

Article IX: Legal safeguards should be established to protect individual free choice in pursuing peaceful, consensual life-extension science, health improvements, body modification, and morphological enhancement. While all individuals should be free to formulate their independent opinions regarding the aforementioned pursuits, no hostile cultural, ethnic, or religious perspectives should be entitled to apply the force of law to erode the safeguards protecting peaceful, voluntary measures intended to maximize the number of life hours citizens possess.

Article X: Sentient entities agree to uphold morphological freedom—the right to do with one's physical attributes or intelligence whatever one wants so long as it does not harm others.

This right includes the prerogative for a sentient intelligence to set forth in advance provisions for how to handle its physical manifestation, should that intelligence enter into a vegetative, unconscious, or similarly inactive state, notwithstanding any legal definition of death. For instance, a cryonics patient has the right to determine in advance that the patient's body shall be cryopreserved and kept under specified conditions, in spite of any legal definition of death that might apply to that patient under cryopreservation. Morphological freedom entails the duty to treat all sapients as individuals instead of categorizing them into arbitrary subgroups or demographics, including as yet undefined subcategorizations that may arise as sapience evolves.

However, the proper exercise of morphological freedom must also ensure that any improvement of the self should not result in involuntary harms inflicted upon others. Furthermore, any sentient entity is also recognized to have the freedom not to modify itself without being subject to negative political repercussions, which include but are not limited to legal and/or socio-economic repercussions.

Article XIL: An altered, augmented, cybernetic, transgenic, anthropomorphic, or avatar sentient entity, whether derived from or edited by science, comprised of or conjoined with technology, has the right to exist, form, and join the neo-civilization.

Article XII: All sentient entities are entitled to reproductive freedom, including through novel means such as the creation of mind clones, monoparent children, or benevolent artificial general intelligence. All sentient entities also have the right to prevent unauthorized reproduction of themselves in both a physical and a digital context. Privacy and security legislation should be enacted to prevent any individual's DNA, data, or other information from being stolen and duplicated without that individual's authorization.

Article XIII: All sentient entities have privacy rights to personal data, genetic material, digital, biographic, physical, and intellectual enhancements, and consciousness. Despite the differences between physical and virtual worlds, equal protections for privacy should apply to both physical and digital environments. Any data, such as footage from a public security camera, archived without the consent of the person(s) about whom the data were gathered and subject to legal retention, shall be removed after a period of seven (7) years, unless otherwise requested by said person(s).

Article XIV: Sousveillance laws should be enacted to ensure that all members of peaceful communities feel safe, to achieve governmental transparency, and to provide counter-balances to any surveillance state. For instance, law-enforcement officials, when interacting with the public, should be required to wear body cameras or similar devices continuously monitoring their activities.

Article XV: All sentient entities, with the exception only of those in legal detention, have the right to private internet access without such access being prohibited or circumvented by either private corporations or governmental bureaucracy.

Article XVI: All sentient entities should be protected from discrimination based on their physical form in the context of business transactions and law enforcement.

Article XVII: All sentient entities have the right to defend themselves from attack, in both physical and virtual worlds.

Article XVIII: Societies of the present and future should afford all sentient entities sufficient basic access to wealth and resources to sustain the basic requirements of existence in a civilized society and function as the foundation for pursuits of self-improvement. Present and future societies should ensure that their members will not live in poverty solely for being born to the wrong parents.

Article XIX: Given the inevitability of technology eventually replacing the need for the labor of sentient entities, all sentient entities should be the beneficiaries of an unconditional universal basic income, whereby the same minimum amount of money or other resources is provided irrespective of a sentient entity's life circumstances, occupations, or other income sources, so as to provide a means for the basic requirements of existence and liberty to be met.

Article XX: Present and future societies should provide education systems accessible and available to all in pursuit of factual knowledge to increase intellectual acuity; promote critical thinking and logic; foster creativity; form an enlightened collective; attain health; secure the bounty of liberty for all sentient entities for our posterity; and forge new ideas, meanings, and values.

Article XXI: All sentient entities are entitled to join their psyches to a collective noosphere in an effort to preserve self-consciousness in perpetuity.

Article XXII: Sentient entities will take every reasonable precaution to prevent existential risks, including those of rogue artificial intelligence, asteroids, plagues, weapons of mass destruction, bioterrorism, war, and global warming, among others.

Article XXIII: All nations and their governments will take all reasonable measures to embrace and fund space travel, not only for the spirit of adventure and to gain knowledge by exploring the universe, but as an ultimate safeguard to its citizens and transhumanity should planet Earth become uninhabitable or be destroyed.

Article XXIV: Transhumanists stand opposed to the post-truth culture of deception. All governments should be required to make decisions and communicate information rationally and in accordance with facts. Lying for political gain or intentionally fomenting irrational fears among the general public should entail heavy political penalties for the officials who engage in such behaviors.

Article XXV: In addition to the rights enumerated herein, this Transhumanist Bill Of Rights hereby incorporates by reference all of the rights expressed in the United Nations Universal Declaration of Human Rights, and hereby extends these rights to all entities encompassed by this. (**Data Source:** Transhumanist Bill of Rights, Version 2.0 (n.d.) In U.S. Transhumanist Party– Official Website. Retrieved June 20, 2018 from https://transhumanist-party.org/tbr-2/)

Chapter 22
Statistical Resultant Analysis of Psychosomatic Survey on Various Human Personality Indicators:
Statistical Survey to Map Stress and Mental Health

Rohit Rastogi
ABES Engineering College, India

Devendra Kumar Chaturvedi
Dayalbagh Educational Institute, India

Pallavi Sharma
ABES Engineering College, India

Vishwas Yadav
ABES Engineering College, India

Sumit Chauhan
ABES Engineering College, India

Muskan Gulati
ABES Engineering College, India

Mayank Gupta
Tata Consultancy Services, India

Parv Singhal
ABES Engineering College, India

ABSTRACT

Machines are getting intelligent day by day. Modern science has gifted us many boons but simultaneously the mental, physical and spiritual disorders have surprisingly disturbed smile, peace and definite attitude and lifestyle of individual and all human beings. The stress has been the biggest challenge against mankind like nuclear weapons, global warming, and epidemics. It leads towards tension, frustration, and depression and ultimately in extreme cases towards the suicide or murder of innocents. The happiness index, safety of individual, living parameters have drastically challenged us and India specially has pathetic situation among global quality of life (QoL) index. This chapter is an effort to define a simulated model and framework for the subjective quality of stress into quantitative parameters and mathematically analyzing it with help of popular machine learning tools and applied methods. Using machine intelligence, authors are trying to establish a framework which may work as an expert system and may help the individual to grow self as better human being.

DOI: 10.4018/978-1-5225-8431-5.ch022

INTRODUCTION

Young People's Health Is Vital and Crucial

Most young people are presumed to be healthy but, as per WHO10, an estimated 2.6 million young people aged 10 to 24 year die each year and a much greater number of young people suffer from illnesses 'behaviors' which hinder their ability to grow and develop to their full potential. Since from many years a behavioral patterns established during the time period of the development, this pattern indicates the health problem of the upcoming youth in the future. As we show from 1990 to till date, many things change like morality, morbidity and the sense of communication. Now we have shifted the focus towards the health and safety scheme. We have to understand the problems of the youth and decide the suitable mechanism for providing the solution for these problems.

COMMON MENTAL DISORDERS

In present time 20% young people are suffer from the mental problems, such as substance abuse, suicidal behaviors, eating disorders, depression and other. [10]A meta-analysis of five psychiatric epidemiological studies yielded an estimated prevalence of mental morbidity including 16 mental and behavioral disorders (classified into eight groups of organic psychosis, schizophrenia, manic affective psychosis, manic depression, endogenous depression, mental retardation, epilepsy, phobia, generalized anxiety, neurotic depression, obsession and compulsion, hysteria, alcohol/drug addiction, somatization, personality disorders and behavioral/emotional disorders) of 22.2 per 1000 population among 15 to 24 years[2].

Data available from community based studies on common mental disorders in India depict a high prevalence among the young people, but comparisons and extrapolations need to be cautiously made due to variations across studies. The prevalence of overall psychiatry morbidity (depression, conduct disorder, social anxiety, panic disorder) among adolescents has varied from 12 to 16.5%[6,8]. Pillai, *et.al.* observed a low prevalence of 1.8% of DSM-IV disorders among adolescents aged 12-16 yr. which was attributed to methodological factors and the presence of protective factors[11]. A six years follow up study in Chandigarh showed the incidence rate of psychiatric disorder to be 0.18% per year among the 10-17 yr. old adolescents[13]. Among the few specific common mental disorders, the prevalence of depression has varied from 0.1 to 18.5%[6,8,14,15,16,17], conduct disorders from 0.2 to 9.2%[20,22,15], and anxiety from 0.1 to 24.4%[6,8,11,15,17,23] across different studies. Two studies showed prevalence of severe and extreme grade of depression in 11.2% of the school dropouts and 3% among the school going adolescents aged 13 to 19 yr. and 18.4% among the 9th standard students using Beck's depression Inventory[14,16]. For responding to a problem and promoting mental health we require counseling services in communities and adolescent-friendly.[24]

TO HEAL YOURSELF THROUGH THOUGHTS ALONE

Today science is trying to explore in every field. Scientists are trying to minimize the use of the drugs and the surgery. Thought in alone about yourself and memorize the positive thoughts is one of the best method to regain the energy and prepare for the upcoming problems[6,13].

Energy Healing Techniques to Heal Your Body, Mind and Soul- Acupuncture, an ancient energy healing art that is used for stimulating the flow of energy of the body back into a more balanced state, Crystal Healing, Quantum Healing, Reiki.

PREVIOUS WORK STUDY

The novel usage arose out of Andlin (2005) and BA UM (1990), experiments. He started to use the term to refer not just to the agent but just to the state of the organism as it responded and adapted to the environment. From the later 1960s academic psychologist started to adopt Selly's concept; they sought to quantify "life stress" by scoring "significant life event", and a larger amount of research was undertaken to examine links between stress and disease of all kinds.(Rastogi, R. 2017a,b).

- Bronfort G. (2004) and Budzynski TH et al. (1969), explored types of role stress present among the engineering and management student of India. Role overload, role stagnation and self-role distance were found to be the major stress experienced by the student. In addition, students may feel unfamiliar situations like nervousness, worry, frustration, abasement, depression, etc. The instability of these emotion easily initiates unusual behaviour, which then affect the learning achievements and adjustment ability of students if appropriate timely counselling is not giving by the institutions, teacher and parents, or if they cannot obtain appropriate concern from their peers or siblings.

- Granella F. (1987) and Hans Selye (1979) of National Institute of Mental Health and Neuron Science (NIMHANS), conducted an appraisal of stress and coping behaviour, on a group of 258 male and female undergraduates. Piekarska (2000) pointed out that the essential factors for the formation of stress are frequent and strong. There is related connection between the results of stress and psychological and personality characteristics. (Rastogi.R, 2019 a,b)
- Kadhiravan S., (2002) and Kohn P. James (1986), Scott, D.S. at al. (1980), constructed college chronic 'Life Stress Survey' and focuses on the frequency of chronic stress in the lives of college students. This scale contains items that persist across time to create stress, such as interpersonal conflicts, self-esteem problems, and the money problems. Rastogi and Chaturvedi (2018a,b,c,d,e,f,g,h,I,j,k) have examined sources of stress among undergraduates through similar studies.
- Miller H. Lyle et al. (2003), Misra Ranjita at al. (2005) and Morgam, King et al. (1986): explained that, the dynamic relationship between a person and the environment, in stress perception and reaction, is especially magnified in college student may differ from those faced by their non-student peers. The most significant stressors were items that are time specific or subject specific which support contention Nandamuri et al. (2006), Peper E and Shaffer F (2010), Rains JC et al. (2005) revealed that learning is a function of time allowed, aptitude, quality of instruction and ability to understand instruction. These core academic stressors were found to be relatively unchanged over time, as observed by Ross, Shannon E,et al. (2008), R Plomin et al. (17 Jun 1994) who compared and academic stressors of their previous study with those experienced eight years later.
- McCrory D, (2001), Mechanic David (1978), found that collegiate stressors included: academics, social relationship, finances, daily hassles (for example, parking and being later) and familiar relationships. Within each domain conflict, insufficient resources, time demands, and new responsibilities had characterized stress. One of the most important techniques is the brain-storming

technique. The brain-storming group Comprise of small number of people who are encouraged to think many ideas as to solve problems of creative nature. It encourages delayed evaluation, because evaluation during production has reducing effect on the members. The brain-storming session may have two or more hours. It is a free-wheeling affair with ideas coming very rapidly from all sources. Checklists are prepared by researchers and they must stimulate the production of ideas.

- Vernon H et al. (1999) parental beliefs about education and child's development and its relationship with school performance by taking an objective to study the difference in academic performance of students in relation to gender, intelligence and culture by taking a sample of 200 students selected through random sampling technique and found that there was difference in the total academic performance of students as well as in their scores in language, science, social science with respect to culture but not gender, parents beliefs about development due to learning as well as cognitive processes were relatively positive to students' intelligence quotient as well as to their academic performance.

- Yadav, Ravindra et al. (2012) in their technique established a modified form of brain-storming technique. He developed a process called 'operational creativity'. In this technique, an abstraction of the problem is presented to the group members instead of detailed specific problems as given in Osborn's brain-storming. His argument is that by presenting an extreme abstraction we may get many ideas that are not ordinarily brought out.

STUDY PLOT- SYSTEM DIFFERENT REQUIREMENTS

The Questionnaire will be planned as per study of Different Books. We will Design a control group which will not participate in experiment and seven experimental groups will be generated lets each of 30 in class of 210 students, these will participate under experiment, in regular touch and their feedback will be recorded.

Observations and readings will be recorded in regular intervals. After some time, interval, calculate their difference level, benefit, deviation based on some set of questionnaires. Tools of Data Collection will be in-Other than Control Group will be undergone by standard or developer defined questionnaire instruments with high level of support, confidence and reliability with depth interview-schedules, case study, ethnography and group interactions which would be used for redefining the very notion of psychic challenges.

Participatory observation would be the technique to explore the relation between gender equality and physical and social infrastructure of NCR. Sources of data will be primary and secondary. Official statistics on the National Capital Region would be used to set the background of the study. For the census survey to measure the prevalence of spiritual tools on psychic awareness in NCR, an adequate number of people would be surveyed cutting across caste, class, religion and location.

Total time period for whole operation that is stress recognition and remedy will be 6 months. For recognition of stress level, Thermal imaging and questionnaire may be used and for remedy we will use meditative techniques and biofeedback therapy. For backup, we will store the data in Google Drive or Hard Disk. Python is an easy to learn powerful programming in machine learning. Our user set contains users of all age and is mainly focused on adolescent. The system will comply with all local regulatory policies.

Product Functions

The stress and psycho analyzer will measure the level of stress of an individual and will give remedy to minimize the stress. Product will have an already fed and defined training set which will contain data base on survey, done on the basis of questionnaires. Questionnaire will have 4 levels. In experiment, more than 1000 people will be requested to participate for the survey and a chart will be made on the basis of data obtained. This chart will show a general data.

Product website will contain the data, chart and questionnaires. Then the data for each individual/participant will be taken and it will be compared with the training set. On the basis of that comparison, remedy will be given to participants. Memory Constraints-2 GB memory is required to run python programs.

Operations

Operations that will be done by user on product are

1. Register to our site if the user is new.
2. After registering, user will be able to login to site anytime.
3. The registered user will go through a questionnaire to test the level of their stress.
4. If they will be given with remedies then they have to follow it.

Machine Learning with Python Language: python is a simple, interpreted, free and open source, high Level, portable, object oriented, extensible language which uses following features for data analysis and training- Numpy and Pandas, Scikit Learn, Model Evaluation and Validation, Training and Testing, Metrics for Evaluation. It has several benefits as most suitable for ML as open source- open software license with GPL compatible and it is highly versatile with scikit-learn machine learning library, pandas for data munging, Numpy for data representation, matplotlib for visualization, Django for web application integration, faster and easier to develop prototypes. Its ssupported by industry for deep learning framework by Google(https://www.tensorflow.org/), and used in Hadoop streaming.

Steps for Windows 7 And Above (32 Or 64 Bit)-Step 1: Download the graphical installer Anaconda for Windows at https://www.continuum.io/downloads#_windows
Step 2: Double-click the .exe file to install Anaconda and follow the instructions on the screen.
Step3: Requires 350MB RAM. (Optional)Add to PATH Environment variable: Anaconda2 Installation
Step 4: Dir \Lib & Anaconda2 Installation Dir \Anaconda2\Scripts
Step 5: Create PYTHONPATH variable and add Anaconda2 installation directory

Anaconda Platform

Anaconda is a freemium open source distribution of the Python and R programming languages for large-scale data processing, predictive analytics, and scientific computing, that aims to simplify package management and deployment. Its package management system is conda. Python forces programmers to produce uniform, regular, and readable code by aligning the code vertically in columns according to its logical structure. Uses Python Console, Idle, Spyder. Python comes equipped with interactive development environment (IDLE).

- **To Run Python:** Select cmd and type IDLE, Spyder -> Select cmd and type spyder, Python implementation for data representation for ML, supervised learning/classification, data visualization, data preprocessing.
- **System Interfaces:** HTML5, CSS3, JavaScript and Bootstrap are used for front end of website. PHP is used for back end of website. XAMPP is used for connectivity of database with web pages of website. Platform that is used for making this site is Sublime Text 3.
- **Hardware Interfaces:** Configurations of system on which our project will work will be operating **System:** Linux, Unix, Windows. Web Server: Apache Web Server, LigHTTPD, IIS (with ISAPI_Rewrite installed) PHP Version: for mysql Editions, PHP 5.3 or above with PHP XML extension enabled. For SQL Server Editions, PHP 5.3 or above with PHP XML extension enabled and Microsoft SQL Server Driver for PHP. Database: MySQL 4.1 or above, Microsoft SQL Server 2005 or above.

Supervised Learning

Classification: An algorithmic method to assign any given new element of the dataset to one of a priori provided classes (categories).

- **Training Set:** Set of data used to train the classification model.
- **Testing Set:** Set of data used to verify how well the model performs.
- It is common practice when performing a (supervised) machine learning experiment to hold out part of the available data as a test set.
- **Pycham Platform:** PyCham is an Integrated Development Environment (IDE) used in computer programming, specifically for the Python language. It is developed by the Czech company Jet Brains. It provides code analysis, a graphical debugger, an integrated unit tester, integration with version control systems (VCSes), and supports web development with Django. PyCharm is cross-platform, with Windows, macOS and Linux versions. The Community Edition is released under the Apache License, and there is also Professional Edition released under a proprietary license.
- **Multinomial Logistic Regression:** Multinomial logistic regression is the generalization of logistic regression algorithm. If the logistic regression algorithm used for the multi-classification task, then the same logistic regression algorithm called as the multinomial logistic regression. The difference in the normal logistic regression algorithm and the multinomial logistic regression is not only about using for different tasks like binary classification or multi-classification task. In much deeper it's all about using the different functions. In the logistic regression, the black function which takes the input features and calculates the probabilities of the possible two outcomes is the Sigmoid Function. Later the high probabilities target class is the final predicted class from the logistic regression classifier. When it comes to the multinomial logistic regression the function is the Softmax Function.

- **Use Case:** Use case model is used to show the functions that can be done by a particular user according to their position. So in this model we can see that a particular participant can login, register on site, can take test, can get a result. An administer can manage the whole database and login on website.
- **Product Perspective:** The framework is based on reports named "Statistical Analysis for Effect of Positive Thinking on Stress Management and Creative Problem Solving for Adolescents" and "Study on the Efficacy of Electromyography and Electroencephalography Biofeedback with Mindful Meditation on Mental Health of Youth". In this, authors will make a website which will contain questionnaires. These questionnaires will be used as a source of testing the level of stress of the participant. Every participant will have to give their answers and on the basis of that answers it will be calculated that what is level of stress and what remedy could be used to minimize or remove the stress. Two types of result would be shown that is specializing as well as general. Specialize result would be result for each participant individually and generalize result would be average result for sample of let say 100 people.

ALGORITHM(S) IMPLEMENTATION RESULTS

Graphs and Tables

Table 1 shows the mean of responses given by 399 participants in the survey.

Table 2 shows the variance and standard deviation of responses given by 399 participants in the survey.

Table 3 shows the covariance of the questions 1 to 5 and input for this is response given by 399 participants in the survey. Table 4 shows the covariance of the questions 6 to 10 and input for this is response given by 399 participants in the survey.

Table 5 shows the covariance of the questions 11 to 15 and input for this is response given by 399 participants in the survey. Table 6 shows the covariance of the questions 16 to 20 and input for this is response given by 399 participants in the survey.

Table 7 shows the covariance of the questions 21 to25 and input for this is response given by 399 participants in the survey. Figure 4 is based on table 1

Figure 1. Use case diagram

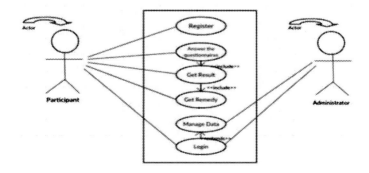

Figure 2. System design and flow chart

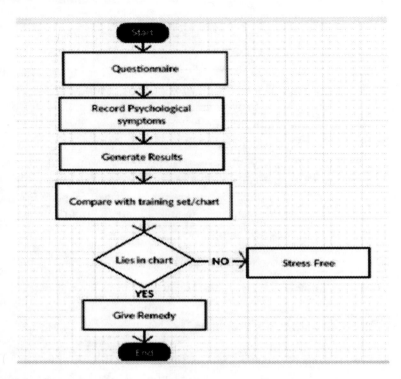

Figure 3. Gantt chart

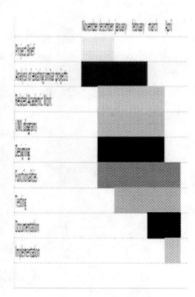

Statistical Resultant Analysis of Psychosomatic Survey on Various Human Personality Indicators

Table 1. Mean

```
q1      3.063063
q2      2.693694
q3      2.828829
q4      2.693694
q5      2.090090
q6      3.648649
q7      3.432432
q8      2.738739
q9      2.027027
q10     2.657658
q11     2.738739
q12     2.234234
q13     2.378378
q14     1.486486
q15     3.486486
q16     1.792793
q17     1.963964
q18     1.324324
q19     2.216216
q20     2.720721
q21     2.297297
q22     1.243243
q23     2.036036
q24     3.108108
q25     2.837838
```

Table 2. Variance and Standard Deviation

Variance = 0.2748672997321667

Standard deviation = 0.5242778840769127

Table 3. Covariance of Question 1 To 5 Table

```
Covariance of question 1 to 5
[[1.20807781 0.45585586 0.58361998 0.5013104  0.43972154]
 [0.45585586 1.35906896 0.62891073 0.45986896 0.63693694]
 [0.58361998 0.62891073 1.50679771 0.64708255 0.61556102]
 [0.5013104  0.45986896 0.64708255 1.45077805 0.6005733 ]
 [0.43972154 0.63693694 0.61556102 0.6005733  1.60999181]]
```

Table 4. Covariance of Question 6 To 10

```
Covariance of question 6 to 10
[[ 1.93906634  0.62604423  0.25282555  0.20958231  0.37862408]
 [ 0.62604423  2.37493857  0.03218673 -0.01179361  0.33120393]
 [ 0.25282555  0.03218673  2.26748567 -0.11105651  0.34610975]
 [ 0.20958231 -0.01179361 -0.11105651  1.64471744  0.37297297]
 [ 0.37862408  0.33120393  0.34610975  0.37297297  1.75446355]]
```

Table 5. Covariance of Question 11 To 15

```
[[ 1.55839476  0.4981163   0.27248157 -0.00010011  0.46461916]
 [ 0.4981163   1.50027191  0.08329238  0.26683047  0.67592138]
 [ 0.27248157  0.08329238  1.49189189 -0.07665848  0.54152334]
 [-0.00010011  0.26683047 -0.07665848  1.21572482  0.05208845]
 [ 0.46461916  0.67592138  0.54152334  0.05208845  1.81572482]]
```

Table 6. Covariance of Question 16 To 20

```
[[1.16676677 0.45610156 0.195086   0.32702703 0.2961507 ]
 [0.45610156 0.94414414 0.16633907 0.40786241 0.27166257]
 [0.195086   0.16633907 0.78476658 0.07469287 0.28230958]
 [0.32702703 0.40786241 0.07469287 1.55282555 0.27002457]
 [0.2961507  0.27166257 0.28230958 0.27002457 1.74856675]]
```

Table 7. Covariance of Question 21 To 25

```
[[1.66535627 0.35428975 0.73464373 0.67665848 0.52137592]
 [0.35428975 0.62211302 0.19115479 0.25528256 0.07616708]
 [0.73464373 0.19115479 1.598696   0.47708698 0.44228044]
 [0.67665848 0.25528256 0.47708698 1.51547912 0.695086  ]
 [0.52137592 0.07616708 0.44228044 0.695086   1.97346437]]
```

Figure 4. Mean

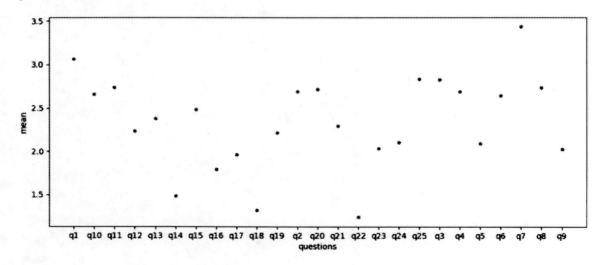

Statistical Resultant Analysis of Psychosomatic Survey on Various Human Personality Indicators

Figure 5 shows the correlation of questions 1 to 25 and is based on table 9. Figure 3 shows the covariance of questions 1 to 25 and is based on table 10.

From figure 7, we analyzed that all the covariance values are positive that is if there is an increase in value of one variable then value of other related variable will also increase. We analyzed that if a person is a worrier then after a point that person will feel extremely sensitive and irritable. If a person feels angry all the time, then he/she will not feel good about themselves. If a person feels extremely sensitive and irritable then he/she will not be able to conduct their point of view in proper and as a result they will feel like other people don't understand them and as the covariance values are positive that means with increase in one symptom there will be an increase in other symptom. From figure 8, we analyzed that if a person spends less time reading newspaper then he is not aware of the latest updates around the world and he is also not interested in his hobbies. Also the person spends more time watching TV for entertainment rather than getting updates and working on his ambition.

From figure 9, we analyzed that if a person is not feeling relaxed then he will suffer from chronic headaches, upset stomach and feel fatigue. Then he will start smoking tobacco to avoid these stress symptoms. From figure 10, we analyzed that if a person has a fight at least once in a week with his coworkers then he is feeling stressed. Fight will occur because he feels like they don't understand him. Then he will also be prone to accidents as because of those fights he will not be able to focus on any other things and will start drinking to avoid these stress symptoms.

From figure 11, we analyzed that if a person is having nightmares or bad dreams then he has trouble falling asleep, so he takes sleeping pills for it. He will always be tired and exhausted.

Figure 5. Correlation (Combine)

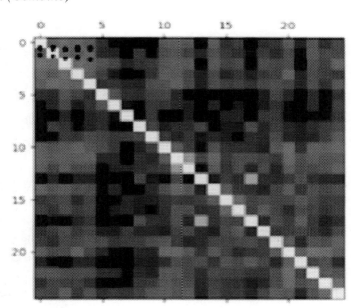

Figure 6. Covariance (Combine)

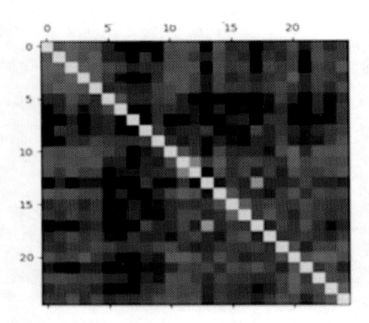

Figure 7. The Covariance of Q1 To 5

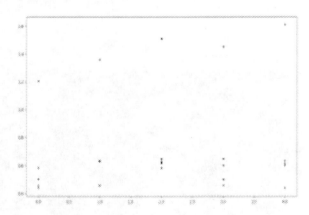

Table 8 Correlation: From table 8 we reached the maximum correlation values and found 6 questions that are highly co related. These questions are Q-3, 5, 10, 20, 21,15. Then we applied logistic regression algorithm on these questions.

Figure 12 shows the graph that came as output of multinomial logistics algorithm which was applied on 6 questions which were highly correlated. These graphs show the classification of test set into three classes that are class 0,1,2 where 0 is low,1 is medium and 2 is high. The train set and the test set are in the ratio 70:30.

Figure 8. Covariance of Question 6 To 10

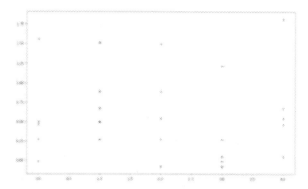

Figure 9. Covariance of 11 To 15

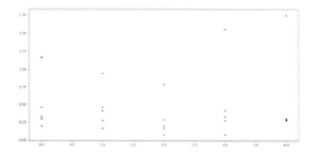

Figure 10. Covariance of 16 To 20

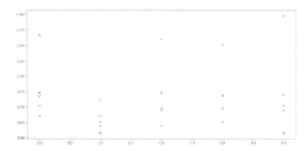

Conclusion of Performance Evaluation

In this algorithm, ratio of train set and test set is 70:30 that is 70% of whole dataset will be train set and 30% will be test set.

After applying algorithm, we got accuracy of both train set and test set. Also we got classification graph in which classification of data set is done among three classes that are 0,1 and 2 where 0 is low, 1 is medium and 2 is high on the basis of features that are those 6 questions.

Figure 11. Covariance of 21 To 25

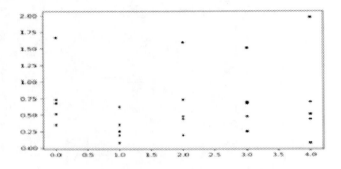

Table 8. Correlation

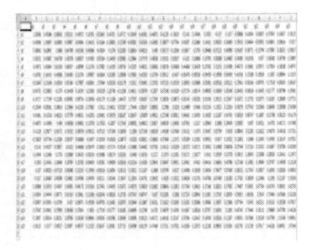

ACCURACY PERCENTAGE

Machine learning can be used to find out the stress level of a person. Machine learning is more accurate way to assign a person to any class of stress level. Hand to hand remedies are given according to stress level. Emotional, Behavioural, Sleep, Physical and Personal indicators which are highly relatable are needed to be cured.

PROJECT LEARNING AND OUTCOME-

Learned python, teamwork, how to break down work into tasks. A person shows certain symptoms through which we can get to know that a person is stressed. The range we selected to classify a person into a level of stress is highly accurate. Symptoms are highly relatable that is feel extremely sensitive, don't feel good, give less than 30 minutes to goal, spend time alone and have trouble falling asleep.

Statistical Resultant Analysis of Psychosomatic Survey on Various Human Personality Indicators

Table 9. Covariance

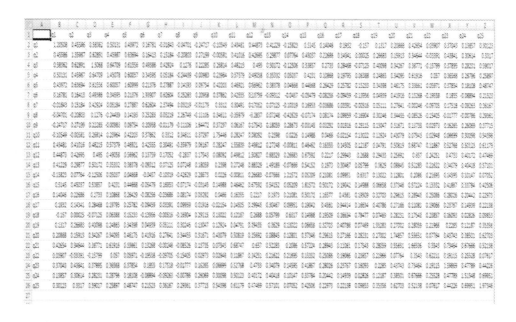

Figure 12

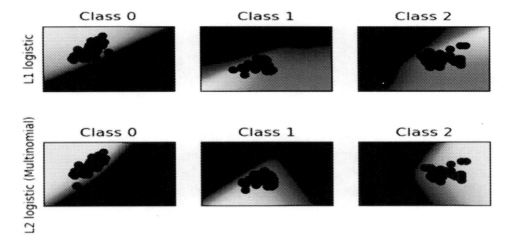

FUTURE DIRECTIONS

Send the result with the remedies to the people through email. Take test of people after regular interval to check if remedies are helpful or not also to check if the remedies are helpful or not. To see that the ranges which we have divided are correct or not.

Figure 13.

```
In percentage
Logistic regression Train Accuracy :: 78.56969247111827
Logistic regression Test Accuracy :: 78.3333333333333
Multinomial Logistic regression Train Accuracy :: 98.92470112727657
Multinomial Logistic regression Test Accuracy :: 97.5
```

NOVELTY IN THE PRESENTED PAPER

The work has been performed with blending and merger of different disciplines and backgrounds like Spirituality, Medical and Computer science engineering with Clinical Psychology. They are merged together for a common interest and that is to make human consciousness uplifted. There are many pros and cons in philosophy but it's interesting to see that the complex concept like Life, personality, human behavior and spiritual growth is being defined mathematically and trying to be quantified. Present time, the psychic challenges are the biggest crisis. Authors have tried to present a quantitative approach for a subjective concept. The mathematical solutions for the human life related issues, spiritual wellbeing has been addressed and will lead to new direction of the study of human intelligence. Use of effect of spiritual practices and bio-statistical Analysis will show significant improvement in many physical, physiological & psychological Parameters.

COMPLEXITY ANALYSIS

The human life, human mind along with human nature, all are very complex in nature. The calculated attributes are subjective and will vary from individual to other list of do's and don'ts may be long and unending so a matter to explore. They are varying and their priority may vary. Also it is so complex phenomena that can be treated as NP complete problem. Still the run time complexity will be finite but very high as all possible combinations of human traits and challenges will be a very large in number.

RECOMMENDATIONS

The given method is the totally new technology to define the human life span, and human complexity, highs and lows of human life, decision making process of human etc. As we all know that the one wrong decision moves the human under stress, tension and other mental disorder. The result of this technology helps in checking the spirituality and decide one's personality and consequently take the important decisions in different circumstances. This is one of the main reasons that it is so important to continually update our skills relating to interview and interrogation, read the latest information on detecting deception studies, knows to deal with persons of psychosomatic disorders, associate with professional organizations on and off-line, read professional trade magazines, and attend formal training courses and academic conferences. Humans are complex. We need keep learning more and more about them.

LIMITATIONS

The framework may work for short no. of parameters, say 30. We have to continuously try for exploration and exploitation for important components contributing in these phenomena. Only global best individual will be allowed to lead at end of each iteration. The traits may be varying. Their priorities may vary so in depth study and defining characteristics of complete human spiritual traits is important.

FUTURE SCOPE AND POSSIBLE APPLICATIONS

One may work on identification of complete parameters and their priorities. Also their correct measurement and representation is important. The more logistic model and simulation structure may be designed and an expert system may be formulated to represent the whole concept livelier.

May be used to identify good coworker, honest employee, life partner or friend for individual. For social reformation, identification of individual characteristics for various decisions making, it may prove useful. The scientific approach to identify the parametric spiritual traits and to define personality and behavior may be used in different ways in almost all walks of life. The results may be obtained through questionnaire and analyzed.

MOTIVATION

Machines are getting intelligent day by day. Almost all the work of inside and out are being executed with their help. Science has worked as boon to solve many complex problems and has made our life simpler, but in spite of this, there are certain issues and challenges, which need to be addressed as soon as possible. One of them is psychological problems of human being like stress, tension, depression, frustration, headache etc. which are now getting common in human personality. Many times, the Human being is having the most deplorable ignorance about his own being.

The proposed project work will be an effort to deal with machine intelligent techniques like python programming on anaconda Platform and SPSS tools using sensor modalities of Bio Feedback therapies to deal with optimized methods of development of noble life in the perspective of Indian scientific philosophy and psychology using various spiritual tools. Humans are complex. We need keep learning more and more about them.

CONCLUSION

To communicate with the database of the present computer system we need mandatory training, from firearms training to domestic violence issues. In present time we need the training on how TO TALK TO PEOPLE so that we can get about maximum information about his psychological condition, mental condition. Generally, we meet with the people at office, school, college, public place etc. and we start judge the people on the basis of their dressing sense bank balance, family background etc. we need to training how we get the maximum information from the people by simple looking their hand moment, talking sense, eye contact, body moment at the time of the talking and many other factors which helpful for ourselves. We need to talk to the people who are under the stress, who are under influence of drugs, who have elevated level of anger, memory issue etc.

The proposed paper is a successful mathematical framework to calculate the human personal spiritual factor and direct the individual for better and noble life. The present work is highlights the problems of present time that are face by the human specially in the youth because they are highly influenced by the drugs, stress, elevated level of the anger, memory problems, injury problem all these problems increase the death rate of the human per day.

Today we need a strong public health community to identify, prepare, integrate and implement the activities that are helpful for today life. We need to launch the various program that are promote the health and healthy life style and establish the mechanism for delivery of population-based intervention along with measuring its impact. We need trained employ that approach to the person which is affected from the psychological problem and provide them solution.

ACKNOWLEDGMENT

Author is a research scholar on domain of scientific spirituality and thankful with gratitude for his guide and co-guides of various prestigious academic institutions to understand the concept well and for showing the path ahead. The Scientific spirituality is the emerging field of future and all spiritual organizations working for betterment of society and humanity in large are acknowledged for their great deeds. The acknowledgement to all those forces which choose us to make this world a better place to live in.

REFERENCES

Andlin-Sobocki, P, Jonsson, B., Wittchen, H.U., & Olesen, J. (2005). Cost of disorders of the brain in Europe. *Eur J Neurol, 1*(12), 13-18.

Baum, A. (1990). Stress, Intrusive Imagery, and Chronic Distress. *Health Psychology, 6*, 653–675. PMID:2286178

Bronfort, G., Nilsson, N., & Haas, M. (2004). Non-invasive physical treatments for chronic/recurrent headache. *Cochrane Database Syst Rev, 3*, 13-18.

Budzynski, T. H., & Stoyva, J. M. (1969). An instrument for producing deep muscle relaxation by means of analog information feedback. *J Appl Behav Anal*, 231-237.

Granella, F., Farina, S., Malferrari, G., & Manzoni, G.C. (1987). Drug abuse in chronic headache: A clinico-epidemiologic study. *Cephalalgia, 7*, 15–19.

James, K. P., & Gragory, F. H. (1986). An Academic Stress Scale: Identification and rated importance of academic stressors. *Psychological Reports*, *59*(2), 415–426. doi:10.2466/pr0.1986.59.2.415

Kadhiravan, S., & Kumar, K. (2002). Stress coping Skills among college students. *Journal of Arts, Science and Commerce, 3*(4).

Lyle, M. H., & Dell Alma, S. (2003). *The Stress Solution*. American Psychological Association.

McCrory, D., Penzien, D., Hasselblad, V., & Gray, R. (2001). *Evidence report: behavioral and physical treatments for tension-type and cervicogenic headache*. Duke University Evidence-based Practice Center. Available at: www.masschiro.org/upload/research/16_0.pdf

Mechanic, D. (1978). *Students under stress; A study in the social psychology of adaption*. Madison, WI: University of Wisconsin Press.

Misra, R., & Castillo, G. L. (2005). Academic stress among college students, comparison of American and international students. *International Journal of Stress Management, 11*(2), 132-148

Morgam, K. (1986). *Weisz and Schopler*. Introduction to Psychology.

Peper, E., & Shaffer, F. (2010). Biofeedback History: An Alternative View. *Biofeedback, 4*(20), 12-22.

Plomin, R., Owen, M. J., & McGuffin, P. (1994, June 17). The genetic basis of complex human behaviors. *Science, 264*(5166), 1733–1739. doi:10.1126cience.8209254 PMID:8209254

Purna, N. P., & Gotham, C. (2006). Stress and The college Students. Oxford, UK: Oxford Brookes University.

Rains, J.C., Penzien, D.B., McCrory, D.C. & Gray, R.N. (2005). Behavioral headache treatment: history, review of empirical literature and methodological critique. *Headache*, 14.

Rastogi, R., Chaturvedi, D. K., Arora, N., Trivedi, P., & Chauhan, S. (2017a). Framework for Use of Machine Intelligence on Clinical Psychology to study the effects of Spiritual tools on Human Behavior and Psychic Challenges. *Proceedings of National System Conference-2017*.

Rastogi, R., Chaturvedi, D. K., Arora, N., Trivedi, P., & Mishra, V. (2017b). Swarm Intelligent Optimized Method Of Development of Noble Life in the perspective of Indian Scientific Philosophy and Psychology. *Proceedings of National System Conference-2017*.

Rastogi, R., Chaturvedi, D. K., Arora, N., Trivedi, P., Singh, P., & Vyas, P. (2018h). Study on Efficacy of Electromyography and Electroencephalography Biofeedback with Mindful Meditation on Mental health of Youths. *Proceedings of the 12th INDIACom*.

Rastogi, R., Chaturvedi, D. K., Satya, S., Arora, N., Bansal, I., & Yadav, V. (2018k). *Intelligent* Analysis for Detection of Complex Human Personality by Clinical Reliable Psychological Surveys on Various Indicators. *The National Conference on 3rd MDNCPDR-2018*.

Rastogi, R., Chaturvedi, D. K., Satya, S., Arora, N., & Chauhan, S. (2018a). *An Optimized Biofeedback Therapy for Chronic TTH between Electromyography and Galvanic Skin Resistance Biofeedback on Audio, Visual and Audio Visual Modes on Various Medical Symptoms*. In The national Conference on 3rd MDNCPDR-2018, Agra, India.

Rastogi, R., Chaturvedi, D. K., Satya, S., Arora, N., Gupta, M., Yadav, V., . . . Sharma, P. (in press). Chronic TTH Analysis by EMG & GSR Biofeedback on Various Modes and Various Medical Symptoms Using IoT, Advances in ubiquitous sensing applications for healthcare. Big Data Analytics for Intelligent Healthcare Management.

Rastogi, R., Chaturvedi, D. K., Satya, S., Arora, N., Saini, H., Verma, H., & Mehlyan, K. (2018j). Comparative Efficacy Analysis of Electromyography and Galvanic Skin Resistance Biofeedback on Audio Mode for Chronic TTH on Various Indicators. *Proceedings of ICCIIoT- 2018*.

Rastogi, R., Chaturvedi, D.K., Satya, S., Arora, N., Saini, H., Verma, H., Mehlyan, K., & Varshney, Y. (2018b). Statistical Analysis of EMG and GSR Therapy on Visual Mode and SF-36 Scores for Chronic TTH. *Proceedings of UPCON-2018*.

Rastogi, R., Chaturvedi, D. K., Satya, S., Arora, N., Singh, P., & Vyas, P. (2018e). Statistical Analysis for Effect of Positive Thinking on Stress Management and Creative Problem Solving for Adolescents. *Proceedings of the 12th INDIACom*.

Rastogi, R., Chaturvedi, D. K., Satya, S., Arora, N., Singhal, P., & Gulati, M. (2018f). Statistical Resultant Analysis of Spiritual & Psychosomatic Stress Survey on Various Human Personality Indicators. *The International Conference proceedings of ICCI 2018*.

Rastogi, R., Chaturvedi, D. K., Satya, S., Arora, N., Sirohi, H., Singh, M., . . . Singh, V. (2018i). Which One is Best: Electromyography Biofeedback Efficacy Analysis on Audio, Visual and Audio-Visual Modes for Chronic TTH on Different Characteristics. *Proceedings of ICCIIoT- 2018*.

Rastogi, R., Chaturvedi, D. K., Satya, S., Arora, N., Trivedi, P., Singh, A., ... Singh, A. (2019a). *Intelligent Analysis for Personality Detection on Various Indicators by Clinical Reliable Psychological TTH and Stress Surveys*. In Proceedings of CIPR 2019 at Indian Institute of Engineering Science and Technology. Springer.

Rastogi, R., Chaturvedi, D. K., Satya, S., Arora, N., Yadav, V., Chauhan, S., & Sharma, P. (2018c). *SF-36 Scores Analysis for EMG and GSR Therapy on Audio, Visual and Audio Visual Modes for Chronic TTH*. Proceedings of the ICCIDA-2018 on Oct. 27-28, CCIS Series, Springer at Gandhi Institute for Technology.

Rastogi, R., Chaturvedi, D. K., Satya, S., Arora, N., Yadav, V., Chauhan, S., & Sharma, P. (2018d). *Analytical Comparison of Efficacy for Electromyography and Galvanic Skin Resistance Biofeedback on Audio-Visual Mode for Chronic TTH on Various Attributes. Proceedings of the ICCIDA-2018 on Oct. 27- 28, CCIS Series, Springer at Gandhi Institute for Technology*.

Rastogi, R., Chaturvedi, D. K., Sharma, S., Bansal, A., & Agrawal, A. (2018g). Audio Visual EMG & GSR Biofeedbac Analysis for Effect of Spiritual Techniques on Human Behavior and Psychic Challenges. *Proceedings of the 12th INDIACom*.

Ravindra, Y., VidinPallavi, K., A., Vainder, S., & Raman, S. (2012). The Interrelationship of positive mental and physical health; A health promoting approach. *The Journal of Positive Psychology, 3*(1), 1–5.

Ross, S. E., Neibling, B. C., & Heckert, T. M. (2008). Source of stress among college students. College Student Journal, 33(2).

Scott, D. S., & Lundeen, T. F. (1980). Myofascial pain involving the masticatory muscles: An experimental model. *Pain, 8*(2), 207–215. doi:10.1016/0304-3959(88)90008-5 PMID:7402684

Selye, H. (1979). The stress of life. In Introduction to psychology. Kolkata, India: Kalyani Publishers.

The American Institute of Stress. (1999). 50 Common Signe and symptoms of Stress. *World Psychology, 469.*

Vernon, H., McDermaid, C.S., & Hagino, C. (1999). Systematic review of randomized clinical trials of complementary/ alternative therapies in the treatment of tension-type and cervicogenic headache. *Complement Ther Med, 7*(14, 13-19.

What is biofeedback? (2008). *Association for Applied Psychophysiology and Biofeedback, 12*(5).

Compilation of References

2045.. 2017). *2045 Initiative*. Retrieved from http://2045.com/

Aberth, J. (2011). Plagues in World History. Lanham, MD: Rowman & Littlefield Publishers.

Abma, T. A., & Widdershoven, G. A. M. (2011). Evaluation as a rationally responsible practice. In N. K. Denzin & Y. S. Lincoln (Eds.), *The Sage handbook of qualitative research* (4th ed.; pp. 669–684). Thousand Oaks, CA: Sage.

Abowd, G. D., & Mynatt, E. D. (2000, March). Charting past, present, and future research in ubiquitous computing. *ACM Transactions on Computer-Human Interaction*, *7*(1), 29–58. doi:10.1145/344949.344988

Abram, S. (2007). Web 2.0, Library 2.0, and Librarian 2.0: Preparing for the 2.0 World. In S. Ricketts, C. Birdie, & E. Isaksson (Eds.), *Library and Information Services in Astronomy V: Common Challenges, Uncommon Solutions* (pp. 161–166). ASP Conference Series. Retrieved from http://adsabs.harvard.edu/full/2007ASPC.377.161A

Acun, R. (2011). Her Dem Yeniden Doğmak: Online Sosyal Ağlar ve Kimlik. *Milli Folklor Dergisi*, *89*, 66–77.

Adams, R. L. (2017). 10 Powerful examples of artificial intelligence in use today. *Forbes*. Retrieved from https://www.forbes.com/sites/robertadams/2017/01/10/10-powerful-examples-of-artificial-intelligence-in-use-today/#3c7c80df420d

Adeboye, D. (2016). *Digital pedagogy: Education, then technology*! Retrieved from https://elearningindustry.com/digital-pedagogy-education-technology

Aeschylus. (1975). *Prometheus Bound* (J. Scully & J. D. Herington, Trans.). Oxford University Press.

Agar, N. (2007). Where to Transhumanism? The Literature Reaches a Critical Mass. *The Hastings Center Report*, *37*(3), 12–17. doi:10.1353/hcr.2007.0034 PMID:17649897

Akbulut, Y. (2009). Investigating Underlying Components of The ICT Indicators Measurement Scale: The Extended Version. *Journal of Educational Computing Research*, *40*(4), 405–427. doi:10.2190/EC.40.4.b

Akbulut, Y., Odabas‚ı, H. F., & Kuzu, A. (2011). Perceptions of preservice teachers regarding the integration of information and communication technologies in Turkish education faculties. *The Turkish Online Journal of Educational Technology*, *10*(3), 175–184.

Aksenov, I. V., & Аксёнов, И. В. (2016). Trans-humanism as an anthropological problem. *Journal of Siberian Federal University. Humanities and Social Sciences*, *3*(9), 678–686.

Akurgal, E., (1995). *Anadolu Uygarlıkları*. İstanbul: Net.

Albeanu, G. (2017). Blockchain technology and education. In G. Albeanu, M. Popovici, R. Jugureanu, A. Adăscăliței, & O. Istrate (Eds.) *Proceedings of the 12th International Conference on Virtual Learning* (pp. 271-275), Bucharest, Romania: Bucharest University Press

Compilation of References

AlDahdouh, A., Osório, A., & Caires, S. (2015). Understanding knowledge network, learning and connectivism. *International Journal of Instructional Technology and Distance Learning, 12*(10), 3–21.

Aleven, V., Popescu, O., Sewall, J., & Xhakaj, F. (2015). *The Beginning of a Beautiful Friendship? Intelligent Tutoring Systems and MOOCs.* Paper presented at International Conference on Artificial Intelligence in Education, Madrid, Spain.

Ali, N. (2014). *Text stylometry for chat bot identification and intelligence estimation.* Academic Press.

Allahar, H. (2014). The Changing Nature of Work, Jobs of the Future, and Strategic Human Resource Framework. *Research Journal of Human Resources*. Retrieved from https://www.researchgate.net/publication/279191690_The_Changing_Nature_of_Work_Jobs_of_the_Future_and_Strategic_Human_Resource_Framework

Allahverdi, N. (2002). *Uzman Sistemler Bir Yapay Zeka Uygulaması.* Ankara, Turkey: Atlas Yayın Dağıtım.

Alpaydın, E. (2016). *Machine learning: The new AI.* MIT Press.

Al-Sheri, S. (2011). Connectivism: A new pathway for theorizing and promoting mobile language learning. *International Journal of Innovation and Leadership in Teaching of Humanities, 1*(2), 10–31.

Amin, S. H., Razmi, J., & Zhang, G. (2011). Supplier selection and order allocation based on fuzzy SWOT analysis and fuzzy linear programming. *Expert Systems with Applications, 38*(1), 334–342. doi:10.1016/j.eswa.2010.06.071

Amish. (2019, Jan. 22). Retrieved from https://en.wikipedia.org/wiki/Amish

ANC. (2018). *American National Corpus Project.* Available: http://www.anc.org

Anderson, P. (2007). What is Web 2.0? Ideas, technologies and implications for education, media and technology. *JISC Technology and Standards Watch*. Retrieved from http://www.jisc.ac.uk/media/documents/techwatch/tsw0701b.pdf

Anderson, T. (2006). *PLE's versus LMS: Are PLEs ready for Prime time?* Available at: http://terrya.edublogs.org/2006/01/09/ples-versus-lms-are-ples-ready-for-prime-time/

Anderson, L. W., Krathwohl, D. R., Airasian, P. W., Cruikshank, K. A., Mayer, R. E., Pintrich, P. R., ... Wittrock, M. C. (2001). *A taxonomy for learning, teaching, and assessing: A revision of Bloom's taxonomy of educational objectives.* New York: Pearson, Allyn & Bacon.

Anderson, T. (2010). Theories for learning with emerging technologies. In G. Veletsianos (Ed.), *Emerging technologies in distance education.* Edmonton, Canada: Athabasca University Press.

Anderson, T., & Dron, J. (2011). Three generations of distance education pedagogy. *International Review of Research in Open and Distance Learning, 12*(3), 80–97. doi:10.19173/irrodl.v12i3.890

Andersson, A., Hatakka, M., Grönlund, Å., & Wiklund, M. (2014). Reclaiming the students–Coping with social media in 1:1 schools. *Learning, Media and Technology, 39*(1), 37–52. doi:10.1080/17439884.2012.756518

Andersson, J. (2018). That Very Big Computer Known as Human Civilisation-Yuval Noah Harari, Homo Deus–A Brief History of Tomorrow. *Archives Européennes de Sociologie, 59*(3), 429–434. doi:10.1017/S0003975618000267

Andlin-Sobocki, P, Jonsson, B., Wittchen, H.U., & Olesen, J. (2005). Cost of disorders of the brain in Europe. *Eur J Neurol, 1*(12), 13-18.

Andolfatto, D. (2018). Blockchain: What it is, what it does, and why you probably don't need one. *Federal Reserve Bank of St. Louis Review, 100*(2), 87–95. doi:10.20955/r.2018.87-95

Andrews, R. (2011). Does e-learning require a new theory of learning? Some initial thoughts. *Journal for Educational Research Online, 3*(1), 104–121.

Anissimov, M. (2007). *Top Ten Transhumanist Technologies*. Retrieved from https://lifeboat.com/ex/transhumanist.technologies

Annas, G. J. (2001). The Man on the Moon, Immortality, and Other Millennial Myths: The Prospects and Perils of Human Genetic Engineering. *Emory Law Journal, 49*, 753–782. PMID:12645561

Annas, G. J. (2002). Protecting the Endangered Human: Toward an International Treaty Prohibiting Cloning and Inheritable Alterations. *American Journal of Law & Medicine, 28*, 151–178. PMID:12197461

Anthony, M. (2003). Visions Without Depth: Michio Kaku's Future. *Journal of Futures Studies, 7*(4), 55-66.

Appadurai, A. (2001). *Globalization*. Durham, NC: Duke University Press. doi:10.1215/9780822383215

Archee, R. (2012). Reflections on personal learning environments: Theory and practice. *Procedia: Social and Behavioral Sciences, 55*, 419–428. doi:10.1016/j.sbspro.2012.09.520

Aroyo, L., Dolog, P., Houben, G.-J., Kravcik, M., Naeve, A., Nilsson, M., & Wild, F. (2006). Interoperability in Personalized Adaptive Learning. *Journal of Educational Technology & Society, 9*(2), 4–18.

Ashburn, E. A., & Floden, R. E. (2006). *Meaningful learning using technology: What educators need to know and do*. New York: Teachers College Press.

Ashby, W. R. (1956). *An Introduction to Cybernetics*. London: Chapman & Hall. doi:10.5962/bhl.title.5851

Ashby, W. R. (1960). *Design for a Brain*. London: Chapman & Hall. doi:10.1007/978-94-015-1320-3

Aslan, A., & Zhu, C. (2017). Investigating variables predicting Turkish pre-service teachers' integration of ICT into teaching practices. *British Journal of Educational Technology, 48*(2), 2017. doi:10.1111/bjet.12437

Attwell, G. (2007). The personal learning environment – the future of learning? *eLearning Papers, 2*(1), 1–8. Retrieved from http://digtechitalia.pbworks.com/w/file/fetch/88358195/Atwell%202007.pdf

Attwell, G. (2010) *Personal learning environments and Vygotsky*. Retrieved from http://www.pontydysgu.org/2010/04/personal-learning-environments-and-vygotsky

Avey, J. B., Reichard, R. J., Luthans, F., & Mhatre, K. H. (2011). Meta-Analysis of the Impact of Positive Psychological Capital on Employee Attitudes, Behaviors and Performance. *Human Resource Development Quarterly, 22*(2), 127–152. doi:10.1002/hrdq.20070

Aydoğan, F., & Akyüz, A. (2010). *Internet in Second Media Era*. İstanbul: Alfa Publishing.

Bach, E. R. (2016). *The Future of Learning*. Franklin Covey whitepaper. Retrieved from http://franklincovey.dk/wp-content/uploads/2017/09/The-Future-of-Learning-Whitepaper-UK.pdf

Bach, J. (2015B). *Why Artificial Intelligence won't just be a bit smarter than humans*. Retrieved from http://bach.ai/why-ai-wont-be-just-a-bit-smarter-than-humans/

Bach, J. (2015A). Modeling motivation in MicroPsi 2. In *International conference on artificial general intelligence* (pp. 3-13). Springer. 10.1007/978-3-319-21365-1_1

Bagade, O. M., Dhole, S. N., Kahane, S. K., Bhosale, D. R., Bhargude, D. N., & Kad, D. R. (2013). Appraisal on preparation and characterization of nanoparticles for parenteral and ophthalmic administration. *International Journal of Research in Pharmaceutical Sciences, 4*(4), 490–503.

Bainbridge, W. (2013). Transavatars. In M. More & N. Vita-More (Eds.), *The Transhumanist Reader: Classical and Contemporary Essays on the Science, Technology, and Philosophy of the Human Future*. Hoboken, NJ: Wiley-Blackwell, John Wiley & Sons, Inc. doi:10.1002/9781118555927.ch9

Bainbridge, W. S. (2010). When virtual worlds expand. In W. S. Bainbridge (Ed.), *Online worlds: Convergence of the real and the virtual* (pp. 237–251). London: Springer. doi:10.1007/978-1-84882-825-4_19

Baker, S. C., Wentz, R. K., & Woods, M. M. (2009). Using virtual worlds in education: Second Life® as an educational tool. *Teaching of Psychology*, *36*(1), 59–64. doi:10.1080/00986280802529079

Bamodu, O., & Ye, X. M. (2013). Virtual Reality and Virtual Reality System Components. *Advanced Materials Research*, *765*, 1169–1172. doi:10.4028/www.scientific.net/AMR.765-767.1169

Bandura, A., & Locke, E. A. (2003). Negative Self-Efficacy and Goal Effects Revisited. *The Journal of Applied Psychology*, *88*(1), 87–99. doi:10.1037/0021-9010.88.1.87 PMID:12675397

Banger, G. (2016). *Endustri 4.0 ve Akilli Isletme*. Ankara, Turkey: Dorlion Yayinevi.

Barak, M. J. (2017). Cloud pedagogy: Utilizing web-based technologies for promotion of social constructivist learning in science teacher preparation courses. *Journal of Science Education and Technology*, *26*(5), 459–469. doi:10.100710956-017-9691-3

Barker, B., Frisbie, A., & Patrick, K. (1989). Broadening the definition of distance education in the light of the new telecommunications technologies. *American Journal of Distance Education*, *3*(1), 20–29. doi:10.1080/08923648909526647

Barnett, J., McPherson, V., & Sandieson, R. M. (2013). Connected teaching and learning: The uses and implications of connectivism in an online class. *Australasian Journal of Educational Technology*, *29*(5), 685–698. doi:10.14742/ajet.243

Barrett, L., Henzi, S. P., & Lusseau, D. (2012). Taking sociality seriously: The structure of multi-dimensional social networks as a source of information for individuals. *Philosophical Transactions of the Royal Society of London. Series B, Biological Sciences*, *367*(1599), 2108–2118. doi:10.1098/rstb.2012.0113 PMID:22734054

Barron, B., & Darling-Hammond, L. (2008). Teaching for meaningful learning: A review of research on inquiry-based and cooperative learning. In L. Darling-Hammond, B. Barron, P.D. Pearson, A.H. Schoenfeld, E.K. Stage, T.D. Zimmerman, G.N. Cervetti, & J.L. Tilson (Eds.), Powerful learning: What we know about teaching for understanding. San Francisco, CA: Jossey-Bass/John Wiley & Sons.

Bashkow. (2004). A Neo-Boasian Conception of Cultural Boundaries. *American Anthropologist, 106*(3), 443-458.

Basic Income. (2018, Nov. 20). Retrieved from https://en.wikipedia.org/wiki/Basic_income

Başöz, T. (2016). Pre-service EFL Teachers' Attitudes towards Language Learning through Social Media. *Procedia: Social and Behavioral Sciences*, *232*, 430–438. doi:10.1016/j.sbspro.2016.10.059

Bates, T. (2018). *Why is innovation in teaching in HE so difficult? Integrating online and distance learning into the mainstream*. Retrieved from https://www.tonybates.ca/2018/08/01/why-is-innovation-in-teaching-in-he-so-difficult-4-integrating-online-and-distance-learning-into-the-mainstream/

Bates, T. (2005). *Technology, E-learning and Distance Education*. New York: Routledge. doi:10.4324/9780203463772

Bauer, K. A. (2012). Transhumanism and its Critics. Fice Arguments against a Posthuman Future. In R. Luppucini (Ed.), *Ethical Impact of Technological Advancements and Applications in Society* (pp. 232–242). Hershey, PA: IGI Global. doi:10.4018/978-1-4666-1773-5.ch018

Bauer, J. M. (2018, May). The internet and income inequality: Socio-economic challenges in a hyperconnected society. *Telecommunications Policy*, *42*(4), 333–343. doi:10.1016/j.telpol.2017.05.009

Baum, A. (1990). Stress, Intrusive Imagery, and Chronic Distress. *Health Psychology*, *6*, 653–675. PMID:2286178

Baumeister, R. F., & Leary, M. R. (1997). Writing narrative literature reviews. *Review of General Psychology*, *1*(3), 311–320. doi:10.1037/1089-2680.1.3.311

Bayne, S. (2014). What's the matter with 'technology enhanced learning'? *Learning, Media and Technology*, *40*(1), 5–20. doi:10.1080/17439884.2014.915851

Bayne, S., & Ross, J. (2013). Posthuman literacy in heterotopic space: A pedagogic proposal. In R. Goodfellow & M. Lea (Eds.), *Literacy in the digital university: Critical perspectives on learning, scholarship, and technology* (pp. 95–110). London: Routledge.

Bayrı, D. (2011). *Gözün Egemenliği Tarihin Sonu mu? Özne: Baudrillard Sayısı, 14*. Kitap.

Bell, F. (2011). Connectivism: Its place in theory-informed research and innovation in technology-enabled learning. *International Review of Research in Open and Distance Learning*, *12*(3), 98. doi:10.19173/irrodl.v12i3.902

Benitti, F. B. V. (2012). Exploring the educational potential of robotics in schools: A systematic review. *Computers & Education*, *58*(3), 978–988. doi:10.1016/j.compedu.2011.10.006

BigThink. (2012). *Michio Kaku Describes Virtual Reality Glasses*. Access: https://bigthink.com/michio-kaku-describes-virtual-reality-glasses

Billinghurst, M. (2002). Augmented reality in education. *New Horizons for Learning*, *12*.

Binkley, M., Erstad, O., Herman, J., Raizen, S., Ripley, M., Miller-Ricci, M., & Rumble, M. (2012). Defining twenty-first century skills. In P. Griffin, B. McGaw, & E. Care (Eds.), *Assessment and teaching of 21st century skills* (pp. 17–66). Dordrecht, The Netherlands: Springer. doi:10.1007/978-94-007-2324-5_2

Bittner, W. S., & Mallory, H. F. (1933). *University Teaching by Mail: A Survey of Correspondence Instruction Conducted by American Universities*. New York: Macmillan.

Black, J. (2013). *Greek mythology and human origins*. Available: https://www.ancient-origins.net/human-origins-folklore/greek-mythology-and-human-origins-0064

Blaschke, L. (2012). Heutagogy and lifelong learning: A review of heutagogical practice and self-determined learning. *International Review of Research in Open and Distance Learning*, *13*(1), 56–71. doi:10.19173/irrodl.v13i1.1076

Blees, I., & Rittberger, M. (2009). Web 2.0 learning environment: concept, implementation, evaluation. *eLearning Papers*, 1–18. Retrieved from http://www.pedocs.de/volltexte/2010/2633/pdf/web20_LE_blees_rittberger_2_D_A.pdf

Bloomberg, J. (2018, April 29). Re: Digitization, digitalization, and digital transformation: confuse them at your peril [web log post]. *Forbes*. Retrieved from https://www.forbes.com/sites/jasonbloomberg/2018/04/29/digitization-digitalization-and-digital-transformation-confuse-them-at-your-peril/#1f02cf102f2c

Bolay, S. H. (2017). Teknoloji Değer Yaratır mı? In Teknoloji ve Değerler (pp.63-83). İstanbul: İmak.

Bonaci, T., Herron, J., Matlack, C., & Chizeck, H. J. (2014). Securing the exocortex: A twenty-first century cybernetics challenge. In *Norbert Wiener in the 21st Century (21CW), 2014 IEEE Conference on* (pp. 1-8). IEEE. 10.1109/NORBERT.2014.6893912

Bostrom, N. (1998). How long before superintelligence? *Int Journal of Future Studies*, *2*.

Compilation of References

Bostrom, N. (1998). How Long Before Superintelligence? *International Journal of Futures Studies, 2*. Retrieved from http://www.nickbostrom.com/superintelligence.html

Bostrom, N. (2001). *Transhumanist Values*. Retrieved from https://nickbostrom.com/tra/values.html

Bostrom, N. (2003). *Ethical Issues in Advanced Artificial Intelligence*. Retrieved from https://nickbostrom.com/ethics/ai.html

Bostrom, N. (2003). Ethical issues in advanced artificial intelligence. *Science Fiction and Philosophy: From Time Travel to Superintelligence*, 277-284.

Bostrom, N. (2003). *The Transhumanist FAQ*. World Transhumanist Association. Retrieved from http://www.transhumanism.org

Bostrom, N. (2005). A history of transhumanist thought. *Journal of Evolution and Technology*. Retrieved from https://nickbostrom.com/papers/history.pdf

Bostrom, N. (2014). Superintelligence: Paths, dangers, strategies. Oxford, UK: Oxford University Press.

Bostrom, N. (2014). *Superintelligence: Paths, Dangers, Strategies*. Retrieved from https://www.researchgate.net/publication/285393594_Nick_Bostrom_Superintelligence_Paths_Dangers_Strategies

Bostrom, N., & Pearce, D. (2007, Dec.). *Transhumanism* (A. Lomena, interviewer) [Audio file transcript]. Retrieved from https://www.hedweb.com/transhumanism/index.html

Bostrom, N. (2002). Existential risks: Analyzing human extinction scenarios and related hazards. *Journal of Evolution and Technology / WTA, 9*.

Bostrom, N. (2003). *The Transhumanist FAQ*. World Transhumanist Association.

Bostrom, N. (2005). A History Of Transhumanist Thought. *Journal of Evolution and Technology / WTA, 14*(1), 1–25.

Bostrom, N. (2005). A history of transhumanist thought. *Journal of Evolution and Technology / WTA, 14*(1).

Bostrom, N. (2005). A History of Transhumanist Thought. *Journal of Evolution and Technology / WTA, 14*(1).

Bostrom, N. (2005). Transhumanist values. *Journal of Philosophical Research, 30*(9999), 3–14. doi:10.5840/jpr_2005_26

Bostrom, N. (2006). *The Future of Human Evolution* (Vol. 2). Death and Anti Death.

Bostrom, N., & Ord, T. (2005). Status quo bias in bioethics: The case for cognitive enhancement. In N. Bostrom & J. Savulescu (Eds.), *Improving Humans*. Oxford, UK: Oxford University Press.

Boulton-Lewis, G. M., & Tam, M. (2012). *Active ageing, active learning. Issues and Challenges*. New York: Springer. doi:10.1007/978-94-007-2111-1

Bowen, J. A. (2012). *Teaching naked: How moving technology out of your college classroom will improve student learning*. San Francisco, CA: Jossey-Bass.

Boyd, D. M., & Ellison, N. B. (2008). Social network sites: Definition, history, and scholarship. *Journal of Computer-Mediated Communication, 13*(1), 210–230. doi:10.1111/j.1083-6101.2007.00393.x

Bozkurt, A. (2015). Kitlesel Açık Çevrimiçi Dersler [Massive Online Open Courses - MOOCs]. *sayısal bilgi çağında yaşamboyu öğrenme fırsatı AUAd, 1*(1), 56-81.

Bozkurt, A. (2016). *Identifying interaction patterns and teacher-learner roles in connectivist massive open online courses* (Doctoral dissertation). Anadolu University, Turkey.

Bozkurt, A., & Aydın, C. H. (2015). *Satisfaction, Preferences and Problems of a MOOC*. Paper presnted at the Association for Educational Communications and Technology (AECT) 2015 International Convention, Indianapolis, IN.

Bozkurt, A., & Göksel, N. (2018). Technology renovates itself: Key concepts on intelligent personal assistants (IPAs). In *Proceedings of 10th International Conference on Education and New Learning Technologies Conference (EDULEARN18)* (pp. 4291-4297). doi: 10.21125/edulearn.2018.1082

Bozkurt, A., Akgün-Özbek, E., & Zawacki-Richter, O. (2017). Trends and patterns in massive open online courses: Review and content analysis of research on MOOCs (2008-2015). *The International Review of Research in Open and Distributed Learning*, *18*(5). doi:10.19173/irrodl.v18i5.3080

Bozkurt, A., Honeychurch, S., Caines, A., Maha, B., Koutropoulos, A., & Cormier, D. (2016). Community Tracking in a cMOOC and Nomadic Learner Behaviour Identification on a Connectivist Rhizomatic Learning Network. *The Turkish Online Journal of Distance Education*, *17*(4), 4–30.

Bozkurt, A., & Keefer, J. (2018). Participatory learning culture and community formation in connectivist MOOCs. *Interactive Learning Environments*, *26*(6), 776–788. doi:10.1080/10494820.2017.1412988

Bozkurt, A., Koseoglu, S., & Singh, L. (2019). An analysis of peer-reviewed publications on openness in education in half a century: Trends and patterns in the open hemisphere. *Australasian Journal of Educational Technology*, *35*(4), 78–97. doi:10.14742/ajet.4252

Braidotti, R. (2014). *İnsan Sonrası* (Ö. Karakaş, Trans.). İstanbul: Kolektif.

Brain Implant. (2018, Sept. 5). Retrieved from https://en.wikipedia.org/wiki/Brain_implant

Brockman, J. (2007). *Gelecek 50 Yıl, Yirmi Birinci Yüzyılın İlk Yarısında Hayat ve Bilim* (N. Elhüseyni, Trans.). İstanbul: NTV.

Bronfort, G., Nilsson, N., & Haas, M. (2004). Non-invasive physical treatments for chronic/recurrent headache. *Cochrane Database Syst Rev, 3*, 13-18.

Brooks, R. (2007). Beden ve Makine Kaynaşması. In Gelecek 50 Yıl içinde (pp. 205-215). İstanbul: NTV.

Brown, J. (2017). *Workforce of the Future: The Competing Forces Shaping 2030*. PricewaterhouseCoopers (PWC). Retrieved from https://www.pwc.com/hu/hu/kiadvanyok/assets/pdf/workforce-of-the-future-the-competing-forces-shaping-2030-pwc.pdf

Brown, E., Cristea, A., Stewart, C., & Brailsford, T. (2005). Patterns in authoring of adaptive educational hypermedia: A taxonomy of learning styles. *Journal of Educational Technology & Society*, *8*(3), 77–90.

Brumfiel, G. (2002). Futurists predict body swaps for planet hops. *Nature International Journal of Science*, *418*, 359. PMID:12140527

Brundage, M. (2015). Taking superintelligence seriously Superintelligence: Paths, dangers, strategies by Nick Bostrom. *Futures*, *72*, 32–35. doi:10.1016/j.futures.2015.07.009

Bruner, J. S. (1966). *Toward a theory of instruction*. Cambridge, MA: Belknap.

Brynjolfsson, E., & Mitchell, T. (2017). What can machine learning do? Workforce implications. *Science*, *358*(6370), 1530–1534. doi:10.1126cience.aap8062 PMID:29269459

Budzynski, T. H., & Stoyva, J. M. (1969). An instrument for producing deep muscle relaxation by means of analog information feedback. *J Appl Behav Anal*, 231-237.

Buesing, D. (2017, July 7). 5 DC Villains Who Destroyed The Justice League. *Comic Book Reader*. Retrieved from https://www.cbr.com/15-dc-villains-who-destroyed-the-justice-league/

Burak, J. L. (2012). Multitasking in the university classroom. *International Journal for the Scholarship of Teaching and Learning*, *6*(2), 1–12. doi:10.20429/ijsotl.2012.060208

Burns, H., & Parlett, J. W. (2014). The evolution of intelligent tutoring systems: Dimensions of design. In H. Burns, C. A. Luckhardt, J. W. Parlett, & C. L. Redfield (Eds.), *Intelligent tutoring systems: Evolutions in design* (pp. 1–13). New York: Psychology Press. doi:10.4324/9781315807492

Bustos, A., Engel, A., Saz, A., & Coll, C. (2012). Integrating personal and institutional virtual learning environments. *Proceedings of EDULEARN12 Conference*, 7425-7433. Retrieved from http://www.academia.edu/download/32785382/ab_ae_as_cc_edulearn12_956.pdf

Butler-Adam, J. (2018). The fourth industrial revolution and education. *South African Journal of Science*, *114*(5-6), 1–1. doi:10.17159ajs.2018/a0271

Cain, M. S., Leonard, J. A., Gabrieli, J. D., & Finn, A. S. (2016). Media multitasking in adolescence. *Psychonomic Bulletin & Review*, *23*(6), 1932–1941. doi:10.375813423-016-1036-3 PMID:27188785

Callaghan, N., & Bower, M. (2012). Learning through social networking sites–The critical role of the teacher. *Educational Media International*, *49*(1), 1–17. doi:10.1080/09523987.2012.662621

Cambria, E., & White, B. (2014). Jumping NLP curves: A review of natural language processing research. *IEEE Computational Intelligence Magazine*, *9*(2), 48–57. doi:10.1109/MCI.2014.2307227

Cameron, K. S., & Caza, A. (2004). Contributions to the Discipline of Positive Organizational Scholarship. *The American Behavioral Scientist*, *47*(6), 731–739. doi:10.1177/0002764203260207

Cameron, K. S., Dutton, J. E., & Quinn, R. E. (2003). *Positive Organizational Scholarship*. San Francisco: Berrett-Koehler.

Campbell, R. J., Robinson, W., Neelands, J., Hewston, R., & Mazzoli, L. (2007). Personalised learning: Ambiguities in theory and practice. *British Journal of Educational Studies*, *55*(2), 135-154. Retrieved from https://www.tandfonline.com/doi/abs/10.1111/j.1467-8527.2007.00370.x?casa_token=VVgLd8UWro8AAAAA:pd7MRCO7mZr3uOCWNws_EEuR_0E0D7qTjq5q53UmALQ8eMIa20JQPHLlJObFNAGBwMglXTEwwwy6njc

Canning, N. (2010). Playing with heutagogy: Exploring strategies to empower mature learners in higher education. *Journal of Further and Higher Education*, *34*(1), 59–71. doi:10.1080/03098770903477102

Cardoso-Leite, P., Kludt, R., Vignola, G., Ma, W. J., Green, C., & Bavelier, D. (2016). Technology consumption and cognitive control: Contrasting action video game experience with media multitasking. *Attention, Perception & Psychophysics*, *78*(1), 218–241. doi:10.375813414-015-0988-0 PMID:26474982

Carneiro, R. (2007). The big picture: Understanding learning and meta-learning challenges. *European Journal of Education*, *42*(2), 151–172. doi:10.1111/j.1465-3435.2007.00303.x

Cartwright, M. (2013, April 20). Prometheus. *Ancient History Encyclopedia*. Retrieved from https://www.ancient.eu/Prometheus/

Carver, D. (2012). Book review - Learning theory and online technologies. *International Review of Research in Open and Distance Learning*, *13*(4), 324–326. doi:10.19173/irrodl.v13i4.1340

Casey, D. M. (2008). The Historical Development of Distance Education through Technology. *TechTrends*, *52*(2), 45–51. doi:10.100711528-008-0135-z

Casquero, O., Ovelar, R., Romo, J., Benito, M., & Alberdi, M. (2016). Students' personal networks in virtual and personal learning environments: a case study in higher education using learning analytics approach. *Interactive Learning Environments*, *24*(1), 49-67. Retrieved from https://www.tandfonline.com/doi/abs/10.1080/10494820.2013.817441?casa_token=5QViK911-dMAAAAA:CYyoHh40XU7vTYH1B_pp5uTE2pHO7tN7eJQ10q6yyNjaJwt61o63n0JnaRH-nUK6AGkeeKONUt63DEUM

Castells, M. (2004). *The network society A cross-cultural perspective*. Edward Elgar.

Castronova, E. (2008). *Exodus to the virtual world: How online fun is changing reality*. New York: Palgrave Macmillan.

Caughill, P. (2017A). *Ray Kurzweil's Most Exciting Predictions About the Future of Humanity*. Access: https://futurism.com/ray-kurzweils-most-exciting-predictions-about-the-future-of-humanity

Caughill, P. (2017B). *Stephen Hawking Believes Humankind Is in Danger of Self-Destruction Due to AI*. Access: https://futurism.com/stephen-hawking-believes-humankind-danger-self-destruction-ai

Cellan-Jones, R. (2014). Stephen Hawking warns artificial intelligence could end mankind. *BBC News*, *2*.

Cephe, P. T., & Balçıkanlı, C. (2012). Web 2.0 tools in language teaching: what student teachers think? *IJONTE*, *3*(1), 1-12. Retrieved from http://www.ijonte.org/FileUpload/ks63207/File/01._cephe.pdf

Chan, D. (2016, April). Mormon Transhumanism and the Immortality Upgrade. *The New Yorker*. Retrieved from https://www.newyorker.com/tech/annals-of-technology/mormon-transhumanism-and-the-immortality-upgrade

Chan, T., Corlett, D., Sharples, M., Ting, J., & Westmancott, O. (2005). Developing interactive logbook: a personal learning environment. *IEEE International Workshop on Wireless and Mobile Technologies in Education (WMTE'05)*, 73–75. Retrieved from https://ieeexplore.ieee.org/abstract/document/1579238

Chang, J.-H. L. (2010). Exploring the Possibility of Using Humanoid Robots as Instructional Tools for Teaching a Second Language in Primary School. *Journal of Educational Technology & Society*, *13*(2), 13–24.

Chan, S., & Yuen, M. (2014). Creativity beliefs, creative personality and creativity-fostering practices of gifted education teachers and regular class teachers in Hong Kong. *Thinking Skills and Creativity*, *14*, 109–118. doi:10.1016/j.tsc.2014.10.003

Chaouchi, H. (Ed.). (2010). The Internet of Things: Connecting Objects to the Web. Wiley–ISTE.

Charisma, D., Suherman, S., Kurniawan, A. B., Yusnilita, N., Susilawati, S., Niawati, N., ... Pambudi, B. D. (2018). The Effectiveness of Using Lyra Personal Assistant in improving Students 'speaking skill. *Community Concern for English Pedagogy and Teaching (CONCEPT)*, *11*(1).

Chatti, M. A. (2007). *PLE links*. Retrieved from http://mohamedaminechatti.blogspot.com/2007/04/ple-links.html

Chatti, M. A., Agustiawan, M. R., Jarke, M., & Specht, M. (2010). Toward a personal learning environment framework. *International Journal of Virtual and Personal Learning Environments*, *1*(4), 66–85. doi:10.4018/jvple.2010100105

Chen, W., Millard, D., & Wills, G. (2008). Mobile VLE vs. Mobile PLE: How informal is mobile learning? *mLearn 2008 Conference: The University of Wolverhampton*. Retrieved from http://eprints.ecs.soton.ac.uk/16158

Chen, B., & Denoyelles, A. (2013). Exploring students' mobile learning practices in higher education. *EDUCAUSE Review*.

Chen, C. J. (2006). The design, development and evaluation of a virtual reality based learning environment. *Australasian Journal of Educational Technology*, *22*(1), 39–63. doi:10.14742/ajet.1306

Chen, C. M. (2008). Intelligent web-based learning system with personalized learning path guidance. *Computers & Education*, *51*(2), 787–814. doi:10.1016/j.compedu.2007.08.004

Chen, E., Heritage, M., & Lee, J. (2005). Identifying and monitoring students' learning needs with technology. *Journal of Education for Students Placed at Risk*, *10*(3), 309–332. doi:10.120715327671espr1003_6

Cheng, K.-H., & Tsai, C.-C. (2012a). Affordances of augmented reality in science learning: Suggestions for future research. *Journal of Science Education and Technology*, *22*(4), 449–462. doi:10.100710956-012-9405-9

Cheng, Y. M., & McInnis, B. (1980). An algorithm for multiple attribute, multiple alternative decision problem based on fuzzy sets with application to medical diagnosis. *IEEE Transactions on Systems, Man, and Cybernetics*, *SMC-10*, 645–650.

Chen, O., Castro-Alonso, J. C., Paas, F., & Sweller, J. (2017). Extending cognitive load theory to incorporate working memory resource depletion: Evidence from the spacing effect. *Educational Psychology Review*, *30*(2), 483–501. doi:10.100710648-017-9426-2

Child Australia. (n.d.). *What is pedagogy? How does it influence our practice?* Retrieved from https://childaustralia.org.au/wp-content/uploads/2017/02/CA-Statement-Pedagogy.pdf

Choe, J., Coffman, B. A., Bergstedt, D. T., Ziegler, M. D., & Phillips, M. E. (2016). Transcranial direct current stimulation modulates neuronal activity and learning in pilot training. *Frontiers in Human Neuroscience*, *10*, 34. doi:10.3389/fnhum.2016.00034 PMID:26903841

Choi, W. W. (2017). Teknoloji ve Hayatın Varlık Boyutunda Bütünleşmesi. In Teknoloji ve Değerler İçinde (pp. 45-55). İstanbul: İmak.

Christensen, C., & Overdorf, M. (2000, March). Meeting the challenge of disruptive change. *Harvard Business Review*.

Christensen, C. (1997). *The innovator's dilemma: When new technologies cause great firms to fail*. Boston: Harvard Business School Press.

Christensson, P. (2010, Jan. 4). *ICT Definition*. Retrieved from http://techterms.com

Churton, A. (1900). *Kant on Education*. Boston: D.C. Heath and Co.

Civelek, M. E. (2009). *İnternet Çağı Dinamikleri*. İstanbul: Beta.

Clark, D. (2013). *MOOCs: taxonomy of 8 types of MOOC*. Retrieved from http://donaldclarkplanb.blogspot.se/2013/04/moocs-taxonomy-of-8- types-of-mooc.html

Clark, D. (2016). *10 ways Blockchain could be used in education*. Retrieved from https://oeb.global/oeb-insights/10-ways-blockchain-could-be-used-in-education

Clark, D. (2015). *Reinventing you and stand out*. Inc. Magazine.

Clauset, A., Newman, M. E., & Moore, C. (2004). Finding community structure in very large networks. *Physical Review. E*, *70*(6), 066111. doi:10.1103/PhysRevE.70.066111 PMID:15697438

Clement, D., & Samara, J. (2003). Young Children and Technology: What Does the Research Say? *National Association for the Education of Young Children.*, *58*(6), 34–40.

Clifford, C. (2016). Elon Musk: robots will take your jobs, government will have to pay your wage. *CNBC.com*, *4*.

Coenen, C. (2014). Transhumanism In Emerging Technoscience As A Challenge For The Humanities And Technology Assessment. *Journal of Teorija in Praksa*, *51*(5), 754.

Coenen, C. (2014). Transhumanism in emerging technoscience as a challenge for the humanities and technology assessment. *Teorija in Praksa*, *51*(5), 754–771. Retrieved from https://www.fdv.uni-lj.si/docs/default-source/tip/tip_05_2014_coenen.pdf

Coffman, T., & Klinger, M. B. (2016). Encouraging innovation through active learning and community building. In *Proceedings of Society for Information Technology & Teacher Education International Conference* (pp. 166-172). Chesapeake, VA: Association for the Advancement of Computing in Education (AACE).

Coffman, T., & Klinger, M. B. (2018). Using microblogging as a cognitive tool in the college classroom. In *Proceedings of Society for Information Technology & Teacher Education International Conference* (pp. 832-839). Washington, DC: Association for the Advancement of Computing in Education (AACE).

Coffman, T., & Klinger, M. B. (2014, July-September). Collaboration and communication in the online classroom through a brain-based approach. *International Journal of Information Communication Technologies and Human Development*, *6*(3), 42–52. doi:10.4018/ijicthd.2014070104

Çolak, M., & İhsan, K. (2017). Prioritization of renewable energy alternatives by using an integrated fuzzy MCDM model: A real case application for Turkey. *Renewable & Sustainable Energy Reviews*, *80*, 840–853. doi:10.1016/j.rser.2017.05.194

Collas, P., & Håkelien, A. M. (2003). Teaching cells new tricks. *Trends in Biotechnology*, *21*(8), 354–361. doi:10.1016/S0167-7799(03)00147-1 PMID:12902172

Collins, A., Brown, J. S., & Holum, A. (1991). Cognitive apprenticeship: Making thinking visible. *American Educator*, *15*(3), 6–11.

Collins, A., & Halverson, R. (2009). *Rethinking education in the age of technology: The digital revolution and schooling in America*. New York: Teachers College Press.

Collins, H. M. (2018). Expert systems, artificial intelligence and the behavioural co-ordinates of skill. In B. P. Bloomfield (Ed.), *The Question of Artificial Intelligence* (pp. 258–281). London: Routledge. doi:10.4324/9780429505331-6

Collis, B., & Moonen, J. (2008). Web 2.0 tools and processes in higher education quality perspectives. *Educational Media International*, *45*(2), 93–106. doi:10.1080/09523980802107179

Comas-Quinn, A. (2011). Learning to teach online or learning to become an online teacher: An exploration of teachers' experiences in a blended learning course. *ReCALL*, *23*(03), 218–232. doi:10.1017/S0958344011000152

Cömert, B. (1972). *Mitoloji ve İkonografi*. Ankara, Turkey: Hacettepe University.

Conde, M. Á., García-Peñalvo, F. J., Alier, M., Casany, M. J., & Piguillem, J. (2013). Mobile devices applied to Computer Science subjects to consume institutional functionalities through a Personal Learning Environment. *International Journal of Engineering Education*, *29*(3), 610-619. Retrieved from http://www.academia.edu/download/42671103/MPLEApplication.pdf

Conole, G. (2014). A new classification schema for MOOCs. *The International Journal for Innovation and Quality in Learning*, *2*(3), 65-77.

Conole, G., & Alevizou, P. (2010). *A literature review of the use of Web 2.0 tools in Higher Education: A report commissioned by the Higher Education Academy*. Milton Keynes, UK: The Open University.

Copeland, M. (2016). *What's the difference between artificial intelligence, machine learning, and deep learning?* Retrieved from https://blogs.nvidia.com/blog/2016/07/29/whats-difference-artificial-intelligence-machine-learning-deep-learning-ai/

Copeland, B. J. (2000). The turing test. *Minds and Machines, 10*(4), 519–539. doi:10.1023/A:1011285919106

Corea, F. (2017). Artificial Intelligence and Exponential Technologies: Business Models Evolution and New Investment Opportunities. New York: Springer. doi:10.1007/978-3-319-51550-2

Cormier, D. (2010). 5 points about PLEs PLNs for PLENK10. *Dave's Educational Blog*.

Cormier, D. (2015). What was #rhizo15. *The Association for Learning Technology (ALT) Newsletter*. Retrieved from https://newsletter.alt.ac.uk/2015/07/what-was-rhizome15/

Cornell University. (2001). *From domesticity to modernity: What was home economics?* Division of Rare and Manuscript Collections, Cornell University.

Cöster, M., Ekenberg, L., Gullberg, C., Westelius, A., & Wettergren, G. (2017). *Organisering och digitalisering: Att skapa värde i det 21a århundradet* [Organization and digitalization: To empower value in the 21st century]. Liber.

Couros, A. (2010). Developing personal learning networks for open and social learning. In G. Veletsianos (Ed.), Emerging technologies in distance education. In T. Anderson (Series Ed.) Issues in Distance Education (pp. 109-128). Edmonton, Canada: AU Press.

Cowen, A. S., Chun, M. M., & Kuhl, B. A. (2014). Neural portraits of perception: Reconstructing face images from evoked brain activity. *NeuroImage, 94*, 12–22. doi:10.1016/j.neuroimage.2014.03.018 PMID:24650597

Craft, A. (2011). *Creativity and education futures: Learning in a digital age*. Stoke-on-Trent, UK: Trentham Books.

Craig, A., Downey, S., Garnett, G., McGrath, R. E., & Myers, J. D. (2009). 12 Immersive Environments for Massive, Multiperson, Online Learning. In B. Cope & M. Kalantzis (Eds.), *In Ubiquitous Learning* (pp. 131–143). Champaign, IL: University of Illinois Press.

Creighton, J. (2014). *The Kardashev Scale – Type I, II, III, IV & V Civilization*. Access: https://futurism.com/the-kardashev-scale-type-i-ii-iii-iv-v-civilization

Creighton. (2018). *The "Father of Artificial Intelligence" Says Singularity Is 30 Years Away*. Access: https://futurism.com/father-artificial-intelligence-singularity-decades-away

Cronin, P., Ryan, F., & Coughlan, M. (2008). Undertaking a literature review: A step-by-step approach. *British Journal of Nursing (Mark Allen Publishing), 17*(1), 38–43. doi:10.12968/bjon.2008.17.1.28059 PMID:18399395

Csikszentmihalyi, M. (2007). Mutluluğun Geleceği. In Gelecek 50 Yıl (pp.107-117). İstanbul: NTV.

Cult of Mac. (2018). *Today in Apple history: Siri debuts on iPhone 4s*. Retrieved from https://www.cultofmac.com/447783/today-in-apple-history-siri-makes-its-public-debut-on-iphone-4s/

Cyborg. (2018, Nov. 21). Retrieved from https://en.wikipedia.org/wiki/Cyborg

Dabbagh, N., & Kitsantas, A. (2012). Personal Learning Environments, social media, and self-regulated learning: A natural formula for connecting formal and informal learning. *The Internet and Higher Education, 15*(1), 3–8. Retrieved from https://www.sciencedirect.com/science/article/abs/pii/S1096751611000467

Dabbagh, N., Benson, A. D., Denham, A., Joseph, R., Al-Freih, M., Zgheib, G., . . . Zhetao, G. (2016). Social media. In *Learning Technologies and Globalization Pedagogical Frameworks and Applications* (pp. 21–26). New York: Springer International Publishing. doi:10.1007/978-3-319-22963-8_4

Dabbgah, N., & Fake, H. (2017). College students' perceptions of personal learning environment through the Lens of digital tools, processes and spaces. *Journal of New Approaches in Educational Research*, *6*(1), 28–38. doi:10.7821/naer.2017.1.215

Dagnelie, G. (2011). *Visual Prosthetics: Physiology, Bioengineering, Rehabilitation*. Berlin: Springer Science & Business Media. doi:10.1007/978-1-4419-0754-7

Dahlin, B. (2012). Our posthuman futures and education: Homo zappiens, cyborgs, and the new Adam. *Futures*, *44*(1), 55–63. doi:10.1016/j.futures.2011.08.007

Dalgarno, B., & Lee, M. J. (2010). What are the learning affordances of 3-D virtual environments? *British Journal of Educational Technology*, *41*(1), 10–32. doi:10.1111/j.1467-8535.2009.01038.x

Dalsgaard, C. (2006). Social software: E-learning beyond learning management systems. *European Journal of Open, Distance and e-learning*, *9*(2). Retrieved from http://www.eurodl.org/index.php?p=archives&year=2006&hal&article=228

Daly, B. M. (2004). *Transhumanism: Toward a brave new world?* Academic Press.

Damberger, T. (2013). A*re pedagogy and transhumanism compatible?* Retrieved from http://indiafuturesociety.org/are-pedagogy-and-transhumanism-compatible/

Dambrot, S. M. (2016). Exocortical Cognition: Heads in the cloud. In *Systems, Man, and Cybernetics (SMC), 2016 IEEE International Conference on* (pp. 004007-004014). IEEE.

Daniel, J. (2015). *Making sense of educational technology: From MOOCs to blended learning: What next? Journal of Open Education Research*.

Daniel, J. S. (1996). *Mega-Universities and Knowledge Media: Technology Strategies for Higher Education*. Abingdon, UK: Psychology Press.

Daradoumis, T., Bassi, R., Xhafa, F., & Caballé, S. (2013). A review on massive e-learning (MOOC) design, delivery and assessment. In *P2P, Parallel, Grid, Cloud and Internet Computing (3PGCIC), 2013 Eighth International Conference on* (pp. 208-213). IEEE.

Daskın, Z. (2017). *A Study of Faculty Members' and Instructors' Awareness, Routines and Use of Web 2.0 Tools in Foreign Language Teaching* (Unpublished Master Thesis). Hacettepe University.

Davies, A., Fidler, D., & Gorbis, M. (2011). *Future Work Skills 2020*. Institute for the Future for the University of Phoenix Research Institute. Retrieved from http://www.iftf.org/uploads/media/SR-1382A_UPRI_future_work_skills_sm.pdf

Davies, A., Fidler, D., & Gorbis, M. (2011). *Future Work Skills 2020*. Institute For the Future For the University of Phoenix Research Institute.

Dawkins, R. (2014). *Gen Bencildir*. Ankara, Turkey: Kuzey.

De Mul, J. (2005). TRANSHUMANISME: de convergentie van evolutie, humanisme en informatietechnologie. *Tydskrif vir Geesteswetenskappe*, *45*(2), 159-176.

de Mul, J. (2010b). Transhumanism: The Convergence of Evolution, Humanism, and Information Technology. In *Cyberspace Odyssey: Towards a Virtual Ontology and Anthropology* (pp. 243–262). Newcastle upon Tyne, UK: Cambridge Scholars Publishing.

Dearstyne. (2007). Blogs, mashups, and wikis: Oh my! *Information Management Journal, 41*(4), 24-33.

Del Aguila, J. W. V., & Solana, E. P. (2015). Transhumanism, neuroethics and human person. *Revista Bioética, 23*(3), 505–512. doi:10.1590/1983-80422015233087

Deleuze, G. (1994). *Difference and Repetition* (P. Patton, Trans.). New York: Columbia University Press.

Deloitte. (2016). *Global Human Capital Trends 2016 – The new organization: Different by design.* Deloitte University Press. Retrieved from https://www2.deloitte.com/content/dam/Deloitte/global/Documents/HumanCapital/gx-dup-global-human-capital-trends-2016.pdf

Demir, A. (2017). Siber Kültür ve Hiper Gerçeklikte Değişen Yaşam. *AJIT-e, 8*(29), 87. doi:10.5824/1309-1581.2017.4.005.x

Demiray, U. (2003). Defining distance education. In A. İşman, M. Barkan, & U. Demiray (Eds.), *Online Distance Education Book*. TOJET. Retrieved from http://www.tojet.net/e-book/ebook.htm

Demiray, U., & İşman, A. (2003). History of distance education. In A. İşman, M. Barkan, & U. Demiray (Eds.), *Online Distance Education Book*. TOJET. Retrieved from http://www.tojet.net/e-book/ebook.htm

Demiray, U., & İşman, A. (2003). History of distance education. In *Online Distance Education Book* (Eds. İşman, A., Barkan, M., & Demiray, U). TOJET. Retrieved from http://www.tojet.net/e-book/ebook.htm

Deng, L., & Yuen, A. H. K. (2011). Towards a framework for educational affordances of blogs. *Computers & Education, 56*(2), 441–451. doi:10.1016/j.compedu.2010.09.005

Department of Education. (1997). *Education White Paper 3: A Programme for the Transformation of Higher Education.* Pretoria: General Notice 1196 of 1997

DeSantis, J., Boyd, R., Marks, K., Putsch, J., & Shepler, T. (2017). Paradigm flip? Investigating technology-integrated history pedagogies. *Social Studies Research & Practice, 12*(3), 258–279. doi:10.1108/SSRP-07-2017-0036

Devedžić, V. (2004). Web intelligence and artificial intelligence in education. *Journal of Educational Technology & Society, 7*(4), 29–39.

Di Cerbo, F., Dodero, G., & Yng, T. L. B. (2011). Bridging the Gap between PLE and LMS. *2011 IEEE 11th International Conference on Advanced Learning Technologies*, 142–146. doi: 10.1109/ICALT.2011.48

Dickson, B. (2017). *How artificial intelligence is shaping the future of education.* Retrieved from https://www.pcmag.com/article/357483/how-artificial-intelligence-is-shaping-the-future-of-educati

Dickson, B. (2018). *AI, big data and the future of humanity.* Access: https://bdtechtalks.com/2018/01/31/yuval-harari-wef-ai-big-data-digital-dictatorship/

Digital Single Market. (2018). *ITC2918, Investing in the future.* Retrieved from https://youtu.be/5UqvCXFjShs

Digital Single Market. (2018, March 19). *Smart cities.* Retrieved from https://ec.europa.eu/digital-single-market/en/policies/smart-cities

Doedo, B. (2009). Transhumanism, Technology and The Future: Posthumanity Emerging or Sub-humanity Descending? *The Appraisal Journal, 7*(3), 39–54.

Dohmen, G. (1967). *Das Fernstudium, Ein neues padagogisches Forschungsund Arbeitsfeld.* Tubingen, Germany: DIFF.

Donald, M. (1991). *Origins of the modern mind: Three stages in the evolution of culture and cognition.* Cambridge, MA: Harvard University Press.

Donald, M. (1993). Precis of Origins of the modern mind: Three stages in the evolution of culture and cognition. *Behavioral and Brain Sciences, 16*(4), 737–748. doi:10.1017/S0140525X00032647

Doswell, J. T. (2006). Context-aware mobile augmented reality architecture for lifelong learning. In *Advanced Learning Technologies, 2006. Sixth International Conference on* (pp. 372-374). IEEE. 10.1109/ICALT.2006.1652448

Doswell, J. T. (2008). Wearable Augmented Reality System Architecture: for Mobile Assistance and Training. In *Proceedings of X Symposium on Virtual and Augmented Reality (SVR 2008), Joao Pessoa, Brazil* (pp. 129-132). Academic Press.

Doswell, J. T., & Skinner, A. (2014). Augmenting human cognition with adaptive augmented reality. In *International Conference on Augmented Cognition* (pp. 104-113). Cham, Switzerland: Springer International Publishing. 10.1007/978-3-319-07527-3_10

Doswell, J. T., Blake, M. B., & Butcher-Green, J. (2006). Mobile augmented reality system architecture for ubiquitous e-learning. In *Wireless, Mobile and Ubiquitous Technology in Education, 2006. WMUTE'06. Fourth IEEE International Workshop on* (pp. 121-123). IEEE. 10.1109/WMTE.2006.261358

Dowell, N. M., Graesser, A. C., & Cai, Z. (2016). Language and discourse analysis with Coh-Metrix: Applications from educational material to learning environments at scale. *Journal of Learning Analytics, 3*(3), 72–95. doi:10.18608/jla.2016.33.5

Downes, S. (2006). *Learning networks and connective knowledge.* Retrieved from http://itforum.coe.uga.edu/paper92/paper92.html

Downes, S. (2007, Feb. 3). *What connectivism is. Half an Hour.* Retrieved from https://halfanhour.blogspot.com/2007/02/what-connectivism-is.html

Downes, S. (2011). About this course affiliation and course registration. *CCK 2011.* Retrieved from http://cck11.mooc.ca/about.htm

Downes, S. (2012). *Connectivism and connective knowledge: Essays on meaning and learning networks.* Retrieved from. http://www.downes.ca/files/books/Connective_Knowledge-19May2012.pdf

Downes, S. (2014, March 10). *The MOOC of One.* Retrieved from https://www.downes.ca/cgi-bin/page.cgi?presentation=336

Downes, S. (2016). Personal and personalized learning. *EMMA Newsletter.* Retrieved from https://us8.campaign-archive.com/?u=17ce08681f559814caf1359d3&id=fa1770e58d&e=6fb1272e29

Dredge, S. (2015). *Artificial intelligence will become strong enough to be a concern, says Bill Gates.* Access: https://www.theguardian.com/technology/2015/jan/29/artificial-intelligence-strong-concern-bill-gates

Driscoll, M. P. (2000). *Psychology of learning for instruction.* Needham Heights, MA: Allyn & Bacon.

Dron, J. (2014). Innovation and change: Changing how we change. In O. Zawacki-Richter & T. Anderson (Eds.), *Online Distance Education: Towards a Research Agenda* (pp. 237–265). Edmonton, Canada: AU Press.

Drucker, P. (2009). *Büyük Değişimler Çağında Yönetim.* İstanbul: Optimist.

D-Transform. (n.d). *Transforming universities for the digital age.* Retrieved from http://www.dtransform.eu/about-us/

Dunleavy, M. & Simmons, B. (2011). *Assessing learning and identity in augmented reality science games.* Academic Press.

Dunleavy, M., Dede, C., & Mitchell, R. (2009). Affordances and limitations of immersive participatory augmented reality simulations for teaching and learning. *Journal of Science Education and Technology, 18*(1), 7–22. doi:10.100710956-008-9119-1

Eagleman, D. (2015). *The Brain: The Story of You*. New York: Pantheon Books.

Ebben, M., & Murphy, J. S. (2014). Unpacking MOOC Scholarly Discourse: A Review of Nascent MOOC Scholarship Learning. *Media and Technology*, *39*(3), 328–345. doi:10.1080/17439884.2013.878352

Eden, A. H., Moor, J. H., Søraker, J. H., & Steinhart, E. (2015). *Singularity Hypotheses*. Springer.

Educause. (2009). 7 things you should know about Personal Learning Environments. *Educause*. Retrieved from http://net.educause.edu/ir/library/pdf/ELI7049.pdf

Edwards, A. & Levin, D. (2012). *Better than well-being: The scope of transhumanism in the context of educational philosophy*. Academic Press.

Edwards, D. (2017a). Thinking Outside the Brain – Why We Need to Build a Decentralized Exocortex - Part 2 [Blog entry]. Retrieved from https://steemit.com/technology/@dana-edwards/thinking-outside-the-brain-why-we-need-to-build-a-decentralized-exocortex-part-2

Edwards, D. (2017b). Personal knowledge management [Blog entry]. Retrieved from https://steemit.com/enigma/@dana-edwards/personal-knowledge-management

Edwards, R. (1995). Different discourses, discourses of difference: Globalisation, distance education, and open learning. *Distance Education*, *16*(2), 241–255. doi:10.1080/0158791950160206

Eguchi, A. (2014). Educational Robotics for Promoting 21st Century Skills. *Journal of Automation. Mobile Robotics & Intelligent Systems.*, *8*, 6–9.

Ehresmann, A., von Ammon, R., Iakovidis, D. K., & Hunter, A. (2012). *Ubiquitous complex event processing in exocortex applications and mathematical approaches*. Retrieved from http://www.complexevents.com/2012/06/17/ubiquitous-complex-event-processing-in-exocortex-applications-and-mathematical-approaches/

Eisenberg, M. (2017a). Self-made: The body as frontier for the maker movement in education. In *Proceedings of the 7th Annual Conference on Creativity and Fabrication in Education (FabLearn '17)* (pp. 1-4). New York: Association for Computing Machinery (ACM). 10.1145/3141798.3141800

Eisenberg, M. (2017b). The binding of fenrir: Children in an emerging age of transhumanist technology. In *Proceedings of the 2017 Conference on Interaction Design and Children (IDC '17)* (pp. 328-333). New York: Association for Computing Machinery (ACM). 10.1145/3078072.3079744

Ekici, E., Ekici, F. T., & Kara, I. (2012). Validity and Reliability Study of ICT Self-Efficacy Perception Scale for Teachers. *Pamukkale University Journal of Education*, *31*(1), 53–65.

Emotiv. (2018). *Emotiv Brainwear*. Retrieved from https://www.emotiv.com/comparison/

End Time. (2018, Nov. 9). Retrieved from https://en.wikipedia.org/wiki/End_time

Endüstri 4.0. (2018). *Kasparov Satranç Oyunu*. Retrieved from https://www.endustri40.com/kasparov-satranc-oyunu-makineye-karsi-insan/

Engelbart, D. C. (1962). *Augmenting human intellect: a conceptual framework*. Retrieved from https://www.dougengelbart.org/pubs/augment-3906.html

Entz, S. (2006). Why pedagogy matters: The importance of teaching in a standards-based environment. *The forum on public policy*. Retrieved from https://files.eric.ed.gov/fulltext/EJ1099138.pdf

Erazo, E., & Derlin, R. (1995). *Distance learning and libraries in the cyberspace age*. Retrieved from http://www.checs.net/95conf/PROCEEDINGS/erazo.html

Ertmer, P. A. (1999). Addressing first-and second-order barriers to change: Strategies for technology integration. *Educational Technology Research and Development*, *47*(4), 47–61. doi:10.1007/BF02299597

Esfandiary, F. M., & FM-2030. (1989). *Are You a Transhuman? Monitoring and Stimulating Your Personal Rate of Growth in a Rapidly Changing World*. Clayton, Australia: Warner Books.

ETC. (2011). *Analytical Writing Sample Essays and Commentaries*. Available: https://www.ets.org/s/gre/accessible/gre_practice_test_2_writing_responses_18_point.pdf

ETC. (2018). *Sample Essay Responses and Rater Commentary for the Argument Task*. Available: https://www.ets.org/gre/revised_general/prepare/analytical_writing/argument/sample_responses

Ettinger, R.C.W. (1972), *Man into superman: The startling potential of human evolution and how to be part of it*. New York: St. Martin's Press.

European Commission. (2018). *Communication from the Commission to the European Parliament, the Council, the European Economic and Social Committee and the Committee of the regions on the digital education action plan*. Brussels: European Commission. COM (2018) 22 final. Retrieved from https://ec.europa.eu/education/sites/education/files/digital-education-action-plan.pdf

Evans, M. H., Fox, C. W., & Prescott, T. J. (2014). Machines learning-towards a new synthetic autobiographical memory. In *Conference on Biomimetic and Biohybrid Systems* (pp. 84-96). Cham, Switzerland: Springer International Publishing. 10.1007/978-3-319-09435-9_8

Everitt, T., Goertzel, B., & Potapov, A. (Eds.). (2017). *Artificial General Intelligence: 10th International Conference, AGI 2017, Melbourne, VIC, Australia, August 15-18, 2017, Proceedings* (Vol. 10414). Springer.

Evers, W. J. G., Brouwers, A., & Tomic, W. (2002). Burnout and self-efficacy: A study on teachers' beliefs when implementing an innovative educational system in the Netherlands. *The British Journal of Educational Psychology*, *72*(2), 227–243. doi:10.1348/000709902158865 PMID:12028610

Eynon, R. (2005). The use of the Internet in higher education. *Aslib Proceedings*, *57*(2), 168-180. Available at http://www.emeraldinsight.com/journals.htm?articleid=1465002

Fahimi, F. (2009). *Autonomous Robots: Modeling, Path Planning, and Control*. New York: Springer. doi:10.1007/978-0-387-09538-7

Fee, K. (2009). *Delivering E-Learning: A Complete Strategy for Design, Application and Assessment*. London: Kogan Page.

Ferguson, R., Sharples, M., & Beale, R. (2015). MOOCs 2030: a future for massive open online learning. In C. J. Bonk, M. M. Lee, T. C. Reeves, & T. H. Reynolds (Eds.), *MOOCs and Open Education around the World* (pp. 315–326). Abingdon, UK: Routledge. doi:10.4324/9781315751108-36

Fishman, B. J. (2006). It's not about the technology. *Teachers College Record*.

Ford, M. (2015). *Rise of the Robots, Technology and the Threat of a Jobless Future*. New York: Basic Books, Perseus Books Group.

Foreman, A. (2011). *Helping our students to develop their personal learning environment*. British Council.

Foster, J., & Yaoyuneyong, G. (2016). Teaching innovation: equipping students to overcome real-world challenges. *Higher Education Pedagogies*, (1), 42-56. doi:10.1080/23752696.2015.1134195

Compilation of References

FreeStyle Libre. (2018). *Şeker Kontrolü*. Retrieved from https://libresensor.com/?utm_source=adwords&utm_medium=google&utm_campaign=171025_Gadwords_NonBranded&utm_content=Parmak_delmeden&gclid=Cj0KCQjw9NbdBRCwARIsAPLsnFYgdUn_wqow2p6aUgYhQJzFExdhkgWlgelLYWJN5tTENnsDvHJBJ_MaAmFOEALw_wcB

Freire, P. (1972). *Pedagogy of the oppressed*. New York: Herder & Herder.

Freitas, R. A. (1998). Exploratory design in medical nanotechnology: A mechanical artificial red cell. *Artificial Cells, Blood Substitutes, and Biotechnology*, 26(4), 411–430. doi:10.3109/10731199809117682 PMID:9663339

Freitas, R. A. (1999). *Basic capabilities*. Georgetown, TX: Landes Bioscience.

Freitas, R. A. (2003). *Nanomedicine volume IIA: Biocompatibility*. Austin, TX: CRC Press. doi:10.1201/9781498712576

Frieadman, T. (2000). *Lexus ve Zeytin Ağacı Küreselleşmenin Geleceği*. İstanbul: Boyner Holding.

Fullan, M., & Langworthy, M. (2014). *A rich seam: How new pedagogies find deep learning*. London: Pearson.

Fullér, R. (1995). *The Lecture Notes, Neural Fuzzy Systems*. Abo Akademi University. Retrieved from http://uni-obuda.hu/users/fuller.robert/ln1.pdf

Gadamer, H. G. (2008). *Philosophical hermeneutics*. Univ of California Press.

Gagné, R. M., Wager, W. W., Golas, K. C., & Keller, J. M. (2005). *Principles of instructional design*. Belmont, CA: Wadsworth/Thomson Learning.

Galeon, D. (2017A). *Ray Kurzweil: AI Will Not Displace Humans, It's Going to Enhance Us*. Access: https://futurism.com/ray-kurzweil-ai-displace-humans-going-enhance

Galeon, D. (2017B). *Stephen Hawking: "I Fear That AI May Replace Humans Altogether"*. Access: https://futurism.com/stephen-hawking-ai-replace-humans

Garnham, A. (2017). *Artificial intelligence: An introduction*. Routledge. doi:10.4324/9780203704394

Garrison, D., & Shale, D. (1987). Mapping the boundaries of distance education: Problems in defining the field. *American Journal of Distance Education*, 1(1), 4–13. doi:10.1080/08923648709526567

Gartner. (2018). *IT Glossary*. Retrieved from https://www.gartner.com/it-glossary/digitization/

Gee, J. (2013). *The anti-education era: Creating smarter students through digital learning*. New York: Palgrave MacMillan.

GEF. (2017). *Global Education Futures*. Retrieved from https://edu2035.org/

Gemuenden, H. G., Lehner, P., & Kock, A. (2017). The Project-Oriented Organization and Its Contribution to Innovation. *International Journal of Project Management*, 2017(Sep). Retrieved from https://www.researchgate.net/publication/319672638_The_project-oriented_organization_and_its_contribution_to_innovation

Geraci, R. M. (2011). There and back again: Transhumanist evangelism in science fiction and popular science. *Implicit Religion*, 14(2), 141–172. doi:10.1558/imre.v14i2.141

Geraci, R. M. (2012). Video games and the transhuman inclination. *Zygon*, 47(4), 735–756. doi:10.1111/j.1467-9744.2012.01292.x

Ghahramani, Z. (2015). Probabilistic machine learning and artificial intelligence. *Nature*, 521(7553), 452–459. doi:10.1038/nature14541 PMID:26017444

Ghazinoory, S., Esmail Zadeh, A., & Memariani, A. (2007). Fuzzy SWOT analysis. *Journal of Intelligent & Fuzzy Systems*, *18*, 99–108.

Ghorbani, M., Velayati, R., & Ghorbani, M. M. (2011). Using Fuzzy TOPSIS to Determine Strategy Priorities by SWOT Analysis. *International Conference on Financial Management and Economics, Proceeding, 11,* 135-139. Retrieved from http://www.ipedr.com/list-36-1.html

Gibson, W. (1984). *Neuromancer.* New York: Ace.

Gibson, I., Rosen, D., & Stucker, B. (2015). *Additive Manufacturing Technologies.* New York: Springer. doi:10.1007/978-1-4939-2113-3

Gibson, W. (1982). Burning Chrome. *Omni (New York, N.Y.)*, *4*(10), 72–77.

Gillet, D., & Bogdanov, E. (2013). Cloud-savvy contextual spaces as agile personal learning environments or informal knowledge management solutions. In *Information Technology Based Higher Education and Training, 2013 International Conference on* (pp. 1-6). IEEE.

Glass. (2018). *Google Glass.* Retrieved from https://www.x.company/glass

GodI. J. (2019, Jan. 28). Retrieved from https://goingfarther.net/common-questions/is-jesus-god/

Goertzel, B. (2007A). *Artificial general intelligence* (vol. 2; C. Pennachin, Ed.). New York: Springer. doi:10.1007/978-3-540-68677-4

Goertzel, B. (2007B). Human-level artificial general intelligence and the possibility of a technological singularity: A reaction to Ray Kurzweil's The Singularity Is Near, and McDermott's critique of Kurzweil. *Artificial Intelligence*, *171*(18), 1161–1173. doi:10.1016/j.artint.2007.10.011

Goktas, Y., Yildirim, Z., & Yildirim, S. (2009). Investigation of K-12 teachers' ICT competencies and the contributing factors in acquiring these competencies. *The New Educational Review*, *17*(1), 276–294.

Gooch, J. (1998). *They Blazed the Trail for Distance Education.* Distance Education Clearinghouse.

Gordon, T. (1990). How Can Correspondence-based distance education be improved? A Survey of attitudes of Students who were not well disposed towards correspondence Study. *Journal of Distance Education*, *5*(1), 16–19.

Gori, M. (2017). *Machine Learning: A Constraint-based Approach.* Burlington, MA: Morgan Kaufmann.

Graesser, A. C., McNamara, D. S., & Kulikowich, J. M. (2011). Coh-Metrix: Providing multilevel analyses of text characteristics. *Educational Researcher*, *40*(5), 223–234. doi:10.3102/0013189X11413260

Graesser, A. C., McNamara, D. S., Louwerse, M. M., & Cai, Z. (2004). Coh-Metrix: Analysis of text on cohesion and language. *Behavior Research Methods, Instruments, & Computers*, *36*(2), 193–202. doi:10.3758/BF03195564 PMID:15354684

Graimann, B., Allison, B., & Pfurtscheller, G. (2009). Brain–computer interfaces: A gentle introduction. In *Brain-Computer Interfaces* (pp. 1–27). Springer Berlin Heidelberg. doi:10.1007/978-3-642-02091-9_1

Granella, F., Farina, S., Malferrari, G., & Manzoni, G.C. (1987). Drug abuse in chronic headache: A clinico-epidemiologic study. *Cephalalgia, 7,* 15–19.

Grech, A., & Camilleri, A. F. (2017). Blockchain in Education. Inamorato dos Santos, A. (Ed.) EUR 28778 EN; doi:10.2760/60649

Guàrdia, L., Maina, M., & Sangrà, A. (2013). MOOC design principles: A pedagogical approach from the learner's perspective. *eLearning Papers*, (33).

Guger. (2017). *Guger Technologies*. Retrieved from http://www.gtec.at/

Gülbahar, Y. (2008). ICT Usage in Higher Education: A Case Study on Preservice Teachers and Instructors. *The Turkish Online Journal of Educational Technology, 7*(1), 32–27.

Gulliksen, J., Lantz, A., Walldius, Å., Sandblad, B., & Åborg, C. (2015). *Digital arbetsmiljö* [Digital work environment]. Report 2015:17: Stockholm (Arbetsmiljöverket). Retrieved from https://www.av.se/globalassets/filer/publikationer/rapporter/digital_arbetsmiljo-rap-2015-17.pdf

Gürdilek. (2016). *Michio Kaku'nun gözünden gelecek 20 yıl*. Access: https://kurious.ku.edu.tr/wp-content/uploads/2016/02/20160212103512-kule_37_michio_kaku.pdf

Gurrin, C., Smeaton, A. F., & Doherty, A. R. (2014). Lifelogging: Personal big data. *Foundations and Trends in Information Retrieval, 8*(1), 1-125.

Gürsakal, N. (2017). *Makine Öğrenmesi ve Derin Öğrenme*. Bursa, Turkey: Dora Basım.

Güzel, E. (2016). Dijital Kültür ve Çevrimiçi Sosyal Ağlarda Rekabetin Aktörü: 'Dijital Habitus'. *Gümüşhane Üniversitesi İletişim Fakültesi Elektronik Dergisi, 4*(1), 83–103.

Habermas, J. (2003). *The future of human nature*. Oxford, UK: Blackwell Polity.

Hall, G. S. (1905). What is pedagogy? *The Pedagogical Seminary, XII*(4), 375–383. doi:10.1080/08919402.1905.10534667

Halverson, L. R., Spring, K. J., Huyett, S., Henrie, C. R., & Graham, C. R. (2017). Blended learning research in higher education and K-12 settings. In M. Spector, B. Lockee, & M. Childress (Eds.), *Learning, Design, and Technology* (pp. 1–30). Cham, Switzerland: Springer. doi:10.1007/978-3-319-17727-4_31-1

Hansell, G. R. (2011). *H+/-: Transhumanism and its Critics*. Xlibris Corporation.

Hansen, B. (2001). Distance learning. *CQ Researcher, 11*(42), 1–24.

Hansen, D., Shneiderman, B., & Smith, M. A. (2010). *Analyzing social media networks with NodeXL: Insights from a connected world*. Burlington, MA: Morgan Kaufmann.

Harari, Y. N. (2018). 21 Lessons for the 21st Century. New York: Spiegel & Grau.

Harari, Y. N. (2018). *21. Yüzyıl İçin 21 Ders*. İstanbul: Kolektif kitap .

Harari, Y. N. (2016). *Homo Deus. A Brief History of Tomorrow*. Harvill Secker.

Harari, Y. N. (2018). *21 Lessons for the 21st Century*. Random House.

Haraway, D. (1991). A cyborg manifesto: Science, technology, and socialist-feminism in the late twentieth century. In D. J. Haraway (Ed.), *Simians, cyborgs, and women: The reinvention of nature* (pp. 149–182). New York: Routledge. (Original work published 1985)

Hardyment, R. (2013). *Future Business: The Four Mega-trends that Every Company Needs to Prepare for*. Corporate Citizenship. Retrieved from https://corporate-citizenship.com/wp-content/uploads/Corporate-Citizenship-Research-and-Futures.pdf

Harel, D., & Koren, Y. (2001). A Fast Multi-Scale Method for Drawing Large Graphs. In *Graph Drawing: 8th International Symposium, GD 2000 Proceedings* (No. 1984, p.183). Springer Science & Business Media. 10.1007/3-540-44541-2_18

Hargreaves, A. (2002). *Teaching in the knowledge society. Education in the age of insecurity*. New York: Teachers College Press. Retrieved from http://citeseerx.ist.psu.edu/viewdoc/download?doi=10.1.1.533.6940&rep=rep1&type=pdf

Harley, J. M., Poitras, E. G., Jarrell, A., Duffy, M. C., & LaJoie, S. P. (2016). Comparing virtual and location-based augmented reality mobile learning: Emotions and learning outcomes. *Educational Technology Research and Development*, *64*(3), 359–388. doi:10.100711423-015-9420-7

Harrison, P., & Wolyniak, J. (2015, Sept. 1). The History of 'Transhumanism. *Notes and Queries*, *62*(3), 465–467. doi:10.1093/notesj/gjv080

Hartley, R. (2018). *What is the role of blockchain in education?* Retrieved from https://edtechnology.co.uk/Blog/what-is-the-role-of-blockchain-in-education/

Hauskeller, M. (2012). Reinventing cockaigne: Utopian themes in Transhumanist Thought. *The Hastings Center Report*, *42*(2), 39–47. doi:10.1002/hast.18 PMID:22733330

Hawking, S. (2016). This is the most dangerous time for our planet. *The Guardian*, *1*.

Hawking, S., & Mlodinow, L. (2017). *The Grand Design*. Academic Press.

Hawking, S., Russel, S., Tegmark, M., & Wilczek, F. (2015, January 5). Stephen Hawking: are we taking artificial intelligence seriously. *The Independent*.

Hebb, D. O. (1949). *The Organization of Behavior -a Neuropsychological Theory*. John What & Sons. Inc. Available at http://s-f-walker.org.uk/pubsebooks/pdfs/The_Organization_of_Behavior-Donald_O._Hebb.pdf

HEC. (2006). *Egitim fakultelerinde uygulanacak yeni programlar hakkında acıklama*. Retrieved from http://www.yok.gov.tr/egitim/ogretmen/yeni_programlar_ve_icerik.htm

Heeter, C. (1992). Being there: The subjective experience of presence. *Presence (Cambridge, Mass.)*, *1*(2), 262–271. doi:10.1162/pres.1992.1.2.262

Hefferon, K., & Boniwell, I. (2011). *Positive Psychology: Theory, Research and Applications*. Open University Press.

Hefferon, K., & Boniwell, I. (2014). *Pozitif Psikoloji*. Ankara, Turkey: Nobel.

Heick, T. (2013). *4 phases of inquiry-based learning: A guide for teachers*. Academic Press.

Heick, T. (2018). *The Difference Between Pedagogy, Andragogy, And Heutagogy*. Retrieved from https://www.teachthought.com/pedagogy/a-primer-in-heutagogy-and-self-directed-learning/

HeideggerM. (2018, Nov. 20). Retrieved from https://en.wikipedia.org/wiki/Martin_Heidegger

Heimlich, R. (2010, Dec. 29). *Baby Boomers Retire*. FactTank. Pew Research Center. Retrieved from http://www.pewresearch.org/fact-tank/2010/12/29/baby-boomers-retire/

Helfer, M. E., Kempe, R. S., & Krugman, R. D. (1997). *The battered child* (5th ed.). Chicago: University of Chicago Press.

Hendrix, A., & Yampolskiy, R. (2017). *Automated IQ Estimation from Writing Samples*. MAICS.

Hennig-Thurau, T., Malthouse, E. C., Friege, C., Gensler, S., Lobschat, L., Rangaswamy, A., & Skiera, B. (2010). The impact of new media on customer relationships. *Journal of Service Research*, *13*(3), 311–330. doi:10.1177/1094670510375460

Henri, F., Charlier, B., & Limpens, F. (2008). Understanding ple as an essential component of the learning process. *Proc. of ED-Media, AACE, Chesapeake*, 3766-3770. Retrieved from https://www.learntechlib.org/p/28906/

Hepp, A. (2010). *Cultural studies und Medienanalyse: eine Einführung*. Springer-Verlag. doi:10.1007/978-3-531-92190-7

Hernaes, C. (2016). *The ethics of transhumanism.* Retrieved from https://techcrunch.com/2016/08/26/the-ethics-of-transhumanism/

Hew, K. F. (2011). Students' and teachers' use of Facebook. *Computers in Human Behavior, 27*(2), 662–676. doi:10.1016/j.chb.2010.11.020

Heydenrych, J. F., & Prinsloo, P. (2010). Revisiting the five generations of distance education: Quo vadis? *Progressio, 32*(1), 5–26.

Hicks, A., & Sinkinson, C. (2014). Critical connections: Personal learning environments and information literacy. *Research in Learning Technology, 23*. doi:10.3402/rlt.v23.21193

Hines, A. (2011). *A Dozen Surprises about the Future of Work.* Wiley Periodicals. Retrieved from https://onlinelibrary.wiley.com/doi/pdf/10.1002/ert.20326

Hines, A. (2018). *Don't Be Surprised by the Future.* Society for Marketing Professional Services. Retrieved from http://www.andyhinesight.com/wp-content/uploads/2018/03/120-Dont-Be-Surprised-by-the-Future_Marketer-February-2018.pdf

Hirschberg, J., & Manning, C. D. (2015). Advances in natural language processing. *Science, 349*(6245), 261–266. doi:10.1126cience.aaa8685 PMID:26185244

Hismanoglu, M. (2012). Prospective EFL Teachers' Perceptions of ICT Integration: A Study of Distance Higher Education in Turkey. *Journal of Educational Technology & Society, 15*(1), 185–196.

Holland, J. H. (2007). Bizi Bekleyen Gelişmeler ve Bunları Tahmin Etme Yolu. In *Gelecek 50 Yıl* (pp. 191–216). İstanbul: NTV.

Holmberg, B. (1985). The feasibility of a theory of teaching for distance education and a proposed theory (ZIFF Papiere 60). Hagen, West Germany: Fern Universität, Zentrales Institute fur Fernstudienforschung Arbeitsbereich. (ERIC Document Reproduction Service No. ED290013)

Holmberg, B. (1977). *Distance Education: A Survey and Bibliography.* London: Kogan Page.

Holmberg, B. (1986). *Growth and structure of distance education* (3rd ed.). London: Croom Helm.

Hololens. (2018). *Microsoft Hololens.* Retrieved from https://www.microsoft.com/en-us/hololens)

Hong, Z. W., Huang, Y. M., Hsu, M., & Shen, W. W. (2016). Authoring robot-assisted instructional materials for improving learning performance and motivation in EFL classrooms. *Journal of Educational Technology & Society, 19*, 337–349.

Horb, M. E., Shen, C. N., Tosh, D., & Slack, J. M. (2003). Experimental conversion of liver to pancreas. *Current Biology, 13*(2), 105–115. doi:10.1016/S0960-9822(02)01434-3 PMID:12546783

Horikawa, T., Tamaki, M., Miyawaki, Y., & Kamitani, Y. (2013). Neural decoding of visual imagery during sleep. *Science, 340*(6132), 639–642. doi:10.1126cience.1234330 PMID:23558170

Horzum, M. B. (2010). An investigation of teachers' awareness, frequency of use and purposes of Web 2.0 tools in terms of different variables. *International Journal of Human Sciences, 7*(1), 603–634.

Hosseini-Nasab, H., Hosseini-Nasab, A., & Milani, A. S. (2011). Coping with imprecision in strategic planning: A case study using fuzzy SWOT analysis. *IBusiness, 3*(1), 23–29. doi:10.4236/ib.2011.31004

Housman, M. (2018). Why 'augmented intelligence' is a better way to describe AI. *AINews.* Retrieved from https://www.artificialintelligence-news.com/2018/05/24/why-augmented-intelligence-is-a-better-way-to-describe-ai/

Houston, B. (2000). *Exocortex.* Retrieved from https://everything2.com/title/exocortex

Hoy, M. B. (2018). Alexa, Siri, Cortana, and More: An Introduction to Voice Assistants. *Medical Reference Services Quarterly*, *37*(1), 81–88. doi:10.1080/02763869.2018.1404391 PMID:29327988

HRL. (2016). *HRL demonstrates the potential to enhance the human intellect's existing capacity to learn new skills*. Retrieved from http://www.hrl.com/news/2016/02/10/hrl-demonstrates-the-potentialto-enhance-the-human-intellects-existing-capacity-to-learn-new-skills

Hsu, Y., Hung, J., & Ching, Y. (2013). Trends of educational technology research: More than a decade of international research in six SSCLI-indexed refereed journals. *Educational Technology Research and Development*, *61*(4), 685–705. doi:10.100711423-013-9290-9

Hughes, J. (2013). Transhumanism and personal identity. *The Transhumanist Reader: Classical And Contemporary Essays On The Science, Technology, And Philosophy Of The Human Future*, 227-233.

Hughes, J. J. (2001). *The Politics of Transhumanism, Version 2.0*. Paper presented at the Annual Meeting of the Society for Social Studies of Science, Cambridge, MA.

Hughes, J. (2004). *Citizen cyborg: Why democratic societies must respond to the redesigned human of the future*. Cambridge, MA: Westview Press.

Hughes, J. (2010). Contradictions from the enlightenment roots of transhumanism. *The Journal of Medicine and Philosophy*, *35*(6), 622–640. doi:10.1093/jmp/jhq049 PMID:21135025

Hughes, J. J. (2006). What comes after Homo sapiens? *New Scientist*, *192*(2578), 70–72. doi:10.1016/S0262-4079(06)61144-5

Hughes, J. J. (2007). The struggle for a smarter world. *Futures*, *39*(8), 942–954. doi:10.1016/j.futures.2007.03.002

Humanity Plus. (2008). *Transhumanist FAQ 3.0*. Retrieved from https://humanityplus.org/philosophy/transhumanist-faq/

Humanity+. (2016). *Transhumanist Declaration*. Retrieved from https://humanityplus.org/philosophy/transhumanist-declaration/

Humanity+. (2017). Philosophy. Retrieved from https://humanityplus.org/philosophy/philosophy-2/

Humanity+. (2018). *Transhumanist Declaration*. Retrieved from https://humanityplus.org/philosophy/transhumanist-declaration/

Humanity+. (2018). *What is the Mission of Humanity+*. Retrieved from https://humanityplus.org/about/mission/.

Husbands, C., & Pearce, J. (2012). *What makes great pedagogy? Nine claims from research*. Nottingham, UK: National College for School Leadership. Retrieved from https://assets.publishing.service.gov.uk/government/uploads/system/uploads/attachment_data/file/329746/what-makes-great-pedagogy-nine-claims-from-research.pdf

Hutchinson, D. (2012). The Future History of Consciousness. Integral Review: A Transdisciplinary & Transcultural Journal for New Thought, Research, &. *Praxis (Bern)*, *8*(1), 62–67.

Huxley, A. (1932). *Brave New World*. London: Chatto & Windus.

Huxley, J. (1927). *Religion without revelation*. London: E. Benn.

Huxley, J. (1957). *New bottles for new wine: Essays*. London: Chatto & Windus.

Huxley, J. (1968). Transhumanism. *Journal of Humanistic Psychology*, *8*(1), 73–76. doi:10.1177/002216786800800107

Hwang G. J., & Tsai, C. C. (2011). Research trends in mobile and ubiquitous learning: A review of publications in selected journals from 2001 to 2010. *Br. J. Educ. Technol.,42*(4). doi:10.1111/j.1467-8535.2011.01183.x

Hwang, G. J. (2014). Definition, framework and research issues of smart learning environments: A context-aware ubiquitous learning perspective. *Smart Learning Environments*, *1*(1), 4. doi:10.118640561-014-0004-5

Hymer, B., Watkins, C., Dawson, E., & Buxton, R. (2015). Embedded voices: Building a non-learning culture within a learning enrichment programme. *Gifted Education International*, *31*(1), 5–24. doi:10.1177/0261429413498487

İçen, D., & Günay S. (2014). Uzman Sistemler ve İstatistik. *İstatistikçiler Dergisi: İstatistik ve Aktüerya, 7*, 37-45.

İlin, M., & Segal, E. (2000). *İnsan Nasıl İnsan Oldu*. İstanbul: Say Yayınları.

imore. (2018). The Secret History of iPhone. Retrieved from https://www.imore.com/history-iphone-original

Inamorato dos Santos, A., Punie, Y., & Castaño-Muñoz, J. (2016). Opening up education: A support framework for higher education institutions. *JRC Science for Policy Report, EUR 27938 EN*. Retrieved from http://publications.jrc.ec.europa.eu/repository/bitstream/JRC101436/jrc101436.pdf

Intelligence Quotient. (2018, Nov. 20). Retrieved from https://en.wikipedia.org/wiki/Intelligence_quotient

İş Dünyasını Değiştirecek Altı Trend. (2012). Retrieved from http://www.ntv.com.tr

Istifci, I. (2014). Perceptions of EFL Students on Educational Use of Facebook. In *Proceedings of the European Conference on Social Media, ECSM* (pp. 219-225). Academic Conferences and Publishing International.

Istifci, I., & Girginer, H. (2011). Prospective English Language Teachers and Web 2.0 Tools. In E-Learning in Turkey, Developments and Applications II (pp. 263-279). Eskişehir, Turkey: Anadolu University Publications.

Istifci, I., Lomidazde, T., & Demiray, U. (2011). An effective role of E-learning technology for the English language teaching by using meta communication actors. *The Turkish Online Journal of Distance Education*, *12*(4), 200–211.

Istvan, Z. (2014). *A New Generation of Transhumanists Is Emerging*. Retrieved from https://www.huffingtonpost.com/zoltan-istvan/a-new-generation-of-trans_b_4921319.html

Istvan, Z. (2015A). *Why I'm running for president—and got a chip implanted in my hand*. Retrieved from https://www.dailydot.com/via/zoltan-istvan-rfid-chip-implant/

Istvan, Z. (2015B). *Transhumanism Is Booming and Big Business Is Noticing*. Retrieved from https://www.huffpost.com/entry/transhumanism-is-becoming_b_7807082

Istvan, Z. (2016). *Why Haven't We Met Aliens Yet? Because They've Evolved into AI*. Retrieved from https://motherboard.vice.com/en_us/article/vv7bkb/why-havent-we-met-aliens-yet-because-theyve-evolved-into-ai

Ivanova, M. (2009). From personal learning environment building to professional learning network forming. *The 5th. International Scientific Conference e Learning and Software For Education*. Bükreş. Retrieved from https://adlunap.ro/else2009/papers/1001.1.Ivanova.pdf

Jackson, R., & Watkin, C. (2004). The Resilience İnventory: Seven Essential Skills for Overcoming Life's Obstacles and Determining Happiness. *Selection and Development Review*, *20*(6), 13–17.

Jahnke, I. (2016). *Digital didactical designs: Teaching and learning in cross action spaces*. New York: Routledge.

James, K. P., & Gragory, F. H. (1986). An Academic Stress Scale: Identification and rated importance of academic stressors. *Psychological Reports*, *59*(2), 415–426. doi:10.2466/pr0.1986.59.2.415

Jasinevičius, R., & Petrauskas, V. (2006). Dynamic SWOT Analysis as a Tool for System Experts. *Engineering Economics, 5*(50), 33-35.

Jewitt, C. (2008). Multimodality and literacy in school classrooms. *Review of Research in Education, 32*(1), 241–267. doi:10.3102/0091732X07310586

Jirgensons, M., & Kapenieks, J. (2018). Blockchain and the future of digital learning credential assessment and management. *Journal of Teacher Education for Sustainability, 20*(1), 145–156. doi:10.2478/jtes-2018-0009

Johnson, M., & Liber, O. (2008). The personal learning environment and the human condition: From theory to teaching practice. *Interactive Learning Environments, 16*(1), 3–15. doi:10.1080/10494820701772652

Johnson, W. L., Rickel, J. W., & Lester, J. C. (2000). Animated pedagogical agents: Face-to-face interaction in interactive learning environments. *International Journal of Artificial Intelligence in Education, 11*(1), 47–78.

Jonassen, D. H., Wilson, B. G., Wang, S., & Grabinger, R. S. (1993). Constructivist uses of expert systems to support learning. *Journal of Computer-Based Instruction, 20*(3), 86–94.

Jordan, M. I., & Mitchell, T. M. (2015). Machine learning: Trends, perspectives, and prospects. *Science, 349*(6245), 255–260. doi:10.1126cience.aaa8415 PMID:26185243

Joy, B. (2000, April). Why the Future Doesn't Need Us. *Wired*. Retrieved from https://www.wired.com/2000/04/joy-2/

Kad, D., & Thorat, S. H. K. (2018). Nanorobotics: Medicine of the future. *World Journal of Pharmacy and Pharmaceutical Sciences, 7*(8), 1393–1416.

Kadhiravan, S., & Kumar, K. (2002). Stress coping Skills among college students. *Journal of Arts, Science and Commerce, 3*(4).

Kaklauskas, A., Amaratunga, D., Haigh, R., & Kuzminske, A. (2016). Intelligent mooc for the disaster resilience dprof programme. In *Proceedings of the 6th International Conference on Building Resilience: building resilience to address the unexpected*. Massey University / The University of Auckland, New Zealand. Retrieved from http://eprints.hud.ac.uk/id/eprint/30295/

Kaku, M. (2017). Discussion question: Are human brains big enough? *Confronting Complexity*, 310.

Kaku, M. (2014). *The Future of the Mind: The Scientific Quest to Understand, Enhance, and Empower the Mind*. New York: Doubleday.

Kaku, M. (2018). *The Future of Humanity: Terraforming Mars*. Penguin.

Kamhi-Stein, L. D. (2000). Looking to the future of TESOL teacher education: Web-based bulletin board discussions in a methods course. *TESOL Quarterly, 34*(3), 423–455. doi:10.2307/3587738

Kanten, P. (2016). Pozitif Örgütsel Davranışın Doğuşu ve Gelişimi. In Örgütlerde Davranışın Karanlık ve Aydınlık Yüzü (pp. 3-62). Ankara, Turkey: Nobel.

Kanwar, A. S., Carr, A., Ortlieb, K., & Mohee, R. (2018). Opportunities and challenges for campus-based universities in Africa to translate into dual-mode delivery. *Distance Education, 39*(2), 140–158. doi:10.1080/01587919.2018.1457944

Kaplan, A. M., & Haenlein, M. (2010). Users of the world, unite! The challenges and opportunities of social media. *Business Horizons, 53*(1), 59–68. doi:10.1016/j.bushor.2009.09.003

Kapoor, A., Shenoy, P., & Tan, D. (2008). Combining brain computer interfaces with vision for object categorization. In *Computer Vision and Pattern Recognition, 2008. CVPR 2008. IEEE Conference on* (pp. 1-8). IEEE. 10.1109/CVPR.2008.4587618

Karaduman, N. (2017). Popüler kültürün oluşmasında ve aktarılmasında sosyal medyanın rolü. *Erciyes Üniversitesi Sosyal Bilimler Enstitüsü Dergisi, 31*(43), 113–133.

Karakoç, E. (2007). *Medya aracılığıyla popüler kültürün aktarılmasında toplumsal değişkenlerin rolü* (Doctoral dissertation). Selçuk Üniversitesi Sosyal Bilimler Enstitüsü.

Karaman, F. (2012). Artificial Intelligence Enabled Search Engines (AIESE) and the Implications. In J. Christophe, I. Biskri, J. G. Ganascia, & M. Roux (Eds.), *Next Generation Search Engines: Advanced Models for Information Retrieval*. Hershey, PA: IGI Publications. doi:10.4018/978-1-4666-0330-1.ch019

Karatop, B., Kubat, C., & Uygun, Ö. (2018). Determining the Strategies on Turkish Automotive Sector Using Fuzzy AHP Based on the SWOT Analysis. *Sakarya University Journal of Science, 22*(5), 1–1. doi:10.16984aufenbilder.298875

Katsevman, M. (2008). *Exploring the exocortex: an approach to optimizing human productivity*. Retrieved from http://logarchy.org/exocortex.pdf

Kaufmann, H. (2003). *Collaborative augmented reality in education*. Imagina Conference 2003, Monaco Mediax, Monaco.

Kay, J., Reimann, P., Diebold, E., & Kummerfeld, B. (2013). *MOOCs: So Many Learners, So Much Potential, AI and Education*. IEEE Computer Society.

Kay, K. N., Naselaris, T., Prenger, R. J., & Gallant, J. L. (2008). Identifying natural images from human brain activity. *Nature, 452*(7185), 352–355. doi:10.1038/nature06713 PMID:18322462

Keegan, D. (1986). *The foundations of distance education*. London: Croom Helm.

Kelly, R. (2012). *Educating for creativity: A global conversation*. Edmonton, Canada: Brush Education.

Kember, D., McNaught, C., Chong, F. C., Lam, P., & Cheng, K. F. (2010). Understanding the ways in which design features of educational websites impact upon student learning outcomes in blended learning environments. *Computers & Education, 55*(3), 1183–1192. doi:10.1016/j.compedu.2010.05.015

Kennedy, J. (2014). Characteristics of massive open online courses (MOOCs): A research review, 2009-2012. *Journal of Interactive Online Learning, 13*(1).

Kerawalla, L., Luckin, R., Seljeflot, S., & Woolard, A. (2006). Making it real: Exploring the potential of augmented reality for teaching primary school science. *Virtual Reality (Waltham Cross), 10*(3-4), 163–174. doi:10.100710055-006-0036-4

Kerawalla, L., Pearce, D., Yuill, N., Luckin, R., & Harris, A. (2008). "I'm keeping those there, are you?" The role of a new user interface paradigm—Separate control of shared space (SCOSS)—In the col- laborative decision-making process. *Computers & Education, 50*(1), 193–206. doi:10.1016/j.compedu.2006.04.007

Kharpal, A. (2017). *Stephen Hawking says A.I. could be 'worst event in the history of our civilization'*. Access: https://www.cnbc.com/2017/11/06/stephen-hawking-ai-could-be-worst-event-in-civilization.html

Khedekar, N. (2013). *WhatsApp overtakes Facebook Messenger to be top mobile messaging app*. Retrieved from http://tech.firstpost.com/news-analysis/whatsapp-overtakes-facebook-messenger-to-be-top-mobile-messaging-app-108826.html

Kheirkhah, A. S., Esmailzadeh, A., & Ghazinoory, S. (2009). Developing strategies to reduce the risk of hazardous materials transportation in Iran using the method of fuzzy SWOT analysis. *Transport, 24*(4), 325–332. doi:10.3846/1648-4142.2009.24.325-332

Kimel, D. V. (2016, May 18). In defense of transhumanism. *The Washington Post*. Retrieved from https://www.washingtonpost.com/news/in-theory/wp/2016/05/18/in-defense-of-transhumanism/?noredirect=on&utm_term=.4418fc5fc27f

King, B. (2016). *Augmented Artırılmış Gerçeklik*. İstanbul: MediaCat Kitapları.

King, F. B., Young, M. F., Drivere-Richmond, K., & Schrader, P. G. (2001). Defining distance learning and distance education. *AACE Journal*, *9*(1), 1–14.

Kinshuk, C., Chen, N.-S., Cheng, I.-L., & Chew, S. W. (2016). Evolution is not enough: Revolutionizing current learning environments to smart learning environments. *International Journal of Artificial Intelligence in Education*, *26*(2), 561–581. doi:10.100740593-016-0108-x

Kirschner, P. A., & Erkens, G. (2006). Cognitive tools and mindtools for collaborative learning. *Journal of Educational Computing Research*, *35*(2), 199–209. doi:10.2190/R783-230M-0052-G843

Kiseleva, J., Williams, K., Hassan Awadallah, A., Crook, A. C., Zitouni, I., & Anastasakos, T. (2016). Predicting user satisfaction with intelligent assistants. In *Proceedings of the 39th International ACM SIGIR conference on Research and Development in Information Retrieval* (pp. 45-54). ACM.

Klichowski, M. (2015). Transhumanism and the idea of education in the world of cyborgs. In H. Krauze-Sikorska & M. Klichowski (Eds.), *The educational and social world of a child. Discourses of communication, subjectivity and cyborgization*. Poznan, Poland: Adam Mickiewicz University Press.

Klinger, M. B., & Coffman, T. (2012). Building knowledge through dynamic meta-communication. In G. Kuruback, U. Demiray, & T. V. Yuzer (Eds.), *Meta-communication for reflective online conversations: Models for distance education*. Hershey, PA: IGI Global. doi:10.4018/978-1-61350-071-2.ch008

Klopfer, E. (2008). *Augmented learning*. Cambridge, MA: MIT press. doi:10.7551/mitpress/9780262113151.001.0001

Klopfer, E., & Squire, K. (2008). Environmental Detectives - the development of an augmented reality platform for environmental simulations. *Educational Technology Research and Development*, *56*(2), 203–228. doi:10.100711423-007-9037-6

Knowles, M. (1990). *The adult learner: A neglected species* (4th ed.). Houston, TX: Gulf Publishing Co.

Knowles, M. S. (1980). *The Modern Practice of Adult Education*. New York: Cambridge Press.

Knowles, M. S. (1984). *Andragogy in Action* (1st ed.). San Francisco: Jossey-Bass.

Koehler, M. J., & Mishra, P. (2005b). What happens when teachers design educational technology? The development of technological pedagogical content knowledge. *Journal of Educational Computing Research*, *32*(2), 131–152. doi:10.2190/0EW7-01WB-BKHL-QDYV

Koehler, M. J., & Mishra, P. (2009). What is technological pedagogical content knowledge? *Contemporary Issues in Technology & Teacher Education*, *9*(1), 60–70.

Kolb, A. Y., & Kolb, D. A. (2005). Learning styles and learning spaces: Enhancing experiential learning in higher education. *Academy of Management Learning & Education*, *4*(2), 193–212. doi:10.5465/amle.2005.17268566

Kommers, P. (2003). Experiential Learning through Constructivist Learning Tools. *International Journal of Computers and Applications*, *25*(1), 8–9. doi:10.1080/1206212X.2003.11441687

Kop, R., & Fournier, H. (2013). Developing a framework for research on personal learning environments. *eLearning Papers*. Retrieved from https://dialnet.unirioja.es/servlet/articulo?codigo=6348049

Compilation of References

Kopcha, T. J. (2012). Teachers' perceptions of the barriers to technology integration and practices with technology under situated professional development. *Computers & Education*, *59*(4), 1109–1121. doi:10.1016/j.compedu.2012.05.014

Koper, R. (2014). Conditions for effective smart learning environments. *Smart Learning Environments*, *1*(1), 5. doi:10.118640561-014-0005-4

Korhonen, A. M., Ruhalahti, S., & Veermans, M. (2018). The online learning process and scaffolding in student teachers' personal learning environments. *Education and Information Technologies*, 1–25. Retrieved from https://link.springer.com/article/10.1007/s10639-018-9793-4

Kose, U. & Arslan, A. (2015).E-Learning experience with artificial intelligence supported software: n International Application on English Language Courses. *Glokalde, 1*(3).

Kose, U. (2015). For an intelligent e-learning: A managerial model suggestion for artificial intelligence supported e-learning content flow. In U. Kose & D. Koc (Eds.), *Artificial intelligence applications in distance education* (pp. 149–160). Hershey, PA: IGI Global. doi:10.4018/978-1-4666-6276-6.ch009

Kose, U. (2015). On the Intersection of Artificial Intelligence and Distance Education. In U. Kose & D. Koc (Eds.), *Artificial Intelligence Applications in Distance Education* (pp. 1–11). Hershey, PA: IGI Global; doi:10.4018/978-1-4666-6276-6.ch001

Kosmyna, N., Tarpin-Bernard, F., & Rivet, B. (2015). Towards brain computer interfaces for recreational activities: Piloting a drone. In *Human-Computer Interaction* (pp. 506–522). Springer International Publishing.

Kosow, H., & Robert Gaßner, R. (2008). *Methods of Future and Scenario Analysis. Studies / Deutsches Institut für Entwicklungspolitik gGmbH. DIE Research Project Development Policy: Questions for the Future*. Bonn, Germany: German Development Institue.

Krashen, S. D. (1988). *Second Language Acquisition and Second Language Learning*. Prentice-Hall International.

Kroop, S. (2013). Evaluation on students' and teachers' acceptance of widget-and cloud-based personal learning environments. *Journal of Universal Computer Science*, *19*(14), 2150–2171. Retrieved from http://jucs.org/jucs_19_14/evaluation_on_students_and/jucs_19_14_2150_2171_kroop.pdf

Kubat, C., (2012). MATLAB: Yapay Zeka ve Mühendislik Uygulamaları. *Beşiz Yayınları*.

Kumar, A., Irsoy, O., Ondruska, P., Iyyer, M., Bradbury, J., Gulrajani, I., ... Socher, R. (2016). Ask me anything: Dynamic memory networks for natural language processing. In *International Conference on Machine Learning* (pp. 1378-1387). New York.

Kurt, S. (2010). Technology use in elementary education in Turkey: A case study. *New Horizons in Education*, *58*(1), 65–76.

Kurzweil, R. (2006). *The Singularity Is Near: When Humans Transcend Biology*. London, UK: Penguin Books.

Kurzweil, R. (2012). *How to Create a Mind: The Secret of Human Thought Revealed*. New York: Viking Penguin.

Kurzweil, R. (2015). Superintelligence and singularity. *Science fiction and philosophy: From time travel to superintelligence*, 146-170.

Kurzweil, R., & Grossman, T. (2004). Fantastic voyage: Live long enough to live forever. Stuttgart, Germany: Holtzbrinck Publishers.

Kurzweil, R. (1999). *The age of spiritual machines*. New York: Viking.

Kurzweil, R. (2000). *The age of spiritual machines: When computers exceed human intelligence*. New York: Penguin.

Kurzweil, R. (2005, Sept. 24). Human 2.0. *New Scientist*, 32–37. PMID:16317855

Kurzweil, R. (2010). *The singularity is near*. Gerald Duckworth & Co.

Kwakernaak, H. (1979). An algorithm for rating multiple-aspect alternatives using fuzzysets. *Automatica*, *15*(5), 615–616. doi:10.1016/0005-1098(79)90010-4

LaForest, M. L. (2015, May). *Guiding transhumanism: The necessity of an ethical approach to transhumanism* (Tennessee Research and Creative Exchange Honors Thesis). Knoxville, TN: University of Tennessee.

LaJoie, S. P., & Derry, S. J. (1993). *Computers as cognitive tools*. New York: Routledge.

Lakhana, A. (2014). What is educational technology? An inquiry into the meaning, use, and reciprocity of technology. *Canadian Journal of Learning and Technology*, *40*(3), 1. doi:10.21432/T2H59S

Lal, A. (2015, May 14). *VR and AR Need Brain-Computer Interfaces to Achieve Their Full Potential*. Retrieved from http://gadgets.ndtv.com/wearables/opinion/vr-and-ar-need-brain-computer-interfaces-to-achieve-their-full-potential-692413

Lanza, R. P., Cibelli, J. B., Blackwell, C., Cristofalo, V. J., Francis, M. K., Baerlocher, G. M., ... Lansdorp, P. M. (2000). Extension of cell life-span and telomere length in animals cloned from senescent somatic cells. *Science*, *288*(5466), 665–669. doi:10.1126cience.288.5466.665 PMID:10784448

Larson, M., & Luthans, F. (2006). Potential Added Value of Psychological Capital in Predicting Work Attitudes. *Journal of Leadership & Organizational Studies*, *13*(2), 76–92. doi:10.1177/10717919070130020601

Laurillard, D. (2012). *Teaching as a design science: Building pedagogical patterns for learning and technology*. London: Routledge.

Lave, J., & Wenger, E. (1991). *Siruared learning. Legitimate peripheral participation*. Cambridge, UK: Cambridge University Press. doi:10.1017/CBO9780511815355

Leadbeater, C., & Wong, A. (2010). *Learning from the extremes: A white paper*. San Jose, Calif., Cisco Systems Inc. Retrieved from www.cisco.com/web/about/citizenship/socio-economic/docs/ Learning fromExtremes_WhitePaper.pdf

Leap, M. (2018). *Magic Leap*. Retrieved from https://www.magicleap.com/

Learning with "e"s. (2018a, Sept. 24). Re: Digital learning in organizations [Web log post]. Retrieved from http://www.steve-wheeler.co.uk/2018/09/digital-learning-in-organisations.html

Learning with "e"s. (2018b, Dec. 14). Re: Humans, machines and learning [Web log post]. Retrieved from http://www.steve-wheeler.co.uk/2018/12/humans-machines-and-learning.html

Lecourt, D. (2003). *İnsan, Post-İnsan, teknik ve yaşam*. Ankara, Turkey: Epos.

LeCun, Y., Bengio, Y., & Hinton, G. (2015). Deep learning. *Nature*, *521*(7553), 436–444. doi:10.1038/nature14539 PMID:26017442

Lee, K. L., & Lin, S. C. (2008). A fuzzy quantified SWOT procedure for environmental evaluation of an international distribution center. *Information Sciences*, *178*(2), 531–549. doi:10.1016/j.ins.2007.09.002

Lee, L. (2005). Using web-based instruction to promote active learning: Learners' perspectives. *CALICO Journal*, *23*(1), 139–156. doi:10.1558/cj.v23i1.139-156

Lee, S. (2013). Current status, opportunities and challenges of augmented reality in education. *Computers & Education*, *62*, 41–49. doi:10.1016/j.compedu.2012.10.024

Compilation of References

Lee, Y.-H. (2015). Facilitating critical thinking using the C-QRAC collaboration script: Enhancing science reading literacy in a computer-supported collaborative learning environment. *Computers & Education*, *88*, 182–191. doi:10.1016/j.compedu.2015.05.004

Lee, Y.-H. (2017). Scripting to enhance university students' critical thinking in flipped learning: Implications of the delayed effect on science reading literacy. *Interactive Learning Environments*, *26*(5), 569–582. doi:10.1080/10494820.2017.1372483

Leong, L. W., Ibrahim, O., Dalvi-Esfahani, M., Shahbazi, H., & Nilashi, M. (2018). The moderating effect of experience on the intention to adopt mobile social network sites for pedagogical purposes: An extension of the technology acceptance model. *Education and Information Technologies*, 1–22. doi:10.100710639-018-9726-2

Leslie, J. (1996). *The end of the world: The ethics and science of human extinction*. London: Routledge.

Licklider, J. C. (1960). Man-computer symbiosis. *IRE Transactions on Human Factors in Electronics*, *1*, 4-11.

Li, J., de Ávila, B. E. F., Gao, W., Zhang, L., & Wang, J. (2017). Micro/nanorobots for biomedicine: Delivery, surgery, sensing, and detoxification. *Science Robotics*, *2*(4), 1–9. doi:10.1126cirobotics.aam6431

Lilley, S. (2013). *Transhumanism and society: The social debate over human enhancement*. New York: Springer. doi:10.1007/978-94-007-4981-8

Lin, P. H., Wooders, A., Wang, J. T. Y., & Yuan, W. M. (2018). Artificial Intelligence, the Missing Piece of Online Education? *IEEE Engineering Management Review*, *46*(3), 25–28. doi:10.1109/EMR.2018.2868068

Liu, D., Huang, R., & Wosinski, M. 2017). *Smart learning in smart cities: Lecture notes in educational technology*. doi:10.1007/978-981-10-4343-7_2

Liu, X., & Pange, J. (2015). Early childhood teachers' perceived barriers to ICT integration in teaching: A survey study in Mainland China. *Journal of Computer Education*, *2*(1), 61–75. doi:10.100740692-014-0025-7

Livingston, K., Schweisfurth, M., Brace, G., & Nash, M. (2017). *Why pedagogy matters: The role of pedagogy in Education 2030 a policy advice paper*. Retrieved from https://www.unesco.org.uk/wp-content/uploads/2017/06/pedagogy.pdf

Livingstone, D. (2015). *Transhumanism. The History of a Dangerous Idea*. Sabilillah Publications.

Liyanagunawardena, T. R., Adams, A. A., & Williams, S. A. (2013). MOOCs: A systematic study of the published literature 2008-2012. *The International Review of Research in Open and Distributed Learning*, *14*(3), 202-227. Retrieved from http://www.irrodl.org/index.php/irrodl/article/view/1455

Lopatovska, I., Rink, K., Knight, I., Raines, K., Cosenza, K., Williams, H., ... Martinez, A. (2018). Talk to me: Exploring user interactions with the Amazon Alexa. *Journal of Librarianship and Information Science*. doi:10.1177/0961000618759414

Loqo, T. (2017). Academic Staff Perceptions and Challenges in Technology Integration: A Case Study of Walter Sisulu University. In *Proceedings of the 16th European Confererence on ELearning* (pp. 318-325). Academic Conferences and Publishing International.

Lorentz, M., Rüßmann, M., Strack, R., Lueth, K., & Bolle, M. (2015). *Man and Machine in Industry 4.0*. Retrieved from https://www.bcg.com/publications/2015/technology-business-transformation-engineered-products-infrastructure-man-machine-industry-4.aspx

Luckin, R., Holmes, W., Griffiths, M., & Forcier, L. B. (2016). Intelligence Unleashed. An argument for AI in Education. London: Pearson.

Luger, G. F. (2002). *Artificial Intelligence: Structures and Strategies for Complex Problem Solving* (4th ed.). Addison-Wesley.

Lukman, R., & Krajnc, M. (2012). Exploring non-traditional learning methods in virtual and real-world environments. *Journal of Educational Technology & Society, 15*(1), 237–247.

Luthans, F. (2002). The Need for and Meaning of Positive Organizational Behavior. *Journal of Organizational Behavior, 23*(6), 695–706. doi:10.1002/job.165

Luthans, F. (2012). *Organizational Behavior*. New York: Mc Graw-Hill Irwin.

Luthans, F., Luthans, K. W., & Luthans, B. C. (2004). Positive Psychological Capital: Beyond Human and Social Capital. *Business Horizons, 47*(1), 45–50. doi:10.1016/j.bushor.2003.11.007

Luthans, F., & Youssef, C. M. (2004). Human, Social and Now Positive Psychological Capital Management: Investing in People for Competitive Advantage. *Organizational Dynamics, 33*(2), 143–160. doi:10.1016/j.orgdyn.2004.01.003

Luthans, F., Youssef, C. M., & Avolio, B. J. (2007). *Psychological Capital: Developing the Human Competitive Edge*. Oxford University Press.

Lyle, M. H., & Dell Alma, S. (2003). *The Stress Solution*. American Psychological Association.

Magda, A. J., & Aslanian, C. B. (2018). *Online college students 2018: Comprehensive data on demands and preferences*. Louisville, KY: The Learning House.

Maharg, P. (2016). Editorial: Learning/Technology. *The Law Teacher, 50*(1), 15–23. doi:10.1080/03069400.2016.1146454

Makridakis, S. (2017). The forthcoming Artificial Intelligence (AI) revolution: Its impact on society and firms. *Futures, 90*, 46–60. doi:10.1016/j.futures.2017.03.006

Malik, A. (2013). Efficacy, Hope, Optimism and Resilience at Workplace–Positive Organizational Behavior. *International Journal of Scientific and Research Publications, 3*(10).

Manso-Vázquez, M., & Llamas-Nistal, M. (2013). Distributed personal learning environments: towards a suitable architecture. *International Journal of Emerging Technologies in Learning (iJET), 8*(2013). Retrieved from https://ieeexplore.ieee.org/abstract/document/6530178

Marlin, D. (2018). Millennials, this is how artificial intelligence will impact your job for better and worse. *Forbes*. Retrieved from https://www.forbes.com/sites/danielmarlin/2018/01/16/millennials-this-is-how-artificial-intelligence-will-impact-your-job-for-better-and-worse/#4a9bad4f4533

Marsh, S. (2018, Oct. 14). *Essays reveal Stephen Hawking predicted race of 'superhumans'*. Retrieved from https://www.theguardian.com/science/2018/oct/14/stephen-hawking-predicted-new-race-of-superhumans-essays-reveal

Masci, D. (2016). Human enhancement: The scientific and ethical dimensions of striving for perfection. *Pew Research Center*. Retrieved from http://www.pewinternet.org/essay/human-enhancement-the-scientific-and-ethical-dimensions-of-striving-for-perfection/

Masten, A. S. (2001). *Resilience Processes in Development*. American Psychological Association, 56(3), 227–238.

Matthews, D. (2017). *What blockchain technology could mean for universities*. Retrieved from https://www.timeshighereducation.com/news/what-blockchain-technology-could-mean-for-universities

Mayer, R. E. (2011). *Multimedia learning*. New York: Cambridge University Press.

Mazzella, N. A. (2011). What are We Learning About Technology Integration and Professional Development? *Educator's Voice*, *4*, 42–49.

McArthur, D. (2018). *Will blockchains revolutionize education?* Retrieved from https://er.educause.edu/articles/2018/5/will-blockchains-revolutionize-education

McArthur, D., Lewis, M., & Bishary, M. (2005). The roles of artificial intelligence in education: Current progress and future prospects. *Journal of Educational Technology*, *1*(4), 42–80.

McAuley, A., Stewart, B., Siemens, G., & Cormier, D. (2010). *Massive open online courses: Digital ways of knowing and learning, The MOOC model for digital practice.* Retrieved from http://www.elearnspace.org/Articles/MOOC_Final.pdf

McAuliffe, M., Hargreaves, D., Winter, A., & Chadwick, G. (2008). Does pedagogy still rule? *Proceedings of the 2008 AAEE Conference.* Retrieved from: http://www.engineersmedia.com.au/journals/aaee/pdf/AJEE_15_1_McAuliffe%202pdf

McCarthy J., Minsky, L., Rochester, N., & Shannon, C. (1955). A Proposal for the Dartmouth Summer Research Project on Artificial Intelligence.

McCarthy, J. (2007). *What is artificial intelligence.* Retrieved from http://www-formal.stanford.edu/jmc/whatisai.html

McCarthy, J. (2007). *What is artificial intelligence? Personal website.* Stanford University.

McCarthy, P. M., & Jarvis, S. (2010). MTLD, vocd-D, and HD-D: A validation study of sophisticated approaches to lexical diversity assessment. *Behavior Research Methods*, *42*(2), 381–392. doi:10.3758/BRM.42.2.381 PMID:20479170

McCrory, D., Penzien, D., Hasselblad, V., & Gray, R. (2001). *Evidence report: behavioral and physical treatments for tension-type and cervicogenic headache.* Duke University Evidence-based Practice Center. Available at: www.masschiro.org/upload/research/16_0.pdf

McDonald, S., & Howell, J. (2012). Watching, creating and achieving: Creative technologies as a conduit for learning in the early years. *British Journal of Educational Technology*, *43*(4), 641–651. doi:10.1111/j.1467-8535.2011.01231.x

McKie, R. (2018, May 6). *No death and an enhanced life: Is the future transhuman?* Retrieved from https://www.theguardian.com/technology/2018/may/06/no-death-and-an-enhanced-life-is-the-future-transhuman

McKie, R. (2018, May 6). No death and an enhanced life: Is the future transhuman? *The Guardian.* Retrieved from https://www.theguardian.com/technology/2018/may/06/no-death-and-an-enhanced-life-is-the-future-transhuman

McLoughlin, C., & Lee, M. J. W. (2010). Personalised and self-regulated learning in the Web 2.0 era: International exemplars of innovative pedagogy using social software. *Australasian Journal of Educational Technology*, *26*(1), 28–43. doi:10.14742/ajet.1100

McNamara, D. S., Crossley, S. A., & McCarthy, P. M. (2010). Linguistic features of writing quality. *Written Communication*, *27*(1), 57–86. doi:10.1177/0741088309351547

McNamara, D. S., Graesser, A. C., McCarthy, P. M., & Cai, Z. (2014). *Automated evaluation of text and discourse with Coh-Metrix.* Cambridge, UK: Cambridge University Press. doi:10.1017/CBO9780511894664

McNeil, W. H. (2007). *Dünya Tarihi.* Ankara, Turkey: İmge.

Mechanic, D. (1978). *Students under stress; A study in the social psychology of adaption.* Madison, WI: University of Wisconsin Press.

Mercer, C. (2014). Religion and transhumanism: The unknown future of human enhancement. Santa Barbara, CA: Praeger.

Merrill, M. D. (2002). First principles of instruction. *Educational Technology Research and Development, 50*(3), 43–59. doi:10.1007/BF02505024

Metin, O., & Karakaya, Ş. (2017). Jean Baudrillard Perspektifinden Sosyal Medya Analizi Denemesi. *Afyon Kocatepe Üniversitesi Sosyal Bilimler Dergisi, 19*(2), 109–121.

Miller, C. (1984). Genre as social action. *The Quarterly Journal of Speech, 70*(2), 151–167. doi:10.1080/00335638409383686

Mills, J. O., Jalil, A., & Stanga, P. E. (2017). Electronic retinal implants and artificial vision: Journey and present. *Eye (London, England), 31*(10), 1383–1398. doi:10.1038/eye.2017.65 PMID:28548648

Minguillon, J., Lopez-Gordo, M. A., & Pelayo, F. (2017). Trends in EEG-BCI for daily-life: Requirements for artifact removal. *Biomedical Signal Processing and Control, 31*, 407–418. doi:10.1016/j.bspc.2016.09.005

Minsky, M. (1994). Will Robots Inherit the Earth? *Scientific American, 271*(4), 108–113. doi:10.1038cientificameric an1094-108 PMID:7939559

Mishra, P., Koehler, M., & Zhao, Y. (2007). *Faculty development by design: Integrating technology in higher education.* Charlotte, NC: Information Age.

Misra, R., & Castillo, G. L. (2005). Academic stress among college students, comparison of American and international students. *International Journal of Stress Management, 11*(2), 132-148

Moore, C. (2015). *Brain Implant Could Help People With Memory Loss.* Retrieved from https://alzheimersnewstoday.com/2015/10/06/brain-implant-help-people-memory-loss/

Moore, M. (1977). On a Theory of Independent Study. Hagen: Fernuniversitat (ZIFF).

Moore's Law. (2018, Nov. 21). Retrieved from https://en.wikipedia.org/wiki/Moore%27s_law

Moore, M. (1973). Toward a theory of independent learning and teaching. *The Journal of Higher Education, 44*(9), 661–679. doi:10.2307/1980599

Moore, M. (1990). Background and overview of contemporary American distance education. In M. Moore (Ed.), *Contemporary issues in American distance education* (pp. xii–xxvi). New York: Pergamon.

Moore, M. G., & Kearsley, G. (2005). *Distance Education: A Systems View* (2nd ed.). Belmont, CA: Thomson Wadsworth.

Moore, M. G., & Kearsley, G. (2011). *Distance Education: A Systems View of Online Learning* (3rd ed.). Belmont, CA: Wadsworth Cengage Learning.

More, M. (1990). Transhumanism: Towards a futurist philosophy. *Extropy*, (6), 6-12.

More, M. (2003). *Principles of Extropy* (3rd ed.). Academic Press.

More, M. (2010). True transhumanism. In H+/-: Transhumanism and Its Critics. Bloomington, IN: XLibris.

More, M. (2013). The Philosophy of Humanism. In Transhumanist Reader: Classical and Contemporary Essays on the Science. Hoboken, NJ: Wiley-Blackwell, A John Wiley & Sons Inc. Publication.

More, M. (2013). The philosophy of transhumanism. *The transhumanist reader: Classical and contemporary essays on the science, technology, and philosophy of the human future*, 3-17.

More, M. (1990). Transhumanism: Towards a futurist philosophy. *Extropy, 6*, 6–12.

More, M. (2010). The overhuman in the transhuman. *Journal of Evolution and Technology / WTA, 21*(1), 1–4.

More, M. (2010). The Overhuman in the Transhuman. *Journal of Evolution and Technology / WTA, 21*(1).

More, M. (2011). *True Transhumanism. In H+/=: Transhumanism and Its Critics*. Metanexus Institute.

More, M. (2013). The philosophy of transhumanism. In M. More & N. Vita-More (Eds.), *The transhumanist reader: Classical and contemporary essays on the science, technology, and philosophy of the human future* (pp. 3–17). Malden, MA: John Wiley & Sons. doi:10.1002/9781118555927.ch1

More, M., & Vita-More, N. (Eds.). (2013). *The transhumanist reader: Classical and contemporary essays on the science, technology, and philosophy of the human future*. John Wiley & Sons. doi:10.1002/9781118555927

Morgam, K. (1986). *Weisz and Schopler*. Introduction to Psychology.

Motiwalla, L. F. (2007). Mobile learning: A framework and evaluation. *Computers & Education, 49*(3), 581–596. doi:10.1016/j.compedu.2005.10.011

Mott, J. (2010). Envisioning the post-LMS era: The open learning network. *EDUCAUSE Quarterly, 33*(1). Retrieved from http://cmapsconverted.ihmc.us/rid=1KCNR85HR-1TZLSG8-VZY/Mott%202010.pdf

Msweli, P. (2012). Mapping the interplay between open distance learning and internationalisation principles. *International Review of Research in Open and Distance Learning, 13*(3), 97–116. doi:10.19173/irrodl.v13i3.1182

Mudry, A., & Mills, M. (2013). The early history of the cochlear implant: A retrospective. *JAMA Otolaryngology-Head & Neck Surgery, 139*(5), 446–453. doi:10.1001/jamaoto.2013.293 PMID:23681026

Multon, K. D., Brown, S. D., & Lent, R. W. (1991). Relation of self-efficacy beliefs to academic outcomes: A meta-analytic investigation. *Journal of Counseling Psychology, 38*(1), 30–38. doi:10.1037/0022-0167.38.1.30

Musk, E. (2017). Making humans a multi-planetary species. *New Space, 5*(2), 46–61. doi:10.1089pace.2017.29009.emu

Mutlu, M. E. (2015e). Öğrenme Deneyimi Portfolyo Sistemi Tasarımı [Design of Learning Experiences Portfolio System]. *Proceedings of INT-E 2015 International Conference on New Horizons in Education*. (in Turkish)

Mutlu, M.E. (2015a). Yaşam Deneyimleri İçin Bir Bağlam Modeli – LECOM (LECOM – A Context Model for Life Experiences). In *AB'15 – XVII. Akademik Bilişim Konferansı*. Anadolu Üniversitesi Eskişehir. (In Turkish)

Mutlu, M.E. (2015c). Öğrenme Deneyimlerinin Yakalanması İçin Çoklu Algılayıcılı Bir Yaşam Günlüğü Sisteminin Geliştirilmesi [Development a Multisensor Lifelogging System for Capturing Learning Experiences]. In *IETC 2015 – 15. Uluslararası Eğitim Teknolojisi Konferansı*. İstanbul Üniversitesi. (in Turkish)

Mutlu, M.E. (2015d). Yaşam Günlüğünün Aktif Kullanımı [Active Usage of Lifelogging]. In *20. Türkiye'de İnternet Konferansı – İnet-Tr'15*. İstanbul Üniversitesi. (in Turkish)

Mutlu, M. E. (2014). Öğrenme Deneyimlerinin Yorumlanması (Interpreting of Learning Experiences). [In Turkish]. *Eğitim ve Öğretim Araştırmaları Dergisi, 3*(4), 21–45.

Mutlu, M. E. (2015b). Design and Development of a Digital Life Logging System for Management of Lifelong Learning Experiences. *Procedia: Social and Behavioral Sciences, 174*, 834–848. doi:10.1016/j.sbspro.2015.01.678

Mutlu, M. E. (2016a). Öğrenme Deneyimlerinin Yönetiminde Üstbilişsel Düzenleme [Meta-cognitive Regulations in Learning Experiences Management]. [In Turkish]. *Eğitim ve Öğretim Araştırmaları Dergisi, 5*(2), 265–288.

Mutlu, M. E. (2016b). Sanal Ortamlardaki Öğrenme Deneyimleri İçin Bir Enformasyon Erişim Sistemi Tasarımı [An Information Retrieval System Design for Learning Experiences in Virtual Environments]. [In Turkish]. *Eğitim ve Öğretim Araştırmaları Dergisi, 5*(2), 395–408.

Mutlu, M. E., Kayabas, I., Kip Kayabas, B., & Peri Mutlu, A. (2015f). Implementation of the Lifelong Learning Experiences Management Approach – Observations on the First Experiences. *Procedia: Social and Behavioral Sciences*, *174*, 849–861. doi:10.1016/j.sbspro.2015.01.680

Nabiyev, V. V. (2010). *Yapay zeka: İnsan bilgisayar etkileşimi*. Seçkin Yayıncılık.

Nadimpalli, M. (2017). Artificial intelligence risks and benefits. *Artificial Intelligence*, *6*(6).

Nance, W. D., & Straub, D. W. (1996). An investigation of task/technology fit and information technology choices in knowledge work. *Journal of Information Technology Management*, *7*, 1–14.

Nasseh, B. (1997). *A Brief History of Distance Education*. Retrieved from http://www.seniornet.org/edu/art/history.html

NeuroSky. (2018). *NeuroSky – Body and Mind Quantified*. Retrieved from http://neurosky.com/

NeuroSky's MindWave. (2018). Retrieved from https://store.neurosky.com/

Neuroweb. (2017). *Neuroweb Iniative*. Retrieved from http://www.globalneuroweb.org/ru/

Ng'ambi, D. (2013). Effective and ineffective uses of emerging technologies: Towards a transformative pedagogical model. *British Journal of Educational Technology*, *44*(4), 652–661. doi:10.1111/bjet.12053

Nielsen, J. (2003). *Voice interfaces: Assessing the potential*. Retrieved from http://www.useit.com/alertbox/20030127.htm

Nietzsche, F. (1885). *Zarathustra*. Academic Press.

Nilsson, N. J. (2010). *The quest for artificial intelligence*. Cambridge, UK: Cambridge University Press.

Nilsson, N. J. (2014). *Principles of artificial intelligence*. Burlington, MA: Morgan Kaufmann.

Nishimoto, S., Vu, A. T., Naselaris, T., Benjamini, Y., Yu, B., & Gallant, J. L. (2011). Reconstructing visual experiences from brain activity evoked by natural movies. *Current Biology*, *21*(19), 1641–1646. doi:10.1016/j.cub.2011.08.031 PMID:21945275

NLTK. (2018). *NLTK Stem Package*. Available: http://www.nltk.org/api/nltk.stem.html

Nolan, C. (Dir.). (2012). *The Dark Knight Rises*. Retrieved from https://www.imdb.com/title/tt1345836/

Now This Future. (2018). *This Start-Up Wants to Upload Your Brain to a Computer*. Retrieved from https://www.facebook.com/NowThisFuture/videos/2008861865821650/

NTV. (2018). *Yapay Zeka Uyarısı*. Retrieved from https://www.ntv.com.tr/galeri/teknoloji/elonmusktanyapay-zeka-uyarisi,REjccX1JVkqq-oyMsZIFbw/NmFwGQ951k-N8OaSkIa15w.

Nunes, M. (1995). Jean Baudrillard in cyberspace: Internet, virtuality, and postmodernity. *Style (Fayetteville)*, 314–327.

O'Reilly, T. (2005). *What is Web 2.0?* Retrieved from http://oreilly.com/web2/archive/what-is-web-20.html

O'Reilly. (2008). *The shape of things to come*. Emerging Technology Conference.

O'Reilly, T. (2007). What is web 2.0: Design patterns and business models for the next generation of software. *Communications & Stratégies*, *65*, 17–37.

Oddee. (2007, Oct. 15). *7 Worst Killer Plagues in History*. Retrieved from https://www.oddee.com/item_90608.aspx

OECD. (2011). *The Future of Families To 2030, Projections, Policy and Options, A Synthesis Report*. International Futures Programme.

OECD. (2013). *OECD skills outlook 2013: first results from the survey of adult skills*. OECD Publishing. doi:10.1787/9789264204256-en

Oliver, P., & Clayes, E. (2014). Issues of Using Information Communication Technologies in Higher Education. In *Proceedings of the European Conference on Social Media*. University of Brighton.

Onah, D. F., & Sinclair, J. E. (2015). Massive open online courses: an adaptive learning framework. In *9th International Technology, Education and Development Conference* (pp. 2-4). Available at https://pdfs.semanticscholar.org/f616/7d7a9acd316fed0e5c7566f5fbdd876100f9.pdf

Önüt, S., Kara, S. S., & Efendigil, T. (2008). A hybrid fuzzy MCDM approach to machine tool selection. *Journal of Intelligent Manufacturing*, *19*(4), 443–453. doi:10.100710845-008-0095-3

Opdebeeck, H. (2017). The challenge of transhumanism in business. *Contributions to Conflict Management. Peace Economics and Development*, *26*, 251–260.

Open and Distance Learning Quality Council. (2012). *Definitions*. Retrieved from http://odlqc.org.uk/odlqc-standards/definitions

Orehovacki, T., Bubas, G., & Konecki, M. (2009). Web 2.0 in education and potential factors of Web 2.0 use by students of information systems. *Proceedings of the ITI 2009 31st Int. Conference on Information Technology Interfaces*. 10.1109/ITI.2009.5196124

Ossiannilsson. (2017a). Leadership in global open, online, and distance learning. In J. Keengwe & P. H. Bull (Eds.), *Handbook of research on transformative digital content and learning technologies* (pp. 345–373). Hershey, PA: IGI Global. Retrieved from https://altc.alt.ac.uk/blog/2017/12/its-time-for-the-next-generation-of-leadership/#comments

Ossiannilsson. (2017b, Dec. 16). Re: It is time for the next generation of leadership [Web log post]. Retrieved from https://altc.alt.ac.uk/blog/2017/12/its-time-for-the-next-generation-of-leadership/#comments

Ossiannilsson. (2018a). Leadership: In a time when learners take ownership of their own learning. In K. Buyuk, S, Kocdar, & A. Bozkurt (Eds.), Administrative leadership in open and distance learning programs (pp. 1–33). Hershey, PA: IGI Global.

Ossiannilsson. (2018b). Visionary leadership for digital transformation: In a time when learners take the ownership of their own learning. *Distance Education in China: An International Forum*, *5*, 22-34.

Ossiannilsson. (2018c, Sept. 26). The case for mobile learning [web log post]. Retrieved from https://virtuallyinspired.org/?s=leadership

Osuagwu, O. E., & Ihedigbo, C. E., & Ndigwe, C. (2015). Integrating Virtual Reality (VR) into traditional instructional design. *West African Journal of Industrial and Academic Research*, *15*(1), 68–77.

Öz, E., & Baykoç, Ö. F. (2004). Tedarikçi Seçimi Problemine Karar Teorisi Destekli Uzman Sistem Yaklaşımı. *Gazi Üniversitesi Mühendislik Mimarlık Fakültesi Dergisi*, *19*(3), 275–286.

Ozel, A. G., & Arıkan, A. (2015). The Use of the Internet and Web 2.0 Tools among EFL Instructors. *Mediterranean Journal of Humanities*, *V*(1), 313–325. doi:10.13114/MJH.2015111386

Öztemel, E. (2003). *Yapay Sinir Ağları*. Papatya yayıncılık.

Öztemel, E. (2009). *Endüstri Mühendisliğine Giriş*. Papatya Yayıncılık.

Öztemel, E. (2010). In L. Benyoucef & B. Grabot (Eds.), *Artificial Intelligence Techniques for Networked Manufacturing Enterprises Management*. Springer-Verlag London Limited.

Pais-Vieira, M., Lebedev, M., Kunicki, C., Wang, J., & Nicolelis, M. A. (2013). A brain-to-brain interface for real-time sharing of sensorimotor information. *Scientific Reports*, *3*(3), 1319. doi:10.1038rep01319 PMID:23448946

Pamuk, S., & Peker, D. (2009). Turkish pre-service science and mathematics teachers' computer related self-efficacies, attitudes, and the relationship between these variables. *Computers & Education*, *53*(2), 454–461. doi:10.1016/j.compedu.2009.03.004

Pane, J. F., Steiner, E. D., Baird, M. D., & Hamilton, L. S. (2015). Continued Progress: Promises Evidence on Personalized Learning. *RAND Corporation*. Retrieved from https://www.rand.org/pubs/research_reports/RR1365.html

Panel, F. O. W. (2016). *Future of Work: 2035 – For Everyone to Shine*. Panel Report. Ministry of Health, Labor and Welfare of Japan. Retrieved from http://www.mhlw.go.jp/file/06-Seisakujouhou-12600000-Seisakutoukatsukan/0000152705.pdf

Pan, Y. (2016). Heading toward artificial intelligence 2.0. *Engineering*, *2*(4), 409–413. doi:10.1016/J.ENG.2016.04.018

Papert, S. (1993). *Mindstorms: Children, computers, and powerful ideas* (2nd ed.). New York: Basic Books.

Papert, S. (1994). *The children's machine: Rethinking school in the age of the computer*. New York: Basic Books.

Pappano, L. (2012). The Year of the MOOC. *The New York Times*. Retrieved from http://www.nytimes.com/2012/11/04/education/edlife/massive-open-online-courses-are-multiplying-at-a-rapid-pace.html

Pappas, C. (2018). *The Top Extended Enterprise Learning Management Systems*. eLearning Industry. Retrieved from https://elearningindustry.com/top-extended-enterprise-learning-management-systems-lms

Paramythis, A., & Loidl-Reisinger, S. (2004). Adaptive learning environments and e-learning standards. *Electronic Journal on e-Learning*, *2*(1), 181-194.

Partnership for 21st Century Learning. (2015). Retrieved from http://www.p21.org/ our-work/p21-framework

Pedagogy. (2018a). In *Cambridge online dictionary*. Retrieved from https://dictionary.cambridge.org/dictionary/english/pedagogy

Pedagogy. (2018b). In *Oxford online dictionary*. Retrieved from https://en.oxforddictionaries.com/definition/pedagogy

Pedagogy. (2018c). In *Merriam-Webster's online dictionary*. Retrieved from https://www.merriam-webster.com/dictionary/pedagogy

Peddie, J. (2017). *Augmented Reality: Where We Will All Live*. Cham, Switzerland: Springer. doi:10.1007/978-3-319-54502-8

Pempek, T. A., Yermolayeva, Y. A., & Calvert, S. L. (2009). College students' so- cial networking experiences on Facebook. *Journal of Applied Developmental Psychology*, *30*(3), 227–238. doi:10.1016/j.appdev.2008.12.010

Peña-López, I. (2010). Personal learning environments: blurring the edges of formal and informal learning. *ICTlogy*. Retrieved from http://ictlogy.net/articles/20101105_ismael_pena-lopez_-_personal_learning_environments_blurring_edges_formal_informal_learning.pdf

Peper, E., & Shaffer, F. (2010). Biofeedback History: An Alternative View. *Biofeedback*, *4*(20), 12-22.

Peters, O. (1973). *Die Didaktische Struktur des Fernunterrich*. Weinheim, Germany: Beltz.

Peters, O. (2014). Foreword. In O. Zawacki-Richter & T. Anderson (Eds.), *Online distance education: Towards a research agenda* (pp. 237–265). Edmonton, Canada: AU Press.

Peterson, C., & Seligman, M. E. P. (2004). *Character Strengths and Virtues: A Handbook and Classification*. New York: Oxford University Press.

Pham, H. L. (2012). Differentiated instruction and the need to integrate teaching and practice. *Journal of College Teaching and Learning*, *9*(1), 13–20. doi:10.19030/tlc.v9i1.6710

Pirim, H. (2006). Yapay Zeka. *Journal of Yasar University*, *1*(1), 81–93.

Pittman, V. V. (1986a). *Pioneering Instructional Radio in the US: Five Years of Frustration at the University of Iowa, 1925-1930*. A Paper for the First International Conference on the History of Adult Education, Oxford, UK.

Pittman, V. V. (1986b). Station WSUI and early days of instructional radio. The days of instructional radio. *The Palimpset*, *67*(2), 38–52.

Plato. (380 B.C.E.). *Protagoras*. Retrieved from http://classics.mit.edu/Plato/protagoras.html

Plomin, R., Owen, M. J., & McGuffin, P. (1994, June 17). The genetic basis of complex human behaviors. *Science*, *264*(5166), 1733–1739. doi:10.1126cience.8209254 PMID:8209254

Pollack, J. (2009). Yapay Zekâ Yükselişe Geçecek. In İyimser Gelecek. İstanbul: NTV.

Postman, N. (2006). *Teknopoli*. İstanbul: Paradigma Yayıncılık.

Prensky, M. (2001). *Digital natives, digital immigrants*. NCB University Press. Available at http://pre2005.flexiblelearning.net.au/projects/resources/Digital_Natives_Digital_Immigrants.pdf

Prensky, M. (2001a). Digital Natives, Digital Immigrants. *On the Horizon*, *9*(5), 1–6. doi:10.1108/10748120110424816

Prensky, M. (2001b). Digital Natives, Digital Immigrants, part 2: Do they really think differently? *On the Horizon*, *9*(6), 6. doi:10.1108/10748120110424843

Prensky, M. (2009). H. Sapiens Digital: From Digital Immigrants and Digital Natives to Digital Wisdom. *Journal of Online Education*, *5*(3).

PricewaterhouseCoopers (PwC). (n.d.). *2019 AI Predictions: Six AI priorities you can't afford to ignore*. PwC. Retrieved from https://www.pwc.com/AI2019#section3

Pring, B., Brown, R. H., Davis, E., Bahl, M., & Cook, M. (2017). 21 Jobs of the Future: A Guide to Getting – and Staying – Employed Over the Next 10 Years. *Cognizant*. Retrieved from https://www.cognizant.com/whitepapers/21-jobs-of-the-future-a-guide-to-getting-and-staying-employed-over-the-next-10-years-codex3049.pdf

Psotka, J. (1995). Immersive training systems: Virtual reality and education and training. *Instructional Science*, *23*(5-6), 405–431. doi:10.1007/BF00896880

Public Broadcasting Service. (2003). *Distance learning week – Timeline: An overview*. Retrieved from http://www.pbs.org/als/dlweek/history/index.html

Puentedura, R. R. (2012). *The SAMR model: Background and exemplars*. Hippasus. Retrieved from http://www.hippasus.com/rrpweblog/archives/2012/08/23/SAMR_BackgroundExemplars.pdf

Pugh, C. (2017). The Disappearing Human: Gnostic Dreams in a Transhumanist World. *Religions*, *8*(81), 1.

Purna, N. P., & Gotham, C. (2006). Stress and The college Students. Oxford, UK: Oxford Brookes University.

Quye, B. J. A. (2011). *Five Trends that Are Dramatically Changing Work and the Workplace*. Knoll Workplace Research.

Radio-Frequency Identification. (2018, Nov. 8). Retrieved from https://en.wikipedia.org/wiki/Radio-frequency_identification

Rahimi, E. (2015). *A design framework for personal learning environments* (Doctoral dissertation). Delft, The Netherlands: Delft University of Technology.

Rahimi, E., van den Berg, J., & Veen, W. (2015). Facilitating student-driven constructing of learning environments using Web 2.0 personal learning environments. *Computers & Education, 81*, 235-246. Retrieved from https://www.sciencedirect.com/science/article/pii/S0360131514002322

Rahimi, E., & Berg, J. (2015). A learning model for enhancing the student's control in educational process using Web 2.0 personal learning environments. *British Journal of Educational Technology, 46*(4), 780–792. doi:10.1111/bjet.12170

Rains, J.C., Penzien, D.B., McCrory, D.C. & Gray, R.N. (2005). Behavioral headache treatment: history, review of empirical literature and methodological critique. *Headache*, 14.

Rajagopal, K., Verjans, S., Costa, C., & Sloep, P. (2012). People in personal learning networks: analysing their characteristics and identifying suitable tools. *Proceedings of the 8th International Conference on Networked Learning 2012*. Retrieved from http://dspace.ou.nl/handle/1820/4224

Ramey, W. (2017). *The AI Podcast, Ep. 1: Deep Learning 101-Computing*. Retrieved from https://soundcloud.com/theaipodcast/ai-podcast-deep-learning-101

Ramirez, S., Liu, X., Lin, P. A., Suh, J., Pignatelli, M., Redondo, R. L., ... Tonegawa, S. (2013). Creating a false memory in the hippocampus. *Science, 341*(6144), 387–391. doi:10.1126cience.1239073 PMID:23888038

Ranisch, R., & Sorgner, R. L. (Eds.). (2014). *Post- and Transhumanism: An Introduction*. New York: Peter Lang.

Rao, R. P., Stocco, A., Bryan, M., Sarma, D., Youngquist, T. M., Wu, J., & Prat, C. S. (2014). A direct brain-to-brain interface in humans. *PLoS One, 9*(11), 1–12. doi:10.1371/journal.pone.0111332 PMID:25372285

Rastogi, R., Chaturvedi, D. K., Arora, N., Trivedi, P., & Chauhan, S. (2017a). Framework for Use of Machine Intelligence on Clinical Psychology to study the effects of Spiritual tools on Human Behavior and Psychic Challenges. *Proceedings of National System Conference-2017*.

Rastogi, R., Chaturvedi, D. K., Arora, N., Trivedi, P., & Mishra, V. (2017b). Swarm Intelligent Optimized Method Of Development of Noble Life in the perspective of Indian Scientific Philosophy and Psychology. *Proceedings of National System Conference-2017*.

Rastogi, R., Chaturvedi, D. K., Arora, N., Trivedi, P., Singh, P., & Vyas, P. (2018h). Study on Efficacy of Electromyography and Electroencephalography Biofeedback with Mindful Meditation on Mental health of Youths. *Proceedings of the 12th INDIACom*.

Rastogi, R., Chaturvedi, D. K., Satya, S., Arora, N., & Chauhan, S. (2018a). *An Optimized Biofeedback Therapy for Chronic TTH between Electromyography and Galvanic Skin Resistance Biofeedback on Audio, Visual and Audio Visual Modes on Various Medical Symptoms*. In The national Conference on 3rd MDNCPDR-2018, Agra, India.

Rastogi, R., Chaturvedi, D. K., Satya, S., Arora, N., Bansal, I., & Yadav, V. (2018k). *Intelligent* Analysis for Detection of Complex Human Personality by Clinical Reliable Psychological Surveys on Various Indicators. *The National Conference on 3rd MDNCPDR-2018*.

Rastogi, R., Chaturvedi, D. K., Satya, S., Arora, N., Gupta, M., Yadav, V., ... Sharma, P. (in press). Chronic TTH Analysis by EMG & GSR Biofeedback on Various Modes and Various Medical Symptoms Using IoT, Advances in ubiquitous sensing applications for healthcare. Big Data Analytics for Intelligent Healthcare Management.

Rastogi, R., Chaturvedi, D. K., Satya, S., Arora, N., Saini, H., Verma, H., & Mehlyan, K. (2018j). Comparative Efficacy Analysis of Electromyography and Galvanic Skin Resistance Biofeedback on Audio Mode for Chronic TTH on Various Indicators. *Proceedings of ICCIIoT- 2018.*

Rastogi, R., Chaturvedi, D. K., Satya, S., Arora, N., Singh, P., & Vyas, P. (2018e). Statistical Analysis for Effect of Positive Thinking on Stress Management and Creative Problem Solving for Adolescents. *Proceedings of the 12th INDIACom.*

Rastogi, R., Chaturvedi, D. K., Satya, S., Arora, N., Sirohi, H., Singh, M., . . . Singh, V. (2018i). Which One is Best: Electromyography Biofeedback Efficacy Analysis on Audio, Visual and Audio-Visual Modes for Chronic TTH on Different Characteristics. *Proceedings of ICCIIoT- 2018.*

Rastogi, R., Chaturvedi, D. K., Sharma, S., Bansal, A., & Agrawal, A. (2018g). Audio Visual EMG & GSR Biofeedback Analysis for Effect of Spiritual Techniques on Human Behavior and Psychic Challenges. *Proceedings of the 12th INDIACom.*

Rastogi, R., Chaturvedi, D.K., Satya, S., Arora, N., Saini, H., Verma, H., Mehlyan, K., & Varshney, Y. (2018b). Statistical Analysis of EMG and GSR Therapy on Visual Mode and SF-36 Scores for Chronic TTH. *Proceedings of UPCON-2018.*

Rastogi, R., Chaturvedi, D. K., Satya, S., Arora, N., Singhal, P., & Gulati, M. (2018f). Statistical Resultant Analysis of Spiritual & Psychosomatic Stress Survey on Various Human Personality Indicators. *The International Conference proceedings of ICCI 2018.*

Rastogi, R., Chaturvedi, D. K., Satya, S., Arora, N., Trivedi, P., Singh, A., ... Singh, A. (2019a). *Intelligent Analysis for Personality Detection on Various Indicators by Clinical Reliable Psychological TTH and Stress Surveys. In Proceedings of CIPR 2019 at Indian Institute of Engineering Science and Technology.* Springer.

Rastogi, R., Chaturvedi, D. K., Satya, S., Arora, N., Yadav, V., Chauhan, S., & Sharma, P. (2018c). *SF-36 Scores Analysis for EMG and GSR Therapy on Audio, Visual and Audio Visual Modes for Chronic TTH. Proceedings of the ICCIDA-2018 on Oct. 27-28, CCIS Series, Springer at Gandhi Institute for Technology.*

Rastogi, R., Chaturvedi, D. K., Satya, S., Arora, N., Yadav, V., Chauhan, S., & Sharma, P. (2018d). *Analytical Comparison of Efficacy for Electromyography and Galvanic Skin Resistance Biofeedback on Audio-Visual Mode for Chronic TTH on Various Attributes. Proceedings of the ICCIDA-2018 on Oct. 27- 28, CCIS Series, Springer at Gandhi Institute for Technology.*

Ratcliffe, A. E. (2014). An exploratory study of the personal learning environments of security and investigation professionals. *Journal of Literacy and Technology, 15*(2), 171–199. Retrieved from https://lra.le.ac.uk/bitstream/2381/29291/1/ar_7 pdf

Ravindra, Y., VidinPallavi, K., A., Vainder, S., & Raman, S. (2012). The Interrelationship of positive mental and physical health; A health promoting approach. *The Journal of Positive Psychology, 3*(1), 1–5.

Rayes, A., & Salam, S. (2017). *Internet of Things – From Hype to Reality.* Cham, Switzerland: Springer. doi:10.1007/978-3-319-44860-2

Reade, W. W. (1910). *The martyrdom of man.* London: Kegan Paul.

Redding, M. (2015, August). Why I Became a Christian Transhumanist. *Motherboard.* Retrieved from https://motherboard.vice.com/en_us/article/9akxm3/why-i-became-a-christian-transhumanist

Redecker, C., & Punie, Y. (2013). The Future of Learning 2025: Developing a Vision for Change. *Future Learning, 1,* 3-7. Retrieved from https://www.researchgate.net/publication/260863799_The_Future_of_Learning_2025_Developing_a_vision_for_change

Redecker, C., Leis, M., Leendertse, M., & Punie, Y. (2011). *The Future of Learning: Preparing for Change.* European Commission JRC Scientific and Technical Reports. Retrieved from http://ftp.jrc.es/EURdoc/JRC66836.pdf

Rees, M. (2003). *Our final hour.* New York: Basic Books.

Regalado, A. (2018). *A startup is pitching a mind-uploading service that is "100 percent fatal".* Retrieved from https://www.technologyreview.com/s/610456/a-startup-is-pitching-a-mind-uploadingservice-that-is-100-percent-fatal/

RemsbergD. (2010). *The benefits and problems of transhumanism.* Retrieved from http://history.msu.edu/hst250-online/2010/04/20/the-benefits-and-problems-of-transhumanism/

Resing, W. C. M., & Blok, J. B. (2002). The classification of intelligence scores. Proposal for an unambiguous system. *The Psychologist, 37*, 244–249.

Rheingold, H. (1993). *The virtual community: Finding commection in a computerized world.* Addison-Wesley Longman Publishing Co., Inc.

Rhisiart, M. (2016). From Foresight to Impact? The 2030 Future of Work Scenarios. *Technological Forecasting and Social Change.* doi:10.1016/j.techfore.2016.11.020

Rienties, B., & Toetenel, L. (2016). The impact of learning design on student behavior, satisfaction and performance: A cross- institutional comparison across 151 modules. *Computers in Human Behavior, 60*, 333–341. doi:10.1016/j.chb.2016.02.074

Rikowski, G. (2002). Education, capital and the transhuman. In D. Hill, P. McLaren, M. Cole, & G. Rikowski (Eds.), *Marxism against postmodernism in educational theory* (pp. 111–143). Lanham, MD: Lexington Books.

Rob, M. (2017). 7 Tips for Machine Learning Success. *PCmag.* Retrieved from https://www.pcmag.com/article/353293/7-tips-for-machine-learning-success

Robbins, J. (2016). When Smart Is Not: Technology and Michio Kaku's The Future of the Mind. *IEEE Technology and Society Magazine, 35*(2), 29–31. doi:10.1109/MTS.2016.2554439

Rogers, B. M., & Stevens, B. E. (2015). Introduction: The Past Is an Undiscovered County. In Classical Traditions in Science Fiction (pp. 1–2). Oxford, UK: Oxford University Press.

Rohse, S., & Anderson, T. (2006). Design patterns for complex learning. *Journal of Learning Design, 1*(3), 82–91. doi:10.5204/jld.v1i3.35

ROLE. (2004). *Responsive Open Learning Environments (ROLE).* Retrieved from http://role-project.archiv.zsi.at/

Roll, I., & Wylie, R. (2016). Evolution and revolution in artificial intelligence in education. *International Journal of Artificial Intelligence in Education, 26*(2), 582–599. doi:10.100740593-016-0110-3

Rosenblum, L. & Robert A. (1997). The challenge of virtual reality. *Visualization & Modeling*, 325-399.

Ross, S. E., Neibling, B. C., & Heckert, T. M. (2008). Source of stress among college students. College Student Journal, 33(2).

Rotolo, D., Hicks, D., & Martin, B. R. (2015, Aug. 9). What is an emerging technology? *Research Policy, 44*(10), 1827–1843. doi:10.1016/j.respol.2015.06.006

Rubin, C. T. (2008). What is Good Humanism. In Medical Enhancement and Posthumanity (pp. 137-156). Berlin: Springer Science and Business Media.

Rubin, C. T. (2008). What is the good of transhumanism? In B. Gordijn & R. Chadwick (Eds.), *Medical Enhancement and Posthumanity* (pp. 137–156). Springer Science.

Rubio, E., Galan, M., Sanchez, M., & Delgado, D. (2011). eProfessional: from PLE to PLWE. *Proceedings of the The PLE Conference 2011*. Retrieved from http://journal.webscience.org/597/

Russell, S. J., & Norvig, P. (2016). *Artificial intelligence: a modern approach*. Pearson Education Limited.

Russell, S., & Norvig, P. (2003). *Artificial intelligence: A modern approach* (2nd ed.). Upper Saddle River, NJ: Pearson Education.

Ryan, R. M., Rigby, C. S., & Przybylski, A. (2006). The motivational pull of video games: A self-determination theory approach. *Motivation and Emotion*, *30*(4), 347–364. doi:10.100711031-006-9051-8

Saavedra, A., & Opfer, V. (2012). *Teaching and learning 21st century skills: Lessons from the learning sciences. A global cities education network report*. New York: Asia Society. Retrieved from http://asiasociety.org/files/rand-0512report.pdf

Saba, F. (2013). *Introduction to distance education: Telecommunications systems*. Retrieved from http://distance-educator.com/in-1962-launch-of-a-beach-ball-sized-satellite-revolutionized-educational-telecommunications/

Saba, F. (2000). Research in distance education: A status report. *International Review of Research in Open and Distance Learning*, *1*(1). doi:10.19173/irrodl.v1i1.4

Saba, F. (2013). Building the Future: A Theoretical Perspective. In M. G. Moore (Ed.), *Handbook of distance education* (pp. 49–65). New York, NY: Routledge. doi:10.4324/9780203803738.ch4

Saettler, P. (1990). *The evolution of American Educational Technology*. Littleton, CO: Libraries Unlimited.

Sahin-Kızıl, A. (2011). EFL teachers' attitudes towards information and communication technologies (ICT). In *5th International Computer & Instructional Technologies Symposium*. Fırat University.

Saka, G. H. (2016). *Bir Ütopya Olarak Teknolojik Ölümsüzlük Sorunsalı: Teknolojik Ölümsüzlük*. V. Türkiye Lisanüstü Çalışmalar Bildiriler Kitabı. doi:10.12658/TLCK.5.4.B015

Sala, N. (2013). Applications of Virtual Reality Technologies in Architecture and in Engineering. *International Journal of Space Technology Management and Innovation*, *3*(2), 78–88. doi:10.4018/ijstmi.2013070104

Salomon, G., & Perkins, D. N. (1989). Rocky roads to transfer: Rethinking mechanisms of a neglected phenomenon. *Educational Psychologist*, *24*(2), 113–142. doi:10.120715326985ep2402_1

Salzman, M. C., Dede, C., Loftin, R. B., & Chen, J. (1999). A model for understanding how virtual real- ity aids complex conceptual learning. *Presence (Cambridge, Mass.)*, *8*(3), 293–316. doi:10.1162/105474699566242

Samson, R. W. (2013). Highly Human Jobs. *The Futurist*, *47*, 29-35. Retrieved from https://issuu.com/worldfuturesociety/docs/the_futurist_2013_may-jun

Samsung Research. (2018). *Artificial Intelligence*. Retrieved from https://research.samsung.com/artificial-intelligence.

Sanakulov, N., & Karjaluoto, H. (2015). Consumer adoption of mobile technologies: A literature review. *International Journal of Mobile Communications*, *13*(3), 244–275. doi:10.1504/IJMC.2015.069120

Sandberg, A., & Bostrom, N. (2008). *Whole brain emulation: a roadmap*. Technical Report #2008-3, Future of Humanity Institute, Oxford, UK: Oxford University. Retrieved from https://www.fhi.ox.ac.uk/brain-emulation-roadmap-report.pdf

Sandu, A., & Terec-Vlad, L. (2016). A Phenomenological Perspective on Transhumanism from the Perspective of the Spoken of Being. *Postmodern Openings*, *7*(1), 67–76. doi:10.18662/po/2016.0701.05

Sang, G., Valcke, M., van Braak, J., Tondeur, J., & Zhu, C. (2011). Predicting ICT integration into classroom teaching in Chinese primary school: Exploring the complex interplay of teacher-related variables. *Journal of Computer Assisted Learning, 27*(2), 160–172. doi:10.1111/j.1365-2729.2010.00383.x

Sang-Hun, C. (2016). Google's Computer Program Beats Lee Se-dol in Go Tournament. *The New York Times*. Retrieved from https://www.nytimes.com/2016/03/16/world/asia/korea-alphago-vs-lee-sedol-go.html

Santos, J., Rodrigues, J. J., Casal, J., Saleem, K., & Denisov, V. (2018). Intelligent personal assistants based on internet of things approaches. *IEEE Systems Journal, 12*(2), 1793–1802. doi:10.1109/JSYST.2016.2555292

SAT. (2014). *SAT Vocabulary Words*. Available: http://www.freevocabulary.com

Savant, M. V. (2018). *Logical Fallacies*. Available: http://marilynvossavant.com/logical-fallacies/

Saygin, A. P., Cicekli, I., & Akman, V. (2000). Turing test: 50 years later. *Minds and Machines, 10*(4), 463–518. doi:10.1023/A:1011288000451

Scalabre, O. (2018). *Embracing Industry 4.0 – and Rediscovering Growth*. Retrieved from https://www.bcg.com/capabilities/operations/embracing-industry-4.0-rediscovering-growth.aspx

Schaffert, S., & Hilzensauer, W. (2008). On the way towards personal learning environments: Seven crucial aspects. *Elearning Papers, 9*(2). doi:10.1.1.167.4083&rep=rep1&type=pdf

Schalk, G., Miller, K. J., Anderson, N. R., Wilson, J. A., Smyth, M. D., Ojemann, J. G., ... Leuthardt, E. C. (2008). Two-dimensional movement control using electrocorticographic signals in humans. *Journal of Neural Engineering, 5*(1), 75–84. doi:10.1088/1741-2560/5/1/008 PMID:18310813

Scheid, K. (1993). *Helping students become strategic learners: Guidelines for teaching*. Cambridge, MA: Brookline Books.

Schlosser, L. A., & Simonson, M. R. (2009). *Distance Education: Definitions and Glossary of Terms* (2nd ed.). Charlotte, NC: Information Age Publishing.

Schoenmakers, S., Barth, M., Heskes, T., & van Gerven, M. (2013). Linear reconstruction of perceived images from human brain activity. *NeuroImage, 83*, 951–961. doi:10.1016/j.neuroimage.2013.07.043 PMID:23886984

Schroeder, R. (1996). *Possible worlds: the social dynamic of virtual reality technology*. Boulder, CO: Westview Press, Inc.

Schunk, D. H., & Pajares, F. (2010). Self-efficacy beliefs. Elsevier Ltd. doi:10.1016/B978-0-08-044894-7.00620-5

Schunk, D. H., & Meece, J. L. (2006). Self-efficacy development in adolescence. *Self-Efficacy Beliefs of Adolescents, 5*, 71–96.

Schwab, K. (2016). *The fourth industrial revolution: what it means, how to respond*. Retrieved from https://www.weforum.org/agenda/2016/01/the-fourth-industrial-revolution-what-it-means-and-how-to-respond?utm_content=buffer8a47b&utm_medium=social&utm_source=facebook.com&utm_campaign=buffer

Schwab, K. (2017). *The fourth industrial revolution*. World Economic Forum.

Schwab, K., Davis, N., & Nadella, S. (2018). *Shaping the fourth industrial revolution*. World Economic Forum.

Sclater, N. (2008). Web 2.0, personal learning environments, and the future of learning management systems. *Research Bulletin, 13*(13), 1–13. Retrieved from https://wiki.oulu.fi/download/attachments/28096837/future+of+LMSs.pdf

Scott, C. L. (2015). *The futures of learning 3: What kind of pedagogies for the 21st century?* UNESCO Education Research and Foresight, Paris. Retrieved from http://unesdoc.unesco.org/images/0024/002431/243126e.pdf

Compilation of References

Scott, D. S., & Lundeen, T. F. (1980). Myofascial pain involving the masticatory muscles: An experimental model. *Pain*, *8*(2), 207–215. doi:10.1016/0304-3959(88)90008-5 PMID:7402684

Self, J. (1999). The defining characteristics of intelligent tutoring systems research: ITSs care, precisely. *International Journal of Artificial Intelligence in Education*, *10*, 350–364.

Seligman, M. E. P. (2005). Positive Psychology, Positive Prevention and Positive Therapy. In Handbook of Positive Psychology (pp. 3-13). Oxford University Press.

Seligman, M. E. P., & Csikszentmihalyi, M. (2000). Positive Psychology: An Introduction. *The American Psychologist*, *55*(1), 5–14. doi:10.1037/0003-066X.55.1.5 PMID:11392865

Sellen, A. J., & Whittaker, S. (2010). Beyond total capture: A constructive critique of lifelogging. *Communications of the ACM*, *53*(5), 70–77. doi:10.1145/1735223.1735243

Selwyn, N. (2007). *Web 2.0 applications as alternative environments for informal learning-a critical review*. Paper for CERI-KERIS International Expert Meeting on ICT and Educational Performance. Retrieved from http://newinbre.hpcf.upr.edu/wp-content/uploads/2017/02/39458556-W2-informal-learning.pdf

Selye, H. (1979). The stress of life. In Introduction to psychology. Kolkata, India: Kalyani Publishers.

Şen, Z. (2009). *Bulanık Mantık İlkeleri ve Modelleme (Mühendislik ve Sosyal Bilimler)*. İstanbul: Su Vakfı Yayınları.

Şeşen, H., & Basım, N. (2012). Birlikte Evrim. In *Örgüt Kuramları* (pp. 221–240). İstanbul: Beta.

Shaikh. (2017). *Deep Learning vs. Machine Learning – the essential differences you need to know!* Retrieved from https://www.analyticsvidhya.com/blog/2017/04/comparison-between-deep-learning-machine-learning/

Shale, D. (1988). Toward a reconceptualization of distance education. *American Journal of Distance Education*, *2*(3), 25–35. doi:10.1080/08923648809526633

Shelly, M. (1818). *Frankenstein or The Modern Prometheus*. London: Lackington, Hughes, Harding, Mavor & Jones.

Shelton, C. (2017). Giving up technology and social media: Why university lecturers stop using technology in teaching. *Technology, Pedagogy and Education*, *26*(3), 303–321. doi:10.1080/1475939X.2016.1217269

Shepherd, C. (2007). PLEs - what are we talking about here? *Clive On Learning*. Retrieved from http://clive-shepherd.blogspot.com/2007/04/ples-what-are-we-talking-about-here.html

Shulman, R. D. (2018, Feb 11). If You Are An Education Entrepreneur In 2018. *Forbes*. Retrieved from https://www.forbes.com/sites/robynshulman/2018/02/11/10-conferences-you-should-attend-if-you-are-an-education-entrepreneur-in-2018/#a1d1cbd36d5d

Shulman, L. (1986). Those who understand: Knowledge growth in teaching. *Educational Researcher*, *15*(2), 4–14. doi:10.3102/0013189X015002004

Shwartz, S., & David, S. (2014). *Understanding Machine Learning: From Theory to Algorithms*. Cambridge, UK: Cambridge University Press. doi:10.1017/CBO9781107298019

Siegel, E. (2017, Oct. 26). Why Exploring Space And Investing in Research Is Non-Negotiable. *Forbes*. Retrieved from https //www.forbes.com/sites/startswithabang/2017/10/26/even-while-the-world-suffers-investing-in-science-is-non-negotiable/#538fabd21647

Siemens, G. (2004). Connectivism: A learning theory for the digital age. *elearnspace*. Retrieved from http://www.elearnspace.org/Articles/connectivism.htm

Siemens, G. (2004). *Connectivism: A learning theory for the digital age.* Retrieved from. http://www.elearnspace.org/Articles/connectivism.htm

Siemens, G. (2007). PLEs - I Acronym, Therefore I Exist. *elearnspace*. Retrieved from http://www.elearnspace.org/blog/2007/04/15/ples-i-acronym-therefore-i-exist/

Siemens, G. (2008). *What is the unique idea in connectivism.* Retrieved from http://www.elearnspace.org/blog/2008/08/06/what-is-the-unique-idea-in-connectivism/

Siemens, G. (2009). *What is Connectivism?* Retrieved from. https://docs.google.com/document/d/14pKVP0_ILdPty6MGMJW8eQVEY1zibZ0RpQ2C0cePIgc/preview

Siemens, G. (2012c). *Designing, developing and running (massive) open online courses.* Retrieved from http://www.slideshare.net/gsiemens/designing-and-running-a-mooc

Siemens, G. (2005). Connectivism: A learning theory for the digital age. *International Journal of Instructional Technology and Distance Learning, 2*(1), 3–10.

Siemens, G., & Conole, G. (2011). Special issue connectivism: Design and delivery of social networked learning. *International Review of Research in Open and Distance Learning, 12*(3), 1–6. doi:10.19173/irrodl.v12i3.1113

Simonton, D. K. (2009). The "other IQ": Historiometric assessments of intelligence and related constructs. *Review of General Psychology, 13*(4), 315–326. doi:10.1037/a0017141

Singh, S. (2017). *Transhumanism and the future of humanity: 7 ways the world will change by 2030.* Retrieved from https://www.forbes.com/sites/unicefusa/2018/07/26/why-migrants-flee-central-america/#2f93dcf1301a

Singh, S. (2017, Nov. 20). *Transhumanism And The Future Of Humanity: 7 Ways The World Will Change By 2030.* Retrieved from https://www.forbes.com/sites/sarwantsingh/2017/11/20/transhumanism-and-the-future-of-humanity-seven-ways-the-world-will-change-by-2030/#498018347d79

Sipilä, K. (2014). Educational use of information and communications technology: Teachers' perspective. *Technology, Pedagogy and Education, 23*(2), 225–241. doi:10.1080/1475939X.2013.813407

Siraj-Blatchford, I., Sylva, K., Muttock, S., Gilden, R., & Bell, D. (2002). *Brief No: 356 Researching Effective Pedagogy in the Early Years.* Retrieved from www.ioe.ac.uk/REPEY_research_brief.pdf

Sirakaya, M. & Cakmak, E. (2018). Investigating Student Attitudes toward Augmented Reality. *Malaysian Online Journal of Educational Technology, 6*(1).

Sisman-Uğur, & Kurubacak, G. (2019). *Handbook of research on learning in the age of transhumanism.* Hershey, PA: IGI Global.

Skinner, A., Russo, C., Baraniecki, L., & Maloof, M. (2014). Ubiquitous augmented cognition. In *International Conference on Augmented Cognition* (pp. 67-77). Cham, Switzerland: Springer.

Skrabut, S. (2008). *Personal learning environments: the natural way of learning.* Retrieved from http://www.uwyo.edu/skrabut/docs/ADED5050_project.pdf

Smith, G. (2008). Newton's *Philosophiae Naturalis Principia Mathematica.* In *The Stanford Encyclopedia of Philosophy.* Retrieved from https://plato.stanford.edu/archives/win2008/entries/newton-principia/

Smith, M. K. (2012). What is pedagogy? In *The encyclopedia of informal education.* Retrieved from http://infed.org/mobi/what-is-pedagogy/

Smoot, F. G. (2009). Cesaret, Çünkü Yarın Daha Kötü Olacak! In İyimser Gelecek (pp. 77-81). İstanbul: NTV.

Snaza, N., Appelbaum, P., Bayne, S., Carlson, D., Morris, M., Rotas, N., ... Weaver, J. A. (2014). Toward a posthumanist education. *Journal of Curriculum Theorizing*, *30*(2), 39–55.

Snyder, C. R., Harris, C., Anderson, J. R., Holleran, S. A., Irving, L. M., Sigmon, S. T., ... Harney, P. (1991). The Will and the Ways: Development and Validation of an Individual Differences Measure of Hope. *Journal of Personality and Social Psychology*, *60*(4), 570–585. doi:10.1037/0022-3514.60.4.570 PMID:2037968

Snyder, C. R., Lopez, S. J., Shorey, H. S., Rand, K. L., & Feldman, D. B. (2003). Hope Theory, Measurements, and Applications to School Psychology. *School Psychology Quarterly*, *18*(2), 122–139. doi:10.1521cpq.18.2.122.21854

Sonwalkar, N. (2013). The first adaptive MOOC: A case study on pedagogy framework and scalable cloud Architecture—Part I. In *MOOCs Forum* (Vol. 1, pp. 22-29). New Rochelle, NY: Mary Ann Liebert, Inc. Retrieved from https://www.liebertpub.com/doi/abs/10.1089/mooc.2013.0007

Sotala, J., & Valpola, H. (2012). Coalescing minds: brain uploading-related group mind scenarios. *International Journal of Machine Consciousness*, *4*(1), 293–312.

Sotala, K. (2012). Advantages of Artificial Intelligences, Uploads, and Digital Minds. *International Journal of Machine Consciousness*, *4*(1), 275–291. doi:10.1142/S1793843012400161

Sotala, K., & Yampolskiy, R. V. (2014). Responses to catastrophic AGI risk: A survey. *Physica Scripta*, *90*(1), 018001. doi:10.1088/0031-8949/90/1/018001

Sourmplis, A., Chatzidaki, E., Koulocheri, E., & Xenos, M. (2011). Implementing an open personal learning environment. *2011 15th Panhellenic Conference on Informatics*, 345–349. Retrieved from http://quality.eap.gr/Publications/XM/Conferences%20Greek/PCI2011_Implementing_an_Open_Personal_Learning_Environment.pdf

Sözen, C., & Gürbüz, S. (2012). Örgütsel Ağlar. In Örgüt Kuramları (pp. 301-326). İstanbul: Beta.

Sparrow, B., Liu, J., & Wegner, D. M. (2011). Google effects on memory: Cognitive consequences of having information at our fingertips. *Science*, *333*(6043), 776–778. doi:10.1126cience.1207745 PMID:21764755

Spector, J. M. (2012). The future of distance learning technology: It's not about the technology and it's not about the distance. In L. Moller & J. B. Huett (Eds.), *The next generation of distance education* (pp. 21–29). Boston, MA: Springer. doi:10.1007/978-1-4614-1785-9_2

Stanford, P., Crowe, M. W., & Flice, H. (2010). Differentiating with technology. *Teaching Exceptional Children Plus*, *6*(4), 2–9.

Stary, C. (2017). Agogic principles in trans-human settings. *Proceedings*, *1*, 236. doi:10.3390/IS4SI-2017-03949

Statistics How To. (2018). *What is a Normal distribution?* Retrieved from https://www.statisticshowto.datasciencecentral.com/probability-and-statistics/normal-distributions/

Steuer, J. (2000). Defining Virtual Reality: Dimensions Determining Telepresence. *Journal of Communication*, *42*(4), 73–93. doi:10.1111/j.1460-2466.1992.tb00812.x

Stewart, V. (2010). A classroom as wide as the world. In H. H. Jacobs (Ed.), *Curriculum 21: Essential education for a changing world* (pp. 97–114). Alexandria, VA: ASCD.

Stross, C. (2004). Elector. *Asimov's Science Fiction*, *4*(9).

Sung, Y. T., Chang, K. E., & Liu, T. C. (2016). The effects of integrating mobile devices with teaching and learning on students' learning performance: A meta-analysis and research synthesis. *Computers & Education*, *94*, 252–275. doi:10.1016/j.compedu.2015.11.008

Suomen Akatemia. (2011). *The Future of Learning, Knowledge and Skills (TULOS)*. Research Programme 2014-2017. Programme memorandum. Retrieved from https://www.aka.fi/globalassets/awanhat/documents/ohjelmat/tulos-tulevaisuuden-oppiminen-ja-osaaminen/ohjelmamuistio_tulos_en.pdf

Superintelligence. (2018, Nov. 20). Retrieved from https://en.wikipedia.org/wiki/Superintelligence

Sutherland, I. E. (1965). The Ultimate Display. *Proceedings of IFIP Congress 2*.

Swan, M. (2012). Sensor mania! The internet of things, wearable computing, objective metrics, and the quantified self 2.0. *Journal of Sensor and Actuator Networks*, *1*(3), 217–253. doi:10.3390/jsan1030217

Tait, A. W. (2018). Education for development: From distance to open education. *The Journal of Learning for Development*, *5*(2), 101-115.

Tang, Y., & Hew, K. F. (2017). Is mobile instant messaging (MIM) useful in education? Examining its technological, pedagogical, and social affordances. *Educational Research Review*, *21*, 85–104. doi:10.1016/j.edurev.2017.05.001

Tanwar, P., Prasad, T. V., & Datta, K. (2014). *An effective reasoning algorithm for question answering system. Editorial Preface*. Retrieved from http://thesai.org/Downloads/SpecialIssueNo9/Paper_8-An_Effective_Reasoning_Algorithm_for_Question_Answering_System.pdf

Tapscott, D. (1999). Educating the Net generation. *Educational Leadership*, *56*, 5, 6–11.

Tapscott, D., & Tapscott, A. (2017). The blockchain revolution and higher education. *EDUCAUSE Review*, *52*(2), 11–24.

Taylan, H. H., & Arklan, Ü. (2008). Medya Ve Kültür: Kültürün Medya Aracıliğıyla Küreselleşmesi. *Sosyal Bilimler Dergisi*, *10*(1), 86.

Taylor, J. C. (2001). *Fifth generation distance education*. Higher Education Division, Department of Education, Training and Youth Affairs.

Tech Terms. (2014). *ICT, Tech Terms*. Available at: http://www.techterms.com/definition/realtime

Technological Determinism. (2018, Nov. 5). Retrieved from https://en.wikipedia.org/wiki/Technological_determinism

Technological Singularity. (2018, Nov. 24). Retrieved from https://en.wikipedia.org/wiki/Technological_singularity

Technological Unemployment. (2018, Nov. 22). Retrieved from https://en.wikipedia.org/wiki/Technological_unemployment

Tegmark, M. (2017). *Life 3.0: Being human in the age of artificial intelligence*. London: Penguin Books.

Tektaş, M., Akbaş, A., & Topuz, V. (2002). *Yapay zeka tekniklerinin trafik kontrolünde kullanilmasi üzerine bir inceleme*. Retrieved from http://www.trafik.gov.tr/SiteAssets/Yayinlar/Bildiriler/pdf/C4-7.pdf

The American Institute of Stress. (1999). 50 Common Signe and symptoms of Stress. *World Psychology*, 469.

The Commonwealth of Learning. (1999). *Planning and Management of Open and Distance Learning*. Vancouver, Canada: The Commonwealth of Learning. Retrieved from http://www.col.org/PublicationDocuments/pub_Planning_Management_03_web.pdf

The Commonwealth of Learning. (2000). *An Introduction to Open and Distance Learning*. Retrieved from http://oasis.col.org/bitstream/handle/11599/138/ODLIntro.pdf?sequence=1&isAllowed=y

Thomas, A. (2017). Super-intelligence and eternal life: transhumanism's faithful follow it blindly into a future for the elite. *The conversation*. Retrieved from http://theconversation.com/super-intelligence-and-eternal-life-transhumanisms-faithful-follow-it-blindly-into-a-future-for-the-elite-78538

Thomas, I. (2014). Special issue-pedagogy for education for sustainability in higher education. *Sustainability*, *6*(4), 1705–1708. doi:10.3390u6041705

Thomas, L. G., & Knezek, D. G. (2008). Information, communications, and educational technology standards for students, teachers, and school leaders. In J. Voogt & G. Knezek (Eds.), *International handbook of information technology in primary and secondary education* (pp. 333–348). New York: Springer. doi:10.1007/978-0-387-73315-9_20

Thompson, J. (2017). Transhumanism: How far is too far? *A Multidisciplinary Journal of Biotechnology and the Body*, *23*(2), 1–14.

Tirosh-Samuelson, H. (2007). *Facing the challenges of transhumanism: Philosophical, religious, and ethical considerations*. Retrieved from http://transhumanism.asu.edu/pdf/2007_news_challenges.pdf

Titmus, C., Buttedahl, P., Ironside, D., & Lengrand, P. (1979). *Terminology of Adult education/Terminol ogie de la Educacion de Adultos/Terminologie de l'Education des Adultes*. Paris: UNESCO.

Toglia, M. P., & Battig, W. F. (1978). Handbook of semantic word norms. Mahwah, NJ: Lawrence Erlbaum.

Tomlinson, C. A. (1999). *The differentiated classroom: Responding to the needs of all learners*. Alexandria, VA: Association for Supervision and Curriculum Development.

Tomlinson, C., & Kalbfleisch, M. L. (1998). Teach me, teach my brain: A call for differentiated classrooms. *Educational Leadership*, 52–55.

Tondeur, J., Van Keer, H., Van Braak, J., & Valcke, M. (2008). ICT integration in the classroom: Challenging the potential of a school policy. *Computers & Education*, *51*(1), 212–223. doi:10.1016/j.compedu.2007.05.003

Tongkaw, A. (2013). Multi Perspective Integrations Information and Communication Technologies (ICTs) in Higher Education in Developing Countries: Case Study Thailand. *Procedia – Social & Behavioral Sciences*, *93*, 1467-72. Available at: http://www.sciencedirect.com/science/article/pii/S1877042813035106

Tooby, J., & Cosmides, L. (1992). The Psychological Foundations of Culture. In J. Barkow, L. Cosmides, & J. Tooby (Eds.), *The Adapted Mind: Evolutionary Psychology and the Generation of Culture* (p. 19). New York: Oxford University Press, Inc.

Törenli, N. (2005). e-Devlet'in ekonomi-politiğine giriş: Kullanıcı dostu ortamlarda "Sanallaşan" kamu hizmetleri. *Ankara Üniversitesi SBF Dergisi*, *60*(01), 191–224.

Tour, E. (2016). *Teachers' personal learning networks (PLNs): exploring the nature of self-initiated professional learning online. Literacy*. Wiley Online Library. doi:10.1111/lit.12101

Transhumanism in higher education: Social implications and institutional roles. (2015, May). *Proceedings of the Symposium on Emerging Technology Trends in Higher Education*. Retrieved from http://epubs.utah.edu/index.php/emerge/article/view/1362

Transhumanist Declaration. (1998). *The Transhumanist Declaration*. Retrieved from https://itp.uni-frankfurt.de/~gros/Mind2010/transhumanDeclaration.pdf

Traxler, J., & Kukulska-Hulme, A. (Eds.). (2016). *Mobile learning: The next generation*. London: Routledge.

Trilling, B., & Fadel, C. (2012). *21st century skills: Learning for life in our times*. Hoboken, NJ: John Wiley & Sons.

Trippett, D. (2018, March 29). Transhumanism: advances in technology could already put evolution into hyperdrive – but should they? *The Conversation*. Retrieved from http://theconversation.com/transhumanism-advances-in-technology-could-already-put-evolution-into-hyperdrive-but-should-they-92694

Trust, T., Krutka, D. G., & Carpenter, J. P. (2016). "Together we are better": Professional learning networks for teachers. *Computers & Education, 102*, 15-34. Retrieved from https://www.sciencedirect.com/science/article/pii/S036013151630135X

Trust, T. (2012). Professional learning networks designed for teacher learning. *Journal of Digital Learning in Teacher Education, 28*(4), 133–138. doi:10.1080/21532974.2012.10784693

Tsang, H. W. C., & Tsui, E. (2017). Conceptual design and empirical study of a personal learning environment and network (PLE&N) to support peer-based social and lifelong learning. *VINE Journal of Information and Knowledge Management Systems, 47*(2), 228–249. doi:10.1108/VJIKMS-03-2017-0010

Tsui, E., & Dragicevic, N. (2018). Use of scenario development and personal learning environment and networks (PLE&N) to support curriculum co-creation. *Management & Marketing, 13*(2), 848-858. Retrieved from https://www.degruyter.com/downloadpdf/j/mmcks.2018.13.issue-2/mmcks-2018-0009/mmcks-2018-0009.pdf

Tsui, E., Wang, W. M., & Sabetzadeh, F. (2014, November). Enacting Personal Knowledge Management & learning with web services interoperability tools. In *Cloud Computing and Intelligence Systems (CCIS), 2014 IEEE 3rd International Conference on* (pp. 491-494). IEEE. Retrieved from https://ieeexplore.ieee.org/abstract/document/7175785

Tsui, M. L., Tsui, E., & See-To, E. W. (2013). Adoption of a personal learning environment & network (PLE&N) to support peer-based lifelong learning. *International Academic Forum (IAFOR)*. Retrieved from http://ira.lib.polyu.edu.hk/bitstream/10397/6290/1/ACSET2013_proceedings_TSUI_Lai_Na_Miriam.pdf

Tu, C. H., Sujo-Montes, M., Blocher, M., Yen, C. J., & Chan, J. Y. (2012). The integrations of personal learning environments & open network learning environments. *TechTrends, 56*(3), 13–19. Retrieved from http://link.springer.com/content/pdf/10.1007%2Fs11528-012-0571-7

Tu, C. H., Yen, C. J. & Sujo-Montes, L. E. (2015). Personal learning environments and self-regulated learning. In *Media Rich Instruction* (pp. 35-48). Springer International Publishing. Retrieved from https://link.springer.com/chapter/10.1007/978-3-319-00152-4_3

Turban, E. (1993). *Decision support systems* (3rd ed.). Upper Saddle River, NJ: Prentice Hall.

Turing, A. M. (1950). Computing machinery and intelligence. *Mind, LIX*(59), 433–460. doi:10.1093/mind/LIX.236.433

Türkçe, B. B. C. (2018). *DERGİ - 6500 yıllık diş dolgusu bulundu*. Retrieved from https://www.bbc.com/turkce/haberler/2016/03/160302_vert_ear_dis_dolgusu

U. S. Department of Commerce. (1926). *Proceedings of the Fourth National Radio Conference and recommendations for regulation of radio*. Washington, DC: Government Printing Office. Retrieved from http://earlyradiohistory.us/1925conf.htm/

Uğur, A., & Kınacı, A. C. (2006). Yapay zeka teknikleri ve yapay sinir ağları kullanılarak web sayfalarının sınıflandırılması. XI. Türkiye'de İnternet Konferansı (inet-tr'06), Ankara, 1-4.

Uğur, S., & Kurubacak, G. (2019). Technology Management Through Artificial Intelligence in Open and Distance Learning. In Handbook of Research on Challenges and Opportunities in Launching a Technology-Driven International University (pp. 338–368). Hershey, PA: IGI Global. doi:10.4018/978-1-5225-6255-9.ch018

Uğur, S. (2018). Transhumanizm ve öğrenmedeki değişim. *Açıköğretim Uygulamaları ve Araştırmaları Dergisi, 4*(3), 58–74.

Uğur, S., Güler, E., Hakan, Y., & Kurubacak, G. (2018). Transhümanist çağda mega açık üniversitelerin yeniden yapılandırılabilmesi için stratejik karar modeli ile bir blokzincir uygulamasının geliştirilmesi. *Açıköğretim Uygulamaları ve Araştırmaları Dergisi, 4*(3), 5–11.

UKCES. (2014). *The Future of Work: Jobs and Skills in 2030*. Evidence Report 84. Retrieved from https://www.gov.uk/government/publications/jobs-and-skills-in-2030

Uludağ İhracatçılar Birliği Genel Sekreterliği. (2017). *Yapay Zekâ*. Retrieved from www.yapayzekâveyeniteknolojiler

UNESCO. (2002). *Open and Distance Learning: trends, policy and strategy consideration*. Paris: UNESCO.

UNESCO. (2010). *ICT transforming education: a regional guide*. Bangkok, Thailand: UNESCO. Retrieved from http://unesdoc.unesco.org/images/0018/001892/189216e.pdf

UNESCO. (2011a). *ICT competency framework for teachers*. Retrieved from http://unesdoc.unesco.org/images/0021/002134/213475e.pdf

UNESCO. (2011b). *Media and information literacy curriculum for teachers*. Retrieved from http://unesdoc.unesco.org/images/0019/001929/192971e.pdf

UNESCO. (2014). *Global monitoring report 2014*. Retrieved from http://unesdoc.unesco.org/images/0022/002256/225660e.pdf

UNESCO. (2015a). *The Incheon Declaration. Education 2030. Towards inclusive and equitable quality lifelong learning for all*. Retrieved from http://unesdoc.unesco.org/images/0023/002338/233813m.pdf

UNESCO. (2015b). Education 2030. The Incheon Declaration and framework for action for sustainable goal 4. Retrieved from http://unesdoc.unesco.org/images/0024/002456/245656E.pdf

UNESCO. (2016, Sept. 9). *Education needs to change fundamentally to meet global development goals*. Retrieved from http://www.unesco.org/new/en/media-services/single-view/news/education_needs_to_change_fundamentally_to_meet_global_devel/

UNESCO. (n.d.). *Sustainable development goal 4 and its targets*. Retrieved from https://en.unesco.org/education2030-sdg4/targets

United Nations. (2018). Sustainable development goal 4. Progress of goal 4 in 2018. Retrieved from https://sustainabledevelopment.un.org/sdg4

Universa Blockchain. (2018). *Blockchain in education*. Retrieved from https://medium.com/universablockchain/blockchain-in-education-49ad413b9e12

Usluel, Y. K., Mazman, S. G., & Arikan, A. (2009). Prospective teachers' awareness of collaborative web 2.0 tools. *The IADIS International Conference WWW/Internet 2009*.

Utecht, J. (2008). *Stages of PLN adoption*. Retrieved from http://www.thethinkingstick.com/?p=652

Valtonen, T., Hacklin, S., Dillon, P., Vesisenaho, M., Kukkonen, J., & Hietanen, A. (2012). Perspectives on personal learning environments held by vocational students. *Computers & Education, 58*(2), 732–739. doi:10.1016/j.compedu.2011.09.025

van Dam, N. H. M. (2017). *21st Century Corporate Learning & Development: Trends and Best Practices*. Retrieved from https://bookboon.com/en/21st-century-corporate-learning-development-ebook

van Erp, J., Lotte, F., & Tangermann, M. (2012). Brain-computer interfaces: Beyond medical applications. *Computer, 45*(4), 26–34. doi:10.1109/MC.2012.107

Van Hilvoorde, I., & Landeweerd, L. (2010). Enhancing disabilities: Transhumanism under the veil of inclusion? *Journal of Disability and Rehabilitation, 32*(26), 2222–2227. doi:10.3109/09638288.2010.491578 PMID:20528168

van Merriënboer, J. J. G. (1997). *Training complex cognitive skills: A four-component instructional design model for technical training*. Englewood Cliffs, NJ: Educational Technology Publications.

Vander Ark, T. (2017a). *Ask about AI: The future of work and learning*. Retrieved from http://www.gettingsmart.com/wp-content/uploads/2018/01/17-EdIn-05-white-paper-rd9-1.pdf

Vander Ark, T. (2017b). *How blockchain will transform credentialing (and education)*. Retrieved from http://www.gettingsmart.com/2017/12/blockchain-will-transform-credentialing-education/

Vander Ark, T. (2018). *20 Ways blockchain will transform (okay, may improve) education*. Retrieved from https://www.forbes.com/sites/tomvanderark/2018/08/20/26-ways-blockchain-will-transform-ok-may-improve-education/#1d4cf0f04ac9

Vanderelst, D., & Winfield, A. (2018). The dark side of ethical robots. In *Proceedings of the 2018 AAAI/ACM Conference on AI, Ethics, and Society* (pp. 317-322). ACM. 10.1145/3278721.3278726

Vasseur, J.-P., & Dunkels, A. (2010). *Interconnecting the Smart Objects with IP*. Burlington, MA: Morgan Kaufmann–Elsevier.

Veletsianos, G., & Shepherdson, P. (2016). A systematic analysis and synthesis of the empirical MOOC literature published in 2013-2015. *The International Review of Research in Open and Distributed Learning, 17*(2), 198–221. doi:10.19173/irrodl.v17i2.2448

Verdoux, P. (2009). Transhumanism, progress and the future. *Journal of Evolution and Technology / WTA, 20*(2), 49–69.

Verdoux, P. (2009). Transhumanism, Progress and the Future. *Journal of Evolution and Technology / WTA, 20*(2), 49–69.

Verduin, J. R. Jr, & Clark, T. A. (1991). *Distance Education: The Foundations of Effective Practice*. San Francisco: Jossey-Bass.

Vernon, H., McDermaid, C.S., & Hagino, C. (1999). Systematic review of randomized clinical trials of complementary/alternative therapies in the treatment of tension-type and cervicogenic headache. *Complement Ther Med, 7*(14, 13-19.

Vigo, J. (2018). *The Ethics Of Transhumanism And The Cult Of Futurist Biotech*. Retrieved from https://www.forbes.com/sites/julianvigo/2018/09/24/the-ethics-of-transhumanism-and-the-cult-of-futurist-biotech/#b3d29b04ac54

Vinge, V. (2003). The Peace War. New York: Tor Books.

Vinge, V. (2013). Technological Singularity. *The Transhumanist Reader*, 365-375.

Vita-More, N. (2013). Aesthetics: bringing the arts & design into the discussion of transhumanism. *The transhumanist reader: Classical and contemporary essays on the science, technology, and philosophy of the human future*, 18-27.

Vita-More, N. (2018). Transhumanism: What is it? Academic Press.

Vita-More, N. (2016). Transhumanism: The growing worldview. In N. Lee (Ed.), *Google It: total information awareness* (pp. 475–487). New York: Springer. doi:10.1007/978-1-4939-6415-4_27

Volery, T., & Lord, D. (2000). Critical success factors in online education. *International Journal of Educational Management, 14*(5), 216–223. doi:10.1108/09513540010344731

Voogt, J., & Roblin, N. P. (2012). A comparative analysis of international frameworks for 21st century competences: Implications for national curriculum policies. *Journal of Curriculum Studies, 44*(3), 299–321. doi:10.1080/00220272.2012.668938

Compilation of References

Vygotsky, L. (1978). *Mind in society: Development of higher psychological processes*. Boston: Harvard University Press.

Vygotsky, L. (1979. (1925). Consciousness as a problem in the psychology of behavior. *Social Psychology, 17*(4), 3–35.

Walker, R., Jenkins, M., & Voce, J. (2017). The rhetoric and reality of technology-enhanced learning developments in UK higher education: Reflections on recent UCISA research findings (2012–2016). *Interactive Learning Environments*, 1–11.

Wallace, B., Bernardelli, A., Molyneux, C., & Farrell, C. (2012). TASC: Thinking actively in a social context. A universal problem-solving process: A powerful tool to promote differentiated learning experiences. *Gifted Education International, 28*(1), 58–83. doi:10.1177/0261429411427645

Walsh, J. P., Meyer, A. D., & Schoonhoven, C. B. (2006). A Future for Organization Theory: Living in and Living with Changing Organizations. *Organization Science, 17*(5), 657–671. doi:10.1287/orsc.1060.0215

Walters, P., & Kop, R. (2009). Heidegger, digital technology, and postmodern education: From being in cyberspace to meeting on MySpace. *Bulletin of Science, Technology & Society, 29*(4), 278–286. doi:10.1177/0270467609336305

Wan, G., & Gut, D. (Eds.). (2011). *Bringing schools into the 21st century*. New York: Springer. doi:10.1007/978-94-007-0268-4

Wang, Y. H. (2017). The effectiveness of integrating teaching strategies into IRS activities to facilitate learning. *Journal of Computer Assisted Learning, 33*(1), 35–50. doi:10.1111/jcal.12164

Ward, L., & Parr, J. M. (2010). Revisiting and Reframing use: Implications for the integration of ICT. *Computers & Education, 54*(1), 113–122. doi:10.1016/j.compedu.2009.07.011

Warschauer, M., & Meskill, C. (2000). Technology and second language learning. In J. Rosenthal (Ed.), *Handbook of undergraduate second language education* (pp. 303–318). Mahwah, NJ: Lawrence Erlbaum.

Warwick, K. (2010). Implications and consequences of robots with biological brains. *Ethics and Information Technology, 12*(3), 223–234. doi:10.100710676-010-9218-6

Watkins, J. & Wilkins, M. (2011). Using YouTube in the EFL classrooms. *Language Education in Asia, 2*(1), 113-119.

Watkins, B. L. (1991). A Quite Radical Idea: The Invention and Elaboration of Collegiate Correspondence Study. In B. L. Watkins & S. J. Wright (Eds.), *The Foundations of American Distance Education: A Century of Collegiate Correspondence Study* (pp. 1–35). Dubuque, IA: Kendall/Hunt.

Wątróbski, J., Ziemba, P., & Wolski, W. (2016). MCDA-based Decision Support System for Sustainable Management – RES Case Study. *Proceedings of the Federated Conference on Computer Science and Information Systems*, 1235–1239. 10.15439/2016F489

WCED. (1987). *Our common future. World commission on environment and development*. Oxford, UK: Oxford University Press.

Weis, R., & Fromherz, P. (1997). Frequency dependent signal transfer in neuron transistors. *Physical Review. E, 55*(1), 877–889. doi:10.1103/PhysRevE.55.877

Weller, M. (2007). My personal work/leisure/learning environment. *The Ed Techie*. Retrieved from http://nogoodreason.typepad.co.uk/no_good_reason/2007/12/my-personal-wor.html

Wenger, E. (2014). *Artificial intelligence and tutoring systems: computational and cognitive approaches to the communication of knowledge*. Burlington, MA: Morgan Kaufmann.

What is biofeedback? (2008). *Association for Applied Psychophysiology and Biofeedback, 12*(5).

Wheeler, S. (2010). *Anatomy of a PLE*. Academic Press.

Wheeler, S. (forthcoming). Digital learning in organisations. London: *Kogan Page*.

Wichmann, A., & Rummel, N. (2013). Improving revision in wiki-based writing: Coordination pays off. *Computers & Education*, *62*, 262–270. doi:10.1016/j.compedu.2012.10.017

Wiley, K. B. (2015). *Mind Uploading and the Question of Life, the Universe, and Everything*. Retrieved from https://ieet.org/index.php/IEET2/more/wiley20150720

Wilkinson, A. (2007). *Managing Tomorrow's People: The Future of Work 2020*. PricewaterhouseCoopers (PWC). Retrieved from https://www.pwc.com/gx/en/managing-tomorrows-people/future-of-work/pdf/mtp-future-of-work.pdf

Wilson, S., Liber, O., Johnson, M. W., Beauvoir, P., Sharples, P., & Milligan, C. D. (2007). Personal learning environments: Challenging the dominant design of educational systems. *Journal of e-Learning and Knowledge Society*, *3*(2), 27-38. Retrieved from https://www.learntechlib.org/p/43419/

Wilson, S. (2008). Patterns of personal learning environments. *Interactive Learning Environments*, *16*(1), 17–34. doi:10.1080/10494820701772660

Windschitl, M. (2002). Framing constructivism in practice as the negotiation of dilemmas: An analysis of the conceptual, pedagogical, cultural, and political challenges facing teachers. *Review of Educational Research*, *72*(2), 131–175. doi:10.3102/00346543072002131

Winn, W. (1997). Advantages of a theory-based curriculum in instructional technology. *Educational Technology*, 34–41.

Winn, W. (2002). Current trends in educational technology research: The study of learning environments. *Educational Psychology Review*, *14*(3), 331–351. doi:10.1023/A:1016068530070

Winter, J. O., Liu, T. Y., Korgel, B. A., & Schmidt, C. E. (2001). Recognition molecule directed interfacing between semiconductor quantum dots and nerve cells. *Advanced Materials*, *13*(22), 1673–1677. doi:10.1002/1521-4095(200111)13:22<1673::AID-ADMA1673>3.0.CO;2-6

Wong, R. (2016, April 5). *Samsung patents smart contact lenses with a built-in camera*. Retrieved from https://www.sciencealert.com/samsung-just-patented-smart-contact-lenses-with-a-built-in-camera

Wood, D. (2018). *Transcending Politics: A Technoprogressive Roadmap to a Comprehensively Better Future*. London: Delta Wisdom.

World Economic Forum. (2016). The fourth industrial revolution: What it means and how to respond.

World Economic Forum. (2017, March 28). *The digital revolution is not about technology – it's about people*. Retrieved from https://www.weforum.org/agenda/2017/03/the-digital-revolution-is-not-about-technology-it-s-about-people/

World Transhumanist Association. (2003). *The Transhumanist Declaration*. Retrieved from http://transhumanism.org/index.php/WTA/declaration/

WTA. (2018). *The Transhumanist FAQ: What is transhumanism?* Retrieved from http://humanityplus.org/philosophy/transhumanist-faq/

Wu, H.-K., Lee, S. W.-Y., Chang, H.-Y., & Liang, J.-C. (2013). *Current status, opportunities and challenges of augmented reality in education*. Academic Press.

Compilation of References

Wu, J. Y., Hsiao, Y. C., & Nian, M. W. (2018). Using supervised machine learning on large-scale online forums to classify course-related Facebook messages in predicting learning achievement within the personal learning environment. *Interactive Learning Environments*, 1–16. doi:10.1080/10494820.2018.1515085

Wu, J.-Y., & Xie, C. (2018). Using time pressure and note-taking to prevent digital distraction behavior and enhance online search performance: Perspectives from the load theory of attention and cognitive control. *Computers in Human Behavior*, *88*, 244–254. doi:10.1016/j.chb.2018.07.008

Wu, P. H., Hwang, G. J., Yang, M. L., & Chen, C. H. (2017). Impacts of integrating the repertory grid into an augmented reality-based learning design on students learning achievements, cognitive load and degree of satisfaction. *Interactive Learning Environments*, *26*(2), 221–234. doi:10.1080/10494820.2017.1294608

Xi, B. D., Su, J., Huang, G. H., Qin, X. S., Jiang, Y. H., Huo, S. L., ... Yao, B. (2010). An integrated optimization approach and multi-criteria decision analysis for supporting the waste-management system of the City of Beijing, China. *Engineering Applications of Artificial Intelligence*, *23*(4), 620–631. doi:10.1016/j.engappai.2010.01.002

Yamamoto, G. T., & Karaman, F. (2005). *A Road-Map For The Development Of The Content Protecting Technologies (CPT) For The Content Based E-Business Models* (Vol. 5). Dubai, UAE: E-Business Review.

Yamamoto, G. T., & Karaman, F. (2006). *ICT, New Working Elite, and Social Implications* (Vol. 6). Dubai, UAE: E-Business Review.

Yampolskiy, R. V. (2012). Leakproofing Singularity-Artificial Intelligence Confinement Problem. *Journal of Consciousness Studies*.

Yampolskiy, R. V. (2015). *Artificial superintelligence: a futuristic approach*. Chapman and Hall/CRC. doi:10.1201/b18612

Yampolskiy, R. V., & Fox, J. (2012). Artificial general intelligence and the human mental model. In *Singularity Hypotheses* (pp. 129–145). Berlin: Springer. doi:10.1007/978-3-642-32560-1_7

Yang, Q. (2018). Machine Learning as a UX Design Material: How Can We Imagine Beyond Automation, Recommenders, and Reminders? *AAAI Spring Symposium Series*.

Yapıcı, I. U., & Hevedanlı, M. (2012). International educational technology conference IETC2012. Preservice biology teachers' attitudes towards ICT using in biology teaching. *Procedia: Social and Behavioral Sciences*, *64*, 633–638. doi:10.1016/j.sbspro.2012.11.074

Yıldırım, S. (2000). Effects of an educational computing course on preservice and inservice teachers: A discussion and analysis of attitudes and use. *Journal of Research on Computing in Education*, *32*(4), 479–495. doi:10.1080/08886504.2000.10782293

Yli-Huumo, J., Ko, D., Choi, S., Park, S., & Smolander, K. (2016). Where is current research on blockchain technology? - A systematic review. *PLoS One*, *11*(10), 1–27. doi:10.1371/journal.pone.0163477 PMID:27695049

Yoo, K. H., Filandrianos, E., Taghados, S., & Park, S. (2013). Non-invasive brain-to-brain interface (BBI): Establishing functional links between two brains. *PLoS One*, *8*(4), e60410. doi:10.1371/journal.pone.0060410 PMID:23573251

Youssef, C. M., & Luthans, F. (2007). Positive Organizational Behavior in the Workplace: The Impact of Hope, Optimism and Resilience. *Journal of Management*, *33*(5), 774–800. doi:10.1177/0149206307305562

Yuen, M., Chan, S., Chan, C., Fung, D. C. L., Cheung, W. M., Kwan, T., & Leung, F. K. S. (2016). Differentiation in key learning areas for gifted students in regular classes: A project for primary school teachers in Hong Kong. *Gifted Education International*, *34*(1), 36–46. doi:10.1177/0261429416649047

Zadeh, L. (1965). Fuzzy Sets. *Information and Control*, *8*(3), 338–353. doi:10.1016/S0019-9958(65)90241-X

Zappa, M. (2012). *Envisioning emerging technology for 2012 and beyond*. Retrieved from http://www.demainlaveille.fr/wp-content/uploads/2012/01/envisioningtech.pdf

Zawacki-Richter, O. (2009). Research areas in distance education: A Delphi study. *International Review of Research in Open and Distributed Learning*, *10*(3), 1–17. doi:10.19173/irrodl.v10i3.674

Zeck, G., & Fromherz, P. (2001). Noninvasive neuroelectronic interfacing with synaptically connected snail neurons immobilized on a semiconductor chip. *Proceedings of the National Academy of Sciences of the United States of America*, *98*(18), 10457–10462. doi:10.1073/pnas.181348698 PMID:11526244

Zeilinger, A. (2009). Bilimin, Dinin ve Teknolojinin Geleceği. In İyimser Gelecek (pp. 37-38). İstanbul: NTV.

Zhang, R., Chen, X., Lu, J., Wen, S., Nepal, S., & Xiang, Y. (2018). *Using AI to Hack IA: A New Stealthy Spyware Against Voice Assistance Functions in Smart Phones*. Retrieved from https://arxiv.org/pdf/1805.06187.pdf

Zhou, P., Wu, F., Zhou, T., Cai, X., Zhang, S., Zhang, X., ... Lan, F. (2016). Simple and versatile synthetic polydopamine-based surface supports reprogramming of human somatic cells and long-term self-renewal of human pluripotent stem cells under defined conditions. *Biomaterials*, *87*, 1–17. doi:10.1016/j.biomaterials.2016.02.012 PMID:26897536

Zhou, Q., Zhao, Y., Hu, J., Liu, Y., & Xing, L. (2010). Pre-service chemistry teachers' attitude toward ICT in Xian. *Procedia: Social and Behavioral Sciences*, *9*, 1407–1414. doi:10.1016/j.sbspro.2010.12.342

Zietsman, G. (2010). *Idiotic Geniuses in Noesis*. Mega Society.

Zigerell, J. (1991). *The use of television in American higher education*. New York: Praeger.

Žubrinic, K., & Kalpic, D. (2008). The web as personal learning environment. *MIPRO*. Retrieved from http://bib.irb.hr/datoteka/357767.576-2219-1-PB-1.pdf

About the Contributors

Serap Sisman–Ugur has been working as a lecturer at the Distance Education Department of Open Education Faculty. She graduated from an undergraduate program in "Computer Education and Instructional Technology" at Anadolu University and the master degree of the same program. She have been studying doctorate in Distance Learning. Since 2017, she has been Social Media Coordinator of Open Education System, which include Open Education Faculty, Faculty of Business Administrator and Faculty of Economics, in Anadolu University. She over twenty years experience in focusing on research and development activities&projects in fields such as e-learning content types, interactivity, digital storytelling, animation, game-based learning, gamification, instructional design, social media and social networks, crosscultural aspects, artificial intelligence, individual differences and human-computer interaction. She interested in technological singularity and transhumanism.

Gulsun Kurubacak is a professor in Distance Education at the College of Open Education of Anadolu University. Dr. Kurubacak undertook graduate studies at Anadolu University, Turkey (MA. Educational Technology) and the University of Cincinnati, USA (Ed.D. Curriculum & Instruction), and also has worked a post-doctoral fellow at the College of Education at New Mexico State University, USA (2001-2002). Dr. Kurubacak earned her B.S. degree in Computer Engineering from the College of Informatics Technologies and Engineering of Hoca Ahmet Yesevi International Turk-Kazakhstani University. Also, she is currently a graduate student in the Department of Computer and Instructional Technologies. Dr. Kurubacak has over thirty-two year experience in focusing on the egalitarian and ecological aspects of distance education; finding new answers, viewpoints and explanations to online communication interactions through critical pedagogy; and improving learner critical thinking skills through project-based online learning, new media and new technologies. She continues to manage and provide pedagogical support for distance learning programs.

* * *

Polina Shafran Abramov received her MS in Computer Science from the department of Computer Engineering and Computer Science at Speed School of Engineering, University of Louisville. She received her BA in Mathematics from Technion - Israel Institute of Technology. She has been working in the software industry since 2004 and has experience developing products ranging from personally tailored, special-case solutions up to large-scale corporate systems. Throughout her career she has developed software solutions for desktop and embedded devices and worked in such industries as Computer Aided Design (CAD) engineering tooling, security and healthcare. Her areas of interest include but are not limited to big data, machine learning and software architecture.

About the Contributors

Okan Aksu graduated from Anadolu University Faculty of Communication Sciences in 2006. Okan continues to work on Aksu HIV / AIDS, Feminism, Human Rights and Social Media.

Hakan Altınpulluk is a Research Assistant Dr in Distance Education at the College of Open Education of Anadolu University, Turkey. He undertook undergraduate studies in the field of Computer Education and Instructional Technologies (CEIT) between the years of 2005-2009 at Anadolu University. He received his Ph.D. Degree in the field of Distance Education in 2018. Hakan Altınpulluk continues to work in the field of Open and Distance Education, Augmented Reality, Virtual Reality, Mobile Learning, Mobile Health, Massive Open Online Courses, Learning Management Systems, Open Educational Resources, Personal Learning Environments, and E-Learning Systems.

Gürcan Banger graduated from METU Electrical Engineering Department. He has an MSc degree. He has established and managed businesses in the hardware, software, electronics and education sectors. He worked as a manager in the vocational chambers and non-governmental organizations. Since 2005, he has served as a corporate consultant and trainer in various organizations on topics like business culture, management, restructuring, clustering, entrepreneurship, strategic planning, Industry 4.0. He teaches part-time at universities. He is currently the cluster coordinator of the Rail Systems Cluster and the project coordinator at the bizobiz.net consulting and training firm. He regularly writes on his blogs. He has books published on different topics. His last books, "Industry 4.0 and Smart Business" and "Industry 4.0 Extra", have appeared in Dorlion Publications. His articles are published in various newspapers, magazines, and blogs.

Işıl Boy Ergül works as a lecturer in the Department of Foreign Languages Education at Yıldız Technical University and as a teacher trainer for Pilgrims Teacher Training in the UK. She has conducted various ICT training courses across Turkey, Europe, and the Middle East since 2010. She holds a BA in TEFL from Istanbul University and an MA in Educational Technology and TESOL from the University of Manchester. Currently she is doing a PhD in Educational Technology at Bahçeşehir University. In 2015, she was selected as an Apple Distinguished Educator. She is also the coordinator of the EdTech Summit (ETZ) and ETZ Academy (www.etz.com.tr).

Aras Bozkurt is a researcher in the Department of Distance Education at Anadolu University, Turkey. He holds MA and Ph.D. degrees in distance education. He conducts empirical studies on online learning through resorting to critical theories including connectivism, rhizomatic learning, and heutagogy. He is interested in emerging research paradigms including social network analysis, sentiment analysis, and data mining.

D. K. Chaturvedi is Sr. professor in the Department of Electrical Engineering at DEI Agra. He has keen interest in Machine Learning and Nano Quantam Computing. He has many laurels to his credit. He has written many books on Electrical Engineering and is presently engaged in books of Human Values and Professional Ethics.

Sumit Chauhan is currently the student of B.Tech. Final Year at ABESEC Ghaziabad and is working extensively in the area of Machine Learning. He has won awards in research paper writing and paper presentations at technical forums.

About the Contributors

Teresa Coffman is a Professor of Education at the University of Mary Washington in Fredericksburg, VA, where she teaches graduate courses in curriculum and instruction, educational theory and research, and technology integration to pre-service teachers as they work toward initial licensure and a Master's degree in Education. Her research interests are in the areas of educational technology, inquiry-based learning and collaboration, distance learning, and global education. She holds a Ph.D. and a Master of Arts in Education. Her professional background includes teaching at the high school level, as well as serving as a technology coordinator and Director of Academic Technology in K-12 education. She has also consulted on technology issues to educators and previously worked in the telecommunications field prior to academia.

Ezgi Doğan graduated from İnönü University, Department of Computer Education and Instructional Technology in 2012. She started her academic career at Van Yüzüncü Yıl University in 2013. She has been working as a research assistant at Anadolu University and continues her PhD education since 2014. Her research interests include virtual reality, gamification, games and technology addiction.

Nil Göksel currently works as an English language instructor at Anadolu University. She received her MA Degree in Distance Education with "Learner -Instructor Interaction within University-Community Partnerships by Giving Samples from Second Life (SL)" in 2009. To pursue her PhD degree, she then completed a research study entitled "Utilizing the Personal Learning Environment for English as a Foreign Language within the Scope of Open and Distance Learning" in 2018. Her research interests lie broadly in online-immersive learning, new learning technologies, Personal Learning Environments (PLEs), educational social networks, virtual interaction, Augmented Reality, Web 2.0 tools used for foreign language teaching and learning, Artificial Intelligence and Intelligent Personal Assistants (IPAs).

Emel Guler is a lecturer in Distance Education at the College of Open Education of Anadolu University. Guler undertook undergraduate (Department of Computer Education & Instructional Technologies, 2004) and graduate studies at Anadolu University, Turkey (Department of Distance Education, 2008). Guler is studying for a PhD in Department of Distance Education. She worked as a ICT teacher in 6 years at the Ministry of National Education (2005- 2011). She is working as a lecturer at the College of Open Education of Anadolu University since 2011. Her research interests are instructional design, educational technology, individual differences and artificial intelligence.

İlknur İstifçi holds both MA and Ph.D. degrees in English Language Teaching. She is currently the head of Modern Languages Department at the School of Foreign Languages, Anadolu University. Her research interests include teacher training, discourse analysis, speech acts, cross-cultural studies, teaching language skills, distance education and using ICTs in ELT.

Zoltan Istvan was born in California and is an Ivy-league educated man yearning to use science, technology, and reason to dramatically remake humanity. Over the last few years, Zoltan has consulted for the US Navy as a futurist, was interviewed to be Libertarian Gary Johnson's Vice President, appeared on the Joe Rogan Experience (and dozens of other shows), and gave many speeches, including at Microsoft, the Global Leaders Forum, Congreso Futuro, and the Financial Times Camp Alphaville (opening Keynote). Zoltan was the only presidential candidate to be interviewed by underground mega-group Anonymous. His award-winning 2013 novel The Transhumanist Wager was a #1 bestseller in Philosophy and also a top 5 Amazon book. It's been compared in reviews to Ayn Rand's work over 1,000 times. It's being taught in various colleges and high schools around the world as a warning and inspiration about the future. Coming out in 2018 is a feature documentary three years in the making called Immortality or Bust, which covers his historic bus tour across America on the Immortality Bus. Zoltan is the founder of the Transhumanist Party, the author of the Transhumanist Bill of Rights, and is a frequently interviewed expert on AI and genetic editing. Before becoming a futurist, he was a journalist for the National Geographic Channel (often an on-camera reporter) and The New York Times Syndicate. Zoltan has traveled to over 100 countries, and he has a degree in Philosophy and Religion from Columbia University. He frequently writes articles for Newsweek, Vice, Wired, HuffPost, TechCrunch, and other major media. He was an endorsed libertarian candidate for California Governor 2018 before being knocked out of the race in the June 5, 2018 statewide primaries.

Şirin Karadeniz is a Professor of Educational Technology and the dean of Faculty of Educational Sciences at Bahcesehir University. Her B.A. in Computer System Education, M.Sc in Computer Education and PhD. in Educational Technology have helped her to develop her interest in developing technology-enhanced learning environments for all ages. Dr. Karadeniz has research interest in digital citizenship, computational thinking, blended learning and technology integration into education. She served as consultant and researcher on national and international projects for Scientific Research Council of Turkey, Ministry of National Education, UNICEF and the European Union. She has published a book and book chapters, articles and proceedings in the field of educational technology.

Faruk Karaman was born in 1971 in Sivas,Turkey. He attended Kayseri Science High School from 1984 to 1987. In 1987, he entered Bosphorus University's Electrical and Electronics Department and graduated in 1993. He then earned MBA and PhD in management from Marmara University. Meanwhile, he worked at investment banking firms such as Korfez Investment, Deniz Investment, Midland Investment and Inter Investment. He also worked at universities like Yeditepe, Istanbul Ticaret, Istanbul Aydın, Gedik, and Okan. Currently, he works at Konya Food and Agriculture University. His research interests are artificial intelligence, futurism, technological singularity and cripto currencies.

Buket Karatop is assistant professor in İstanbul University-Cerrahpasa. Dr. Karatop undertook graduate degree in Industrial Engineering from Yıldız Technical University, and her Ph.D. in industrial Engineering from Sakarya University. She has worked in various positions at Alarko and Şişecam companies. Dr. Karatop has also worked as an academician in Erciyes University, Atatürk University, Süleyman Demirel University, department of Industrial Engineering. She has served as coordinator of engineering education accreditation (MÜDEK) and Quality Development coordinator in these universities. As the Quality Development Director of the Faculty of Open and Distance Education of Istanbul University, he managed the faculty's institutionalization process and received ISO: 9001: 2008 certificate for distance education. She managed the institutionalization process of Istanbul University Open and Distance Education Faculty As the Director of Quality Development, and received ISO: 9001: 2008 certificate for distance education. It has been awarded through the EFQM assessment in distance education. Dr. Karatop worked as a consultant about "process design and institutionalization of the remote health education system under ISO 9001 and EFQM conditions" at the Turkish Ministry of Health. She continues her academic studies on Strategic Management, Quality Management, MCDM, Artificial Intelligence and distance learning.

About the Contributors

Mary Beth Klinger is a Professor of Business and Management at the College of Southern Maryland in Leonardtown, MD, where she teaches undergraduate courses in business, management, leadership, organizational behavior, small business and entrepreneurship, and marketing. Her research interests are in the areas of knowledge management, leadership, innovation, and global education. She holds a Ph.D. in Organization and Management, a Master's in Business Administration, and a Master's in International Management. Her professional background includes educational consulting, employment in private industry in logistics, as well as federal service in the U.S. Office of Personnel Management.

Pradeep Kumar Misra is a Professor in Education in the Chaudhary Charan Singh University, Meerut, India. He has also held the posts of Dean, Faculty of Education and Head, Department of Education. His research specializations are teacher education, educational technology, and lifelong learning. Dr. Misra has received a number of prestigious international research scholarships that include the Commonwealth Academic Fellowship of CSC, UK; Erasmus Mundus Visiting Scholar Scholarship of the European Commission; Doctoral and Senior Researcher Scholarship of DAAD, Germany; Research Exchange Scholarship of FMSH, France; and National Scholarship of Slovak Republic. Dr. Misra also served as a visiting scholar in Arhus University's School of Education, Copenhagen, Denmark, in 2009 for International Masters in Lifelong Learning: Policy and Management Program. Dr. Misra has authored a number of publications in journals of international repute; two books-The Trioka of Adult Learners, Lifelong Learning, and Mathematics; and, Educational Television in Germany; and a number of R&D projects and educational media programs.

Mehmet Emin Mutlu is associate professor at the Faculty of Open Education of the Anadolu University, Turkey. He has a degree in Mathematical Engineering, M.Sc. in Industrial Engineering, PhD in Operational Research in the area of Management of e-Learning Production. His research field is e-learning, open and distance learning, lifelong learning, personal learning environments, lifelogging and personal knowledge management.

Erdem Ongun is the chair of Public Relations and Advertising Department at KYCUBYO School of Applied Sciences of Trakya University, Edirne, Turkey. His main interest areas of study center around social media and information technologies. He has written numerous articles and book chapters in the related field.

Ebba Ossiannilsson is the Vice President for the Swedish Association for Distance Education and for the Swedish Association for E-Competence. She is the CEO of her company on Quality in Open Online Learning. She was awarded the EDEN Fellow title in 2014 and became Open Education Europa (OEE) Fellow in 2015, and an Ambassador for OEE in 2017. Since 2016 she is ambassador for GLOBE the Community of digital learning. Since 2018, she is in the Council of EDEN Fellows. She is a researcher, guest professor, reviewer, advisor and consultant within the area of open, online, flexible, and technology-enabled teaching and learning (OOFAT) and quality. Since 2000, she worked at Lund University, Sweden, as an e-learning, open online learning expert, and advisor with special focus on quality. She is frequently invited as keynote speaker. She is board member in international associations. She is in the

ICDE Quality Network, and Chair and is an ambassador in the ICDE OER Advocacy Committee, and ICDE ON BOLDIC. She has conducted several research studies and national overview reports within the area of OOFAT. Her PhD at Oulu University, Finland in 2012 was on Benchmarking e-learning in higher education. Her dissertation had a large outreach and is often cited. She has over 200 publications.

Rohit Rastogi received his B.E. degree in Computer Science and Engineering from C.C.S.Univ. Meerut in 2003, the M.E. degree in Computer Science from NITTTR-Chandigarh (National Institute of Technical Teachers Training and Research-affiliated to MHRD, Govt. of India), Punjab Univ. Chandigarh in 2010. He is pursuing his Ph.D. in computer science from Dayalbagh Educational Institute, Agra, under renowned professor of Electrical Engineering Dr. D.K. Chaturvedi in area of spiritual consciousness. Dr. Santosh Satya of IIT-Delhi and Dr. Navneet Arora of IIT-Roorkee have happily consented him to co supervise. He is also working presently with Dr. Piyush Trivedi of DSVV Hardwar, India in center of Scientific spirituality. He is an Associate Professor of CSE Dept. in ABES Engineering. College, Ghaziabad (U.P.-India), affiliated to Dr. A.P. J. Abdul Kalam Technical Univ. Lucknow (earlier Uttar Pradesh Tech. University). Also, he is preparing some interesting algorithms on Swarm Intelligence approaches like PSO, ACO and BCO etc. Rastogi is involved actively with Vichaar Krnati Abhiyaan and strongly believes that transformation starts within self.

Ferhan Şahin graduated from Çukurova University, Department of Computer Education and Instructional Technology, in 2012 and received his MS in the same department from Anadolu University in 2016. He has been working as a research assistant at Anadolu University since 2014 and continues his PhD education since 2016. His research interests include technology acceptance and use, innovativeness, games, problematic use of technology.

Pallavi Sharma is pursuing her B.Tech from ABESEC, Ghaziabad. She is working hard in data mining and machine learning domain. Her hobbies are singing, cooking and dancing.

Ramesh Chander Sharma holds a Ph.D. in Education (Educational Technology) and is currently working as an Associate Professor of Educational Technology and Learning Resources in the Educational Technology and Publishing (ETP) Unit at Wawasan Open University, Malaysia. He has been to the Universidade do Estado da Bahia (UNEB), Salvador, Bahia, Brazil, and University of Fiji, Fiji, as a Visiting Professor; Commonwealth of Learning as Director of the Commonwealth Educational Media Centre for Asia, New Delhi; Indira Gandhi National Open University, India; and University of Guyana, Guyana. He is the co-Editor of the 'Asian Journal of Distance Education'. In addition, he has been associated with several peer reviewed journals as Reviewer, Editor and Editorial Advisory Board member in the field of Open and Distance Learning such as "Distance Education", "International Review of Research in Open and Distributed Learning (IRRODL)", "International Journal of Distance Education Technologies (IJDET)", and "Indian Journal of Open Learning (IJOL)". He is also on the Editorial Advisory Board and is an author for the "Encyclopedia of Distance Learning (4 volumes), 2005" (https://www.igi-global.com/book/encyclopedia-distance-learning/351).

About the Contributors

Hasan Ucar is an instructor at Bilecik Seyh Edebali University, Turkey. He received his Ph.D. (2016) and Master's Degree (2012) in Distance Education from Anadolu University, Turkey. Hasan's current research agenda is the motivational design of instruction in online learning environments. Additional areas of research include distance learning and teaching, online learning, instructional design/technology, teaching and learning in online technologies, motivation and engagement of online learners, and online academic procrastination.

Suzan Urgan was born in Eskişehir, Turkey, in 1972. She received the bachelor degree in faculty of economics and administrative sciences from the Anadolu University, Eskişehir, Turkey, in 1998, and the master's degree in department of management of health institutions from the Selçuk University, Konya, in 2011, and the Ph.D. degree in business from the Dumlupınar University, Kütahya, in 2018. Since 2016, she has been working as a manager at Yunus Emre State Hospital. Her current research interests include Organizational Behavior, Management Organization, International Health Facilities, Cultural Intelligence, Social and Psychological Capital.

Natasha Vita-More is Executive Director of Humanity+, Inc., a Professor, University of Advancing Technology, a Fellow, Institute for Ethics & Emerging Technologies, and Lead Scientific Researcher on the C. Elegans Memory Project. She is an internationally known speaker on the future of humanity who advocates technological enhancement. Natasha received celebrity status by innovating the future human body for superlongevity, "Primo Posthuman". Wired magazine called her the "early adapter of revolutionary changes" and the New York Times publicized her as the "first female philosopher of transhumanism". Vita-More is featured in over 24 televised documentaries. Vita-More is co-author and co-editor of the book The Transhumanist Reader: on the Science, Technology and Philosophy of the Human Future (Wiley-Blackwell).

Vishwas Yadav is B.Tech. Final Year student of CSE in ABESEC, Ghaziabad, He is working presently on Human consciousness with machine Learning. His hobbies are playing cricket and watching movies. He is young and has a dynamic personality.

Roman V. Yampolskiy is a Tenured Associate Professor in the department of Computer Engineering and Computer Science at the Speed School of Engineering, University of Louisville. He is the founding and current director of the Cyber Security Lab and an author of many books, including "Artificial Superintelligence: a Futuristic Approach". Dr. Yampolskiy is a Senior member of IEEE and AGI; Member of Kentucky Academy of Science, and Research Advisor for MIRI, and Associate of GCRI. He holds a PhD degree from the University at Buffalo and was a recipient of a four year NSF (National Science Foundation) IGERT (Integrative Graduate Education and Research Traineeship) fellowship. Before beginning his doctoral studies, Dr. Yampolskiy received a BS/MS (High Honors) combined degree in Computer Science from Rochester Institute of Technology, New York.

Index

A

AGI 26
AI (Artificial Intelligence) 9-10, 21-23, 25-26, 29, 87, 90, 96, 100-102, 104-105, 107, 112, 115, 121, 161-163, 224-226, 228-232, 238, 242-244, 247, 250, 291, 294, 299, 301, 354
Anaconda 367, 379
Andragogy 263-265, 272
Android 189, 229, 308, 347, 357
artificial general intelligence 3-4, 7, 26, 54, 160, 352
Artificial Intelligence (AI) 1-4, 7, 9-12, 21, 29, 55-56, 79, 81, 83-84, 87, 96, 100-101, 115-117, 121-124, 126-129, 157-159, 161-165, 167-168, 172, 176, 187, 189, 191, 194, 197-198, 200, 204, 206, 224-226, 228-229, 236, 238, 242-244, 250, 291, 294, 298-300, 307-309, 319, 322, 326, 328-329, 331-332, 334, 347, 349, 351, 354
artificial superintelligence 2-4, 7-8, 10-12
Augmented Human 160-161, 168
augmented reality 1-2, 7, 12, 56, 64, 164, 199, 291, 294, 296-297, 308-309, 311-312, 317-318, 320

B

Basic Income 30, 102, 115, 353
Big Data 59, 101, 115, 121, 227, 242, 310, 320, 322
Blended Learning 97, 119, 241, 250
Blockchain Technology 242, 244-247, 250
body enhancement 191, 196
Brain Implant 47, 105, 115
Business Ecosystem 309, 311, 314-315, 317-321, 323, 326
Business Learning 321-324, 326
Business Management 126, 307, 309, 311, 315, 320-322, 326
Business Model 82, 206, 311-314, 327
Business Skill 327

C

Cognitive Capacity 156
Communities of Practice 156, 209
Complex Cognitive Processing 136, 143, 147, 156
Computer Interface 51
Connectivism 205, 209, 211, 223, 264, 266-267, 272
Constructivist 296-297
Content Co-Creation 139, 156
Cooperative 50, 136, 139, 205, 212, 318-319
Cryonics 79, 84, 294, 330, 348, 357, 360
cyber culture 1, 4-5, 12
Cybernetics 50, 79, 84, 308, 349
Cyborg 7, 105-107, 115, 176, 189, 308, 347-348, 351, 357

D

Deep Learning 103, 129, 224-227, 236, 242, 367
Demand of pedagogies 171, 176
digital culture 4
digital technologies 4, 87, 89, 135-136, 138, 140-141, 144, 146-147, 179, 196, 242, 298
Digital Transformation 78-80, 82-83, 86-87, 91, 96, 117, 206
Digitalization 80-83, 86-87, 96, 167, 310, 316, 322
Digitization 79-80, 82-83, 87, 96
Disruption 96
Distance Education (DE) 96, 116, 125, 209, 232, 237-243, 245, 247, 250, 252-253, 256-261, 272, 277
Dual Mode University 250

E

Electronic Learning (E-Learning) 97, 208-209, 240, 258, 272-273, 300
ELT Education 280-281, 286
Eschatology 357

Index

Ethics 26, 80, 87, 90, 98, 109-110, 112, 146, 313-314, 353
Eugenics 349, 354, 357
Exponential Technology 25, 309, 327
Extropy 171, 292, 348, 358

G

Giga University 272
Global 5, 8, 20-22, 24, 55, 80-81, 84, 90-91, 111, 134, 136-137, 140, 143-148, 173, 177-178, 188, 237-238, 252, 311-315, 319, 323, 333, 350-351, 363, 379

H

H+ 78, 97, 161, 164, 168
Heutagogy 263-265, 272
Human Enhancement 20, 194, 204, 291, 293, 349, 354
Humanity+ 159-161, 242-243, 291

I

ICT Integration 274, 276-278, 280, 285-286
ICT Self-Efficacy 274, 277-278, 280, 284, 286
Immersion 139, 186, 200, 204, 295
Industrial Revolution 10, 78-80, 84-85, 87, 158
Information and Communication Technologies (ICTs) 205, 237, 250
Innovative Leadership 78, 91, 96
Intelligent Learning Environments 236
Intelligent Personal Assistant 228, 236
intelligent personal assistants 225, 228
Intelligent Tutoring System 125, 231, 236
Internet of Things (IoT) 96
IQ 30, 32-33, 35-36, 39-43, 105, 115

L

Leadership 18-19, 21, 24, 78-82, 84-85, 87, 91-92, 96, 296, 312
Learning Experiences Management 47-48, 56-59, 61, 63, 66, 68, 71-72
Learning Management Systems (LMS) 206, 223

M

Machine Learning 10, 44, 52, 63, 69, 71, 121, 129, 162, 206, 224-227, 236, 238, 244, 299, 307, 309, 319, 363, 366-367, 376

Massive Open Online Courses (MOOCs) 241, 250
Max More 160, 171
Mega University 272
Meta-cognitive Regulation 62
Mind enhancement 193, 195-196, 198
Mixed Reality 64, 69
Mobile Learning (M-Learning) 272
Mobile Phones 164-165, 206, 279, 284, 297
Mobile Technologies 1-2, 139, 142, 156, 164, 272
MOOCs 116-121, 124-129, 241, 250
Myths 18-19, 21-22, 158, 347

N

Nano Robot 204
nanotechnology 6, 79, 159-160, 171-172, 175, 187, 189, 194-195, 204, 242, 294
Natural Language Processing 32, 37, 121, 224-228, 236, 331
Networked Environment 135, 139, 142, 156
Nick Bostrom 56, 354
NLP 32, 224-225, 227-228

O

Online Learning 96, 121, 232, 238, 240-241, 250, 315, 317
Open and Distance Learning (ODL) 125-126, 206-207, 209-210, 217, 223, 238, 252-253, 259-263, 266-267, 272
Open University 239, 272
Openness (in Education) 272
Optimism 175, 177, 180, 328-329, 337-338, 340-341
Organizational Behavior 328-329, 334-338, 341

P

Personal Learning Environment (PLE) 223
Personal Learning Network (PLN) 210, 223
Personalized Learning 88, 125, 142, 156, 207, 209
Positive Psychological Capital 328-329, 335-337, 339
Post-Human 56, 72, 160-161, 185, 187-189, 195, 198, 204, 347-348, 350-351, 353
Pre-Service Teachers 274-275, 277-280, 282-286
Python 37, 39, 366-368, 376, 379

Q

Quality in Open Online Learning 96

R

Reflective Learning Process 61
Resilience 277, 328-329, 337-341
RFID 115
Rhizomatic Learning 264, 266, 273
robotics 8, 79, 103, 105, 175-176, 242, 294, 300
Role of pedagogies 171, 175, 180

S

Sapient 346-347, 351, 353, 358
Self-Efficacy 140-141, 147, 274, 277-278, 280, 284, 286, 298, 328-329, 337-341
Sentience 351
Single Mode University 250
Singularity 7-8, 55, 103-104, 115, 160, 188-189, 204
Smart Learning 78-80, 85, 87-90, 97
Social Media 5, 11-12, 88-89, 136-138, 156, 179, 206-207, 278
Social Networks 4-5, 79, 84, 87, 137, 140, 142-143, 205-207, 212, 217, 223
Social Revolution 78-81, 83, 87, 91
Somatic 196, 199, 354, 358
Stress 110, 363, 365-367, 373, 376, 378-380
Student-centered 298
Superhuman 330, 355
Synthetic Recollection 70-71

T

Teacher Education 274, 277, 285
Teaching 86, 89, 96, 102, 116, 125-126, 134-136, 142, 145-146, 172-173, 178, 180, 198-199, 209, 216, 238-242, 247, 250, 252, 254, 258-259, 261-263, 267, 272, 274, 276-278, 280, 282, 284-286, 291-294, 297-300, 321, 323

Technological Singularity 103-104, 115
Three-Dimensional Virtual World 204
Transhuman 8, 12, 29-30, 55-56, 72, 100-102, 109, 161, 172, 178-181, 186-187, 348-349
Transhuman age 178-181
Transhumanism 2, 6-7, 9, 18, 25, 28-30, 55, 78-84, 86-88, 91-92, 97-101, 103-107, 109-113, 115-116, 124-125, 134-135, 137, 140-141, 144-145, 147, 157, 159-162, 164-168, 171-172, 174-182, 185-191, 193-194, 197-199, 237-238, 291-292, 294-296, 298, 301, 307-309, 327-330, 334-335, 340-341, 347-350, 354-355, 358
Transhumanism (H+ or h+) 97
transhumanist 1, 5-10, 12, 21-22, 25, 29-30, 80, 82, 86-87, 109-111, 135, 140, 144, 146-147, 161, 164, 170-171, 175, 180, 182, 185, 187-190, 238-239, 242, 251, 291, 294-295, 299, 301, 307-311, 317, 319, 329, 333, 339, 342, 346-348, 350-355, 359
transhumanist culture 1, 5-6, 8, 12
Transparent Tool 135, 156

U

Ubiquitous Learning (U-Learning) 273
Unemployment 99, 102, 105, 115, 316-317, 334
UNESCO 81, 84, 90, 173, 275-276

V

Variance 369
virtual reality 1-2, 5, 7-8, 186, 189-190, 192-193, 200, 291, 294-296, 339

W

Web 2.0 205-210, 212, 217, 223, 277-278, 284-285, 346

Purchase Print, E-Book, or Print + E-Book

IGI Global books are available in three unique pricing formats:
Print Only, E-Book Only, or Print + E-Book. Shipping fees apply.

www.igi-global.com

Recommended Reference Books

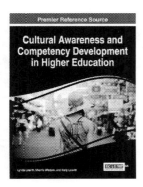

ISBN: 978-1-5225-2145-7
© 2017; 408 pp.
List Price: $210

ISBN: 978-1-5225-2334-5
© 2017; 375 pp.
List Price: $195

ISBN: 978-1-5225-1718-4
© 2017; 457 pp.
List Price: $270

ISBN: 978-1-5225-0672-0
© 2017; 678 pp.
List Price: $295

ISBN: 978-1-5225-2630-8
© 2018; 209 pp.
List Price: $145

ISBN: 978-1-5225-1621-7
© 2017; 173 pp.
List Price: $135

Do you want to stay current on the latest research trends, product announcements, news and special offers?
Join IGI Global's mailing list today and start enjoying exclusive perks sent only to IGI Global members.
Add your name to the list at **www.igi-global.com/newsletters.**

Publisher of Peer-Reviewed, Timely, and Innovative Academic Research

Ensure Quality Research is Introduced to the Academic Community

Become an IGI Global Reviewer for Authored Book Projects

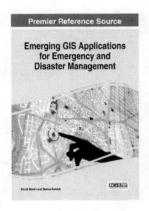 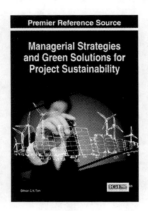  

The overall success of an authored book project is dependent on quality and timely reviews.

In this competitive age of scholarly publishing, constructive and timely feedback significantly expedites the turnaround time of manuscripts from submission to acceptance, allowing the publication and discovery of forward-thinking research at a much more expeditious rate. Several IGI Global authored book projects are currently seeking highly qualified experts in the field to fill vacancies on their respective editorial review boards:

Applications may be sent to:
development@igi-global.com

Applicants must have a doctorate (or an equivalent degree) as well as publishing and reviewing experience. Reviewers are asked to write reviews in a timely, collegial, and constructive manner. All reviewers will begin their role on an ad-hoc basis for a period of one year, and upon successful completion of this term can be considered for full editorial review board status, with the potential for a subsequent promotion to Associate Editor.

If you have a colleague that may be interested in this opportunity, we encourage you to share this information with them.

www.igi-global.com

Celebrating 30 Years of Scholarly Knowledge Creation & Dissemination

InfoSci®-Books

A Collection of 4,000+ Reference Books Containing Over 87,000 Full-Text Chapters Focusing on Emerging Research

This database is a collection of over 4,000+ IGI Global single and multi-volume reference books, handbooks of research, and encyclopedias, encompassing groundbreaking research from prominent experts worldwide. These books are highly cited and currently recognized in prestigious indices such as: Web of Science™ and Scopus®.

Librarian Features:
- No Set-Up or Maintenance Fees
- Guarantee of No More Than A 5% Annual Price Increase
- COUNTER 4 Usage Reports
- Complimentary Archival Access
- Free MARC Records

Researcher Features:
- Unlimited Simultaneous Users
- No Embargo of Content
- Full Book Download
- Full-Text Search Engine
- No DRM

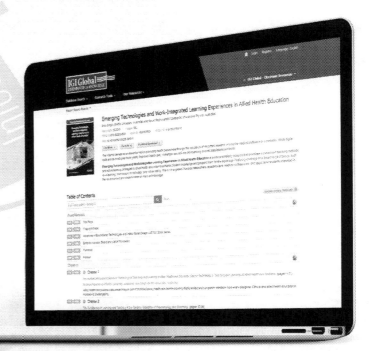

To Find Out More or To Purchase This Database:
www.igi-global.com/infosci-books

eresources@igi-global.com • Toll Free: 1-866-342-6657 ext. 100 • Phone: 717-533-8845 x100

Are You Ready to Publish Your Research?

IGI Global offers book authorship and editorship opportunities across 11 subject areas, including business, healthcare, computer science, engineering, and more!

Benefits of Publishing with IGI Global:

- Free one-to-one editorial and promotional support.
- Expedited publishing timelines that can take your book from start to finish in less than one (1) year.
- Choose from a variety of formats including: Edited and Authored References, Handbooks of Research, Encyclopedias, and Research Insights.
- Utilize IGI Global's eEditorial Discovery® submission system in support of conducting the submission and blind-review process.
- IGI Global maintains a strict adherence to ethical practices due in part to our full membership to the Committee on Publication Ethics (COPE).
- Indexing potential in prestigious indices such as Scopus®, Web of Science™, PsycINFO®, and ERIC – Education Resources Information Center.
- Ability to connect your ORCID iD to your IGI Global publications.
- Earn royalties on your publication as well as receive complimentary copies and exclusive discounts.

Get Started Today by Contacting the Acquisitions Department at:
acquisition@igi-global.com

Available to Order Now

Order through www.igi-global.com with **Free Standard Shipping**.

The Premier Reference for Information Science & Information Technology

100% Original Content
Contains 705 new, peer-reviewed articles with color figures covering over 80 categories in 11 subject areas

Diverse Contributions
More than 1,100 experts from 74 unique countries contributed their specialized knowledge

Easy Navigation
Includes two tables of content and a comprehensive index in each volume for the user's convenience

Highly-Cited
Embraces a complete list of references and additional reading sections to allow for further research

Included in: **InfoSci-Books**

Encyclopedia of Information Science and Technology Fourth Edition
A Comprehensive 10-Volume Set

Mehdi Khosrow-Pour, D.B.A. (Information Resources Management Association, USA)
ISBN: 978-1-5225-2255-3; © 2018; Pg: 8,104; Release Date: July 2017

For a limited time, receive the complimentary e-books for the First, Second, and Third editions with the purchase of the *Encyclopedia of Information Science and Technology, Fourth Edition* e-book.*

The **Encyclopedia of Information Science and Technology, Fourth Edition** is a 10-volume set which includes 705 original and previously unpublished research articles covering a full range of perspectives, applications, and techniques contributed by thousands of experts and researchers from around the globe. This authoritative encyclopedia is an all-encompassing, well-established reference source that is ideally designed to disseminate the most forward-thinking and diverse research findings. With critical perspectives on the impact of information science management and new technologies in modern settings, including but not limited to computer science, education, healthcare, government, engineering, business, and natural and physical sciences, it is a pivotal and relevant source of knowledge that will benefit every professional within the field of information science and technology and is an invaluable addition to every academic and corporate library.

Scan for Online Bookstore

Pricing Information
Hardcover: **$5,695**   E-Book: **$5,695**   Hardcover + E-Book: **$6,895**

Both E-Book Prices Include:
- *Encyclopedia of Information Science and Technology, First Edition E-Book*
- *Encyclopedia of Information Science and Technology, Second Edition E-Book*
- *Encyclopedia of Information Science and Technology, Third Edition E-Book*

*Purchase the Encyclopedia of Information Science and Technology, Fourth Edition e-book and receive the first, second, and third e-book editions for free. Offer is only valid with purchase of the fourth edition's e-book through the IGI Global Online Bookstore.

Recommend this Title to Your Institution's Library: www.igi-global.com/books

www.igi-global.com/infosci-ondemand

 InfoSci®-OnDemand

Continuously updated with new material on a weekly basis, InfoSci®-OnDemand offers the ability to search through thousands of quality full-text research papers. Users can narrow each search by identifying key topic areas of interest, then display a complete listing of relevant papers, and purchase materials specific to their research needs.

Comprehensive Service
- Over 110,800+ journal articles, book chapters, and case studies.
- All content is downloadable in PDF format and can be stored locally for future use.

No Subscription Fees
- One time fee of $37.50 per PDF download.

Instant Access
- Receive a download link immediately after order completion!

"It really provides an excellent entry into the research literature of the field. It presents a manageable number of highly relevant sources on topics of interest to a wide range of researchers. The sources are scholarly, but also accessible to 'practitioners'."

– Lisa Stimatz, MLS, University of North Carolina at Chapel Hill, USA

"It is an excellent and well designed database which will facilitate research, publication and teaching. It is a very very useful tool to have."

– George Ditsa, PhD, University of Wollongong, Australia

"I have accessed the database and find it to be a valuable tool to the IT/IS community. I found valuable articles meeting my search criteria 95% of the time."

– Lynda Louis, Xavier University of Louisiana, USA

Recommended for use by researchers who wish to immediately download PDFs of individual chapters or articles.

www.igi-global.com/e-resources/infosci-ondemand

www.igi-global.com

Printed in the United States
By Bookmasters